CCH
a Wolters Kluwer business

Attestation and Other Special Engagements

by J. Russell Madray

Highlights

Attestation and Other Special Engagements shows practitioners the most cost-effective approach for conducting the many types of attestation and other special engagements. The book is filled with practical explanations of the most common types of engagements, reducing the technical language of official pronouncements to easy-to-read and easy-to-understand advice and procedures. This book is designed to enhance the quality of your practice, and it presents an approach that will help you perform your engagements effectively and efficiently.

Throughout *Attestation and Other Special Engagements* you will find engagement efficiency, effectiveness, and cost-saving measures to help you complete your engagements profitably. These pages include numerous practice aids—checklists, questionnaires, workpapers, sample correspondence, and sample reports—that will take you through an engagement from the initial evaluation of a client to issuance of the appropriate report.

2006 Edition

The 2006 Edition of *Attestation and Other Special Engagements* has been updated throughout with the very latest information on:

- PCAOB Auditing Standard No. 2 (AS-2) (An Audit of Internal Control over Financial Reporting Performed in Conjunction with an Audit of Financial Statements)
- PCAOB Staff Q&As on Auditing Standard No. 2
- Interpretation No. 6 of Chapter 1 (Attest Engagements) of SSAE-10 (AT 101) (Reporting on Attestation Engagements Performed in Accordance with Government Auditing Standards)
- SSARS-13 (AR 110) (Compilation of Specified Elements, Accounts, or Items of a Financial Statement)

- SSARS-14 (AR 120) (Compilation of Pro Forma Financial Information)
- New chapter on marketing special engagements to clients
- New chapter on pre-engagement considerations
- New chapter on specified elements, accounts, or items of a financial statement
- New chapter on management's discussion and analysis

You'll also receive all the timesaving checklists, questionnaires, workpapers, sample correspondence, and sample reports you'll need to perform a thorough attestation engagement on the free companion CD-ROM.

CCH Learning Center: The Solution to Your Professional Development and CPE Needs

CCH's goal is to provide you with the clearest, most concise, and up-to-date accounting and auditing information to help further your professional development, as well as a convenient method to help you satisfy your continuing professional education requirements. The CCH Learning Center* offers a complete line of self-study courses covering complex and constantly evolving accounting and auditing issues. We are continually adding new courses to the library to help you stay current on all the latest developments. The CCH Learning Center courses are available 24 hours a day, seven days a week. You'll get immediate exam results and certification. To view our complete accounting and auditing course catalog, go to: **http://cch.learningcenter.com.**

03/06

For questions concerning this shipment, billing, or other customer service matters, call our Customer Service department at 1 800 248 3248.

*CCH is registered with the National Association of State Boards of Accountancy (NASBA) as a sponsor of continuing professional education on the National Registry of CPE Sponsors. State boards of accountancy have final authority on the acceptance of individual courses for CPE credit. Complaints regarding registered sponsors may be addressed to the National Registry of CPE Sponsors, 150 Fourth Avenue North, Suite 700, Nashville, TN 37219-2417. Telephone: 615-880-4200.

*CCH is registered with the National Association of State Boards of Accountancy (NASBA) as a Quality Assurance Service (QAS) sponsor of continuing professional education. Participating state boards of accountancy have final authority on the acceptance of individual courses for CPE credit. Complaints regarding QAS program sponsors may be addressed to NASBA, 150 Fourth Avenue North, Suite 700, Nashville, TN 37219-2417. Telephone: 615-880-4200.

2006

Attestation and Other Special Engagements

J. Russell Madray

CCH
a Wolters Kluwer business

ISBN: 0-8080-9018-6

4025 W. Peterson Avenue
Chicago, IL 60646-6085
1 800 248 3248
http://cchgroup.com

a Wolters Kluwer business

Portions of this work were published in a previous edition.

Printed in the United States of America

Contents

Preface

Client needs drive the opportunity to provide any professional service, including nontraditional services. In order to successfully tap into attestation and other special engagements, you must be proficient at uncovering client needs. *Attestation and Other Special Engagements* helps you uncover those client needs and shows you the most cost-effective approach for conducting high-quality, profitable nontraditional services.

So, what exactly are special engagements? The term "special engagements" encompasses any engagement other than the traditional compilation, review, or audit of financial statements. Examples of special engagements covered in *Attestation and Other Special Engagements* include

- Agreed-upon procedures
- Financial forecasts and projections
- Reports on internal control
- Audits, reviews, and compilations of specified financial statement elements, accounts, or items
- Reports on pro forma financial information

The primary advantage of being able to provide special engagements is that they give you the flexibility to meet the needs of your clients. You are often able to meet specific client needs in a cost-effective manner, reducing the possibility that the client may go to another professional for the service. Special engagements also provide opportunities to establish relationships with potential new clients. In addition, nontraditional engagements are often perceived by clients as value-added services (as opposed to traditional financial statement compilations, reviews, and audits, which are viewed as a commodity). This means nontraditional engagements can be more profitable than traditional engagements.

Attestation and Other Special Engagements reduces the technical language of official pronouncements to easy-to-read and easy-to-understand advice and procedures. It is designed to enhance the quality of your practice, and it presents an approach that will help you perform your attestation engagements effectively and efficiently.

Throughout *Attestation and Other Special Engagements* you will find various engagement efficiency, effectiveness, and cost-saving measures to help you complete your nontraditional engagements profitably. At the same time, it includes numerous practice aids—checklists, questionnaires, workpapers, sample correspondence, and sample reports—that will take you through an engagement from the initial evaluation of a client to issuance of the appropriate report.

The 2006 edition of *Attestation and Other Special Engagements* has been expanded to 14 chapters and covers all major topics and types of attestation and other special engagements, including

- An overview of the professional standards applicable to attestation engagements
- How to market special engagements
- Pre-engagement considerations
- Unique planning and administration issues for attestation engagements
- Step-by-step guidance to examination engagements
- How to execute review engagements
- How to perform agreed-upon procedures engagements
- Step-by-step guidance for compliance engagements
- Detailed guidance on internal control engagements for both public and nonpublic entities
- How to perform engagements related to specified elements of a financial statement
- Step-by-step guidance for due diligence engagements
- Detailed guidance on prospective financial information engagements, including forecasts and projections
- Illustrations and applications of a variety of forms, checklists, and practice aids

Attestation and Other Special Engagements comes with a CD-ROM that contains all of the correspondence letters, practice aids, forms, checklists, and reports found in the text.

The 2006 edition of *Attestation and Other Special Engagements* has been updated for new auditing and attestation pronouncements and reflects the most current guidance from the AICPA, the SEC, and the Public Company Accounting Oversight Board (PCAOB). In addition, this edition has been significantly expanded beyond attestation engagements and now includes many of the most common types of nontraditional engagements requested by clients. Specifically, this edition contains the following new material:

- A new chapter that provides an overview of the marketing of attestation and other special engagements, including methods of identifying potential clients along with methods for marketing and selling nontraditional services to these clients.
- A new chapter on general pre-engagement considerations for attestation and other special engagements.
- A new chapter that discusses the various types of engagements related to specified elements, accounts, or items of a

financial statement, including engagements to compile or audit specified elements.

- A new detailed discussion in Chapter 11 on internal control engagements, which includes audits of public companies' internal control over financial reporting.
- A new detailed discussion in Chapter 12 that includes compilations of pro forma financial information.
- A new chapter that discusses the types of attestation engagements related to management's discussion and analysis under AT 701.

The following is just a sample of some of the hundreds of nontraditional engagements you can provide to your clients with *Attestation and Other Special Engagements:*

- Cash forecasts for cash management purposes
- Cash flow projections for loan proposals
- Assurance on nonfinancial performance metrics
- Assurance on compliance with laws or regulations
- Assistance in compiling a schedule of specific financial statement items (e.g., accounts receivable, inventory, property, plant, and equipment, cost of goods sold, operating expenses, etc.)
- Assurance on a schedule of specific financial statement items (e.g., accounts receivable, inventory, property, plant, and equipment, cost of goods sold, operating expenses, etc.)
- Assurance on effectiveness of internal control
- Specific procedures applied to verify financial statement items (e.g., accounts receivable or cost of goods sold)
- Specific procedures applied to verify lease calculations
- Assurance on calculations for lease payments
- Assurance on calculations for royalty payments
- Assurance on calculations for profit participation
- Assurance on federal and state income tax provisions included in financial statements
- Assurance on operating or customer service measures to aid in client marketing
- Local government business license fee compliance
- Ballot counting or contest result assurance
- Specific procedures to inspect documents for evidence of certain types of transactions or characteristics (e.g., inspect shipment dates for a sample of shipping documents to determine whether any such dates were subsequent to year-end)

- Specific procedures to confirm information with third parties
- Specific procedures to compare documents, schedules, or analyses with certain specified attributes (e.g., compare the amounts of invoices included in each column of an accounts receivable aging to the amount and invoice date shown on the outstanding invoice)
- Specific procedures to perform mathematical computations (e.g., calculate specified debt covenant ratios and verify that the resulting ratios agree with those reported in a specified schedule)
- Specific procedures to trace all outstanding checks appearing on a bank reconciliation as of a certain date to checks that cleared the bank statement of the subsequent month
- Specific procedures to calculate the number of miles of streets paved shown on a contractor's certificate of completion
- Specific procedures to calculate the rate of return on a specified investment
- Specific procedures to assist management in connection with the acquisition of another company
- Recommendations on improvements to a client's system of internal control
- Assistance in compiling pro forma financial information to show the effects of a proposed transaction (e.g., business combination, change in capitalization, or change in the form of business organization)
- Assurance on pro forma financial information to show the effects of a proposed transaction (e.g., business combination, change in capitalization, or change in the form of business organization)
- Assistance with investigation and analysis of an acquisition target
- Assistance with preparation of budget information

The author welcomes comments, suggestions, and recommendations to improve the book which will be considered for incorporation in future revisions of the guide. Please send your comments to Anita Rosepka, Executive Editor, at rosepkaa@cch.com.

Accounting Research Manager™

Accounting Research Manager is the most comprehensive, up-to-date, and objective online resource of financial reporting literature. It includes all authoritative and proposed accounting, auditing, and SEC literature, plus independent, expert-written interpretive guidance.

And, in addition to our standard accounting and SEC libraries, you can enjoy the full spectrum of financial reporting with our Audit library.

The Audit library covers auditing standards, attestation engagement standards, accounting and review services standards, audit risk alerts, and other vital auditing-related guidance. You will also have online access to our best-selling *GAAS Practice Manual, Audit Procedures, Compilations & Reviews, CPA's Guide to Effective Engagement Letters, CPA's Guide to Management Letter Comments*, and be kept up-to-date on the latest authoritative literature via the *GAAS Update Service*.

With **Accounting Research Manager,** you maximize the efficiency of your research time, while enhancing your results. Learn more about our content, our experts, and how you can request a FREE trial by visiting us at **www.accountingresearchmanager.com.**

Acknowledgments

Thanks are due to the publishing staff for their constructive input and diligent efforts in producing this book. The author would also like to thank his wife, Beth, and his family for their encouragement, support, and understanding as he developed *Attestation and Other Special Engagements*.

Russ Madray
Greenville, South Carolina

About the Author

J. Russell Madray is president of The Madray Group, Inc., which specializes in knowledge transfer. Through a combination of technical writing, training, and targeted consulting, The Madray Group helps businesses, accounting firms, and other organizations understand and implement technical accounting and auditing issues.

Mr. Madray earned a B.S. in Accounting from Clemson University in 1986 and a Master of Professional Accountancy from Clemson University in 1988. He is a certified public accountant, a certified internal auditor, a certified management accountant, and a certified financial manager. He is a past member of the AICPA's Accounting and Review Services Committee and a past member of the Board of Directors of the South Carolina Association of CPAs.

Mr. Madray has more than 18 years of professional experience, including ten years in public practice. He also serves as a senior lecturer at Clemson University's School of Accountancy and Legal Studies.

Mr. Madray is the author of numerous publications and articles on accounting and auditing topics, including many of the AICPA's Audit Risk Alert series. In addition, he speaks to hundreds of groups each year on accounting and auditing topics and has made presentations in more than 40 states.

CHAPTER 1
OVERVIEW OF ATTESTATION AND OTHER SPECIAL ENGAGEMENTS

CONTENTS

OVERVIEW

This chapter provides an overview of attestation engagements and other related engagements that a practitioner might perform. The levels of assurance are discussed, along with the form and content of the Statements on Standards for Attestation Engagements (SSAEs). In addition, other engagements are discussed, which are not the subject of this guide.

OVERVIEW OF SPECIAL ENGAGEMENTS

The term "special engagements" as used in this guide, encompasses any engagement other than the traditional compilation, review, or audit of financial statements. Examples of special engagements covered in this guide are

- Agreed-upon procedures
- Financial forecasts and projections
- Reports on internal control
- Audits, reviews, and compilations of specified financial statement elements, accounts, or items
- Reports on pro forma financial information

> **OBSERVATION:** Special engagements may also be called "nontraditional" engagements or services.

Clients often request traditional accounting or audit services. Some clients, however, have particular needs that cannot be met by traditional financial statement audits, reviews, or compilations. In those situations, a special engagement, such as one of those mentioned above, is often the best solution.

Occasionally a client specifically requests a special engagement (such as a report on internal control). More often, though, a request for a traditional engagement provides an opportunity to perform a special engagement that better meets the client's needs. For example, a small-business owner may request an audit of the business's financial statements when he or she is actually interested in specific procedures being applied to an item such as accounts receivable. Or a lender may request a review of a client's financial statements when he or she really only needs assurance on the client's inventory that serves as collateral for a loan.

The primary advantage of being able to provide special engagements is that they give the practitioner the flexibility to meet the needs of his or her clients. The practitioner is often able to meet specific client needs in a cost-effective manner, reducing the possibility that the client may go to another professional for the service. Special engagements also provide opportunities to establish relationships with potential new clients. In addition, nontraditional engagements are often perceived by clients as value-added services (as opposed to traditional financial statement compilations, reviews, and audits, which are viewed as a commodity). This means nontraditional engagements can be more profitable than traditional engagements.

OVERVIEW OF ATTESTATION ENGAGEMENTS

An attest engagement is one in which a practitioner, by virtue of issuing a report, provides assurance on information that is the responsibility of another party. The term *attest* and its variants, such as *attesting* and *attestation*, are used in a number of state accountancy laws and in regulations issued by state boards of accountancy under such laws for different purposes and with different meanings from those intended by the SSAEs. Consequently, the definition of "attestation" as used in the SSAEs should not be understood as defining these terms and similar terms for purposes other than for application of the SSAEs.

The term "attest" is broad and encompasses a variety of specific engagements. In fact, the traditional financial statement audit is an attest service in that a practitioner (auditor), by virtue of issuing a report (audit opinion), provides assurance on the information (financial statements) that is the responsibility of another party (management). However, for practical purposes the term has evolved in the accounting profession to mean an engagement or service that provides assurance on information other than historical financial statements.

Attestation engagements are performed under the AICPA's Statements on Standards for Attestation Engagements. The attestation standards provide guidance and establish a broad framework for a variety of attest services. SSAEs are issued by senior technical bodies of the AICPA designated to issue pronouncements on attestation matters. Attestation Interpretations are recommendations on the application of SSAEs in specific circumstances, including engagements for entities in specialized industries, issued under the authority of AICPA senior technical bodies.

The purpose of the first attestation standards, issued in 1986, was to provide guidance on performing and reporting on attest engagements. However, changes in the business environment began to create problems in the way that the standards could be applied in practice. The issuance of SSAE-10 (Attestation Standards: Revision and Recodification), was intended to address the practical application of the attest standards. SSAE-10 supersedes all preceding SSAEs. Although most of the guidance from those previous standards has been carried forward, significant portions of SSAE-1 have been replaced or rewritten.

OBSERVATION: The Statements on Standards for Attestation Engagements (SSAEs) have been codified into the AICPA Professional Standards, Volume 1, as AT sections 101 through 701. References in this book to AT sections refer to those standards.

Chapter 1 of SSAE-10 is the umbrella standard. The primary purpose of Chapter 1 of SSAE-10 (AT 101) is to provide a basic framework for performing attest engagements and for the ongoing development of related standards. Underneath the umbrella standard are specific standards for certain subject matter and application of the standards to agreed-upon procedures engagements. The specific guidance follows the basic framework outlined in Chapter 1 of SSAE-10. However, important differences exist for certain types of engagements. Exhibit 1-1 illustrates some of these important differences.

Specific attestation standards have been developed in the chapters of SSAE-10 in the following areas:

- Chapter 2, "Agreed-Upon Procedures Engagements" (AT 201)—An agreed-upon procedures engagement is one in which a practitioner is engaged to issue a report of findings based on specific procedures agreed to by the users and the practitioner.
- Chapter 3, "Financial Forecasts and Projections" (AT 301)—A forecast presents an entity's expected financial position, results of operations, and cash flows based on the client's assumptions about conditions that are expected to exist and the course of action that it is expected to be taken. In contrast, a projection is based on one or more hypothetical assumptions and, in that sense, attempts to answer the question "What would happen if . . .?" Chapter 3 provides guidance for compilations, examinations, and agreed-upon procedures of prospective financial statements.
- Chapter 4, "Reporting on Pro Forma Financial Information" (AT 401)—The objective of pro forma financial information is to show what the significant effects on historical financial information might have been had a consummated or proposed transaction (or event) occurred at an earlier date. Chapter 4 provides guidance for the examination or review of pro forma financial information.
- Chapter 5, "Reporting on an Entity's Internal Control over Financial Reporting" (AT 501)—Chapter 5 provides guidance on engagements to examine the effectiveness of an entity's internal control over financial reporting, and it addresses examinations only. Engagements to provide limited assurance (review) on internal control are explicitly prohibited.
- Chapter 6, "Compliance Attestation" (AT 601)—The engagements covered in Chapter 6 include those related to either (1) examination of or agreed-upon procedures pertaining to an entity's compliance with requirements of specified laws, regulations, rules, contracts, or grants, or (2) agreed-upon procedures pertaining to only the effectiveness of an entity's internal control over compliance with specified requirements (an examination-level service on this subject would be covered by AT 101).
- Chapter 7, "Management's Discussion and Analysis" (AT 701)—Public companies are required by the SEC to include a Management's Discussion and Analysis (MD&A) in

their annual reports and other documents. Chapter 7 of the attestation standards applies to practitioners who are engaged to report on the MD&A prepared using the rules and regulations adopted by the SEC. Chapter 7 provides guidance on examinations and reviews of MD&A.

LEVELS OF ASSURANCE

Although the standards vary depending on the nature of the subject matter, in general, the attestation standards allow the CPA to provide four different levels of service:

1. *Examination* An examination is analogous to a financial statement audit. When engaged to perform an examination, the CPA expresses an opinion as to whether the subject matter or assertion about the subject matter is in conformity with given criteria. In other words, the CPA provides positive assurance in an examination.
2. *Review* A review is analogous to a review of historical financial statements. When engaged to perform a review, the CPA states a conclusion about whether any information came to his or her attention to indicate that the subject matter or assertion about the subject matter is not in conformity with given criteria. This conclusion is referred to as negative assurance.
3. *Agreed-Upon Procedures* In an agreed-upon procedures engagement, the CPA issues a report of findings based on specific procedures performed on the subject matter.
4. *Compilation of Prospective Information* A compilation is defined in Chapter 3 of SSAE-10 (AT 301.12) as a professional service that involves assembling the prospective financial statements based on the responsible party's assumptions, performing the required compilation procedures, and issuing a compilation report. Compilations of prospective financial statements is the only type of compilation covered by the attestation standards, and it was included when the already existing standard on forecasts and projections was absorbed into the attestation standards.

ASSURANCE SERVICES

The AICPA Special Committee on Assurance Services was created in 1994 to explore the expansion of audit-like services into new areas. This Committee defined "assurance services" as follows:

> Assurance services are independent professional services that improve the quality of information, or its context, for decision makers.

"Assurance services" is a broad concept that encompasses both audit and attest services. These services can involve financial or nonfinancial information. The information may be internal or external to the user, and might involve discrete data or entire systems.

Today's business environment is marked by increased competition and the need for quicker and better information for decisions. In addition, the complexity of systems and the anonymity of the Internet present barriers to growth. Businesses and their customers need independent assurance that the information that decisions are based on is reliable. By virtue of their training, experience, and reputation for integrity, CPAs are the logical choice to provide this assurance.

The AICPA's movement into developing additional assurance services began with the 1993 Audit/Assurance Conference. The conference had been concerned with the decline in the demand for audits and other attest services, and the users of assurance services had expressed dissatisfaction with their scope and utility. It analyzed why the audit and assurance function had come to this juncture and developed a broad plan for shaping the future of assurance to enhance its value.

The AICPA authorized the Special Committee on Assurance Services to investigate the issues and what could be done to reposition CPAs for the future. The Committee's report, *The Report of the Special Committee on Assurance Services,* was issued in 1997. The report called for the development of additional services to serve the needs of clients.

The Committee research identified a number of new service opportunities and the AICPA has actively developed the following assurance services:

- *SysTrust Services* As more organizations become dependent on information technology to run their businesses, produce products and services, and communicate with customers and business partners, it is critical that their systems be secure, available when needed, and consistently able to produce accurate information. An unreliable system can trigger a chain of business events that negatively affect a company and its customers, suppliers, and business partners. SysTrust responds to this business need by providing suitable criteria and a process that enables a CPA to provide assurance that a system is, in fact, reliable.
- *WebTrust Services* During a WebTrust engagement, the practitioner "audits" a company's online business practices to verify compliance matters such as privacy, security, availability, confidentiality, consumer redress for complaints, and business practices. WebTrust provides suitable criteria for practitioners as well as a licensing process that enables CPAs to provide assurance on Web sites.

- *ElderCare Services* The Committee defines ElderCare Services as a service designed to provide assurance to family members that care goals are achieved for elderly family members no longer able to be totally independent. The service relies on the expertise of other professionals, with the CPA serving as the coordinator and assurer of quality of services based on criteria and goals set by the client. The purpose of the service is to provide assurance in a professional, independent, and objective manner to third parties (children, family members, or other concerned parties) that the needs of the elderly person to whom they are attached are being met. ElderCare Services can involve three kinds of services: direct services, assurance services, and consulting services. Direct services entail the more traditional aspects of accounting and financial services. Assurance services involve the measuring and reporting on prescribed goals against stated criteria. Consulting services include planning and evaluation of client needs.
- *Performance View Services* This service enables CPAs to use the skills they have traditionally used to handle the financial portion of a client's business to address the nonfinancial aspects as well. This service identifies critical success factors that lead to measures that can be tracked over time. These measures are then used to assess progress in achieving specific targets linked to an entity's vision and performance.
- *Risk Advisory Services* The CPA profession has taken a leading role in the field of risk, and firms increasingly include risk management in the wide range of services they provide to their clients. Risk Advisory Services provide the CPA with:
  - — A common language and framework for understanding and communicating risk management issues.
  - — A series of practice guides describing tools, techniques, and training that support the risk management process.

OBSERVATION: Although SysTrust and WebTrust differ in minor respects such as structure and style, in substance they are very similar. (For instance, both services address the need for assurance about security and availability.) After assessing the objectives of SysTrust and WebTrust, the AICPA has concluded that the next step in the evolution of these standards is to harmonize the underlying Principles and Criteria where they share commonalities and to conform the presentation and wording of the standards. It is not the goal or intent of the AICPA to change the SysTrust or WebTrust services or to introduce additional branded services at this time.

The performance of these new services may or may not be subject to the attestation standards, depending on how an engagement is

EXHIBIT 1-1
COMPARISON OF ATTESTATION, ASSURANCE, AND CONSULTING SERVICES

	Attestation	Assurance	Consulting
Result:	Written conclusion about the reliability of the written assertions of another party	Better information for decision-makers; recommendations might be a by-product	Recommendations based on the objectives of the engagement
Objective:	Reliable information	Better decision making	Better outcomes
Parties to the engagement:	Not specified, but generally three (the third party is usually external); CPA generally paid by the preparer	Generally three (although the other two might be employed by the same entity); CPA paid by the preparer or user	Generally two; CPA paid by the user
Independence:	Required by standards	Included in definition	Not required
Substance of CPA output:	Conformity with established or stated criteria	Assurance about reliability or relevance of information; criteria might be established, stated, or unstated	Recommendations; not measured against formal criteria
Form of CPA output:	Written	Some form of communication	Written or oral
Critical information developed by:	Asserter	Either CPA or asserter	CPA
Information content determined by:	Preparer (client)	Preparer, CPA, or user	CPA
Level of assurance:	Examination, review, or agreed-upon procedures	Flexible, for example, it might be compilation level, explicit assurance about usefulness of the information for intended purpose, or implicit from the CPA's involvement	No explicit assurance

developed and performed. As discussed in Chapter 3, the attestation standards apply whenever a CPA is engaged to issue or does issue an examination, review, or agreed-upon procedures report on subject matter (or an assertion about the subject matter) that is the responsibility of another party. This definition is engagement-oriented and, therefore, the CPA must take care to define the nature of the services to be provided and whether they are intended to provide assurance.

ENGAGEMENTS INCLUDED IN THIS GUIDE

This guide is written specifically to address the most common types of attestation and other special engagements, including engagements covered by the Statements on Standards for Attestation Engagements.

Attestation Engagements

The SSAEs apply to all engagements in which a certified public accountant in the practice of public accounting is engaged to issue or does issue an examination, review, or agreed-upon procedures report on subject matter, or an assertion about the subject matter, that is the responsibility of another party. Specifically, the following attestation engagements are included in this guide:

- Examination engagements (Chapter 5)
- Review engagements (Chapter 6)
- Agreed-upon procedures engagements (Chapter 7)
- Compliance engagements (Chapter 9)
- Internal control engagements (Chapter 10)
- Pro forma financial information engagements (Chapter 11)
- Prospective financial statement engagements (Chapter 12)
- Management's discussion and analysis engagements (Chapter 13)

Other Special Engagements

In addition to attestation engagements, this guide includes the most common types of other nontraditional engagements:

- Audits of specified financial statement elements, accounts, or items (Chapter 8)

- Compilations of specified financial statement elements, accounts, or items (Chapter 8)
- Due diligence engagements (Chapter 11)

ENGAGEMENTS NOT COVERED BY THIS GUIDE

Other engagements that may be similar to attestation engagements, include audit engagements, compilation engagements, review engagements, and consulting engagements. These types of engagements are not covered by this guide.

Frequently, a practitioner will choose between performing an engagement under the attestation standards and another set of professional standards. The key factors to consider when deciding which type of engagement is most appropriate are the nature of the information presented and the primary beneficiaries of the service. Exhibit 1-2 summarizes these considerations for engagements performed under the attestation standards and those performed under other professional standards. (See also Exhibit 1-3.)

Audit Engagements

Audits of historical financial statements are conducted in accordance with Statements on Auditing Standards (SASs). In an audit, the practitioner performs tests of financial statement assertions to form an opinion on the financial statements taken as a whole. The objective of an audit is to provide a reasonable basis for expressing an opinion as to whether the financial statements are fairly presented in accordance with generally accepted accounting principles (or an other comprehensive basis of accounting).

Compilation and Review Engagements

Compilation and review engagements are performed in accordance with Statements on Standards for Accounting and Review Services (SSARSs). SSARSs apply to services on unaudited financial statements of nonpublic entities. The standards establish the two services that practitioners can apply to such financial statements—compilation and review. In a SSARS compilation, the practitioner presents in the form of financial statements information that is the representation of management, without undertaking to express any assurance on the financial statements. In a SSARS review, the practitioner performs inquiries and analytical procedures on the financial statement data to provide him or her with a reasonable basis for expressing limited assurance on the financial statements. The objective in a SSARS review is to provide a reasonable basis for stating that there are no material modifications that should be made to the financial statements in order for them to be in conformity with generally accepted accounting principles (or an other comprehensive basis of accounting).

When the practitioner submits unaudited financial statements of a nonpublic entity, he or she is required to either compile or review them in accordance with SSARS. The standards define "submission of financial statements" as presenting to a client or third parties financial statements that the practitioner has prepared either manually or through the use of computer software.

Fourteen SSARS have been issued to date:

- SSARS-1 (Compilation and Review of Financial Statements) (December 1978)—Replaced the former unaudited engagement standards contained in SAS-1. SSARS-1 provides guidance to CPAs concerning the standards and procedures applicable to engagements to compile or review financial statements. It does not establish standards or procedures for other services (e.g., tax return or bookkeeping services).
- SSARS-2 (Reporting on Comparative Financial Statements) (October 1979)—Applies to reports on any comparative financial statements that include current period compiled or reviewed financial statements of an entity that is nonpublic as of the current period. Otherwise SASs would apply.
- SSARS-3 (Compilation Reports on Financial Statements Included in Certain Prescribed Forms) (December 1981)—Amends SSARS-1 and SSARS-2 to provide for an alternative form of standard compilation report on prescribed forms that call for departures from GAAP. SSARS-3 applies to any standard preprinted form designed or adopted by the body to which it is submitted (e.g., a bank).
- SSARS-4 (Communications between Predecessor and Successor Accountants) (December 1981)—Provides guidance to a successor who decides to communicate with a predecessor. It does not require communication. It does require the predecessor to respond if authorized by the client.
- SSARS-5 (Reporting on Compiled Financial Statements) (July 1982) (Deleted November 1992 by the issuance of SSARS-7)—All of the former SSARS-5 requirements are now included in SSARS-1, SSARS-2, and SSARS-3.
- SSARS-6 (Reporting on Personal Financial Statements Included in Written Personal Financial Plans) (September 1986)—Provides an optional exemption from SSARS-1 if the accountant establishes an understanding with the client, preferably in writing, that the financial statements:
  - Will be used solely to assist the client and the client's advisors to develop the client's personal financial goals and objectives.

  - Will not be used to obtain credit or for any other purpose.
  - Nothing comes to the CPA's attention during the engagement that causes him or her to believe that the financial statements will be used to obtain credit or for other purposes.

- SSARS-7 (Omnibus Statement on Standards for Accounting and Review Services—1992) (November 1992)—Contains a number of technical amendments.
- SSARS-8 (Amendment to SSARS No. 1) (October 2000)—Amends SSARS-1 to create a management-use-only compilation and make other changes.
- SSARS-9 (Omnibus Statement on Standards for Accounting and Review Services—2002) (November 2002)—Contains a number of technical amendments.
- SSARS-10 (Performance of Review Engagements) (May 2004)—Amends SSARS-1 to modify the inquiry and analytical procedures in a review engagement.
- SSARS-11 (Standards for Compilation and Review Engagements) (May 2004)—Establishes a "SSARS hierarchy" and contains a technical amendment to SSARS-2.
- SSARS-12 (Omnibus Statement on Standards for Accounting and Review Services—2005) (June 2005)—Amends SSARS-1 by:
  - Requiring the accountant to establish an understanding with the client, preferably in writing, that the accountant will report to the appropriate level of management any evidence or information that comes to the accountant's attention during the performance of compilation or review procedures that fraud or an illegal act may have occurred. (However, the accountant need not report matters regarding illegal acts that are clearly inconsequential, and may reach agreement in advance with the entity on the nature of any such matters to be communicated.)
  - Providing guidance on when an accountant should obtain an updated representation letter from management.
  - Providing guidance to the accountant on restricting the use of reports issued pursuant to SSARS.

  SSARS-12 also amends SSARS-2 to enable a successor accountant to report on a restatement adjustment of prior-period financial statements and indicate that a predecessor accountant reported on the financial statements of the prior period before the restatement.
- SSARS-13 (Compilation of Specified Elements, Accounts, or Items of a Financial Statement) (June 2005)—Expands the applicability of SSARS to situations in which an accountant is

engaged to compile or issues a compilation report on one or more specified elements, accounts, or items of a financial statement.

- SSARS-14 (Compilation of Pro Forma Financial Information) (June 2005)—Expands the applicability of SSARS to situations in which an accountant is engaged to compile or issues a compilation report on pro forma financial information.

Consulting Engagements

Consulting engagements are performed in accordance with Statements on Standards for Consulting Services (SSCS). SSCSs apply to engagements in which the practitioner develops the findings, conclusions, and recommendations presented. The practitioner does not attest to someone else's assertion but is the one who develops the final presentation. In a consulting engagement, the practitioner's role is solely to assist the client, or engagements in which a practitioner is engaged to testify as an expert witness in accounting, auditing, taxation, or other matters, given certain stipulated facts.

Consulting services include consultations, advisory services, implementation services, transaction services, staff and other support services, and product services. They do not include any of the services described in SASs, SSARSs, or SSAEs.

EXHIBIT 1-2
KEY DIFFERENCES BETWEEN STANDARDS

	SSAEs	SASs & SSARSs	SSCSs
Nature of information reported on	Can accommodate historical, nonhistorical, financial, or nonfinancial.	Must be both historical and financial.	Can accommodate historical, nonhistorical, financial, or nonfinancial.
Beneficiary of service	Third parties benefit by receiving assurance about the reliability of information for decision making.	Third parties benefit by receiving assurance about the reliability of information for decision making.	The client is the primary beneficiary of all recommendations and advice.

EXHIBIT 1-3
COMPARISON OF REQUIREMENTS FOR ATTESTATION ENGAGEMENTS

Requirements	Exam.	Rev.	AUP	Fin. Fore & Proj.	Pro Forma Fin. Info.	I C	Comp.	MD&A
Conditions for engagement acceptance?	No	No	Yes	No	Yes	Yes	Yes	Yes
Written assertion required?	No[1]	No[2]	No	No	No	Yes, except AUP engage-ments	Yes	Yes
Examination-level service permitted?	Yes	N/A	N/A	Yes	Yes	Yes	Yes	Yes
Review-level service permitted?	N/A	Yes	N/A	No	Yes	No	No	Yes
Provides guidance on compilations?	No	No	No	Yes	No	No	No	No
Provides guidance on AUP?	No	No	Yes	Yes	No	No	Yes	No
Certain specified procedures required?	No	No	No	No	Yes	No	Yes	Yes
Written representation letter required?	Yes	Yes	No	Yes	Yes	Yes	Yes	Yes
Requirements for restricting use of report?	No	No	Yes	Yes	No	No	No	No

[1] If the client is the responsible party, not obtaining a written assertion will result in a qualified opinion, disclaimer of opinion, or withdrawal from the engagement.

[2] If the client is the responsible party, not obtaining a written assertion will result in withdrawal from the engagement.

CHAPTER 2
MARKETING SPECIAL ENGAGEMENTS

CONTENTS

OVERVIEW

This chapter provides an overview of marketing of attestation and other special engagements. The methods of identifying potential clients are discussed, along with methods for marketing and selling nontraditional services to these clients.

IDENTIFYING POTENTIAL CLIENTS

One of the biggest problems CPA firms face in marketing is that they wait for their clients to approach them about additional service needs rather than seeking out their clients' needs proactively. This is unfortunate because there are more ways a CPA can help his or her clients than ever before. There are reasons why the wait-and-see approach to being more profitable does not work:

- Clients do not walk around thinking about their CPAs. So, when a problem arises, the CPA is not foremost in their mind as the one to solve it, and they look elsewhere.
- Often clients do not know what other services their CPA could provide, because their CPA has not told them or they forgot. So, they buy services somewhere else—from a competitor or outside consultant.
- Clients do not take the time to sit down and evaluate how they can be more profitable or effective.

In the end, practitioners succeed by satisfying current clients and acquiring new ones. The key to this success is a constant focus on the client, through innovation and marketing. Innovation is helping clients solve their problems through the application of nontraditional services. Successful marketing necessitates understanding client concerns and goals and adapting services to help them meet their needs.

AICPA research indicates that the most common source of additional services is direct, unsolicited requests from existing clients. Practitioners can, however, actively market additional services, often more profitably than traditional accounting, auditing, or tax services. AICPA research also shows that many clients would welcome more input from their CPAs. But practitioners need to take the initiative to learn what their clients need—and then inform the clients about the services they can provide to meet those needs.

The AICPA has used focus groups to elicit clients' opinions of what they value in their adviser. The participants in the focus groups were clients of small to midsize CPA firms that purchased nontraditional services from their CPAs. The information obtained from the focus groups indicated that three factors influence clients to obtain additional services:

1. *Client interaction.* Clients put a premium on responsiveness and dependability. This means the CPA
   — Is easily accessible.
   — Follows through; does what it takes to get the job done and does what he or she says will be done.
   — Offers innovative, creative solutions. CPAs have to overcome the perceived stereotype as bean counters whose job is to say no to everything. Clients want CPAs to figure out how to help them achieve their goals, not tell them what cannot be done.
2. *Knowledge and skills.* Clients expect CPAs to have technical accounting and auditing or tax skills. What they look for when seeking nontraditional services is
   — Extensive knowledge of the company and the industry, as well as of the client's own goals and operating philosophies.
   — A CPA with a broad perspective who can answer their questions or link them to an excellent referral network.
   — Wisdom gleaned from work with many different organizations in a variety of situations. They want suggestions for improvement and information about how other organizations have solved similar problems.
3. *Personal characteristics.* Some personalities seem better suited to nontraditional services. The typical CPA is a master technician who seeks perfection in his or her work. The CPA who provides nontraditional service has to be comfortable in uncharted territory where there are often no standards, rules or right answers.

Practitioners can market new services to existing clients or they can attempt to identify new clients. However, it is far more efficient to target existing clients. In fact, research shows that the top business producers in the accounting profession generate approximately 25% to 40% of their new, incremental business from the sales of additional services to their existing clients. The major difference between selling services to new clients and selling to existing satisfied clients is that selling to satisfied clients is much easier.

Exhibit 2-1, based on an AICPA committee study on assurance services, provides suggestions for identifying opportunities with existing clients.

Existing, satisfied clients have already made the decision to do business with the CPA—and that is the hardest hurdle to overcome in any sale. The CPA already has a trusting relationship with his or her clients, who are also prospective buyers of services. In addition,

EXHIBIT 2-1
IDENTIFYING OPPORTUNITIES WITH EXISTING CLIENTS

1. Build opportunities for enhanced services into checklists used in standard accounting, auditing and tax services. Appendix 2A is a sample checklist.
2. Consider offering a small service (such as review of a tax return the client prepares) gratis to demonstrate genuine interest and to build the relationship.
3. Monitor the effectiveness of relationships with quality assurance interviews conducted by someone outside the firm or by a senior-level person not involved with the client. Meet periodically with clients to discuss the relationship and identify unmet needs.
4. Encourage partners and staff to spend time at the client's office to gain a better understanding of the business. It is ironic that many firms' billing routines work against this, discouraging a gesture that clients value highly.
5. Respond quickly to relationship problems when they surface. Be willing to change a partner assignment if necessary. Many firms' cultures are not readily amenable to such changes.
6. Communicate to all employees, from receptionists to senior partners, that they have a responsibility to market the firm's services. Train them to be aware of the spectrum of services the firm offers.
7. Develop a system for capturing and following up opportunities identified during audits and tax season.
8. Help firm members develop and practice people skills, such as interviewing, coaching, presenting, and selling. Ask partners who are experienced and comfortable in these areas to provide mentoring.
9. Invite current and prospective clients to an open house or an industry-specific seminar to introduce the firm's key players and services.
10. Conduct client research on how to improve current services and generate ideas for new ones.

[Source: "What Do Clients Want," by Don M. Pallais and Ellen L. Good, *Journal of Accountancy*, December 1996.]

the CPA has access to information about existing clients that a salesperson would value highly, information that includes whether the client can afford to purchase additional services, who the decision-makers are, and how they usually make decisions.

Typical Characteristics of Potential Clients

Clients with specific immediate needs are the most likely buyers of nontraditional services. For example, a client that recently discovered inventory theft may want a review of its internal control; a client that is considering an acquisition may want an analysis of the potential target's financial condition. When there are no apparent existing client needs, however, there may be opportunities to provide nontraditional services to existing clients.

The most likely buyers of nontraditional services tend to have the following characteristics:

- The company is profitable and wants to grow. The clients' top management values what the CPA has to offer. This is not the client who wants everything done as quickly as possible and then complains about the bill.
- The client is open-minded. The company leaders are not only willing to try new things but they are also always looking for new ideas.
- They ask questions and they know that the CPA needs information to be helpful; thus, the CPA is allowed access to key decision makers and information.
- The company leaders are honest, fair, upbeat, and innovative. They are probably people the CPA would enjoy working with more closely because there is already a good chemistry.

Client Perception of CPA

Clients who receive more than traditional accounting, auditing, and tax work tend to see their CPAs as trusted business advisers. The AICPA focus groups showed that clients relate to people, not firms. When participants discussed their relationships with the CPA firms, they invariably spoke in terms of specific individuals in those firms—generally the partner on the engagement. This suggests, of course, that excessive or unexplained staff changes can have a detrimental effect on the client relationship.

An important component of the relationship is chemistry. Relationships with the right chemistry usually involve a partner who takes a genuine interest in the client and his or her business. Both the client and the CPA are comfortable enough with each other to allow for a free exchange of information and ideas. It is when this special chemistry between partner and client is missing that staff changes should be made—until the relationship works for everyone.

Conversely, the AICPA focus groups showed that clients respond negatively to CPAs who

- Do not take the time to understand the client and the business other than in a narrow way.
- Are sloppy about details and do not think situations through.

- Are unenthusiastic, with a tendency to dismiss ideas before hearing them out.
- Do not follow through on commitments.
- Offer only textbook or packaged solutions, without much creativity or customization.

IDENTIFYING CLIENT SERVICES

Clients generally want relevant and reliable information in order to make decisions and accomplish goals. Therefore, it is critical to understand both the client's goals and the obstacles that keep the client from accomplishing them.

Identifying Client Needs

Client needs drive the opportunity to provide any professional service, including nontraditional services. In order to successfully expand nontraditional services, practitioners must be proficient at uncovering client needs.

The AICPA's nonauthoritative publication *Attestation Services: How to Perform Successful Agreed-Upon Procedures and Other Attestation Engagements* provides the following suggestions for identifying client needs.

Client needs drive the opportunity to provide any professional service, including attestation engagements. In order to successfully expand attestation services, practitioners must be proficient at uncovering client needs.

Listen, Don't Talk

Identifying client needs is an exercise in listening. The objective of initial contact with a client is to gather as much information as possible. In order to succeed in this pursuit, the practitioner should ask questions rather than give answers. Tips for this include the following:

- Ask open-ended questions, which extend rather than restrict conversation.
- Listen to the prospective client just to learn about the organization.
- Avoid the temptation to become a talker, even when a problem is uncovered in which the practitioner has expertise.

Ask "What," not "Why"

Questions that ask "why" tend to put people on the defensive and seem to demand an explanation. These questions can cause frustration or anxiety in the person being asked the question. "What" questions, in contrast, encourage introspection and more free-flowing thoughts. Examples of "why" versus "what" questions are as follows:

Why (Worse)	What (Better)
Why do you feel that way? Why did you make that decision?	What led to your feeling that way? What were the factors in your decision?

Focus on Outcomes, not Problems

Most people have a tendency to focus on solving problems rather than on defining desired outcomes. The difference may seem small, but the distinction is powerful, as the following table indicates:

Problems (Worse)	Outcomes (Better)
Can you describe the problem?	What are you trying to accomplish?
What is causing the low morale?	What result do you want to achieve by increasing morale?
What complaints are you hearing that you want to address?	What do you want your customers to notice or not notice about your service?

In general, clients are far more interested in achieving desired outcomes than in merely solving a problem. When a practitioner asks outcome-oriented questions, clients become more excited and focused on possibilities. Problem-oriented questions are useful at times, but they often only amplify what is wrong. Uncovering a client's desired outcomes enables the practitioner to diagnose what is preventing the optimum results and enables him or her to gain insights about what the client wants to achieve.

Understand the History of the Situation

Questions aimed at uncovering the history of a situation can help a practitioner gain a better understanding of an organization, avoid suggestions that have already been tried, and contribute to generating new ideas. Sample questions include the following:

- What alternative forms of reporting (e.g., agreed-upon procedures) have you tried in the past?

- What has been the reaction of bankers or other third parties when you've suggested reports other than traditional financial statement audits?

Ask Value-Based Questions

Value-based questions help to uncover what is really important to the client. Often, clients need help prioritizing and focusing on their main issues and concerns. Value-based questions help a client zero in on a point or issue. They are especially helpful for clients who ramble or who are overwhelmed by their situation or task. Examples of value-based questions are as follows:

- What is important to you about . . . ?
- What concerns you about . . . ?
- If you had to name one (priority, outcome, objective, concern), what would it be?

Identifying Obstacles to Client Goals

One of the best ways of identifying client needs is to understand the client's concerns and the obstacles to meeting their goals. The following are common client concerns:

- Regulation
  - — Tax planning and compliance
  - — Compliance with industry regulations
  - — Legal risks (e.g., product liability, employee, and environmental concerns)
  - — Impact of future legislation
- Access to capital
  - — Planning for future needs
  - — Cost of capital
- Marketplace
  - — Customer retention
  - — Market expansion
  - — Competitive challenges
  - — Product advantages
  - — Industry change and innovation
  - — Profitability analysis
  - — Marketing effectiveness
  - — Client satisfaction

- Internal processes
  - — Efficiency
  - — Reliability
  - — Employee satisfaction
  - — Employee recruitment and retention
  - — Succession planning
- Supplier relationships
  - — Raw material quality
  - — Dependability

Identifying Service Benefits

Many times, the value of nontraditional services is not obvious to the client. Therefore, it is important to demonstrate in a tangible way the benefits of the potential services. In describing the potential benefits, the CPA should focus on the client's needs. The benefits should be described in simple, direct terms, relating directly to the client's concerns. Most clients are not as familiar with nontraditional engagements as they are with audits, reviews, and compilations. Therefore, the client may have trouble conceptualizing the service, its results, or how it can help meet his or her needs. The client's understanding may be helped by presenting him or her with a prototype. For example, for an agreed-upon procedures engagement, it might be helpful to walk the client through a hypothetical engagement.

Pricing

To overcome a client's initial resistance to a new service, the CPA might offer to perform the initial service for free or according to a different pricing method. The following are common pricing methods other than standard hourly rates:

- *Value pricing* With value pricing, the charge is based on the value of the services to the client rather than on how much it costs the CPA to provide them. The charge for many engagements should be based on what the client thinks they are worth instead of the actual time spent doing the work. Keep in mind a simple truth: Most clients value CPA services higher than the CPA does. Value pricing is particularly appropriate for value-added services or when monetary savings or the extra revenues produced for clients are visible to them and measurable. If the value of the services is above standard, the CPA should charge above-standard rates. Clients will accept value pricing if it is discussed with them before performing the services.

- *Results pricing* Results pricing is the practice of agreeing with the client in advance to charge based on the results obtained, regardless of the amount of the CPA's time that is involved. It is not a gratuity to add on for extra special service after an engagement has been completed.
- *Fixed-price agreements* Fixed-price agreements transfer the risk of cost overruns from the client to the CPA. In return for assuming such risk, the CPA can charge a premium to the client. Given a choice, many clients prefer to pay more in return for having a ceiling on their price. Fixed-price agreements communicate competence, confidence, and experience on the CPA's part. However, when using them, be careful of scope creep, a phenomenon in which a project expands beyond its original conception because the client keeps asking for additional services and the accountant provides them because he or she has not set clear boundaries on the engagement.

DETERMINING WHICH TYPE OF ENGAGEMENT TO PERFORM

The client's needs ultimately determine the type of engagement that the CPA will perform. A preliminary discussion with the client is beneficial and is necessary for the CPA to become familiar with the client's needs and the services that are required. The discussion should include consideration of the following:

1. Does the client need assurance? Is an examination or review essential for the intended use? Does the client understand the differing scopes, levels of assurance, and cost of the different engagements?
2. What is the expected use of the report? Is the report needed to meet the requirements of a third party, such as a government agency, or to meet contractual requirements?
3. Does the client want only advice and recommendations? If an examination or review is not needed, will a consulting engagement meet the client's needs?
4. When is the report needed? Does the reporting date allow sufficient time to perform the necessary engagement?

Professional standards do not provide guidance on choosing the best type of engagement to perform. However, based on the client's needs, the following issues should be considered:

- *Historical financial statements* Audit and review engagements are used to provide assurance to users about the reliability of historical financial statements. If the information is

EXHIBIT 2-2
DETERMINING WHICH TYPE OF ENGAGEMENT TO PERFORM

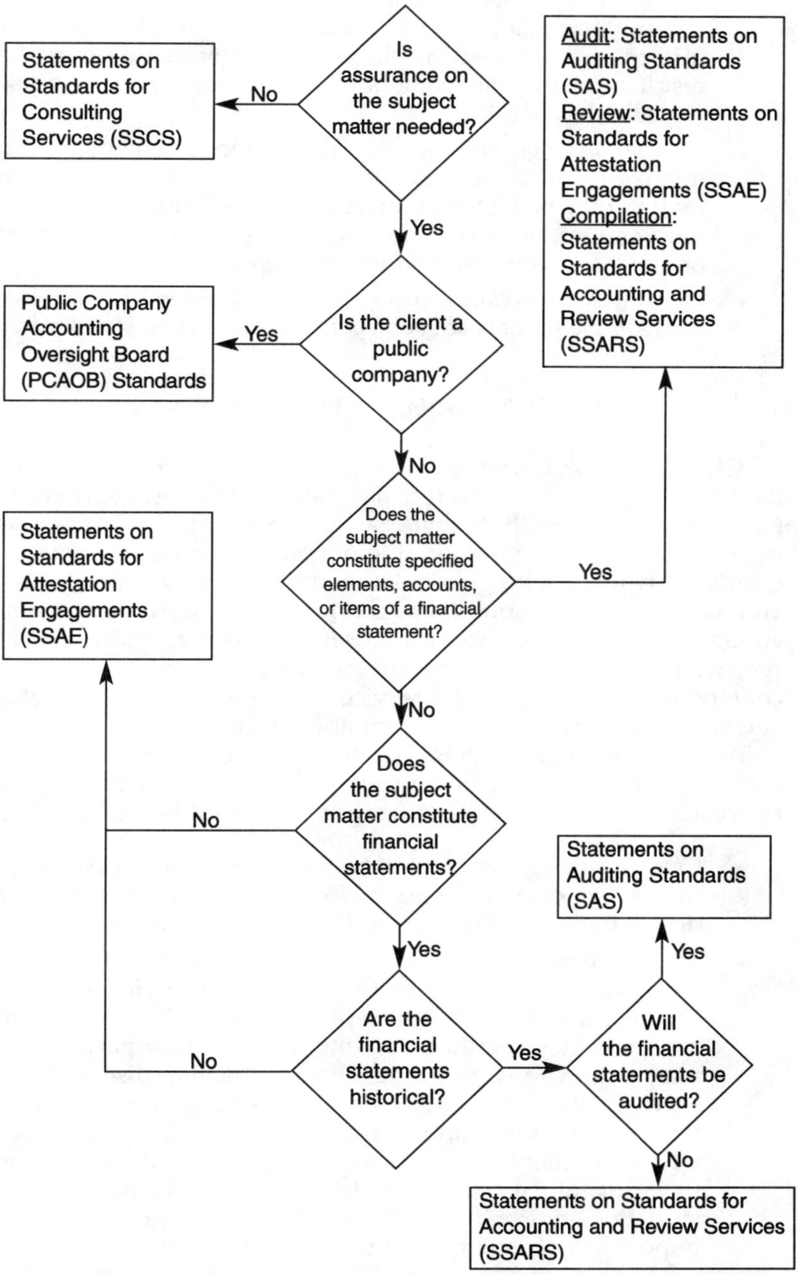

pro forma, prospective, or nonfinancial in nature, the SASs and SSARSs do not apply.

- *Consulting engagements* A consulting engagement may involve financial or nonfinancial information, and this information may be historical or prospective. However, in a consulting engagement, no assurance is provided on the information. Instead, findings and recommendations that result from the engagement are communicated to the user (usually the client).
- *Attestation engagements* An attestation engagement may involve financial or nonfinancial information and this information may be historical or prospective. Unlike a consulting engagement, however, the objective is to provide assurance on the information in the form of a report.
- *Agreed-upon procedures engagements* All agreed-upon procedures engagements are subject to the attestation standards.

MARKETING SPECIAL ENGAGEMENTS

As CPA firms look for new ways to grow their practice and ensure their ongoing success, marketing has become an increasingly critical part of their business. But what exactly is marketing? What marketing means for CPA firms is finding out what existing and potential clients really need, letting them know the firm has what they need, and, ultimately, delivering those services to them. Accountants are adept at selling compliance-related services such as audits and tax preparation; however, because the prospective client must first be convinced that nontraditional services are beneficial, the marketing and selling of these services present unique challenges.

The first step in persuading a prospective client is recognizing the challenges inherent in selling a professional service. The following approach is used by many CPA firms to market additional services:

- *Create a missing services checklist* Build a menu of services the firm offers or could render. Use this as a diagnostic tool to determine what services the client is and is not buying.
- *Target a client to market to* Select a client the firm has a good working relationship with. On the missing services checklist, list the services that client now buys from the firm and the products they should be buying. Enroll senior partners and managers who work on the client in helping discover what services the firm could be providing a specific client. Personnel on the front line may have some great ideas about where the client's weaknesses lie (e.g., internal control, cash flow, inventory control, strategic plans, and financial services). Engaging staff in this kind of initiative teaches them the importance of selling additional services to clients.

- *Set an appointment* Contact the client. Ask the client about the specific areas on the missing services checklist. Are they pleased with their internal controls? Do they suspect theft? Why? How about their cash flow? Let the client do most of the talking. Limit the conversation to one or two specific services; do not overwhelm them.

Instead of merely asking "How's business?" or "Is there anything we can be doing for you?," being specific about what to address with the client creates an environment for them to think in a direct manner. If the client does perceive a problem or thinks something could be improved, jump on the opportunity immediately, before they forget about the conversation. Explain to the client how the firm can help tighten up their internal controls, inventory control—or solve the problem, whatever it is—and what it would cost. Set the appointment to start the work now.

Key Elements of a Marketing Plan

Even if the CPA firm does not have a formal marketing plan in place, chances are the firm is involved in some form of marketing that communicates a message to clients. For example, even something as ordinary as business cards and letterhead conveys messages about the firm.

Although there are many different approaches to marketing, every successful marketing approach addresses four basic essentials: Product, audience, awareness, and delivery. To determine the best marketing strategy for the firm, start with a detailed self-evaluation:

- What are the firm's strengths?
- What are the firm's weaknesses?
- How do clients perceive the firm?
- How does the competition perceive the firm?
- How does the firm perceive its competition?

As these questions are contemplated, also think about the future and the goals the firm wants to set. What does the firm want to accomplish in the next six months? Twelve months? Five years?

Next, consider the four essentials:

1. *Product* What services does the firm offer? How are they different from the competitors? How are they better?
2. *Audience* Who is the target audience? How can the firm reach them?
3. *Awareness* What do people think of the firm's services? How can the firm increase their awareness?

4. *Delivery* How are the firm's services delivered? How responsive is the firm to clients?

Once the firm has considered where it is and where it wants to go, the marketing plan should be put in writing. Putting the ideas in writing allows the organization of thoughts into precisely formulated strategies. A written plan provides the firm with a means for measuring progress along the way and for making adjustments as they become necessary.

Identify Core Products, Services, and Target Audience

In developing a marketing plan, it is important to clearly define the core services the firm wants to market—and the target audience. Identifying a particular market and offering that market a specialized service is the definition of niche marketing. Whether it is the restaurant industry or the health-care profession, offering a service that fills a particular need for a particular audience allows the firm to open up a new potential market, with ready-made prospects.

The key to success is to avoid a one-size-fits-all marketing strategy and to target specific markets with particular services. A market can be segregated according to any set of criteria, whether it is income level, demographics, industry, specialization, or even specific hobbies. The more CPAs know about their audience, the more they can target their marketing efforts.

Create Awareness

A successful awareness effort requires planning, imagination, and persistence. The following are three things to keep in mind:

1. *Focus efforts* Concentrate on reaching that share of the audience most likely to respond positively to the firm's efforts.
2. *Choose media imaginatively* Do not limit efforts to just one strategy or one medium. Do not be afraid to be unconventional.
3. *Consistency and persistence count* The CPA's audience is already being bombarded with messages from other companies. The most important facet of the message should be emphasized and repeated over and over again. Do not expect an immediate response from the first effort. Rather, realize that name recognition and image are established over time through repetition and consistency.

Effective Advertising

It is important to make sure that the advertising reaches the target audience. And again, consistency and repetition are important. Studies show that for a message to be communicated via an ad, whether in print, on radio, or on television, it generally takes seven times for it to register with the general consumer audience.

Here are some tips to make sure print advertising captures readers' attention:

- *Limit the amount of text* Especially in today's fast-paced society, people tend to skim through reading materials, so the message should be simple and direct. If an ad is filled with too much text, readers will just move on to something less overwhelming.
- *Make the ad stand out* Bold lines, color, layout, or font should be used in a distinctive way to draw attention. Look at other ads as a source of ideas for features to use in your ad.
- *Choose images carefully* Often a graphic, illustration, or photograph does not reproduce well.

If you have no experience in advertising, working with professionals such as advertising agencies or art directors can result in a better ad.

Direct Mail

One commonly used marketing method is direct mail. If done properly, direct mail can be one of the most efficient, cost-effective forms of marketing. For a direct mail piece to be successful, it must look professional, be easy to respond to, and the mailing list must be accurate and up-to-date. Direct marketing pieces should include a clear call to action. Mailers should not be sent simply to educate people about the firm's services—the recipients should be asked to do something; it can be as easy as completing a reply card to get more information about the firm.

Online Marketing

Online marketing involves the use of the Internet to deliver marketing messages to the target audience. Compared to traditional offline marketing, online marketing is very different and at the same time, very much the same. The tools traditionally used by CPAs are print advertising, direct mail solicitations, newsletters, and free seminars.

The new tools that are available to the online marketer are different, including

- Web sites
- E-mail
- Hotlinks

Many classic marketing principles apply no matter what medium or marketing tool is being employed; for instance

- The marketing message must reach the appropriate target.
- The marketing message must be clear, easy to understand, and relevant to the target audience.
- The tone and manner of the message and the entire marketing communication piece must be appropriate to the nature of the marketer, the target audience, and the subject at hand.

Integrating Online and Offline Marketing

An essential truth of marketing any type of product or service is that to be effective, the imagery and messages contained with all pieces need to be consistent and integrated. This consistency applies to online marketing as well.

E-Mail Tips

E-mail can be an effective, powerful, and highly affordable marketing tool. The benefits include

- No cost for postage.
- The elimination of printing and paper costs.
- A significant reduction in the time needed to create and launch a campaign.
- A process for communicating frequently.
- A method for reaching the intended recipient rather than an assistant who serves as a gatekeeper.
- A system for getting messages to recipients the same day they are sent.
- A method that allows recipients to respond quickly and easily.
- A mechanism for encouraging recipients to visit the firm's Web site by clicking on a link included in the e-mail message.

The ease and simplicity of creating and sending e-mail messages allows CPA firms to engage in direct marketing and formalized client communications more frequently than with traditional marketing methods. Whenever a firm has new and important information for its clients, regarding tax law changes, the firm's services, or on some other topic, e-mail offers an opportunity to communicate that information in an efficient, professional manner.

Seminars and Speeches

In addition to advertising, mailings and other promotions, client seminars, and presenting speeches to groups are effective ways to market nontraditional services. The key is to make sure that the topic is relevant to the audience and the services the firm can provide. Ideally, speaking engagements should be before groups that best represent the target audience. When making any kind of presentation, the CPA should be as dynamic as possible. In addition, the CPA should be available after the presentation to answer questions individually. Leaving immediately after making a speech is to miss opportunities for making new client contacts.

Handouts should be available at presentations for attendees to take with them. The handouts can include a summary of the remarks, information about the firm, biographies of presenters and firm partners, and brochures imprinted with the firm's name. Handouts provide a way to communicate the firm's strengths and qualifications—and provide the audience with a means to contact the firm after the presentation.

SELLING STRATEGIES

There is no such thing as a natural born salesperson. Successful selling is a constant learning experience. Before trying to sell anything, the salesperson must identify the target audience and the services to be sold. Once these two matters are determined, a unique selling proposition needs to be developed. Precisely defined, developing a selling proposal entails knowing what unique characteristics about the firm's core business services will most appeal to clients and prospective clients. In developing the unique selling proposition it is important to include the "CPA difference"—or what sets the CPA apart from other accountants and business advisors. CPAs have met stringent education and experience requirements, their work must be performed in accordance with high-quality technical and professional standards, and they must adhere to a strict code of professional ethics.

Existing Client Base

The easiest place to increase the potential client base and sales is an area that's overlooked the most—the firm's existing client base.

The CPA already has credibility with those clients; that credibility can be used to build new business. This can be done as follows:

- *Take an inventory of clients* What does the firm do for each client? What other needs does each client have that are not being met? Do any of the firm's services meet those needs? What additional assistance can be provided to each client given the firm's level of knowledge about them?
- *Ask questions and listen* Ask clients open-ended questions—questions that require more than a simple yes or no answer. This allows the CPA to learn about their goals, needs, and challenges.
- *Follow up* Follow up with clients about how the firm can help with their needs and assist them in meeting their goals. Following up is the key element in sales and customer service.

APPENDIX 2A
NEW SERVICE OPPORTUNITY CHECKLIST

The American Institute of CPAs Special Committee on Assurance Services developed the following set of questions for use in identifying new service opportunities. Clients make decisions based on information. The information might be financial or nonfinancial, relate to data or systems, or come from internal or external sources. Often the information clients actually use is not directly relevant to their problems or reliable, but they use it because better information has not been developed or because they have not linked their decision needs with the range of available information. Assisting clients in identifying information needs and then finding or developing the information can be a high-value service.

The following questions should be asked during a typical client service engagement. Depending on the relationship with the client, the CPA might ask these questions during a formal meeting or informal lunch with the controller, chief financial officer, chief executive officer, or other executive. In any case, notes should be taken in order to communicate to the client the importance of the discussion and to assist in follow-up discussions and, later, documentation of the CPA's suggestions:

- What important business decisions keep you awake at night?
- For each type of decision, what kind of information is most helpful to you in making the decision?
- Who provides it?
- Is it adequate or do you feel you're flying blind? How do you know whether the information is accurate?
- Is the information useful in the format you get it in?
- What other information would be helpful that you can't or don't get?

- Is the information you need about operations readily, regularly, and quickly available?
- Is it adequate to
  — Compare with prior periods?
  — Measure against goals and benchmarks?
  — Compare with competitors?
- Do you need information from outsiders, such as customers or suppliers?
- Can you easily obtain the information?
- Is it reliable?
- What information do you need about
  — Relationships (for example, suppliers, customers, partners, labor)?
  — Outputs (for example, product quality, customer satisfaction)?
  — Markets (for example, competitors, market share, customer preferences, technologies)?
- How do you obtain it?
- What would make the information more useful or valuable to you?

APPENDIX 2B
POTENTIAL ENGAGEMENTS

Client needs drive the opportunity for any professional service, including nontraditional engagements. In order to successfully expand nontraditional services, practitioners must be proficient at uncovering client needs. Clients generally want relevant and reliable information to make decisions and accomplish goals. Exhibit 2-3 lists the most common types of nontraditional engagements performed by pracitioners and a cross reference to the chapter in this guide where the engagement is discussed.

EXHIBIT 2-3
COMMON TYPES OF NONTRADITIONAL ENGAGEMENTS

Engagement	**Chapter in *Attestation and Other Special Engagements***
Cash forecasts for cash management purposes	13
Cash flow projections for loan proposals	13
Assurance on nonfinancial performance metrics	6 & 7

Engagement	Chapter in ***Attestation and Other Special Engagements***
Assurance on compliance with laws or regulations	10
Assistance in compiling a schedule of specific financial statement items (e.g., accounts receivable, inventory, property, plant, and equipment, cost of goods sold, operating expenses, etc.)	8
Assurance on a schedule of specific financial statement items (e.g., accounts receivable, inventory, property, plant, and equipment, cost of goods sold, operating expenses, etc.)	8
Assurance on effectiveness of internal control	11
Specific procedures applied to verify financial statement items (e.g., accounts receivable or cost of goods sold)	9
Specific procedures applied to verify lease calculations	9
Assurance on calculations for lease payments	8
Assurance on calculations for royalty payments	8
Assurance on calculations for profit participation	8
Assurance on federal and state income tax provisions included in financial statements	8
Assurance on operating or customer service measures to aid in client marketing	6 & 7
Local government business license fee compliance	6, 7 & 10
Ballot counting or contest result assurance	6 & 7
Specific procedures to inspect documents for evidence of certain types of transactions or characteristics (e.g., inspect shipment dates for a sample of shipping documents to determine whether any such dates were subsequent to year-end)	9
Specific procedures to confirm information with third parties	9
Specific procedures to compare documents, schedules, or analyses with certain specified attributes (e.g., compare the amounts of invoices included in each column of an accounts receivable aging to the amount and invoice date shown on the outstanding invoice)	9
Specific procedures to perform mathematical computations (e.g., calculate specified debt covenant ratios and verify that the resulting ratios agree with those reported in a specified schedule)	9

Engagement	**Chapter in *Attestation and Other Special Engagements***
Specific procedures to trace all outstanding checks appearing on a bank reconciliation as of a certain date to checks that cleared the bank statement of the subsequent month	9
Specific procedures to calculate the number of miles of streets paved shown on a contractor's certificate of completion	9
Specific procedures to calculate the rate of return on a specified investment	9
Specific procedures to assist management in connection with the acquisition of another company	9
Recommendations on improvements to a client's system of internal control	11
Assist management in compiling pro forma financial information to show the effects of a proposed transaction (e.g., business combination, change in capitalization, or change in the form of business organization)	12
Assurance on pro forma financial information to show the effects of a proposed transaction (e.g., business combination, change in capitalization, or change in the form of business organization)	12
Assistance with investigation and analysis of an acquisition target	12
Assist management with preparation of budget information	13

APPENDIX 2C
TEN PHRASES FOR POSITIVE CLIENT COMMUNICATION

Words can be very powerful. The right words can immediately put a client at ease. The wrong ones can raise their defenses and their stress level just as quickly. The following 10 phrases facilitate effective communication with clients:

1. How may I help?
2. I can solve that problem.
3. I will take responsibility.
4. I don't know the answer, but I'll find out.
5. There will be no unpleasant surprises.

6. I will keep you updated.
7. I will deliver it on time.
8. It will be just what you requested.
9. The job will be complete.
10. I appreciate your business.

APPENDIX 2D
TEN SUGGESTED USES FOR BROCHURES

Brochures produced by CPA marketing firms can increase a firm's visibility in the client community. Brochures can be mailed to potential and existing clients, used as handouts when giving speeches, and displayed in a firm's office reception area. Here are 10 specific suggestions on how to use brochures to assist in marketing nontraditional services:

1. Give some brochures, with a business card attached, to clients and vendors who are likely to make referrals, and ask them to pass them on to individuals or business owners they know who may need a CPA.
2. Send copies of brochures to the media along with a letter describing the topics that the firm could provide information on.
3. Send brochures to clients after tax season with a letter describing additional non-tax services that the firm offers.
4. Distribute brochures to participants at seminars or meetings that a member of the firm speaks at.
5. Send brochures to bankers and attorneys the firm is acquainted with along with a cover letter highlighting key services.
6. Give brochures to other individuals who are potential referral sources for the firm.
7. Use brochures as part of a direct-mail campaign to prospective clients.
8. Provide copies of brochures to members and/or leaders of organizations that members of the firm volunteer for.
9. Leave brochures in the reception area of the firm's office.
10. Use brochures as a handout when making career presentations before high school and college students.

CHAPTER 3
PROFESSIONAL STANDARDS FOR THE CPA AND THE FIRM

CONTENTS

OVERVIEW

This chapter discusses the background and professional standards that provide specific guidance for the individual CPA and the CPA firm in the performance of attestation engagements.

Some of the standards that CPAs follow in performing attestation engagements were specifically established to provide guidance in such engagements; others are general in nature. The standards discussed here include the AICPA Code of Professional Conduct, Statements on Standards for Attestation Engagements (SSAEs), SSAE Interpretations, and Statements on Quality Control Standards (SCQSs); SSARSs and SASs are also discussed.

THE AICPA CODE OF PROFESSIONAL CONDUCT

The AICPA Code of Professional Conduct (the Code) provides guidance for the CPA to conduct his or her professional practice. A CPA must observe all of the rules and interpretations in the Code. The Code consists of two sections: (1) the Principles and (2) the Rules. The Principles provide the framework for the Rules, which govern the performance of professional services by CPAs. The Council of the AICPA is authorized to designate bodies to promulgate technical standards under the Rules.

The Code was adopted by the membership of the AICPA to provide guidance and rules to all members—in public practice, in industry, in government, and in education—in the performance of their professional responsibilities.

Compliance with the Code of Professional Conduct, as with all standards in an open society, depends primarily on members' understanding and voluntary actions, secondarily on reinforcement by peers and public opinion, and ultimately on disciplinary proceedings, when necessary, against members who fail to comply with the Rules. The Code applies to all service performed by a practitioner while holding out as a CPA. According to the Code, a practitioner holds out as a CPA if he or she informs others of his or her status as a CPA or AICPA-accredited specialist. This includes, for example

- Oral or written representation to another regarding CPA status.
- Use of CPA designation on business cards or letterhead.
- The display of a certificate evidencing the CPA designation.
- Listing as a CPA in local telephone directories.

The Code also applies to other people in the practitioner's firm. An Ethics Interpretation states:

> A member may be held responsible for compliance with the rules by all persons associated with him or her in the practice of public accounting whom the member has the authority or capacity to control.
>
> A member shall not permit others to carry out on his or her behalf, either with or without compensation, acts which, if carried out by the member, would place the member in violation of the rules.

FORM AND CONTENT

The Code of Professional Conduct consists of four parts: (1) principles, (2) rules, (3) interpretations, and (4) rulings. Principles of professional conduct provide the framework for the Code's specific rules. Rules of conduct govern the performance of professional services. The AICPA Council establishes the rules and can designate bodies to establish technical standards under the rules. The rules consist of the following:

- Rule 101: Independence
- Rule 102: Integrity and Objectivity
- Rule 201: General Standards
- Rule 202: Compliance with Standards
- Rule 203: Accounting Principles
- Rule 301: Confidential Client Information
- Rule 302: Contingent Fees

- Rule 501: Acts Discreditable
- Rule 502: Advertising and Other Forms of Solicitation
- Rule 503: Commissions and Referral Fees
- Rule 505: Form of Organization and Name

Rule 201: General Standards

Rule 201 of the Code is concerned with general standards, including guidance on organizational structure, that the CPA must observe in the performance of all professional services, including attestation engagements:

> A member shall comply with the following standards and with any interpretations thereof by bodies designated by Council.
>
> A. *Professional Competence.* Undertake only those professional services that the member or the member's firm can reasonably expect to be completed with professional competence.
>
> B. *Due Professional Care.* Exercise due professional care in the performance of professional services.
>
> C. *Planning and Supervision.* Adequately plan and supervise the performance of professional services.
>
> D. *Sufficient Relevant Data.* Obtain sufficient relevant data to afford a reasonable basis for conclusions or recommendations in relation to any professional services performed.

Professional Competence

The professional competence standard under Rule 201 is similar to the first general standard for attestation engagements, which requires that attestation engagements be performed by practitioners having adequate technical training and proficiency in the attest function. "Adequate technical training" means that the CPA is thoroughly familiar with financial accounting standards, with procedures relevant to the performance of an attestation engagement, and with attestation standards. "Proficiency" refers to practical experience. That is, a CPA in charge of an attestation engagement should have sufficient practical experience to execute the engagement successfully in accordance with professional standards.

Due Professional Care

The general standard of due professional care requires the CPA to perform the attestation engagement in a manner appropriate for a professional accountant. If due professional care is not exercised, an entity that sustains a financial loss may have grounds for bringing legal action against the CPA.

Due professional care can be evaluated only in the context of a specific engagement. For this reason, the CPA must approach each attestation engagement with the appropriate degrees of skepticism and creativity. Skepticism means that the CPA approaches the subject matter of the engagement with an inquisitive mind. Creativity on the part of the CPA will facilitate the successful performance of an attestation engagement. Attestation engagements cover a broad range of subject matter. Regardless of the number of standards promulgated, the CPA must approach each engagement as unique and be prepared to respond in a meaningful way to the issues that arise from the attestation procedures.

Planning and Supervision

Like all professional engagements, attestation engagements need proper planning and supervision to be effective. The planning and supervision standard under Rule 201 is similar to the first standard of fieldwork of the attestation standards, which requires that the work be adequately planned and that assistants be properly supervised.

Proper planning allows the CPA to understand the needs of the client and the demands of the attestation engagement. In addition, adequate planning requires that the CPA firm consider the staffing requirements and assign personnel whose technical training and proficiency match the demands of the specific engagement. In fact, determining whether appropriate staff are available for an engagement is an important element in determining whether an attestation engagement should even be accepted.

Staff accountants for an attestation engagement should be properly supervised. As part of its organizational structure, an accounting firm should implement an adequate system of review and supervision for attestation engagements. The level of supervision will vary with each engagement depending in part on the complexity of the engagement and the technical and experience of the assistants.

Sufficient Relevant Data

Before a CPA can issue an attestation report, he or she must collect sufficient relevant data to support the conclusions. The sufficient relevant data standard under Rule 201 is similar to the second standard of fieldwork of the attestation standards, which requires the practitioner to obtain sufficient evidence to provide a reasonable basis for the conclusion that is expressed in the report.

Rule 202: Compliance with Standards

Rule 202 of the Code of Professional Conduct, reproduced below, addresses compliance with standards that the CPA must observe in the performance of all professional services:

> A member who performs auditing, review, compilation, management consulting, tax, or other professional services shall comply with standards promulgated by bodies designated by Council.

The AICPA has designated the Accounting and Review Services Committee (ARSC), the Auditing Standards Board (ASB), and the Consulting Services Executive Committee (CSEC), jointly, to establish professional standards for attestation engagements. Statements on Standards for Attestation Engagements and SSAE Interpretations have been issued under the authority established by Rule 202.

Interpretations of Rules of Conduct

Interpretations of Rules of Conduct consist of interpretations that have been adopted (after exposure to state societies, state boards, practice units, and other interested parties) by the professional ethics division's executive committee to provide guidelines on the scope and application of the Rules of Conduct but are not intended to limit such scope or application. A CPA who departs from such guidelines has the burden of justifying such departure in the event of a disciplinary hearing.

Ethics Rulings

Ethics Rulings consist of formal rulings made by the AICPA's professional ethics division's executive committee after exposure to state societies, state boards, practice units, and other interested parties. Ethics Rulings summarize the application of Rules of Conduct and Interpretations to particular sets of factual circumstances. CPAs who depart from such rulings in similar circumstances will be requested to justify such departures.

STATEMENTS ON STANDARDS FOR ATTESTATION ENGAGEMENTS

Statements on Standards for Attestation Engagements (SSAEs) are issued by senior technical bodies that the AICPA has designated to issue pronouncements on attestation matters. Rule 202 of the Code of

Professional Conduct requires CPAs who perform attest engagement (practitioners) to comply with such pronouncements. Practitioners should have sufficient knowledge of the SSAEs to identify those that are applicable to his or her attestation engagement, and he or she should be prepared to justify departures from the SSAEs.

Purpose of the Standards

Attestation standards enable engagements in which the practitioner provides credibility on information other than historical financial information. Attestation engagements may be appropriate when the subject matter has one or more of the following characteristics:

- It is nonfinancial.
- It is nonhistorical.
- It may be the responsibility of another party, that is, one who is not the client.

The purpose of the first attestation standards, issued in 1986, was to provide guidance on performing and reporting on attest engagements. Changes in the business environment gradually created problems in the way the standards could be applied in practice. To address the practical application of the attest standards, SSAE-10 (Attestation Standards: Revision and Recodification) was released. SSAE-10 supersedes all preceding SSAEs.

Application of SSAEs

SSAEs apply whenever a practitioner is engaged to issue or does issue an examination, review, or agreed-upon procedures report on a subject matter (or an assertion about the subject matter) that is the responsibility of another party. Technically, this definition encompasses services such as audits and reviews of financial statements. However, the SSAEs state that they do not supersede any guidance in the SASs or SSARSs. The SSAEs provide for four levels of services: (1) examination, (2) review, (3) agreed-upon procedures, and (4) compilation of prospective financial information.

Organization of the Standards

Chapter 1 of SSAE-10 (AT 101) is the umbrella standard. Its primary purpose is to provide a basic framework for performing attest engagements and for the ongoing development of related standards. Chapter 1 of SSAE-10 (AT 101) comprises specific standards for certain subject matters and the application of the standards to agreed-upon procedures engagements. This specific guidance generally follows the basic framework outlined in Chapter 1 of SSAE-10 (AT 101). However, important differences exist for certain types of engagements. Exhibit 1-3 lists some of these important differences.

SSAE Interpretations

Attestation Interpretations are recommendations on the application of SSAEs in specific circumstances, including engagements for entities in specialized industries, that are issued under the authority of AICPA senior technical bodies. If the practitioner does not apply the attestation guidance included in an applicable attestation interpretation, he or she should be prepared to explain how he or she complied with the SSAE provisions addressed by the Interpretation.

Interpretations of Chapter 1 of SSAE-10

1. *Defense Industry Questionnaire on Business Ethics and Conduct* According to this Interpretation, when a practitioner is engaged by a defense contractor to provide an examination or a review report on the contractor's written responses to the Defense Industry Questionnaire, such an engagement involves subject matter that is the responsibility of the defense contactor. Consequently, Chapter 1 of SSAE-10 (AT 101) applies to such engagements. This Interpretation also provides illustrative examination and review reports to be used in such engagements.
2. *Responding to Requests on Matters Relating to Solvency* According to this Interpretation, a practitioner should not provide any form of assurance, through examination, review, or agreed upon procedures, that an entity
   - Is not insolvent at the time the debt is incurred or would not be rendered insolvent by incurring the debt.
   - Does not have unreasonably small capital.
   - Has the ability to pay its debts as they mature.
3. *Applicability of Attestation Standards to Litigation Services* Chapter 1 of SSAE-10 (AT 101) does not apply to litigation services that involve pending or potential proceedings before a court, regulatory body, or governmental authority (or the agent of any of these) such as a grand jury or an arbitrator (mediator) when the
   - Practitioner has not been engaged to issue and does not issue an examination, review, or agreed-upon procedures report on a subject matter, or an assertion about the subject matter that is the responsibility of another party.

- Practitioner is an expert witness or a "trier of fact" (or an agent for one).
- Practitioner's work is subject to detailed analysis and challenge by each party to the dispute.
- Practitioner is engaged by an attorney and is protected by the attorney's work product privilege.

4. *Providing Access to or Copies of Attest Documentation to a Regulator* This Interpretation states that the guidance in Interpretation No. 1 (Providing Access to or Copies of Audit Documentation to a Regulator) of AU Section 339 (Audit Documentation) is applicable to attestation engagements. The Interpretation also provides illustrative letters to regulators in these circumstances.
5. *Attest Engagements on Financial Information Included in XBRL Instance Documents* This Interpretation defines the terms "XBRL" and "XBRL instance document" and describes the matters that practitioners should consider when engaged to examine and report on whether an instance document accurately reflects the financial information. The Interpretation also provides illustrative examination reports for reporting on either the subject matter or management's assertion.
6. *Reporting on Attestation Engagements Performed in Accordance with Government Auditing Standards* This Interpretation explains how an attestation report should be modified for attestation engagements performed pursuant to generally accepted government auditing standards (GAGAS).

Interpretations of Chapter 5 of SSAE-10

1. *Pre-Award Surveys* This Interpretation states that a practitioner may not issue a report on a pre-award survey by management about the effectiveness of the design of an entity's internal control based solely on the consideration of internal control in an audit of the entity's financial statements. In order to issue such a report, the practitioner should follow the guidance in Chapter 5 of SSAE-10 (AT 501) and perform an examination or apply agreed-upon procedures to management's assertion about the effectiveness of the design of the entity's internal control.

Technical Practice Aids

Inquires and replies based on selected practice problems received by the staff of the Technical Information Service are published each year in the AICPA Technical Practice Aids. The replies to practitioner's inquires are not official positions of the AICPA or any of its committees.

STATEMENTS ON STANDARDS FOR ACCOUNTING AND REVIEW SERVICES

Statements on Standards for Accounting and Review Services (SSARS) are issued to provide basic guidance for the performance of a compilation or review engagement. Broadly speaking, these statements supply fundamental definitions and descriptions of compilations and reviews, discuss procedures to be used in the engagement, and provide guidance for the preparation of the compilation or review report. The information in the SSARS is fairly nonspecific, however, and leaves many issues for the accountant to resolve through professional judgment.

SSARS Hierarchy

SSARS-11 (Standards for Accounting and Review Services), issued in 2004, establishes a SSARS hierarchy. The hierarchy is beneficial to practitioners by making them aware of the appropriate literature and the various publications' standing in the SSARS hierarchy. The hierarchy is as follows.

Level 1: Statements on Standards for Accounting and Review Services

The ARSC develops and issues standards in the form of Statements on Standards for Accounting and Review Services (SSARS) through a due process that includes deliberations in meetings open to the public, public exposure of proposed SSARS, and a formal vote. The SSARS are codified. The accountant should have sufficient knowledge of the SSARS to identify those that are applicable to his or her engagement. The nature of the SSARS requires an accountant to exercise professional judgment in applying them. The accountant should be prepared to justify departures from the SSARS.

Level 2: Interpretative Publications

Interpretative publications consist of compilation and review Interpretations of the SSARS and appendixes to the SSARS. Interpretative publications are not standards for accounting and review services. Interpretative publications are recommendations on the application of the SSARS in specific circumstances, including engagements for entities in specialized industries. Interpretative publications are included in the Codification of Statements on Standards for Accounting and Review Services. An interpretative publication is issued after all ARSC members have been provided an opportunity to consider and comment on whether the proposed interpretative publication is consistent with the SSARS. The accountant should be aware of and consider interpretive publications applicable to his or her compilation or review. If the accountant does not apply the guidance included in an applicable interpretive publication, the accountant should be prepared to explain how he or she complied with the SSARS provisions addressed by such guidance.

Level 3: Other Publications

Other compilation and review publications include AICPA accounting and review publications not referred to above; AICPA's annual *Compilation and Review Alert*; compilation and review articles in the *Journal of Accountancy* and other professional journals; compilation and review articles in the AICPA *CPA Letter*; continuing professional education programs and other instruction materials, textbooks, guide books, compilation and review programs, and checklists; and other compilation and review publications from state CPA societies, other organizations, and individuals. Other compilation and review publications have no authoritative status; however, they may help the accountant understand and apply the SSARS. If an accountant applies the guidance included in another compilation and review publication, he or she should be satisfied that, in his or her judgment, it is both relevant to the circumstances of the engagement, and appropriate. In determining whether a nonauthoritative compilation and review publication is appropriate, the accountant may wish to consider the degree to which the publication is recognized as being helpful in understanding and applying the SSARS and the degree to which the issuer or author is recognized as an authority in compilation and review matters. Other compilation and review publications published by the AICPA that have been reviewed by the AICPA Audit and Attest Standards staff are presumed to be appropriate.

According to Rules 201 and 202 of the AICPA Code of Professional Conduct, a CPA must be prepared to explain and justify any aspect of a compilation or review engagement that is not consistent with the standards established in Statements on Standards for Accounting and Review Services (SSARS).

STATEMENTS ON AUDITING STANDARDS

An independent auditor plans, conducts, and reports the results of an audit in accordance with generally accepted auditing standards

(GAAS). Auditing standards provide a measure of audit quality and the objectives to be achieved in an audit. Auditing procedures differ from auditing standards. Auditing procedures are acts that an auditor performs during the course of an audit to comply with auditing standards.

Auditing Standards

The general, fieldwork, and reporting standards (the 10 standards) approved and adopted by the membership of the AICPA, as amended by the AICPA Auditing Standards Board (ASB), are as follows.

General Standards

Audits are to be performed by a person or persons having adequate technical training and proficiency as an auditor.

In all matters relating to the assignment, an independence in mental attitude is to be maintained by the auditor or auditors.

Due professional care is to be exercised in the performance of the audit and the preparation of the report.

Standards of Fieldwork

The work is to be adequately planned and assistants, if any, are to be properly supervised.

A sufficient understanding of internal control is to be obtained to plan the audit and to determine the nature, timing, and extent of tests to be performed.

Sufficient competent evidential matter is to be obtained through inspection, observation, inquiries, and confirmations to afford a reasonable basis for an opinion regarding the financial statements under audit.

Standards of Reporting

The report shall state whether the financial statements are presented in accordance with generally accepted accounting principles (GAAP).

The report shall identify those circumstances in which such principles have not been consistently observed in the current period in relation to the preceding period.

Informative disclosures in the financial statements are to be regarded as reasonably adequate unless otherwise stated in the report.

The report shall contain either an expression of opinion regarding the financial statements taken as a whole or an assertion to the effect that an opinion cannot be expressed. When an overall opinion cannot be expressed, the reasons for this should be stated. In all cases where an auditor's name is associated with financial statements, the report should contain a clear-cut indication of the character of the auditor's work, if any, and the degree of responsibility the auditor is taking.

Rule 202 requires an AICPA member who performs an audit (the auditor) to comply with standards promulgated by the Auditing Standards Board (ASB). The ASB develops and issues standards in the form of Statements on Auditing Standards (SASs) through a due process that includes deliberation in meetings open to the public, public exposure of proposed SASs, and a formal vote. The SASs are codified within the framework of the 10 standards.

The auditor should have sufficient knowledge of the SASs to identify those that are applicable to his or her audit. The nature of the 10 standards and the SASs requires the auditor to exercise professional judgment in applying them. Materiality and audit risk also underlie the application of the 10 standards and the SASs, particularly those related to fieldwork and reporting. The auditor should be prepared to justify departures from the SASs.

Interpretive Publications

Interpretive publications consist of auditing Interpretations of the SASs, auditing guidance included in AICPA Audit and Accounting Guides, and AICPA auditing Statements of Position. Interpretive publications are not auditing standards. Interpretive publications are recommendations on the application of the SASs in specific circumstances, including engagements for entities in specialized industries. An interpretive publication is issued under the authority of the ASB after all ASB members have been provided an opportunity to consider and comment on whether the proposed interpretive publication is consistent with the SASs.

The auditor should be aware of and consider interpretive publications applicable to his or her audit. If the auditor does not apply the auditing guidance included in an applicable interpretive publication, the auditor should be prepared to explain how he or she complied with the SAS provisions addressed by such auditing guidance.

Other Auditing Publications

Other auditing publications include AICPA auditing publications not referred to above; auditing articles in the *Journal of Accountancy* and other professional journals; auditing articles in the AICPA *CPA*

Letter; continuing professional education programs and other instruction materials, textbooks, guide books, audit programs, and checklists; and other auditing publications from state CPA societies, other organizations, and individuals. Other auditing publications have no authoritative status; however, they may help the auditor understand and apply the SASs.

If an auditor applies the auditing guidance included in another auditing publication, he or she should be satisfied that, in his or her judgment, it is both relevant to the circumstances of the audit and appropriate. In determining whether a nonauthoritative auditing publication is appropriate, the auditor may wish to consider the degree to which the publication is recognized as being helpful in understanding and applying the SASs and the degree to which the issuer or author is recognized as an authority in auditing matters. Other auditing publications published by the AICPA that have been reviewed by the AICPA Audit and Attest Standards staff are presumed to be appropriate.

IMPACT OF SARBANES-OXLEY ACT OF 2002

On July 30, 2002, President George W. Bush signed into law the Sarbanes-Oxley Act of 2002. The act, which applies in general to publicly held companies and their audit firms, dramatically affects the accounting profession.

Title II of the Sarbanes-Oxley Act (the Act) prohibits most "consulting" services outside the scope of practice of auditors. These services are prohibited even if they are preapproved by the issuer's audit committee. Prohibited services include:

- Bookkeeping and related services
- Design and implementation of financial information systems
- Appraisal or valuation services (including fairness opinions and contribution-in-kind reports)
- Actuarial services
- Internal audit outsourcing
- Services that provide any management or human resources
- Investment or broker/dealer services
- Legal and "expert services unrelated to the audit"
- Any other service that the board determines, by regulation, is impermissible

Firms, however, may provide tax services or other services that are not listed, provided the firm receives pre-approval from the audit committee. Presumably, most attestation and other special engagements would be allowed.

In accordance with Section 404 of the Act, the Securities and Exchange Commission (SEC) issued rules requiring that each annual report of a publicly held company contain an internal control report that

- States that it is the responsibility of management to establish and maintain an adequate internal control structure and procedures for financial reporting.
- Contains an assessment, as of the end of the most recent fiscal year, of the effectiveness of the internal control structure and procedures.

In addition, Section 404 of Sarbanes-Oxley requires public companies' external auditors to attest to, and report on, the internal control assessment made by the management of the issuer in accordance with the standards for attestation engagements adopted by the Public Company Accounting Oversight Board (PCAOB), which the Act established.

In June 2003, the SEC issued its Final Rule: Management's Reports on Internal Control Over Financial Reporting and Certification of Disclosure in Exchange Act Periodic Reports, Securities and Exchange Commission Release No. 33-8238, related to Section 404. The Final Rule requires the management of public companies to assess the effectiveness of the company's internal control over financial reporting, as of the end of the company's most recent fiscal year. Section 404 also requires management to include in the company's annual report management's conclusion as a result of that assessment about whether the company's internal control is effective.

In June 2004, the SEC approved the PCAOB AS-2 (An Audit of Internal Control over Financial Reporting Performed in Conjunction with an Audit of Financial Statements), which addresses both the work that is required in order to audit internal control over financial reporting and the relationship of that audit to the audit of the financial statements. An audit of internal control includes, among other things, evaluating the process used by management to perform its assessment of internal control effectiveness, evaluating the effectiveness of both the design and operation of the internal control, and forming an opinion about whether internal control over financial reporting is effective.

Companies considered accelerated filers (seasoned U.S. companies with public float exceeding $75 million) were required to comply with the internal control reporting and disclosure requirements of Section 404 of the Sarbanes-Oxley Act for fiscal years ending on or after November 15, 2004. Accordingly, auditors engaged to audit the financial statements of such companies for fiscal years ending on or after November 15, 2004, are also required to audit and report on the company's internal control over financial reporting as of the end of that fiscal year. Other companies (including smaller companies, foreign private issuers, and companies with only registered debt securities) had until fiscal years ending on or after July 15, 2005, to comply with these internal control reporting and disclosure requirements as well as the requirement for audit reporting on internal control.

An audit of internal control performed under AS-2 closely resembles the examination engagement detailed in Chapter 11 "(Internal Control Engagements)." However, the audit of internal control under AS-2 can only be performed in conjunction with an audit of a company's financial statements.

IMPLICATIONS OF PCAOB STANDARDS

In October 2003, the AICPA's Governing Council recognized the PCAOB's authority to discipline auditors of issuers by adopting a policy that allows the AICPA's professional ethics division to discipline an AICPA member without investigation when the PCAOB disciplines the member for a violation of PCAOB standards. In May 2004, the Governing Council designated the PCAOB as a body with the authority to promulgate auditing and related attestation standards, quality control, ethics, independence, and other standards relating to the preparation and issuance of audit reports for issuers. (The term "issuer" means an issuer (as defined in Section 3 of the Securities Exchange Act of 1934, as amended) whose securities are registered under Section 12 of the Securities Exchange Act of 1934 or who is required to file reports under Section 15(d) of the 1934 Act or who files or has filed a registration statement that has not yet become effective under the Securities Act of 1933 and that the issuer has not withdrawn.) The Governing Council's policy enables the AICPA's ethics division to discipline members under Rule 201 (General Standards) and Rule 202 (Compliance with Standards) of the AICPA Code of Professional Conduct after the PCAOB has taken action. The AICPA's Auditing Standards Board (ASB) continues to set auditing and quality control standards, and the AICPA's Professional Ethics Executive Committee continues to set ethics and independence standards for audits of non-issuers.

Practice Issues

During 2004, the PCAOB issued the following standards:

- Auditing Standard No. 1 (AS-1) (References in Auditors' Report to the Standards of the PCAOB)
- Auditing Standard No. 2 (AS-2) (An Audit of Internal Control over Financial Reporting Performed in Conjunction with an Audit of Financial Statements)
- Auditing Standard No. 3 (AS-3) (Audit Documentation)

The following are three broad practice issues to consider if a non-issuer requests a practitioner to perform services (such as an attestation engagement) pursuant to the auditing and related professional practice standards of the PCAOB:

1. The applicability of generally accepted auditing standards as established by the AICPA's ASB
2. The applicable PCAOB standards that are to be followed
3. The applicable provisions of the Sarbanes-Oxley Act that should be applied by the non-issuer

Applicability of Generally Accepted Auditing Standards

The ASB is the body designated by AICPA's Governing Council with the authority to set performance and reporting standards for audits of financial statements of non-issuers. If a non-issuer follows the PCAOB standards, both the auditing standards promulgated by the ASB and the applicable auditing and related professional practice standards promulgated by the PCAOB must be followed.

SAS-58 (AU 508) (Reports on Audited Financial Statements) requires the auditor to state in the auditor's report that the audit was conducted in accordance with generally accepted auditing standards and identify the United States of America as the country of origin of those standards. However, an auditor may indicate that the audit was also conducted in accordance with another set of auditing standards. According to Interpretation No. 18 of SAS-58 (AU 508), if the auditor conducted the audit in accordance with generally accepted auditing standards *and* the auditing standards of the PCAOB, the auditor may state in the auditor's report that the audit was conducted in accordance with both sets of standards.

Exhibit 3-1 is an example of additional language provided by Interpretation No. 18 of SAS-58 (AU 508). This language may be included in the auditor's report to state that an audit was conducted in accordance with both generally accepted auditing standards and the PCAOB's auditing standards, and to clarify that the purpose and extent of the auditor's testing of internal control over financial reporting was to determine the auditor's procedures and that it was not sufficient to express an opinion on the effectiveness of internal control. To clarify the source of generally accepted auditing standards in a dual reference reporting situation, the auditor may indicate that the audit was conducted in accordance with generally accepted auditing standards as established by the ASB.

Applicability of PCAOB Standards

PCAOBAS-1 (References in Auditors' Reports to the Standards of the Public Company Accounting Oversight Board) states that the

EXHIBIT 3-1
ILLUSTRATIVE AUDIT REPORT

Independent Auditor's Report

[*Same first paragraph as the standard report*]

We conducted our audit in accordance with generally accepted auditing standards as established by the Auditing Standards Board (United States) and in accordance with the auditing standards of the Public Company Accounting Oversight Board (United States). Those standards require that we plan and perform the audit to obtain reasonable assurance about whether the financial statements are free of material misstatement. The Company is not required to have, nor were we engaged to perform, an audit of its internal control over financial reporting. Our audit included consideration of internal control over financial reporting as a basis for designing audit procedures that are appropriate in the circumstances, but not for the purpose of expressing an opinion on the effectiveness of the Company's internal control over financial reporting. Accordingly we express no such opinion. An audit also includes examining, on a test basis, evidence supporting the amounts and disclosures in the financial statements, assessing the accounting principles used and significant estimates made by management, as well as evaluating the overall financial statement presentation. We believe that our audit provides a reasonable basis for our opinion.

[*Same opinion paragraph as the standard report*]

standard audit report of an issuer is to read as follows: "We conducted our audits in accordance with the standards of the Public Company Accounting Oversight Board (United States)." PCAOB Release No. 2003-06 defines "Interim Professional Auditing Standards" to include five rules:

1. Rule 3200T: Interim Auditing Standards
2. Rule 3300T: Interim Attestation Standards
3. Rule 3400T: Interim Quality Control Standards
4. Rule 3500T: Interim Ethics Standards
5. Rule 3600T: Interim Independence Standards

Questions have arisen as to whether an accounting firm (whether registered with the PCAOB or not) that performs audit or attest services for a non-issuer in accordance with the standards of the PCAOB must follow the foregoing five rules. Examples of differences between these PCAOB standards and generally accepted auditing standards are as follows:

- *Reporting* PCAOB AS-1 requires that the audit report include the following statement: "We conducted our audits in accordance with the standards of the Public Company Accounting Oversight Board (United States)."
- *Concurring partner* PCAOB Rule 3400T requires the establishment of policies and procedures for a concurring review.
- *Affiliated firms* PCAOB Rule 3400T requires registered firms that are part of an international association to seek adoption of policies and procedures by the international organization or individual foreign associated firms consistent with PCAOB standards.
- *Partner rotation* PCAOB Rule 3600T requires compliance with the SEC's independence rules which include partner rotation.
- *Independence matters* PCAOB Rule 3600T requires compliance with the SEC independence rules and Standards No. 1, 2, and 3 and interpretations 99-1, 00-1, and 00-2 of the Independence Standards Board.

According to a PCAOB Staff Q&A document *Audits of Financial Statements of Non-Issuers Performed Pursuant to the Standards of the PCAOB* (PCAOB Q&A), a reference to "the auditing standards of the Public Company Accounting Oversight Board (United States)" or to "the standards of the Public Company Accounting Oversight Board (United States)" in an auditor's report on the financial statements of a non-issuer does not imply that the non-issuer is subject to, or otherwise complied with, some or all of the provisions of the Sarbanes-Oxley Act and other securities laws or the SEC's rules and regulations thereunder.

In addition, the PCAOB Q&A states that an audit of the financial statements of a non-issuer does not become subject to PCAOB inspection solely because the auditor performed and reported on the audit in accordance with the standards of the PCAOB. Auditors of the financial statements of non-issuers may, nevertheless, be subject to various forms of state and federal oversight, such as review by federal banking regulators, the U.S. General Accounting Office, or a state board of accountancy.

If a non-issuer elects to have its financial statements audited pursuant to the PCAOB's standards, it does not have to have its internal control over financial reporting audited pursuant to PCAOB AS-2 (An Audit of Internal Control Over Financial Reporting Performed in Conjunction with An Audit of Financial Statements) according the PCAOB Q&A. Only certain issuers that are subject to Section 404 of the Sarbanes-Oxley Act are required to include within the scope of the audit an audit of internal control over financial reporting. Although the PCAOB's standards provide for an integrated audit of financial statements and internal control for those issuers that are subject to Section 404 of the Sarbanes-Oxley Act, the PCAOB's standards also permit auditors to conduct a financial statement-only audit under circumstances, for example, when Section 404 of the Sarbanes-Oxley Act is not applicable.

Also, according to the PCAOB Q&A, if an auditor refers to either "the standards of the Public Company Accounting Oversight Board (United States)" or "the auditing standards of the Public Company Accounting Oversight Board (United States)" in an audit report on an audit of the financial statements of a non-issuer, the auditor is not required to subject the audit to a "concurring partner review" as required by the PCAOB's adoption of certain of the requirements of the AICPA's former Securities and Exchange Commission Practice Section (SECPS). Although the PCAOB may at some time adopt a standard requiring the performance of a second partner review, at this time, the interim quality control standards only require registered firms that were members of the SECPS as of April 16, 2003, to have a concurring partner review on audits of issuers.

According to the PCAOB Q&A, auditors of the financial statements of non-issuers, including nonprofit organizations, government agencies, and municipalities and other governments, should look to relevant state and federal laws and regulations relating to auditor independence. The PCAOB Q&A further states that by referring to "the auditing standards of the Public Company Accounting Oversight Board (United States)" or to "the standards of the Public Company Accounting Oversight Board (United States)" in an audit report on the financial statements of a non-issuer, the auditor does not represent that he or she has complied with the SEC's auditor independence requirements.

Applicability of the Sarbanes-Oxley Act

It is clear from the Sarbanes-Oxley Act that its rules and those of the SEC together with the PCAOB's standards provide for a complete system of regulation for the registered accounting firm and the issuer. The public's perception could be that a non-issuer that is audited in accordance with PCAOB standards is also subject to this entire system of regulations when, for example, the non-issuer's management might not have certified its financial statements or established an independent audit committee. The ASB and other committees are just beginning to deliberate this issue.

However, according to the PCAOB Q&A, the Sarbanes-Oxley Act requires only that those public accounting firms that prepare or issue, or participate in the preparation or issuance of, audit reports on the financial statements of issuers be registered with the PCAOB.

STATEMENTS ON QUALITY CONTROL STANDARDS

Statements on Quality Control Standards (SQCSs) are a framework for quality control in a CPA firm that applies to both the functional and technical aspects of attestation engagements as well as other types of engagements.

The following SQCSs have been issued by the Auditing Standards Board:

- SQCS-1 (System of Quality Control for a CPA Firm) [superseded by SQCS-2]
- SQCS-2 (System of Quality Control for a CPAFirm's Accounting and Auditing Practice)
- SQCS-3 (Monitoring a CPA Firm's Accounting and Auditing Practice)
- SQCS-4 (System of Quality Control for a CPA Firm's Accounting and Auditing Practice)
- SQCS-5 (The Personnel Management Element of a Firm's System of Quality Control—Competencies Required by a Practitioner in Charge of an Attest Engagement)
- SQCS-6 (Amendment to SQCS-2)

The standards established by the SQCSs apply to a firm's accounting and auditing practice, which SQCS-2 defines as follows:

> Accounting and auditing practice refers to all audit, attest, accounting and review, and other services for which standards have been established by the AICPA Auditing Standards Board or the AICPA Accounting and Review Services Committee under Rules 201 or 202 of the AICPA Code of Professional Conduct.

Elements of a Quality Control System

The fundamental elements of a quality control system are

- Independence, integrity, and objectivity
- Personnel management
- Acceptance and continuance of clients and engagements
- Engagement performance
- Monitoring

Although these elements are discussed separately in the following analysis, an effective system of quality control recognizes that all of the elements are interrelated.

Independence, Integrity, and Objectivity

Policies and procedures should be established to reasonably ensure that personnel are independent. For example, a firm may distribute a client list periodically to personnel and have them acknowledge whether they have a financial interest or whether any of their relatives hold a key position with any client on the list.

Independence is the foundation of the attest function. Third-party users rely on the CPA's opinion in an audit or attest engagement because they believe the conclusion is impartial and unbiased. Chapter 1 of SSAE-10 (AT 101) states, "The practitioner should maintain the intellectual honesty and impartiality necessary to reach an unbiased conclusion about the subject matter or the assertion."

The only attestation engagement allowed for a CPA who is not independent is a compilation of prospective financial statements (see Chapter 13, "Prospective Financial Information").

Personnel Management

Policies and procedures related to personnel management should encompass "hiring, assigning personnel to engagements, professional development, and advancement activities." The quality control standards specifically state that policies and procedures should be designed to reasonably assure that the following are achieved:

- Those hired possess the appropriate characteristics to enable them to perform competently.
- Work is assigned to personnel who have the degree of technical training and proficiency required in the circumstances.
- Personnel participate in general and industry-specific continuing professional education and other professional development activities that enable them to fulfill assigned responsibilities and satisfy applicable continuing professional education requirements of the AICPA and regulatory agencies.
- Personnel selected for advancement have the qualifications necessary to fulfill the responsibilities they will be called on to assume.

Acceptance and Continuance of Clients and Engagements

Policies and procedures should be in place to determine whether the firm should continue to be associated with clients and prospective clients. These policies and procedures should be designed to assess the integrity of a client's management. For example, a firm may require a thorough investigation of the integrity of the principals associated with existing and prospective clients. Although the firm must be concerned with the integrity of management, the evaluation performed by the firm does not vouch for the integrity of management.

The standards also require that policies and procedures be established to provide reasonable assurance that the following objectives related to an engagement are achieved:

- Undertake only those engagements that the firm can reasonably expect to be completed with professional competence.
- Appropriately consider the risk associated with providing professional services in the particular circumstances.

Engagement Performance

Quality control policies and procedures should be designed to reasonably assure that an engagement is performed in a manner that satisfies "professional standards, regulatory requirements, and the firm's standards of quality." These policies and procedures should encompass all phases of the engagement, from its initial acceptance to the preparation of the accountant's report. An integral part of engagement performance is consultation, which ranges from referring to authoritative literature to holding discussions with personnel who have expertise relevant to the engagement.

Monitoring

Policies and procedures should be established to determine whether the auditing firm is observing the quality control policies and procedures discussed above.

Administration of the Quality Control System

Once established, policies and procedures can achieve their objectives only with an effective system of administration. SQCS-2 lists the following as elements that should be considered in the design of an effective system of administration:

- *Assignment of responsibilities* The responsibility for the design and maintenance of quality control policies and procedures should be assigned to a competent individual, along with adequate authority to administer the quality control system.
- *Communication* A firm must communicate its quality control policies and procedures (as well as changes to those policies and procedures) to its personnel on a timely and comprehensive basis.

- *Documentation of quality control policies and procedures* The specific policies and procedures related to the documentation of quality control policies and procedures adopted by a firm are dependent on the characteristics of the firm and its practice.

  OBSERVATION: SQCS-2 does not require that quality control policies and procedures be documented, only that the documentation requirements be a reflection of the "size, structure, and nature of the practice of the firm." In addition, the standard states that "although communication is ordinarily enhanced if it is in writing, the effectiveness of a firm's system of quality control is not necessarily impaired by the absence of documentation of established quality control policies and procedures."

- *Documentation of compliance with quality control policies and procedures* Firm personnel must document their compliance with quality control policies and procedures established by the firm. The specific form of documentation is dependent on the characteristics of the firm and its practice.

  OBSERVATION: Although SQCS-2 does not require a listing of the specific quality control policies and procedures used, the standard does require documentation that policies and procedures were observed.

Monitoring a Firm's System of Quality Control

SQCS-2 specifically states that monitoring a firm's system of quality control encompass the following:

- Relevance and adequacy of the firm's policies and procedures.
- Appropriateness of the firm's guidance materials and any practice aids.
- Effectiveness of professional development activities.
- Compliance with the firm's policies and procedures.

Although the specific procedures that constitute effective monitoring of a firm's system of quality control depend on "the firm's management philosophy and the environment in which the firm practices," SQCS-3 states that such procedures may include (1) inspection procedures and (2) pre-issuance or post-issuance review of selected engagements.

Inspection Procedures

Specific inspection procedures adopted as part of the monitoring activity should be designed to determine whether the auditing firm's personnel are in fact observing the firm's quality control policies and procedures. Inspection procedures should include the review of administrative and personnel records, review of working papers, and conversations with firm personnel. SQCS-3 notes that inspection procedures may encompass (1) a periodic summarization of weaknesses discovered as part of the monitoring process, (2) recommendations to eliminate or minimize the occurrence of such weaknesses in the future, (3) communication of weaknesses and related recommendations to appropriate firm management personnel, and (4) follow-up procedures conducted by appropriate firm management personnel to ensure that recommendations are implemented on a timely basis.

Pre-Issuance or Post-Issuance Review of Selected Engagements

Monitoring procedures could include a review of an engagement either before or after the report is issued. Review procedures are considered inspection procedures if they meet the following criteria:

- The review is sufficiently comprehensive to enable the firm to assess compliance with all applicable professional standards and the firm's quality control policies and procedures.
- Findings of reviews that might indicate the need to improve compliance with or modify the firm's quality control policies and procedures are periodically summarized, documented, and communicated to the firm's management personnel having the responsibility and authority to make changes in the policies and procedures.
- The firm's management personnel consider on a timely basis the systemic causes of findings that indicate improvements are needed and plans appropriate actions to be taken.
- On a timely basis, the firm implements planned actions, communicates changes to personnel who might be affected, and follows up to verify that the planned actions were taken.

For reviews to be considered monitoring procedures, they must be conducted by reviewers who "are not directly associated with the performance of the engagement"—with one exception: If a firm has a "limited number of qualified management-level individuals," a postissuance review may be conducted by the person with final responsibility for the engagement. Although SQCS-3 allows this exception, it does note that reviewing one's own work is generally not as effective as a review performed by someone who was not associated with the engagement. For this reason, SQCS-3 suggests that firms consider hiring someone outside of the firm to perform inspection procedures.

OBSERVATION: Although a peer review is not a substitute for a firm's monitoring procedures, SQCS-3 states that a peer review that satisfies the standards established by the AICPA may substitute for "some or all of [the firm's] inspection procedures for the period covered by the review."

Practitioner-in-Charge

QC Section 20 (System of Quality Control for a CPA Firm's Accounting and Auditing Practice) provides that a CPA firm shall have a system of quality control for its accounting and auditing practice that should encompass the following elements:

- Independence, integrity, and objectivity
- Personnel management
- Acceptance and continuance of clients and engagements
- Engagement performance
- Monitoring

Personnel Management

Personnel management encompasses hiring, assigning personnel to engagements, professional development, and advancement activities. Accordingly, policies and procedures should be established to provide the firm with reasonable assurance that

1. Those hired possess the appropriate characteristics to enable them to perform competently. Examples of such characteristics may include meeting minimum academic requirements established by the firm, maturity, integrity, and leadership traits.
2. Work is assigned to personnel having the degree of technical training and proficiency required in the circumstances.
3. Personnel participate in general and industry-specific continuing professional education and other professional development activities that enable them to fulfill their assigned responsibilities and satisfy applicable continuing professional education requirements of the AICPA and regulatory agencies.
4. Personnel selected for advancement have the qualifications necessary for fulfillment of the responsibilities they will be called on to assume.

QC Section 40 clarifies the requirements of the personnel management element of a firm's system of quality control. In light of the significant responsibilities during the planning and performance of accounting, auditing, and attestation engagements of individuals who are responsible for supervising accounting, auditing, and attestation engagements and signing or authorizing an individual to sign the accountant's report on such engagements, a firm's policies and procedures related to the items noted above should be designed to provide a firm with reasonable assurance that such individuals possess the kinds of competencies that are appropriate given the circumstances of individual client engagements. For purposes of QC Section 40, such an individual is referred to as the practitioner-in-charge of the engagement.

Competencies

Competencies are the knowledge, skills, and abilities that enable a practitioner-in-charge to be qualified to perform an accounting, auditing, or attestation engagement. A firm is expected to determine the kinds of competencies that are necessary in the individual circumstances. Competencies are not measured by periods of time, because such a quantitative measurement might not accurately reflect the kinds of experiences gained by a practitioner in any given time period. Accordingly, for purposes of QC Section 40, a measure of overall competency is qualitative rather than quantitative.

Gaining Competencies

A firm's policies and procedures would ordinarily require a practitioner-in-charge of an engagement to gain the necessary competencies through recent experience in accounting, auditing, and attestation engagements. In some cases, however, a practitioner-in-charge will have obtained the necessary competencies through disciplines other than the practice of public accounting, such as in relevant industry, governmental, and academic positions. If necessary, the experience of the practitioner-in-charge should be supplemented by continuing professional education (CPE) and consultation. The following are examples:

- A practitioner-in-charge of an engagement whose recent experience has consisted primarily in providing tax services may acquire the competencies necessary in the circumstances to perform a compilation or review engagement by obtaining relevant CPE.
- A practitioner-in-charge of an engagement who did not have any experience in auditing the financial statements of a public company and only possessed recent prior experience in auditing the financial statements of nonpublic entities may develop the necessary competencies by obtaining relevant

CPE related to SEC rules and regulations and consulting with other practitioners who possess relevant knowledge related to SEC rules and regulations.

- A practitioner-in-charge of an engagement who did not have any experience in auditing the financial statements of a public company but possessed prior public accounting practice experience auditing financial statements of nonpublic entities and who also has relevant experience as the controller of a public company may have the necessary competencies in the circumstances.
- A practitioner-in-charge of an engagement whose actual experience consists of performing review and compilation engagements may be able to obtain the necessary competencies to perform an audit by becoming familiar with the industry the client operates in, obtaining continuing professional education relating to auditing and/or using consulting sources during the course of performing the audit engagement.
- A person in academia might obtain the necessary competencies to perform accounting, auditing or attestation engagements by (1) obtaining specialized knowledge through teaching or authorship of research projects or similar papers and (2) a rigorous self-study program or by engaging a consultant to assist on such engagements.

Regardless of the manner in which a particular competency is gained, a firm's quality control policies and procedures should be adequate to provide reasonable assurance that a practitioner-in-charge of an engagement possesses the competencies necessary to fulfill his or her engagement responsibilities.

The nature and extent of competencies established by a firm that are expected of the practitioner-in-charge of an engagement should be based on the characteristics of a particular client, industry, and the kind of service being provided. For example, the following should be considered:

- The competencies expected of a practitioner-in-charge of an engagement to compile financial statements would be different than those expected of a practitioner engaged to review or audit financial statements.
- Supervising engagements and signing or authorizing others to sign reports for clients in certain industries or engagements, such as financial services, governmental, or employee benefit plan engagements, would require different competencies than what would be expected in performing attest services for clients in other industries.
- The practitioner-in-charge of an engagement to audit the financial statements of a public company would be expected

to have certain technical proficiency in SEC reporting requirements, whereas a practitioner-in-charge who is not assigned to the audits of public companies would not need to be proficient in this area. This would include, for example, experience in the industry and appropriate knowledge of SEC and ISB rules and regulations, including accounting and independence standards.

- The practitioner-in-charge of an attestation engagement to examine management's assertion about the effectiveness of an entity's internal control over financial reporting would be expected to have certain technical proficiency in understanding and evaluating the effectiveness of controls, while a practitioner-in-charge of an attestation engagement to examine investment performance statistics would be expected to have different competencies, including an understanding of the subject matter of the underlying assertion.

Competencies Expected in Performing Accounting, Auditing, and Attestation Engagements

In practice, the kinds of competency requirements that a firm should establish for the practitioner-in-charge of an engagement are necessarily broad and varied in both their nature and number. However, the firm's quality control policies and procedures should ordinarily address the following competencies for the practitioner-in-charge of an engagement. Firms policies and procedures should also address other competencies as necessary in the circumstances. The following is a list of competencies that could be included:

1. *Understanding of the role of a system of quality control and the AICPA's Code of Professional Conduct* Practitioners-in-charge of an engagement should possess an understanding of the role of a firm's system of quality control and the AICPA's Code of Professional Conduct, both of which play critical roles in assuring the integrity of the various kinds of accountant's reports.
2. *Understanding of the service to be performed* Practitioners-in-charge of an engagement should possess an understanding of the performance, supervision, and reporting aspects of the engagement, which is normally gained through actual participation in that kind of engagement under appropriate supervision.
3. *Technical proficiency* Practitioners-in-charge of an engagement should possess an understanding of the applicable accounting, auditing, and attest professional standards, including those standards directly related to the industry the

client operates in and the kinds of transactions the client engages in.

4. *Familiarity with the industry* To the extent required by professional standards applicable to the kind of service being performed, practitioners-in-charge of an engagement should possess an understanding of the industry the client operates in. In performing an audit or review of financial statements, this understanding would include an industry's organization and operating characteristics sufficient to identify areas of high or unusual risk associated with an engagement and to evaluate the reasonableness of industry-specific estimates.
5. *Professional judgment* Practitioners-in-charge of an engagement should possess skills that indicate sound professional judgment. In performing an audit or review of financial statements, such skills would typically include the ability to exercise professional skepticism and identify areas requiring special consideration, including, for example, the evaluation of the reasonableness of estimates and representations made by management and the determination of the kind of report necessary in the circumstances.
6. *Understanding the organization's information technology systems* Practitioners-in-charge of an audit engagement should have an understanding of how the organization is dependent on or enabled by information technologies; and the manner in which information systems are used to record and maintain financial information.

Interrelationship of Competencies and Other Elements of a Firm's System of Quality Control

The competencies listed above are interrelated and gaining one particular competency may be related to achieving another. For example, familiarity with the client's industry interrelates with a practitioner's ability to make professional judgments relating to the client.

In establishing policies and procedures related to the nature of competencies needed by the practitioner-in-charge of an engagement, a firm may need to consider the requirements of policies and procedures established for other elements of quality control. For example, a firm would consider its requirements related to engagement performance in determining the nature of any competency requirements that assess the degree of technical proficiency necessary in a given set of circumstances.

The Relationship of the Competency Requirement of the Uniform Accountancy Act to the Personnel Management Element of Quality Control

The Uniform Accountancy Act (UAA) is a model legislative statute and related administrative rules that the AICPA and the National Association of State Boards of Accountancy (NASBA) designed in order to provide a uniform approach to the regulation of the accounting profession. CPAs are not required to follow the provisions of the UAA itself but, rather, the accountancy laws of the individual licensing jurisdictions in the United States governing the practice of public accounting, which may have adopted the UAA in whole or in part. The UAA provides that "any individual licensee who is responsible for supervising attest or compilation services and signs or authorizes someone to sign the accountant's report on the financial statements on behalf of the firm shall meet the competency requirements set out in the professional standards for such services." A firm's compliance with QC Section 40 is intended to enable a practitioner who performs the services described in the preceding sentence on the firm's behalf to meet this competency requirement; however, QC Section 40's applicability is broader than what is required by the UAA because the definition of an accounting and auditing practice in quality control standards encompasses a wider range of attest engagements.

PEER REVIEW

Quality control is concerned with establishing policies and procedures that encourage an accounting firm and its members to perform services consistent with professional standards. An integral part of an effective system of quality control is peer review, which enables a firm to evaluate its system of quality control to determine strengths and weaknesses and take corrective action where appropriate.

History of Peer Review

The AICPAPeer Review Program (PRP) was put in place to monitor the profession and establish a layer of public protection by identifying CPA firms that have inadequate systems of quality control, detecting nonperformance in accordance with professional standards in all material respects, imposing remedial action to correct deficiencies, and improving firms' accounting and auditing practices. The approved practice-monitoring programs are the AICPA's PRP and the AICPA's Center for Public Company Audit Firms

(CPCAF) (formerly the SEC Practice Section peer review program). In 2003 the AICPA's SEC Practice Section peer review program was expected to be supplanted by the Public Company Accounting Oversight Board's inspection program. The AICPA Peer Review Program requires a peer review of firms' accounting and auditing practice every three years.

Since its inception, the peer review program has been amended several times to expand its reach and strengthen its effectiveness. The PRP continues to evolve in response to changing market needs:

- 1977: Voluntary AICPA peer review program established.
- 1988: AICPA bylaw approved requiring all AICPA members active in the practice of public accounting to be associated with a firm that is enrolled in an AICPA approved practice monitoring program.
- 2000: AICPA bylaw amendment approved requiring *individual* CPAs to enroll in an AICPA-approved practice-monitoring program if they perform compilation services in firms or organizations not eligible to enroll in such a program.
- 2001: AICPA Standards for Performing and Reporting on Peer Reviews revised to include three different tiers of peer reviews: (1) system, (2) engagement, and (3) report reviews discussed below.

Objectives of Peer Review

Firms that perform engagements under the Statements on Auditing Standards (SASs), *Government Auditing Standards* (the Yellow Book), and/or examinations of prospective financial information under the Statements on Standards for Attestation Engagements (SSAEs) must undergo a System Review, in which independent peers periodically evaluate their system of quality control. These reviews are system- and compliance-oriented, with the objectives of evaluating whether

- The reviewed firm's system of quality control for its accounting and auditing practice has been designed to meet the requirements of the Quality Control Standards established by the AICPA.
- The reviewed firm's quality control policies and procedures are adhered to, providing the firm with reasonable assurance that it is complying with professional standards.

Firms that perform compilations (except as noted below) or review services under SSARSs and/or services under the SSAEs not included in system reviews must undergo an Engagement Review.

The objectives of an engagement review are to provide the peer reviewer with a reasonable basis for expressing limited assurance that

- The financial statements or information, and the related accountant's report on the accounting and review engagements and attestation engagements submitted for review, conform in all material respects with the requirements of professional standards.
- The reviewed firm's documentation conforms with the requirements of SSARSs and the SSAEs applicable to those engagements in all material respects.

Firms that only perform compilation engagements under SSARS where the firm has compiled financial statements that omit substantially all disclosures undergo peer reviews called report reviews. The objective of a report review is to enable the reviewed firm to improve the overall quality of its compilations that omit substantially all disclosures. The reviewer provides comments and recommendations based on whether the submitted financial statements and related accountant's reports conform with the requirements of professional standards in all material respects.

Strategies for Peer Review

The integration of peer review into a CPA firm's practice should be viewed as an opportunity to improve the profession. A negative attitude toward peer review will impede the growth and development of the firm. Although each firm must adopt its own strategies for implementing peer review, the following guidelines should be helpful to firms that are just beginning to address the issue.

Philosophy at the Top

If the key partners and other supervisory personnel of the firm approach the peer review process with a positive attitude, the firm will have an excellent opportunity for growth and improvement.

The starting point for developing a positive attitude is the initial planning for a peer review. Someone, presumably the managing partner, should embrace the concept and meet with key personnel. During the meeting, he or she should make it clear that peer review is an opportunity and not a necessary evil. Perhaps the best strategy for a successful peer review is to show how peer review fits into the firm's overall plans for development. For example, the managing partner may show how peer review could generate a valuable assessment of current policies and procedures, provide insight into the level of staff expertise, and afford an opportunity to talk candidly with an outside professional about the strengths and weaknesses of the firm.

Communicate the Philosophy

Once the key personnel of the firm have developed a consensus about the peer review process, it is important to communicate that position to the staff—both formally and informally. The formal aspect includes a staff meeting and a memorandum. Perhaps more important, however, are informal, sincere expressions of support by top management; that is, in day-to-day conversations with staff, key personnel should fully explain and stress the benefits of peer review.

Identify a Coordinator

The firm should assign one individual the responsibility of coordinating the peer review. The selection of a coordinator sends a signal to other staff members that the firm is fully committed to the peer review process. Thus, the coordinator should be highly competent and committed to the project.

Once the coordinator is identified, an internal review should begin. The coordinator, perhaps with assistants, should begin to catalog policies and procedures related to the five quality control elements. If policies and procedures are vague, it may be necessary to develop a list of perceived policies and procedures and submit those to key personnel in the firm for confirmation or modification.

Next, existing forms, checklists, programs, and other, similar documents should be identified. If documentary forms appear to be out of date or inappropriate, new forms should be designed, with appropriate feedback from staff.

Institute an Internal Inspection Process

An ongoing internal inspection process should be instituted before an external peer review is conducted. As noted earlier, an internal inspection is essential to a well-designed quality control system. CPA firms that are comfortable with the internal inspection process are better able to take full advantage of an external peer review.

Prepare for the Recommendations

The peer review process is by nature somewhat contentious, so key personnel of the firm must encourage the attitude that the results are recommendations, not criticisms. It is crucial that the firm be enthusiastic about the recommendations and see them as opportunities to strengthen the firm. If the peer review team is competent, that is exactly what the firm will receive: an opportunity to grow.

Peer Review Follow-Up

Once the external peer review is completed, the CPA firm should be prepared to make the best use of the peer evaluation. Again, this response should be orchestrated by the coordinator and may include staff meetings and individual assessment conferences with staff members. The firm should be prepared to read, evaluate, and implement the recommendations of the peer review team as quickly as possible; delayed response decreases the likelihood that the full benefit of the process will be achieved. Finally, peer review should be seen as a continuous process, not something to be endured every three years. Firm members should meet periodically to discuss quality control issues (including peer review). At every opportunity, key personnel of the firm should remind the staff that the key to growth is quality work and that a strong quality control system benefits the firm as a whole and the staff members individually.

CHAPTER 4
PRE-ENGAGEMENT CONSIDERATIONS

CONTENTS

OVERVIEW

Some of the procedures a CPA should perform as part of accepting an engagement are broad in nature. They apply to a structure that should be in place within the accounting firm to evaluate each prospective engagement, and they should take into consideration relevant portions of the AICPA Code of Professional Conduct and the firm's quality control system. Other procedures should be directed at the specific prospective client and include, for example, evaluating the prospective client's integrity, determining who will use the financial statements, and determining the level of service required. Procedures should be in place to ensure that the CPA and the client establish, preferably in writing, a clear understanding about the services to be performed. This chapter discusses these concepts in detail. Chapter 5, "Planning and Administration for Attestation Engagements," contains further discussion of planning issues that are unique to attestation engagements.

CLIENT ACCEPTANCE AND RETENTION

Rule 201 of the AICPA Code of Professional Conduct specifically states that the CPA should "undertake only those professional services that the member or the member's firm can reasonably expect to be completed with professional competence." This standard does not necessarily preclude a CPA firm from accepting an engagement that the firm is not fully qualified to execute at the time of acceptance as long as the CPA obtains the necessary expertise before the engagement is completed.

Ethical Considerations

Independence

Although an accountant may have adequate technical training and proficiency to conduct an engagement, he or she must also be without bias with respect to the client. As noted in SAS-95 (AU 150) (Generally Accepted Auditing Standards), the second general standard states that "in all matters relating to the assignment, an independence in mental attitude is to be maintained by the auditor or auditors." The auditor must be independent both in fact and in appearance. The accountant must also be independent in order to perform an attest engagement. Even though an accountant may perform a compilation engagement when he or she is not independent, he or she must indicate that he or she is not independent. Therefore, as a preliminary step before the engagement is accepted, the accounting firm should make inquiries of its professional staff to determine whether there is any relationship between a staff member and the client that might impair the firm's independence.

Management Integrity

The CPA is required to plan and perform an audit with an attitude of professional skepticism. In other words, the auditor neither assumes that management is dishonest nor assumes unquestioned honesty. In difficult audit areas that are subject to an increased level of professional judgment, the auditor should recognize the increased importance of factors that bear on management integrity. A lack of management integrity has been found to exist in the great majority of significant accountants' liability cases. The following are questions that the CPA should consider asking:

- Are there significant disagreements or lawsuits among the owners?
- What is the reputation of top management and/or majority owners in the business community?
- Is there any significant pending litigation against the entity?
- Is there high turnover in key financial positions?

- Does top management lack the experience necessary to operate the business?

Professional Competency and Staff Availability

A prospective client may be in an industry that is not familiar to the accountant, may have a sophisticated accounting system that requires a high level of expertise, or may be subject to stringent requirements of regulatory agencies (e.g., the Securities and Exchange Commission) that the accountant is not familiar with. When determining whether an engagement should be accepted, the accountant should assess the level and quality of staffing needed to complete the engagement. The level of staffing needed is based on the size and complexity of the engagement. The accountant should make preliminary estimates of the number of staff hours needed to complete the engagement and the period of time when the engagement will be executed. The accountant must determine whether appropriate skilled personnel will be available at the proper time to work on the engagement.

CLIENT ACCEPTANCE PROCEDURES

Chapter 3, SQCS-2 (System of Quality Control for a CPA Firm's Accounting and Auditing Practice) states that an accounting firm should establish procedures to determine whether a client should be accepted, rejected, or retained and whether or not a specific engagement for that client should be performed. SQCS-2 highlights the fact that the accountant should exercise due professional care in the initial contact with, and evaluation of, prospective clients and in determining whether to continue a client relationship. The purpose of the SQCS-2 quality control requirement is to minimize the probability of a CPA associating with a client whose management lacks integrity. When making client acceptance and continuance decisions, the accountant should carefully consider taking the following steps:

- Evaluate prospective clients.
- Identify intended users of the subject matter.
- Assess the firm's capabilities.
- Consider the firm's independence.

OBSERVATION: The presentation of client acceptance procedures in this chapter is extensive, and may be more elaborate than is necessary for all engagements. Depending on the risk assessment and the size of the client, the CPA may need only meet with the client, look over the client's records, obtain a copy of the current financial statement and tax return, and speak with the intended third-party user, if any.

Evaluate Prospective Clients

After the initial contact by a prospective client—but before the terms of the engagement are negotiated—the CPA should evaluate the prospective client. This screening process should determine whether the prospective client fits with the type of practice that the accounting firm is developing. A variety of factors are relevant to the screening process. The following are the more basic steps that should be taken:

- Interview the prospective client.
- Develop a preliminary understanding of the form of the prospective client's records.
- Perform a preliminary evaluation of staff competencies.
- Contact third parties familiar with the prospective client.

Interview the Prospective Client

After the prospective client initially contacts the CPA, arrangements should be made for the two parties to meet, allowing the CPA the opportunity to speak directly with key management personnel or owners and get a feeling for the skill level of personnel and the types of personalities in the client's company. Other areas that should be explored during the interview are

- Why the prospective client wants the engagement
- What limitations, if any, the prospective client may impose on the engagement
- A brief history of the prospective client, including identification of the principals involved and the management team
- A summary of turnover of key personnel, including financial staff
- Identification and description of pending or threatened litigation
- Any conflict of interest between the accounting firm and the prospective client

Develop a Preliminary Understanding of the Prospective Client's Records

Unlike the standards for audits, the standards that are applicable to other engagements do not require the CPA to understand and evaluate the client's internal control; however, the CPA should develop some understanding of the prospective client's records. Ordinarily, this understanding includes identification of the types of journals and ledgers used, the manner in which data are processed (manually, by machine, or electronically), the use of outside data processing services, and the training and level of education of the client's personnel. A basic understanding of the prospective client's records should alert the CPA to whether additional services are needed before an engagement can be performed. In some instances, the records may be so poorly designed and maintained that the CPA will decide that an engagement cannot be performed or that the potential for encountering problems is so great that it would be better not to accept the engagement.

Contact Third Parties Familiar with the Prospective Client

The CPA should also consider contacting other parties familiar with the prospective client, including other accountants (including the predecessor CPA), bankers, the prospective client's attorney, and other business associates. In making such contacts, the CPA must be careful not to breach any confidential relationships between the prospective client and other parties. It is a good idea for the CPA to get the prospective client's permission before beginning any discussions with third parties.

Identify Intended Users of the Subject Matter

As part of client acceptance, the CPA should determine the purpose of the report, which might be intended for use by management, governmental regulatory authorities, or external parties such as banks and other creditors.

Although the specific engagement procedures do not depend on the users of the subject matter, the CPA should assess the risk associated with each engagement—whether the final users of the report are internal or external parties.

Assess the Firm's Capabilities

Once the CPA has discussed the engagement with the prospective client and has identified the users of the report, the next step for the CPA is to assess his or her firm's ability to complete the engagement successfully. Beyond having the prerequisite expertise, the CPA firm should consider a number of other factors. Initially, the CPA firm should determine whether staff members are available for the prospective engagement. If it appears that the engagement will involve two or more offices of the firm, all offices involved must have the capacity to perform the engagement. In order to satisfy the standard of due professional care in the engagement, the firm must have adequate resources at its disposal.

The firm must also consider whether the CPA handling the engagement will need to obtain training and/or technical materials for a specialized industry that CPA has had little or no exposure to.

OTHER ENGAGEMENT ACCEPTANCE CONSIDERATIONS

Recognizing Danger Signs

Screening prospective and existing clients is a valuable component of the accountant's malpractice-defense program. Warning signs of potentially troublesome clients are

- Fee and time pressures
- Financial or organizational difficulty
- Involvement in suspicious transactions
- Lack of cooperation by key management and accounting personnel
- Refusal to sign engagement and representation letters

The following is a summary of the key danger signs that may be relevant to the accountant in deciding whether or not to accept a new client or retain an existing one:

- Financial or organizational difficulty:
  - — Dependence on a few customers or vendors
  - — Difficulty in collecting receivables from customers
  - — Economic slump
  - — Excessive inventory buildup relative to sales
  - — High level of debt
  - — High turnover in key positions
  - — Increased competition, domestic or foreign
  - — Industry experiencing business failures
  - — Insufficient working capital and inadequate liquid resources
  - — Limited sources of capital
  - — Material IRS adjustments
  - — Pending or threatened litigation
  - — Problems with, or investigations by, regulatory agencies
  - — Restrictive debt covenants

  - Significant losses from operations
  - Uncalculated or uncontrolled expansion
- Management practices and characteristics:
  - Compensation tied to financial results or specific transactions
  - Failure to file income tax returns for several years
  - Frequent change of auditors toward year-end
  - High staff turnover
  - Inadequate employee training and evaluation
  - Key management known to have criminal or questionable background
  - Personal financial stress
  - Poor hiring practices
- Nature of accounting transactions:
  - Large, numerous, and unusual year-end transactions
  - Significant number of transactions with related parties
  - Unusual number of audit adjusting entries identified
  - Unusually large expenditures to lawyers, consultants, agents, and related parties
  - Weaknesses in, or absence of, internal controls
- Unrealistic expectations and lack of cooperation:
  - Frequent fee pressures and disputes
  - Refusal to provide necessary documents and records on time
  - Threats to switch auditors
  - Unrealistic expectations of the time needed to complete the engagement
  - Unwillingness to correct material weaknesses in internal control or to follow up on comments raised by the auditor in the management letter
  - Vague, guarded, or evasive responses to inquiries

Valuable Lessons from Litigation

In response to the persistent and significant allegations CPAs have faced in litigation, the following reminders are offered:

- The CPA should exercise great care in deciding to accept and, equally important, retain clients. The CPA should consider having discussions with the prospective client's banker, legal counsel, and key personnel before accepting the client. Similarly, the CPA should carefully evaluate a continuing client's request for new levels of service in light of the firm's expertise and ability to deliver those services.

- The CPA should evaluate high turnover in key management positions, which can result in poor recordkeeping, weak internal controls, and increased risk.
- The CPA should be realistic in assessing the risks associated with the engagement. For example, weak internal controls, coupled with an aggressive management team or questionable management integrity, greatly heighten risk.
- The CPA should determine whether there is adequate board oversight of the client environment. For example, when a company gets into financial difficulties and shareholders and creditors learn that top executives have treated airplanes and vacation homes as personal entitlements, they are quick to blame the CPA. Such abuse of company resources is likely to be controlled and minimized if the client has an effective oversight board.
- The CPA firm and its staff should possess adequate training, competence, and proficiency to complete the engagement in accordance with professional standards. All engagement team members should try to evaluate the significance of the issues they face. This is even more important for supervisory personnel, particularly engagement partners. If the client operates in a specialized industry, the CPA should be knowledgeable about the specific requirements and issues facing the industry.
- The CPA should allocate adequate time and effort to high-risk, complex, and unusual transactions. The time records and summaries should be complete and accurate.
- The CPA should adequately document in the workpapers the work performed and the conclusions reached, including why certain factors were considered more relevant and persuasive than others in reaching the conclusions. In general, the workpapers for an audit must demonstrate that the standards of fieldwork have been achieved and that the accounting records agree or reconcile with the financial statements being reported on.
- The CPA should obtain timely representations and confirmations from management, client legal counsel, and other third parties (where required).

Documentation

The acceptance of an engagement should be well documented. The documentation should clearly show that the necessary pre-engagement planning procedures were properly completed, and it should include copies of communications with the client, a memorandum of the exchanges of information between the predecessor and successor accountants, and other pertinent information concerning pre-engagement planning.

Once an engagement is accepted, the professional relationship between the client and the CPA should be evaluated annually. This monitoring is critical for recognizing clients who may be developing into risks to the CPA's practice. The requirement of periodic evaluation of client retention is explicitly mandated by SQCS-2. Therefore, the CPA should continue to evaluate the integrity of management and periodically determine his or her ability to serve the client.

Appendix 4B is a client acceptance and retention evaluation form, which the CPA can use to document his or her screening of prospective new clients and to evaluate the retention of existing clients. The form is only a guide: the CPA should exercise professional judgment in revising or adding questions where appropriate. This form should be updated at least annually, and the engagement executive should review it to determine whether to accept a particular engagement and whether to retain or terminate clients.

INDEPENDENCE CONSIDERATIONS

Independence is the foundation of the attest function. Third-party users rely on the CPA's opinion in an audit or attest engagement because they believe the conclusion is impartial and unbiased. A compilation report can be issued even if there is an impairment of independence; however, under this circumstance the compilation report must state that the CPA is not independent. Thus, before accepting the engagement the CPA should evaluate a prospective client to determine whether there is an independence problem. If there is an independence problem, the CPA and the prospective client should discuss the situation, and the prospective client should understand that the compilation report to be issued will contain a reference to a lack of independence.

Determining independence is a matter of professional judgment, and CPAs should use the guidelines found in the AICPA Code of Professional Conduct. The AICPA's Code provides guidance in Rule 101 (Independence), Interpretations of Rule 101, and Ethics Rulings on Independence. Rule 101 is reproduced in Appendix 4A. A summary of guidelines for determining independence on the basis of Interpretations of Rule 101 are also presented in Appendix 4A, as is a list of circumstances that could affect independence.

In May 1999, the AICPA Professional Ethics Executive Committee revised Ethics Interpretation 101-3 and issued a new Interpretation 101-3 (Performance of Other Services), which provides numerous examples of types of services being performed in today's practice environment and the impact they have on the accountant's independence. In 2003, the Professional Ethics Executive Committee adopted significant revisions to the Interpretation 101-3 (renamed "Performance of Nonattest Services").

The revised AICPA rules clarify the general requirements for performing nonattest services and include a pre-engagement documentation requirement. Restrictive rules apply to certain services such as financial information system design and implementation and appraisal, valuation, and actuarial services.

> **OBSERVATION:** The pre-engagement documentation requirement applies to any nonattest services (e.g., bookkeeping, tax or consulting services) performed by the CPA for an attest client. While the rule requires that the understanding with the client must be in writing, the form of documentation is left to the CPA's discretion. The method of documentation is not as important as the content of the documentation. For example, if the CPA performs a consulting engagement for an attest client, the CPA may decide to document the required elements with respect to the consulting engagement in the attest engagement letter, but the understanding could also be documented, for example, in a separate engagement letter specific to the consulting service engagement, in a memo to the attest engagement files, or in a checklist that the CPA completes as part of the attest engagement. If a client engages the CPA to perform tax services, the understanding could be documented in a tax organizer or in a memo contained in the tax working papers. Other methods of documentation such as a memo of understanding maintained in the CPA's billing or correspondence files (i.e., separate from the client work paper files) would also satisfy this requirement.

One of the key principles underlying the AICPA rules on nonattest services is that the accountant may not serve—or even appear to serve—as a member of a client's management. For example, the accountant may not

- Make operational or financial decisions for the client
- Perform management functions for the client
- Report to the board of directors on behalf of management

> **OBSERVATION:** The AICPA reminds CPAs that state societies, state boards of accountancy, and state regulatory agencies may have additional requirements for assessing whether independence has been compromised.

Understanding the Nature of the Services

A CPA should discuss with the client the nature of the compilation, review, audit, or attest engagement (called here "attest engagements") and other services (nonattest services) the client has requested the CPA to perform. This discussion should include (1) the objectives and limitations of the requested attest engagement and (2) the responsibilities of both the CPA and management. Interpretation 101-3 states that it is preferable that this understanding be part of the engagement letter and that it be made clear that the CPA "will not perform management functions or make management decisions."

Evaluating the Client's Understanding of Its Responsibilities

It is not sufficient to document an understanding of the services in an engagement letter. The CPA should also evaluate the client to determine whether management has an understanding of its responsibility to

- Designate a management-level individual or individuals to be responsible for overseeing the services being provided.
- Evaluate the adequacy of the services performed and any findings that result.
- Make management decisions, including accepting responsibility for the results of the other services.
- Establish and maintain internal controls, including monitoring ongoing activities.

The determination of whether the CPA's independence is impaired because of the performance of other services in an attest engagement is a matter of professional judgment. However, Interpretation 101-3 does provide general guidance by listing services that would impair independence in an attest engagement:

- Authorizing, executing, or consummating a transaction or otherwise exercising authority on behalf of a client
- Preparing source documents or originating data, in electronic or other form, evidencing the occurrence of a transaction
- Having custody of client assets
- Supervising client employees in the performance of their normal activities
- Determining which recommendations of the CPA should be implemented
- Reporting to the board of directors on behalf of management
- Serving as a client's stock transfer or escrow agent, registrar, or general counsel or its equivalent

A CPA may perform a variety of services that are not part of an attest engagement. Some of the more common services are

- Bookkeeping
- Payroll and other disbursement

- Benefit plan administration
- Investment advising or investment managing
- Corporate finance consulting or advising
- Appraisal, valuation, or actuarial
- Executive or employee search
- Business risk consulting
- Information system design, installation, or integration

Bookkeeping

Routine bookkeeping activities such as recording properly approved transactions and preparing financial statements from a trial balance do not impair independence. However, Interpretation 101-3 notes that the following activities do impair independence in a compilation or review engagement:

- Determining or changing journal entries, account coding or classification for transactions, or other accounting records without obtaining client approval
- Authorizing or approving transactions
- Preparing source documents or originating data
- Making changes to source documents without client approval

The AICPA independence rules prohibit accountants from acting as client management in all circumstances. Accordingly, an accountant may provide bookkeeping services provided that the client effectively oversees the services and, among other tasks, performs all management functions and makes all management decisions in connection with the services. For example, if an accountant is engaged to provide bookkeeping services that will result in a set of financial statements, the client must

- Approve all account classifications.
- Provide source documents to the accountant so that the accountant can prepare journal entries.
- Take responsibility for the results of the accountant's services (e.g., financial statements).
- Establish and maintain internal controls over the accountant's bookkeeping activities.

Payroll and Other Disbursement

Activities such as processing approved payroll information or making electronic payroll tax payments, "assuming the client has made arrangements for its financial institution to limit such payments to a named payee," do not impair independence. When activities include authorizing payments, cosigning client checks, maintaining custody over a client's cash account, or approving vendor invoices for payment, the CPA assumes the role of management and thus impairs his or her independence.

Benefit Plan Administration

Benefit plan administrative duties may include communicating summary plan data to a plan trustee or preparing participant statements based on data provided by management. Interpretation 101-3 notes that the following activities impair independence in a compilation or review engagement:

- Making disbursements to participants
- Serving as a fiduciary as defined by ERISA
- Making policy decisions related to the plan

Investment Advising and Investment Managing

A CPA may develop expertise in investment planning and management, and his or her independence is not impaired when his or her activities include recommending an asset allocation strategy to the client and transmitting approved investment transactions to a broker. Activities that do impair independence include executing transactions and assuming custody over investment assets.

Corporate Finance Consulting and Advising

Often clients seeking compilation or review engagements have limited expertise in corporate finance. The CPA's performance of activities such as assisting in the development of corporate strategies or participating in transaction negotiations is acceptable if the CPA does not assume a managerial role. Interpretation 101-3 notes that the following activities impair the CPA's independence:

- Negotiating on behalf of the client or its owners with potential investors and sources of capital
- Distributing private placement memoranda or offering documents to potential investors
- Acting as an underwriter, broker, agent, distributor, or guarantor regarding client securities
- Soliciting investors or promoting client securities
- Maintaining custody of client securities

Appraisal, Valuation, and Actuarial

A CPA may be hired to perform services related to the appraisal or valuation of accounts or the determination of actuarial valuations. However, the CPA should have the expertise necessary to perform these services, and the work product should be carefully considered by the client. The CPA cannot assume responsibility for determining amounts that appear in the financial statements, because that role belongs strictly to management. Interpretation 101-3 illustrates this guidance with the following descriptions of acceptable services:

- Testing the reasonableness of the value placed on an asset or liability included in a client's financial statements by preparing a separate valuation of that asset or liability
- Performing a valuation of a client's business when all significant matters of judgment are determined or approved by the client and the client is in a position to have an informed judgment on the results of the valuation

If a CPA determines a valuation based on his or her judgment that is not approved by the client, the CPA's independence is impaired.

Executive and Employee Search

A CPA is often able to provide valuable services in the recruitment of employees. These services do not impair independence if they include activities such as screening prospective employees based on client-approved criteria or recommending a job description to the client. The hiring or firing of employees are activities that do impair independence.

Business Risk Consulting

A CPA can assist the client in activities such as assessing business risk and recommending strategies to manage risk without impairing independence.

Information System Design, Installation, and Integration

CPAs typically develop strong information systems skills, and Interpretation 101-3 has identified the following related activities as not impairing independence:

- Installing or integrating a client's financial information system that was not designed or developed by the accountant (e.g., an off-the-shelf accounting package).

- Assisting in setting up the client's chart of accounts and financial statement format with respect to the client's financial information system.
- Designing, developing, installing, or integrating a client's information system that is unrelated to the client's financial statements or accounting records.
- Providing training and instruction to client employees on an information and control system.

Activities that do impair independence include designing or developing a client's financial information system, making other than insignificant modifications to source code underlying a client's existing financial information system, supervising client personnel in the daily operation of their information system, and operating a client's local area network (LAN) system.

> **OBSERVATION:** In order for a CPA to prevent his or her impairment of independence, if he or she is offered employment by a client or seeks employment with a client during an engagement, he or she should remove him- or herself from the engagement until the employment offer is rejected or employment is no longer being sought.

COMMUNICATION WITH THE PREDECESSOR CPA

Audit Engagements

In evaluating a potential client that has been audited previously by another auditor, the predecessor auditor is a primary source of information about the client. SAS-84 (AU 315) (Communications Between Predecessor and Successor Auditors) requires the successor auditor to communicate with the predecessor auditor. However, Rule 301 of the AICPA Code of Professional Conduct prohibits an auditor from disclosing confidential information except when the client agrees to the disclosure. To reconcile the requirements of AU 315 with Rule 301, the successor auditor should ask the prospective client to grant permission to discuss the impending engagement with the predecessor auditor. If the successor auditor cannot obtain required information from the predecessor auditor because of client restrictions, the successor auditor should carefully consider the implications of such restrictions in evaluating whether to accept the engagement.

The initiative for communicating rests with the successor auditor, and the form of such communication between the successor auditor and the predecessor auditor may be oral or written (although the communication must be documented whether oral or written). The successor auditor's main objective in communicating is to find out any information that is relevant to his or her decision on whether to accept the client. Therefore, the questions raised by the successor auditor should be sufficiently specific to help determine whether he or she should accept the engagement.

AU 315.09 states that matters subject to inquiry should include

- Information that might bear on the integrity of management
- Disagreements with management over the application of accounting principles, auditing procedures, or other similarly significant matters
- Communications to audit committees or others with equivalent authority and responsibility (e.g., board of directors or the owner in a small business) regarding fraud, illegal acts by clients, and internal-control-related matters
- The predecessor auditor's understanding of the reasons for the change of auditors

The successor auditor should request the client to authorize the predecessor auditor to allow a review of the predecessor's working papers. In an effort to reduce potential misunderstandings about the scope of the communications being authorized, the predecessor auditor might wish to request a consent and acknowledgment letter from the client to document this authorization. Appendix 4C is an illustrative client consent and acknowledgment letter.

AU 315.11 states that, ordinarily, the predecessor auditor should permit the successor to review working papers, including documentation of planning, internal control, audit results, and other matters of continuing accounting and auditing significance such as the working paper analyses of balance sheet accounts and those relating to contingencies. The extent, if any, to which a predecessor auditor permits access to the working papers is a matter of professional judgment. Before permitting access to the working papers, the predecessor auditor may wish to obtain a written communication from the successor auditor as to the use of the working papers. Appendix 4D is an illustrative successor auditor acknowledgment letter.

Compilation Engagements

SSARS-4 (AR 400.02) (Communication Between Predecessor and Successor Accountants) provides the following definitions:

- *Successor accountant* An accountant who has been invited to make a proposal for an engagement to compile or review financial statements and is considering accepting the engagement or an accountant who has accepted such an engagement.
- *Predecessor accountant* An accountant who (1) has reported on the most recent compiled or reviewed financial statements or was engaged to perform but did not complete a compilation or review of the financial statements and (2) has

resigned, declined to stand for reappointment, or been notified that his or her services have been, or may be, terminated.

The successor accountant may (but is not required to) communicate with the predecessor accountant (with the prospective client's permission) to determine whether a compilation engagement should be accepted. AR 400.05 notes that the inquiries "should be specific and reasonable regarding matters that will assist the successor accountant in determining whether to accept the engagement" and may include areas of inquiry such as the following:

- Management (owner's) integrity
- Disagreements concerning accounting principles, the performance of engagement procedures, or "similarly significant matters"
- Management cooperation with requests for additional or revised information
- Fraud or illegal acts
- The reason for the change of accountants

Generally the predecessor accountant should respond promptly and fully with inquiries posed by the successor accountant except in the case of unusual circumstances such as litigation. When the response is limited, the predecessor accountant should inform the successor accountant of this.

Attestation Engagements

Although the attestation standards do not address the issue of communication with other accountants, guidance may be found in the SASs and SSARS. The CPA should obtain the prospective client's permission for communicating with the predecessor or primary accountant. Exhibit 4-1 is a sample information release form. If the prospective client refuses to provide this permission, the CPA may consider turning down the engagement.

Inquiries of the predecessor or primary accountant may include the following:

- Facts that might bear on the integrity of management
- Significant disagreements with management
- Communications with the entity regarding fraud or illegal acts and internal control matters
- Whether the current CPA refused to provide the attestation service and, if so, why
- The predecessor's understanding of the reasons for a change in accountants, if applicable

EXHIBIT 4-1
INFORMATION RELEASE FORM

July 17, 20XX

John Doe, CPA
123 Main Street
Greenville, SC 29601

We have engaged Able, Baker, and Charles, CPAs to perform certain attestation [agreed-upon procedures] services for our company. In connection with these services, they would like to make inquires and examine certain of your documentation for the [audit, compilation, review, consulting] engagement for the [*period(s)*] ended [*date(s)*]. We hereby authorize you to respond fully and without limitation to their requests.

Please allow Able, Baker, and Charles, CPAs to copy any information needed from files related to your engagements for us (unless proprietary in nature) and bill our company for the reproduction costs.

You will be contacted by Mr. Will Baker concerning these matters.

Yours truly,

[*officer's signature and title*]

ESTABLISHING AN UNDERSTANDING WITH THE CLIENT

Audit Engagements

SAS-83 (AU 310) (Establishing an Understanding with the Client) requires the auditor to establish an understanding with the client regarding the services to be performed for each engagement. Such an understanding reduces the risk that either the auditor or the client may misinterpret the needs or expectations of the other party. The understanding should include the objectives of the engagement, management's responsibilities, the auditor's responsibilities, and limitations of the engagement. The auditor should document the understanding in the working papers, preferably through a written communication with the client. If the auditor believes that an understanding with the client has not been established, he or she should decline to accept or to perform the engagement.

AU 310.06 states that an understanding with the client generally includes the following matters:

- The objective of the audit is the expression of an opinion.

- Management is responsible for the entity's financial statements.
- Management is responsible for establishing and maintaining effective internal control over financial reporting.
- Management is responsible for identifying and ensuring that the entity complies with the laws and regulations applicable to its activities.
- Management is responsible for making all financial records and related information available to the auditor.
- At the conclusion of the audit, management will provide the auditor with a letter that confirms certain representations made during the audit.
- The auditor is responsible for conducting the audit in accordance with generally accepted auditing standards. Those standards require that the auditor obtain reasonable, rather than absolute, assurance about whether the financial statements are free of material misstatement, whether caused by error or by fraud. Accordingly, a material misstatement may remain undetected. Also, an audit is not designed to detect error or fraud that is immaterial to the financial statements. If for any reason the auditor is unable to complete the audit or is unable to form or has not formed an opinion, he or she may decline to express an opinion or decline to issue a report as a result of the engagement.
- An audit includes obtaining an understanding of internal control sufficient to plan the audit and determine the nature, timing, and extent of the audit procedures to be performed. An audit is not designed to provide assurance on internal control or to identify reportable conditions. However, the auditor is responsible for ensuring that the audit committee or others with equivalent authority or responsibility are aware of all reportable conditions that come to his or her attention.
- Management is responsible for adjusting the financial statements to correct material misstatements and for affirming to the auditor in the representation letter that the effects of any uncorrected misstatements, resulting from errors or fraud, aggregated by the auditor during the current engagement and pertaining to the latest period presented are immaterial, both individually and in the aggregate, to the financial statements taken as a whole.

In addition to the required matters discussed above, AU 310.07 states that an understanding with the client also may include other matters, such as the following:

- Arrangements concerning the conduct of the engagement, such as timing, client assistance regarding the preparation of schedules, and the availability of documents

- Arrangements regarding involvement of specialists or internal auditors, if applicable
- Arrangements involving a predecessor auditor
- Arrangements regarding fees and billings
- Any limitation of, or other arrangements regarding, the liability of the auditor or the client, such as indemnification of the auditor against liability arising from knowing misrepresentations to the auditor by management
- Conditions under which access to the auditor's working papers may be granted to others
- Additional services to be provided relating to regulatory requirements
- Arrangements regarding other services to be provided in connection with the engagement

The auditor may communicate the understanding with the client and the matters discussed above in an engagement letter to the client. Although not required by generally accepted auditing standards, the use of engagement letters is a common and sound business practice.

The engagement letter is intended to achieve the following primary objectives:

- Document the contractual duties agreed to by the auditor and the client.
- Explain the auditor's and the client's responsibilities.
- Explain the nature of the services to be rendered by the auditor and establish that the financial statements are the responsibility of the client.
- Avoid misunderstandings with the client and among the staff.
- Protect the auditor from legal liability.

The engagement letter is normally addressed to the board of directors, the audit committee, the partners, the proprietor, or the chief executive officer. The engagement letter should identify the period under audit, describe the financial statement element that will be audited (e.g., accounts receivable or inventory), and identify the type of report the auditor expects to issue.

In addition, the auditor should mention that in the event of unforeseen circumstances or conditions the client will be notified in writing about the revised terms of the engagement. For example, the auditor may be unable to express an opinion on the financial statement element without extensive additional procedures because the internal controls were found to be ineffective or because of the poor condition of the accounting records.

Exhibit 4-2 is a checklist of engagement letter dos and don'ts that the auditor can refer to when writing engagement letters.

EXHIBIT 4-2
DOS AND DON'TS IN ENGAGEMENT LETTERS

DO

- State the purpose of the engagement.
- Define the scope of the engagement (i.e., specifically what you will and will not do).
- Specify known negative conditions or adverse situations.
- Note client instructions, responsibilities, and delivery dates.
- Note reliance on facts provided by client.
- Outline terms of fee collections and the consequences of late payment.
- Request the client's signature and instruct the client to return the signed letter.
- Explain inherent limitations of the internal control.
- Explain limitations regarding financial statement distribution.
- Explain conditions for engagement termination procedures.

DON'T

- Use absolutes, superlatives, and words that expand rather than limit your responsibilities.
- Use legal jargon or ambiguous terms, abbreviations, or words only a CPA would understand.
- Include forms of marketing or promotional information. The engagement letter is a contract and should be composed accordingly.
- Make adverse comments about other auditors.

Compilation Engagements

A compilation engagement may be performed for a client who lacks a high degree of accounting sophistication. For this reason, it is important that the CPA and the client reach an understanding on what service(s) will be performed. AR 100.05 states that, preferably, the understanding with the client should be in writing and should include

- A description of the scope and the limitations of the compilation engagement
- A description of the compilation report that the CPA expects to issue

- A statement that the compilation engagement cannot be relied upon to disclose errors, fraud, or illegal acts
- A statement that the CPA will inform the appropriate level of management of (1) any material errors that come to the CPA's attention and (2) any fraud or illegal acts that come to the CPA's attention, unless they are clearly inconsequential

Although the understanding with the client is not required to be in writing, it should be documented adequately in the compilation workpapers. If the understanding is in writing, the best form of documentation is an engagement letter. If the understanding is not in writing, other documentation methods may be used to summarize the understanding between the client and the CPA.

Scope of the Engagement

Before accepting a compilation engagement, the CPA should make clear to the prospective client the scope of the engagement as the CPA perceives it. Once the CPA has a clear picture of the necessary scope of the engagement, he or she can design specific compilation procedures.

> **OBSERVATION:** Reaching an understanding with the client does not imply that the client determines the scope of the compilation engagement. The understanding between the CPA and the client simply facilitates the execution of a successful compilation engagement. When a CPA cannot perform the procedures deemed appropriate in a compilation engagement, no compilation report can be issued.

Engagement Letters

Generally, SSARS do not require that the accountant obtain an engagement letter to formalize the understanding with the client. However, to avoid a misunderstanding with the client and to reduce liability risk exposure, the CPA should prepare an engagement letter before accepting a compilation engagement. (Best practice dictates that if no letter is obtained, this fact should be documented.)

These procedures should be repeated for each subsequent compilation engagement with the client. The CPA should be sensitive to any circumstances that would require a change in a subsequent engagement letter.

The following elements are ordinarily covered in an engagement letter:

- A description of the nature of the service to be performed and the limitations of the service

- A description of any additional services to be performed, such as tax return preparation or bookkeeping services
- An indication of the time period covered by the engagement
- An example of the report the accountant expects to render
- An indication of the frequency with which the service will be rendered, especially when different services will be rendered with different frequencies
- An indication of the client's responsibilities during the engagement, such as responsibility for the preparation of account analyses
- Fees for the service and billing arrangements
- A statement that the engagement cannot be relied on to disclose errors, fraud, or illegal acts
- A statement that the accountant will inform the appropriate level of management of any material errors that come to his or her attention and any irregularities or illegal acts that come to his or her attention, unless they are clearly inconsequential

Although most compilation engagement letters include basically the same text, the CPA should word the letter carefully to conform to the individual characteristics of each engagement.

Other Documentation Methods

If the understanding with the client is not documented in an engagement letter, the understanding should be documented in the compilation workpapers. The documentation can take a variety of forms, including a checklist or questionnaire or a memorandum based on the discussions with the client. The workpaper documentation should state the basic understanding with the client.

Attestation Engagements

Chapter 1 of SSAE-10 (AT 101) requires the practitioner to establish an understanding with the client regarding the services to be performed for each attestation engagement. That understanding should include

- *The objectives of the engagement* The practitioner should address the objectives of the engagement and any limitations of the engagement. For example, the objective of an examination engagement is to express an opinion as to whether the assertion or subject matter is fairly stated in all material respects based on the stated criteria.

- *Management's responsibilities* In an examination engagement, management must select the criteria and determine that it is appropriate for its purposes. If the client is the responsible party, the client is also responsible for the subject matter (or related assertion) that the practitioner will perform his or her procedures on.
- *Practitioner's responsibilities* The practitioner's responsibility is to perform the engagement in accordance with professional standards. More specifically, the practitioner should describe the services that he or she will provide as precisely as possible to avoid misunderstandings.
- *Limitations of the engagement* The limitations that should be addressed relate to two aspects of the engagement: (1) limitations of the type of services to be performed and (2) use limitations based on the type of service. For example, the practitioner may wish to document that the engagement does not provide absolute assurance. In addition, the client should understand that in some cases the use of the report would be limited. For example, if a written assertion is not obtained from the responsible party, the practitioner's report would be restricted.

Other matters that practitioners should consider discussing with the client are

- *Subject matter* The practitioner should determine specifically the subject matter to be reported on. This understanding should be used to determine that the practitioner has, or can acquire, sufficient expertise to perform the engagement.
- *Criteria* The criteria to be used must be both suitable and available to users.
- *Users of the report* Knowing who the potential users are helps the practitioner assess the risks in the engagement and provides him or her with information regarding the appropriateness of the service he or she is to provide.
- *Logistics* The practitioner should determine whether the client has the necessary personnel and expertise to develop the subject matter. In addition, this understanding should include arrangements concerning the conduct of the engagement, such as timing, client assistance, and the availability of documents. Additional matters might include arrangements concerning involvement of specialists and conditions under which access to the working papers may be granted to others.
- *Fees* The practitioner should determine that the fee and billing arrangements are appropriate.

Engagement Letters

The attestation standards require the practitioner to establish an understanding with the client. The standards state that a written engagement letter is preferred but not necessarily required. Although not specifically required by the SSAEs, a written engagement letter is strongly recommended. Most practitioners believe that a written engagement letter can effectively reduce misunderstandings between the practitioner and the client over the nature and limitations of the engagement. Engagement letters are particularly important in attestation engagements because of the increased risk of misunderstanding the nature of the practitioner's responsibilities (while clients may be familiar with traditional financial statement audits, they might not understand the nature and limitations of attestation engagements). The written engagement letter commonly includes the items discussed in the preceding section. When a written engagement letter is not obtained, the understanding of the engagement should be obtained and documented in the workpapers.

APPENDIX 4A
RULE 101 OF THE AICPA CODE OF PROFESSIONAL CONDUCT

Rule 101: Independence

A member in public practice shall be independent in the performance of professional services as required by standards promulgated by bodies designated by Council.

SUMMARY GUIDELINES FOR INTERPRETATIONS OF RULE 101

Independence shall be considered to be impaired if, for example, a member had any of the following transactions, interests, or relationships:

A. During the period of a professional engagement or at the of expressing an opinion, a member or a member's firm:
   1. Had or was committed to acquire any direct or material financial interest in the enterprise.
   2. Was a trustee of any trust or executor or administrator of estate if such trust or estate had or was committed to acquire direct or material indirect financial interest in the enterprise.
   3. Had any joint, closely held business investment with the or with any officer, director, or principal stockholders that was material in relation to the member's net worth or to net worth of the member's firm.

4. Had any loan to or from the enterprise or any officer, director, or principal stockholder of the enterprise, except for those allowed under Interpretation 101-5.

B. During the period covered by the financial statements, during the period of the professional engagement, or at the time of expressing an opinion, a member or a member's firm:

1. Was connected with the enterprise as a promoter, underwriter, or voting trustee, as a director or officer, or in any capacity equivalent to that of a member of management or of an employee.
2. Was a trustee for any pension or profit-sharing trust of the enterprise.

The above examples are not intended to be all-inclusive.

Prior to 1988, Interpretation 101-1 was part of Rule 101. Rule 101 is reproduced here in its entirety.

Interpretation 101-2: Former Practitioners and Firm Independence

The term "member or a member's firm" does not include a former member of the firm if the following conditions are satisfied:

- Payments made to the former member of the firm do not raise doubts about the continued existence of the firm.
- Amounts due to the former member are (1) fixed, (2) based on a specific schedule of payments, (3) to be paid over a reasonable period, (4) and carry a reasonable rate of interest.
- There is no participation by the former member in the operations of the firm except over a reasonable transition period.
- The name of the former member is not used in a way that would suggest that the member participates in or is otherwise associated with the firm.
- The former member of the firm may have an office in the firm's suite of offices and other amenities, provided the former member does not have a position of significant influence with the firm's clients.

Interpretation 101-3: Performance of Nonattest Services

The CPA should not perform management functions or make management decisions for the attest client. However, the CPA may provide advice, research materials, and recommendations to assist the client's management in performing its functions and making decisions.

The client must agree to perform the following functions in connection with the engagement to perform nonattest services:

- Make all management decisions and perform all management functions;

- Designate a competent employee, preferably within senior management, to oversee the services;
- Evaluate the adequacy and results of the services performed;
- Accept responsibility for the results of the services; and
- Establish and maintain internal controls, including monitoring ongoing activities.

The CPA should be satisfied that the client will be able to meet all of these criteria and make an informed judgment on the results of the CPA's nonattest services. In assessing the competency of the client's designated employee, the CPA should be satisfied that such individual understands the services to be performed sufficiently to oversee them. In cases where the client is unable or unwilling to assume these responsibilities (for example, the client does not have an individual with the necessary competence to oversee the nonattest services provided, or is unwilling to perform such functions due to lack of time or desire), the CPA's provision of these services would impair independence.

Before performing nonattest services, the CPA should establish and document in writing his or her understanding with the client (board of directors, audit committee, or management, as appropriate in the circumstances) regarding the following:

- Objectives of the engagement
- Services to be performed
- Client's acceptance of its responsibilities
- Member's responsibilities
- Any limitations of the engagement

The documentation requirement does not apply to certain routine activities performed by the CPA such as providing advice and responding to the client's technical questions as part of the normal client-CPA relationship.

To avoid impairing independence, the CPA, according to the interpretation, should not perform any management function or make management decisions for the client. The interpretation provides the following examples (not all inclusive) of activities that impair independence.

- Authorizing, executing, or consummating a transaction, or otherwise exercising authority on behalf of a client (e.g., negotiating a transaction), or having authority to do so.
- Preparing source documents (e.g. purchase orders, payroll time records, and customer orders) or originating data, in electronic form evidencing the occurrence of a transaction.
- Having custody of client assets.
- Supervising client employees in the performance of their normal recurring activities.
- Determining which recommendations of the CPA should be implemented.
- Reporting to the board of directors on behalf of management.

- Serving as a client's stock transfer or escrow agent, registrar, general counsel, or its equivalent.

The interpretation also includes additional examples (categorized by type of service) of activities that would and would not impair independence.

Interpretation 101-4: Honorary Directorships and Trusteeships

Independence for a firm is not impaired when a CPA permits his or her name to be identified as a director or trustee of a nonprofit entity while being associated with the entity's financial statements if the following conditions are observed:

- The position is purely honorary.
- The position is identified as honorary on all letterheads and in material externally circulated by the entity.
- The CPA's participation is restricted to the use of his or her name.
- The entity's governing body is large enough to allow the CPA to perform in a purely honorary fashion.

Interpretation 101-5: Loans from Financial Institution Clients and Related Terminology

Loans that are not considered impairments of independence are (1) grandfathered loans and (2) other permitted loans:

- Grandfathered loans: The following loans from financial institutions do not impair independence:
  - — Home mortgages
  - — Loans that are secured (the collateral must at least be equal to the amount of the loan as of January 1, 1992, and for all subsequent dates)
  - — Loans considered immaterial to the CPA's net worth

The above loans must have been made under normal lending conditions established by a financial institution and must meet one of the following conditions:

- Existed as of January 1, 1992
- Obtained from a financial institution prior to that institution becoming a review or audit client
- Obtained from a financial institution for which independence was not required but was sold to a financial institution for which independence was required
- Obtained from a financial institution for which independence was required but the loan was made to an individual before that individual became a member of the CPA firm

Loans that are considered grandfathered must be and remain current, and the terms of such loans must not be renegotiated after the latest of the dates expressed or implied in the four circumstances listed above.

- Other permitted loans: The following personal loans from a financial institution requiring independence will not, if made under the normal lending practices, impair independence:
  - — Loans or leases for automobiles when collateralized by the automobile
  - — Loans based on the surrender value of an insurance policy
  - — Loans fully collateralized by cash deposits held at the same financial institution
  - — Cash advances from checking accounts and credit cards with total unpaid current balances of $5,000 or less.

Personal loans must remain current at all times in order not to be considered impairments of independence.

Interpretation 101-6: The Effect of Actual or Threatened Litigation on Independence

- Litigation, actual or threatened, brought by the client against the CPA may impair independence.
- Litigation, actual or threatened, brought by securities holders against the CPA would normally not impair independence.
- Litigation, actual or threatened, brought by creditors or insurers against the CPA would normally not impair independence.

Interpretation 101-7 (withdrawn)

Interpretation 101-8: Effect on Independence of Financial Interests in Nonclients Having Investor or Investee Relationships with a Member's Client

Financial interests in a nonclient that has a relationship with the client should be considered to determine whether independence is impaired. In evaluating a relationship between a client and a nonclient, Interpretation 101-8 establishes the following definitions:

- *Client* The person or entity with whose financial statements the member or the member's firm is associated.
- *Investor* Either (a) a parent, (b) a general partner, or (c) a natural person or corporation that has the ability to exercise significant influence. [Note: *Significant influence* is defined in APB-18 (The Equity Method of Accounting for Investments in Common Stock).]
- *Investee* Either (a) a subsidiary or (b) an entity over which an investor has the ability to exercise significant influence.

The following relationships are discussed in Interpretation 101-8:

- Client investor has a *material* interest in a nonclient investee, a direct financial interest, or a material indirect financial interest by the CPA in the nonclient investee.
- Client has an *immaterial* interest in a nonclient investee.
- Nonclient investor has a *material* interest in a client investee, a direct interest, or a material indirect financial interest by the CPA in the nonclient investor.
- Nonclient investor has an *immaterial* interest in a client investee.
- Brother-sister common control relationship exists and interest is immaterial.
- Brother-sister common control relationship exists and interest is material.
- Joint venture relationship.
- Other relationships with nonclient entities could exist that may impair independence.

Interpretation 101-9: The Meaning of Certain Independence Terminology and the Effect of Family Relationships on Independence

- The following would be considered to be encompassed by the phrase "he and his firm":
  - — Members of the firm who perform services for the client and who require independence
  - — All the partners and shareholders of the CPA firm
  - — All professional employees who participate in the engagement
  - — All managerial employees located in an office that performs a significant portion of the engagement
  - — Any entity whose operating, financial, or accounting polices can be significantly influenced by a person described in the above four categories
  - — Spouses and dependent persons who are in a position to exert significant influence over the client's policies or who are in an audit-sensitive position

Interpretation 101-10: The Effect on Independence of Relationships Proscribed by Rule 101 and Its Interpretations with Nonclient Entities Included with a Member's Client in the Financial Statements of a Governmental Reporting Entity

- The following guidelines should be followed when the client is a governmental entity made up of an oversight entity and one or more component units:
  - — The CPA for the reporting entity must be independent with respect to the oversight unit and all component units, although exceptions are provided for certain related organizations.

— The CPA for a material fund type, fund, account group, or component unit (but not the primary government) must be independent with respect to all of theses entities; however, independence is not required with respect to other accounting entities and account groups if (a) financial accountability is not present or (b) significant influence cannot be exerted.

— The CPA for one or more fund type, fund, account group, or component unit (but not the primary government) that is immaterial in relationship to the general-purpose financial statements must be independent with respect to the entity audited and should not be associated with the primary government in a way described in Interpretation 101-B.

Interpretation 101-11: Independence and the Performance of Professional Services under the Statements on Standards for Attestation Engagements and Statement on Auditing Standards No. 75, Engagements to Apply Agreed-Upon Procedures to Specified Elements, Accounts, or Items of a Financial Statement

- Interpretation 101-11 applies to the SSAE series and SAS-75 only if "the report issued states that its use is to be restricted to identified parties and the member [of the AICPA] reasonably expects that the report will be restricted to those parties."

Interpretation 101-12: Independence and Cooperative Arrangement with Clients

- Independence is impaired when a member's firm and a client the firm jointly engage in business activity (cooperative arrangements) when the arrangement is material to the member's firm or to the client. Generally, however, joint action with a client would not be considered a cooperative arrangement if the following conditions exist:
  — The participation by each party (the member's firm and the client) is governed by a separate agreement or understanding.
  — The member's firm is not responsible for the activities of the client and the client is not responsible for the activities of the member's firm.
  — Neither the member's firm nor the client has the authority to act as the agent/representative of the other.

Relationships that are considered inappropriate under Interpretation 101-12 include a joint venture to market a service and the "bundling of services offered by the two participants whereby there is reference to both parties."

Interpretation 101-13: Extended Audit Services

[Withdrawn]

Interpretation 101-14: The Effect of Alternative Practice Structures on the Applicability of Independence Rules

In the past, professional services have been performed by a CPA firm or a sole practitioner. In some states, alternative practice structures (APS) are being created in order to deliver attest and nonattest services. Although a variety of APS may evolve over time, Interpretation 101-14 currently describes an APS as one in which "a substantial (the nonattest) portion of a member's practice is conducted under public or private ownership, and the attest portion of the practice is conducted through a separate firm owned and controlled by the member." As these structures have been created over the past few years, the question of whether Rule 101 and other standards established by the AICPA apply to CPAs that practice in these arrangements has arisen. The Interpretation concludes that the established standards do apply.

Although the AICPA wrote the guidance for APS in the context of a specific structure, it noted that "the concepts expressed herein be applied, in spirit and in substance, to variations of the example structure as they develop." Below is the example used by the Interpretation.

The example APS in this Interpretation is one where an existing CPA practice ("Oldfirm") is sold by its owners to another (possibly public) entity ("PublicCo"). PublicCo has subsidiaries or divisions such as a bank, insurance company, or broker-dealer, and it also has one or more professional service subsidiaries or divisions that offer to clients nonattest professional services (e.g., tax, personal financial planning, and management consulting). The owners and employees of Oldfirm become employees of one of PublicCo's subsidiaries or divisions and may provide those nonattest services.

In addition, the owners of Oldfirm form a new CPA firm ("Newfirm") to provide attest services. CPAs, including the former owners of Oldfirm, own a majority of Newfirm (as to vote and financial interests). Attest services are performed by Newfirm and are supervised by its owners. The arrangement between Newfirm and PublicCo (or one of its subsidiaries or divisions) includes the lease of employees, office space, and equipment; the performance of back-office functions such as billing and collections; and advertising. Newfirm pays a negotiated amount for these services.

The Interpretation requires Rule 101 as well as the following additional guidance to be observed by an APS:

- The term "member or member's firm" (Member) in an APS any person (leased or employed) or entity included in the definition of a member in Interpretation 101-9, as described in paragraph 1 of the Interpretation. In addition, these standards apply to Other PublicCo Entities, which are defined to include entities consolidated in the PublicCo financial statements and (1) not included in the definition of Member and (2) not subject to the same rules as Member because they are not entities over whose activities a Direct Superior can exercise significant influence.
- Indirect Superiors and Other PublicCo Entities may not have a relationship contemplated by Interpretation 101-1.A (e.g., investments, loans, etc.) with an attest client of Newfirm that is material.

- Financial relationships of Indirect Superiors or Other PublicCo Entities should not allow such persons or entities to exercise significant influence (as defined in Interpretation 101-9) over the attest client.
- Neither Other PublicCo Entities nor any of their employees may be connected with an attest client of Newfirm as a promoter, underwriter, voting trustee, director, or officer.
- Except as noted above, Indirect Superiors and Other PublicCo Entities may provide services to an attest client of Newfirm that would impair independence if performed by, for example, the Member.

Direct Superiors include those persons located in an office participating in a significant portion of the attest engagement and who are so closely associated with (1) an owner of Newfirm or (2) a person with a managerial position employed or leased by Newfirm that such persons can directly control the activities of the owner or managerial employee.

Indirect Superiors and Other PublicCo Entities include those persons who are one or more levels above the persons included in Direct Superiors.

DETERMINING INDEPENDENCE ON THE BASIS OF AICPA ETHICS RULINGS: MISCELLANEOUS CIRCUMSTANCES

- Independence may be impaired if a CPA receives more than a token gift from a client.
- Independence is not impaired if a CPA is a member of a client/trade association, as long as the CPA is not a member of the association's management.
- Independence is not impaired when the CPA's spouse is the client's bookkeeper, assuming the spouse's duties are limited to those of a bookkeeper.
- Independence is not impaired when the CPA performs extensive management advisory services.
- Independence is impaired when the CPA performs "employee duties" for a creditor's committee in control of a debtor client.
- Independence is impaired when a CPA is an elective legislator of a municipality, even when the city manager is an elected official.
- Independence is impaired with respect to a corporation when the CPA serves as the executor and trustee of the estate of a person who has majority ownership of the corporation.
- Independence is impaired with respect to a charitable foundation and the estate that made the foundation its sole beneficiary when a CPA serves as a trustee of the foundation.
- Independence is not impaired with respect to various nonprofit organizations when the CPA is a director or officer of a local fund that raises money for various nonprofit organizations, provided the fund does not exercise managerial control over the various nonprofit organizations.

- Independence is impaired with respect to a nonprofit social club when a CPA serves on the board of directors of the club.
- Independence is not impaired with respect to a country club when a CPA as part of the membership requirements acquires a rata share of equity in the club, as long as the CPA does not participate in the management of the club.
- Independence is impaired when the CPA serves on the client's committee that administers the client's deferred compensation program and the duties of the CPA include general supervisory services.
- Independence is not impaired with respect to a county government when the CPA serves on a citizens' committee that is studying the restructuring of the county and the financial status of the state in which the county is located.
- Independence is impaired with respect to an entity's profit-sharing trust when the CPA serves as a director of the entity.
- Independence is impaired when the CPA acquires bonds of a municipal authority.
- Independence is impaired when the CPA owns a unit in a cooperative, condominium association, planned unit development, homeowners association, timeshare development, or other common realty association.
- Independence is not impaired when the CPA owns shares in regulated mutual investment fund and the fund owns shares of clients of the CPA, if the relationship does not create an indirect mutual financial interest.
- Independence is impaired with respect to a client in which an investment club hold shares when the CPA is a member of the investment club.
- Independence is not impaired with respect to a bank or trust department when the CPA and the bank serve as cofiduciaries an estate or trust, assuming that the assets of the estate or trust were not material to the bank and/or the trust department.
- Independence is not impaired when the CPA serves in an engagement requiring independence with respect to an insurance company that has been funding a retirement for the CPA and in which the insurance company manages the contribution made by the CPA in a pooled separate account, provided that funds held for the benefit of the CPA are not material in relation to the net worth of the insurance company.
- Independence is impaired when a CPA who is a full- or part-time member of the faculty is engaged by the university whereby the following conditions exist: (1) the basic faculty-administrator-student relationship exists, (2) the university acts as a collection agent for student fees, and (3) an official of the administration must sign student senate checks.
- Independence is impaired for a current engagement if fees have not been collected for services rendered more than a year before the date of the current report.
- Independence is impaired with respect to an employee benefit plan when the CPA is not independent of the employer.

- Independence is impaired with respect to a fund-raising foundation whose sole purpose is to raise funds for an agency for which the CPA is a member of the board, unless the board membership honorary.
- Independence would be impaired when the CPA's retirement or savings plan has a direct or material indirect financial interest in a CPA's client.
- Independence is not impaired if a loan prohibited by Interpretation 101 is serviced by a client, if there is no possibility of a material loss accruing to the client.
- Independence is impaired when a direct financial interest in a client is held in a blind trust.
- Independence is impaired with respect to a limited partnership when a CPAhas a material interest in another limited partnership and both partnerships have the same general partner.
- Independence is not impaired with respect to a client that is a financial institution where the CPA has a checking account or other deposits, if the items are fully insured or if uninsured items are not material with respect to the CPA.
- Independence is impaired if a CPA uses members of another firm and that firm is not independent with respect to the CPA's client.
- Independence is impaired if a CPA serves as a member of a client's advisory board, unless (1) the board is in-fact "advisory in nature," (2) the board has no authority to make managerial decisions, and (3) those having authority to make managerial decisions are separate from the advisory board.
- When independence is impaired, a CPA cannot issue a review or an audit report; however, a compilation report may be issued and must disclose the lack of independence.
- Independence is not impaired with respect to a credit union when the CPA firm and its employees are members of the credit if (1) acceptance as a member is based on the established criteria and not simply due to the professional relationship, (2) CPA does not have significant influence over the policies of the credit union, (3) loans to the members of the CPA firm do not violate professional standards and are based on normal lending practices, and (4) deposits with the credit union satisfy the ruling five items previous regarding checking accounts or other deposits.
- A CPA should not participate in an engagement requiring independence if he or she has been offered a position by the client or is seeking employment with the client until the offer has been rejected or until the CPA no longer is seeking a position. (If the CPA learns that a member of the firm was considering or had accepted a position with the client during the engagement, the CPA should decide whether it is necessary to perform additional procedures to ensure that the firm's staffperson's work was performed with objectivity and integrity.)
- Independence is impaired when a CPA has a direct financial interest in a partnership that invests in a client, if the CPA functions as a general partner; however, if the CPA serves as a limited partner the

relationship is an indirect interest and the interest must be material in order for independence to be impaired.

- Independence is impaired when a CPA is a general partner (with direct financial interest) in a partnership that invests in a client of the CPA's firm; however, when the CPA is a limited partner (with indirect financial interest), independence is impaired only if the interest in the client is material to the CPA.
- Independence is impaired in a limited partnership arrangement (including a master limited partnership), if the CPA is a limited partner and a client is a general partner, with respect to (1) the limited partnership; (2) the client, if the investment is material to the client; and (3) any subsidiary of the limited partnership, if the investment is material to the CPA. (See Interpretation 101-1.A.3 for guidance when the CPA and the client individually or together can control the limited partnership.)
- A CPA who serves as the campaign treasurer of the campaign organization of a candidate for mayor is independent with respect to the political party and the municipality but not with respect to the campaign organization.
- Independence is not impaired when a CPA in public practice serves as a bank director; however, if the CPA has clients that are also customers of the bank, the CPA should consider complications arising from (1) Rule 301 (Confidential Client Information) and (2) Interpretation 102-2 (Conflict of Interest).
- Independence is not impaired if a CPA(lessee) leases property from a client and at the time of the transaction the lease would not be considered a capital lease as defined by FAS-13 (Accounting for Leases) and the lease is made under normal leasing arrangements. Independence would be impaired if the lease is considered a capital lease, unless the lease transaction is in compliance with Interpretation 101-1.A.4 and Interpretation 101-5.
- When a CPA has a joint investment in a vacation home with an officer, director, or principal stockholder of a client that uses services that require independence, the relationship is a "joint closely held business investment" under Interpretation 101-1.A.3.
- When a CPA is a director or officer of a local United Way (or similar organization) that operates as a federated fund-raising entity and dispenses funds to clients of the member, a conflict of interest does not arise if any significant relationships are disclosed and consent is obtained from appropriate parties.
- Independence is not impaired when a client agrees to include in an engagement letter a clause stating the client will not hold the member liable for any damages arising from misrepresentations knowingly made by management.
- Independence is not impaired when a CPA and a client enter into a predispute agreement to use alternative dispute resolution (ADR) techniques (rather than litigation) to settle future disagreements.
- Independence generally is not impaired when an ADR proceeding is begun; however, if the proceeding is similar to the litigation process,

the CPA and the client are placed in a position of "material adverse interests" and the guidance established by Interpretation 101-6 should be observed.

- Independence is impaired with respect to a client when a nonclient subsidiary (of the client) makes a loan to the CPA(assuming the loan is not grandfathered or permitted under Interpretation 101-5); however, independence is not impaired with respect to a client when a nonclient parent (of the client) makes a loan to the CPA(assuming the subsidiary is not material to the parent).
- Integrity and objectivity may be impaired when a CPA has been requested by a company to perform personal financial planning or tax services for its executives and the advice given by the CPA may be detrimental to the company.
- A CPA may re-sign or consent to the use of his or her report that was initially issued when the CPA was independent but subsequently lost independence with respect to the client if no "postaudit" work was performed during the period of independence impairment. Post-audit work does not include "inquiries of successor auditors, reading of subsequent financial statements, or such procedures as may be necessary to assess the effect of subsequently discovered facts on the financial statements covered by the member's previously issued report."
- A CPA is not considered an advocate of a client (as discussed in Interpretation 102-6) when he or she serves as an expert witness for the client.
- Independence is impaired when a CPA agrees to "indemnify the client for damages, losses, or costs arising from lawsuits, claims, or settlements that relate, directly or indirectly, to client acts."
- Independence is not impaired when a CPA performs an attestation engagement to report on a client's assertion regarding the effectiveness of its internal control over financial reporting and provides an extended audit service (as defined in Interpretation 101-13, Extended Audit Services) if the following conditions are satisfied:
  - — The guidance established by Interpretation 101-13 is observed.
  - — The client's management has assumed responsibility for establishing and maintaining internal control
  - — Management has not relied on the CPA's services as the primary basis for developing the assertion, and in this regard has evaluated both the results of its ongoing monitoring procedures and the member's findings, if any.
- Independence is not impaired when, as part of an extended audit engagement, a CPA is requested to evaluate the effectiveness and/or efficiency of a client's processes, if during the engagement the CPA does not act or appear to act as an employee or a member of management and the client is responsible for determining whether to accept the CPA's recommendations or conclusions.
- The frequency with which a specific audit procedure is performed (as part of procedures performed in extended audit services) does not affect independence if (a) the guidance established by Interpretation

101-13 (Extended Audit Services) is observed and (b) the procedures performed are "separate evaluations of effectiveness of the ongoing control and monitoring activities/procedures that are built into the client's normal recurring activities."

- Independence is impaired with respect to a client when a CPA has significant influence (as defined in Interpretation 101-9) over an entity that has significant influence over the client.
- Independence is impaired with respect to the client and the health and welfare plan when a CPA participates in the plan sponsored by the client. If the participation in the plan is (a) based on a member's spouse or cohabitant's relationship with the plan (and the conditions established by Interpretation 101-9 are satisfied), and (b) normally provided to all employees of similar status, independence is not impaired.
- Independence is impaired with respect to the client and the plan when a CPA participates in a retirement, savings, or similar plan sponsored by the client or when the plan invests in a client. Independence is also impaired with respect to any of the CPA's clients when the plan invests in these other clients. Independence is not impaired if the participation in the plan is based on a CPA's spouse or cohabitant's relationship with the plan (and the conditions established by Interpretation 101-9 are satisfied), and all of the following conditions are satisfied: (a) the plan is normally provided to all employees of similar status, (b) under the terms of the plan, the spouse has selected investments options that do not involve any of the CPA's clients, (c) under the terms of the plan, an investment must be made in a client but "the right of possession exists" and the investment in a client is promptly withdrawn, and (d) a right of possession does not exist but the investment is considered "an indirect financial interest and is not material to the CPA's net worth."
- Independence is impaired when a CPA uses a nonclient financial services company to make investments in a client or clients if the CPA "has the ability to direct and does direct his or her investment through a financial services product into a client."
- Independence is impaired when a CPA is an officer, director, or principal shareholder of an entity that has a loan to or a loan from a client if the CPA has control over the entity unless the loan from the client is specifically allowed under Interpretation 101-5.
- Independence is impaired with respect to a benefit plan when a CPA provides asset management or investment services for a client's employee benefit plan. Also, independence with respect to the client is impaired if the plan is a defined benefit plan and if "the assets under management or in the custody of the member are material to the plan or the client sponsor."

APPENDIX 4B
CLIENT ACCEPTANCE AND RETENTION EVALUATION FORM

Client Name: ____

Date of Financial Statements: ____________________________

Instructions

This form should be used to document the screening of prospective new clients/engagements and for evaluating the retention of existing clients/engagements. This form is only a guide: the CPA should exercise professional judgment in revising or adding questions where appropriate. This form should be updated at least annually, and the engagement executive should review it to determine whether to accept a particular engagement and whether to retain or terminate clients.

Section I: Background and Basic Information

1. Entity legal name: ____________________________________
2. Key contact name and title: _____________________________
3. Entity address, telephone number, fax number, e-mail address, and Web site address:

   ____

   ____

   ____

4. Type of entity (e.g., partnership, subchapter S, public):

   ____

5. Fiscal year-end:

   ____

6. Principal stockholders, officers, and directors:

Name	Position

7. Describe how contact was initially established:

____

____

____

8. Entity's attorneys:

Name ______________________________________

Address ____________________________________

____

9. Entity's banking relationships:

Name ______________________________________

Address ____________________________________

____

10. Describe the nature of the entity's business and products or services provided, including any economic dependence or concentrations.

____

____

____

11. Explain management's reasons for changing CPA firms and how frequently the entity has changed CPA firms.

____

____

____

12. Describe what services and reports are requested and their required completion dates.

____

____

____

13. Describe why the entity desires the engagement and what parties may potentially rely on the report.

____

____

____

Section II: Entity Financial Condition and Nature of Transactions

Any "Yes" answers to the following questions indicate a higher than normal level of risk, and the CPA should expand on those answers.

		Yes	No	N/A
1.	Is cash flow or working capital inadequate to meet operating requirements, debt payments, dividends, etc.?	____	____	____
2.	Are there significant demands for new debt or equity capital?	____	____	____
3.	Have loan agreement covenants been waived or violated?	____	____	____
4.	Is there any doubt about the ability of the entity to continue in existence?	____	____	____
5.	Have sales, gross margins, or income trends deteriorated significantly in recent years?	____	____	____
6.	Is the entity's industry unfavorable, unusually litigious, or considered risky (e.g., construction companies)?	____	____	____
7.	Does the entity engage in significant related-party transactions?	____	____	____
8.	Does the entity usually engage in significant unusual transactions during the year or near year-end?	____	____	____
9.	Is there evidence of complex accounting issues or transactions that are difficult to audit?	____	____	____
10.	Is financing by third parties contingent on the entity's meeting certain minimum financial ratios?	____	____	____
11.	Does the company engage in the use of derivatives?	____	____	____

Section III: Management Integrity and Business Risk Exposure

Any "Yes" answers to the following questions indicate a higher than normal level of risk, and the CPA should expand on those answers.

		Yes	No	N/A
1.	Has the entity or any of its principals ever been charged with violations of any federal, state, or local laws?	____	____	____
2.	Is there any pending litigation or investigation against the entity or any of its principals?	____	____	____

	Yes	No	N/A
3. Is there disagreement among/between the owners?	____	____	____
4. Are any mergers, acquisitions, or dispositions planned or likely?	____	____	____
5. Has there been a high turnover of key management?	____	____	____
6. Is the entity dependent on one major customer for most of its revenue or on one major supplier for most of its products?	____	____	____
7. Does management have a reputation for taking unusual or unnecessary risks?	____	____	____
8. Is management reluctant to provide necessary documents regarding major transactions or generally uncooperative or unreasonable?	____	____	____
9. Is management unwilling to correct material misstatements in the financial statements?	____	____	____
10. Is there any indication that management representations are not reliable?	____	____	____
11. Does management place undue pressure on meeting financial goals or reducing income taxes?	____	____	____
12. Are key management employees compensated based on the results of the entity's operations?	____	____	____
13. Is management aware of any instances of fraud or illegal acts?	____	____	____

Section IV: Communication with Predecessor Accountants

Any "Yes" answers to the following questions indicate a higher than normal level of risk, and the CPA should expand on those answers.

	Yes	No	N/A
1. Are you aware of any situations that might bear on the integrity of management?	____	____	____
2. Have you had any significant disagreements with management over the application of accounting principles, practices, or financial statement disclosures?	____	____	____
3. Has management ever attempted to restrict or direct the scope of the audit?	____	____	____

		Yes	No	N/A
4.	Are you aware of any incidents of management intervention in, or circumvention, of the company's internal control?	____	____	____
5.	Is management unwilling to accept primary responsibility for the content of the financial statements?	____	____	____
6.	Does management discourage its key employees from cooperating fully with the independent auditor?	____	____	____
7.	Have you had any communications with management regarding fraud, illegal acts, or internal control related matters?	____	____	____

8. Inquire of the predecessor auditor about his or her understanding of reasons for change in auditors and summarize:

____

____

____

9. Name, address, and phone number of predecessor accountant:

____

10. Name and position of person inquired of:

____

11. Date of inquiry:

____

Section V: Auditability and Ability to Provide Services Requested

		Yes	No	N/A
1.	Does the entity appear to have appropriate completeness procedures to ensure that accounting transactions enter into the accounting system?	____	____	____
2.	Does the accounting system appear to provide records sufficient to permit application of cost-effective audit procedures?	____	____	____
3.	Does our firm have the required technical skills and expertise in the entity's field?	____	____	____

	Yes	No	N/A
4. Does our firm or any of its staff have any existing relationship with the entity or conflicts of interest that would impair our independence?	_____	_____	_____
5. Does top management lack experience necessary to operate the business?	_____	_____	_____
6. Are there any indications that our firm might have a problem billing or collecting its fees?	_____	_____	_____

Section VI: Additional Comments

Use this section to elaborate on any of the answers above or to provide additional comments about matters that increase the overall engagement risk.

____

____

Section VII: Conclusion

Prepared by: ______________________ Date: ______________

Acceptance decision:

☐ YES ☐ NO

Partner's signature: ______________________ Date: ______________

Concurring Partner's signature: ______________ Date: ______________

Updated in subsequent years as follows:

Year	Updated by	Date

APPENDIX 4C
ILLUSTRATIVE CLIENT CONSENT AND ACKNOWLEDGEMENT LETTER

[*date*]

Upstate Event and Race Promotions, Inc.
123 Main Street
Greenville, SC 29601

You have given your consent to allow [*name of successor CPA firm*], as successor independent auditors for Upstate Event and Race Promotions, Inc., access to our working papers for our audit of the December 31, 20X5 financial statements of Upstate Event and Race Promotions, Inc. You also have given your consent to us to respond fully to [*name of successor CPA firm*] inquiries. You understand and agree that the review of our working papers is undertaken solely for the purpose of obtaining an understanding about Upstate Event and Race Promotions, Inc. and certain information about our audit to assist [*name of successor CPA firm*] in planning the audit of the [*identify the subject matter; for example,* the schedule of accounts receivable] of Upstate Event and Race Promotions, Inc.

Please confirm your agreement with the foregoing by signing and dating a copy of this letter and returning it to us.

Attached is the form of the letter we will furnish [*name of successor CPA firm*] regarding the use of the working papers.

Very truly yours,

[*predecessor auditor*]

By: ______________________

Accepted:

Upstate Event and Race Promotions, Inc.

By: ______________________ Date: ______________

APPENDIX 4D
ILLUSTRATIVE SUCCESSOR AUDITOR ACKNOWLEDGEMENT LETTER

[*date*]

[*successor auditor*]

[*address*]

We have previously audited, in accordance with generally accepted auditing standards, the December 31, 20X5 financial statements of Upstate Event and Race Promotions, Inc. We rendered a report on those financial statements and have not performed any audit procedures subsequent to the audit report date. In connection with your audit of Upstate Event and Race Promotions, Inc.'s [*identify subject matter; for example,* schedule of accounts receivable], you have requested access to our working papers prepared in connection with that audit. Upstate Event and Race Promotions, Inc. has authorized our firm to allow you to review those working papers.

Our audit, and the working papers prepared in connection therewith, of Upstate Event and Race Promotions, Inc.'s financial statements were not planned or conducted in contemplation of your review. Therefore, items of possible interest to you may not have been specifically addressed. Our use of professional judgement and the assessment of audit risk and materiality for the purpose of our audit mean that matters may have existed that would have been assessed differently by you. We make no representation as to the sufficiency or appropriateness of the information in our working papers for your purposes.

We understand that the purpose of your review is to obtain information about Upstate Event and Race Promotions, Inc. and our 20X5 audit results to assist you in planning your 20X6 audit of Upstate Event and Race Promotions, Inc. For that purpose only, we will provide you with access to our working papers that relate to that objective.

Upon request, we will provide copies of these working papers that provide factual information about Upstate Event and Race Promotions, Inc. You agree to subject any such copies or information otherwise derived from our working papers to your normal policy for retention of working papers and protection of confidential client information. Furthermore, in the event of a third-party request for access to your working papers prepared in connection with your audits of Upstate Event and Race Promotions, Inc., you agree to obtain our permission before voluntarily allowing any such access to our working papers or information otherwise derived from our working papers, and to obtain on our behalf any releases that you obtain from such third party. You agree to advise us promptly and provide us with a copy of any subpoena, summons, or other court order for access to your working papers that include copies of our working papers or information otherwise derived therefrom.

Because your review of our working papers is undertaken solely for the purpose described above and may not entail a review of all of our working papers, you agree that (1) the information obtained from the review will not be used by you for any other purpose, (2) you will not comment, orally or in writing, to anyone as a result of that review as to whether our audit was performed in accordance with generally accepted auditing standards, (3) you will not provide expert testimony or litigation support services or otherwise accept an engagement to comment on issues relating to the quality of our audits, and (4) you will not use the audit procedures or the results thereof documented in our working papers as evidential matter in rendering your opinion on the [*identify subject matter; for example,* schedule of accounts receivable] of Upstate Event and Race Promotions, Inc., except as contemplated in Statement on Auditing Standards No. 84.

Please confirm your agreement with the foregoing by signing and dating a copy of this letter and returning it to us.

Very truly yours,

[*predecessor auditor*]

By: ______________________________

Accepted:

[*successor auditor*]

By: ______________________________

APPENDIX 4E
INFORMATION RELEASE FORM

July 17, 20XX

John Doe, CPA
123 Main Street
Greenville, SC 29601

We have engaged Able, Baker, and Charles, CPAs to perform certain attestation [agreed-upon procedures] services for our company. In connection with these services, they would like to make inquires and examine certain of your documentation for the [audit, compilation, review, consulting] engagement for the [*period(s)*] ended [*date(s)*]. We hereby authorize you to respond fully and without limitation to their requests.

Please allow Able, Baker, and Charles, CPAs to copy any information needed from files related to your engagements for us (unless proprietary in nature) and bill our company for the reproduction costs.

You will be contacted by Mr. Will Baker concerning these matters.

Yours truly,

[*officer's signature and title*]

CHAPTER 5
PLANNING AND ADMINISTRATION FOR ATTESTATION ENGAGEMENTS

CONTENTS

OVERVIEW

This chapter discusses the unique planning for and administration issues that pertain to attestation engagements. Although there are many different kinds of attestation engagements, there are certain definitions, standards, and criteria that apply to all. Key concepts that are covered in this chapter are "subject matter," "assertion," and "responsible party." In addition, the eleven attestation standards are discussed, which cover the general standards, standards of fieldwork, and reporting standards.

DEFINITION OF AN ATTEST ENGAGEMENT

Chapter 1 of SSAE-10 (AT 101.01) defines an attest engagement as one "in which a certified public accountant in the practice of public accounting (hereinafter referred to as a practitioner) is engaged to issue or does issue an examination, review, or an agreed-upon procedures report on subject matter, or an assertion about the subject matter (hereafter referred to as the assertion), that is the responsibility of another party." Several key terms are used in the definition of an attestation engagement that the CPA must understand.

Subject Matter

The subject matter is the information that is the foundation of what the CPA is attesting to—it is what the CPA applies procedures to. Unlike the auditing standards (which are limited to historical financial statements as subject matter), the attestation standards are designed to accommodate a wide variety of subject matter. The subject matter may or may not be financial or numeric in nature. In fact, there is no limit to what might be considered subject matter in an attest engagement.

Chapter 1 of SSAE-10 (AT 101.07) provides the following examples of subject matter:

- Historical or prospective performance or condition (for example, historical or prospective financial information, performance measurements, and backlog data)
- Physical characteristics (for example, narrative descriptions, square footage of facilities)
- Historical events (for example, the price of a market basket of goods on a certain date)
- Analyses (for example, break-even analyses)
- Systems and processes (for example, internal control)
- Behavior (for example, corporate governance, compliance with laws and regulations, and human resource practices)

The subject matter may be as of a point in time or for a period of time. The subject matter may or may not be reduced to writing. For example, subject matter such as a break-even analysis might be in writing and accompany the CPA's report. Other subject matter, such as behavior, might not be in writing. Generally, it is easier to test subject matter if it has been reduced to writing.

Assertion

An assertion is any declaration or set of declarations about whether the subject matter is based on or in conformity with the criteria selected. For example, in an engagement to test the effectiveness of internal control, the subject matter is the client's system of internal control; the assertion is that the system is effective based on criteria such as the COSO criteria. The Committee of Sponsoring Organizations (COSO) of the Tread way Commission developed criteria to be used in evaluating an entity's system of internal control. (See Chapter 11, "Internal Control Engagements," for a discussion of internal control engagements.) In an audit, the subject matter is the financial statements and the assertion is that the financial statements are fairly presented in accordance with generally accepted accounting principles (the criteria). The accountant may report on a written assertion or may report directly on the subject matter.

> **OBSERVATION:** Previous attestation standards required a written assertion in order for the CPA to perform the engagement. SSAE-10 removes this requirement for certain engagements.

An example of a written assertion is as follows: "The Company maintained effective internal control over financial reporting as of December 31, 20XX, based on criteria established in the COSO Report."

Chapter 1 of SSAE-10 (AT 101.09) states that the accountant, "should ordinarily obtain a written assertion in an examination or review engagement." The phrase "should ordinarily" means that it is highly recommended that the CPA obtain a written assertion, but he or she is not *required* to do so. There may be situations where it is impractical or impossible to obtain a written assertion. There are several implications, however, of not obtaining a written assertion in an attest engagement:

- The attest standards allow the CPA to report either directly on the subject matter or on a written assertion. If a written assertion is not obtained, then the report should be directly on the subject matter.
- On some engagements, the client is the responsible party. The attestation standards presume that if the client is the responsible party, it will be capable of providing the CPA with a written assertion regarding the subject matter. If a written assertion is not obtained when the client is the responsible party, then a scope limitation exists:
  - — *Examination* When a CPA is engaged to perform an examination engagement, a scope limitation will require the CPA to either (1) qualify or disclaim the opinion or (2) withdraw from the engagement.
  - — *Review* When a CPA is engaged to perform a review engagement, a scope limitation results in an incomplete review. A review that is incomplete is not an adequate basis for issuing a review report and, accordingly, the CPA should withdraw from the engagement.
- In other situations, the client is not the responsible party. In such a case, the CPA may be able to conclude that he or she does, in fact, have sufficient evidence to form a conclusion and issue a report about the subject matter without obtaining a written assertion from the nonclient responsible party. If a report is issued in this situation, it should be restricted to the client and the responsible party.

EXHIBIT 5-1
REPORTING IMPLICATIONS WHEN WRITTEN ASSERTION IS NOT OBTAINED

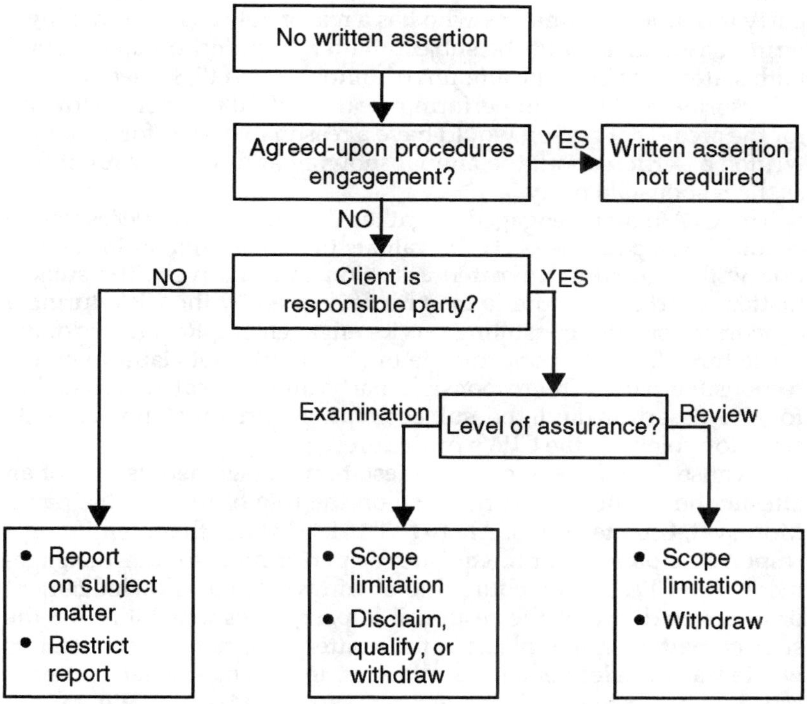

OBSERVATION: Chapter 1 of SSAE-10 describes several ways in which a written assertion can be presented to a CPA, including in a narrative description, within a schedule, or as part of a representation letter appropriately identifying what is being presented and the period or point in time covered.

Responsible Party

The responsible party is defined as the person or persons, either as individuals or as representatives of the entity, responsible for the subject matter. In other words, this is the party who is to be held accountable for the subject matter. Sometimes the nature of the subject matter is such that no such party exists. For example, suppose that the Ski Valley Ski Resort made the assertion that "on average, we have over 120 inches of snow a year." The subject matter is the number of inches of snow in a year, but no person or persons can be held accountable for the snowfall. In such a situation, a responsible party is defined as someone who has a reasonable basis for making a written assertion about the subject matter. In order to make a good faith statement about the amount of annual snowfall, someone at the ski resort would have to perform research into the historic snowfall for the area. That person would have a reasonable basis for making a written assertion about the annual snowfall and could be identified as the responsible party.

The CPA may be engaged to gather the information necessary to enable the responsible party to evaluate the subject matter in connection with providing a written assertion. Alternatively, the subject matter, assertion, or criteria may be developed by the CPA during a concurrent or prior consulting service engagement. Regardless of the procedures the CPA performs, he or she should not claim to be the responsible party. The responsible party must accept responsibility for the assertion and the subject matter and must not base its assertion solely on the CPA's procedures.

Because the CPA's role in an attestation engagement is that of an attester, he or she should not take on the role of responsible party. Moreover, Chapter 1 of SSAE-10 (AT 101.13) states that identifying a responsible party is a prerequisite for performing an attest engagement. The CPA is also required to obtain written acknowledgement or other evidence of the responsible party's responsibility for the subject matter, or, if applicable, the written assertion. Generally, this written acknowledgement is obtained in an engagement letter, a representation letter, or the written assertion. If the CPA cannot obtain direct written acknowledgement of the responsibly party's responsibility, other evidence, such as reference to legislation, a regulation, or a contract, may be sufficient.

When the Client Is Not the Responsible Party

The attestation standards recognize that the responsible party might not always be the client of the CPA. Nevertheless, a CPA may accept an attestation engagement when the responsible party is not the client. In that case, the CPA needs to obtain evidence of the third party's responsibility for the subject matter, which may be obtained through

- The engagement letter.
- The representation letter.

- A statement within the presentation of the subject matter.
- A separate written assertion.
- Contracts or correspondence between the client and the third party.
- Relevant laws or regulations.

Chapter 1 of SSAE-10 requires the CPA to obtain evidence of the responsible party's responsibility for the subject matter. In a two party engagement, this evidence is typically obtained in the form of an engagement letter, representation letter, or written assertion. However, if the responsible party is not the CPA's client, the responsible party might be unwilling to provide such a written acknowledgement.

Case Study 5-1: Nonclient Responsible Party

Facts

In the state of South Carolina, attorneys are subject to a law that requires them to obtain and report at least forty hours of continuing legal education (CLE) each year. Individual attorneys are responsible for reporting the CLE information to the South Carolina State Bar each year.

The Bar would like to obtain assurance that the CLE hours are being reported accurately. They would also like to convey a message to the attorneys that the CLE information is being scrutinized. The law in South Carolina requiring CLE also allows the Bar to periodically analyze the evidence of attorneys' continuing education reporting to determine whether the CLE hours have been properly reported. The Bar engages John Doe, CPA, to help them in this analysis.

Analysis

In this example, the subject matter is the CLE hours reported by the attorneys. The Bar is John Doe's client. However, the Bar cannot be held accountable for the CLE hours reported by the attorneys, nor could anyone on the Bar's staff have a reasonable basis for providing a written assertion about the CLE hours. The individual attorneys are the responsible parties, thus, this is a three-party engagement: John Doe (the CPA), the Bar (the client), and the individual attorneys (the responsible parties). If an individual attorney were unwilling to sign a statement indicating that he or she was responsible for the CLE hours, John Doe, CPA, would simply use the state law as evidence that the attorney was, in fact, responsible.

Case Study 5-2: Subject Matter and Responsible Party

Facts

The City of Greenville, like most cities, requires all businesses to pay a business license fee each year based on their annual gross receipts. The ordinance establishing the business license fee allows the city to "periodically analyze the books and records" of business establishments to determine whether the license fee has been properly calculated. The City Council would like to obtain assurance that the revenues reported and license fees paid to the city are accurate. The council would also like to convey a message to the businesses that the information they provide to the city is being scrutinized. The city council engages a CPA to help them in this endeavor.

Analysis

In this example, the subject matter is the business license fee paid to the city, which is based on the amount of annual gross receipts collected by the businesses. The City of Greenville is the client of the CPA; however, the city cannot be held accountable for the gross receipts of the businesses, nor could anyone at the city have a reasonable basis for providing a written assertion about the gross receipts. The individual businesses are the responsible parties.

Evidence of Responsibility

AT101.13 requires the practitioner to obtain evidence of the responsible parties' responsibility for the subject matter. In a two-party engagement, this evidence is typically obtained in the form of an engagement or representation letter or a written assertion. However, when the responsible party is not the client (a three-party engagement), the responsible party might be unwilling to provide such a written acknowledgement. If a business owner is unwilling to sign a statement indicating that he or she is responsible for the business license fee, the practitioner could simply use the city ordinance as evidence that the business owner was, in fact, responsible. Evidence of the responsible party's responsibility for the subject matter may be provided in various forms.

APPLICABILITY OF THE STANDARDS

As discussed in Chapter 3, "Professional Standards of the CPA and the Firm," all attestation engagements are subject to SSAEs. SSAEs apply whenever a CPA is engaged to issue or does issue an examination, review, or agreed-upon procedures report on a subject matter (or an assertion about a subject matter) that is the responsibility of another party. This definition is engagement-oriented and, therefore, the CPA must take care to define the nature of the services to be provided and whether they are intended to provide assurance. The language in SSAE-10 means that attest standards normally only apply when a CPA is specifically engaged to provide an attest report. However, CPAs who issue examination, review, or agreed-upon procedures reports are subject to the standards, even if they are not specifically engaged to do so.

SSAE-10 (AT 101.06) provides further guidance:

> Any professional service resulting in the expression of assurance must be performed under AICPA professional standards that provide for the expression of such assurance. Reports issued by the practitioner in connection with other professional standards should be written to be clearly distinguishable from and not to be confused with attest reports.

There are only three sets of professional standards that provide for the expression of assurance: Statements on Auditing Standards (SASs), Statements on Standards for Accounting and Review Services (SSARS), and Statements on Standards for Attestation Engagements (SSAEs). Therefore, any report expressing assurance should be issued in conformity with the applicable standards. More importantly, when a CPAissues a report under a set of professional standards that do not provide for the expression of assurance, he or she should be careful in the wording of the report. That is, the report should not convey assurance or be confused with an attest report. More specifically, the report should not (1) refer to the service as an examination or review, (2) provide any form of positive or negative assurance about the subject matter, or (3) claim to comply with AICPA standards. (Note, however, that according to SSAE-10 (AT 101.06), a report that merely excludes the words "was conducted in accordance with attestation standards established by the American Institute of Certified Public Accountants" but is otherwise similar to an examination, a review, or an agreed-upon procedures attest report may be inferred to be an attest report.)

Case Study 5-3: Applicability of Attestation Standards

Facts

A CPA is engaged to perform an engagement that is intended solely to assist an organization in improving its controls over the privacy of client data (a consulting engagement). The CPA is not engaged to examine and report on (1) the suitability of the design or (2) the operating effectiveness of such controls.

Analysis

The CPA may issue a report, but is not required to do so by the consulting standards. The report should not use the words "examination" or "review," should not claim to comply with AICPA professional standards, and should not provide any form of assurance as to the suitability or effectiveness of these controls.

DETERMINING WHICH TYPE OF ENGAGEMENT TO PERFORM

The client's needs ultimately determine the type of engagement that the CPA is to perform. A preliminary discussion with the client is beneficial and may be necessary to become familiar with the client's needs and the services that are required. The discussion should include consideration of the following:

- Does the client need assurance? Is an examination or review essential for the intended use? Does the client understand the differing scopes, levels of assurance, and cost of the different engagements?
- What is the expected use of the report? Is the report needed to meet the requirements of a third party, such as a government agency or to meet contractual requirements?
- Does the client want only advice and recommendations? If an examination or review is not needed, will a consulting engagement meet the client's needs?
- When is the report needed? Does the reporting date allow sufficient time to perform the necessary engagement?

The attestation standards do not provide guidance on choosing the best type of engagement to perform. However, based on the client's needs, the following issues should be considered:

- *Historical financial statements* Audit and review engagements are used to provide assurance to users about the reliability of historical financial statements. If the information is pro forma, prospective, or nonfinancial in nature, the SASs and SSARSs do not apply.
- *Consulting engagements* A consulting engagement may involve financial or nonfinancial information and this information

may be historical or prospective. However, in a consulting engagement, no assurance is provided on the information. Instead, findings and recommendations are communicated to the user (usually the client).

- *Attestation engagements* An attestation engagement may involve financial or nonfinancial information and this information may be historical or prospective. Unlike a consulting engagement, however, the objective is to provide assurance on the information in the form of a report.
- *Agreed-upon procedures engagements* All agreed-upon procedures engagements are subject to the attestation standards.

OBSERVATION: SAS-93 (Omnibus Statement on Auditing Standards—2000) withdrew SAS-75 (Engagements to Apply Agreed-Upon Procedures to Specified Elements, Accounts, or Items of a Financial Statement). The relevant guidance on agreed-upon procedures for financial statement elements, accounts, or items has been integrated into Chapter 2 of SSAE-10.

Case Study 5-4: Type of Engagement

Facts

Chandler Company is a provider of office technology (printers, copiers, etc.). Customers of the company demand high reliability from this equipment. In the event of malfunction, customers demand quick response time from Chandler Company representatives.

The management of Chandler Company would like to develop a set of nonfinancial performance measures to help them assess their operational effectiveness in this key area of its operations. In addition, the marketing department believes that these measurements would be a useful marketing tool to sell potential customers on the reliability of the company's products.

Analysis

The practitioner has potentially two separate engagements, both of which involve nonfinancial information.

Chandler Company's first need is to develop a set of measures to assess the reliability of the company's equipment. The practitioner could assist Chandler Company. Because this service is for the benefit of the company itself and the practitioner would not be attesting to the reliability of the information to third parties, the engagement could be structured and performed as a consulting engagement.

Based on the consulting engagement, the practitioner may recommend two metrics: (1) the time the company's equipment runs reliably (as a percentage of total time the customers run the equipment) and (2) the average response time to a service call.

Once the company is able to take these measurements, it would like to share this information with third parties (i.e., prospective customers). For example, the marketing department could tell potential customers that Chandler Company equipment ran reliably 97% of the time for the year ended December 31, 20X7, and that if there was a malfunction, the average response time for a service call was only 2 hours.

To meet this need, Chandler Company could engage the practitioner to perform an engagement under the attestation standards, because the standards allow the practitioner (assuming the criteria are suitable and available) to provide assurance on the measurements.

THE ELEVEN ATTESTATION STANDARDS

The attestation standards are a natural extension of the ten generally accepted auditing standards. Like the auditing standards, the attestation standards deal with the need for technical competence, independence in mental attitude, due professional care, adequate planning and supervision, sufficient evidence, and appropriate reporting. However, they are much broader in scope. The 11 attestation standards are listed below.

General Standards

1. The engagement shall be performed by a practitioner having adequate technical training and proficiency in the attest function.
2. The engagement shall be performed by a practitioner having adequate knowledge of the subject matter.
3. The practitioner shall perform the engagement only if he or she has reason to believe that the subject matter is capable of evaluation against criteria that are suitable and available to users.
4. In all matters relating to the engagement, an independence in mental attitude shall be maintained by the practitioner.
5. Due professional care shall be exercised in the planning and performance of the engagement.

EXHIBIT 5-2
DETERMINING WHICH TYPE OF ENGAGEMENT TO PERFORM

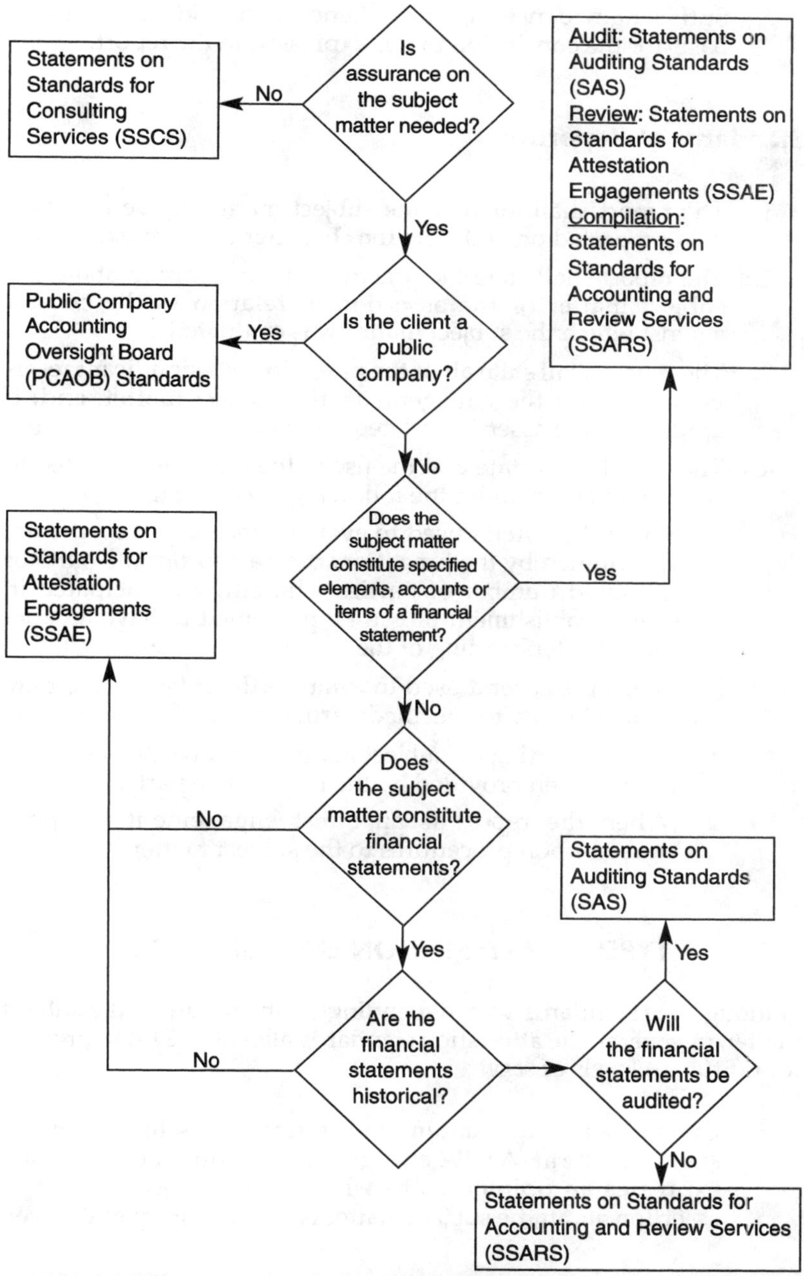

Standards of Fieldwork

1. The work shall be adequately planned and assistants, if any, shall be properly supervised.
2. Sufficient evidence shall be obtained to provide a reasonable basis for the conclusion that is expressed in the report.

Standards of Reporting

1. The report shall identify the subject matter or the assertion being reported on and state the character of the engagement.
2. The report shall state the practitioner's conclusion about the subject matter or the assertion in relation to the criteria against which the subject matter was evaluated.
3. The report shall state all of the practitioner's significant reservations about the engagement, the subject matter, and, if applicable, the assertion related thereto.
4. The report shall state that the use of the report is restricted to specified parties under the following circumstances:
   a. When the criteria used to evaluate the subject matter are determined by the practitioner to be appropriate only for a limited number of parties who either participated in their establishment or can be presumed to have an adequate understanding of the criteria.
   b. When the criteria used to evaluate the subject matter are available only to specified parties.
   c. When reporting on subject matter and a written assertion has not been provided by the responsible party.
   d. When the report is an attest engagement to apply agreed-upon procedures to the subject matter.

TYPES OF ATTESTATION ENGAGEMENTS

Although the standards vary depending on the nature of the subject matter, in general, the attestation standards allow the CPA to provide four different levels of service:

1. *Examination* An examination is analogous to a financial statement audit. A CPA engaged to perform an examination expresses an opinion as to whether the subject matter or assertion about the subject matter is in conformity with given

criteria. In other words, the CPA provides positive assurance in an examination.

2. *Review* A review is analogous to a review of historical financial statements. A CPA engaged to perform a review states a conclusion about whether any information came to his or her attention to indicate that the subject matter or assertion about the subject matter is not in conformity with given criteria. This conclusion is referred to as negative assurance.
3. *Agreed-upon procedures* In an agreed-upon procedures engagement, the CPA issues a report of findings based on specific procedures performed on the subject matter.
4. *Compilation of prospective information* A compilation is defined in Chapter 3 of SSAE-10 (AT 301.12) as a professional service that involves assembling the prospective financial statements based on the responsible party's assumptions, performing the required compilation procedures, and issuing a compilation report. A compilation of prospective financial statements is the only type of compilation covered by the attestation standards, and it was included when the already-existing standard on forecasts and projections was absorbed into the attestation standards.

ACCEPTANCE OF AN ENGAGEMENT: GENERAL

The general requirements to be considered in deciding whether or not to accept an attestation engagement apply to any examination or review attestation engagement. Similar engagement-specific requirements must be considered before accepting other types of attestation engagements (agreed-upon procedures, compilation, etc.) and are discussed in subsequent chapters.

Competence

The first general standard requires the CPA to have adequate technical training and proficiency in the attest function. Performing attest services is different from simply preparing and presenting subject matter or an assertion, which involves collecting, classifying, summarizing, and communicating information; this usually entails reducing a mass of detailed data to a manageable and understandable form. Attest services, on the other hand, involve gathering evidence to support the subject matter or the assertion and objectively assessing the measurements and communications of the responsible party. To summarize, attest services are analytical, critical, investigative, and are concerned with the basis and support for the subject matter or the assertion.

In addition, the performance of an attestation engagement requires the CPA to be skilled in effective communications and the exercise of unbiased judgment. Auditors typically possess these skills and generally these skills do not present a significant barrier to performing an attestation service. However, auditors should recognize that the communication and judgment required for an attest engagement may be different from the requirements of an audit.

The AICPA's nonauthoritative Practice Aid *New Standards, New Services: Implementing the Attestation Standards* states that CPAs should be aware of the following communication and judgment issues encountered in attestation engagements.

Communications

CPAs should consider the need to formally or informally communicate to the client the following:

- *Nature of the attest engagement* Clients might be familiar with attestation to historical financial information (audits and reviews), but might not be aware of attest engagements and how they differ from audits, reviews, and consulting engagements.
- *Limitations of the attest engagement* Clients who are familiar with audits might have certain expectations that are not warranted for an attest engagement. For example, an auditor of financial statements is required to gain an understanding of the client's internal control. Depending on the subject matter, a CPA performing an attest engagement might not be required to understand internal control.
- *Assertions* Ordinarily, a written assertion is required in an examination or review engagement. The CPA might need to explain to the responsible party the definition of an assertion and why it is necessary to have one in writing. In addition, the CPA should explain the consequences for the report if a written assertion is not obtained.
- *Reporting* Clients might be familiar with audit, review, and compilation reports, but the CPA might need to explain the meaning of reports prepared under the attestation standards, particularly agreed-upon procedures reports, which present a list of findings rather than an opinion.

Judgment

Auditors are accustomed to exercising judgment in a wide variety of areas. When performing an attest engagement, the CPA will be required to exercise judgment in several areas not included in an audit:

- *Suitable and available criteria* In order to perform an attest engagement, the CPA must believe that the subject matter is capable of evaluation against suitable and available criteria. In an audit, the criteria are GAAP or an other comprehensive basis of accounting (OCBOA). In an attest engagement, there are no limits to the subject matter, which may conform to any number of criteria.
- *Materiality* As with an audit, materiality plays a role in attest engagements. However, because the subject matter may include nonfinancial information, it can be difficult to determine what is considered material. (Materiality is discussed in Chapter 6, "Examination Engagements.")

The second general standard requires the CPA to have adequate knowledge of the subject matter. This knowledge can be obtained through formal or continuing education or practical experience. How much knowledge of a subject matter is adequate varies with the type of engagement, from common sense to complex subjects, such as actuarial data. In general, the knowledge of the subject matter should be sufficient to allow the CPA to form an objective conclusion about the subject matter.

SSAE-10 (AT 101.22) clarifies that a CPA does not have to personally acquire all of the knowledge in the subject matter to be qualified to express a conclusion. The knowledge requirement can be met, in part, through the use of one or more specialists on a particular attest engagement if the CPA has sufficient knowledge of the subject matter to

- Communicate the objectives of the work to the specialist; and
- Evaluate the specialist's work to determine whether objectives were met.

Criteria

The third general standard for attest engagements states that a CPA should perform an engagement only if he or she has reason to believe that "the subject matter is capable of evaluation against criteria that are suitable and available to users."

OBSERVATION: The former attestation standards required that the criteria be "reasonable" and provided guidance that was drawn mostly from the accounting literature. SSAE-10 now requires that the criteria be "suitable." The change in language is intended to be more user-friendly, and it is also consistent with international assurance standards.

In a financial statement audit, the auditor forms an opinion that the financial statements are fairly presented, in all material respects, in conformity with GAAP. In the audit, GAAP represent suitable criteria that the financial statements can be judged against. The subject matter of an audit is limited to historical financial statements. Attestation engagements, however, can deal with a much wider range of subject matter, which might not be historical or financial in nature. For many types of subject matter, criteria comparable to GAAP do not exist. Therefore, establishing these criteria, or benchmarks, becomes critical to performing an attest engagement.

Suitability

In order to perform an attestation engagement, the criteria used to judge the subject matter must be suitable. In order to be considered suitable, the criteria must have all of the following attributes:

- *Objectivity* Criteria should be free from bias.
- *Measurability* Criteria should permit reasonably consistent measurements, qualitative or quantitative, of subject matter.
- *Completeness* Criteria should be sufficiently complete so that relevant factors that would alter a conclusion about subject matter are not omitted.
- *Relevance* Criteria should be relevant to the subject matter.

The attestation standards require that all four attributes of suitability—objectivity, measurability, completeness, and relevance—be present in order for criteria to be considered suitable. However, the attributes may be present in varying proportions. For example, financial statements are judged against the criteria of GAAP or an other comprehensive basis of accounting (OCBOA), such as the cash basis. From an objectivity standpoint, the cash basis is preferable to GAAP because it does not involve many of the estimates and judgments required for GAAP. GAAP on the other hand, might be considered more relevant to certain users because it captures information about noncash assets and liabilities. Both sets of criteria are suitable for financial statements, yet there is a trade-off in the proportions of the attributes of suitability. As long as all four attributes are present in some amount, the criteria can be considered to be suitable. The relative importance of each attribute is a matter of the CPA's judgment.

In addition, there may be more than one set of suitable criteria for a given subject matter. For example, in an attest engagement to express assurance about customer satisfaction, a responsible party might select as a criterion for customer satisfaction that all customer complaints are resolved to the customer's satisfaction. However, another responsible party might select a different criterion, such as the number of repeat purchases in the three months following the initial purchase.

> **OBSERVATION:** The attestation standards require that the CPA establish that the criteria are suitable, but they do not require that the CPA determine which set of criteria is the *most* suitable. However, caution should be exercised in undertaking an engagement when a client selects a particular set of criteria despite the fact that a more suitable set of criteria is available.

Chapter 1 of SSAE-10 (AT 101.25) provides guidance on determining the suitability of certain types of criteria:

- Criteria promulgated by a body designated by the AICPA Governing Council are, by definition, considered to be suitable.
- Criteria that are established or developed by groups composed of experts that follow due process procedures, including exposure of the proposed criteria for public comment, ordinarily should be considered suitable.
- Criteria that are established or developed by others (client, responsible party, industry associations, etc.) that do not follow due process procedures or do not as clearly represent the public interest, may be considered suitable if all attributes are present.

Case Study 5-5: Suitability of Criteria

Facts

The National Society of Industrial Realtors (NSIR) is a trade association whose purpose is to protect and promote the interests of industrial real estate agents. The NSIR has established criteria for measuring square footage of industrial properties. For example, the criteria establish standards for what portions of industrial facilities should be included in square footage calculations and how to determine the calculation. The criteria were established by a panel of industrial realtors whose primary goal was to provide conformity to the ways in which realtors were marketing their properties.

Industrial Properties is an industrial real estate broker. For the properties they list, they would like to include the square footage along with the attestation of a CPA to assure prospective buyers that the calculations were made in accordance with standards established by the NSIR.

Analysis

The NSIR is a trade association that does not clearly represent the public interest, and it is unlikely that the panel of realtors exposed their standards to due process and public comment. For these reasons, a practitioner cannot assume that the organization's criteria are suitable. In order for the NSIR criteria to be suitable criteria for an attest engagement, they must possess each of the four attributes listed in AT 101.24 (i.e., objectivity, measurability, completeness, and relevance).

Reasonably Consistent Measurement

In evaluating the measurability attribute, the CPA should consider whether the criteria are sufficiently precise to permit people having competence in and using the same measurement method to be able to ordinarily obtain materially similar measurements. CPAs should not perform an attest engagement when the criteria are so subjective or vague that reasonably consistent measurements cannot be obtained.

For the purpose of assessing whether the use of particular criteria can be expected to yield reasonably consistent measurement and evaluation, consideration should be given to the nature of the subject matter. For example, soft information, such as forecasts and projections, would be expected to have a wider range of reasonable estimates than hard data, such as the calculated investment performance of a defined portfolio of managed investment products.

Judgment is required in order to determine whether the subject matter is capable of reasonably consistent measurements. The AICPA's nonauthoritative Practice Aid *New Standards, New Services: Implementing the Attestation Standards* offers the following issues that should be considered in making that judgment:

- *Suitability of the criteria* Assertions that use highly subjective language probably will not be capable of evaluation against suitable and available criteria. For example, a company that wishes to report on the best software package probably will not be able to develop criteria that are capable of reasonably consistent measurement, because there are a wide variety of reasonable determinations of what is meant by "best." Even terms that do not on their surface appear subjective might, in fact, be too subjective to form the basis for an attest engagement. In situations where the subject matter is highly subjective, the CPA may only be able to perform the engagement if the parties to the engagement agree to the criteria that will be used to measure the subject matter (which would require a restricted-use report).
- *Measurements chosen strictly for marketing purposes* CPAs should be skeptical of metrics that have been developed by an entity strictly to achieve a marketing purpose.

- *Significant discretion in choosing the relevant standard* CPAs should use caution when there is wide array of ways to measure the subject matter. For example, a company might claim that its car is "fastest in its class." There might be several ways to measure the speed of a car. Further, what criteria are used to constitute a particular class of cars?

Case Study 5-6: Suitability of Criteria: Reasonably Consistent Measurement

Facts

Radio station WETH AM 680 has an all-weather format modeled after the Weather Channel on cable TV. The radio station wishes to emphasize this matter in its advertising by making the claim that "We give you more weather in an hour than any other radio station in the tri-state area." They wish to engage a CPA to attest to this assertion.

Analysis

In this case, the subject matter involves the amount of weather presented by a radio station in one hour. But what is the definition of "weather"? Is it limited to weather forecasts? Does it include human-interest "storm stories" and other items? Would a call-in talk show on current weather events be considered weather or entertainment? Reasonable people may have different answers to these questions, which raises doubts about whether the subject matter—weather—is capable of reasonably consistent measurement.

It may be possible for the radio station to restate its assertion and still obtain the desired effect. For example, it may want to claim that "We offer fewer commercial minutes per hour than any other radio station in the tri-state area." Unlike the definition of "weather," the definition of "commercial minutes" is widely known within the industry. Changing the assertion to a more objective assertion would allow the CPA to perform an attest engagement.

Case Study 5-7: Suitability of Criteria: Reasonably Consistent Measurement

Facts

Discount Foods is a retail grocer in a highly competitive market. The company has determined that price is the single biggest reason why customers frequent a particular grocer. In order to encourage customers to shop at its stores, Discount Foods runs print ads claiming that its prices are the lowest in town. It compares the total for a "shopping list for a typical family of four" at its stores with the total for the list at several of its competitors. In order to add credibility to its ads, Discount Foods wishes to engage a CPA to attest to its claim.

Analysis

As stated, the criteria probably are not capable of reasonably consistent evaluation. What would be included in a "shopping list for a typical family of four?" Who makes that determination? Is the determination made at a point in time or is it an average over a period of time? There is too much discretion in the criteria to allow different individuals to reach a materially similar conclusion.

Responsibility for Determining Suitable Criteria

Regardless of who establishes or develops the criteria, the responsible party or the client is responsible for selecting the criteria and the client is responsible for determining that the criteria are appropriate for its purposes. However, it is clear from the attest standards that the CPA has the explicit responsibility to assess the criteria and determine that they are suitable.

In some cases, the criteria are appropriate only for a limited number of parties, who either

- Participated in the establishment of the criteria; or
- Can be presumed to have an adequate understanding of the criteria.

For example, criteria set forth in a lease agreement for override payments might be appropriate only for reporting to the parties to the agreement because of the likelihood that such criteria would be misunderstood or misinterpreted by parties other than those who have specifically agreed to the criteria. In this case, the users may agree on the criteria they believe is useful for their purposes, even if the CPA is not satisfied that they meet the four-part test for suitability. However, the presentation and report should be restricted to the use of those who agreed on the criteria or to those whom the CPA can presume to have an adequate understanding of the criteria.

Finally, the need for suitable criteria is unrelated to the level of service performed. Consequently, the CPA should not perform a review engagement if he or she concludes that the criteria is not suitable for an examination engagement. Therefore, the CPA cannot solve the problem of unsuitable criteria simply by providing a lower level of service. The only options available in this situation would be to

- Select a better set of criteria that is suitable; or
- Obtain the user's agreement with the criteria and restrict the report to those users.

Availability

Chapter 1 of SSAE-10 (AT 101.33) states that the criteria should be available to users in one or more of the following ways:

- Available publicly (for example, available on the Internet, in libraries, or for purchase).
- Available to all users through inclusion in a clear manner in the presentation of the subject matter or in the assertion (for example, when an attest report is published on the Internet, the criteria may be made available via a link from the report).
- Available to all users through inclusion in a clear manner in the CPA's report.
- Well understood by most users, although not formally available (for example, "the distance between points A and B is twenty feet"—the criterion of distance measured in feet is considered to be well understood).
- Available only to specified parties (for example, terms of a contract or criteria issued by an industry association that are available only to those in the industry).

If criteria are only available to specified parties, the CPA's report should be restricted to those parties who have access to the criteria. The attestation standards recognize that CPAs have no control over their client's distribution of a report. Therefore, in those situations, the report should contain a separate paragraph alerting the reader that the report is not intended to be, and should not be, used by anyone other than the specified parties. In addition, this restriction on use should also be addressed in the engagement letter.

Case Study 5-8: Suitability of Criteria: Objectivity

Facts

Chandler Digital wishes to engage a practitioner to attest to its claim that "in a national survey, 88% of those surveyed preferred our cell phone to any other brand." The survey was based on existing

Chandler Digital customers and compared the company's new cell phone to other "prior generation" models.

Analysis

Because the criteria to determine preference are based on comparing Chandler Digital's new cell phone to other "prior generation" models, they are not objective. Those surveyed would undoubtedly have a bias toward using the company's product because it has newer and improved features from older generation models. This lack of objectivity makes the criteria unsuitable and would preclude the practitioner from performing the attest engagement.

Case Study 5-9: Suitability of Criteria: Measurability

Facts

High Tech "R" Us operates in a rapidly changing industry that is known for extremely short product life cycles and is quickly becoming subject to sweeping changes in the government regulatory structure. In order to raise capital, High Tech "R" Us has prepared a financial forecast of its expected financial position, results of operations, and cash flows for the next 10 years. The company wishes to engage a practitioner to provide some level of assurance on the forecast.

Analysis

The company operates in a highly volatile, rapidly changing environment in which there are many significant uncertainties about the future. Given the facts and circumstances presented, it is doubtful that High Tech "R" Us will have a reasonable basis to forecast its financial position, results of operations, and cash flows that far in advance with any degree of reasonable consistency. That is, the criteria do not possess the measurability attribute and would not be suitable.

Case Study 5-10: Suitability of Criteria: Completeness

Facts

Offtrack Railways has recently endured a great deal of public criticism over the lack of on-time performance of its scheduled trains. Therefore, the company has compiled statistics that indicate that over 78% of its trains that depart during the business week arrive at their scheduled destinations on time. The company would like to publicize this statistic and seeks to engage a practitioner provide reliability through an attest engagement.

Analysis

The practitioner should consider whether the criteria for measuring "on time" are complete. The criteria measure only trains that depart during the business week, but what about scheduled trains that are cancelled or weekend trains? The omission of this information could very well alter the conclusion reached by a decision maker about the reliability of the trains. A lack of completeness renders criteria unsuitable for an attest engagement.

Case Study 5-11: Choice of Criteria

Facts

Connor Products emphasizes customer service. The company has developed two different metrics for assessing whether they have been successful at meeting customer expectations. The first metric is based on a survey of customers that is used to measure their "satisfaction index." This index is based on a large number of perceptions the customers have about the company and its level of service.

The second metric is based on the number of repeat purchases in the three months following an initial purchase. The company believes that only highly satisfied customers will return for additional purchases within a short period of time. Connor Products wishes to engage a CPA to perform an attest engagement relating to customer service.

Analysis

The practitioner may perform an attest engagement using either set of criteria, as long as they contain each of the four required attributes (objectivity, measurability, completeness, and relevance). Determining which set of criteria to use is a matter of professional judgment that depends largely on which set is most useful to decision makers. The second set of criteria is objective and can be measured with greater precision than the first set of criteria, which depends on customers' answers to survey questions. However, the first set of criteria might be more complete because it attempts to measure different attributes of customer service. Therefore, the two sets of criteria present a tradeoff; greater measurability versus a more complete measurement process.

Independence

Independence is the foundation of the attest function. Third-party users rely on the CPA's opinion in an audit or attest engagement because they believe the conclusion is impartial and unbiased. Chapter 1 of SSAE-10 (AT 101.36) states, "The practitioner should maintain the intellectual honesty and impartiality necessary to reach an unbiased conclusion about the subject matter or the assertion."

In the final analysis, independence in mental attitude means objective consideration of facts, unbiased judgments, and honest neutrality on the part of the CPA in forming and expressing conclusions. Independence in mental attitude presumes an undeviating concern for an unbiased conclusion about the subject matter or an assertion no matter what the subject matter or assertion may be.

The independence rules for CPAs can be found in the AICPA's Code of Professional Conduct. Section 101 of the Code contains Rule 101, "Independence," and various interpretations and rulings. This guidance has been established to guard against the appearance of the loss of independence. Appearance is stressed because the possession of intrinsic independence is a matter of personal quality rather than of rules that formulate certain objective tests.

As with many rules and standards of the profession, the guidance for independence is continually changing to meet the developments and pressures facing the profession. Nevertheless, CPAs and their firms should take steps to ensure they meet the independence requirements before performing any attest service for a client.

OTHER ENGAGEMENT ACCEPTANCE CONSIDERATIONS

A decision of whether or not to accept an engagement is a matter of the CPA's professional judgment. The decision is generally based on a consideration of the potential risks and rewards associated with the engagement. Risks generally arise from

- Clients of questionable integrity.
- Highly subjective subject matter.
- Highly subjective criteria.

While the last two items are a matter of judgment in the conduct of the attest engagement, the issue of the client's integrity is a risk that can be minimized by having effective client acceptance procedures.

SQCS-2 requires CPA firms to establish policies and procedures to minimize the likelihood of accepting or continuing association with a client whose management lacks integrity. Although there are no specific requirements in the attestation standards on the depth of investigation of potential clients, the AICPA's *Guide for Establishing and Maintaining a System of Quality Control for a CPA Firm's Accounting and Auditing Practice* suggests the following sources of information:

- Specific inquiry of the prospective client's lawyer, banker, and others having a business relationship with the entity.
- Review of available financial information about a prospective client, such as recent financial statements, income tax returns, reports to regulatory agencies, and credit reports.
- Specific inquiry of former accountants who have provided services to the entity.

OTHER ADMINISTRATIVE CONSIDERATIONS

Change in the Level of Service

Occasionally, during the course of an engagement, clients request the CPA to change the nature of the engagement. This change may be from a review to an examination or vice versa. The attestation standards do not address changes in the level of service other than to state that it is not appropriate to change an engagement from an examination to a review if the CPA has determined that the examination cannot be performed because the subject matter is not capable of evaluation against criteria that are suitable and available to users. Guidance from SSARS, however, is helpful. Generally, a change from a review to an examination poses no dangers to the CPA. The CPA must

- Determine what additional procedures and standards are required for the examination.
- Determine whether it is possible and practical to perform the procedures and comply with the standards.
- Revise the understanding with the client.

If the request is to change from an examination to a review, the SSARS guidance suggests that the CPA consider the following:

- The reason given for the client's request, particularly the implications of a restriction on the scope of the examination.
- The additional effort required to complete the examination.
- The estimated additional cost to complete the examination.

A client request to change from an examination or review to an agreed-upon procedures engagement generally does not a present a problem because, in an agreed-upon procedures engagement, the users specify the procedures to be performed and are responsible for the sufficiency of the procedures.

Withdrawal from the Engagement

The CPA should consider withdrawing from an engagement if any of the following conditions exist:

- The CPA has doubts about the integrity of the client.
- The client refuses to provide a signed representation letter.
- The CPA determines that he or she does not have and cannot obtain sufficient knowledge of the subject matter.
- The CPA determines that he or she is not independent with respect to the entity.
- There have been substantial limitations in the scope of the engagement that cannot be resolved (withdrawal is required in a review engagement).
- The CPA has significant reservations about the subject matter in an examination or review.

Exhibit 5-3 is a sample engagement resignation letter.

EXHIBIT 5-3
ENGAGEMENT RESIGNATION LETTER

July 30, 20XX

ABC Company
123 Main Street
Greenville, SC 29601

Dear [*name of client*]:

Effective [*date*], we will cease our services as your accountants. We have reached this conclusion after substantial deliberation because [*insert short description of reason for resignation*].

We wish to remind you that you have unpaid invoices totaling $[*amount*]. This does not include our services rendered since [*date*], which will be included in an invoice to be sent to you shortly. We expect full payment of all invoices. If you are not in a position to make full payment, please contact us so that we may discuss payment arrangements.

Subject to your making appropriate arrangements for the payment of your outstanding invoices, we will cooperate with your new accountants in addressing these and other matters. To facilitate that process, please send us a letter authorizing us to make disclosures to your new accountants. Without such written authorization, we are prohibited by our Code of Conduct from communicating with others regarding your company's affairs.

We look forward to helping you make a smooth transition with your new accountants.

Yours truly,

Able, Baker, and Charles, CPAs

By [*engagement partner*]

APPENDIX 5A
FREQUENTLY ASKED QUESTIONS

1. May a practitioner report on an assertion when a written assertion has not been provided by the responsible party?

   Answer: No. A practitioner may only report on the subject matter when a written assertion has not been obtained. Furthermore, when reporting on subject matter and a written assertion has not been provided by the responsible party, the use of the practitioner's report should be restricted.

2. What are some services that are typically provided by practitioners under the attestation standards?

   Answer: Services that typically are provided by practitioners under the attestation standards include:

   - Examining, compiling, or performing agreed-upon procedures related to a management financial forecast or projection.
   - Examining or performing agreed-upon procedures related tomanagement's assertion about the effectiveness of internal controls over financial reporting.
   - Examining or performing agreed-upon procedures related to management's assertion about compliance with specified legal, contractual, and regulatory requirements.

3. What are some services that are provided by practitioners that would not be considered attest engagements?

   Answer: Examples of professional services typically provided by that would not be considered attest engagements include:

   - Management consulting engagements whereby the practitioner provides advice or recommendations to a client.
   - Engagements to advocate a client's position, for example, tax matters being reviewed by the Internal Revenue Service.

- Tax engagements involving the preparation of tax returns or providing tax advice.
- Compilations or reviews of financial statements.
- Engagements in which the practitioner's role is solely to assist the client, for example, acting as the company's accountant in preparing information other than financial statements.
- Engagements to testify as an expert witness in accounting, auditing, taxation, or other matters.
- Engagements to provide an expert opinion on certain points of principle, such as the application of tax laws or accounting standards, given certain stipulated facts provided by another party as long as the expert opinion does not express a conclusion about the reliability of the facts provided by another party.

4. Are practitioners required to comply with quality control standards when performing attest engagements?

   Answer: Yes. Practitioners, in the conduct of a firm's attest practice, need to comply with quality control standards. Therefore, a firm should establish quality control policies and procedures to provide it with reasonable assurance of conforming with attestation standards in its attest engagements. While attestation standards relate to the conduct of individual attest engagements, quality control standards relate to the conduct of a firm's attest practice as a whole. Therefore, attestation standards and quality control standards are related and the quality control policies and procedures that a firm adopts may affect both the conduct of individual attest engagements and the conduct of a firm's attest practice as a whole.

5. What is the difference between an examination and a review attest engagement?

   Answer: The fundamental difference is that an examination is designed to provide positive assurance, that is to say an opinion, on the subject matter or the assertion. It requires the practitioner to accumulate sufficient evidence to reduce to an appropriately low level the risk that his or her procedures will result in an improper assurance. The standards and procedures for performing an examination are in many ways analogous to those for performing an audit.

   A review, on the other hand, offers only a limited level of assurance. The practitioner's objective in such an engagement is to accumulate evidence to limit his or her attestation risk to a moderate level. Generally, inquiries and analytical procedures will be sufficient to accomplish this objective.

6. May a practitioner use a specialist in connection with acquiring knowledge in the subject matter of the assertion to be reported on?

   Answer: Yes. A practitioner may use a specialist on a particular attest engagement as long as he or she has sufficient knowledge of the subject matter to achieve both of the following:

   - Communicate to the specialist the objectives of the work.
   - Evaluate the specialist's work to determine if the objectives achieved.

7. What are considered "suitable criteria" against which a practitioner can evaluate the subject matter in an attest engagement?

   Answer: Criteria issued by regulatory agencies and other bodies composed of experts that follow due-process procedures, including procedures for broad distribution of proposed criteria for public comment, normally should be considered suitable criteria. Criteria promulgated by a body designated by the AICPA's Governing Council are, by definition, considered to be suitable. Examples include the Financial Accounting Standards Board (FASB), the Governmental Accounting Standards Board (GASB), and the Federal Accounting Standards Advisory Board (FASAB).

8. What effect do restrictions on the scope of an attest engagement have on the practitioner's report?

   Answer: When there are restrictions on the scope of an attest engagement, whether imposed by the client or other circumstances, the practitioner should (a) qualify the assurance provided, (b) disclaim any assurance, or (c) withdraw from the examination or review engagement. Generally a disclaimer of opinion or withdrawal from an examination engagement is appropriate under the following circumstances:

   - If the scope limitation is imposed by the client or the responsible party.
   - If the potential effects of the scope limitation are pervasive to the subject matter or the assertion.
   - In a review engagement, the practitioner should withdraw from the attest engagement under the following circumstances:
   - When the practitioner is unable to perform the inquiry and the analytical, or other, procedures deemed necessary to achieve the limited assurance contemplated by a review.
   - When the client is the responsible party and does not provide the practitioner with a written assertion.

9. Is a practitioner responsible for controlling a client's distribution of restricted-use reports?

   Answer: No. The statement provided in a restricted-use report indicating that the report is not intended to be and should not be used by anyone other than the specified parties is sufficient.

APPENDIX 5B
COMPARISON BETWEEN ATTESTATION STANDARDS AND GENERALLY ACCEPTED AUDITING STANDARDS

Attestation Standards	**Generally Accepted Auditing Standards**
General Standards	
1. The engagement shall be performed by a practitioner having adequate technical training and proficiency in the attest function.	1. The audit is to be performed by a person or persons having adequate technical training and proficiency as an auditor.

2. The engagement shall be performed by a practitioner having adequate knowledge of the subject matter.	
3. The practitioner shall perform the engagement only if he or she has reason to believe that the subject matter is capable of evaluation against criteria that are suitable and available to users.	
4. In all matters relating to the engagement, an independence in mental attitude shall be maintained by the practitioner.	2. In all matters relating to the assignment, an independence in mental attitude is to be maintained by the auditor or auditors.
5. Due professional care shall be exercised in the planning and performance of the engagement.	3. Due professional care is to be exercised in the planning and performance of the audit and the preparation of the report.

Standards of Field Work

1. The work shall be adequately planned and assistants, if any, shall be properly supervised.	1. The work is to be adequately planned and assistants, if any, are to be properly supervised.
2. Sufficient evidence shall be obtained to provide a reasonable basis for the conclusion that is expressed in the report.	2. A sufficient understanding of internal control is to be obtained to plan the audit and to determine the nature, timing, and extent of tests to be performed.

Standards of Reporting

1. The report shall identify the subject matter or the assertion being reported on and state the character of the engagement.	1. The report shall state whether the financial statements are presented in accordance with generally accepted accounting principles.
2. The report shall state the practitioner's conclusion about the subject matter or the assertion in relation to the criteria against which the subject matter was evaluated.	2. The report shall identify those circumstances in which such principles have not been consistently observed in the current period in relation to the preceding period.
3. The report shall state all of the practitioner's significant reservations about the engagement, the subject matter, and, if applicable, the assertion related thereto.	3. Informative disclosures in the financial statements are to be regarded as reasonably adequate unless otherwise stated in the report.

4. The report shall state that the use of the report is restricted to specified parts under the following circumstances:
   - When the criteria used to evaluate the subject matter are determined by the practitioner to be appropriate only for a limited number of parties who either participated in the establishment, or can be presumed to have an adequate understanding, of the criteria.
   - When the criteria used to evaluate the subject matter are available only to specified parties.
   - When reporting on subject matter and a written assertion has not been provided by the responsible party.
   - When the report is on an attest engagement to apply agreed-upon procedures to the subject matter.

4. The report shall either contain an expression of opinion regarding the financial statements, taken as a whole, or an assertion to the effect that an opinion cannot be expressed. When an overall opinion cannot be expressed, the reasons therefor should be stated. In all cases where an auditor's name is associated with financial statements, the report should contain a clear-cut indication of the character of the auditor's work, if any, and the degree of responsibility the auditor is taking.

CHAPTER 6
EXAMINATION ENGAGEMENTS

CONTENTS

OVERVIEW

An examination is the highest level of service under the SSAEs. An examination is analogous to a financial statement audit. In an examination, the practitioner expresses an opinion on whether the subject matter or assertion about the subject matter is in conformity with given criteria. In this sense, the practitioner provides positive assurance in an examination. The examination requires the practitioner to reduce the risk of undetected material misstatement to a low level, and it involves substantial gathering of evidence.

ENGAGEMENT ACCEPTANCE

Identifying the Responsible Party

The responsible party is defined as the person or persons, either as individuals or as representatives of the entity, responsible for the subject matter. Sometimes the nature of the subject matter is such that no such party exists. For example, suppose that the Ski Valley Ski Resort made the assertion that "on average, we have over 120 inches of snow a year." The subject matter is the number of inches of snow in a year, but no person or persons can be held accountable for the snowfall. In such a situation, a responsible party is defined as someone who has a reasonable basis for making a written assertion about the subject matter. In order to make a good faith statement about the amount of annual snowfall, someone at the ski resort would have to perform research into the historic snowfall for the area. That person would have a reasonable basis for making a written assertion about the annual snowfall and could be identified as the responsible party.

The CPA may be engaged to gather the information necessary to enable the responsible party to evaluate the subject matter in connection with providing a written assertion. Alternatively, the subject matter, assertion, or criteria may be developed by the CPA during a concurrent or prior consulting service engagement. Regardless of the procedures the CPA performs, he or she should not claim to be the responsible party. The responsible party must accept responsibility for the assertion and the subject matter and must not base its assertion solely on the CPA's procedures.

Because the CPA's role in an attestation engagement is that of an attester, he or she should not take on the role of the responsible party. Moreover, Chapter 1 of SSAE-10 (AT 101.13) states that identifying a responsible party is a prerequisite for performing an attest engagement. The CPA is also required to obtain written acknowledgement or other evidence of the responsible party's responsibility for the subject matter, or, if applicable, the written assertion. Generally, this written acknowledgement is obtained in an engagement letter, a representation letter, or the written assertion. If the CPA cannot obtain direct written acknowledgement of the responsibly party's responsibility, other evidence, such as reference to legislation, a regulation, or a contract, may be sufficient.

When the Client Is Not the Responsible Party

The attestation standards recognize that the responsible party might not always be the client of the CPA. Nevertheless, a CPA may accept an attestation engagement when the responsible party is not the client. In that case, the CPA needs to obtain evidence of the third party's responsibility for the subject matter, which may be obtained through

- The engagement letter.
- The representation letter.
- A statement within the presentation of the subject matter.
- A separate written assertion.
- Contracts or correspondence between the client and the third party.
- Relevant laws or regulations.

Chapter 1 of SSAE-10 (AT 101.14) requires the CPA to obtain evidence of the responsible party's responsibility for the subject matter. In a two-party engagement, this evidence is typically obtained in the form of an engagement letter, representation letter, or written assertion. However, if the responsible party is not the CPA's client, the responsible party may be unwilling to provide such a written acknowledgement.

Case Study 6-1: Nonclient Responsible Party

Facts

In the state of South Carolina, attorneys are subject to a law that requires them to obtain and report at least 40 hours of continuing legal education (CLE) each year. Individual attorneys are responsible for reporting the CLE information to the South Carolina State Bar each year.

The Bar would like to obtain assurance that the CLE hours are being reported accurately. They would also like to convey a message to the attorneys that the CLE information is being scrutinized. The law in South Carolina requiring CLE also allows the Bar to periodically analyze the evidence of attorneys' continuing education reporting to determine whether the CLE hours have been properly reported. The Bar engages John Doe, CPA, to help them in this analysis.

Analysis

In this example, the subject matter is the CLE hours reported by the attorneys. The State Bar is John Doe's client. However, the Bar cannot be held accountable for the CLE hours reported by the attorneys, nor could anyone on the Bar's staff have a reasonable basis for providing a written assertion about the CLE hours. The individual attorneys are the responsible parties, thus, this is a three-party engagement: John Doe (the CPA), the State Bar (the client), and the individual attorneys (the responsible parties). If an individual attorney was unwilling to sign a statement saying that he or she was responsible for the CLE hours, John Doe, CPA, would simply use the state law as evidence that the attorney was, in fact, responsible.

Case Study 6-2: Responsibility for Subject Matter

Facts

The marketing department of Legal Prep, a law school entrance exam prep company, has obtained information from the exam administrator about the median exam score of persons taking Legal Prep's exam prep classes. The marketing department believes that this score speaks favorably about the high quality of exam preparation offered by Legal Prep, and the department would like to publish it in literature that it distributes to college students.

Recently, an investigative reporter turned up evidence of several exam prep companies manufacturing such information in order to attract new students. Although Legal Prep was not one of the companies identified by the reporter, the marketing department is concerned that their test score may be viewed with some skepticism as a result of the recent bad publicity. In order to provide some assurance on the median exam score it will publish, Legal Prep engages a CPA to perform an attestation engagement.

The exam administration organization collected the original data and calculated the median exam score, so the CPA identifies them as the responsible party. However, in attempting to obtain a written assertion, the CPA discovers that the personnel at the exam administration organization are unwilling to make a written assertion about the median exam score. Although the administrator believes the information is accurate, she also believes that organization policy prohibits her from making that statement in writing. The administrator could obtain a waiver of this policy, but the process would likely take two to three months.

The marketing department cannot wait two to three months because by that time, the recruiting season will be over, and the information will no longer be useful. The administrator finally agrees to provide the information with a letter that says: "Enclosed is the median exam score for the law school entrance exam you requested."

Analysis

In this example, the responsible party refuses to provide a written assertion. AT 101.09 states that the practitioner should ordinarily obtain a written assertion in an examination or review engagement. This does not mean that the CPA is prevented from performing an attest engagement in these circumstances.

If the CPA believed that the unwillingness to provide a written assertion was caused by the administrator's belief that the reported exam scores were false or inaccurate, then good business practice would dictate that the CPA decline the engagement because of the risk involved.

The administrator is qualified to make an assertion about the exam score. However, the statement "Enclosed is the median exam score for the law school entrance exam you requested," does not establish the administrator's responsibility for the subject matter or assertion. The administrator is merely presenting information without claiming responsibility.

The fact that the responsible party is unwilling to provide a written assertion in an examination or review engagement has significant reporting ramifications. As a result, restrictions on the use of the report and possible scope restrictions are not likely to meet Legal Prep's purpose, which was to provide credibility to certain information presented to third parties (i.e., potential students). Although the CPA could perform an agreed-upon procedures engagement, the report would be restricted as to use; once again, such a report is not likely to meet Legal Prep's original purpose.

Therefore, it is wise for the practitioner to communicate the importance of a written assertion (and resulting consequences if it cannot be provided) to the client at the time of engagement acceptance.

Required Understanding

SSAE-10 (AT 101.46) requires the practitioner to establish an understanding with the client regarding the services to be performed for each engagement. The understanding should include:

- *The objectives of the engagement* The practitioner should address the objectives of the engagement and any limitations of the engagement. For example, the objective of an examination engagement is to express an opinion as to whether the assertion or the subject matter is fairly stated, in all material respects, based on the stated criteria.
- *Management's responsibilities* In an examination engagement, management must select the criteria and determine that it is appropriate for its purposes. If the client is the responsible party, the client is also responsible for the subject matter (or related assertion) that the practitioner is to perform his or her procedures on.
- *Practitioner's responsibilities* The practitioner's responsibility is to perform the engagement in accordance with professional standards. More specifically, in order to avoid misunderstandings, the practitioner should describe the services that he or she will provide as precisely as possible.
- *Limitations of the engagement* The limitations that should be addressed relate to two aspects of the engagement: (1) limitations of the type of services to be performed and (2) use limitations based on the type of service. For example, the practitioner may wish to document that the engagement does not provide absolute assurance. In addition, the client should understand that in some cases the use of the report would be limited. For example, if a written assertion is not obtained from the responsible party, the practitioner's report would be restricted.

Other matters that practitioners should consider discussing with the client include:

- *Subject matter* The practitioner should determine specifically the subject matter to be reported on. This understanding should be used to determine whether the practitioner has, or can acquire, sufficient expertise to perform the engagement.
- *Criteria* The criteria to be used must be both suitable and available to users (see discussion in Chapter 4, "Pre-Engagement Considerations").

- *Users of the report* Knowing who the potential users are helps the practitioner assess the risks in the engagement and also provides information regarding the appropriateness of the service to be provided.
- *Logistics* The practitioner should determine whether the client has the necessary personnel and expertise to develop the subject matter. In addition, this understanding should include arrangements concerning the conduct of the engagement, such as timing, client assistance, and the availability of documents. Additional matters might include arrangements concerning involvement of specialists and conditions under which access to the workpapers may be granted to others.
- *Fees* The practitioner should determine that the fee and billing arrangements are appropriate.

Engagement Letters

The attestation standards require the practitioner to establish an understanding with the client. The standards state that a written engagement letter is preferred but not required. Although it is not specifically required by the SSAEs, a written engagement letter is strongly recommended. Most practitioners believe that a written engagement letter can effectively reduce misunderstandings between the practitioner and the client over the nature and limitations of the engagement. Engagement letters are particularly important in attestation engagements because of the increased risk of misunderstanding the nature of the practitioner's responsibilities (although clients might be familiar with traditional financial statement audits, they might not understand the nature and limitations of attestation engagements). The written engagement letter commonly includes the items discussed in the preceding section. An illustrative engagement letter for an examination engagement is included in Appendix 6A. When a written engagement letter is not obtained, the understanding of the engagement should be obtained and documented in the workpapers.

Understanding the Subject Matter

The second general standard for attestation engagements requires the practitioner to have adequate knowledge of the subject matter he or she is to report on. This includes understanding both its nature and the transactions or events that give rise to its measurement. It can also involve understanding the client's industry and how its business operates. The practitioner's understanding of the subject matter should be sufficient to allow him or her to form a conclusion about the subject matter in good faith.

SSAE-10 (AT 101.22) clarifies that the practitioner is not required to possess all of the necessary knowledge. He or she may rely on the work of a specialist as long as the knowledge of the subject matter is sufficient to allow the practitioner to

- Communicate to the specialist the objectives of the work; and
- Evaluate the specialist's work to determine whether the objectives were achieved.

The section titled "Use of a Specialist" (later in this chapter) provides additional guidance on using a specialist in an examination engagement.

ENGAGEMENT PLANNING

Materiality

The concept of materiality for an attest engagement is the same as that for an audit of financial statements prepared in conformity with generally accepted auditing standards (GAAS). SSAE-10 (AT 101.67) states:

> In expressing a conclusion, the practitioner should consider an omission or a misstatement to be material if the omission or misstatement—individually or when aggregated with others—is such that a reasonable person would be influenced by the omission or misstatement.

The relative, rather than absolute, size of an omission or misstatement determines whether it is material in a given situation. In addition, the practitioner should consider both quantitative and qualitative aspects of omissions and misstatements. Generally, materiality is considered at two phases of the engagement: the planning stage and the evaluation stage.

The following steps summarize how the practitioner should apply the materiality concept to the engagement:

1. Establish preliminary judgment about materiality during the initial planning stage of the engagement. This is referred to as "planning materiality."
2. Relate the planning materiality to the scope of tests. This is referred to as "tolerable misstatement."
3. Summarize total misstatements. This step includes (a) known misstatements (i.e., the amounts of errors specifically identified when performing attest procedures) and (b) likely misstatements (i.e., an estimate or projection of actual errors

because only a sample, rather than the entire population, is tested).

4. Compare total misstatements with materiality at the end of the engagement and evaluate whether attest procedures have been sufficient to detect material misstatements.
5. If significantly lower materiality levels become appropriate in evaluating the findings, the practitioner should reevaluate the sufficiency of the attest procedures that he or she has performed.

Steps 1 and 2 are performed in the planning stage, before attest procedures are applied, and are discussed below. Steps 3 and 4 are performed in the evaluation stage, after the attest procedures are applied, and are discussed in the "Evaluation of Results" section later in this chapter.

Case Study 6-3: Materiality

Facts

In its marketing and recruiting literature, Law Ready publishes the median score of its students on the four most recent law school entrance exams. In its upcoming literature, Law Ready plans to publish information showing the median exam scores for its students for the last four exams were (out of a possible 1,000) 680, 678, 683, and 681.

Law Ready engages a CPA to perform an attest engagement relating to all four of these published exam scores. During the course of her engagement, the practitioner discovers the methodology used by Law Ready inadvertently failed to include a certain segment of the population in the calculation of the averages. When this segment is included in the population, the actual averages for the last four years are 670, 667, 665, and 663.

Analysis

As a percentage of the originally calculated median exam scores, the misstatements vary from1% to 3%. As a purely quantitative measure, one might argue that this variation is not material. However, the correct amounts do affect the trend of the information. Under the first calculation, the median exam scores for Law Ready students appear to be fairly constant. When the calculation is corrected, it appears that the median exam score may be slipping, because median exam scores have gotten progressively lower over the past four years. In these circumstances, the practitioner may consider the misstatement to be material.

Planning Materiality

In the planning stage, the practitioner evaluates materiality in order to plan the attestation procedures necessary to detect material misstatements. Materiality in the evaluation stage is used to determine whether the subject matter is materially misstated. Ordinarily it is not feasible to anticipate all of the circumstances that may ultimately influence the practitioner's judgment about materiality, therefore the amount that the practitioner considers material at the end of the engagement may differ from planning materiality.

Based on a preliminary estimate of the subject matter, the practitioner decides what level would be considered material to the presentation. Because materiality is relative, rather than absolute, it is necessary to have bases for establishing whether misstatements are material. The practitioner calculates planning materiality by applying an appropriate percentage to a relevant base. The practitioner specifies the base to be used, calculates the amount of the base from the client's data, specifies an appropriate percentage, and computes planning materiality by applying the percentage to the base.

For subject matters expressed in financial amounts, the matrix presented in Exhibit 6-1 can generally be used for estimating planning materiality. When the subject matter is not expressed in financial amounts but is nonetheless numeric (for example, the number of widgets produced), Exhibit 6-1 can still be used. Although the table is based on judgments regarding financial statements, the overall

EXHIBIT 6-1
GUIDELINES TO CALCULATE PLANNING MATERIALITY

If the total dollar amount of the subject matter (the "base") is:		***Planning materiality is:***
Over	**But less than**	**Amount + (percent x base)**
$0	$50,000	0 + 5.5%
$50,000	$100,000	1, 250 + 3.0%
$100,000	$500,000	2, 250 + 2.0%
$500,000	$1 million	7, 500 + 1.0%
$1 million	$5 million	9, 500 + 0.8%
$5 million	$10 million	19, 500 + 0.6%
$10 million	$50 million	40, 000 + 0.4%
$50 million	$100 million	115, 000 + 0.25%
$100 million		185, 000 + 0.18%

percentages are also considered appropriate for determining materiality for numeric subject matter.

Subject matter that is not numeric (for example, customer satisfaction) presents more complex materiality judgments. In such cases, the practitioner may try to quantify some aspect of the subject matter as a basis for a materiality judgment. For example, the practitioner may be able to quantify a tolerable rate (such as failures per 1,000 transactions).

> **OBSERVATION:** Materiality is related to the subject matter rather than the level of service. Therefore, the same materiality measures apply to both examination and review engagements. The difference is the nature and extent of procedures applied.

Qualitative Aspects of Materiality

There is no definitive guidance on the qualitative factors to consider when assessing materiality. However, the following issues may be relevant in making this determination:

- The effect of the misstatement or omission on trends.
- The potential effect of the misstatement or omission on the company's compliance with debt covenants, other contractual agreements, and regulatory provisions.
- The significance of the misstatement or omission relative to known user needs.
- The precision with which the element of the subject matter can be measured.

Attestation Risk

Attestation risk is the risk that the practitioner will not detect a material misstatement in the subject matter. This is analogous to the concept of audit risk explained in SAS-47 (AU 312) (Audit Risk and Materiality in Conducting an Audit). In an examination engagement, the practitioner is required to reduce attestation risk to a low level.

Attestation risk (AR), like audit risk, is made up of:

- *Inherent risk* (IR) The susceptibility of the subject matter to material misstatement.
- *Control risk* (CR) The risk that a material misstatement that did occur would not be prevented or detected.

- *Detection risk* (DR) The risk that a material misstatement that eludes the client will also elude the practitioner.

This combination is multiplicative and is usually stated as follows:

$$AR = IR \times CR \times DR$$

Inherent Risk

Inherent risk is the susceptibility of the subject matter to material misstatement, assuming there are no related controls. Inherent risk is a measure of the practitioner's assessment of expectation of material misstatement before considering the entity's internal control.

Control Risk

Control risk is the risk that a material misstatement that could occur in the subject matter will not be prevented or detected on a timely basis by the entity's internal control. Control risk is a measure of the practitioner's assessment of the effectiveness of an entity's internal control in preventing or detecting material misstatements. Control risk, like inherent risk, is beyond the practitioner's control.

Detection Risk

Detection risk is the risk that the practitioner will not detect a material misstatement that exists in the subject matter. Detection risk is a measure of the risk that attestation procedures will fail to detect material misstatements. The practitioner controls detection risk through selection and application of tests. Detection risk arises because not all items that make up the subject matter are examined (sampling error) and attest procedures are not properly applied (nonsampling error). Restating the above formula illustrates the importance of detection risk (DR) as it relates to the performance of the engagement:

$$DR = \frac{AR}{IR \times CR}$$

Whereas inherent risk (IR) and control risk (CR) are not under the control of the practitioner, detection risk can be controlled because it relates to attest procedures, which can be changed at the practitioner's discretion. Inherent risk and control risk exist, and the practitioner can only assess them. If the assessments of inherent risk and control risk are high, the practitioner's tests must be more effective to reduce detection risk and adequately control attestation risk (AR). When the risks are lower, the practitioner may perform correspondingly less work to reduce detection risk.

Inherent risk and control risk can be assessed separately or in combination. Also, they be assessed quantitatively or qualitatively. While both approaches are acceptable, the approach used in this book is qualitative because it is considered highly effective and efficient. As such, the practitioner can use the matrix in Exhibit 6-2 to express the combined assessments of inherent risk and control risk in qualitative terms: maximum, moderate, or low.

EXHIBIT 6-2
COMBINING INHERENT RISK AND CONTROL RISK

Inherent Risk	×	Control Risk	=	Risk of Material Misstatement
High		Maximum		High
High		Moderate		High
High		Low		Moderate
Moderate		Maximum		Moderate
Moderate		Moderate		Low
Moderate		Low		Low
Low		Maximum		Moderate
Low		Moderate		Low
Low		Low		Low

Evidential Matter

The second standard of fieldwork states, "Sufficient evidence shall be obtained to provide a reasonable basis for the conclusion that is expressed in the report." Selecting and applying procedures that will accumulate evidence that is sufficient in the circumstances to provide a reasonable basis for the level of assurance to be expressed in the examination report requires careful exercise of professional judgment. A wide variety of procedures may be applied in an attest engagement. According to SSAE-10 (AT 101.52), in establishing the proper combination of procedures to appropriately restrict attestation risk, the practitioner should consider the following presumptions, keeping in mind that they are not mutually exclusive and may be subject to exceptions:

- Evidence obtained from independent sources outside an entity provides greater assurance about the subject matter or the assertion than evidence secured solely from within the entity.
- Information obtained from the independent attester's direct personal knowledge (such as through physical examination,

observation, computation, operating tests, or inspection) is more persuasive than information obtained indirectly.

- The more effective the controls over the subject matter, the more assurance they provide about the subject matter or the assertion.

Therefore, in the hierarchy of available attest procedures, those that involve search and verification (e.g., inspection, confirmation, or observation), particularly when using independent sources outside the entity, are generally more effective in restricting attestation risk than those involving internal inquiries and comparisons of internal information (e.g., analytical procedures and discussions with individuals responsible for the subject matter or assertion). However, the latter are generally less costly to apply.

Planning the Procedures

As noted earlier, in the hierarchy of available attest procedures, those that involve search and verification (e.g., inspection, confirmation, and observation), particularly when using independent sources outside the entity, are generally more effective in restricting attestation risk than those involving internal inquiries and comparisons of internal information (e.g., analytical procedures and discussions with individuals responsible for the subject matter or assertion). The extent to which attestation procedures are to be performed should be based on the level of assurance to be provided and the practitioner's consideration of

- The nature and materiality of the information to be tested to the subject matter or the assertion taken as a whole.
- The likelihood of misstatements.
- Knowledge obtained during current and previous engagements.
- The responsible party's competence in the subject matter.
- The extent to which the information is affected by the asserter's judgment.
- Inadequacies in the responsible party's underlying data.

As part of the attestation procedures, the practitioner considers the written assertion ordinarily provided by the responsible party. If a written assertion cannot be obtained from the responsible party, the practitioner should consider the effects on his or her ability to obtain sufficient evidence to form a conclusion about the subject matter. When the client is not the responsible party and a written assertion is not provided, the practitioner may be able to conclude that he or she has sufficient evidence to form a conclusion about the subject matter.

OBSERVATION: When the client is the responsible party, it is presumed that the client will be capable of providing the practitioner with a written assertion regarding the subject matter. Failure to provide the written assertion in this circumstance is a client-imposed scope limitation on the practitioner's evidence-gathering efforts. In an examination, the practitioner should modify the report for the scope limitation.

Planning and Supervision

The first standard of fieldwork states "The work shall be adequately planned and assistants, if any, shall be properly supervised." Proper planning and supervision contribute to the effectiveness of attest procedures. Proper planning directly influences the selection of appropriate procedures, and proper supervision helps to ensure that planned procedures are appropriately applied. In planning the attest engagement, the objective is to establish an overall strategy for

- How the engagement is to be conducted.
- The scope of the procedures.

To develop this strategy, the practitioner should seek to understand the events, transactions, and practices that, in their judgment, have a significant effect on the subject matter or assertion. SSAE-10 (AT 101.45) lists the following factors to be considered in planning an attest engagement:

- The criteria to be used.
- Preliminary judgments about attestation risk and materiality for attest purposes.
- The nature of the subject matter or items within the assertion that are likely to require revision or adjustment.
- Conditions that may require extension or modification of attest procedures.
- The nature of the report expected to be issued.

The nature, extent, and timing of planning varies with the nature and complexity of the subject matter or the assertion and the practitioner's prior experience with management. As part of the planning process, the practitioner should consider the nature, extent, and timing of the work to be performed to accomplish the objectives of the attest engagement. Nevertheless, as the engagement progresses, changed conditions may make it necessary to modify planned procedures.

Although the attestation standards describe what should be considered in planning the engagement, they do not state how to gather this information to make these planning decisions. SAS-22 (AU 311) (Planning and Supervision) provides useful guidance on engagement planning, even though it does not apply to attestation engagements. SAS-22 (AU 311) suggests the following procedures (modified for attestation engagements):

- Review correspondence files, prior-year workpapers and reports, and permanent files.
- Discuss matters that might affect the engagement with other firm personnel familiar with the entity (or those familiar with the responsible party, subject matter, or assertion).
- Inquire about current developments affecting the entity.
- Read current-year financial statements (or relevant financial and nonfinancial information related to the subject matter).
- Discuss the type, scope, and timing of the engagement with entity's management, board of directors, or audit committee (and, if applicable, the responsible party).
- Consider the effects of any recent changes in the subject matter or criteria.
- Coordinate the assistance of client or responsible party personnel in data preparation.
- Determine the extent of involvement, if any, of consultants, specialists, or others in the engagement.
- Establish the timing of the engagement.
- Establish and coordinate the staffing requirements.

Supervision involves directing the efforts of assistants who participate in accomplishing the objectives of the attest engagement and determining whether those objectives were accomplished. Elements of supervision include the following:

- Instructing assistants.
- Staying informed of significant problems encountered.
- Reviewing the work performed.
- Dealing with differences of opinion among personnel.

LEVEL OF TESTING

In an examination engagement, the practitioner performs sufficient testing to reduce the risk of an undetected misstatement to an appropriately low level. Therefore, the level of testing in an examination engagement is similar to that of an audit of financial statements. Although it is useful to draw analogies from the audit literature, keep in mind that audit requirements in the SASs generally do not apply to attestation engagements.

Internal Control

The attestation standards do not incorporate any specific requirements to gain an understanding of internal control. However, the subject matter of an attestation engagement is a product of the client's information system. In order to examine and report on such information, the practitioner should consider the sources of the information and how it was derived. The guidance in SAS-55 (AU 319) (Consideration of Internal Control in a Financial Statement Audit) (as amended by SAS-78 (AU 319, AU 324) and SAS-94 (AU 319)) is helpful in an examination engagement.

SAS-78 (AU 319, AU 324) defines internal control as follows:

> Internal control is a process, effected by an entity's board of directors, management and other personnel, designed to provide reasonable assurance regarding the achievement of objectives in the following categories:
>
> - Reliability of financial reporting
> - Effectiveness and efficiency of operations
> - Compliance with applicable laws and regulations

SAS-78 (AU 319, AU 324) states that an entity's internal control consists of the following five interrelated components:

a. Control Environment—The control environment refers to the "tone of the organization" with respect to the importance of internal control within an entity. This refers to management's attitudes, actions, and awareness about the importance of presenting reliable subject matter.

b. Risk Assessment—Risk assessment is the entity's identification and analysis of relevant risks to achievement of its objectives, forming a basis for determining how the risks should be managed. This refers to the process of identifying potential risks relevant to misstatements in an organization's subject matter and developing plans to address those risks.

c. Control Activities—Control activities are the policies and procedures that help ensure management directives are carried out. To successfully address risks and achieve its objectives, management must institute various control activities, such as reviews, comparisons, and segregation of duties.

d. Information and Communication—Information and communication systems support the identification, capture, and exchange of information in a form and timeframe that enable people to carry out their responsibilities.

e. Monitoring—Like all processes, an entity's system of internal control must be monitored.

Although not a requirement in an attestation engagement, the practitioner might consider applying the minimum requirements discussed in SAS-55 (AU 319), as amended. The practitioner should understand the components of internal control to sufficiently

- Understand the areas of increased risk.
- Understand the types of misstatements that could occur.
- Design tests to detect material misstatements.

Testing Controls

Although not required by the attestation standards and not commonly done in an attestation engagement, testing of controls should be considered. If the client's controls are effective and it is cost-effective to test them, conducting the tests can be an efficient approach to the engagement. To be effective, the controls must be designed to prevent or detect misstatements and they should be in effect for the period that affects the assertions. In order to test controls, the practitioner may apply inquiry, observation, inspection, or reperformance procedures to determine how, by whom, and how consistently a control procedure was applied.

Detection Procedures

The practitioner should identify the test objectives when designing procedures to test the subject matter. SAS-31 (AU 326) (Evidential Matter), as amended by SAS-80 (AU 326), provides guidance for deriving five test objectives in an attestation engagement, as follows:

1. *Existence or occurrence* The information included in the subject matter actually exists or the underlying events actually occurred.
2. *Completeness* The information includes everything it purports to.
3. *Rights and obligations* The information is what it purports to be.
4. *Valuation or allocation* The amounts or value judgments about the information are appropriate.
5. *Presentation and disclosure* The presentation and disclosure is in conformity with the criteria.

For all assertions, the foregoing five objectives should be addressed. The nature and extent of procedures applied to any given objective varies depending on the practitioner's assessment of risk of misstatement. When there is a low risk of misstatement for one or more of the objectives, either because the nature of the assertion does not lend itself to misstatement (inherent risk) or because tests of controls indicate that the client's procedures would prevent or detect misstatements (control risk), the level of testing for those objectives can be lower.

Nature of Tests

Some procedures are more effective in reducing attestation risk than others. SSAE-10 (AT101.53) describes two basic classes of procedures:

1. *Search and verification* Procedures include inspection, confirmation, and observation. Search and verification procedures are most effective when sources outside the entity are used or when the practitioner has direct knowledge of the subject matter (e.g., through physical examination, observation, computation, operating tests, or inspection).
2. *Inquiry and comparison of internal information* Procedures include analytical procedures and discussions with individuals responsible for the subject matter or assertion. Although these procedures are typically less costly to apply, they provide less assurance about the subject matter or the assertion than search and verification procedures.

The foregoing two classes of procedures are not mutually exclusive, and the practitioner chooses among the various types of detection procedures, choosing those that are most effective.

Case Study 6-4: Nature of Tests

Facts

The Metro School of Law engaged a CPA to perform an attest engagement related to the median score of its incoming freshman class on a law school entrance exam. An independent third party administers the exam and calculates the scores. Prospective students authorize this third party to report their scores directly to the Metro School of Law. Metro accumulates this data and calculates the median and average of its incoming freshmen.

Analysis

Because each student's exam is administered, graded, and reported to Metro by an independent third party, the CPA may determine that the combined inherent and control risk related to the raw exam score data for each student is rather low. The CPA would perform some tests to validate this data, but, because the risk of material misstatement is low, these tests will not be extensive. Also, the calculation of the median is not complex, and the risk of material misstatement is low. The CPA would limit tests in this area, as well.

However, the CPA might determine that issues related to defining the population of exam scores to be included in the population require an element of judgment by Metro. For example, the CPA might discover that the population of students is constantly changing. Students who accept enrollment subsequently change their mind; individuals on the waiting list are added. As the first day of class approaches, the population becomes more fixed. However, in order to meet the needs of the recruiting department, the calculation of averages must be done several months before the start of the academic year.

Because of these uncertainties and other judgments required of the admissions department, the CPA might consider the completeness of the population to be the area most vulnerable to misstatement and, therefore, the area that will receive the most extensive and effective tests.

The exam score received from the third party that administers the exam is probably quite reliable. Vouching the information included in Metro's calculation to the information from the outside organization that administered the exam would be a highly effective procedure that most likely would be performed as part of an examination engagement. Similarly, tracing the names of students included in the population to outside sources documenting their enrollment might also be performed in an examination engagement.

EXTENT OF TESTS

The extent of tests to be applied depends on the risk of material misstatement. This, in turn, depends on the measure of materiality. The practitioner's judgment on materiality varies based on whether the subject matter is numeric or nonnumeric.

Numeric Information

When the subject matter is numeric, the practitioner can use Exhibit 6-1 to determine materiality. The approach described in this section is more effective for testing overstatement than understatement. If the client's assertion is such that the primary concern is understatement, the practitioner's judgment of materiality may need to be based on a reciprocal population.

The following is a step-by-step approach for determining the extent of tests of numeric information. A planning worksheet for substantive testing is included in Appendix 6B. This worksheet can be used to document the decision regarding the extent of testing:

1. Determine tolerable misstatement. This is the maximum amount of misstatement that the practitioner can accept in a population and still conclude that it is not materially misstated. Rules of thumb in practice are to estimate tolerable misstatement as a percentage within 50% to 75% of planning materiality.
2. Identify the individually significant items in the population. To establish a cutoff amount for individually significant items, a rule of thumb is to divide tolerable misstatement by a factor ranging from three to six, depending on how much reliance is placed on the procedures being applied. These items are tested individually.
3. Identify unusual items. Identify any other unusual items in the population that should be examined individually because they are unlike the rest of the population or present increased risk.
4. Consider the remaining population. Subtract the amounts identified in steps 2 and 3 from the population. If the remainder is greater than tolerable misstatement, additional testing is generally necessary. This may involve application of analytical procedures, selecting more individually significant items, or sampling from the remaining population.

SAS-39 (AU 350) (Audit Sampling) and the AICPA Auditing Practice Release *Audit Sampling* provide useful guidance on the extent of tests in an attestation engagement. Based on that guidance, if the remaining population (i.e., the residual amount from step 4 above) is to be sampled, the following approach may be useful:

1. Divide the remaining population by the tolerable misstatement. This establishes the basic sample size:

$$\frac{\text{Sampling Population}}{\text{Tolerable Misstatement}} = \text{Basic Sample Size}$$

2. Apply a risk factor. Multiply the result of step 1 by the appropriate factor shown in Exhibit 6-3. This adjusts the sample size for (a) the risk of material misstatement and (b) the risk that other procedures, if any, that the practitioner plans to apply to the same amounts will fail to detect a material misstatement. Other procedures risk is inversely related to the effectiveness of the other procedures. That is, the more effective the other procedure, the lower the risk assessment. If no other procedures are planned, other procedures risk should be assessed as high.

$$\text{Basic Sample Size} \times \text{Risk Factor} = \text{Sample Size}$$

EXHIBIT 6-3
RISK FACTORS

Risk of Material Misstatement	Risk That Other Procedures Will Fail to Detect a Material Misstatement		
	High	**Moderate**	**Low**
High	3.0	2.3	1.9
Moderate	2.3	1.6	1.2
Low	1.9	1.2	0.9

3. Consider stratification. If the population is not stratified (i.e., not segregated into relatively homogeneous groups, such as by size or other attributes), increase the result from step 2 by a factor to recognize increased risk. An expansion factor of 1.2 to 1.5 (i.e., 20% to 50%) can generally be used to compensate for a lack of stratification:

$$\text{Sample Size (from step 2)} \times \text{Expansion Factor (1.2 to 1.5)} = \text{Adjusted Sample Size}$$

The sample items should be selected in such a way that all items have an opportunity of being selected. Common representative sampling methods include the following:

- *Random selection* A random selection provides each item in the population an equal chance of being selected. A random number table or generator is required. Random sampling is required only when statistical sampling is used.
- *Systemic sampling* Systemic sampling consists of determining a uniform interval and selecting throughout the population one item at each of the uniform intervals from the starting point.
- *Haphazard selection* Haphazard selection consists of a selection that is made without any special reason for including or excluding a given item from the sample.

Evaluating the Sample Results

The practitioner may use one of several methods to project the sample misstatement to the population. The AICPA Auditing Practice Release *Audit Sampling* presents two methods from which methods can be derived for use in attestation engagements.

Ratio Method

The ratio of the sample quantity (the total of all items selected) to the population quantity (the total of the population from which the sample is selected) is used to project the sample misstatement as follows:

$$\frac{\text{Amount of sample misstatement}}{\text{Sample quantity}} \times \text{Population quantity} = \text{Projected population misstatement}$$

Difference Method

The average amount of misstatement in the sample is calculated and multiplied by the number of items in the population to project the sample misstatement as follows:

$$\frac{\text{Sample misstatement}}{\text{Sample items}} \times \text{Population items} = \text{Projected population misstatement}$$

One of these methods should be selected based on whether there is a reason to expect a relationship between the amount of the misstatement and the amount of the item:

Factor	**Method**
Misstatement relates to size of the item	Ratio method
Misstatement relatively constant for all items	Difference method

The practitioner should calculate the projected misstatement separately for each individual group used. The projected misstatement for each group should then be added to determine the projected misstatement for the sample. The practitioner should also give adequate consideration to the qualitative aspects of misstatements, including the possible relationship of the misstatements to other phases of the engagement. The nature and cause of the misstatements should be considered, including (1) whether they are errors caused by fraud or (2) whether they are due to misunderstandings of instructions, carelessness, intentional failure to perform procedures, or other factors. The discovery of fraud generally requires more attention from the practitioner than the discovery of an error.

Nonnumeric Information

When the information is not numeric, the sampling approach cannot be based solely on a numeric measure of materiality. In that case, attribute sampling may be used, as follows:

1. Determine the amount of assurance needed to be provided by the test. The necessary level of assurance increases when the

item being tested is very important. It decreases when other tests are expected to provide additional information about the information being tested. It also decreases if controls over development of the information are tested and found to be effective, or if the subject matter involves a relatively lower level of inherent risk. This assessment does not need to be quantified, and the practitioner may assess it in qualitative terms, such as low, moderate, or high.

2. Estimate deviations. Estimate the number of deviations expected to be found in the population. The practitioner makes this estimate based on past experience or based on other factors, such as his or her assessment of the overall control environment.
3. Determine the sample size. The sample size can be determined based on the table in Exhibit 6-4.

Evaluation of Results

After applying the examination procedures, the practitioner should evaluate the results. If, based on the tests, the practitioner believes

EXHIBIT 6-4
MATRIX FOR DETERMINING SAMPLE SIZE FOR ATTRIBUTE SAMPLING

Expected Number of Deviations	Degree of Assurance Needed: High	Moderate	Low
0	60	45	35
1	95	80	65
2	125	110	90
3	155	135	110

This table is based on a tolerable deviation rate (materiality) of 5% and a confidence level as follows:

High degree of assurance needed	95%
Moderate degree of assurance needed	90%
Low degree of assurance needed	85%

For example, if a sample of 60 items is tested and no deviations are found, the practitioner can be 95% sure that the deviation rate does not exceed 5%.

that the subject matter is materially misstated, he or she should have the subject matter corrected or modify the examination report.

Numeric Information

If the subject matter consists of multiple items, the practitioner must consider the effect of the aggregate misstatement on individual items, totals, and subtotals within the subject matter. In the case of multiple items, the considerations are analogous to an audit of financial statements. Usually, however, only one item is involved and it is tested primarily by applying tests of details. In the case of a single item, the evaluation should consist of the following:

- Quantitative considerations
- Qualitative considerations
- Consideration of risk of further misstatement

Quantitative Considerations

First, all known and likely misstatements should be aggregated. Known misstatements consist of those that were specifically identified by performing examination procedures. For example, misstatements detected in items that were tested 100% (individually significant items) are known misstatements. Likely misstatements are determined when the practitioner uses certain sampling or analytical procedures. A projection of sample results is an example of likely misstatement.

Total known and likely misstatement should then be compared to the amount considered material to the subject matter. When only a single amount is being presented, this amount (evaluation materiality) is generally the same as planning materiality. If the total of known and likely misstatement exceeds the amount considered material to the subject matter, the practitioner should have the subject matter corrected or modify the examination report. If the total of known and likely misstatement is less than the amount considered material to the subject matter, then the practitioner should consider the qualitative aspects of the misstatement and consider the risk of further misstatement.

Qualitative Considerations

The practitioner must recognize that otherwise immaterial misstatements might be qualitatively material. In many instances, qualitative factors are more important than the quantitative guidelines. The intended uses and nature of the subject matter must be carefully evaluated, because certain types of misstatements are likely to be more important to certain users than others. Examples are as follows:

- *Error versus fraud* Amounts involving fraud generally are considered more critical than unintentional errors of equal dollar amounts. This is because fraud reflects on the integrity of the client.
- *Considerations of contractual obligations* Misstatements that are otherwise minor may be material if adverse consequences are likely to arise from contractual obligations.

Risk of Further Misstatement

As the aggregate effect of misstatements gets closer to the amount that the practitioner considers material, the practitioner should give more consideration to possible further undetected misstatements. If the practitioner believes that the risk of further undetected misstatements is too high, he or she should perform additional examination procedures to support the examination report.

USE OF A SPECIALIST

The practitioner may need specialized assistance on an engagement, and may decide to rely on the work of an expert. When the practitioner uses the work of a specialist, the attestation standards require that he or she have sufficient knowledge of the subject matter to (1) communicate to the specialist the objectives of the work and (2) evaluate the specialist's work to determine whether the objectives were achieved.

Before using and relying on the work of a specialist, the practitioner should be satisfied with the specialist's qualifications in the particular field. For guidance on using the work of a specialist, the practitioner may consider the guidance in SAS-73 (AU 336) (Using the Work of a Specialist). SAS-73 (AU 336) recommends that the practitioner consider the following in connection with his or her evaluation of the specialist's qualifications:

- The professional certification, license, or other recognition of the competence of the specialist.
- The reputation and standing of the specialist in the views of peers and others familiar with his or her work.
- The specialist's experience in the type of work that the practitioner is considering using the specialist for.

If the specialist is related to the client, the practitioner should assess the risk that the specialist's objectivity might be impaired. If the practitioner believes the specialist's objectivity might be impaired, he or she should either:

- Engage another specialist who is unrelated to the client; or
- Perform additional procedures to test the specialist's assumptions, methods, or findings (or engage another specialist to do so).

REPRESENTATION LETTERS

During an attest engagement, the responsible party makes many representations to the practitioner, both oral and written, in response to specific inquiries or through presentation of the subject matter or an assertion. Such representations from the responsible party are part of the evidential matter that the practitioner obtains. Although the attestation standards do not require a written representation letter, it is highly advisable to obtain one from the responsible party. Written representations from the responsible party ordinarily confirm representations explicitly or implicitly made to the practitioner, state and document the continuing appropriateness of such representations, and reduce the possibility of misunderstanding concerning the matters that are the subject of the representations. Examples of matters that might appear in a written representation letter are as follows:

- A statement acknowledging responsibility for the subject matter and, when applicable, the assertion.
- A statement acknowledging responsibility for selecting the criteria, where applicable.
- A statement acknowledging responsibility for determining that such criteria are appropriate for its purposes, where the responsible party is the client.
- The assertion about the subject matter based on the criteria.
- A statement that all known matters contradicting the assertion and any communication from regulatory agencies affecting the subject matter or assertion have been disclosed to the practitioner.
- Availability of all records relevant to the subject matter.
- A statement that any known events subsequent to the period (or point in time) of the subject matter being reported on that would have a material effect on the subject matter (or, if applicable, the assertion) have been disclosed to the practitioner.
- Other matters as the practitioner deems appropriate.

The representation letter should be dated no earlier than the date of the practitioner's report, which should coincide with the end of fieldwork. The letter should be addressed to the practitioner and signed by members of management whom the practitioner believes are responsible for and knowledgeable, directly or through others in the organization, about the matters covered by the representations. Normally, the CEO should sign the letter. It should also be signed by the highest ranking officer under whose responsibility the subject matter falls. For example, if the subject matter is financial, the CFO should also sign the letter.

When the client is not the responsible party, the practitioner should nevertheless consider obtaining a representation letter from the client. Examples of matters that might appear in such a representation letter are as follows:

- A statement that any known events subsequent to the period (or point in time) of the subject matter being reported on that would have a material effect on the subject matter (or, if applicable, the assertion) have been disclosed to the practitioner.
- A statement acknowledging the client's responsibility for selecting the criteria, where applicable.
- A statement acknowledging the client's responsibility for determining that such criteria are appropriate for its purposes.
- Other matters as the practitioner deems appropriate.

If the responsible party or the client refuses to furnish all written representations that the practitioner deems necessary, the practitioner should consider the effects of such a refusal on his or her ability to issue a conclusion about the subject matter. If the practitioner believes that the representation letter is necessary to obtain sufficient evidence to issue a report, the responsible party's or the client's refusal to furnish such evidence in the form of written representations constitutes a limitation on the scope of an examination sufficient to preclude an unqualified opinion and ordinarily is sufficient to cause the practitioner to disclaim an opinion or withdraw from the engagement. However, based on the nature of representations not obtained or the circumstances of the refusal, the practitioner may conclude that a qualified opinion is appropriate. Further, the practitioner should consider the effects of the refusal on his or her ability to rely on other representations.

Appendix 6G and Appendix 6H are illustrative representation letters for examination engagements.

SUBSEQUENT EVENTS

Events or transactions that have a material effect on the subject matter sometimes occur subsequent to the point in time or period of time of the subject matter being tested but prior to the date of the practitioner's report. These occurrences are referred to as subsequent events. The practitioner has no responsibility to detect subsequent events. However, he or she should inquire of the responsible party (and his or her client if the client is not the responsible party) as to whether they are aware of any subsequent events, through the date of the practitioner's report, that would have a material effect on the subject matter or assertion. If the practitioner has obtained a representation letter, the letter would ordinarily include a representation concerning subsequent events.

Two types of subsequent events require consideration by the practitioner:

1. Events that provide additional information with respect to conditions that existed at the point in time or during the period of time of the subject matter being tested: This information should be used by the practitioner in considering whether the subject matter is presented in conformity with the criteria and may affect the presentation of the subject matter, the assertion, or the examination report.
2. Events that provide information with respect to conditions that arose subsequent to the point in time or period of time of the subject matter being tested that are of such a nature and significance that their disclosure is necessary to keep the subject matter from being misleading: This type of information does not normally affect the practitioner's report if the information is appropriately disclosed.

The practitioner has no responsibility to keep informed of events subsequent to the date of his or her report. However, the practitioner might later become aware of conditions that existed at that date that might have affected his or her report had he or she been aware of them. In such circumstances, the practitioner should consider the guidance in AU Section 561 (Subsequent Discovery of Facts Existing at the Date of the Auditor's Report).

DOCUMENTATION

Attest documentation is the principal record of attest procedures applied, information obtained, and conclusions or findings reached by a practitioner in an engagement. The quantity, type, and content of attest documentation are matters of the practitioner's professional judgment. Attest documentation serves mainly to

- Provide the principal support for the practitioner's report, including the representation regarding observance of the standards of fieldwork, which is implicit in the reference in the report to attestation standards.

- Aid the practitioner in the conduct and supervision of the attest engagement.

Attest documentation should be sufficient to (1) enable members of the engagement team with supervision and review responsibilities to understand the nature, timing, extent, and results of attest procedures performed and the information obtained and (2) identify the engagement team member(s) who performed and reviewed the work.

Examples of attest documentation are work programs, analyses, memoranda, letters of confirmation and representation, abstracts and copies of entity documents, and schedules or commentaries prepared or obtained by the practitioner. Ordinarily, attest documentation includes

- Documentation of the engagement acceptance or continuance decision.
- An engagement letter.
- A planning form documenting the practitioner's knowledge of the client and consideration of attestation risk.
- Documentation of the procedures performed.
- Support for data in the presentation.
- A discussion of unusual matters encountered and their resolution.
- A representation letter.
- Copies of reports from other accountants, if any, who have examined a component of the subject matter.
- Documentation that the workpapers were reviewed.

Attest documentation may be in paper form, electronic form, or other media.

The practitioner has an ethical, and in some situations a legal, obligation to maintain the confidentiality of client information or information of the responsible party. Because attest documentation often contains confidential information, the practitioner should adopt reasonable procedures to maintain the confidentiality of that information. The practitioner should also adopt reasonable procedures to prevent unauthorized access to attest documentation.

EXAMINATION REPORTS

A practitioner who accepts an attest engagement should issue a report on the subject matter or the assertion or withdraw from the engagement. If the practitioner is reporting on the assertion, the assertion should be bound with or accompany the practitioner's report or be clearly stated in the practitioner's report.

When expressing an opinion, the practitioner should clearly state whether, in his or her opinion, (1) the subject matter is based on (or in conformity with) the criteria in all material respects or (2) the assertion is presented (or fairly stated), in all material respects, based on the criteria. The form of the report depends on whether the practitioner opines on the subject matter or the assertion.

In general, deciding on whether to report on the assertion or directly on the subject matter is a matter of personal preference. Some practitioners believe that reporting directly on the subject matter is more desirable because users of the information will find the conclusion easier to understand.

However, there are two instances when the attestation standards prohibit the practitioner from reporting on an assertion and require reporting directly on the subject matter:

1. When the responsible party does not provide a written assertion: As discussed in Chapter 4, "Pre-Engagement Considerations," the practitioner must report directly on the subject matter when a written assertion is not obtained. The form of the report will vary depending on the circumstances, and its use should be restricted.
2. When the responsible party asserts that the subject matter is not in accordance with the stated criteria: SSAE-10 (AT 101.84) states that the practitioner should report directly on the subject matter whenever the subject matter deviates from or is materially misstated in relation to the criteria.

The attestation standards state that the practitioner may examine the assertion and opine on the subject matter. That is, the introductory paragraph may refer to the assertion, while the opinion paragraph refers to the subject matter directly.

SSAE-10 (AT 101.85) requires the examination report to include the following elements:

1. A title that includes the word "independent."
2. An identification of the subject matter and the responsible party. (When reporting on an assertion, the report should identify the assertion rather than the subject matter. If the assertion does not accompany the report, the first paragraph of the report should also contain a statement of the assertion.)
3. A statement that the subject matter (or, if reporting on an assertion, the assertion) is the responsibility of the responsible party.
4. A statement that the practitioner's responsibility is to express an opinion on the subject matter (or, if reporting on an assertion, the assertion) based on his or her examination.

5. A statement that the examination was conducted in accordance with attestation standards established by the American Institute of Certified Public Accountants, and, accordingly, included procedures that the practitioner considered necessary in the circumstances.
6. A statement that the practitioner believes the examination provides a reasonable basis for his or her opinion.
7. The practitioner's opinion on whether the subject matter is based on (or is in conformity with) the criteria in all material respects (or, if reporting on an assertion, whether the assertion is presented, or fairly stated, in all material respects based on the criteria).
8. Under the following circumstances, a statement restricting the use of report to specified parties:
   a. When the criteria used to evaluate the subject matter are determined by the practitioner to be appropriate only for a limited number of parties who either participated in their establishment or can be presumed to have an adequate understanding of the criteria.
   b. When the criteria used to evaluate the subject matter are available only to the specified parties.
   c. When a written assertion has not been provided by the responsible party (the practitioner should also include a statement to that effect in the introductory paragraph of the report).
9. The manual or printed signature of the practitioner's firm.
10. The date of the examination report.

Exhibit 6-5 is an example of an examination report on a subject matter. Exhibit 6-6 is an example of an examination report on an assertion about a subject matter.

EXHIBIT 6-5
ILLUSTRATIVE EXAMINATION REPORT: EXAMINATION OF SUBJECT MATTER

Independent Accountant's Report

To the Board of Directors of
[*client name*]
[*city, state*]

We have examined the [*identify the subject matter; for example,* the accompanying schedule of investment returns of XYZ Company for the year ended

December 31, 20XX]. XYZ Company's management is responsible for the schedule of investment returns. Our responsibility is to express an opinion based on our examination.

Our examination was conducted in accordance with attestation standards established by the American Institute of Certified Public Accountants and, accordingly, including examining, on a test basis, evidence supporting [*identify the subject matter; for example,* XYZ Company's schedule of investment returns] and performing such other procedures as we considered necessary in the circumstances.We believe that our examination provides a reasonable basis for our opinion.

[*Additional paragraph(s) may be added to emphasize certain matters relating to the attest engagement or the subject matter.*]

In our opinion, the schedule referred to above presents, in all material respects, [*identify the subject matter; for example,* the accompanying schedule of investment returns of XYZ Company for the year ended December 31, 20XX] based on [*identify criteria; for example,* the ABC criteria set forth in Note 1].

[*signature of accountant*]

[*date*]

EXHIBIT 6-6
ILLUSTRATIVE EXAMINATION REPORT: EXAMINATION OF ASSERTION ABOUT THE SUBJECT MATTER

Independent Accountant's Report

To the Board of Directors of
[*client name*]
[*city, state*]

We have examined management's assertion that [*identify the assertion; for example,* the accompanying schedule of investment returns of XYZ Company for the year ended December 31, 20XX is presented in accordance with ABC criteria set forth in Note 1]. XYZ Company's management is responsible for the assertion. Our responsibility is to express an opinion on the assertion based on our examination.

Our examination was conducted in accordance with attestation standards established by the American Institute of Certified Public Accountants and, accordingly, including examining, on a test basis, evidence supporting management's assertion and performing such other procedures aswe considered necessary in the circumstances. We believe that our examination provides a reasonable basis for our opinion.

[*Additional paragraph(s) may be added to emphasize certain matters relating to the attest engagement or the assertion.*]

In our opinion, management's assertion referred to above is fairly stated, in all material respects, based on [*identify established or stated criteria; for example,* the ABC criteria set forth in Note 1].

[*signature of accountant*]

[*date*]

The report should be dated as of the end of fieldwork. That is the date that the practitioner's procedures are substantially complete.

Emphasis of a Matter

In some circumstances, even though the practitioner issues an unqualified examination opinion, he or she wishes to draw the reader's attention to an important matter regarding the attest engagement, the subject matter, or the assertion. This information might include, for example, inherent limitations of the data so that it is not misinterpreted; emphasis of certain aspects of the data, such as the interpretations made in applying the criteria; or uncertainties, such as pending legislation that might affect the assertions in the future.

A separate paragraph should be used to emphasize a matter, and the paragraph should not be referred to in the opinion paragraph. An emphasis of a matter paragraph is not a substitute for

- Lack of appropriate disclosure.
- A modified opinion.

> **OBSERVATION:** Emphasis-of-a-matter paragraphs are never required but may be added solely at the practitioner's discretion.

Modified Examination Reports

There are three types of modified examination reports: (1) qualified opinion, (2) adverse opinion, and (3) disclaimer of opinion.

Qualified Opinion

A qualified opinion states that "except for" the effects of a certain matter, the subject matter is in conformity with the criteria in all material respects. If conditions exist that individually or in combination result in one or more material misstatements or deviations from the criteria, the practitioner should modify the report and, ordinarily, in order to most effectively communicate with the reader of the report, express his or her conclusion directly on the subject matter.

When a practitioner expresses a qualified opinion, he or she should disclose all of the substantive reasons for the qualification in an explanatory paragraph preceding the opinion paragraph. The opinion paragraph should also include the appropriate qualifying language and a reference to the explanatory paragraph.

Adverse Opinion

An adverse opinion states that the subject matter is not in conformity with the criteria, which includes the adequacy of the disclosure of material matters. Such an opinion is expressed when the practitioner believes that the departures from the criteria are so material and pervasive that the information presented is grossly misstated or misleading.

When the practitioner expresses an adverse opinion, he or she should disclose all of the substantive reasons in an explanatory paragraph preceding the opinion paragraph. The practitioner should state the principal effects of the matter that gave rise to the adverse opinion on the subject matter. The opinion paragraph should then make reference to the explanatory paragraph.

Disclaimer of Opinion

A disclaimer of opinion states that the practitioner does not express an opinion on the subject matter. A disclaimer is appropriate when the engagement has not been performed in sufficient scope to allow the practitioner to form an opinion. A disclaimer is not appropriate when the practitioner believes that the subject matter is materially misstated in relation to the criteria.

When a practitioner disclaims an opinion, he or she should state in a separate explanatory paragraph the reasons why the scope of the engagement was restricted. The practitioner should also state in the disclaimer-of-opinion paragraph, which should refer to the explanatory paragraph, that the scope of the engagement was not sufficient to warrant the expression of an opinion. The report should not include a scope paragraph. The introductory paragraph of the report must also reflect the disclaimed of opinion.

Case Study 6-5: Emphasis of a Matter

Facts

Slugger Baseball manufactures baseball equipment, including baseball bats, baseballs, and other related equipment. The company has conducted extensive tests on the trajectory and distance for the flight of baseballs hit with the bats that it manufactures. The trajectory has been measured based on the angle of flight at the time the ball was hit; the distance has been measured in meters. The company wishes to engage a CPA to perform an attest engagement related to these measurements.

During the course of the engagement, the practitioner discovers that the tests were performed with specially designed baseball hitting robots. These robots were designed and approved by the Baseball Equipment Manufacturers Association as a means to ensure accuracy and comparability in the reporting of tests on baseballs and bats.

The practitioner also discovers that the company conducted its tests in the city of Denver, with an elevation of 5,280 feet above sea level. It is common knowledge that the thin air at such an altitude results in baseballs flying higher and farther than they would at sea level. The practitioner considers this fact to be significant for the users of the information.

Analysis

This case underscores the importance of the practitioner having a good understanding of the subject matter and the criteria. The practitioner's first consideration is whether the criteria used are suitable. If the criteria are not suitable, then the practitioner would be prohibited from performing the engagement.

In this case, the ball's trajectory is based on the angle of flight, and the distance is measured in meters. These criteria meet the suitability criteria described in AT 101.24. As such, another company could perform the same tests and reach materially similar measurements.

However, the matter of the test conditions (i.e., the tests were performed at an altitude of 5,280 feet above sea level) should also be considered. In this regard, the practitioner should consider whether the location of the company's test has been adequately disclosed. If the matter has not been adequately disclosed, and if the practitioner considered the matter material (i.e, its inclusion would influence a reasonable person), then he or she should modify the examination opinion.

If the matter has been adequately disclosed, the practitioner may still want to draw the reader's attention to it by including an emphasis-of-a-matter paragraph in the standard examination report. This paragraph would not modify the practitioner's opinion, but it would serve to alert the reader that the company conducted its tests under conditions that significantly affected the results.

Scope Limitations

The third standard of reporting states "The report shall state all of the practitioner's significant reservations about the engagement, the subject matter, and if applicable, the assertion thereto." The phrase "reservations about the engagement" refers to any unresolved problem that the practitioner had in complying with the attestation standards or interpretive standards. These types of problems are typically referred to as "scope limitations."

Scope limitations fall into two categories: (1) those imposed by the client or the responsible party and (2) those imposed by other circumstances:

1. *Client- and responsible party-imposed scope limitations* When the client or responsible party imposes a scope limitation, the practitioner should generally qualify or disclaim an opinion or withdraw from the engagement.
2. *Other scope limitation* When a scope limitation is imposed by circumstances beyond the control of the client or responsible party, then the practitioner may issue a qualified opinion or a disclaimer of opinion, depending on the nature and magnitude of the potential effects of the matters in question and on their significance to the subject matter or assertion.

Case Study 6-6: Scope Limitations

Facts

The Snow Valley Ski Resort wishes to publicize the area's outstanding winter weather. In an effort to attract skiers, the resort would like to claim that "on average, the area receives over 300 inches of snow per year." For the past 25 years, the resort has been collecting data on its snowfall, and this information was used to calculate the average inches of snow per year. The actual calculation came to 301.5 inches per year. In order to provide assurance on this data, the resort engages a CPA to perform an attest engagement.

While performing the engagement procedures, the practitioner discovers that five years of weather reports were destroyed in a fire and, therefore, are unavailable for testwork.

Analysis

The inability to perform tests on five years of data constitutes a scope limitation that may affect the report. The practitioner should first determine the potential effect this limitation has on the assertion. For example, is it possible that the data could have changed the calculated average enough so that the resort's assertion would be false? In this case, the calculated average is 301.5 inches of snowfall per year, and the resort's assertion states "over 300 inches." It is possible that the five missing years could have brought the average below 300 inches. If the calculated average was, say, 330 inches, it is unlikely that the five missing years would affect the practitioner's conclusion about the assertion. In that case, he or she may have been able to express an unqualified opinion.

Assume that the practitioner concludes that the inability to test five of the 25 years does, in fact, affect the ability to express assurance. The question now becomes whether the practitioner should qualify the opinion, disclaim an opinion, or withdraw from the engagement. The attestation standards state that generally the practitioner should disclaim an opinion or withdraw from the engagement when the client or responsible party has imposed the scope restriction. That is not the case here, because the inability to examine the records was caused by a fire that destroyed the records.

Therefore, the practitioner may issue either a qualified opinion or disclaim an opinion. In this case, the nature of the scope limitation is relatively minor and limited to a small number of items. Because it is not pervasive to the assertion, the practitioner would most likely qualify the opinion.

A possible alternative would be for the practitioner to discuss with the client the possibility of modifying the assertion or the criteria in such a way that the practitioner could provide an unqualified opinion. For example, if all of the data and evidential matter is available for the past 18 years, the client could make an assertion about the average snowfall for the past 18 years, instead of 25 years.

Reservations about the Subject Matter or the Assertion

The phrase "reservations about the subject matter or the assertion" refers to any unresolved reservation about the conformity of the subject matter with the criteria, including the adequacy of the disclosure of material matters. These reservations may relate to the measurement, form, arrangement, content, or underlying judgments and assumptions applicable to the subject matter and its appended notes. Examples are reservations about

- The terminology used.
- The amount of detail given.
- The classification of items.
- The bases of amounts set forth.

The existence of these reservations can result in either a qualified or an adverse opinion, depending upon the materiality of the departures from the criteria.

Report Restrictions

A general use report is one that is not restricted to specified parties. The need for restriction on the use of a report may result from a number of circumstances, including the purpose of the report, the criteria used in preparation of the subject matter, the extent to which the procedures performed are known or understood, and the potential for the report to be misunderstood when taken out of the context in which it was intended to be used. According to SSAE-10, the examination report is required to carry a use restriction in the following circumstances:

- When the criteria used to evaluate the subject matter are determined by the practitioner to be appropriate only for a limited number of parties who either participated in their establishment or can be presumed to have an adequate understanding of the criteria
- When the criteria used to evaluate the subject matter are available only to specified parties
- When reporting on subject matter and a written assertion has not been provided by the responsible party

> **OBSERVATION:** The attestation standards describe situations in which a practitioner is required to restrict the use of a report, but the standards do not preclude the practitioner from restricting the use of any report.

An examination report that is restricted as to use should contain a separate paragraph at the end of the report that includes the following elements:

- A statement stating that the report is intended solely for the information and use of the specified parties.
- An identification of the specified parties to whom use is restricted.
- A statement that the report is not intended to be and should not be used by anyone other than the specified parties.

An example of such a paragraph is the following:

> This report is intended solely for the information and use of [*the specified parties*] and is not intended to be and should not be used by anyone other than these specified parties.

The practitioner should inform his or her client that restricted-use reports are not intended for distribution to nonspecified parties, regardless of whether they are included in a document containing a separate general-use report. However, the practitioner is not responsible for controlling a client's distribution of restricted-use reports.

OBSERVATION: The practitioner should consider adding language to the engagement letter to obtain the client's agreement that the client and the specified parties will not distribute the report to parties other than those identified in the report.

OTHER INFORMATION IN A CLIENT-PREPARED DOCUMENT

A client may publish various documents that contain information in addition to the practitioner's examination report. The practitioner's responsibility with respect to the other information does not extend beyond the information identified in the examination report, and the practitioner has no obligation to perform any procedures to corroborate any other information contained in the document. However, the practitioner should read the other information not covered by the examination report and consider whether it, or the manner of its presentation, is materially consistent with the information appearing in the examination report.

If the practitioner believes that the other information is inconsistent with the information appearing in the examination report, he or she should

- Consider whether the examination report requires revision; or
- Request the client to revise the other information to eliminate the inconsistency.

If the other information is not revised to eliminate the inconsistency, the practitioner should consider other actions, such as:

- Revising the examination report to include an explanatory paragraph describing the material inconsistency.
- Withholding the use of the examination report.
- Withdrawing from the engagement.

If, while reading the other information, the practitioner becomes aware of information that he or she believes is a material misstatement of fact that is not a material inconsistency as described above, the practitioner should discuss the matter with the client. If, after discussing the matter, the practitioner concludes that a material misstatement of fact remains, the action the practitioner takes will depend on his or her judgment in the circumstances. The practitioner should consider steps such as notifying the client's management and audit committee in writing of his or her views concerning the information and consulting his or her legal counsel about further appropriate action in the circumstances.

ATTEST SERVICES AS PART OF A CONSULTING SERVICES ENGAGEMENT

When a practitioner determines that an attest service is to be provided as part of a consulting service engagement, he or she should inform the client of the relevant differences between the two types of services and obtain concurrence that the attest service is to be performed in accordance with the appropriate professional requirements. The practitioner should issue separate reports on the attest engagement and the consulting service engagement and, if they are presented in a common binder, the report on the attest engagement should be clearly identified and segregated from the report on the consulting service engagement.

APPENDIX 6A
ILLUSTRATIVE ENGAGEMENT LETTER

[*date*]

[*client's name*]
[*address*]

Dear [*client name*],

We are pleased to confirm our understanding of the services we are to provide for [*client's legal name*].

We will examine the [*describe subject matter or related assertion*] of [*client's name*] as of [*date*]. Our examination will be conducted in accordance with attestation standards established by the American Institute of Certified Public Accountants. Accordingly, it will include tests of your records and other procedures we consider necessary to enable us to express an opinion as to whether your [*describe subject matter*] is presented, in all material respects, in conformity with [*describe criteria*] or whether [describe assertion] is fairly stated, in all material respects based on conformity with [*describe criteria*]. If, for any reason, we are unable to complete the examination, we will not issue a report as a result of this engagement.

[*Describe restrictions on the use of the report, if any.*]

Our engagement will not include a detailed inspection of every transaction and cannot be relied upon to disclose all material errors, fraud, or other illegal acts that may exist. However, we will inform you of any material errors or fraud that comes to our attention. We will also inform you of any other illegal acts that come to our attention, unless they are clearly inconsequential.

We understand that you will provide us with the basic information required for our examination and that you are responsible for the accuracy and completeness of that information. We may advise you about appropriate criteria or assist in the development of the subject matter, but the responsibility for the subject matter remains with you. At the end of the engagement, we will require a representation letter from management.

We expect to begin our examination on approximately [*date*]. We estimate that our fees for these services will range from $_____ to $_____. You will also be billed for travel and other out-of-pocket costs such as report production, typing, postage, etc. Additional expenses are estimated to be $_____. The fee estimate is based on anticipated cooperation from your personnel and the assumption that unexpected circumstances will not be encountered during the examination. If significant additional time is necessary, we will discuss it with you and arrive at a new fee estimate before we incur the additional costs. Our invoices for these services will be rendered each month as work progresses and are payable on presentation. In accordance with our firm policies, work may be suspended if your account becomes _____ days or more overdue and will not be resumed until your account is paid in full. If we elect to terminate our services for nonpayment, our engagement will be deemed to have been completed upon written notification of termination, even if we have not completed our report. You will be obligated to compensate us for all time extended and to reimburse us for all out-of-pocket expenditures through the date of termination.

We appreciate the opportunity to be of service to you and believe this letter accurately summarizes the significant terms of our engagement. If you have any questions, please let us know. If you agree with the terms of our engagement as described in this letter, please sign the enclosed copy and return it to us.

Very truly yours,

[*CPA firm's name*]

Response

This letter correctly sets forth the understanding of [*client's name*].

By:

Title:

Date:

APPENDIX 6B
PLANNING MATERIALITY CALCULATION FORM

Client Name: ________________ Date of Subject Matter: _____________

Completed by: ________________ Date Completed: __________________

Instructions

The purpose of this form is to determine and document the materiality amount that will be considered suitable for planning purposes. For engagements related to financial or numeric subject matter, complete Part 1 of this form to determine planning materiality and tolerable misstatement. Part 1 should be completed using amounts as of the date of the subject matter. For nonfinancial and nonnumeric subject matter, complete Part 2 of this form to document the assessed tolerable rate of misstatement or noncompliance for the subject matter. This form should be prepared by the engagement personnel in charge of fieldwork (senior or supervisory staff) and reviewed and approved by the engagement executive for all attestation engagements.

Part 1: Procedures Related to Financial or Numeric Subject Matter

If the total dollar amount of the subject matter (the "base") is:		***Planning materiality is:***
Over	**But less than**	**Amount + (Percent x Base)**
$0	$50,000	0 + 5.5%
$50,000	$100,000	1,250 + 3.0%
$100,000	$500,000	2,250 + 2.0%
$500,000	$1 million	7,500 + 1.0%
$1 million	$5 million	9,500 + 0.8%
$5 million	$10 million	19,500 + 0.6%
$10 million	$50 million	40,000 + 0.4%
$50 million	$100 million	115,000 + 0.25%
$100 million		185, 000 + 0.18%

Example: If the base amount is $5.5 million, then the planning materiality would be determined as follows:

$19,500 + (.006 × $5,500,000) = $52,500

Calculations

1. Planning Materiality

Amount from Table	+	(Percentage from Table	×	Base Amount)	=	Planning Materiality
________		(________	×	________)	=	________

2. Tolerable Misstatement

Tolerable misstatement is used in computing sample sizes and in making other scope decisions. As a rule of thumb, tolerable misstatement can be calculated as follows:

Planning Materiality From Above	×	Factor	=	Tolerable Misstatement
____________	×	.75	=	________

3. Individually Significant Items

The amount used to determine individually significant items can be any amount up to tolerable misstatement.

Part 2: Nonfinancial and Nonnumeric Subject Matter

For nonfinancial and nonnumeric subject matter, materiality is considered to be a tolerable rate of ____ %. (The sampling approach in discussed in this chapter uses a tolerable rate of 5%.)

APPENDIX 6C
EXAMINATION PROCEDURES CHECKLIST

Client Name: ______________ Date of Subject Matter: ______________

Completed by: ______________ Date Completed: __________________

		Completed by	N/A
1.	Complete the Client Acceptance and Retention Evaluation Form.	________	______
2.	Establish and document an understanding with the client, preferably in an engagement letter. If an engagement letter will not be obtained, the oral understanding should be documented in a memo.	________	______
3.	Obtain an understanding of the client and the engagement.	________	______
4.	If the client is not the responsible party, obtain evidence of the responsible party's responsibility for the subject matter.	________	______
5.	Obtain an understanding of the subject matter.	________	______
6.	Perform any additional services needed to assist the responsible party in developing the subject matter or related assertion.	________	______
7.	Determine that the scheduling and staffing are adequate to perform the engagement.	________	______
8.	Complete the Planning Materiality Calculation Form.	________	______
9.	Obtain the engagement partner's approval of the overall engagement plan.	________	______
10.	If other services have been performed for the responsible party, review relevant		

	Completed by	N/A
workpapers and any related reports for indications of matters that contradict the subject matter or related assertion.	______	______
11. Develop and perform procedures necessary to evaluate the subject matter based on the criteria (attach a program or memo to this checklist).	______	______
12. Review the results of the preceding procedures and evaluate whether the subject matter is presented in conformity with the criteria. If the procedures reveal omissions or misstatements, assess the significance of those omissions or misstatements and their effect on the examination report.	______	______
13. Consider whether events have occurred after the date of the subject matter but before the end of fieldwork that affect the presentation of the subject matter.	______	______
14. Obtain a representation letter from the responsible party (and the client, if the client is not the responsible party).	______	______
15. Draft the examination report.	______	______
16. Read other information in a client-prepared document that contains the examination report for inconsistencies with the report and material misstatements of fact.	______	______
17. If any situations have occurred that require consultation, determine that such consultation has been properly documented.	______	______
18. If there were differences of professional opinion among members of the engagement team or between the engagement team and a specialist, determine that the differences were properly resolved and documented.	______	______
19. Determine that all questions, exceptions, or notes, if any, posed during the engagement have been followed up and resolved.	______	______
20. Determine that all required forms, questionnaires, and checklists have been completed.	______	______
21. Ensure that the workpapers and examination report have been reviewed in accordance with firm policy.	______	______
22. Obtain engagement partner's review and approval for issuance of report.	______	______

APPENDIX 6D
SAMPLING WORKSHEET FOR SUBSTANTIVE TESTS

Client Name: ________________ Date of Subject Matter: ____________

Completed by: ________________ Date Completed: ________________

Instructions

This worksheet is designed to assist the practitioner in planning, performing, and evaluating a nonstatistical sample for substantive tests. This form should be prepared by the engagement personnel in charge of fieldwork (senior or supervisory staff) and reviewed and approved by the engagement executive for all attestation engagements.

Part 1: Initial Calculation

1. Identify the amount for individually significant items. As a rule of thumb, consider using 33 1/3% of tolerable misstatement. However, any amount up to tolerable misstatement is acceptable.
2. Identify unusual items not included in Step 1 that are individually significant by their nature.
3. Calculate the remaining balance and percent of coverage:

	Number of Items	Amount
A. Total		$
B. Individually significant items [1/3 of $____________ tolerable misstatement = $ __________]		$
C. Unusual items (other than those in B. Briefly describe the nature of the unusual items:		$
D. Remaining balance [A – (B + C)]		$
E. Percent of coverage [(B + C) / A]		%
F. Tolerable misstatement		

4. After completing the initial calculation, if the remaining balance (D) is greater than tolerable misstatement (F), go to Part 2. If D is less than F, additional testing of D might not be necessary. If this is the case, go to Part 3. However, this is a matter of professional judgment.

Part 2: Consideration of Remaining Balance

1. If the remaining balance (D) is greater than tolerable misstatement (F), decide what additional procedures, if any, are needed to test D. Select one or more of the following options:
   a. No further testing of D: Consider this option only if (1) the assessed risk of material misstatement of D is low, and (2) the

percent of coverage (E) represents a substantial portion of the balance (such as 65% or more).

b. Applying analytical procedures: Consider using analytical procedures if sufficiently effective procedures can be designed and they provide adequate assurance with respect to D.

c. Relying on other substantive procedures: If other planned substantive tests in this area contribute to achieving the same objective, consider whether those other procedures provide adequate assurance with respect to D.

d. Sampling: Consider sampling D if (1) D consists of numerous items (such as 100 items or more), and (2) the expected misstatement of D does not exceed one-third of tolerable misstatement.

e. Testing more individually significant items: Consider this option if (1) analytical procedures and/or other substantive procedures do not provide adequate assurance, and (2) sampling is impractical.

If option e. is selected, complete Step 2. Otherwise go to Part 3.

2. Recalculate the remaining balance and percent of coverage using a lower amount for individually significant items. The amount should be based on the desired percentage of coverage.

	Number of Items	Amount
A. Total		$
B. Individually significant items. Amount used: $__________		$
C. Unusual items		$
D. Remaining balance [A – (B + C)]		$
E. Percent of coverage [(B + C) / A]		%
F. Tolerable misstatement		$

3. If D exceeds F, reconsider the options in Step 1. If D is less than F, additional testing of D may not be necessary. Document this decision by completing Part 3.

Part 3: Summary of Testing to Be Performed

1. Briefly describe the procedures to be applied to the individually significant items.
2. Briefly describe the procedures, if any, to be applied to the remaining balance (D from Part 1 or Part 2, above). If sampling will be used, complete the Sampling Planning and Evaluation Form: Substantive Tests.

APPENDIX 6E
SAMPLING PLANNING AND EVALUATION FORM

Client Name: ________________ Date of Subject Matter: ____________

Completed by: ________________ Date Completed: ________________

Instructions

This worksheet can be used in the examination of subject matter presented in financial or numeric form. It has been developed for financial subject matter, but can be modified for use with numeric (nonfinancial) subject matter.

Part 1: Planning

1. Describe the population being tested

	Units	Amount
a. Items to be examined 100% (individually significant items)	______	______
b. Population being sampled	______	______
c. Total	______	______

2. Briefly describe the test to be performed:
3. Describe the sampling unit:
4. Describe how completeness of the population will be considered:
5. Describe what will be considered a misstatement:
6. Sample selection method to be used:

   Haphazard_____ Random_____ Systemic_____

Expected Misstatement

7. Tolerable misstatement $___________
8. One-third of tolerable misstatement $___________
9. Expected misstatement (amount of projected misstatement expected in the population) $___________

Sample Size Calculation

10. Compute sample size, as follows:

Sampling Population / Tolerable Misstatement = Basic Sample Size

(Step 1b.) $______ / $_____________ =

Basic Sample Size × Risk Factor = Adjusted Sample Size

___________ × ________ = ____________

This adjusts the sample size for (a) the risk of material misstatement and (b) the risk that other procedures, if any, that the practitioner plans to apply to the same amounts will fail to detect a material misstatement. Other procedures risk is inversely related to the effectiveness of the other procedures. That is, the more effective the other procedure, the lower the risk assessment. If no other procedures are planned, other procedures risk should be assessed as high.

	Risk That Other Procedures Will Fail to Detect a Material Misstatement		
Risk of Material Misstatement	**High**	**Moderate**	**Low**
High	3.0	2.3	1.9
Moderate	2.3	1.6	1.2
Low	1.9	1.2	0.9

11. If it is not practical to stratify the population, multiply the sample size in Step 10 by 1.20 or other appropriate amount. ______

Part 2: Evaluation

Projection of Misstatement: If population is stratified, misstatement should be projected by stratum and added together. If the population is not stratified, use Stratum #1 column.

	Stratum #1	**Stratum #2**	**Total**
12. Dollar amount of misstatements noted in the sample	______	______	
13. Dollar amount of the sample	______	______	
14. Population being sampled	______	______	
15. Projected misstatement [(12/13) × 14]	______	______	______
16. Dollar amount of misstatements noted in items tested 100%			______
17. Total known and projected misstatement			______

Evaluation of Test Results

18. Explain reasons for misstatements:
19. Does the level of sampling risk appear acceptable? (Compare the amount in Step 15 to the amounts in Steps 8 and 9)
20. Describe how the sampling results affect the engagement:

APPENDIX 6F
ATTRIBUTE PLANNING AND EVALUATION FORM

Client Name: ________________ Date of Subject Matter: ____________

Completed by: ________________ Date Completed: ________________

Instructions

This form can be used to document tests applied to nonnumeric subject matter. It can also be used for numeric subject matter if the practitioner is concerned with the rate of misstatements rather than the amount of misstatements.

1. Describe the test to be performed:

   Test to Be Performed Sampling Unit Deviation Definition

2. Describe the population being tested and how the completeness of the population was considered:
3. Assess the degree of assurance needed from this test:
   a. High ___
   b. Moderate ___
   c. Low ___
4. Determine the required sample size using the following table.

   Sample size ________________

Matrix for Determining Sample Size for Attribute Sampling

Expected Number of Deviations	Degree of Assurance Needed: High	Moderate	Low
0	60	45	35
1	95	80	65
2	125	110	90
3	155	135	110

5. Document the sample selection method:
   a. Haphazard ___
   b. Random ___
   c. Systemic ___
6. Document the results of the tests

   Number of deviations detected: __________

   Describe deviations below:

   Deviation Cause

7. Compare the number of deviations detected to the number of expected deviations and the degree of assurance needed from the test. The practitioner should make a qualitative assessment of the nature and cause of any deviations detected before reaching a conclusion about the presentation of the subject matter in conformity with the criteria. Document the conclusion.

APPENDIX 6G
ILLUSTRATIVE REPRESENTATION LETTER

[*date—No earlier than date of the accountant's report*]

[*CPA firm's name*]
[*address*]

In connection with your examination of the [*describe subject matter*] as of [*date of subject matter*], for the purpose of expressing an opinion that the [*describe subject matter*] is presented, in all material respects, in conformity with [*describe criteria*] or [*describe assertion*] is fairly stated, in all material respects, based on [*describe criteria*], we confirm, to the best of our knowledge and belief, the following representations made to you during the course of your examination:

- We are responsible for the [*describe subject matter*] and for our assertion that is presented in conformity with [*describe criteria*].
- We are responsible for selecting the criteria and for determining that the criteria are appropriate for our purposes.
- As of [*date of subject matter*], the [*describe subject matter*] is presented in conformity with [*describe criteria*].
- We have disclosed to you all information we are aware of that may contradict the [*describe subject matter*], and we have disclosed to you all communications from regulatory agencies affecting [*describe subject matter*].
- We have disclosed to you all events subsequent to [*date of subject matter*] that would have a material effect on [*describe subject matter*].
- We have made available to you all records relevant to [*describe subject matter*].
- We intend to distribute your report only to [*describe restrictions, if any*].

Signature:	Signature:
Title:	Title:

APPENDIX 6H
CLIENT REPRESENTATION LETTER: CLIENT IS NOT THE RESPONSIBLE PARTY

[*date—No earlier than date of the accountant's report*]

[*CPA firm's name*]
[*address*]

In connection with your examination of the [*describe subject matter*] as of [*date of subject matter*], for the purpose of expressing an opinion that the [*describe subject matter*] is presented, in all material respects, in conformity with [*describe criteria*] or [*describe assertion*] is fairly stated, in all material respects, based on [*describe criteria*], we confirm, to the best of our knowledge and belief, the following representations made to you during the course of your examination:

- We have disclosed to you all events subsequent to [*date of subject matter*] that would have a material effect on [*describe subject matter*].
- We are responsible for selecting the criteria and for determining that the criteria are appropriate for our purposes.
- We intend to distribute your report only to [*describe restrictions, if any*].

Signature:

Title:

APPENDIX 6I
STANDARD EXAMINATION REPORT ON SUBJECT MATTER

Independent Accountant's Report

To the Board of Directors of
XYZ Company
[*city, state*]

We have examined the [*identify the subject matter; for example,* the accompanying schedule of investment returns of XYZ Company for the year ended December 31, 20XX]. XYZ Company's management is responsible for the schedule of investment returns. Our responsibility is to express an opinion based on our examination.

Our examination was conducted in accordance with attestation standards established by the American Institute of Certified Public Accountants and, accordingly, including examining, on a test basis, evidence supporting [*identify the subject matter; for example,* XYZ Company's schedule of investment returns] and performing such other procedures as we considered necessary in the circumstances. We believe that our examination provides a reasonable basis for our opinion.

[*Additional paragraph(s) may be added to emphasize certain matters relating to the attest engagement or the subject matter.*]

In our opinion, the schedule referred to above presents, in all material respects, [*identify the subject matter; for example,* the accompanying schedule of investment returns of XYZ Company for the year ended December 31, 20XX] based on [*identify criteria; for example,* the ABC criteria set forth in Note 1].

[*firm's signature*]

[*city, state*]

[*date*]

APPENDIX 6J
STANDARD EXAMINATION REPORT ON AN ASSERTION

Independent Accountant's Report

To the Board of Directors of
XYZ Company
[*city, state*]

We have examined management's assertion that [*identify the assertion; for example,* the accompanying schedule of investment returns of XYZ Company for the year ended December 31, 20XX is presented in accordance with ABC criteria set forth in Note 1]. XYZ Company's management is responsible for the assertion. Our responsibility is to express an opinion on the assertion based on our examination.

Our examination was conducted in accordance with attestation standards established by the American Institute of Certified Public Accountants and, accordingly, including examining, on a test basis, evidence supporting management's assertion and performing such other procedures as we considered necessary in the circumstances. We believe that our examination provides a reasonable basis for our opinion.

[*Additional paragraph(s) may be added to emphasize certain matters relating to the attest engagement or the assertion.*]

In our opinion, management's assertion referred to above is fairly stated, in all material respects, based on [*identify established or stated criteria; for example,* the ABC criteria set forth in Note 1].

[*firm's signature*]

[*city, state*]

[*date*]

APPENDIX 6K
STANDARD EXAMINATION REPORT: EXAMINATION OF AN ASSERTION; OPINION ON SUBJECT MATTER

Independent Accountant's Report

To the Board of Directors of
XYZ Company
[*city, state*]

We have examined management's assertion that [*identify the assertion; for example,* the accompanying schedule of investment returns of XYZ Company for the year ended December 31, 20XX is presented in accordance with ABC criteria set forth in Note 1]. XYZ Company's management is responsible for the assertion. Our responsibility is to express an opinion based on our examination.

Our examination was conducted in accordance with attestation standards established by the American Institute of Certified Public Accountants and, accordingly, including examining, on a test basis, evidence supporting [*identify the subject matter; for example,* XYZ Company's schedule of investment returns] and performing such other procedures as we considered necessary in the circumstances.We believe that our examination provides a reasonable basis for our opinion.

[*Additional paragraph(s) may be added to emphasize certain matters relating to the attest engagement or the assertion.*]

In our opinion, the schedule referred to above presents, in all material respects, [*identify the subject matter; for example,* the accompanying schedule of investment returns of XYZ Company for the year ended December 31, 20XX] based on [*identify criteria; for example,* the ABC criteria set forth in Note 1].

[*firm's signature*]

[*city, state*]

[*date*]

APPENDIX 6L
EXAMINATION REPORT: DISCLAIMER OF OPINION BECAUSE OF A SCOPE LIMITATION

Independent Accountant's Report

To the Board of Directors of
XYZ Company
[*city, state*]

We were engaged to examine the accompanying schedule of investment returns of XYZ Company for the year ended December 31, 20XX. XYZ Company's management is responsible for the schedule of investment returns.

[*Include paragraph to describe scope limitations.*]

Because management [*describe scope limitations*], the scope of our work was not sufficient to enable us to express, and therefore we do not express, an opinion on whether the schedule referred to above presents, in all material respects, [*identify the subject matter; for example,* the investment returns of XYZ Company for the year ended December 31, 20XX] based on [*identify criteria; for example,* the ABC criteria set forth in Note 1].

[*firm's signature*]

[*city, state*]

[*date*]

APPENDIX 6M
EXAMINATION REPORT: RESTRICTED BECAUSE THE CRITERIA ARE AVAILABLE ONLY TO SPECIFIED PARTIES

Independent Accountant's Report

To the Board of Directors of
XYZ Company
[*city, state*]

We have examined the [*identify the subject matter; for example,* the accompanying schedule of investment returns of XYZ Company for the year ended December 31, 20XX]. XYZ Company's management is responsible for the schedule of investment returns. Our responsibility is to express an opinion based on our examination.

Our examination was conducted in accordance with attestation standards established by the American Institute of Certified Public Accountants and, accordingly, including examining, on a test basis, evidence supporting [*identify the subject matter; for example,* XYZ Company's schedule of investment returns] and performing such other procedures as we considered necessary in the circumstances.We believe that our examination provides a reasonable basis for our opinion.

[*Additional paragraph(s) may be added to emphasize certain matters relating to the attest engagement or the subject matter.*]

In our opinion, the schedule referred to above presents, in all material respects, [*identify the subject matter; for example,* the accompanying schedule of investment returns of XYZ Company for the year ended December 31, 20XX] based on [*identify criteria; for example,* the ABC criteria set forth in Note 1].

This report is intended solely for the information and use of XYZ Company and [*identify other specified parties*] and is not intended to be and should not be used by anyone other than these specified parties.

[*firm's signature*]

[*city, state*]

[*date*]

APPENDIX 6N
EXAMINATION REPORT: QUALIFIED FOR MATERIAL MISSTATEMENTS OR DEVIATIONS FROM THE CRITERIA

Independent Accountant's Report

To the Board of Directors of
XYZ Company
[*city, state*]

We have examined the [*identify the subject matter; for example,* the accompanying schedule of investment returns of XYZ Company for the year ended December 31, 20XX]. XYZ Company's management is responsible for the schedule of investment returns. Our responsibility is to express an opinion based on our examination.

Our examination was conducted in accordance with attestation standards established by the American Institute of Certified Public Accountants and, accordingly, including examining, on a test basis, evidence supporting [*identify the subject matter; for example,* XYZ Company's schedule of investment returns] and performing such other procedures as we considered necessary in the circumstances. We believe that our examination provides a reasonable basis for our opinion.

Our examination disclosed the following [*describe condition(s) that, individually or in the aggregate, resulted in a material misstatement or deviation from the criteria*].

In our opinion, except for the material misstatement [*or* deviation from the criteria] described in the third paragraph, the schedule referred to above presents, in all material respects, [*identify the subject matter; for example,* the accompanying schedule of investment returns of XYZ Company for the year ended December 31, 20XX] based on [*identify criteria; for example,* the ABC criteria set forth in Note 1].

[*firm's signature*]

[*city, state*]

[*date*]

APPENDIX 6O
EXAMINATION REPORT: RESTRICTED BECAUSE NO WRITTEN ASSERTION PROVIDED BY THE NONCLIENT RESPONSIBLE PARTY

Independent Accountant's Report

To the Board of Directors of
XYZ Company
[*city, state*]

We have examined the [*identify the subject matter; for example,* the accompanying schedule of investment returns of XYZ Company for the year ended

December 31, 20XX]. XYZ Company's management is responsible for the schedule of investment returns. XYZ management did not provide us a written assertion about their schedule of investment returns for the year ended December 31, 20XX. Our responsibility is to express an opinion based on our examination.

Our examination was conducted in accordance with attestation standards established by the American Institute of Certified Public Accountants and, accordingly, including examining, on a test basis, evidence supporting [*identify the subject matter; for example,* XYZ Company's schedule of investment returns] and performing such other procedures as we considered necessary in the circumstances. We believe that our examination provides a reasonable basis for our opinion.

[*Additional paragraph(s) may be added to emphasize certain matters relating to the attest engagement or the subject matter.*]

In our opinion, the schedule referred to above presents, in all material respects, [*identify the subject matter; for example,* the accompanying schedule of investment returns of XYZ Company for the year ended December 31, 20XX] based on [*identify criteria; for example,* the ABC criteria set forth in Note 1].

This report is intended solely for the information and use of the management and board of directors of XYZ Company and is not intended to be and should not be used by anyone other than these specified parties.

[*firm's signature*]

[*city, state*]

[*date*]

CHAPTER 7
REVIEW ENGAGEMENTS

CONTENTS

OVERVIEW

This chapter discusses performing and reporting on a review engagement. Key concepts that this chapter covers are engagement acceptance, engagement planning, review procedures, and review reports. In addition, the question of whether a review engagement should be performed is discussed. This chapter covers many of the key concepts previously discussed in Chapter 6, "Examination Engagements," as they also apply to review engagements.

A review performed under the attestation standards is analogous to a review of historical financial statements. A CPA engaged to perform a review states a conclusion about whether any information came to his or her attention to indicate that the subject matter or assertion about the subject matter is not in conformity with given criteria. This conclusion is referred to as negative assurance. In a review engagement, the objective is to accumulate sufficient evidence to restrict attestation risk to a moderate level.

Decision by the Practitioner to Perform a Review Engagement

Although the attestation standards allow review engagements in all situations in which examination engagements can be performed, some practitioners avoid performing review engagements in most cases. Common reasons cited by practitioners are

- Inability to define a level of procedures that provides a moderate level of assurance that differs significantly from the procedures that would be performed in an examination.
- Fear that a review report would be misunderstood by users.
- Lack of a market demand for such services.

However, if a review engagement is to be performed, the practitioner should make sure that the users are able to understand the practitioner's report and the level of responsibility that the practitioner assumes.

ENGAGEMENT ACCEPTANCE

Identifying the Responsible Party

The responsible party is defined as the person or persons, either as individuals or as representatives of the entity, responsible for the subject matter. Sometimes the nature of the subject matter is such that no such party exists. For example, suppose that the Ski Valley Ski Resort made the assertion that "on average, we have over 120 inches of snow a year." The subject matter is the number of inches of snow in a year, but no person or persons can be held accountable for the snowfall. In such a situation, a responsible party is defined as someone who has a reasonable basis for making a written assertion about the subject matter. In order to make a good faith statement about the amount of annual snowfall, someone at the ski resort would have to perform research into the historic snowfall for the area. That person would have a reasonable basis for making a written assertion about the annual snowfall and could be identified as the responsible party.

The CPA may be engaged to gather the information necessary to enable the responsible party to evaluate the subject matter in connection with providing a written assertion. Alternatively, the subject matter, assertion, or criteria may be developed by the CPA during a concurrent or prior consulting service engagement. Regardless of the procedures the CPA performs, he or she should not claim to be the responsible party. The responsible party must accept responsibility for the assertion and the subject matter and must not base its assertion solely on the CPA's procedures.

Because the CPA's role in an attestation engagement is that of an attester, he or she should not take on the role of the responsible party. Moreover, Chapter 1 of SSAE-10 (AT 101.13) states that identifying a responsible party is a prerequisite for performing an attest engagement. The CPA is also required to obtain written acknowledgement or other evidence of the responsible party's responsibility for the subject matter or, if applicable, the written assertion. Generally, this written acknowledgement is obtained in an engagement letter, a representation letter, or the written assertion. If the CPA cannot obtain direct written acknowledgement of the responsibly party's responsibility, other evidence, such as reference to legislation, a regulation, or a contract, may be sufficient.

When the Client Is Not the Responsible Party

The attestation standards recognize that the responsible party might not always be the client of the CPA. Nevertheless, a CPA may accept an attestation engagement when the responsible party is not the client. In that case, the CPA needs to obtain evidence of the third party's responsibility for the subject matter. Evidence of the third party's responsibility for the subject matter may be obtained through:

- The engagement letter.
- The representation letter.
- A statement within the presentation of the subject matter.
- A separate written assertion.
- Contracts or correspondence between the client and the third party.
- Relevant laws or regulations.

Case Study 7-1: Nonclient Responsible Party

Facts

In the state of South Carolina, attorneys are subject to a law that requires them to obtain and report at least 40 hours of continuing legal education (CLE) each year. Individual attorneys are responsible for reporting the CLE information to the South Carolina State Bar each year.

The Bar would like to obtain assurance that the CLE hours are being reported accurately. They would also like to convey a message to the attorneys that the CLE information is being scrutinized. The law in South Carolina requiring CLE also allows the Bar to periodically analyze the evidence of attorneys' continuing education reporting to determine if the CLE hours have been properly reported. The Bar engages John Doe, CPA, to help them in this analysis.

Analysis

In this example, the subject matter is the CLE hours reported by the attorneys. The State Bar is John Doe's client. However, the Bar cannot be held accountable for the CLE hours reported by the attorneys, nor could anyone on the Bar's staff have a reasonable basis for providing a written assertion about the CLE hours. The individual attorneys are the responsible parties, thus, this is a three-party engagement: John Doe (the CPA), the State Bar (the client), and the individual attorneys (the responsible parties).

Chapter 1 of SSAE-10 (AT 101.14) requires the CPA to obtain evidence of the responsible party's responsibility for the subject matter. In a two-party engagement, this evidence is typically obtained in the form of an engagement letter, representation letter, or written assertion. However, if the responsible party is not the CPA's client, the responsible party might be unwilling to provide such a written acknowledgement. If an individual attorney was unwilling to sign a statement saying that he or she was responsible for the CLE hours, John Doe, CPA, would simply use the state law as evidence that the attorney was, in fact, responsible.

Case Study 7-2: Responsibility for Subject Matter

Facts

The marketing department of Legal Prep, a law school entrance exam prep company, has obtained information from the exam administrator about the median exam score of persons taking Legal Prep's exam prep classes. The marketing department believes that this score speaks favorably about the high quality of exam preparation offered by Legal Prep, and the department would like to publish it in literature that it distributes to college students.

Recently, an investigative reporter turned up evidence of several exam prep companies manufacturing such information in order to attract new students. Although Legal Prep was not one of the companies identified by the reporter, the marketing department is concerned that their test score may be viewed with some skepticism as a result of the recent bad publicity. In order to provide some assurance on the median exam score it will publish, Legal Prep engages a CPA to perform an attestation engagement.

The exam administration organization collected the original data and calculated the median exam score, so the CPA identifies them as the responsible party. However, in attempting to obtain a written assertion, the CPA discovers that the personnel at the exam administration organization are unwilling to make a written assertion about the median exam score. Although the administrator believes the information is accurate, she also believes that organization policy prohibits her from making that statement in writing. The administrator could obtain a waiver of this policy, but the process would likely take two to three months.

The marketing department cannot wait two to three months because by that time, the recruiting season will be over, and the information will no longer be useful. The administrator finally agrees to provide the information with a letter that says: "Enclosed is the median exam score for the law school entrance exam you requested."

Analysis

In this example, the responsible party refuses to provide a written assertion. AT 101.09 states that the practitioner should ordinarily obtain a written assertion in an examination or review engagement. This does not mean that the CPA is prevented from performing an attest engagement in these circumstances.

If the CPA believed that the unwillingness to provide a written assertion was caused by the administrator's belief that the reported exam scores were false or inaccurate, then good business practice would dictate that the CPA decline the engagement because of the risk involved.

The administrator is qualified to make an assertion about the exam score. However, the statement "Enclosed is the median exam score for the law school entrance exam you requested," does not establish the administrator's responsibility for the subject matter or assertion. The administrator is merely presenting information without claiming responsibility.

The fact that the responsible party is unwilling to provide a written assertion in an examination or review engagement has significant reporting ramifications. As a result, restrictions on the use of the report and possible scope restrictions are not likely to meet Legal Prep's purpose, which was to provide credibility to certain information presented to third parties (i.e., potential students). Although the CPA could perform an agreed-upon procedures engagement, the report would be restricted as to use; once again, such a report is not likely to meet Legal Prep's original purpose.

Therefore, it is wise for the practitioner to communicate the importance of a written assertion (and resulting consequences if it cannot be provided) to the client at the time of engagement acceptance.

Required Understanding

SSAE-10 (AT 101.16) requires the practitioner to establish an understanding with the client regarding the services to be performed for each engagement. That understanding should include:

- *The objectives of the engagement* The practitioner should address the objectives of the engagement and any limitations of the engagement. For example, the objective of a review engagement is to express a conclusion as to whether any information came to the practitioner's attention on the basis of the work performed that indicates that the subject matter is not based on the criteria or the assertion is not presented in material respects based on the criteria.
- *Management's responsibilities* In a review engagement, management must select the criteria and determine that it is appropriate for its purposes. If the client is the responsible party, the client is also responsible for the subject matter (or related assertion) to which the practitioner will perform his or her procedures.
- *Practitioner's responsibilities* The practitioner's responsibility is to perform the engagement in accordance with professional standards. More specifically, in order to avoid misunderstandings, the practitioner should describe as precisely as possible the services that he or she will provide.
- *Limitations of the engagement* The limitations that should be addressed relate to two aspects of the engagement: (1) limitations of the type of services to be performed and (2) use limitations based on the type of service. For example, the practitioner may wish to document that the engagement does not provide absolute assurance. In addition, the client should understand that, in some cases, the use of the report would be limited. For example, if a written assertion is not obtained from the responsible party, the practitioner's report would be restricted.

Other matters that practitioners should consider discussing with the client include:

- *Subject matter* The practitioner should determine specifically the subject matter to be reported on. This understanding should be used to determine that the practitioner has, or can acquire, sufficient expertise to perform the engagement.

- *Criteria* The criteria to be used must be both suitable and available to users (see discussion in Chapter 5, "Planning and Administration for Attestation Engagements").
- *Users of the report* Knowing who the potential users are helps the practitioner assess the risks in the engagement and also provides information regarding the appropriateness of the service to be provided.
- *Logistics* The practitioner should determine whether the client has the necessary personnel and expertise to develop the subject matter. In addition, this understanding should include arrangements concerning the conduct of the engagement, such as timing, client assistance, and the availability of documents. Additional matters might include arrangements concerning involvement of specialists and conditions under which access to the workpapers may be granted to others.
- *Fees* The practitioner should determine that the fee and billing arrangements are appropriate.

Engagement Letters

The attestation standards require the practitioner to establish an understanding with the client. The standards state that a written engagement letter is preferred, but not necessarily required. Although it is not specifically required by the SSAEs, a written engagement letter is strongly recommended. Most practitioners believe that a written engagement letter can effectively reduce misunderstandings between the practitioner and the client over the nature and limitations of the engagement. Engagement letters are particularly important in attestation engagements because of the increased risk of misunderstanding the nature of the practitioner's responsibilities (although clients may be familiar with traditional financial statement audits, they might not understand the nature and limitations of attestation engagements). The written engagement letter commonly includes the items discussed in the preceding section. Appendix 7A is an illustrative engagement letter for a review engagement. When a written engagement letter is not obtained, the understanding of the engagement should be obtained and documented in the workpapers.

Understanding the Subject Matter

The second general standard for attestation engagements requires the practitioner to have adequate knowledge of the subject matter on which he or she is to report. This includes understanding both its nature and the transactions or events that give rise to its measurement.

It might also involve understanding the client's industry and how its business operates. The practitioner's understanding of the subject matter should be sufficient to allow him or her to form a conclusion about the subject matter in good faith.

SSAE-10 (AT 101.22) clarifies that the practitioner is not required to possess all of the necessary knowledge. He or she may rely on the work of a specialist as long as the knowledge of the subject matter is sufficient to allow the practitioner to

- Communicate to the specialist the objectives of the work; and
- Evaluate the specialist's work to determine whether the objectives were achieved.

The section titled "Use of a Specialist," later in this chapter, provides additional guidance on using a specialist in a review engagement.

ENGAGEMENT PLANNING

Materiality

The concept of materiality for an attest engagement is the same as that for an audit of financial statements prepared in conformity with generally accepted accounting standards (GAAP). SSAE-10 (AT 101.67) states:

> In expressing a conclusion, the practitioner should consider an omission or a misstatement to be material if the omission or misstatement—individually or when aggregated with others—is such that a reasonable person would be influenced by the omission or misstatement.

The relative, rather than absolute, size of an omission or misstatement determines whether it is material in a given situation. In addition, the practitioner should consider both quantitative and qualitative aspects of omissions and misstatements. Generally, materiality is considered at two phases of the engagement: (1) the planning stage and (2) the evaluation stage.

The following steps summarize how the practitioner should apply the materiality concept to the engagement:

1. Establish preliminary judgment about materiality during the initial planning stage of the engagement. This is referred to as "planning materiality."
2. Relate the planning materiality to the scope of tests. This is referred to as "tolerable misstatement."
3. Summarize total misstatements. This step includes (a) known misstatements (i.e., the amounts of errors specifically identified

when performing attest procedures) and (b) likely misstatements (i.e., an estimate or projection of actual errors because only a sample, rather than the entire population, is tested).

4. Compare total misstatements with materiality at the end of the engagement and evaluate whether attest procedures have been sufficient to detect material misstatements.
5. If significantly lower materiality levels become appropriate in evaluating the findings, the practitioner should reevaluate the sufficiency of the attest procedures that he or she has performed.

Steps 1 and 2 are performed in the planning stage, before attest procedures are applied, and are discussed here. Steps 3 and 4 (discussed in the section titled "Evaluation of Results," later in this chapter) are performed in the evaluation stage, after the attest procedures are applied.

Planning Materiality

In the planning stage, the practitioner evaluates materiality in order to plan the attestation procedures necessary to detect material misstatements. Materiality in the evaluation stage is used to determine whether the subject matter is materially misstated. Therefore, the amount that the practitioner considers material at the end of the engagement may differ from planning materiality because ordinarily it is not feasible to anticipate all of the circumstances that may ultimately influence the practitioner's judgment about materiality.

Based on a preliminary estimate of the subject matter, the practitioner decides what level would be considered material to the presentation. Because materiality is relative, rather than absolute, it is necessary to have bases for establishing whether misstatements are material. The practitioner calculates planning materiality by applying an appropriate percentage to a relevant base. The practitioner specifies the base to be used, calculates the amount of the base from the client's data, specifies an appropriate percentage, and computes planning materiality by applying the percentage to the base.

When the subject matter is expressed in financial amounts, the table presented in Exhibit 6-1 can generally be used for estimating planning materiality. When the subject matter is not expressed in financial amounts but is nonetheless numeric (for example, the number of widgets produced), Exhibit 6-1 can still be used. Although the table is based on judgments regarding financial statements, the overall percentages are also considered appropriate for determining materiality for numeric subject matter.

> **OBSERVATION:** Materiality is related to the subject matter, rather than the level of service. Therefore, the same materiality

measures apply to both examination and review engagements. The difference is the nature and extent of procedures applied.

Qualitative Aspects of Materiality

There is no definitive guidance on the qualitative factors a practitioner must consider when assessing materiality. However, the following issues may be relevant in making this determination:

- The effect of the misstatement or omission on trends.
- The potential effect of the misstatement or omission on the company's compliance with debt covenants, other contractual agreements, and regulatory provisions.
- The significance of the misstatement or omission relative to known user needs.
- The precision with which the element of the subject matter can be measured.

Case Study 7-3: Materiality

Facts

In its marketing and recruiting literature, Law Ready publishes the median score of its students on the four most recent law school entrance exams. In its upcoming literature, Law Ready plans to publish information showing the median exam scores for its students for the last four exams were (out of a possible 1,000) 680, 678, 683, and 681.

Law Ready engages a CPAto perform an attest engagement relating to all four of these published exam scores. During the course of her engagement, the practitioner discovers the methodology used by Law Ready inadvertently failed to include a certain segment of the population in the calculation of the averages. When this segment is included in the population, the actual averages for the last four years are 670, 667, 665, and 663.

Analysis

As a percentage of the originally calculated median exam scores, the misstatements vary from1% to 3%. As a purely quantitative measure, one might argue that this variation is not material. However, the correct amounts do affect the trend of the information. Under the first calculation, the median exam scores for Law Ready students appear to be fairly constant. When the calculation is corrected, it appears that the median exam score may be slipping, because median exam scores have gotten progressively lower over the past four years. In these circumstances, the practitioner may consider the misstatement to be material.

Attestation Risk

Attestation risk is the risk that the practitioner will not detect a material misstatement in the subject matter. This is analogous to the concept of audit risk explained in SAS-47 (AU 312) (Audit Risk and Materiality in Conducting an Audit). In a review engagement, the practitioner is required to reduce attestation risk to a moderate level.

Attestation risk (AR), like audit risk, is made up of

- *Inherent risk* (IR) The susceptibility of the subject matter to material misstatement.
- *Control risk* (CR) The risk that a material misstatement that did occur would not be prevented or detected.
- *Detection risk* (DR) The risk that a material misstatement that eludes the client will also elude the practitioner.

This combination is multiplicative and is usually stated as follows:

$$AR = IR \times CR \times DR$$

Inherent Risk

Inherent risk (IR) is the susceptibility of the subject matter to material misstatement, assuming there are no related controls. Inherent risk is a measure of the practitioner's assessment of expectation of material misstatement before considering the entity's internal control.

Control Risk

Control risk (CR) is the risk that a material misstatement that could occur in the subject matter will not be prevented or detected on a timely basis by the entity's internal control. Control risk is a measure of the practitioner's assessment of the effectiveness of a entity's internal control in preventing or detecting material misstatements. Control risk, like inherent risk, is beyond the practitioner's control.

Detection Risk

Detection risk (DR) is the risk that the practitioner will not detect a material misstatement that exists in the subject matter. Detection risk is a measure of the risk that attestation procedures will fail to detect material misstatements. The practitioner controls detection risk through selection and application of tests. Detection risk arises because all items that make up the subject matter are not reviewed (sampling error) and attest procedures are not properly applied (nonsampling error). Restating the above formula illustrates the importance of detection risk (DR) as it relates to the performance of the engagement:

$$\text{DR} = \frac{\text{AR}}{\text{IR} \times \text{CR}}$$

Whereas inherent risk (IR) and control risk (CR) are not under the control of the practitioner, detection risk can be controlled because it relates to attest procedures, which can be changed at the practitioner's discretion. Inherent risk and control risk exist, and the practitioner can only assess them. If the assessments of inherent risk and control risk are high, the practitioner's tests must be more effective to reduce detection risk and adequately control attestation risk (AR). When the risks are lower, the practitioner may perform correspondingly less work to reduce detection risk.

Inherent risk and control risk can be assessed separately or in combination. Also, they can be assessed quantitatively or qualitatively. Although both approaches are acceptable, the approach used in this book is qualitative because it is considered highly effective and efficient. As such, the practitioner can use the matrix in Exhibit 6-2 to express the combined assessments of inherent risk and control risk in qualitative terms: maximum, moderate, or low.

Evidential Matter

The second standard of fieldwork states, "Sufficient evidence shall be obtained to provide a reasonable basis for the conclusion that is expressed in the report." Selecting and applying procedures that will accumulate evidence that is sufficient in the circumstances to provide a reasonable basis for the level of assurance to be expressed in the review report requires careful exercise of professional judgment. A wide variety of procedures may be applied in an attest engagement. According to SSAE-10 (AT 101.52), in establishing the proper combination of procedures to appropriately restrict attestation risk, the practitioner should consider the following presumptions, keeping in mind that they are not mutually exclusive and may be subject to exceptions:

- Evidence obtained from independent sources outside an entity provides greater assurance about the subject matter or the assertion than evidence secured solely from within the entity.

- Information obtained from the independent attester's direct personal knowledge (such as through physical examination, observation, computation, operating tests, or inspection) is more persuasive than information obtained indirectly.
- The more effective the controls over the subject matter, the more assurance they provide about the subject matter or the assertion.

In a review engagement, the objective is to restrict attestation risk to a moderate level. To accomplish this, the types of procedures performed are generally limited to inquiries and analytical procedures (rather than also including search and verification procedures).

Planning the Procedures

The extent to which attestation procedures are to be performed should be based on the level of assurance to be provided and the practitioner's consideration of

- The nature and materiality of the information to be tested to the subject matter or the assertion taken as a whole.
- The likelihood of misstatements.
- Knowledge obtained during current and previous engagements.
- The responsible party's competence in the subject matter.
- The extent to which the information is affected by the asserter's judgment.
- Inadequacies in the responsible party's underlying data.

As part of the attestation procedures, the practitioner considers the written assertion ordinarily provided by the responsible party. If a written assertion cannot be obtained from the responsible party, the practitioner should consider the effects on his or her ability to obtain sufficient evidence to form a conclusion about the subject matter. When the client is not the responsible party and a written assertion is not provided, the practitioner might be able to conclude that he or she has sufficient evidence to form a conclusion about the subject matter.

> **OBSERVATION:** When the client is the responsible party, it is presumed that the client will be capable of providing the practitioner with a written assertion regarding the subject matter. Failure to provide the written assertion in this circumstance is a client-imposed scope limitation on the practitioner's evidence-gathering efforts. In a review engagement,

such a scope limitation results in an incomplete review and the practitioner should withdraw from the engagement.

Planning and Supervision

The first standard of fieldwork states "The work shall be adequately planned and assistants, if any, shall be properly supervised." Proper planning and supervision contribute to the effectiveness of attest procedures. Proper planning directly influences the selection of appropriate procedures, and proper supervision helps to ensure that planned procedures are appropriately applied. In planning an attest engagement, the objective is to establish an overall strategy for

- How the engagement will be conducted.
- The scope of the procedures.

To develop this strategy, the practitioner should seek to understand the events, transactions, and practices that, in his or her judgment, have a significant effect on the subject matter or assertion. SSAE-10 (AT 101.45) lists the following factors to be considered in planning an attest engagement:

- The criteria to be used.
- Preliminary judgments about attestation risk and materiality for attest purposes.
- The nature of the subject matter or items within the assertion that are likely to require revision or adjustment.
- Conditions that may require extension or modification of attest procedures.
- The nature of the report expected to be issued.

The nature, extent, and timing of planning will vary with the nature and complexity of the subject matter or the assertion and the practitioner's prior experience with management. As part of the planning process, the practitioner should consider the nature, extent, and timing of the work to be performed to accomplish the objectives of the attest engagement. Nevertheless, as the engagement progresses, changed conditions may make it necessary to modify planned procedures.

Although the attestation standards describe what should be considered in planning the engagement, they do not indicate how to gather this information to make these planning decisions. However, SAS-22 (AU 311) (Planning and Supervision) provides useful guidance on engagement planning even though it does not apply to attestation engagements. SAS-22 (AU 311) suggests the following procedures (modified for attestation engagements):

- Review correspondence files, prior-year workpapers and reports, and permanent files.
- Discuss matters that might affect the engagement with other firm personnel familiar with the entity (or those familiar with the responsible party, subject matter, or assertion).
- Inquire about current developments affecting the entity.
- Read current-year financial statements (or relevant financial and nonfinancial information related to the subject matter).
- Discuss the type, scope, and timing of the engagement with entity's management, board of directors, or audit committee (and, if applicable, the responsible party).
- Consider the effects of any recent changes in the subject matter or criteria.
- Coordinate the assistance of client or responsible party personnel in data preparation.
- Determine the extent of involvement, if any, of consultants, specialists, or others in the engagement.
- Establish the timing of the engagement.
- Establish and coordinate the staffing requirements.

Supervision involves directing the efforts of assistants who participate in accomplishing the objectives of the attest engagement and determining whether those objectives were accomplished. Elements of supervision include:

- Instructing assistants.
- Staying informed of significant problems encountered.
- Reviewing the work performed.
- Dealing with differences of opinion among personnel.

LEVEL OF TESTING

In a review engagement, the practitioner performs sufficient testing to reduce the risk of an undetected misstatement to an appropriately moderate level. Therefore, the level of testing in a review engagement is similar to that of a review of historical financial statements. Although it is useful to draw analogies from the audit literature, keep in mind that audit requirements in the SASs and review requirements in SSARSs generally do not apply to attestation engagements.

Internal Control

The attestation standards do not incorporate any specific requirements for practitioners to gain an understanding of internal control. However, the subject matter of an attestation engagement is a product of the client's information system. In order to review and report on such information, the practitioner should consider the sources of the information and how the information was derived. The guidance in SAS-55 (AU 319) (Consideration of Internal Control in a Financial Statement Audit) (as amended by SAS-78 (AU 319, AU 324) and SAS-94 (AU 319)), is helpful in a review engagement.

SAS-78 (AU 319, AU 324) defines internal control as follows:

> Internal control is a process, effected by an entity's board of directors, management, and other personnel, designed to provide reasonable assurance regarding the achievement of objectives in the following categories:
>
> - Reliability of financial reporting
> - Effectiveness and efficiency of operations
> - Compliance with applicable laws and regulations

SAS-78 (AU 319, AU 324) states that an entity's internal control consists of the following five interrelated components:

a. Control Environment—The control environment refers to the "tone of the organization" with respect to the importance of internal control within an entity. This refers to management's attitudes, actions, and awareness about the importance of presenting reliable subject matter.

b. Risk Assessment—Risk assessment is the entity's identification and analysis of relevant risks to achievement of its objectives, forming a basis for determining how the risks should be managed. This refers to the process of identifying potential risks relevant to misstatements in an organization's subject matter and developing plans to address those risks.

c. Control Activities—Control activities are the policies and procedures that help ensure management directives are carried out. To successfully address risks and achieve its objectives, management must institute various control activities, such as reviews, comparisons, and segregation of duties.

d. Information and Communication—Information and communication systems support the identification, capture, and exchange of information in a form and timeframe that enable people to carry out their responsibilities.

e. Monitoring—Like all processes, an entity's system of internal control must be monitored.

Although it is not a requirement in an attestation engagement, the practitioner may want to consider applying the minimum requirements discussed in SAS-55 (AU 319), as amended. The practitioner should understand the components of internal control to sufficiently

- Understand the areas of increased risk.
- Understand the types of misstatements that could occur.
- Design tests to detect material misstatements.

Testing Controls

It would be unusual to test controls in a review engagement. In a review, the procedures are generally limited to inquiries and analytical procedures, and the testing of controls does not provide a meaningful reduction of those procedures. However, the attestation standards do allow tests of controls in a review engagement. The practitioner might consider testing controls if they make the engagement more efficient by allowing him or her to apply the inquiry and analytical procedures to more aggregated data.

Nature of Procedures

Some procedures are more effective in reducing attestation risk than others. SSAE-10 (AT101.53) describestwobasic classes of procedures:

1. Search and verification procedures include inspection, confirmation, and observation. Search and verification procedures are most effective when sources outside the entity are used or when the practitioner has direct knowledge of the subject matter (e.g., through physical examination, observation, computation, operating tests, or inspection).
2. Inquiry and comparison of internal information procedures include analytical procedures and discussions with individuals responsible for the subject matter or assertion. Although these procedures are typically less costly to apply, they provide less assurance about the subject matter or the assertion than search and verification procedures.

In a review engagement, the objective is to restrict attestation risk to a moderate level. To accomplish this, the types of procedures performed are generally limited to inquiries and analytical procedures (rather than also including search and verification procedures).

EXTENT OF PROCEDURES

Generally, in a review engagement, procedures consist of inquiries and analytical procedures. Normally, it is not necessary to obtain independent confirmations or apply inspection or observation procedures. However, these types of procedures are not prohibited and can be efficient in some situations.

Inquiries and Analytical Procedures

The practitioner's inquiries and analytical procedures generally consist of the following:

- Inquiries concerning the client's interpretation and application of the criteria.
- Inquiries concerning the client's sources of the information for the subject matter and procedures for how the information was derived.
- Analytical procedures designed to identify relationships and individual items that appear to be unusual. These procedures may consist of:
  - — Comparisons of data with similar data from previous periods.
  - — Comparison of data with anticipated results (such as budgets).
  - — Study of relationships that would be expected to conform to a predictable pattern based on the client's experience.
- Inquiries concerning actions taken at meetings of stockholders, board of directors, committees of board of directors, or comparable meetings that might affect the subject matter.
- Reading the subject matter to consider whether it appears to conform to the criteria.
- Obtaining reports from other practitioners, if any, who have been engaged to examine or review the subject matter for significant portions of the entity, its subsidiaries, or other investees.
- Inquiries of persons having responsibility for the subject matter concerning (1) whether the subject matter has been prepared in conformity with the criteria, consistently applied, (2) changes in the entity's business activities or application of the criteria, (3) matters for which questions have arisen in the course of applying the foregoing procedures, and (4) events subsequent to the date of the subject matter that would have a material effect on the presentation of the subject matter.

However, there are circumstances in which inquiry and analytical procedures (1) cannot be performed, (2) are deemed less efficient than other procedures, or (3) yield evidence indicating that the subject matter or the assertion is incomplete or inaccurate. In the first circumstance, the practitioner should perform other procedures that he or she believes can provide him or her with a level of assurance equivalent to that which inquiries and analytical procedures would have provided. In the second circumstance, the practitioner may perform other procedures that he or she believes would provide him or her with a level of assurance equivalent to that which inquires and analytical procedures would provide. In the third circumstance, the practitioner should perform additional procedures.

If the practitioner does not believe that the inquiries and analytical procedures provide the level of assurance needed to provide a conclusion in the review report, he or she should apply more effective procedures, such as those involving search and verification.

Appendix 7C provides a procedures checklist for a review engagement. It should be supplemented with specific inquiries and analytical procedures to be applied to the engagement.

Case Study 7-4: Extent of Procedures

Facts

The Metro School of Law engaged a CPA to perform an attest engagement related to the median score of its incoming freshman class on a law school entrance exam. An independent third party administers the exam and calculates the scores. Prospective students authorize this third party to report their scores directly to the Metro School of Law. Metro accumulates this data and calculates the median and average of its incoming freshmen.

Analysis

Because each student's exam is administered, graded, and reported to Metro by an independent third party, the CPA might determine that the combined inherent and control risk related to the raw exam score data for each student is rather low. The CPA would perform some tests to validate this data, but, because the risk of material misstatement is low, these tests would not be extensive. Also, the calculation of the median is not complex and the risk of material misstatement is low. The CPA would limit tests in this area as well.

However, the CPA may determine that issues related to defining the population of exam scores to be included in the population require an element of judgment by Metro. For example, the CPA might discover that the population of students is constantly changing. Students who accept enrollment subsequently change their mind; individuals on the waiting list are added. As the first day of class approaches, the population becomes more fixed. However, in order to meet the needs of the recruiting department, the calculation of averages must be done several months before the start of the academic year.

Because of these uncertainties and other judgments required of the admissions department, the CPA may consider the completeness of the population to be the area most vulnerable to misstatement and, therefore, the area that will receive the most extensive and effective tests.

If the CPA is engaged to perform a review, his or her procedures would be limited to inquiries and analytical procedures. For example, the CPA might inquire of admissions department personnel about the procedures used to ensure the integrity of the population or compare the calculated averages to historical averages of the school or comparable institutions.

REPRESENTATION LETTERS

During an attest engagement, the responsible party makes many representations to the practitioner, both oral and written, in response to specific inquiries or through presentation of the subject matter or an assertion. Such representations from the responsible party are part of the evidential matter that the practitioner obtains.

Although the attestation standards do not require a written representation letter, it is highly advisable to obtain a representation letter from the responsible party. Written representations from the responsible party ordinarily confirm representations explicitly or implicitly made to the practitioner, state and document the continuing appropriateness of such representations, and reduce the possibility of misunderstanding concerning the matters that are the subject of the representations. Examples of matters that might appear in a written representation letter include the following:

- A statement acknowledging responsibility for the subject matter and, when applicable, the assertion.
- A statement acknowledging responsibility for selecting the criteria, where applicable.
- A statement acknowledging responsibility for determining that such criteria are appropriate for its purposes, where the responsible party is the client.
- The assertion about the subject matter based on the criteria.
- A statement that all known matters contradicting the assertion and any communication from regulatory agencies affecting the subject matter or assertion have been disclosed to the practitioner.
- Availability of all records relevant to the subject matter.
- A statement that any known events subsequent to the period (or point in time) of the subject matter being reported on that

would have a material effect on the subject matter (or, if applicable, the assertion) have been disclosed to the practitioner.

- Other matters as the practitioner deems appropriate.

The representation letter should be dated no earlier than the date of the practitioner's report, which should coincide with the end of fieldwork. The letter should be addressed to the practitioner and signed by members of management whom the practitioner believes are responsible for and knowledgeable about, directly or through others in the organization, about the matters covered by the representations. Normally, the CEO should sign the letter. It should also be signed by the highest ranking officer under whose responsibility the subject matter falls. For example, if the subject matter is financial, the CFO should also sign the letter.

When the client is not the responsible party, the practitioner should also consider obtaining a representation letter from the client. Examples of matters that might appear in such a representation letter are as follows:

- A statement that any known events subsequent to the period (or point in time) of the subject matter being reported on that would have a material effect on the subject matter (or, if applicable, the assertion) have been disclosed to the practitioner.
- A statement acknowledging the client's responsibility for selecting the criteria, where applicable.
- A statement acknowledging the client's responsibility for determining that such criteria are appropriate for its purposes.
- Other matters as the practitioner deems appropriate.

If the responsible party or the client refuses to furnish all written representations that the practitioner deems necessary, the practitioner should consider the effects of such a refusal on his or her ability to issue a conclusion about the subject matter. If the practitioner believes that the representation letter is necessary to obtain sufficient evidence to issue a report, the responsible party's or the client's refusal to furnish such evidence in the form of written representations constitutes a limitation on the scope of the engagement, in which case the practitioner should withdraw from the engagement.

Appendix 7D and Appendix 7E are illustrative representation letters for review engagements.

SUBSEQUENT EVENTS

Events or transactions that have a material effect on the subject matter sometimes occur subsequent to the point in time or period of time of the subject matter being tested but prior to the date of the practitioner's report. These occurrences are referred to as subsequent events. The practitioner has no responsibility to detect subsequent events. However, he or she should inquire of the responsible party (and his or her client if the client is not the responsible party) as to whether they are aware of any subsequent events, through the date of the practitioner's report, that would have a material effect on the subject matter or the assertion. If the practitioner has obtained a representation letter, the letter would ordinarily include a representation concerning subsequent events.

Two types of subsequent events require consideration by the practitioner:

1. Events that provide additional information with respect to conditions that existed at the point in time or during the period of time of the subject matter being tested. This information should be used by the practitioner in considering whether the subject matter is presented in conformity with the criteria and might affect the presentation of the subject matter, the assertion, or the review report.
2. Events that provide information with respect to conditions that arose subsequent to the point in time or period of time of the subject matter being tested that are of such a nature and significance that their disclosure is necessary to keep the subject matter from being misleading. This type of information does not normally affect the practitioner's report if the information is appropriately disclosed.

The practitioner has no responsibility to keep informed of events subsequent to the date of his or her report. However, the practitioner might later become aware of conditions that existed at that date that might have affected the practitioner's report had he or she been aware of them. In such circumstances, the practitioner might consider the guidance in AU Section 561 (Subsequent Discovery of Facts Existing at the Date of the Auditor's Report).

DOCUMENTATION

Attest documentation is the principal record of attest procedures applied, information obtained, and conclusions or findings reached by the practitioner in an engagement. The quantity, type, and content of attest documentation are matters of the practitioner's professional judgment. Attest documentation serves mainly to

- Provide the principal support for the practitioner's report, including the representation regarding observance of the standards of fieldwork, which is implicit in the reference in the report to attestation standards.

- Aid the practitioner in the conduct and supervision of the attest engagement.

Attest documentation should be sufficient to (1) enable members of the engagement team with supervision and review responsibilities to understand the nature, timing, extent, and results of attest procedures performed and the information obtained and (2) identify the engagement team member(s) who performed and reviewed the work.

Examples of attest documentation are work programs, analyses, memoranda, letters of confirmation and representation, abstracts or copies of entity documents, and schedules or commentaries prepared or obtained by the practitioner. Ordinarily, attest documentation includes:

- Documentation of the engagement acceptance or continuance decision.
- An engagement letter.
- A planning form documenting the practitioner's knowledge of the client and consideration of attestation risk.
- Documentation of the procedures performed.
- Support for data in the presentation.
- A discussion of unusual matters encountered and their resolution.
- A representation letter.
- Copies of reports from other accountants, if any, who have examined a component of the subject matter.
- Documentation that the workpapers were reviewed.

Attest documentation may be in paper form, electronic form, or other media. The practitioner has an ethical, and in some situations a legal, obligation to maintain the confidentiality of client information or information of the responsible party. Because attest documentation often contains confidential information, the practitioner should adopt reasonable procedures to maintain the confidentiality of that information. The practitioner should also adopt reasonable procedures to prevent unauthorized access to attest documentation.

REVIEW REPORTS

The practitioner who accepts an attest engagement should issue a report on the subject matter or the assertion or withdraw from the engagement. If the practitioner is reporting on the assertion, the assertion should be bound with or accompany the practitioner's report or be clearly stated in the practitioner's report.

In general, deciding on whether to report on the assertion or directly on the subject matter is a matter of personal preference. Some practitioners believe that reporting directly on the subject matter is more desirable because users of the information will find the conclusion easier to understand.

However, there are two instances when the attestation standards prohibit the practitioner from reporting on an assertion and require reporting directly on the subject matter:

1. When the responsible party does not provide a written assertion. As discussed in Chapter 5, the practitioner must report directly on the subject matter when a written assertion is not obtained. The form of the report will vary depending on the circumstances, and its use should be restricted.
2. When the responsible party asserts that the subject matter is not in accordance with the stated criteria. SSAE-10 (AT 101.84) states that the practitioner should report directly on the subject matter whenever the subject matter deviates from or is materially misstated in relation to the criteria.

SSAE-10 (AT 101.89) requires the review report to include the following elements:

- A title that includes the word "independent."
- An identification of the subject matter and the responsible party. (When reporting on the assertion, the report should identify the assertion rather than the subject matter. If the assertion does not accompany the report, the first paragraph of the report should also contain a statement of the assertion.)
- A statement that the subject matter (or, if reporting on the assertion, the assertion) is the responsibility of the responsible party.
- A statement that the review was conducted in accordance with attestation standards established by the American Institute of Certified Public Accountants.
- A statement that a review is substantially less in scope than an examination, the objective of which is an expression of an opinion on the subject matter, and accordingly, no such opinion is expressed.
- A statement about whether the practitioner is aware of any material modifications that should be made to the subject matter in order for it to be based on (or in conformity with), in all material respects, the criteria, other than those modifications, if any, stated in his or her report.
- A statement restricting the use of report to specified parties under the following circumstances:
  - When the criteria used to evaluate the subject matter are determined by the practitioner to be appropriate only for

a limited number of parties who either participated in their establishment or can be presumed to have an adequate understanding of the criteria.

— When the criteria used to evaluate the subject matter are available only to the specified parties.

— When a written assertion has not been provided by the responsible party. (The practitioner should also include a statement to that effect in the introductory paragraph of the report.)

- The manual or printed signature of the practitioner's firm.
- The date of the review report.

Exhibit 7-1 is an example of a review report on a subject matter. Exhibit 7-2 is an example of a review report on an assertion about a subject matter.

The report should be dated as of the end of fieldwork. That is the date that the practitioner's procedures are substantially complete.

EXHIBIT 7-1
ILLUSTRATIVE REVIEW REPORT: REVIEW OF SUBJECT MATTER

Independent Accountant's Report

To the Board of Directors of
[*client name*]
[*city, state*]

We have reviewed the [*identify the subject matter; for example*, the accompanying schedule of investment returns of XYZ Company for the year ended December 31, 20XX]. XYZ Company's management is responsible for the schedule of investment returns.

Our review was conducted in accordance with attestation standards established by the American Institute of Certified Public Accountants. A review is substantially less in scope than an examination, the objective of which is the expression of an opinion on [*identify the subject matter; for example*, XYZ Company's schedule of investment returns]. Accordingly, we do not express such an opinion.

[*Additional paragraph(s) may be added to emphasize certain matters relating to the attest engagement or the subject matter.*]

Based on our review, nothing came to our attention that caused us to believe that [*identify the subject matter; for example*, the accompanying schedule of investment returns of XYZ Company for the year ended December 31,

20XX] is not presented, in all material respects, in conformity with [*identify criteria; for example,* the ABC criteria set forth in Note 1].

[*signature of accountant*]

[*date*]

EXHIBIT 7-2
REVIEW REPORT: REVIEW OF ASSERTION ABOUT THE SUBJECT MATTER

Independent Accountant's Report

To the Board of Directors of
[*client name*]
[*city, state*]

We have reviewed management's assertion that [*identify the assertion; for example,* the accompanying schedule of investment returns of XYZ Company for the year ended December 31, 20XX is presented in accordance with ABC criteria set forth in Note 1]. XYZ Company's management is responsible for the assertion.

Our review was conducted in accordance with attestation standards established by the American Institute of Certified Public Accountants. A review is substantially less in scope than an examination, the objective of which is the expression of an opinion on management's assertion. Accordingly, we do not express such an opinion.

[*Additional paragraph(s) may be added to emphasize certain matters relating to the attest engagement or the assertion.*]

Based on our review, nothing came to our attention that caused us to believe that management's assertion referred to above is not fairly stated, in all material respects, based on [*identify criteria; for example,* the ABC criteria set forth in Note 1].

[*signature of accountant*]

[*date*]

Emphasis of a Matter

The review report may include additional commentary or information. This information might include, for example, inherent limitations of the data so that it is not misinterpreted; emphasis of certain aspects of the data, such as the interpretations made in applying the criteria; or uncertainties, such as pending legislation that might affect the assertions in the future. A separate paragraph should be used to emphasize a matter and the paragraph should not be referred to in the conclusion paragraph.

> **OBSERVATION:** Emphasis-of-a-matter paragraphs are never required but may be added solely at the practitioner's discretion.

Modified Review Reports

When a report is modified because of a material misstatement (i.e., deviation from the criteria), it should express a conclusion on the subject matter, rather than on the assertion. SSAE-10 (AT 101.66) states that this is a more effective form of communication for modified review reports.

Case Study 7-5: Emphasis of a Matter

Facts

Slugger Baseball manufactures baseball equipment, including baseball bats, baseballs, and other related equipment. The company has conducted extensive tests on the trajectory and distance of flight of baseballs hit with the bats that it manufactures. The trajectory has been measured based on the angle of flight at the time the ball was hit; the distance has been measured in meters. The company wishes to engage a CPA to perform an attest engagement related to these measurements.

During the course of the engagement, the practitioner discovers that the tests were performed with specially designed baseball hitting robots. These robots were designed and approved by the Baseball Equipment Manufacturers Association as a means to ensure accuracy and comparability in the reporting of tests on baseballs and bats.

The practitioner also discovers that the company conducted its tests in the city of Denver, with an elevation of 5,280 feet above sea level. It is common knowledge that the thin air at such an altitude results in baseballs flying higher and farther than they would at sea level. The practitioner considers this fact to be significant for the users of the information.

Analysis

This case underscores the importance of the practitioner having a good understanding of the subject matter and the criteria. The practitioner's first consideration is whether the criteria used are suitable. If the criteria are not suitable, then the practitioner would be prohibited from performing the engagement.

In this case, the ball's trajectory is based on the angle of flight, and the distance is measured in meters. These criteria meet the suitability criteria described in AT 101.24. As such, another company could perform the same tests and reach materially similar measurements.

However, the matter of the test conditions (i.e., the tests were performed at an altitude of 5,280 feet above sea level) should also be considered. In this regard, the practitioner should consider whether the location of the company's test has been adequately disclosed. If the matter has not been adequately disclosed, and if the practitioner considered the matter material (i.e., its inclusion would influence a reasonable person), then he or she should modify the review report.

If the matter has been adequately disclosed, the practitioner may still want to draw the reader's attention to it by including an emphasis-of-a-matter paragraph in the standard review report. This paragraph would not modify the practitioner's conclusion, but it would serve to alert the reader that the company conducted its tests under conditions that significantly affected the results.

Report Restrictions

A general use report is one that is not restricted to specified parties. The need for restriction on the use of a report may result from a number of circumstances, including the purpose of the report, the criteria used in preparation of the subject matter, the extent to which the procedures performed are known or understood, and the potential for the report to be misunderstood when taken out of the context in which it was intended to be used. According to SSAE-10 (AT 101.78), a review report is required to carry a use restriction in the following circumstances:

- When the criteria used to evaluate the subject matter are determined by the practitioner to be appropriate for only a limited number of parties who either participated in their establishment or can be presumed to have an adequate understanding of the criteria.
- When the criteria used to evaluate the subject matter are available only to specified parties.
- When reporting on subject matter and a written assertion has not been provided by the responsible party.

OBSERVATION: The attestation standards describe situations in which a practitioner is required to restrict the use of a report, but the standards do not preclude practitioners from restricting the use of any report.

A review report whose use is restricted should contain a separate paragraph at the end that includes the following elements:

- A statement saying that the report is intended solely for the information and use of the specified parties.
- An identification of the specified parties to whom use is restricted.
- A statement that the report is not intended to be and should not be used by anyone other than the specified parties.

An example of such a paragraph is the following:

> This report is intended solely for the information and use of [*the specified parties*] and is not intended to be and should not be used by anyone other than these specified parties.

The practitioner should inform his or her client that restricted-use reports are not intended for distribution to nonspecified parties, regardless of whether they are included in a document containing a separate general-use report. However, the practitioner is not responsible for controlling a client's distribution of restricted-use reports.

> **OBSERVATION:** The practitioner should consider adding language to the engagement letter to obtain the client's agreement that the client and the specified parties will not distribute the report to parties other than those identified in the report.

OTHER INFORMATION IN A CLIENT-PREPARED DOCUMENT

A client may publish various documents that contain information in addition to the practitioner's review report. The practitioner's responsibility with respect to the other information does not extend beyond the information identified in the review report, and the practitioner has no obligation to perform any procedures to corroborate any other information contained in the document. However, the practitioner should read the other information not covered by the review report and consider whether it, or the manner of its presentation, is materially consistent with the information appearing in the review report.

If the practitioner believes that the other information is inconsistent with the information appearing in the review report, the practitioner should

- Consider whether the review report requires revision; or
- Request the client to revise the other information to eliminate the inconsistency.

If the other information is not revised to eliminate the inconsistency, the practitioner should consider other actions, such as

- Revising the review report to include an explanatory paragraph describing the material inconsistency.
- Withholding the use of the review report.
- Withdrawing from the engagement.

If, while reading the other information, the practitioner becomes aware of information that he or she believes is a material misstatement of fact that is not a material inconsistency as described above, the practitioner should discuss the matter with the client. If, after discussing the matter, the practitioner concludes that a material misstatement of fact remains, the action taken by the practitioner will depend on his or her judgment in the circumstances. The practitioner should consider steps such as notifying the client's management and audit committee in writing of his or her views concerning the information and consulting his or her legal counsel about further appropriate action in the circumstances.

ATTEST SERVICES AS PART OF A CONSULTING SERVICES ENGAGEMENT

When the practitioner determines that an attest service is to be provided as part of a consulting service engagement, the practitioner should inform the client of the relevant differences between the two types of services and obtain concurrence that the attest service is to be performed in accordance with the appropriate professional requirements. The practitioner should issue separate reports on the attest engagement and the consulting service engagement and, if presented in a common binder, the report on the attest engagement should be clearly identified and segregated from the report on the consulting service engagement.

APPENDIX 7A ILLUSTRATIVE ENGAGEMENT LETTER

[*date*]

[*client's name*]
[*address*]

We are pleased to confirm our understanding of the services we are to provide for [*client's legal name*].

We will review the [*describe subject matter or related assertion*] of [*name of client*] as of [*date*]. Our review will be conducted in accordance with attestation standards established by the American Institute of Certified Public Accountants. Accordingly, it will consist primarily of inquiries of company personnel and the application of analytical procedures to data, and we will require a representation letter from management. We will not perform an examination, the objective of which is the expression of an opinion [*describe subject matter*]. Accordingly, we will not express such an opinion.

[*Describe restrictions on the use of the report, if any.*]

Our report on the [*describe subject matter*] as of [*date*] is currently expected to read as follows:

> We have reviewed the [*describe subject matter*] as of [*date*]. [*Name of responsible party*] is responsible for the [*describe subject matter*].
>
> Our review was conducted in accordance with attestation standards established by the American Institute of Certified Public Accountants. A review is substantially less in scope than an examination, the objective of which is the expression of an opinion on [*describe subject matter*]. Accordingly, we do not express such an opinion.
>
> Based on our review, nothing came to our attention that caused us to believe that [*describe subject matter*] is not presented, in all material respects, in conformity with [*identify criteria*].

If, for any reason, we are unable to complete the review, we will not issue a report as a result of this engagement. Our engagement cannot be relied upon to disclose all material errors, fraud, or other illegal acts that may exist. However, we will inform you of any material errors or fraud that comes to our attention. We will also inform you of any other illegal acts that come to our attention, unless clearly inconsequential.

We understand that you will provide us with the basic information required for our review and that you are responsible for the accuracy and completeness of that information. We may advise you about appropriate criteria or assist in the development of the subject matter, but the responsibility for the subject matter remains with you. At the end of the engagement, we will require a representation letter from management.

We expect to begin our review on approximately [*date*]. We estimate that our fees for these services will range from $_____ to $_____. You will also be billed for travel and other out-of-pocket costs such as report production, typing, postage, etc. Additional expenses are estimated to be $_____. The fee estimate is based on anticipated cooperation from your personnel and the assumption that unexpected circumstances will not be encountered during the review. If significant additional time is necessary, we will discuss it with you and arrive at a new fee estimate before we incur the additional costs. Our invoices for these services will be rendered each month as work progresses and are payable on presentation. In accordance with our firm policies, work may be suspended if your account becomes _____ days or more overdue and will not be resumed until your account is paid in full. If we elect to terminate our services for nonpayment, our engagement will be deemed to have been completed upon written notification of termination, even if we have not completed our report. You will be obligated to compensate us for all time extended and to reimburse us for all out-of-pocket expenditures through the date of termination.

We appreciate the opportunity to be of service to you and believe this letter accurately summarizes the significant terms of our engagement. If you have any questions, please let us know. If you agree with the terms of our engagement as described in this letter, please sign the enclosed copy and return it to us.

Very truly yours,

[*CPA firm's name*]

Response:

This letter correctly sets forth the understanding of [*client's name*].

By:

Title:

Date:

APPENDIX 7B
PLANNING MATERIALITY CALCULATION FORM

Client Name: ____________________ Date of Subject Matter: ______________

Completed by: ___________________ Date Completed: ___________________

Instructions

The purpose of this form is to determine and document the materiality amount that will be considered suitable for planning purposes. For engagements related to financial or numeric subject matter, complete Part 1 of this form to determine planning materiality and tolerable misstatement. Part 1 should be completed using amounts as of the date of the subject matter. For nonfinancial and nonnumeric subject matter, complete Part 2 of this form to document the assessed tolerable rate of misstatement or noncompliance for the subject matter. This form should be prepared by the engagement personnel in charge of fieldwork (senior or supervisory staff) and reviewed and approved by the engagement executive for all attestation engagements.

Part 1: Procedures Related to Financial or Numeric Subject Matter

If the total dollar amount of the subject matter (the "base") is:		*Planning materiality is:*
Over	**But less than**	**Amount + (Percent x Base)**
$0	$50,000	0 + 5.5%
$50,000	$100,000	1,250 + 3.0%
$100,000	$500,000	2,250 + 2.0%
$500,000	$1 million	7,500 + 1.0%
$1 million	$5 million	9,500 + 0.8%
$5 million	$10 million	19,500 + 0.6%
$10 million	$50 million	40,000 + 0.4%
$50 million	$100 million	115,000 + 0.25%
$100 million		185,000 + 0.18%

Example: If the base amount is $5.5 million, then the planning materiality would be determined as follows:

$\$19,500 + (.006 \times \$5{,}500{,}000) = \$52{,}500$

Calculations

1. Planning Materiality

Amount from Table	+	(Percentage from Table	×	Base Amount)	=	Planning Materiality
________		(________	×	________)	=	________

2. Tolerable Misstatement

Tolerable misstatement is used in computing sample sizes and in making other scope decisions. As a rule of thumb, tolerable misstatement can be calculated as follows:

Planning Materiality From Above	×	Factor	=	Tolerable Misstatement
________	×	.75	=	________

3. Individually Significant Items

The amount used to determine individually significant items can be any amount up to tolerable misstatement.

Part 2: Nonfinancial and Nonnumeric Subject Matter

For nonfinancial and nonnumeric subject matter, materiality is considered to be a tolerable rate of ____ %. (The sampling approach in discussed in this chapter uses a tolerable rate of 5%.)

APPENDIX 7C
REVIEW PROCEDURES CHECKLIST

Client Name: ____________________ Date of Subject Matter: ______________

Completed by: ____________________ Date Completed: ____________________

	Completed by	N/A
1. Complete the Client Acceptance and Retention Evaluation Form.	________	________
2. If the engagement was originally intended to be an examination, document the considerations of:		
a. The reasons given for the client's request to change the engagement to a review, particularly the implications of a restriction on the scope of the examination, whether imposed by the client or circumstances.	________	________
b. The additional effort required to complete the examination.	________	________
c. The estimated additional cost to complete the examination.	________	________
3. Establish and document an understanding with the client, preferably in an engagement letter. If an engagement letter will not be obtained, the oral understanding should be documented in a memo.	________	________
4. Obtain an understanding of the client and the engagement.	________	________
5. If the client is not the responsible party, obtain evidence of the responsible party's responsibility for the subject matter.	________	________
6. Obtain an understanding of the subject matter.	________	________
7. Perform any additional services needed to assist the responsible party in developing the subject matter or related assertion.	________	________
8. Determine that the scheduling and staffing are adequate to perform the engagement.	________	________
9. Complete the Planning Materiality Calculation Form.	________	________

	Completed by	N/A
10. Obtain the engagement partner's approval of the overall engagement plan.	________	________
11. If other services have been performed for the responsible party, review relevant workpapers and any related reports for indications of matters that contradict the subject matter or related assertion.	________	________
12. Develop and perform procedures necessary to provide moderate assurance that the subject matter is presented in conformity with the criteria (attach a program or memo to this checklist).	________	________
13. If there is an indication that the subject matter may be incomplete or inaccurate, perform additional procedures, as deemed necessary.	________	________
14. Read the subject matter and:		
a. Determine that it includes all of the disclosures required to keep it from being misleading.	________	________
b. Determine that it is appropriate in form.	________	________
c. Determine that it is free of obvious arithmetical or clerical mistakes.	________	________
d. Determine that it is free of obvious measurement departures from the criteria.	________	________
15. If disclosures required to keep the subject matter from being misleading have been omitted, include the omitted disclosures in the review report if the information required to be disclosed has been determined. If this information has not been determined, either revise the subject matter to correct the departure or modify the review report. If neither alternative is acceptable, consider withdrawing from the engagement.	________	________
16. If the subject matter is not in appropriate form or free of obvious material error or if it contains departures from the criteria, either revise the subject matter to correct the departure or modify the review report. If neither alternative is acceptable, consider withdrawing from the engagement.	________	________
17. If any circumstances were encountered that precluded performance of the inquiries and analytical procedures as deemed necessary, consider whether these circumstances		

	Completed by	N/A
result in an incomplete review and thus an inadequate basis for issuing a review report.	________	________
18. Consider whether events have occurred after the date of the subject matter, but before the end of fieldwork, that affect the presentation of the subject matter.	________	________
19. Obtain a representation letter from the responsible party (and the client, if not the responsible party).	________	________
20. Draft the review report.	________	________
21. Read other information in a client-prepared document that contains the review report for inconsistencies with the report and material misstatements of fact.	________	________
22. If any situations have occurred that require consultation, determine that such consultation has been properly documented.	________	________
23. If there were differences of professional opinion among members of the engagement team or between the engagement team and a specialist, determine that the differences were properly resolved and documented.	________	________
24. Determine that all questions, exceptions, or notes, if any, posed during the engagement have been followed up and resolved.	________	________
25. Determine that all required forms, questionnaires, and checklists have been completed.	________	________
26. Ensure that the workpapers and review report have been reviewed in accordance with firm policy.	________	________
27. Obtain engagement partner's review and approval for issuance of report.	________	________

APPENDIX 7D
ILLUSTRATIVE REPRESENTATION LETTER

[*date*]

[*CPA firm's name*]
[*address*]

In connection with your review of the [*describe subject matter*] as of [*date of subject matter*], for the purpose of expressing limited assurance that nothing came to your attention that caused you to believe that the [*describe subject matter*] is not presented, in all material respects, in conformity with [*describe *criteria*], we confirm, to the best of our knowledge and belief, the following representations made to you during the course of your review:

- We are responsible for the [*describe subject matter*] and for our assertion that is presented in conformity with [*describe criteria*].
- We are responsible for selecting the criteria and for determining that the criteria are appropriate for our purposes.
- As of [*date of subject matter*], the [*describe subject matter*] is presented in conformity with [*describe criteria*].
- We have disclosed to you all information of which we are aware that may contradict the [*describe subject matter*], and we have disclosed to you all communications from regulatory agencies affecting [*describe subject matter*].
- We have disclosed to you all events subsequent to [*date of subject matter*] that would have a material effect on [*describe subject matter*].
- We have made available to you all records relevant to [*describe subject matter*].
- We intend to distribute your report only to [*describe restrictions, if any*].

Signature:	Signature:
Title:	Title:

APPENDIX 7E
CLIENT REPRESENTATION LETTER: CLIENT NOT RESPONSIBLE PARTY

[*date—No earlier than date of the accountant's report*]

[*CPA firm's name*]
[*address*]

In connection with your review of the [*describe subject matter*] as of [*date of subject matter*], for the purpose of expressing limited assurance that nothing came to your attention that caused you to believe that the [*describe subject matter*] is not presented, in all material respects, in conformity with [*describe criteria*], we confirm, to the best of our knowledge and belief, the following representations made to you during the course of your review:

- We have disclosed to you all events subsequent to [*date of subject matter*] that would have a material effect on [*describe subject matter*].
- We are responsible for selecting the criteria and for determining that the criteria are appropriate for our purposes.
- We intend to distribute your report only to [*describe restrictions, if any*].

Signature:

Title:

APPENDIX 7F
STANDARD REVIEW REPORT ON SUBJECT MATTER

Independent Accountant's Report

To the Board of Directors of
XYZ Company
[*city, state*]

We have reviewed the [*identify the subject matter; for example,* the accompanying schedule of investment returns of XYZ Company for the year ended December 31, 20XX]. XYZ Company's management is responsible for the schedule of investment returns.

Our review was conducted in accordance with attestation standards established by the American Institute of Certified Public Accountants. A review is substantially less in scope than an examination, the objective of which is the expression of an opinion on [*identify the subject matter; for example,* XYZ Company's schedule of investment returns]. Accordingly, we do not express such an opinion.

[*Additional paragraph(s) may be added to emphasize certain matters relating to the attest engagement or the subject matter.*]

Based on our review, nothing came to our attention that caused us to believe that [*identify the subject matter; for example,* the accompanying schedule of investment returns of XYZ Company for the year ended December 31, 20XX] is not presented, in all material respects, in conformity with [*identify criteria; for example,* the ABC criteria set forth in Note 1].

[*firm's signature*]

[*city, state*]

[*date*]

APPENDIX 7G
STANDARD REVIEW REPORT ON AN ASSERTION

Independent Accountant's Report

To the Board of Directors of
XYZ Company
[*city, state*]

We have reviewed management's assertion that [*identify the assertion; for example,* the accompanying schedule of investment returns of XYZ Company for the year ended December 31, 20XX is presented in accordance with ABC criteria set forth in Note 1]. XYZ Company's management is responsible for the assertion.

Our review was conducted in accordance with attestation standards established by the American Institute of Certified Public Accountants. A review is substantially less in scope than an examination, the objective of which is the expression of an opinion on management's assertion. Accordingly, we do not express such an opinion.

[*Additional paragraph(s) may be added to emphasize certain matters relating to the attest engagement or the assertion.*]

Based on our review, nothing came to our attention that caused us to believe that management's assertion referred to above is not fairly stated, in all material respects, based on [*identify criteria; for example,* the ABC criteria set forth in Note 1].

[*firm's signature*]

[*city, state*]

[*date*]

APPENDIX 7H REVIEW REPORT: RESTRICTED BECAUSE NO WRITTEN ASSERTION PROVIDED BY THE NONCLIENT RESPONSIBLE PARTY

Independent Accountant's Report

To the Board of Directors of
XYZ Company
[*city, state*]

We have reviewed the [*identify the subject matter; for example,* the accompanying schedule of investment returns of XYZ Company for the year ended December 31, 20XX]. XYZ Company's management is responsible for the schedule of investment returns. XYZ Company's management did not provide us with a written assertion about their schedule of investment returns for the year ended December 31, 20XX.

Our review was conducted in accordance with attestation standards established by the American Institute of Certified Public Accountants. A review is substantially less in scope than an examination, the objective of which is the expression of an opinion on [*identify the subject matter; for example,* XYZ Company's schedule of investment returns]. Accordingly, we do not express such an opinion.

[*Additional paragraph(s) may be added to emphasize certain matters relating to the attest engagement or the subject matter.*]

Based on our review, nothing came to our attention that caused us to believe that [*identify the subject matter; for example,* the accompanying schedule of investment returns of XYZ Company for the year ended December 31, 20XX] is not presented, in all material respects, in conformity with [*identify criteria; for example,* the ABC criteria set forth in Note 1].

This report is intended solely for the information and use of [*party that engaged the practitioner; for example,* DEF Company], and is not intended to be and should not be used by anyone other than this specified party.

[*firm's signature*]

[*city, state*]

[*date*]

CHAPTER 8
SPECIFIED ELEMENTS, ACCOUNTS, OR ITEMS OF A FINANCIAL STATEMENT

CONTENTS

OVERVIEW

This chapter discusses types of engagements related to specified elements, accounts, or items of a financial statement. The focus of this chapter is on engagements to compile or audit specified elements, accounts, or items of a financial statement. This chapter also discusses review engagements and agreed-upon procedures engagements.

INTRODUCTION

Elements, accounts, or items of a financial statement constitute accounting information that is part of, but less than, a financial statement. Such information also encompasses accounting information contained in the client's accounts that supports the elements, accounts, or items presented in the financial statements. Although accounting information is usually expressed in monetary amounts (or percentages derived from monetary amounts), it may also include quantitative information derived from accounting records that is not expressed in monetary amounts.

> **OBSERVATION:** In this chapter, the term "specified element" is used in place of the term "specified elements, accounts, or items of a financial statement."

Specified elements may be taken directly from an entity's financial statements (or notes). They may also represent any component or combination of components derived from financial statements. Specified elements may be individual financial statement line items or a combination of several line items. They may also be general ledger accounts that make up all or part of a financial statement line item. The following are examples of specified element presentations:

- Total sales from the income statement
- Summary of all amounts included in property, plant and, equipment at a specified date
- Schedule of accounts receivable at a specified date
- Schedule of balances in cash accounts at a specified date
- Schedule of construction costs incurred

Incomplete Presentations versus Specified Elements

Elements, accounts, or items of a financial statement constitute accounting information that is part of, but less than, a financial statement. Incomplete presentations, on the other hand, are regarded as financial statements even though certain items are excluded. Thus, when an auditor is asked to report on incomplete presentations, the measurement of materiality for purposes of expressing an opinion should be related to the presentations taken as a whole. Further, the presentations should differ from complete financial statements only to the extent necessary to meet the special purposes they were prepared for. The following are examples of incomplete presentations:

- Schedule of gross income and certain expenses to meet a regulatory requirement
- Statement of assets sold and liabilities transferred to comply with a contractual agreement

Incomplete presentations are not addressed in this chapter. For additional guidance on reporting on incomplete presentations, see *Audit Procedures* and *Compilations & Reviews*.

Supplementary Information versus Specified Elements

SAS-29 (AU 551) (Reporting on Information Accompanying the Basic Financial Statements in Auditor-Submitted Documents) defines "supplementary information" as additional details or explanations of items in or related to the basic financial statements, consolidating information, historical summaries of items extracted from basic financial statements, statistical data, other material, some of which may be from sources outside the accounting system or outside the entity. Basic financial statements include the balance sheet, statement of income, statement of retained earnings or changes in stockholders' equity, and statement of cash flows. In addition, the following presentations are considered part of the basic financial statements:

- descriptions of accounting policies
- notes to financial statements
- schedules and explanatory material that are identified as being part of the basic financial statements

Supplementary information is included with the basic financial statements but is presented outside the basic financial statements and is not considered necessary for presentation of financial position, results of operations, or cash flows in conformity with generally accepted accounting principles.

The purpose of an audit of basic financial statements in accordance with generally accepted auditing standards is to form an opinion on those statements taken as a whole. When reporting on information accompanying the basic financial statements, the measurement of materiality is the same as that used in forming an opinion on the basic financial statements taken as a whole. Accordingly, the auditor need not apply procedures as extensive as would be necessary to express an opinion on the information presented as a separate specified element.

Reporting on supplementary information is not addressed in this chapter. For additional guidance on reporting on incomplete presentations, see *Audit Procedures* and *Compilations & Reviews*.

TYPES OF ENGAGEMENTS

There are four types of engagements that CPAs can perform on specified elements:

1. Audit
2. Review
3. Compilation
4. Agreed-upon procedures

Audit Engagements

An auditor may express an opinion on one or more specified elements, accounts, or items of a financial statement. In such an engagement, the specified element(s) may be presented in the report or in a document accompanying the report. Examples of specified elements that an auditor may report on based on an audit made in accordance with generally accepted auditing standards are rentals, royalties, profit participation, and provisions for income taxes. Authoritative guidance for auditing specified elements is found in SAS-62 (AU 623) (Special Reports) (AU 623) and is discussed later in this chapter.

Review Engagements

An accountant may be engaged to perform a review of a specified element. When engaged to perform a review, the CPA states a conclusion about whether any information came to his or her attention to indicate that the specified element is not in conformity with generally accepted accounting principles. This conclusion is referred to as "negative assurance." Authoritative guidance for reviewing specified elements is found in Chapter 1 of SSAE-10 (AT 101). In a review engagement, the objective is to accumulate sufficient evidence to restrict attestation risk to a moderate level. Review engagements are covered in Chapter 7, "Review Engagements," of this guide.

Compilation Engagements

An accountant may prepare or assist a client in preparing a schedule of one or more specified elements, accounts, or items of a financial statement. A compilation of a specified element is limited to presenting financial information that is the representation of management without undertaking to express any assurance on that information. When the information is likely to be used by a third party, the accountant should consider how such a presentation of specified elements will be used. The accountant should consider the potential of being associated with the schedule and the likelihood that the user may inappropriately infer, through that association, an unintended level of assurance. If the accountant believes that he or she will be associated with the information, he or she should consider issuing a compilation report so a user will not infer a level of assurance that does not exist. Examples of specified elements, accounts, or items of a financial statement that an accountant may compile are schedules of rentals, royalties, profit participation, and provisions for income taxes. Compiling specified elements is discussed later in this chapter, and authoritative guidance is found in SSARS-13 (AR 110) (Compilation of Specified Elements, Accounts, or Items of a Financial Statement).

Agreed-Upon Procedures Engagements

In an agreed-upon procedures engagement a practitioner is engaged by a client to issue a report of findings based on specific procedures performed on a specified element. The client engages the practitioner to assist specified parties in evaluating the specified element as a result of the needs of the specified parties. Because the specified parties require that findings be independently derived, a practitioner performs procedures and reports on his or her findings. The specified parties and the practitioner agree upon the procedures to be performed. These are the procedures that the specified parties believe are appropriate. Because the needs of the specified parties can vary widely, the nature, timing, and extent of the procedures can vary as well. Consequently, the specified parties assume responsibility for the sufficiency of the procedures because they best understand their own needs. Agreed-upon procedures engagements are covered in Chapter 9, "Agreed-Upon Procedures Engagements," of this guide, and authoritative guidance for agreed-upon procedures engagements is found in Chapter 2 of SSAE-10 (AT 201).

AUDITING SPECIFIED ELEMENTS, ACCOUNTS, OR ITEMS OF A FINANCIAL STATEMENT

An auditor may be requested to express an opinion on one or more specified elements, accounts, or items of a financial statement, such as rentals, royalties, a profit participation, or provisions for income taxes. The auditor may undertake such engagement either in conjunction with an audit of financial statements or as a separate engagement. If the engagement is performed in conjunction with an audit of financial statements, the auditor should consider the effect that any departure, including any additional explanatory language, from the standard report on the audited financial statements might have on the report on a specified element, account, or item.

Authoritative guidance for auditing specified elements is found in SAS-62 (AU 623). However, the engagement must also be performed in accordance with generally accepted auditing standards (GAAS). Therefore the same general, fieldwork, and reporting standards apply to audits of specified elements as apply to audits of financial statements, including such matters as audit planning, audit risk and materiality, consideration of internal control, consideration of fraud, and reporting. Provided here is an overview of the major considerations and steps in auditing a specified element. For a complete discussion of GAAS and the audit process, see *Miller Audit Procedures*.

If a specified element, account, or item is, or is based on, an entity's net income or stockholders' equity (or the equivalent thereof), the auditor should audit the complete financial statements to express an opinion on the specified element, account, or item.

Engagement Planning

Materiality

Because, in engagements to audit specified elements, the auditor expresses an opinion on the specified elements encompassed by the auditor's report, the measurement of materiality must be related to each such item reported on rather than to the financial statements taken as a whole.

The relative, rather than absolute, size of an omission or misstatement determines whether it is material in a given situation. In addition, the auditor should consider both quantitative and qualitative aspects of omissions and misstatements. Generally, materiality is considered at two phases of the engagement: the planning stage and the evaluation stage.

The following steps summarize how the auditor should apply the materiality concept to an engagement:

1. Establish preliminary judgment about materiality during the initial planning stage of the engagement. This is referred to as "planning materiality."
2. Relate the planning materiality to the scope of tests. This is referred to as "tolerable misstatement."

3. Summarize total misstatements. This step includes (a) known misstatements (i.e., the amounts of errors specifically identified when performing audit procedures) and (b) likely misstatements (i.e., an estimate or projection of actual errors because only a sample, rather than the entire population, is tested).
4. Compare total misstatements with materiality at the end of the engagement and evaluate whether audit procedures have been sufficient to detect material misstatements.
5. If significantly lower materiality levels become appropriate in evaluating the findings, the auditor should reevaluate the sufficiency of the audit procedures that he or she has performed.

Step 1 and Step 2 are performed in the planning stage, before audit procedures are applied, and are discussed here. Step 3 and Step 4 are performed in the evaluation stage, after the audit procedures are applied, and are discussed in the "Evaluation of Results" section later in this chapter.

Planning Materiality

In the planning stage, the auditor evaluates materiality in order to plan the audit procedures necessary to detect material misstatements. Materiality in the evaluation stage is used to determine whether the specified element is materially misstated. Therefore, the amount that the auditor considers material at the end of the engagement may differ from planning materiality, because ordinarily it is not feasible to anticipate all of the circumstances that may ultimately influence the auditor's judgment about materiality.

Based on a preliminary estimate of the specified element, the auditor decides what level would be considered material to the presentation. Since materiality is relative, rather than absolute, it is necessary to have bases for establishing whether misstatements are material. The auditor calculates planning materiality by applying an appropriate percentage to a relevant base. The auditor specifies the base to be used, calculates the amount of the base from the client's data, specifies an appropriate percentage, and computes planning materiality by applying the percentage to the base.

The matrix presented in Exhibit 8-1 can be used for estimating planning materiality. When the specified element is not expressed in financial amounts but is nonetheless numeric (for example, the number of widgets produced), the table in Exhibit 8-1 can still be used. Although the table is based on judgments regarding financial statements, the overall percentages are also considered appropriate for determining materiality for specified elements.

EXHIBIT 8-1
GUIDELINES TO CALCULATE PLANNING MATERIALITY

If the total dollar amount of the subject matter (the "base") is:		***Planning materiality is:***
Over	**But less than**	**Amount + (percent x base)**
\$0	\$50,000	0 + 5.5%
\$50,000	\$100,000	1, 250 + 3.0%
\$100,000	\$500,000	2, 250 + 2.0%
\$500,000	\$1 million	7, 500 + 1.0%
\$1 million	\$5 million	9, 500 + 0.8%
\$5 million	\$10 million	19, 500 + 0.6%
\$10 million	\$50 million	40, 000 + 0.4%
\$50 million	\$100 million	115, 000 + 0.25%
\$100 million		185, 000 + 0.18%

Qualitative Aspects of Materiality

There is no definitive guidance on the qualitative factors to consider when assessing materiality. However, the following issues may be relevant in making this determination:

- The effect of the misstatement or omission on trends
- The potential effect of the misstatement or omission on the company's compliance with debt covenants, other contractual agreements, and regulatory provisions
- The significance of the misstatement or omission relative to known user needs
- The precision with which the specified element can be measured

Audit Risk

Audit risk is the risk that the auditor will not detect a material misstatement in the specified element. Audit risk is explained in SAS-47 (AU 312) (Audit Risk and Materiality in Conducting an Audit). In an audit engagement, the auditor is required to reduce audit risk to a low level.

Audit risk (AR) is made up of

- *Inherent risk* (IR) The susceptibility of the specified element to material misstatement.
- *Control risk* (CR) The risk that a material misstatement that did occur would not be prevented or detected.
- *Detection risk* (DR) The risk that a material misstatement that eludes the client will also elude the auditor.

This combination is multiplicative, and it is usually stated as follows:

$$AR = IR \times CR \times DR$$

Inherent Risk

Inherent risk is the susceptibility of the specified element to material misstatement, assuming there are no related controls. Inherent risk is a measure of the auditor's assessment of expectation of material misstatement before considering the entity's internal control.

Control Risk

Control risk is the risk that a material misstatement that could occur in the specified element will not be prevented or detected on a timely basis by the entity's internal control. Control risk is a measure of the auditor's assessment of the effectiveness of an entity's internal control in preventing or detecting material misstatements. Control risk, like inherent risk, is beyond the auditor's control.

Detection Risk

Detection risk is the risk that the auditor will not detect a material misstatement that exists in the specified element. Detection risk is a measure of the risk that audit procedures will fail to detect material misstatements. The auditor controls detection risk through selection and application of tests. Detection risk arises because all items that make up the specified element are not examined (sampling error) and audit procedures are not properly applied (nonsampling error). A different way of stating the formula above illustrates its importance as it relates to the performance of the engagement:

$$DR = \frac{AR}{IR \times CR}$$

Whereas inherent risk and control risk are not under the control of the auditor, detection risk can be controlled by the auditor because it

EXHIBIT 8-2
COMBINING INHERENT RISK AND CONTROL RISK

Inherent Risk	×	Control Risk	=	Risk of Material Misstatement
High		Maximum		High
High		Moderate		High
High		Low		Moderate
Moderate		Maximum		Moderate
Moderate		Moderate		Low
Moderate		Low		Low
Low		Maximum		Moderate
Low		Moderate		Low
Low		Low		Low

relates to audit procedures, which can be changed at the auditor's discretion. Inherent risk and control risk exist, and the auditor can only assess them. If the assessment of inherent risk and control risk is high, the auditor's tests must be more effective to reduce detection risk and adequately control audit risk. When they are lower, the auditor may do correspondingly less work to reduce detection risk.

Inherent risk and control risk can be assessed separately or in combination. Also, they be assessed quantitatively or qualitatively. While both approaches are acceptable, the approach used in this book is qualitative because it is considered highly effective and efficient. As such, the auditor can use the matrix in Exhibit 8-2 to express the combined assessments of inherent risk and control risk in qualitative terms: maximum, moderate, or low.

Evidential Matter

Selecting and applying procedures that will accumulate evidence that is sufficient in the circumstances to provide a reasonable basis for the level of assurance to be expressed in the audit report requires careful exercise of professional judgment. A wide variety of procedures may be applied in an audit engagement. In establishing the proper combination of procedures to appropriately restrict audit risk, the auditor should consider the following presumptions, keeping in mind that they are not mutually exclusive and may be subject to exceptions:

- Evidence obtained from independent sources outside an entity provides greater assurance about the specified element than evidence secured solely from within the entity.

- Information obtained from the independent auditor's direct personal knowledge (such as through physical examination, observation, computation, operating tests, or inspection) is more persuasive than information obtained indirectly.
- The more effective the controls over the specified element, the more assurance they provide about the specified element.

Therefore, in the hierarchy of available audit procedures, those that involve search and verification (e.g., inspection, confirmation, or observation), particularly when using independent sources outside the entity, are generally more effective in restricting audit risk than those involving internal inquiries and comparisons of internal information (e.g., analytical procedures and discussions with individuals responsible for the specified element). However, the latter are generally less costly to apply.

Planning the Procedures

As noted earlier, in the hierarchy of available audit procedures, those that involve search and verification (e.g., inspection, confirmation, or observation), particularly when using independent sources outside the entity, are generally more effective in restricting audit risk than those involving internal inquiries and comparisons of internal information (e.g., analytical procedures and discussions with individuals responsible for the specified element). The extent to which audit procedures will be performed should be based on the level of assurance to be provided and the auditor's consideration of

- The nature and materiality of the information to be tested to the specified element taken as a whole.
- The likelihood of misstatements.
- Knowledge obtained during current and previous engagements.
- Management's competence.
- The extent to which the information is affected by management's judgment.
- Inadequacies in management's underlying data.

Planning and Supervision

The first standard of fieldwork states "The work shall be adequately planned and assistants, if any, shall be properly supervised." Proper planning and supervision contribute to the effectiveness of audit procedures. Proper planning directly influences the selection of appropriate procedures and proper supervision helps to ensure that planned procedures are appropriately applied. In planning the audit engagement, the objective is to establish an overall strategy for

- How the engagement will be conducted
- The scope of the procedures

To develop this strategy, the auditor should seek to understand the events, transactions, and practices that, in their judgment, have a significant effect on specified element. The nature, extent, and timing of planning will vary with the nature and complexity of the specified element and the auditor's prior experience with management. As part of the planning process, the auditor should consider the nature, extent, and timing of the work to be performed to accomplish the objectives of the audit engagement. Nevertheless, as the engagement progresses, changed conditions may make it necessary to modify planned procedures.

SAS-22 (AU 311) (Planning and Supervision) provides guidance on engagement planning. SAS-22 suggests the following procedures:

1. Review correspondence files, prior-year workpapers and reports, and permanent files.
2. Discuss matters that may affect the engagement with other firm personnel familiar with the entity.
3. Inquire about current developments affecting the entity.
4. Read current-year financial statements (or relevant financial and nonfinancial information related to the specified element).
5. Discuss the type, scope, and timing of the engagement with entity's management, board of directors or audit committee.
6. Consider the effects of any recent changes in the specified element.
7. Coordinate the assistance of client or responsible party personnel in data preparation.
8. Determine the extent of involvement, if any, of consultants, specialists, or others in the engagement.
9. Establish the timing of the engagement.
10. Establish and coordinate the staffing requirements.

Supervision involves directing the efforts of assistants who participate in accomplishing the objectives of the audit engagement and determining whether those objectives were accomplished. Elements of supervision include

- Instructing assistants
- Staying informed of significant problems encountered.

- Reviewing the work performed.
- Dealing with differences of opinion between personnel

Internal Control

The second standard of fieldwork requires the auditor gain an understanding of internal control sufficient to plan the audit and to determine the nature, timing, and extent of tests to be performed. The guidance in SAS-55 (AU 319) (Consideration of Internal Control in a Financial Statement Audit) (as amended by SAS-78 and SAS-94), provides guidance for gaining this understanding.

SAS-78 (AU 319.06) defines internal control as follows:

> Internal control is a process, effected by an entity's board of directors, management and other personnel, designed to provide reasonable assurance regarding the achievement of objectives in the following categories:
>
> - Reliability of financial reporting
> - Effectiveness and efficiency of operations
> - Compliance with applicable laws and regulations

SAS-78 (AU 319.07) states that an entity's internal control consists of the following five interrelated components:

1. *Control environment* The control environment refers to the tone of the organization with respect to the importance of internal control within an entity. This refers to management's attitudes, actions, and awareness about the importance of presenting reliable financial statements.
2. *Risk assessment* Risk assessment is the entity's identification and analysis of relevant risks to achievement of its objectives, forming a basis for determining how the risks should be managed. This refers to the process of identifying potential risks relevant to misstatements in an organization's financial statements and developing plans to address those risks.
3. *Control activities* Control activities are the policies and procedures that help ensure that management directives are carried out. To successfully address risks and achieve its objectives, management must institute control activities, such as reviews, comparisons, and segregation of duties.
4. *Information and communication* Information and communication systems support the identification, capture, and exchange of information in a form and time frame that enables people to carry out their responsibilities.
5. *Monitoring* Like all processes, an entity's system of internal control must be monitored.

The auditor should understand the components of internal control to sufficiently:

- Understand the areas of increased risk
- Understand the types of misstatements that could occur
- Design tests to detect material misstatements

Testing Controls

If the client's controls are effective and it is cost-effective to test controls, then this may be an efficient approach to the audit engagement. To be effective, the controls must be designed to prevent or detect misstatements, and they should be in effect for the period that affects the assertions.

In order to test controls, the auditor may apply inquiry, observation, inspection, or reperformance procedures to determine how, by whom, and how consistently a control procedure was applied.

Detection Procedures

The auditor should identify the test objectives when designing procedures to test the specified element. SAS-31 (AU 326) (Evidential Matter) as amended by SAS-80, provides guidance for deriving test objectives, as follows:

1. *Existence or occurrence* The information included in the specified element actually exists or the underlying events actually occurred.
2. *Completeness* The information includes everything it purports to.
3. *Rights and obligations* The information is what it purports to be.
4. *Valuation or allocation* The amounts or value judgments about the information are appropriate.
5. *Presentation and disclosure* The presentation and disclosure is in conformity with generally accepted accounting principles.

For any assertion, the foregoing five objectives should be addressed. The nature and extent of procedures applied to any given objective will vary depending on the auditor's assessment of risk of misstatement. When there is a low risk of misstatement for one or more of the objectives, either because the nature of the assertion does not lend itself to misstatement (inherent risk) or because tests of controls indicate that the client's procedures would prevent or detect misstatements (control risk), the level of testing for those objectives can be lower.

Nature of Tests

A misrepresentation of any of the five financial statement assertions could cause a material misstatement in the financial statements. The auditor should consider the risk of material misstatement for each assertion, and then obtain evidence to support the financial statement assertions to reduce the risk of material misstatement to an acceptably low level. To determine what type of evidence to obtain, the auditor should develop specific audit objectives for each assertion.

In determining audit objectives, the auditor should evaluate each of the five assertions as they relate to the specific account balance or class of transactions being examined. For example, if the auditor is attempting to gather evidence on the assertion of existence of inventory, the objective would be to gather evidence that inventory included in the balance sheet physically existed at the balance sheet date.

Exhibit 8-3 is an example of the relationship between financial statement assertions and audit objectives for inventory.

Audit Tests

After the auditor has determined the audit objectives, the method of achieving the objectives should be selected. These methods are referred to by different names, such as audit procedures, audit techniques, and audit tests. They are all evidence-gathering methods auditors use. The basic requirement for determining audit procedures, according to SAS-31, is that

> . . . the procedures adopted should be adequate to achieve the audit objectives developed by the auditor, and the evidential matter obtained should be sufficient for the auditor to form conclusions concerning the validity of the individual assertions embodied in the components of the financial statements. . . .

Some audit procedures can satisfy a combination of audit objectives for a given account balance or class of transactions. For example, the observation of a physical inventory count can provide evidence that inventories physically exist and that inventory quantities include all products, materials, and supplies on hand.

Audit procedures can be classified or categorized in a variety of ways. The most common classifications are by purpose of the test or type of test. Exhibit 8-4 shows the relationship between audit tests by purposes and audit tests by type.

EXHIBIT 8-3
RELATIONSHIP OF ASSERTIONS AND OBJECTIVES FOR INVENTORY

Financial Statement Assertion	Illustrative Audit Objective
Existence or occurrence	• Inventories included in the balance sheet physically exist. • Inventories represent items held for sale in the normal course of business.
Completeness	• Inventory quantities include all products, materials, and supplies on hand. • Inventory listings are accurately compiled and the totals are properly included in the inventory accounts. • Inventory quantities include all products, materials, and supplies owned by the client that are in transit or stored at outside locations.
Rights and obligations	• The entity has legal title or similar rights of ownership to the inventory. • Inventories exclude items billed to customers or owned by others.
Valuation or allocation	• Inventories are properly stated at cost (except when market is lower). • Slow-moving, excess, defective, or obsolete items included in inventories are properly identified and valued.
Presentation and disclosure	• Inventories are properly classified in the balance sheet as current assets. • The major categories or inventories and their bases of valuation are adequately disclosed in the financial statements. • The pledge or assignment of inventories is appropriately disclosed.

Purpose of the Test

According to SAS-55 (AU 319), there are two possible purposes of audit tests:

1. To obtain evidential matter about the effectiveness of both the design and operation of a control that supports a control risk

EXHIBIT 8-4
MATRIX OF AUDIT TESTS BY TYPE AND PURPOSE

	Purpose of Test	
Type of Test	Substantive test	Test of controls
Analytical procedures	Yes (Example A)	Not applicable
Observation and inquiry	Yes (Example B)	Yes (Examples C & D)
Tests of transactions	Yes (Example E)	Yes (Examples F & G)
Tests of balances	Yes (Example H)	Not applicable

Examples

A. Compare this year's expenses with last year's expenses, and investigate unusual fluctuations.
B. Inquire about subsequent events.
C. Observe that cash is deposited daily by a specific clerk.
D. Inquire about who deposits cash and how often.
E. Examine invoices to support additions (specific transactions) to fixed assets account during year.
F. Examine sales invoices to see if initials of credit manager are there to indicate a credit file and credit approval (inspection test).
G. Vouch from sales invoices to credit files to see if customer has a credit file and has been approved for credit (reperformance test).
H. Confirm year-end balances in accounts receivable.

assessment below the maximum level. These tests are called tests of controls.

2. To determine whether material dollar or disclosure misstatements exist in the financial statements. These tests are called substantive tests.

If the objective in designing a procedure is to evaluate whether a control operated effectively, the procedure is considered a test of controls even if the results of the procedure also provide evidence of material misstatements in the financial statements. If the objective in designing and performing a procedure is to detect material misstatements in the financial statements, the procedures is considered a substantive test even if the results of the test also provide some assurance relative to the control risk assessment.

Some audit tests are designed to achieve the purposes of both tests of controls and substantive procedures. Those tests are classified as dual-purpose tests. However, to be considered a dual-purpose test, the test should be designed and performed at a time and to the extent necessary to achieve the objectives of both substantive tests and tests of controls. Tests that are specifically designed and performed to serve both purposes provide the auditor with information sufficient to reach conclusions regarding their anticipated control risk assessment as well as information sufficient to reach conclusions regarding the validity and propriety of the accounting treatment of transactions and balances.

Often control risk is assessed at maximum. If a decision is made to assess control risk below the maximum, the auditor evaluates how the controls improve the reliability of financial information and thus the probability that financial statement assertions are adequately supported. In other words, if the auditor plans to assess control risk below the maximum, the control that supports the lower assessed level of control risk should be linked to specific financial statement assertions. In addition, the auditor should consider how the control improves the reliability of financial information and decreases the likelihood of a material misstatement regarding the specific financial statement assertion. As a result, the auditor may be able to reduce substantive testing. If a control cannot be linked to a specific assertion, tests of controls are inefficient, because the control cannot be relied upon to reduce substantive testing. However, the auditor may still perform tests of controls for client-service reasons.

Type of Test

Auditors perform four types of tests:

1. Analytical procedures
2. Observation and inquiry
3. Tests of transactions
4. Tests of balances

Analytical Procedures

Analytical procedures consist of evaluations of financial information made by a study of plausible relationships between both financial and nonfinancial data. They focus on the reasonableness of the relationships and the identification of unusual fluctuations in data. Analytical procedures are required in the planning and final review phases of all audits.

Analytical procedures can be used as a substantive test because they can identify potential material misstatements in the financial statements. For example, a significant increase in the gross margin percentage from the previous year could be caused by an overcounting or overpricing of ending inventory. When a potential misstatement is identified, it should be investigated and satisfactorily resolved.

Observation and Inquiry

Compliance with controls that leave no audit trail of documentary evidence can often be tested by observation and inquiry. Auditors make inquiries of different individuals and conduct observation tests to determine who performs a particular activity or how and when the activity is performed. For example, the auditor may ask different individuals about who posts to the receivables ledger, observe who prepares the bank reconciliation, or observe when cash is deposited in the bank.

Observation and inquiry can also be used as substantive tests. For example, an audit procedure such as observation of a physical asset to determine that is exists it a substantive test related to the existence assertion. Likewise, inquiries regarding subsequent events would be a substantive test because they provide evidence regarding the adequacy of disclosures in the financial statements.

Tests of Transactions

Tests of transactions consist of the examination of the documents and accounting records involved in the processing of specific transactions. Such tests can accomplish both tests of controls and substantive objectives and are sometimes used as dual-purpose tests.

Tests of controls objectives are accomplished when the auditor examines transaction documentation to determine whether controls have been applied as prescribed. Tests of controls on transactions can be classified as either inspection tests or reperformance tests. If the auditor examines documentation, the compliance test is classified as an inspection test. Alternatively, if the auditor repeats a control activity performed by the client, the test is classified as a reperformance test. For example, a control activity may require employees to match vendors' invoices with purchase orders and receiving reports and then initial the invoices to indicate that the procedure was performed. If the auditor tests the control by examining the invoices for initials, the test is an inspection test. If he or she tests the control by comparing vendors' invoices with purchase orders and receiving reports, the test is a reperformance test. Regardless of whether the auditor tests by inspection or reperformance, the test is a test of controls over transactions.

The substantive purpose of test of transactions is accomplished when the auditor examines transaction documentation to determine whether dollar errors exist in a balance. For example, if the auditor examines documentation supporting individual charges (debits) to an equipment account to determine whether the account balance is fairly stated, the test is classified as a substantive test of transactions.

Tests of Balances

Tests of balances consist of examination of evidential matter directly supporting the ending balance in an account. Tests of balances are substantive tests designed to identify misstatements by a direct test of the ending balance rather than by testing the transactions that make up that balance.

Substantive tests of transactions and tests of balances are interrelated in that each class of transactions affects a related account balance. Because financial statement amounts are the accumulation of transactions, the auditor may test the transactions, the account balance, or both.

Linking Audit Procedures to Objectives

To design an audit program, the auditor should select audit procedures that achieve specific audit objectives developed from the five broad assertions for the specified element.

In selecting audit procedures to achieve the audit objectives developed, the auditor should consider the following, according to SAS-31 (AU 326):

- The risk of material misstatement of the specified element
- The assessed level of control risk
- The expected efficiency and effectiveness of possible audit procedures
- The nature and materiality of the items being tested
- The kinds and competence of available evidential matter
- The nature of the audit objective to be achieved

Extent of Tests

The extent of tests to be applied depends on the risk of material misstatement. This, in turn, depends on the measure of materiality. The approach described in this section is more effective for testing overstatement than understatement. If the client's assertion is such that the primary concern is understatement, the auditor's judgment of materiality may need to be based on a reciprocal population.

The following is a step-by-step approach for determining the extent of tests. A "Sampling Worksheet for Substantive Tests" is included in Appendix 8E. This worksheet can be used to document the decision regarding the extent of testing:

1. *Determine tolerable misstatement* Tolerable misstatement is the maximum amount of misstatement that the auditor can accept in a population and still conclude that it is not materially misstated. A rule of thumb in practice are to estimate tolerable misstatement as a percentage within 50% to 75% of planning materiality.
2. *Identify the individually significant items in the population* To establish a cutoff amount for individually significant items, a rule of thumb is to divide tolerable misstatement by a factor ranging from three to six, depending on how much reliance is placed on the procedures being applied. These items will be tested individually.
3. *Identify unusual items* Identify any other unusual items in the population that should be examined individually because they are unlike the rest of the population or because they present increased risk.
4. *Consider the remaining population* Subtract the amounts identified in steps 2 and 3 from the population. If the remainder is greater than tolerable misstatement, additional testing is generally necessary. This may involve application of analytical procedures, selecting more individually significant items, or sampling from the remaining population.

SAS-39 (AU 350) (Audit Sampling) and the AICPA Auditing Practice Release *Audit Sampling* provide guidance on the extent of tests in an audit engagement. Based on that guidance, if the remaining population (i.e., the residual amount from step 4, above) is to be sampled, the following approach may be useful:

1. Divide the remaining population by the tolerable misstatement. This establishes the basic sample size:

$$\frac{\text{Sampling Population}}{\text{Tolerable Misstatement}} = \text{Basic Sample Size}$$

2. Apply a risk factor. Multiply the result of step 1 by the appropriate factor shown in Exhibit 8-5. This adjusts the sample size for (a) the risk of material misstatement and (b) the risk that other procedures, if any, that the auditor plans to apply

to the same amounts will fail to detect a material misstatement. Other procedures risk is inversely related to the effectiveness of the other procedures. That is, the more effective the other procedure, the lower the risk assessment. If no other procedures are planned, other procedures risk should be assessed as high:

Basic Sample Size × Risk Factor = Sample Size

3. Consider stratification. If the population is not stratified (i.e., not segregated into relatively homogeneous groups, such as size or other attributes), increase the result from step 2 by a factor to recognize increased risk. An expansion factor of 1.2 to 1.5 (i.e., 20% to 50%) generally can be used to compensate for a lack of stratification:

Sample Size (from step 2)	×	Expansion Factor (1.2 to 1.5)	=	Adjusted Sample Size

The sample items should be selected in such a way that all items have an opportunity of being selected. Common representative sampling methods are as follows:

- *Random selection* A random selection provides each item in the population with an equal chance of being selected. A random number table or generator is required. Random sampling is required only when statistical sampling is used.
- *Systemic sampling* Systemic sampling consists of determining a uniform interval and selecting throughout the population one item at each of the uniform intervals from the starting point.
- *Haphazard selection* Haphazard selection consists of a selection that is made without any special reason for including or excluding a given item from the sample.

EXHIBIT 8-5
RISK FACTORS

Risk of Material Misstatement	**Risk That Other Procedures Will Fail to Detect a Material Misstatement**		
	High	Moderate	Low
High	3.0	2.3	1.9
Moderate	2.3	1.6	1.2
Low	1.9	1.2	0.9

Evaluating the Sample Results

The auditor may use one of several methods to project the sample misstatement to the population. The AICPA Auditing Practice Release *Audit Sampling* presents two methods, which are discussed here.

Ratio Method

The ratio of the sample quantity (the total of all items selected) to the population quantity (the total of the population from which the sample is selected) is used to project the sample misstatement as follows:

$$\frac{\text{Amount of sample misstatement}}{\text{Sample quantity}} \times \text{Population quantity} = \text{Projected population misstatement}$$

Difference Method

The average amount of misstatement in the sample is calculated and multiplied by the number of items in the population to project the sample misstatement as follows:

$$\frac{\text{Sample misstatement}}{\text{Sample items}} \times \text{Population items} = \text{Projected population misstatement}$$

One of these methods should be selected based on whether there is a reason to expect a relationship between the amount of the misstatement and the amount of the item:

Factor	Method
Misstatement relates to size of the item	Ratio method
Misstatement relatively constant for all items	Difference method

The auditor should calculate the projected misstatement separately for each individual group used. The projected misstatement for such groups should then be added to determine the projected misstatement for the sample. The auditor should also give adequate consideration to the qualitative aspects of misstatements, including the possible relationship of the misstatements to other phases of the engagement. The nature and cause of the misstatements should be considered, including (1) whether they are errors caused by fraud and (2) whether they are due to misunderstandings of instructions, carelessness, intentional failure to perform procedures, or other factors. The discovery of fraud generally requires more attention from the auditor than the discovery of an error.

Evaluation of Results

After applying the audit procedures, the auditor should evaluate the results. If, based on the tests, the auditor believes that the specified element is materially misstated, he or she should have the information corrected or modify the audit report.

The auditor must also consider the effect of the aggregate misstatement on individual items, totals, and subtotals within the specified element. In that case, the evaluation should consist of the following:

- Quantitative considerations
- Qualitative considerations
- Consideration of risk of further misstatement

Quantitative Considerations

First, all known and likely misstatements should be aggregated. Known misstatements consist of those that were specifically identified by performing audit procedures. For example, misstatements detected in items tested 100% (individually significant items) are known misstatements. Likely misstatements are determined when the auditor uses certain sampling or analytical procedures. The projection of sample results is an example of likely misstatement.

Total known and likely misstatement should then be compared to the amount considered material to the specified element. When only a single amount is being presented, this amount (evaluation materiality) will generally be the same as planning materiality. If total known and likely misstatement exceeds the amount considered material to the specified element, his or her auditor should have the information corrected or modify the audit report. If total known and likely misstatement is less than the amount considered material to the specified element, then the auditor should consider the qualitative aspects of the misstatement and consider the risk of further misstatement.

Qualitative Considerations

The auditor must recognize that otherwise immaterial misstatements may be qualitatively material. In many instances, qualitative factors are more important than the quantitative guidelines. The intended uses and nature of the specified element must be carefully evaluated, Because certain types of misstatements are likely to be more important to certain users than others. Examples are as follows:

- *Error versus fraud* Amounts involving fraud are generally considered more critical than unintentional errors of equal dollar amounts. This is because fraud reflects on the integrity of the client.

- *Considerations of contractual obligations* Misstatements that are otherwise minor may be material if adverse consequences are likely to arise from contractual obligations.

Risk of Further Misstatement

As the aggregate effect of misstatements gets closer to the amount that the auditor considers material, the auditor should give more consideration to possible further undetected misstatements. If the auditor believes that the risk of further undetected misstatements is too high, he or she should perform additional audit procedures to support the audit report.

Use of a Specialist

The auditor may need specialized assistance on the engagement and decide to rely on the work of an expert. When an auditor uses the work of a specialist, the audit standards require that he or she have sufficient knowledge of the specified element to (1) communicate to the specialist the objectives of the work and (2) evaluate the specialist's work to determine whether the objectives were achieved.

Before using and relying on the work of a specialist, the auditor should be satisfied with the specialist's qualifications in the particular field. For guidance on using the work of a specialist, the auditor should consider the guidance in SAS-73 (AU 336) (Using the Work of a Specialist). SAS-73 recommends that the auditor consider the following in connection with his or her evaluation of the specialist's qualifications:

- The professional certification, license, or other recognition of the competence of the specialist.
- The reputation and standing of the specialist in the views of peers and others familiar with his or her work.
- The specialist's experience in the type of work the auditor is considering using the specialist for.

If the specialist is related to the client, the auditor should assess the risk that the specialist's objectivity may be impaired. If the auditor believes the specialist's objectivity may be impaired, he or she should either

- Engage another specialist that is unrelated to the client or
- Perform additional procedures to test the specialist's assumptions, methods, or findings (or engage another specialist to do so).

Representation Letters

During an audit engagement, management makes many representations to the auditor, both oral and written, in response to specific inquiries or through presentation of the specified element. Such representations from management are part of the evidential matter that the auditor obtains.

Written representations from management ordinarily confirm representations explicitly or implicitly made to the auditor, indicate and document the continuing appropriateness of such representations, and reduce the possibility of misunderstanding concerning the matters that are the subject of the representations. SAS-85 (AU 333.05) (Management Representations) requires the auditor to obtain written representations from management for all financial statements and periods covered by the auditor's report.

The specific written representations that the auditor obtains will depend on the circumstances of the engagement and the nature and basis of presentation of the element. SAS-85 (AU 333.06), as amended, states that specific representations ordinarily relate to the following matters:

- Management's acknowledgment of its responsibility for the fair presentation in the financial statements of financial position, results of operations, and cash flows in conformity with GAAP
- Management's belief that the financial statements are fairly presented in conformity with GAAP
- Availability of all financial records and related data
- Completeness and availability of all minutes of the meetings of stockholders, directors, and committees of directors
- Communications from regulatory agencies concerning noncompliance with or deficiencies in financial reporting practices
- Absence of unrecorded transactions
- Management's belief that the effects of any uncorrected financial statement misstatements aggregated by the auditor during the current engagement and pertaining to the latest period presented are immaterial, both individually and in the aggregate, to the financial statements taken as a whole. (A summary of such items should be included in or attached to the representation letter.)
- Management's acknowledgment of its responsibility for the design and implementation of programs and controls to prevent and detect fraud
- Management's knowledge of any fraud or suspected fraud affecting the entity involving (a) management, (b) employees who have significant roles in the internal control, or (c) others where the fraud could be material

- Management's knowledge of any allegations of fraud or suspected fraud affecting the entity that is received in communications from employees, former employees, analysts, regulators, short sellers, or others
- Plans or intentions that may affect the carrying value or classification of assets and liabilities
- Information concerning related-party transactions and amounts receivable from or payable to related parties
- Guarantees, whether written or oral, that the company is contingently liable for
- Significant estimates and material concentrations known to management that are required to be disclosed in accordance with the AICPA's SOP 94-6 (Disclosure of Certain Significant Risks and Uncertainties)
- Violations or possible violations of laws or regulations whose effects should be considered for disclosure in the financial statements or as a basis for recording a loss contingency
- Unasserted claims or assessments that the entity's lawyer has advised are probable of assertion and must be disclosed in accordance with FAS-5 (Accounting for Contingencies)
- Other liabilities and gain or loss contingencies that are required to be accrued or disclosed by FAS-5
- Satisfactory title to assets, liens or encumbrances on assets, and assets pledged as collateral
- Compliance with aspects of contractual agreements that may affect the financial statements
- Information concerning subsequent events

OBSERVATION: The items listed above would be included in a representation letter in an audit of a specified element only to the extent they are relevant. For example, if the auditor is reporting on revenue, the representation letter generally would not mention items such as stock options or compensating balance arrangements. However, it would mention availability of financial records, fraud and illegal acts, related-party transactions, and other relevant matters.

The representation letter should be dated no earlier than the date of the auditor's report, which should coincide with the end of fieldwork. The letter should be addressed to the auditor and signed by members of management whom the auditor believes are responsible for and knowledgeable, directly or through others in the organization, about the matters covered by the representations. Normally, the CEO and CFO should sign the letter. Appendix 8G an illustrative representation letter.

Documentation

Audit documentation is the principal record of audit procedures applied, information obtained, and conclusions or findings reached by the auditor in the engagement. The quantity, type, and content of audit documentation are matters of the auditor's professional judgment. Audit documentation serves mainly to

- Provide the principal support for the auditor's report, including the representation regarding observance of the standards of fieldwork, which is implicit in the reference in the report to generally accepted auditing standards.
- Aid the audit in the conduct and supervision of the audit engagement.

Audit documentation should be sufficient to (1) enable members of the engagement team with supervision and review responsibilities to understand the nature, timing, extent, and results of audit procedures performed and the information obtained and (2) identify the engagement team member(s) who performed and reviewed the work.

Examples of audit documentation are work programs, analyses, memoranda, letters of confirmation and representation, abstracts or copies of entity documents, and schedules or commentaries prepared or obtained by the auditor. Ordinarily, audit documentation includes the following:

- Documentation of the engagement acceptance or continuance decision
- An engagement letter
- A planning form documenting the auditor's knowledge of the client and consideration of audit risk (including fraud risk)
- Support for judgments about materiality
- Documentation of the procedures performed
- Support for data in the presentation, including relating it to the accounting records and financial statements
- A discussion of unusual matters encountered and their resolution
- A representation letter
- Copies of reports from other auditors, if any, who have audited a component of the specified element
- Documentation that the workpapers were reviewed

Audit documentation may be in paper form, electronic form, or other medium.

The auditor has an ethical, and in some situations a legal, obligation to maintain the confidentiality of client information. Because audit documentation often contains confidential information, the auditor should adopt reasonable procedures to maintain the confidentiality of that information. The auditor should also adopt reasonable procedures to prevent unauthorized access to attest documentation.

If the audit of the specified element is performed at, or near, the same time as the audit of the financial statements, the auditor may use some of the documentation prepared for the financial statement audit to document the audit of the specified element.

Reporting

An auditor's report on one or more specified elements, accounts, or items of a financial statement should include the following:

1. A title that includes the word "independent."
2. A paragraph stating that
    a. The specified elements, accounts, or items were audited. If the audit was in conjunction with an audit of the entity's financial statements, the paragraph should so state and indicate the date of the auditor's report on those financial statements. Also, any departure from the standard report on those statements should be disclosed if considered relevant;
    b. The specified elements, accounts, or items are the responsibility of the company's management; and
    c. The auditor is responsible for expressing an opinion on the specified elements, accounts, or items based on the audit.
3. A paragraph stating that
    a. The audit was conducted in accordance with GAAS, and an identification of the United States of America as the country of origin of those standards [for audits performed in accordance with PCAOB standards, a statement that the audit was conducted "in accordance with the standards of the Public Company Accounting Oversight Board (United States)"];
    b. GAAS require that the auditor plan and perform the audit to obtain reasonable assurance about whether the specified elements, accounts, or items are free of material misstatement;
    c. An audit includes
        (1) Examining, on a test basis, evidence supporting the amounts and disclosures in the specified elements, accounts, or items
        (2) Assessing the accounting principles used and significant estimates made by management

    (3) Evaluating the overall presentation of the specified elements, accounts, or items

  d. The auditor believes that the audit provides a reasonable basis for his or her opinion.

4. A paragraph describing
   a. The basis on which the specified elements, accounts, or items are presented and on, if applicable, agreements specifying the basis if the presentation is not prepared in conformity with GAAP; and
   b. If necessary, significant interpretations and their sources, if any, made by management that relate to the provisions of a relevant agreement.
5. A paragraph that expresses the auditor's opinion, or disclaims an opinion, on whether the specified elements, accounts, or items are presented fairly, in all material respects, in conformity with the basis of accounting described. If the auditor concludes that such items are not presented fairly on the basis of accounting described, or if there has been a limitation on the scope of the audit, the auditor should
   a. Disclose, in an explanatory paragraph preceding the opinion paragraph of the report, all the substantive reasons for his or her conclusion and
   b. Include in the opinion paragraph the appropriate modifying language and a reference to the preceding explanatory paragraph.
6. If the specified element, account, or item is prepared to comply with the requirements or financial reporting provisions of a contract or agreement that results in a presentation that is not in conformity with either GAAP or OCBOA, a separate paragraph at the end of the report stating that its use is restricted to those within the entity and the parties to the contract or agreement and that it should not be used by anyone other than these specified parties.
7. Manual or printed signature of the auditor's firm.
8. Date of the audit report (i.e., date of completion of fieldwork).
9. For audits in accordance with the standards of the Public Company Accounting Oversight Board, the city and state (or city and country, for non-U.S. auditors) where the auditor's report has been issued.

Piecemeal Opinions

The auditor should not express an opinion on specified elements, accounts, or items included in financial statements that he or she has expressed an adverse opinion on or disclaimed an opinion on based on an audit. Such reporting would be the same as expressing a piecemeal opinion on the financial statements. However, an auditor would be able to express an opinion on one or more specified elements, accounts, or items of a financial statement if the matters to be reported on and the related scope of the audit were not intended to, and did not, encompass so many elements, accounts, or items as to constitute a major portion of the financial statements.

Appendixes 8I, 8J, 8K, 8L, and 8M are examples of audit reports on specified elements.

COMPILING SPECIFIED ELEMENTS, ACCOUNTS, OR ITEMS OF A FINANCIAL STATEMENT

SSARS-13 (AR 110) (Compilation of Specified Elements, Accounts, or Items of a Financial Statement) provides guidance concerning the standards and procedures applicable when an accountant is engaged to compile or issues a compilation report on a specified element. However, the engagement must also follow the general compilation performance requirements found in SSARS-1 (AR 100) (Compilation and Review of Financial Statements). This section provides an overview of the major considerations and steps in compiling a specified element. For a complete discussion of compilation engagements, including checklists and practice aids that can be adapted to specified elements, see *Miller Compilations & Reviews*.

Although SSARS-13 (AR 110) provides guidance for compiling specified elements, nothing precludes an accountant from preparing or assisting in the preparation of a specified element and submitting such a presentation to the client without the issuance of a compilation report.

> **OBSERVATION:** When the accountant is engaged to compile a specified element, he or she is required to report on the compiled specified elements.

A compilation of a specified element is limited to presenting financial information that is the representation of management (or the owners) without undertaking to express any assurance on that information. However, the accountant might consider it necessary to perform other accounting services in order to compile the financial information.

Examples of specified elements that an accountant may compile are schedules of rentals, royalties, profit participation, and provision for income taxes.

Conditions for Compiling Specified Elements

If an accountant prepares or assists a client in preparing a schedule of a specified element, he or she should consider how the presentation of specified elements, accounts, or items will be used. The accountant should consider the potential for being associated with the schedule and the likelihood of the user inappropriately inferring, through that association, an unintended level of assurance. If the accountant believes that he or she will be associated with the information, he or she should consider issuing a compilation report so that users will not infer a level of assurance that does not exist.

An engagement to compile one or more specified elements, accounts, or items of a financial statement may be undertaken as a separate engagement or in conjunction with a compilation of financial statements.

Establishing an Understanding with the Entity

When engaged to compile a specified element, the accountant should establish an understanding with the entity, preferably in writing, regarding the services to be performed. The understanding should include a description of the nature and limitations of the services to be performed and a description of the report. The understanding should also state

- That the engagement cannot be relied upon to disclose errors, fraud, or illegal acts and
- That the accountant will inform the appropriate level of management of any material errors and any evidence or information that comes to the accountant's attention during the engagement that fraud or an illegal act may have occurred.

OBSERVATION: The accountant need not report any matters regarding illegal acts that may have occurred that are clearly inconsequential and may reach agreement in advance with the entity on the nature of any such matters to be communicated.

OBSERVATION: "Fraud" is an intentional act that results in a misstatement in compiled specified elements, accounts, or items of a financial statement. "Illegal acts" are violations of laws or government regulations excluding fraud.

OBSERVATION: Whether an act is, in fact, fraudulent or illegal is a determination that is normally beyond the accountant's professional competence. According to SSARS-13 (AR 110), in reporting on specified elements, an accountant presents him- or herself as one who is proficient in accounting and compilation services. The accountant's training, experience, and understanding of the client and its industry may provide a basis for recognition that some client acts coming to his or her attention may be fraudulent or illegal. However, the determination of whether a particular act is fraudulent or illegal is generally based on the advice of an informed expert qualified to practice law or it might have to await final determination by a court of law.

Responsibility for Fraud and Illegal Acts

When an accountant is engaged to compile a specified element and evidence or information comes to his or her attention during the engagement that fraud or an illegal act may have occurred, he or she must adhere to the communication requirements contained in SSARS-1 (AR 100.61–.62), as amended.

AR 100.61 states that when evidence or information comes to the accountant's attention during the performance of compilation procedures that fraud or an illegal act may have occurred, the matter should be brought to the attention of the appropriate level of management. The accountant is not required to report matters regarding illegal acts that are clearly inconsequential and may reach agreement in advance with the client on the nature of such items to be communicated.

When the fraud or illegal act involves senior management, the accountant should report the matter to an individual or group at a higher level within the entity, such as the manager (owner) or the board of directors. The communication may be oral or written. If the communication is oral, the accountant should document it. When the fraud or illegal act involves an owner of the business, the accountant should consider resigning from the engagement. Additionally, the accountant should consider consulting with his or her legal counsel and insurance provider whenever any evidence or information comes to his or her attention during the performance of compilation procedures that fraud or an illegal act may have occurred, unless the illegal act is clearly inconsequential.

The disclosure to parties other than the client's senior management (or the client's board of directors, if applicable) of any evidence or information that comes to the accountant's attention during the performance of compilation procedures that fraud or an illegal act may have occurred is ordinarily not part of the accountant's responsibility and ordinarily would be precluded by the accountant's ethical or legal obligations of confidentiality. The accountant should recognize, however, that in the following circumstances a duty to disclose to parties outside of the entity might exist:

- To comply with certain legal and regulatory requirements
- To a successor accountant when the successor decides to communicate with the predecessor accountant in accordance with SSARS-4 (AR 400) (Communications Between Predecessor and Successor Accountants), as amended, regarding acceptance of

an engagement to compile or review the financial statements of a nonpublic entity

- In response to a subpoena

Because potential conflicts between the accountant's ethical and legal obligations for confidentiality of client matters may be complex, the accountant may wish to consult with legal counsel before discussing matters regarding fraud or illegal acts with parties outside the client.

Performance Requirements

When an accountant is engaged to compile or issues a compilation report on one or more specified elements, accounts, or items of a financial statement, he or she must adhere to the compilation performance requirements contained in SSARS-1 (AR 100.07–.11), as amended. These requirements include the following:

- The accountant should possess a level of knowledge of the accounting principles and practices of the industry in which the entity operates that will enable him or her to compile the specified element that is appropriate in form for an entity operating in that industry. An accountant is not precluded from accepting a compilation engagement for an entity in an industry that the accountant has no previous experience in. It does, however, place upon the accountant a responsibility to obtain the required level of knowledge. The accountant may do so, for example, by consulting AICPA guides, industry publications, financial statements of other entities in the industry, textbooks and periodicals, or individuals knowledgeable about the industry.
- To compile a specified element, the accountant should possess a general understanding of the nature of the entity's business transactions, the form of its accounting records, the stated qualifications of its accounting personnel, the accounting basis that the specified element is to be presented on, and the form and content of the specified element. The accountant ordinarily obtains knowledge of these matters through experience with the entity or inquiry of the entity's personnel. On the basis of that understanding, the accountant should consider whether it will be necessary to perform other accounting services (such as assist in adjusting the books of account or consult on accounting matters) when he or she compiles the specified element.
- The accountant is not required to make inquiries or perform other procedures to verify, corroborate, or review information supplied by the entity. However, the accountant may have

made inquiries or performed other procedures. The results of such inquiries or procedures, knowledge gained from prior engagements, or the specified element on its face may cause the accountant to become aware that information supplied by the entity is incorrect, incomplete, or otherwise unsatisfactory. If any evidence or information comes to the accountant's attention regarding fraud or an illegal act that may have occurred, the accountant should request that management consider the effect of the matter on the specified element. Additionally, the accountant should consider the effect of the matter on his or her compilation report. In circumstances where the accountant believes that the specified element is materially misstated, the accountant should obtain additional or revised information. If the entity refuses to provide additional or revised information, the accountant should withdraw from the engagement.

- Before issuing his or her compilation report on one or more specified elements, accounts, or items of a financial statement, the accountant should read the compiled specified elements and consider whether the information appears to be appropriate in form and free of obvious material errors. In this context, the term "error" refers to mistakes in the compilation of the specified element, including arithmetical or clerical mistakes, and mistakes in the application of accounting principles, including disclosures, if presented.

Reporting Requirements

When an accountant is engaged to perform a compilation and issue a compilation report on one or more specified elements, accounts, or items of a financial statement, the basic elements of the report are as follows:

- A statement that the specified element(s), account(s), or item(s) identified in the report were compiled. If the compilation was performed in conjunction with a compilation of the company's financial statements, the paragraph should state this and state the date of the accountant's compilation report on those financial statements. Furthermore, departures from the standard report on those statements should also be disclosed if the accountant considers them relevant to the presentation of the specified element(s), account(s), or item(s).
- A statement that the compilation was performed in accordance with Statements on Standards for Accounting and Review Services issued by the American Institute of Certified Public Accountants.
- A description of the basis that the specified element(s), account(s), or item(s) are presented on if the basis is not

generally accepted accounting principles and if the basis of presentation is a comprehensive basis of accounting other than generally accepted accounting principles.

- A statement that a compilation is limited to presenting financial information that is the representation of management (owners).
- A statement that the specified element(s), account(s), or item(s) have not been audited or reviewed and, accordingly, the accountant does not express an opinion or any other form of assurance on it (them).
- A signature of the accounting firm or the accountant as appropriate. (The signature could be manual, stamped, electronic, or typed.)
- The date of the compilation report. (The date of completion of the compilation should be used as the date of the accountant's report.)

Any other procedures that the accountant might have performed before or during the compilation engagement should not be described in the report.

Each page of the compiled specified elements should include a reference, such as "See Accountant's Compilation Report."

An accountant is not precluded from issuing a compilation report on a specified element for an entity that the accountant is not independent of. If the accountant is not independent, he or she should specifically disclose the lack of independence. However, the reason for the lack of independence should not be described. When the accountant is not independent, the following should be included as the last paragraph of the report:

> I am (we are) not independent with respect to XYZ Company.

Appendix 8N and Appendix 8O are examples of compilation reports on specified elements.

APPENDIX 8A
ILLUSTRATIVE ENGAGEMENT LETTER: AUDIT OF SPECIFIED ELEMENTS, ACCOUNTS, OR ITEMS OF A FINANCIAL STATEMENT

[*date*]

Mr. Robert Evans, President
Upstate Event and Race Promotions, Inc.
123 Main Street
Greenville, SC 29601

Dear Mr. Evans

We are pleased to confirm our understanding of the services we are to provide for Upstate Event and Race Promotions, Inc. for the year ended December 31, 20X6. We will audit the [*identify specified element; for example,* schedule of accounts receivable] of Upstate Event and Race Promotions, Inc. as of December 31, 20X6.

Our audit will be made in accordance with U.S. generally accepted auditing standards and will include tests of the accounting records of Upstate Event and Race Promotions, Inc. and other procedures we consider necessary to enable us to express an unqualified opinion that the [*identify specified element; for example,* schedule of accounts receivable] is fairly presented, in all material respects, in conformity with accounting principles generally accepted in the United States. If our opinion is other than unqualified, we will fully discuss the reasons with you in advance. If, for any reason, we are unable to complete the audit, we will not issue a report as a result of this engagement.

Our procedures will include tests of documentary evidence that support the transactions recorded in the accounts and direct confirmation of cash, investments, and certain other assets and liabilities by correspondence with creditors and financial institutions. We will request written representations from your attorneys as part of the engagement, and they may bill you for responding to that inquiry. At the conclusion of our audit, we will also request certain written representations from you about the [*identify subject matter; for example,* schedule of accounts receivable] and related matters.

An audit includes examining, on a test basis, evidence supporting the amounts and disclosures in the [*identify specified element; for example,* schedule of accounts receivable]; therefore, our audit will involve judgment about the number of transactions to be examined and the areas to be tested. Our audit is designed to provide reasonable, rather than absolute, assurance of detecting misstatements that, in our judgment, could have a material effect on the [*identify specified element; for example,* schedule of accounts receivable]. Consequently, our audit will not necessarily detect misstatements less than this materiality level that might exist due to error, fraudulent financial reporting, or misappropriation of assets.

Our audit is not specifically designed and cannot be relied on to disclose reportable conditions, that is, significant deficiencies in the design or operation of the internal control. However, during the audit, if we become aware of such reportable conditions or ways that we believe management practices can be improved, we will communicate them to you in a separate letter. By your signature below, you acknowledge that you are responsible for the design and implementation of programs and controls to prevent and detect fraud, and for informing us about all known or suspected fraud affecting the company that involves management, employees who have significant roles in internal control, and others where the fraud could have a material effect on the financial statements. You are also responsible for informing us of your knowledge of any allegations of fraud or suspected fraud affecting the company received in communications from employees, former employees, regulators, or others. You agree that you will confirm your understanding of your responsibilities as defined in this letter to us in your management representation letter. Our responsibility as auditors is limited to the period covered by our audit and does not extend to matters that might arise during any later periods for which we are not engaged as auditors.

We understand that you will provide us with the basic information required for our audit and that you are responsible for the accuracy and completeness of that information. We will advise you about appropriate accounting principles and their application and will assist in the preparation of your [*identify specified element; for example,* schedule of accounts receivable], but the responsibility for the [*identify specified element; for example,* schedule of accounts receivable] remains with you. You acknowledge that management is responsible for adjusting the [*identify specified element; for example,* schedule of accounts receivable] to correct material misstatements and for confirming to us in the management representation letter that the effects of any uncorrected misstatements aggregated by us during the current engagement and pertaining to the latest period presented are immaterial, both individually and in the aggregate, to the [*identify specified element; for example,* schedule of accounts receivable]. Other management responsibilities include maintaining adequate records and related internal control policies and procedures, selecting and applying accounting principles, and safeguarding assets.

We understand that your employees will type all confirmations we request and will locate any documents or invoices selected by us for testing.

We expect to begin our audit on approximately [*date*] and issue our report no later than [*date*].

Our fees for these services will be based on the actual time spent at our standard hourly rates, plus travel and other out-of-pocket costs, such as report production, typing, and postage. Our standard hourly rates vary according to the degree of responsibility involved and the experience level of the personnel assigned to your audit. Our invoices for these fees will be rendered each month as work progresses and are payable upon presentation. Payment is due [*number*] days after invoice date. Work may be suspended if your account becomes [*number*] days or more overdue and will not be resumed until your account is paid in full. Based on our preliminary estimates, the fee should approximate $[*amount*]. That estimate is based on anticipated cooperation from your personnel and the assumption that unexpected circumstances will not be encountered during the audit. If significant additional time is necessary, we will discuss it with you and arrive at a new fee estimate before we incur the additional costs.

We appreciate the opportunity to be of service to Upstate Event and Race Promotions, Inc. and believe this letter accurately summarizes the significant terms of our engagement. If you have any questions, please let us know. If you agree with the terms of our engagement as described in this letter, please sign the enclosed copy and return it to us.

Very truly yours,

____

Jim Ashley
Ashley & Company, CPAs

Approval:

____

Robert Evans
Upstate Event and Race Promotions, Inc.

____

Title

____

Date

APPENDIX 8B ILLUSTRATIVE ENGAGEMENT LETTER: COMPILATION OF SPECIFIED ELEMENTS, ACCOUNTS, OR ITEMS OF A FINANCIAL STATEMENT

[*date*]

Mr. Robert Evans, President
Upstate Event and Race Promotions, Inc.
123 Main Street
Greenville, SC 29601

Dear Mr. Evans:

This letter is to confirm our understanding of the terms and objectives of our engagement and the nature and limitations of the services we will provide.

We will perform the following services:

We will compile, from information you provide, [identify specified element, account, or item of the financial statement, e.g., schedule of accounts receivable or schedule of depreciation-income tax basis] of Upstate Event and Race Promotions, Inc. as of December 31, 20X6.

We will compile the [identify specified element, account, or item of the financial statement] and issue an accountant's report thereon in accordance with Statements on Standards for Accounting and Review Services. A compilation is limited to presenting financial information that is the representation of management (owners). We will not audit or review the [identify specified element, account, or item of the financial statement] and, accordingly, will not express an opinion or any other form of assurance on it.

Our engagement cannot be relied upon to disclose errors, fraud, or illegal acts that may exist. However, we will inform the appropriate level of management of any material errors, and of any evidence or information that comes to our attention during the performance of our compilation procedures, that fraud may have occurred. In addition, we will report to you any evidence or information that comes to our attention during the performance of our compilation procedures regarding illegal acts that may have occurred, unless they are clearly inconsequential.

As part of our engagement, we will also (list any nonattest services to be performed, if applicable, such as income tax preparation and bookkeeping services).

You are responsible for:

(a) Making all management decisions and performing all management functions;

(b) Designating an individual who possesses suitable skill, knowledge, and/or experience, preferably within senior management, to oversee the services;

(c) Evaluating the adequacy and results of the services performed;

(d) Accepting responsibility for the results of the services; and

(e) Establishing and maintaining internal controls, including monitoring ongoing activities.

If, for any reason, we are unable to complete the compilation of your [identify specified element, account, or item of the financial statement], we will not issue a report on such schedule as a result of this engagement.

Our fees for this work will be at our regular hourly rates for the individuals involved plus direct out-of-pocket expenses. Payment for service is due when rendered, and interim billings may be submitted as work progresses and expenses are incurred.

Billings become delinquent if not paid within [*number*] days of the invoice date. If billings are past due in excess of [*number*] days, we will stop all work until your account is brought current, or withdraw from this engagement. Upstate Event and Race Promotions, Inc. acknowledges and agrees that we are not required to continue work in the event of Upstate Event and Race Promotions, Inc.'s failure to pay on a timely basis for services rendered as required by this engagement letter. Upstate Event and Race Promotions, Inc. further acknowledges and agrees that in the event we stop work or withdraw from this engagement as a result of Upstate Event and Race Promotions, Inc.'s failure to pay on a timely basis for services rendered as required by this engagement letter, we shall not be liable to Upstate Event and Race Promotions, Inc. for any damages that occur as a result of our ceasing to render services.

We will require a retainer of $[*amount*], which will be applied to current billings as registered.

We shall be pleased to discuss this letter with you at any time.

If the foregoing is in accordance with your understanding, please sign the copy of this letter in the space provided and return it to us.

Sincerely,

____

Jim Ashley
Ashley & Company, CPAs

Acknowledged:

____

Robert Evans
Upstate Event and Race Promotions, Inc.

____

Date

APPENDIX 8C
PLANNING MATERIALITY CALCULATION FORM

Client Name: ________________ Date of Presentation: ________________

Completed by: ________________ Date Completed: ________________

Instructions

The purpose of this form is to determine and document the materiality amount that will be considered suitable for planning purposes. Complete this form to determine planning materiality and tolerable misstatement using amounts as of the date of the presentation. This form should be prepared by the engagement personnel in charge of fieldwork (senior or supervisory staff) and reviewed and approved by the engagement executive for all audit engagements.

If the total dollar amount of the subject matter (the "base") is:		*Planning materiality is:*
Over	**But less than**	**Amount + (Percent x Base)**
$0	$50,000	0 + 5.5%
$50,000	$100,000	1,250 + 3.0%
$100,000	$500,000	2,250 + 2.0%
$500,000	$1 million	7,500 + 1.0%
$1 million	$5 million	9,500 + 0.8%
$5 million	$10 million	19,500 + 0.6%

If the total dollar amount of the subject matter (the "base") is:		***Planning materiality is:***
Over	**But less than**	**Amount + (Percent x Base)**
$10 million	$50 million	40,000 + 0.4%
$50 million	$100 million	115,000 + 0.25%
$100 million		185, 000 + 0.18%

Example: If the base amount is $5.5 million, then the planning materiality would be determined as follows:

$19,500 + (.006 × $5,500,000) = $52,500

Calculations

1. Planning Materiality

Amount from Table	+	(Percentage from Table	×	Base Amount)	=	Planning Materiality
________		(________	×	________)	=	________

2. Tolerable Misstatement

Tolerable misstatement is used in computing sample sizes and in making other scope decisions. As a rule of thumb, tolerable misstatement can be calculated as follows:

Planning Materiality From Above	×	Factor	=	Tolerable Misstatement
________	×	.75	=	________

3. Individually Significant Items

The amount used to determine individually significant items can be any amount up to tolerable misstatement.

APPENDIX 8D
AUDIT PROCEDURES CHECKLIST

Client Name: ____________________ Date of Presentation: ______________

Completed by: ____________________ Date Completed: ______________

	Completed by or N/A
1. Complete the Client Acceptance and Retention Evaluation Form.	________

		Completed by or N/A
2.	Establish and document an understanding with the client, preferably in an engagement letter. If an engagement letter will not be obtained, the oral understanding should be documented in a memo.	________
3.	Obtain an understanding of the client and the engagement.	________
4.	Obtain an understanding of the specified element.	________
5.	Determine that the scheduling and staffing are adequate to perform the engagement.	________
6.	Complete the Planning Materiality Calculation Form.	________
7.	Obtain the engagement partner's approval of the overall engagement plan.	________
8.	If other services have been performed for the client, review relevant workpapers and any related reports for indications of matters that contradict the assertions.	________
9.	Develop and perform procedures necessary to evaluate the specified element (attach a program or memo to this checklist).	________
10.	Review the results of the preceding procedures and evaluate whether the specified element is presented in conformity with generally accepted accounting principles. If the procedures reveal omissions or misstatements, assess the significance of those omissions or misstatements and their effect on the audit report.	________
11.	Consider whether events have occurred after the date of the specified element but before the end of fieldwork that affect the presentation of the specified element.	________
12.	Obtain a representation letter from management.	________
13.	Draft the audit report.	________
14.	Read other information in a client-prepared document that contains the audit report for inconsistencies with the report and material misstatements of fact.	________
15.	If any situations have occurred that require consultation, determine that such consultation has been properly documented.	________
16.	If there were differences of professional opinion among members of the engagement team or between the engagement team and a specialist, determine that the differences were properly resolved and documented.	________
17.	Determine that all questions, exceptions, or notes, if any, posed during the engagement have been followed up and resolved.	________

	Completed by or N/A
18. Determine that all required forms, questionnaires, and checklists have been completed.	________
19. Ensure that the workpapers and audit report have been reviewed in accordance with firm policy.	________
20. Obtain engagement partner's review and approval for issuance of report.	________

APPENDIX 8E
SAMPLING WORKSHEET FOR SUBSTANTIVE TESTS

Client Name: ________________ Date of Presentation: ____________

Completed by: ________________ Date Completed: ____________

Instructions

This worksheet is designed to assist the practitioner in planning, performing, and evaluating a nonstatistical sample for substantive tests. This form should be prepared by the engagement personnel in charge of fieldwork (senior or supervisory staff) and reviewed and approved by the engagement executive for all audit engagements.

Part 1: Initial Calculation

1. Identify the amount for individually significant items. As a rule of thumb, consider using $33^1/3\%$ of tolerable misstatement. However, any amount up to tolerable misstatement is acceptable.
2. Identify unusual items not included in Step 1 that are individually significant by their nature.
3. Calculate the remaining balance and percent of coverage:

	Number of Items	Amount
A. Total		$
B. Individually significant items [1/3 of $__________ tolerable misstatement = $ ________]		$
C. Unusual items (other than those in B. Briefly describe the nature of the unusual items:		$
D. Remaining balance [A – (B + C)]		$
E. Percent of coverage [(B + C) / A]		%
F. Tolerable misstatement		

4. After completing the initial calculation, if the remaining balance (D) is greater than tolerable misstatement (F), go to Part 2. If D is less than F, additional testing of D might not be necessary. If this is the case, go to Part 3. However, this is a matter of professional judgment.

Part 2: Consideration of Remaining Balance

1. If the remaining balance (D) is greater than tolerable misstatement (F), decide what additional procedures, if any, are needed to test D. Select one or more of the following options:
   a. No further testing of D: Consider this option only if (1) the assessed risk of material misstatement of D is low, and (2) the percent of coverage (E) represents a substantial portion of the balance (such as 65% or more).
   b. Applying analytical procedures: Consider using analytical procedures if sufficiently effective procedures can be designed and they provide adequate assurance with respect to D.
   c. Relying on other substantive procedures: If other planned substantive tests in this area contribute to achieving the same objective, consider whether those other procedures provide adequate assurance with respect to D.
   d. Sampling: Consider sampling D if (1) D consists of numerous items (such as 100 items or more), and (2) the expected misstatement of D does not exceed one-third of tolerable misstatement.
   e. Testing more individually significant items: Consider this option if (1) analytical procedures and/or other substantive procedures do not provide adequate assurance, and (2) sampling is impractical.

If option e. is selected, complete Step 2. Otherwise go to Part 3.

2. Recalculate the remaining balance and percent of coverage using a lower amount for individually significant items. The amount should be based on the desired percentage of coverage.

	Number of Items	Amount
A. Total		$
B. Individually significant items Amount used: $ ________		$
C. Unusual items		$
D. Remaining balance [A – (B + C)]		$
E. Percent of coverage [(B + C) / A]		%
F. Tolerable misstatement		$

3. If D exceeds F, reconsider the options in Step 1. If D is less than F, additional testing of D may not be necessary. Document this decision by completing Part 3.

Part 3: Summary of Testing to Be Performed

1. Briefly describe the procedures to be applied to the individually significant items.
2. Briefly describe the procedures, if any, to be applied to the remaining balance (D from Part 1 or Part 2, above). If sampling will be used, complete the Sampling Planning and Evaluation Form: Substantive Tests.

APPENDIX 8F
SAMPLING PLANNING AND EVALUATION FORM

Client Name: ________________ Date of Presentation: ___________

Completed by: ________________ Date Completed: ______________

Instructions

This worksheet can be used in the audit of specified elements presented in financial or numeric form. It has been developed for financial subject matter, but can be modified for use with numeric (nonfinancial) specified elements.

Part 1: Planning

1. Describe the population being tested

	Units	Amount
a. Items to be examined 100% (individually significant items)	_____	_____
b. Population being sampled	_____	_____
c. Total	_____	_____

2. Briefly describe the test to be performed:
3. Describe the sampling unit:
4. Describe how completeness of the population will be considered:
5. Describe what will be considered a misstatement:
6. Sample selection method to be used:

   Haphazard____ Random____ Systemic____

Expected Misstatement

7. Tolerable misstatement $__________
8. One-third of tolerable misstatement $__________
9. Expected misstatement (amount of projected misstatement expected in the population) $__________

Sample Size Calculation

10. Compute sample size, as follows:

Sampling Population / Tolerable Misstatement			=	Basic Sample Size
(Step 1b.) $______ / $__________			=	
Basic Sample Size	×	Risk Factor	=	Adjusted Sample Size
______	×	_____	=	______

This adjusts the sample size for (a) the risk of material misstatement and (b) the risk that other procedures, if any, that the practitioner plans to apply to the same amounts will fail to detect a material misstatement. Other procedures risk is inversely related to the effectiveness of the other procedures. That is, the more effective the other procedure, the lower the risk assessment. If no other procedures are planned, other procedures risk should be assessed as high.

	Risk That Other Procedures Will Fail to Detect a Material Misstatement		
Risk of Material Misstatement	**High**	**Moderate**	**Low**
High	3.0	2.3	1.9
Moderate	2.3	1.6	1.2
Low	1.9	1.2	0.9

11. If it is not practical to stratify the population, multiply the sample size in Step 10 by 1.20 or other appropriate amount. ______

Part 2: Evaluation

Projection of Misstatement: If population is stratified, misstatement should be projected by stratum and added together. If the population is not stratified, use Stratum #1 column.

	Stratum #1	**Stratum #2**	**Total**
12. Dollar amount of misstatements noted in the sample			
13. Dollar amount of the sample	____	____	
14. Population being sampled	____	____	
15. Projected misstatement [(12/13) × 14]	____	____	____
16. Dollar amount of misstatements noted in items tested 100%			____
17. Total known and projected misstatement			____

Evaluation of Test Results

18. Explain reasons for misstatements:
19. Does the level of sampling risk appear acceptable? (Compare the amount in Step 15 to the amounts in Steps 8 and 9)
20. Describe how the sampling results affect the engagement:

APPENDIX 8G
ILLUSTRATIVE MANAGEMENT REPRESENTATION LETTER: AUDIT OF A SPECIFIED ELEMENT, ACCOUNT, OR ITEM OF A FINANCIAL STATEMENT

OBSERVATION: Some of the items in the representation letter below would be included in representation letter for an audit of a specified element only to the extent they are relevant. For example, if the auditor is reporting on revenue, the representation letter generally would not mention items such as stock options or compensating balance arrangements. However, it would mention availability of financial records, fraud and illegal acts, related-party transactions, and other relevant matters.

[*Prepared on client's letterhead*]

[*date—No earlier than date of the accountant's report*]

To [*independent auditor*]

We are providing this letter in connection with your audit(s) of the [*identify specified element; for example,* schedule of accounts receivable] of [*name of entity*] as of [*dates*] and for the [*periods*] then ended, for the purpose of expressing an opinion as to whether the [*identify specified element; for example,* schedule of accounts receivable] is fairly presented, in all material respects, in conformity with accounting principles generally accepted in the United States of America. We confirm that we are responsible for the fair presentation of the [*identify specified element; for example,* schedule of accounts receivable] in conformity with generally accepted accounting principles.

Certain representations in this letter are described as being limited to matters that are material. Items are considered material, regardless of size, if they involve an omission or misstatement of accounting information that, in the light of surrounding circumstances, makes it probable that the judgment of a reasonable person relying on the information would be changed or influenced by the omission or misstatement.

We confirm, to the best of our knowledge and belief, as of [*date of auditor's report*], the following representations made to you during your audit(s):

1. The [*identify specified element; for example,* schedule of accounts receivable] referred to above is fairly presented in conformity with accounting principles generally accepted in the United States of America.
2. We have made available to you all:
   a. Financial records and related data.
   b. Minutes of the meetings of stockholders, directors, and committees of directors, or summaries of actions of recent meetings for which minutes have not yet been prepared.

3. There have been no communications from regulatory agencies concerning noncompliance with or deficiencies in financial reporting practices.
4. There are no material transactions that have not been properly recorded in the accounting records underlying the [*identify specified element; for example,* schedule of accounts receivable].
5. We believe that the effects of the uncorrected misstatements in the [*identify specified element; for example,* schedule of accounts receivable] summarized in the attached schedule and aggregated by you during the current engagement are immaterial, both individually and in the aggregate, to the [*identify specified element; for example,* schedule of accounts receivable].
6. We acknowledge our responsibility for the design and implementation of programs and controls to prevent and detect fraud.
7. We have no knowledge of any fraud or suspected fraud affecting the entity involving (a) management, (b) employees who have significant roles in internal controls, or (c) others where the fraud could have a material effect on the [*identify specified element; for example,* schedule of accounts receivable].
8. We have no knowledge of any allegations of fraud or suspected fraud affecting the entity received in communications from employees, former employees, analysts, regulators, short sellers, or others.
9. The Company has no plans or intentions that may materially affect the carrying value or classification of assets and liabilities.
10. The following have been properly recorded or disclosed in the financial statements:
    a. Related-party transactions, including sales, purchases, loans, transfers, leasing arrangements, and guarantees, and amounts receivable from or payable to related parties.
    b. Guarantees, whether written or oral, under which the Company is contingently liable.
    c. Significant estimates and material concentrations known to management that are required to be disclosed in accordance with the AICPA's Statement of Position 94-6 (Disclosure of Certain Significant Risks and Uncertainties). Significant estimates are estimates at the balance-sheet date that could change materially within the next year. Concentrations refer to volumes of business, revenues, available sources of supply, or markets or geographic areas for which events could occur that would significantly disrupt normal finances within the next year.
11. There are no:
    a. Violations or possible violations of laws or regulations whose effects should be considered for disclosure in the [*identify specified element; for example,* schedule of accounts receivable] or as a basis for recording a loss contingency.
    b. Unasserted claims or assessments that our lawyer has advised are probable of assertion and must be disclosed in accordance with Financial Accounting Standards Board (FASB) Statement No. 5 (Accounting for Contingencies).

   c. Other liabilities or gain or loss contingencies that are required to be accrued or disclosed by FASB-5.

12. The Company has satisfactory title to all owned assets, and there are no liens or encumbrances on such assets nor has any asset been pledged as collateral.

13. We have complied with all aspects of contractual agreements that would have a material effect on the [*identify specified element; for example,* schedule of accounts receivable] in the event of noncompliance.

14. We represent to you the following for the Company's fair value measurements and disclosures:

    a. The underlying assumptions are reasonable and they appropriately reflect management's intent and ability to carry out its stated courses of action.

    b. The measurement methods and related assumptions used in determining fair value are appropriate in the circumstances and have been consistently applied.

    c. The disclosures related to fair values are complete, adequate, and in conformity with GAAP.

    d. There are no subsequent events that require adjustments to the fair value measurements and disclosures included in the [*identify specified element; for example,* schedule of accounts receivable].

[*Add additional representations that are unique to the entity's business or industry.*]

To the best of our knowledge and belief, no events have occurred subsequent to the [*identify specified element; for example,* schedule of accounts receivable] date and through the date of this letter that would require adjustment to or disclosure in the aforementioned [*identify specified element; for example,* schedule of accounts receivable].

____

(Name of Chief Executive Officer and Title)

____

(Name of Chief Financial Officer and Title)

APPENDIX 8H
COMPILATION ENGAGEMENT PROGRAM

Use the following procedures as a guide for performing a compilation of a specified element. This compilation program is only a guide; professional judgment should be exercised to determine whether the procedures in this program should be adding to or revised.

Initial and date each procedure as it is completed. If a procedure is not relevant to this particular compilation engagement, place "N/A" (not applicable) in the space provided for initials and cross-reference the omitted procedure to another workpaper that explains why it was omitted.

Client Name: ______________________________

Date of Presentation: ______________________________

	Initials	Date
1. Acquire an adequate understanding of the accounting principles and practices of the client's industry.	____	____
2. Develop a general understanding of the nature of the client's business transactions.	____	____
3. Develop a general understanding of the stated qualifications of the client's accounting personnel.	____	____
4. Develop a general understanding of the accounting basis used to prepare the specified element.	____	____
5. Develop a general understanding of the form and content of the specified element.	____	____
6. Consider whether other professional services are needed in order to complete the compilation engagement.	____	____
7. If any evidence or information regarding fraud or an illegal act that may have occurred is discovered:		
a. Request that management consider the effect of the matter on the specified element and	____	____
b. Consider the effect of the matter on the compilation report.	____	____
8. Read the specified element.	____	____
9. On the basis of information collected using other compilation procedures and/or information that otherwise has come to our attention, consider whether additional or revised information must be obtained.	____	____
10. Other compilation procedures used:	____	____

____

____

____

Reviewed by: ______________________________

Date: ____________

APPENDIX 8I
AUDITOR'S REPORT ON ACCOUNTS RECEIVABLE

Independent Auditor's Report

[*for accounting firms registered with the PCAOB, the title should read* "Report of Independent Registered Public Accounting Firm"]

Board of Directors and Stockholders
ABC Company

We have audited the accompanying schedule of accounts receivable of ABC Company as of December 31, 20X2. This schedule is the responsibility of the Company's management. Our responsibility is to express an opinion on this schedule based on our audit.

We conducted our audit in accordance with auditing standards generally accepted in the United States of America [*for audits performed in accordance with PCAOB standards,* "in accordance with the standards of the Public Company Accounting Oversight Board (United States)"]. Those standards require that we plan and perform the audit to obtain reasonable assurance about whether the schedule of accounts receivable is free of material misstatement. An audit includes examining, on a test basis, evidence supporting the amounts and disclosures in the schedule of accounts receivable. An audit also includes assessing the accounting principles used and significant estimates made by management, as well as evaluating the overall schedule presentation. We believe that our audit provides a reasonable basis for our opinion.

In our opinion, the schedule of accounts receivable referred to above presents fairly, in all material respects, the accounts receivable of ABC Company as of December 31, 20X2, in conformity with accounting principles generally accepted in the United States of America.

[*signature*]

[*city and state for U.S. auditors; city and country for non-U.S. auditors*]

[*date*]

APPENDIX 8J
AUDITOR'S REPORT ON AMOUNT OF SALES FOR THE PURPOSE OF COMPUTING RENTAL

Independent Auditor's Report

[*for accounting firms registered with the PCAOB, the title should read* "Report of Independent Registered Public Accounting Firm"]

Board of Directors and Stockholders
XYZ Stores Corporation

We have audited the accompanying schedule of gross sales (as defined in the lease agreement dated March 4, 20X1, between ABC Company, as lessor, and XYZ Stores Corporation, as lessee) of XYZ Stores Corporation at its Main Street store, [*city*], [*state*], for the year ended December 31, 20X2. This schedule is the responsibility of XYZ Stores Corporation's management. Our responsibility is to express an opinion on this schedule based on our audit.

We conducted our audit in accordance with auditing standards generally accepted in the United States of America [*for audits performed in accordance with PCAOB standards,* "in accordance with the standards of the Public Company Accounting Oversight Board (United States)"]. Those standards require that we plan and perform the audit to obtain reasonable assurance about whether the schedule of gross sales is free of material misstatement. An audit includes examining, on a test basis, evidence supporting the amounts and disclosures in the schedule of gross sales. An audit also includes assessing the accounting principles used and significant estimates made by management, as well as evaluating the overall schedule presentation. We believe that our audit provides a reasonable basis for our opinion.

In our opinion, the schedule of gross sales referred to above presents fairly, in all material respects, the gross sales of XYZ Stores Corporation at its Main Street store, [*city*], [*state*], for the year ended December 31, 20X2, as defined in the lease agreement referred to in the first paragraph.

This report is intended solely for the information and use of the boards of directors and managements of XYZ Stores Corporation and ABC Company and is not intended to be and should not be used by anyone other than these specified parties.

[*signature*]

[*city and state for U.S. auditors; city and country for non-U.S. auditors*]

[*date*]

APPENDIX 8K
AUDITOR'S REPORT ON ROYALTIES

Independent Auditor's Report

[*for accounting firms registered with the PCAOB, the title should read* "Report of Independent Registered Public Accounting Firm"]

Board of Directors and Stockholders
ABC Company

We have audited the accompanying schedule of royalties applicable to engine production of the Q Division of ABC Company for the year ended December 31, 20X2, under the terms of a license agreement dated May 14, 20X1, between XYZ Corporation and ABC Company. This schedule is the responsibility of ABC Company's management. Our responsibility is to express an opinion on this schedule based on our audit.

We conducted our audit in accordance with auditing standards generally accepted in the United States of America [*for audits performed in accordance with PCAOB standards,* "in accordance with the standards of the Public Company Accounting Oversight Board (United States)"]. Those standards require that we plan and perform the audit to obtain reasonable assurance about whether the schedule of royalties is free of material misstatement. An audit includes examining, on a test basis, evidence supporting the amounts and disclosures in the schedule of royalties. An audit also includes assessing the accounting principles used and significant estimates made by management, as well as evaluating the overall schedule presentation. We believe that our audit provides a reasonable basis for our opinion.

We have been informed that, under ABC Company's interpretation of the agreement referred to in the first paragraph, royalties were based on the number of engines produced after giving effect to a reduction for production retirements that were scrapped but without a reduction for field returns that were scrapped, even though the field returns were replaced with new engines without charge to customers.

In our opinion, the schedule of royalties referred to above presents fairly, in all material respects, the number of engines produced by the Q Division of ABC Company during the year ended December 31, 20X2, and the amount of royalties applicable thereto, under the license agreement referred to above.

This report is intended solely for the information and use of the boards of directors and managements of ABC Company and XYZ Corporation and is not intended to be and should not be used by anyone other than these specified parties.

[*signature*]

[*city and state for U.S. auditors; city and country for non-U.S. auditors*]

[*date*]

APPENDIX 8L
AUDITOR'S REPORT ON PROFIT PARTICIPATION

Independent Auditor's Report

[*for accounting firms registered with the PCAOB, the title should read* "Report of Independent Registered Public Accounting Firm"]

Board of Directors and Stockholders
ABC Company

We have audited, in accordance with auditing standards generally accepted in the United States of America, the financial statements of ABC Company for the year ended December 31, 20X2, and have issued our report thereon dated March 5, 20X3. We have also audited ABC Company's schedule of John Smith's profit participation for the year ended December 31, 20X2. This schedule is the responsibility of the Company's management. Our responsibility is to express an opinion on this schedule based on our audit.

We conducted our audit of the schedule in accordance with auditing standards generally accepted in the United States of America [*for audits performed in accordance with PCAOB standards,* "in accordance with the standards of the Public Company Accounting Oversight Board (United States)"]. Those standards require that we plan and perform the audit to obtain reasonable assurance about whether the schedule of profit participation is free of material misstatement. An audit includes examining, on a test basis, evidence supporting the amounts and disclosures in the schedule. An audit also includes assessing the accounting principles used and significant estimates made by management, as well as evaluating the overall schedule presentation. We believe that our audit provides a reasonable basis for our opinion.

We have been informed that the documents that govern the determination of John Smith's profit participation are (a) the employment agreement between John Smith and ABC Company dated February 1, 20X1, (b) the production and distribution agreement between ABC Company and Television Network Incorporated dated March 1, 20X1, and (c) the studio facilities agreement between ABC Company and QRX Studios dated April 1, 20X1, as amended November 1, 20X1.

In our opinion, the schedule of profit participation referred to above presents fairly, in all material respects, John Smith's participation in the profits of ABC Company for the year ended December 31, 20X2, in accordance with the provisions of the agreements referred to above.

This report is intended solely for the information and use of the boards of directors and managements of ABC Company and John Smith and is not intended to be and should not be used by anyone other than these specified parties.

[*signature*]

[*city and state for U.S. auditors; city and country for non-U.S. auditors*]

[*date*]

APPENDIX 8M
AUDITOR'S REPORT ON FEDERAL AND STATE INCOME TAXES INCLUDED IN FINANCIAL STATEMENTS

Independent Auditor's Report

[*for accounting firms registered with the PCAOB, the title should read* "Report of Independent Registered Public Accounting Firm"]

Board of Directors and Stockholders
ABC Company

We have audited, in accordance with auditing standards generally accepted in the United States of America, the financial statements of ABC Company for the year ended June 30, 20X2, and have issued our report thereon dated August 13, 20X2. We have also audited the current and deferred provision for the Company's federal and state income taxes for the year ended June 30, 20X2, included in those financial statements, and the related asset and liability tax accounts as of June 30, 20X2. This income tax information is the responsibility of the Company's management. Our responsibility is to express an opinion on it based on our audit.

We conducted our audit of the income tax information in accordance with auditing standards generally accepted in the United States of America [*for audits performed in accordance with PCAOB standards,* "in accordance with the standards of the Public Company Accounting Oversight Board (United States)"]. Those standards require that we plan and perform the audit to obtain reasonable assurance about whether the federal and state income tax accounts are free of material misstatement. An audit includes examining, on a test basis, evidence supporting the amounts and disclosures related to the federal and state income tax accounts. An audit also includes assessing the accounting principles used and significant estimates made by management, as well as evaluating the overall presentation of the federal and state income tax accounts. We believe that our audit provides a reasonable basis for our opinion.

In our opinion, the Company has paid or, in all material respects, made adequate provision in the financial statements referred to above for the payment of all federal and state income taxes and for related deferred income taxes that could be reasonably estimated at the time of our audit of the financial statements of ABC Company for the year ended June 30, 20X2.

[*signature*]

[*city and state for U.S. auditors; city and country for non-U.S. auditors*]

[*date*]

APPENDIX 8N
COMPILATION REPORT ON ACCOUNTS RECEIVABLE

Board of Directors and Stockholders
XYZ Company

I (we) have compiled the accompanying schedule of accounts receivable of XYZ Company as of December 31, 20XX, in accordance with Statements on Standards for Accounting and Review Services issued by the American Institute of Certified Public Accountants.

A compilation is limited to presenting financial information that is the representation of management (owners). I (we) have not audited or reviewed the accompanying schedule of accounts receivable and, accordingly, do not express an opinion or any other form of assurance on it.

[*signature*]

[*date*]

APPENDIX 8O
COMPILATION REPORT ON A SCHEDULE OF DEPRECIATION: INCOME TAX BASIS

Board of Directors and Stockholders
XYZ Company

I (we) have compiled the accompanying schedule of depreciation—income tax basis of XYZ Company as of December 31, 20XX, in accordance with Statements on Standards for Accounting and Review Services issued by the American Institute of Certified Public Accountants. The schedule of depreciation—income tax basis has been prepared on the accounting basis used by the Company for federal income tax purposes, which is a comprehensive basis of accounting other than generally accepted accounting principles.

A compilation is limited to presenting financial information that is the representation of management (owners). I (we) have not audited or reviewed the accompanying schedule of depreciation—income tax basis and, accordingly, do not express an opinion or any other form of assurance on it.

[*signature*]

[*date*]

CHAPTER 9
AGREED-UPON PROCEDURES ENGAGEMENTS

CONTENTS

OVERVIEW

This chapter discusses the agreed-upon procedures engagement. Conditions for engagement acceptance are covered, along with specific engagement performance requirements. In addition, reporting requirements are discussed, including standard and common examples of the agreed-upon procedures report.

INTRODUCTION

Definition of an Agreed-Upon Procedures Engagement

An agreed-upon procedures engagement is one in which a practitioner is engaged by a client to issue a report of findings based on specific procedures performed on subject matter. The client engages the practitioner to assist specified parties in evaluating subject matter or an assertion as a result of a need or needs of the specified parties. Because the specified parties require that findings be independently derived, the services of a practitioner are obtained to perform procedures and report on his or her findings. The specified parties and the practitioner agree upon the procedures to be performed. These are the procedures that the specified parties believe are appropriate. Because the needs of the specified parties can vary widely, the nature, timing, and extent of the procedures can vary as well. Consequently, the specified parties assume responsibility for the sufficiency of the procedures since they best understand their own needs.

In an agreed-upon procedures engagement, the practitioner does not perform an examination or a review and does not provide an opinion or negative assurance. Instead, the practitioner's report should be in the form of procedures and findings.

When the SSAEs Apply

SSAE-10 Chapter 2 (AT 201) (Agreed-Upon Procedures Engagements) sets forth the standards and provides the guidance concerning performance and reporting in all agreed-upon procedures engagements. The practitioner should also refer to the following chapters of SSAE-10, which provide additional guidance for certain types of agreed-upon procedures engagements:

- SSAE-10 Chapter 6 (AT 601) (Compliance Attestation), which is discussed in Chapter 10, "Compliance Engagements."
- SSAE-10 Chapter 3 (AT 301) (Financial Forecasts and Projections), which is discussed in Chapter 13, "Prospective Financial Information."

Major Changes from Previous Standards

The principal differences between the current Chapter 2 of SSAE-10 (AT 201) and the previous guidance on agreed-upon procedures engagements (which was contained in SSAE-4) are that the new standard

- Does not require a written assertion from the responsible party.
- Covers engagements to apply agreed-upon procedures to elements, accounts, or items of a financial statement (prior to SSAE-10, these engagements were covered by the now withdrawn SAS-75).
- Changes the elements of the standard reports to conform to those elsewhere in the attestation standards.

OBSERVATION: Prior to the issuance of SSAE-10, agreed-upon procedures engagements were covered by two separate standards. SAS-75 (Applying Agreed-Upon Procedures to Specified Elements, Accounts, or Items of a Financial Statement) covered agreed-upon procedures applied to elements, accounts, or items of a financial statement. SAS-75 allowed the practitioner to perform the engagement without obtaining a separate written assertion. SSAE-4 covered the application of agreed-upon procedures to all other types of data. Because SSAE-10 revised SSAE-4 to eliminate the principal differences between that standard and SAS-75, particularly the requirement in SSAE-4 for a separate written assertion, two separate standards were no longer needed. Consequently, SAS-93 (AU 315, AU 411, AU 508, AU 622) (Omnibus Statement on Auditing Standards—2000) withdrew SAS-75. Chapter 2 of SSAE-10 now covers all agreed-upon procedures engagements.

Definitions and Terms

Several key terms are used in the definition of an agreed-upon procedures engagement that the CPA must understand.

Subject Matter

The subject matter of an agreed-upon procedures engagement may take many different forms and it may be at a single point in time or cover a period of time. In an agreed-upon procedures engagement, it is to the specific subject matter that the agreed-upon procedures are applied using the criteria selected. Even though the procedures are agreed upon between the practitioner and the specified parties, the subject matter and criteria must still meet the conditions set forth in the third general standard:

> The practitioner shall perform the engagement only if he or she has reason to believe that the subject matter is capable of evaluation against criteria that are suitable and available to users.

See Chapter 5, "Planning and Administration for Attestation Engagements," for a discussion of criteria and the characteristics of suitability and availability. The criteria against which the specific subject matter needs to be measured may be recited within the procedures enumerated or referred to in the practitioner's report.

Assertion

An assertion is any declaration or set of declarations about whether the subject matter is based on or in conformity with the criteria selected. A written assertion is generally not required in an agreed-upon procedures engagement unless it is specifically required by another attest standard (for example, compliance attestation or engagements related to management's discussion and analysis).

> **OBSERVATION:** If the practitioner requests the responsible party to provide an assertion, the assertion may be presented in a representation letter or another written communication from the responsible party, such as in a statement, narrative description, or schedule appropriately identifying what is being presented and the point in time or the period of time covered.

Specified Parties

The client engages the practitioner to assist other interested parties in evaluating subject matter or an assertion as a result of a need or needs of the parties. The parties, including the client, are referred to as "specified parties." As a consequence of the role of the specified parties in agreeing upon the procedures performed or to be performed, a practitioner's report on such engagements should clearly state that its use is restricted to those specified parties.

Responsible Party

The responsible party is someone other than the practitioner who takes responsibility for the subject matter. The responsible party is defined as the person or persons, either as individuals or as representatives of the entity, responsible for the subject matter. In other words, this is the party who will be held accountable for the subject matter. The responsible party might or might not be the practitioner's client.

When to Perform an Agreed-Upon Procedures Engagement

Like other attestation engagements, an agreed-upon procedures engagement is appropriate for situations where users want information on subject matter that is nonfinancial or not in the form of a financial statement. (Financial statement audits and reviews provide assurance on a set of financial statements.) However, certain engagements are specifically excluded from the standards for agreed-upon procedures.

Exhibit 9-1 provides examples of situations in which an agreed-upon procedures engagement would be appropriate. Exhibit 9-2 summarizes engagements that are excluded from agreed-upon procedures.

EXHIBIT 9-1
SITUATIONS IN WHICH AN AGREED-UPON PROCEDURES ENGAGEMENT MIGHT BE APPROPRIATE

Nature of the Subject Matter	Users may desire information about
Nonfinancial	• Qualities of the documentation supporting loans in a loan portfolio • Effectiveness of internal controls • Quantity of inventory on hand • Dimensions of an asset
Financial	• Existence of documentation supporting revenue recognized during the period • Accuracy of an inventory report • Aging of accounts receivable • Amount of cash held by an organization

EXHIBIT 9-2
ENGAGEMENTS EXCLUDED FROM THE STANDARDS FOR AGREED-UPON PROCEDURES

Excluded Engagement	Source of Authoritative Guidance
Specified compliance requirements based solely on an audit	SAS-62 (AU 623) (Special Reports)
Compliance auditing in audits of governmental entities and recipients of governmental financial assistance	SAS-74 (AU 801) (Compliance Auditing Considerations in Audits of Governmental Entities and Recipients of Governmental Financial Assistance)
Reporting on service organizations	SAS-70 (AU 324) (Service Organizations)
Letters for underwriters	SAS-72 (AU 634) (Letters for Underwriters and Certain Other Requesting Parties)
Consulting engagements	SSCS-1 (CS 100) (Consulting Services—Definitions and Standards)

Agreed-Upon Procedures Engagement versus a Consulting Engagement

When a practitioner is engaged by a client to perform certain procedures, the practitioner might be unsure of whether the engagement should be structured as an agreed-upon procedures engagement or a consulting engagement. Because the standards for performing the two types of engagements are very different, it is important that the engagement be structured appropriately. Most clients are not familiar with the differences in the two types of engagements and the practitioner must explain the types of available services and assist the client in determining the best type of service that suits the client's needs.

In determining the most appropriate type of engagement, the practitioner should consider both the needs of the client and the conditions for engagement performance. Generally, in an agreed-upon procedures engagement, the practitioner is engaged to perform procedures that add reliability to the subject matter. Although the practitioner does not provide assurance on the subject matter, the client and other specified parties usually expect enhanced credibility of the subject matter, because of the procedures performed. In addition, a consulting engagement usually involves only two parties—the practitioner and the client (although the consulting standards do not prohibit use by third parties). In an agreed-upon procedures engagement, there are usually three parties involved—the practitioner, the responsible party (which might or might not be the client), and other interested parties (the specified parties in the report).

In general, if any of the following is true, an attestation engagement (such as an agreed-upon procedures engagement) should be performed:

- Users require an attestation engagement
- There is a third-party user of the report
- The engagement can easily be structured to meet the attestation requirements

ENGAGEMENT PLANNING AND ADMINISTRATION

Appropriateness of Procedures

The procedures that the practitioner and specified parties agree upon may be as limited or as extensive as the specified parties desire. However, mere reading of an assertion or specified information about the subject matter does not constitute a procedure sufficient to allow the practitioner to report on the results of applying agreed-upon procedures. In addition, the practitioner should not agree to perform procedures that are overly subjective and thus possibly open to varying interpretations. Terms of uncertain meaning (such as "general review," "limited review," "check," or "test") should not be used in describing the procedures unless such terms are defined within the agreed-upon procedures.

Engagement Acceptance

The general, fieldwork, and reporting standards for attestation engagements as discussed in Chapter 5, "Planning and Administration for Attestation Engagements," together with interpretive guidance regarding their application as addressed throughout Chapter 2 of SSAE-10 (AT 201) should be followed by the practitioner. Chapter 2 of SSAE-10 (AT 201.06) also sets forth several conditions that must exist whenever a practitioner performs an agreed-upon procedures engagement.

Conditions

The practitioner may perform an agreed-upon procedures engagement provided that

- The practitioner is independent.
- One of the following conditions is met:
  - The party wishing to engage the practitioner is responsible for the subject matter or has a reasonable basis for providing a written assertion about the subject matter when the nature of the subject matter is such that a responsible party does not otherwise exist (see discussion in Chapter 5, "Planning and Administration for Attestation Engagements").
  - The party wishing to engage the practitioner is not responsible for the subject matter but is able to provide the practitioner, or have a third party who is responsible for the subject matter provide the practitioner, with evidence of the third party's responsibility for the subject matter.
- The practitioner and the specified parties agree upon the procedures performed or to be performed by the practitioner.
- The specified parties take responsibility for the sufficiency of the agreed-upon procedures for their purposes.
- The specific subject matter to which the procedures are to be applied is subject to reasonably consistent measurement.
- Criteria to be used in the determination of findings are agreed upon between the practitioner and the specified parties.

- The procedures to be applied to the specific subject matter are expected to result in reasonably consistent findings using the criteria.
- Evidential matter related to the specified subject matter that the procedures are applied to is expected to exist to provide a reasonable basis for expressing the findings in the practitioner's report.
- Where applicable, the practitioner and the specified parties agree on any materiality limits for reporting purposes.
- Use of the report is restricted to the specified parties.
- For agreed-upon procedures engagements on prospective financial information, the prospective financial statements include a summary of significant assumptions (see Chapter 13, "Prospective Financial Information").

Assessment of Required Services

It is important for the practitioner to discuss the engagement with the prospective client to become familiar with the services that will be required. This allows the practitioner to consider whether the firm is capable of performing the required level of service. This discussion should include consideration of the following:

- *Nature of the procedures* Are the procedures appropriate for an agreed-upon procedures engagement? Are the procedures too subjective? Would a consulting engagement more appropriately meet the needs of the client?
- *Use of the report* How will the report be used and by whom? Are all specified parties identified?
- *Type of engagement* Does the client understand the differences in scope, levels of assurance, and costs associated with examinations, reviews, and agreed-upon procedures engagements?
- *Timing* Is the report needed by a particular date to meet the client's needs? Does the practitioner have the resources needed to meet the client's reporting deadlines?

Competence

The first general standard requires the practitioner to have adequate technical training and proficiency in the attest function. Performing attest services is different from simply preparing and presenting subject matter or an assertion, which involves collecting, classifying, summarizing, and communicating information, a process that usually entails reducing a mass of detailed data to a manageable and understandable form. Attest services, on the other hand, involve gathering evidence to support the subject matter or the assertion and objectively assessing the measurements and communications of the responsible party.

In addition, the second general standard requires that the practitioner have adequate knowledge of the subject matter. This knowledge can be obtained through formal or continuing education or through practical experience. Knowledge of the subject matter varies with the type of engagement, from common sense to complex subjects, such as actuarial data. In general, the knowledge of the subject matter should be sufficient to allow the practitioner to form an objective conclusion about it.

SSAE-10 (AT 101.22) clarifies that the practitioner does not have to personally acquire all of the knowledge in the subject matter to be qualified to apply agreed-upon procedures to the subject matter. The knowledge requirement can be met in part through the use of one or more specialists on a particular engagement if the practitioner has sufficient knowledge of the subject matter to:

- Communicate the objectives of the work to the specialist; and
- Evaluate the specialist's work to determine whether objectives were met.

See also the discussion later in this chapter concerning the involvement of specialists in an agreed-upon procedures engagement.

Independence

Independence is the foundation of the attest function. Third-party users rely on the CPA's opinion in an audit or attest engagement because they believe the conclusion is impartial and unbiased. Chapter 1 of SSAE-10 (AT 101.36) states, "The practitioner should maintain the intellectual honesty and impartiality necessary to reach an unbiased conclusion about the subject matter or the assertion."

In the final analysis, independence in mental attitude means objective consideration of facts, unbiased judgments, and honest neutrality on the part of the CPA in forming and expressing conclusions. Independence in mental attitude presumes an undeviating concern for an unbiased conclusion about the subject matter or an assertion no matter what the subject matter or assertion may be.

Subject Matter, Criteria, and Procedures

The agreed-upon procedures should be applied to the specific subject matter using the criteria selected. Even though the procedures are agreed upon between the practitioner and the specified parties, the engagement should be performed only if the subject matter is capable of evaluation against criteria that are suitable and available to users. However, in an agreed-upon procedures engagement, the criteria merely have to be agreed upon between the practitioner and the specified parties. Chapter 1 of SSAE-10 (AT 101.31) states that

> Some criteria may be suitable for only a limited number of parties who either participated in their establishment or can be presumed to have an adequate understanding of the criteria . . . Such criteria can be agreed upon directly by the parties or through a designated representative.

Therefore, the practitioner can evaluate the subject matter against any criteria that the specified parties find useful for their purposes, keeping in mind that the report must be restricted to the used of the specified parties.

Establishing the Terms of the Engagement

Chapter 2 of SSAE-10 (AT 201.10) requires the practitioner to establish an understanding with the client regarding the services to be performed. That understanding should include the following:

- The nature of the engagement. The practitioner should address the nature of the engagement and any limitations of the engagement. For example, the nature of an agreed-upon procedures engagement is to present the results of applying agreed-upon procedures to specific subject matter in the form of findings.
- Identification of the subject matter, the responsible party, and the criteria to be used.
- Identification of specified parties.
- Specified parties' acknowledgement of their responsibility for the sufficiency of the procedures.
- Practitioner's responsibilities. The practitioner's responsibility is to carry out the procedures and report the findings in accordance with the general, fieldwork, and reporting standards.
- Reference to attestation standards established by the American Institute of Certified Public Accountants.
- Agreement on procedures by enumerating (or referring to) the procedures.
- Disclaimers expected to be included in the practitioner's report.
- Use restrictions.

- Assistance to be provided to the practitioner. The practitioner should determine whether the client has the necessary personnel and expertise to develop the subject matter. In addition, this understanding should include arrangements concerning the conduct of the engagement, such as timing, client assistance, and the availability of documents.
- Involvement of a specialist.
- Agreed-upon materiality limits.

Engagement Letters

The attestation standards require the practitioner to establish an understanding with the client. The standards state that a written engagement letter is preferred but not required. Although not specifically required by the SSAEs, a written engagement letter is strongly recommended. Most practitioners believe that a written engagement letter can effectively reduce misunderstandings between the practitioner and the client over the nature and limitations of the engagement. Engagement letters are particularly important in attestation engagements because of the increased risk of misunderstanding the nature of the practitioner's responsibilities (while clients may be familiar with traditional financial statement audits, they might not understand the nature and limitations of attestation engagements). The written engagement letter commonly includes the items discussed in the preceding section. Appendix 9A is an illustrative engagement letter for an agreed-upon procedures engagement. When a written engagement letter is not obtained, the understanding of the engagement should be obtained and documented in the workpapers.

> **OBSERVATION:** When a written engagement letter is used, it should be addressed to the client, and in some circumstances also to all specified parties.

Agreement on and Sufficiency of Procedures

To satisfy the requirements that the practitioner and the specified parties agree upon the procedures performed or to be performed and that the specified parties take responsibility for the sufficiency of the agreed-upon procedures for their purposes, ordinarily the practitioner should communicate directly with and obtain affirmative acknowledgement from each of the specified parties.

> **OBSERVATION:** This agreement may be accomplished by meeting with the specified parties or by distributing a draft of

the anticipated report or a copy of an engagement letter to the specified parties and obtaining their agreement.

If the practitioner is not able to communicate directly with all of the specified parties, he or she may satisfy these requirements by applying any one or more of the following or similar procedures:

- Compare the procedures to be applied and written requirements of the specified parties.
- Discuss the procedures to be applied with appropriate representatives of the specified parties.
- Review relevant contracts with or correspondence from the specified parties.

The practitioner should not report on an engagement when specified parties do not agree upon the procedures performed or to be performed and do not take responsibility for the sufficiency of the procedures for their purposes.

See Appendix 9C for an illustrative letter that may be used to request the specified parties' comments on the agreed-upon procedures.

Case Study 9-1: Agreement on Sufficiency of Procedures

Facts

A staff person of the firm sends the following e-mail to the partner in charge of attestation engagements:

> I got a voice mail message from a potential client today who said he wanted one of our reports "just like the one you did for Chandler Corporation across the street." When I returned the call and asked him what he wanted us to do he said, "Just do the usual stuff. I'm sure that whatever you did for Chandler Corp. was fine. We need the same thing." When I asked him whether he had seen the report we issued for Chandler Corp., he said, "No."

Analysis

The firm should not begin this engagement. The attestation standards require that the practitioner establish a clear understanding with the client regarding the procedures to be performed. What is described in the e-mail is not sufficient. Instead, the specified parties must

- Agree to the procedures to be performed; and
- Take responsibility for the sufficiency of these procedures.

Typically, this understanding is established in writing. The receipt of a rather vague e-mail from a potential client does not satisfy this requirement.

Adding Specified Parties

Subsequent to the completion of an agreed-upon procedures engagement, the practitioner may be asked to consider the addition of another party as a specified party (referred to as a "nonparticipant party"). The practitioner may agree to add a nonparticipant party based on the consideration of such factors as the identity of the nonparticipant party and the intended use of the report.

> **OBSERVATION:** When considering whether to add a nonparticipant party, the guidance in SAS-1 (AU 530) (Dating of the Independent Auditor's Report) is helpful.

If the practitioner does agree to add the nonparticipant party, he or she should obtain affirmative acknowledgement, preferably in writing, from the nonparticipant party agreeing to the procedures performed and of its taking responsibility for the sufficiency of the procedures. If the nonparticipant party is added after the report is issued, the report may be reissued or the practitioner may provide other written acknowledgement that the nonparticipant party has been added as a specified party. If the practitioner provides written acknowledgement that the nonparticipant party has been added as a specified party, such written acknowledgement should state that no additional procedures have been performed subsequent to the date of the report.

The illustrative letter in Appendix 9C, "Request for Specified Party's Comments on Procedures," may be used to obtain affirmative acknowledgement from the nonparticipant party of responsibility and sufficiency of procedures.

> **OBSERVATION:** If the report is reissued, the original report date should not be changed.

ENGAGEMENT PERFORMANCE

Designing Procedures

The specified parties are responsible for the sufficiency (nature, timing, and extent) of the agreed-upon procedures because they best understand their own needs. The specified parties assume the risk that such procedures might be insufficient for their purposes. In addition, the specified parties assume the risk that they might misunderstand or otherwise inappropriately use the findings properly reported by the practitioner.

The practitioner assumes the risk that misapplication of the procedures might result in the reporting of inappropriate findings. Furthermore, the practitioner assumes the risk that appropriate findings might not be reported or might be reported inaccurately. The practitioner's risks can be reduced through adequate planning and supervision and due professional care in performing the procedures, determining the findings, and preparing the report.

The practitioner has no responsibility to determine the differences between the agreed-upon procedures to be performed and the procedures that the practitioner would have determined to be necessary had he or she been engaged to perform another form of attest engagement. The procedures that the practitioner agrees to perform may be more or less extensive than the procedures that he or she would determine to be necessary to perform another form of engagement.

Appropriate Procedures

The procedures that the practitioner and the specified parties agree upon may be as limited or as extensive as the specified parties desire. In some circumstances, the procedures evolve or are modified over the course of the engagement. The practitioner may want to consider using an addendum to the agreement reached in the original engagement letter to document the modified or additional procedures. Appendix 9B is an illustrative engagement letter addendum. In general, there is flexibility in determining the procedures as long as the specified parties acknowledge responsibility for the sufficiency of such procedures for their purposes. Matters that should be agreed upon include the nature, timing, and extent of the procedures.

The practitioner should obtain evidential matter by applying the agreed-upon procedures to provide a reasonable basis for the finding or findings expressed in his or her report, but he or she need not perform additional procedures outside the scope of the engagement to gather additional evidential matter.

Examples of appropriate procedures are as follows:

- Execution of a sampling application after agreeing on relevant parameters.
- Inspection of specified documents evidencing certain types of transactions or detailed attributes thereof.
- Confirmation of specific information with third parties.
- Comparison of documents, schedules, or analyses with certain specified attributes.

- Performance of specific procedures on work performed by others (including the work of internal auditors).
- Performance of mathematical computations.

Inappropriate Procedures

The procedures that the practitioner and specified parties agree upon may be as limited or as extensive as the specified parties desire. However, mere reading of an assertion or specified information about the subject matter does not constitute a procedure sufficient to permit a practitioner to report on the results of applying agreed-upon procedures. In addition, the practitioner should not agree to perform procedures that are overly subjective and thus possibly open to varying interpretations. Terms of uncertain meaning (such as "general review," "limited review," "check," or "test") should not be used in describing the procedures unless such terms are defined within the agreed-upon procedures.

The following are examples of inappropriate procedures:

- Mere reading of the work performed by others solely to describe their findings.
- Evaluating the competency or objectivity of another party.
- Obtaining an understanding about a particular subject.
- Interpreting documents outside the scope of the practitioner's professional expertise.

Case Study 9-2: Appropriateness of Procedures

The procedures performed in an agreed-upon procedures engagement must be precisely defined in a way that leaves no room for any misunderstanding or any other interpretation. The following table lists examples of inappropriate procedures and more appropriate revisions of these procedures:

Inappropriate	More Appropriate
Test year-end shipping cutoff for propriety.	Inspect shipping dates for a sample (agreed-upon) of specified shipping documents. Determine whether any such dates were subsequent to year-end.
Check accounts receivable aging for proper calculation.	Compare the amounts of invoices included in each column of accounts receivable aging of a specific customer as of a certain

	date to the amount and invoice date shown on the outstanding invoice. Recalculate the number of days outstanding and compare this calculation to the description at the top of the column.
Review client's calculation of debt covenant ratios.	Calculate the specified debt covenant ratios (according to an agreed-upon formula) and verify that the resulting ratios agree to those reported in a specified schedule.

Materiality

The concept of materiality is normally not relevant in an agreed-upon procedures engagement. In an agreed-upon procedures engagement, the practitioner is engaged to perform specific procedures that are requested by the specified parties and the practitioner should report all findings from application of these procedures. Materiality levels used in performing the procedures should be determined by the specified parties, agreed to in the engagement letter, and described in the practitioner's report.

Knowledge of Matters Outside of the Agreed-Upon Procedures

The practitioner need not perform procedures beyond the agreed-upon procedures. However, in connection with the application of the agreed-upon procedures, if matters come to the practitioner's attention by other means that significantly contradict the subject matter (or the written assertion) referred to in the practitioner's report, the practitioner should include that matter in his or her report.

Matters Outside of the Agreed-Upon Procedures

In the course of applying agreed-upon procedures regarding an entity's system of internal control, the practitioner becomes aware of a material weakness by means other than performance of the agreed-upon procedures. In this case, the practitioner should include this matter in his or her report.

Reference to the Modified Audit Report

Assume the practitioner has audited the entity's financial statements and that the auditor's report on the financial statements includes a departure from a standard report. If the practitioner is performing agreed-upon procedures on an element, account, or item of a financial statement which relate to the audited financial statements, he or she should consider including a reference to the auditor's report and the departure from the standard report in his or her agreed-upon procedures report.

Change in Type of Engagement

A practitioner who has been engaged to perform another form of attest engagement or a nonattest service engagement might, before the engagement's completion, be requested to change the engagement to an agreed-upon procedures engagement. A request to change the engagement might result from a change in circumstances affecting the client's requirements, a misunderstanding about the nature of the original services or the alternative services originally available, or a restriction on the performance of the original engagement, whether imposed by the client or caused by circumstances.

Before a practitioner changes the engagement to an agreed-upon procedures engagement, he or she should consider the following:

- The possibility that certain procedures performed as part of another type of engagement are not appropriate for inclusion in an agreed-upon procedures engagement.
- The stated reason for the request, particularly the implications of a restriction on the scope of the original engagement or the matters to be reported.
- The additional effort required to complete the original engagement.
- If applicable, the reasons for changing from a general-use report to a restricted-use report.

If the specified parties acknowledge agreement to the procedures performed or to be performed and assume responsibility for the sufficiency of the procedures to be included in the agreed-upon procedures engagement, either of the following would be considered a reasonable basis for requesting a change in the engagement:

- A change in circumstances that requires another form of engagement.
- A misunderstanding concerning the nature of the original engagement or the available alternatives.

In all circumstances, if the original engagement procedures are substantially complete or the effort to complete such procedures is relatively insignificant, the practitioner should consider the propriety of accepting a change in the engagement.

If the practitioner concludes based on his or her professional judgment that there is reasonable justification to change the engagement, and provided he or she complies with the standards applicable to an agreed-upon procedures engagement, the practitioner should issue an appropriate agreed-upon procedures report.

> **OBSERVATION:** The report should not refer to either the original engagement or the performance limitations that resulted in the changed engagement.

Documentation

Documentation of the agreed-upon procedures engagement is the principal record of procedures applied, information obtained, and findings reached by the practitioner in the engagement. The quantity, type, and content of documentation are matters of the practitioner's professional judgment. Documentation serves mainly to

- Provide the principal support for the practitioner's report, including the representation regarding observance of the standards of fieldwork, which is implicit in the reference in the report to attestation standards.
- Aid the practitioner in the conduct and supervision of the engagement.

Documentation should be sufficient to (1) enable members of the engagement team with supervision and review responsibilities to understand the nature, timing, extent, and results of procedures performed and the information obtained and (2) identify the engagement team member(s) who performed and reviewed the work.

Examples of documentation are work programs, analyses, memoranda, letters of confirmation and representation, abstracts or copies of entity documents, and schedules or commentaries prepared or obtained by the practitioner. Ordinarily, documentation includes

- Documentation of the engagement acceptance or continuance decision.
- An engagement letter.
- Documentation of how the specified parties determined the procedures to be performed.
- Documentation for planning considerations.
- Procedures checklist.
- A list of the procedures agreed to with a cross reference to documentation of performance.
- Summary of findings.
- Agreed-upon procedures report.

- A discussion of unusual matters encountered and their resolution.
- A representation letter.
- Documentation that the workpapers were reviewed.

Documentation may be in paper form, electronic form, or other media. The practitioner has an ethical, and in some situations a legal, obligation to maintain the confidentiality of client information or information of the responsible party. Because documentation often contains confidential information, the practitioner should adopt reasonable procedures to maintain the confidentiality of that information. The practitioner should also adopt reasonable procedures to prevent unauthorized access to documentation.

Representation Letters

A practitioner may find a representation letter to be a useful and practical means of obtaining representations from the responsible party. Although the attestation standards do not require a written representation letter, it is highly advisable to obtain a representation letter from the responsible party. Written representations from the responsible party ordinarily confirm representations that are explicitly or implicitly made to the practitioner, state and document the continuing appropriateness of such representations, and reduce the possibility of misunderstanding concerning the matters that are the subject of the representations. The following are examples of matters that might appear in a written representation letter:

- A statement acknowledging responsibility for the subject matter and, when applicable, the assertion.
- A statement acknowledging responsibility for selecting the criteria and for determining that the criteria are appropriate for their purposes.
- The assertion about the subject matter based on the criteria selected.
- A statement that all known matters contradicting the subject matter or the assertion and any communication from regulatory agencies affecting the subject matter or assertion have been disclosed to the practitioner.
- Availability of all records relevant to the subject matter and the agreed-upon procedures.
- Other matters as the practitioner deems appropriate.

The representation letter should be dated no earlier than the date of the practitioner's report, which should coincide with the end of fieldwork. The letter should be addressed to the practitioner and signed by members of management whom the practitioner believes are responsible for and knowledgeable, directly or through others in the organization, about the matters covered by the representations. Normally, the CEO should sign the letter. It should also be signed by the highest ranking officer under whose responsibility the subject matter falls. For example, if the subject matter is financial, the CFO should also sign the letter.

When the client is not the responsible party, the practitioner should also consider obtaining a representation letter from the client. Examples of matters that might appear in such a representation letter are as follows:

- A statement that any known events subsequent to the period (or point in time) of the subject matter being reported on that would have a material effect on the subject matter (or, if applicable, the assertion) have been disclosed to the practitioner.
- A statement acknowledging the client's responsibility for selecting the criteria.
- A statement acknowledging the client's responsibility for determining that such criteria are appropriate for its purposes.
- Other matters as the practitioner deems appropriate.

The responsible party's refusal to furnish written representations determined by the practitioner to be appropriate for the engagement constitutes a limitation on the performance of the engagement. In such circumstances, the practitioner should do one of the following:

- Disclose in his or her report the inability to obtain representations from the responsible party.
- Withdraw from the engagement.
- Change the engagement to another form of engagement.

Appendix 9F and Appendix 9G are illustrative representation letters for agreed-upon procedures engagements.

Involvement of a Specialist

In certain circumstances, it is appropriate to involve a specialist to assist the practitioner in the performance of one or more procedures. The following are examples of such circumstances:

- An attorney might provide assistance concerning the interpretation of legal terminology involving laws, regulations, rules, contracts, or grants.
- A medical specialist might provide assistance in understanding the characteristics of diagnosis codes documented in patient medical records.

- An environmental engineer might provide assistance in interpreting environmental remedial action regulatory directives that might affect the agreed-upon procedures applied to an environmental liabilities account in a financial statement.
- A geologist might provide assistance in distinguishing between varying physical characteristics of a generic minerals group related to information to which agreed-upon procedures are applied.

The practitioner and the specified parties should explicitly agree to the involvement of the specialist in the performance of an agreed-upon procedures engagement. This agreement may be reached when obtaining agreement on the procedures performed or to be performed and acknowledgement of responsibility for the sufficiency of the procedures, as discussed earlier. The practitioner's report should describe the nature of the assistance provided by the specialist.

A practitioner may agree to apply procedures to the report or work product of a specialist that does not constitute assistance by the specialist to the practitioner. For example, the practitioner may make reference to information contained in a report of a specialist in describing an agreed-upon procedure. However, it is inappropriate for the practitioner to agree to merely read the specialist's report solely to describe or repeat the findings, or to take responsibility for all or a portion of any procedures performed by a specialist or the specialist's work product.

Internal Auditors and Other Personnel

According to Chapter 2 of SSAE-10 (AT 201.22), the agreed-upon procedures to be enumerated or referred to in the practitioner's report are to be performed entirely by the practitioner. However, internal auditors or other client personnel may prepare schedules and accumulate data or provide other information for the practitioner's use in performing the agreed-upon procedures. Also, internal auditors may perform and report separately on procedures that they have carried out. Such procedures may be similar to the procedures that the practitioner performs.

A practitioner may agree to perform procedures on information documented in the workpapers of internal auditors. For example, the practitioner may agree to:

- Repeat some or all of the procedures.
- Determine whether the internal auditors' workpapers contain documentation of procedures performed and whether the findings documented in the workpapers are presented in a report prepared by the internal auditors.

However, it is inappropriate for the practitioner to:

- Agree to merely read the internal auditors' report solely to describe or repeat their findings.
- Take responsibility for all or a portion of any procedures performed by internal auditors by reporting those findings as the practitioner's own.
- Report in any manner that implies shared responsibility for the procedures with the internal auditors.

REPORTING

Content of the Report

The practitioner's report on agreed-upon procedures should be in the form of procedures and findings. The practitioner's report should contain the following elements:

- A title that includes the word "independent."
- Identification of the specified parties.
- Identification of the subject matter (or the written assertion) and the character of the engagement.
- Identification of the responsible party.
- A statement that the subject matter is the responsibility of the responsible party.
- A statement that the procedures performed were those agreed to by the specified parties identified in the report.
- A statement that the agreed-upon procedures engagement was conducted in accordance with attestation standards established by the AICPA.
- A statement that the sufficiency of the procedures is solely the responsibility of the specified parties and a disclaimer of responsibility for the sufficiency of those procedures.
- A list of the procedures performed (or reference thereto) and related findings.
- Where applicable, a description of any agreed-upon materiality limits.
- A statement that the practitioner was not engaged to and did not conduct an examination of the subject matter, the objective of which would be an expression of an opinion, a disclaimer of opinion on the subject matter, and a statement that if the practitioner had performed additional procedures, other matters might have come to his or her attention that would have been reported.

- A statement of restrictions on the use of the report because it is intended to be used solely by the specified parties.
- Where applicable, reservations or restrictions concerning procedures or findings.
- Where applicable, a description of the nature of the assistance provided by a specialist.
- The manual or printed signature of the practitioner's firm.
- The date of the report.

Appendix 9H, Appendix 9I, and Appendix 9J are illustrative reports for agreed-upon procedures engagements.

Identifying the Subject Matter

In an agreed-upon procedures engagement, the subject matter may accompany the report or be presented only in the representation letter. However, regardless of how the subject matter is presented, the report should describe the subject matter and explain that the subject matter is the responsibility of the responsible party.

Nature of Conclusions

The practitioner should present the results of applying the agreed-upon procedures to specific subject matter in the form of findings. The practitioner should report all findings from application of the agreed-upon procedures and he or she should avoid vague or ambiguous language in reporting the findings. Examples of appropriate and inappropriate descriptions of findings resulting from the application of certain agreed-upon procedures are presented in Exhibit 9-3.

EXHIBIT 9-3
DESCRIPTION OF FINDINGS

Procedures Agreed Upon	Appropriate Description of Findings	Inappropriate Description of Findings
Inspect the shipment dates for a sample (agreed-upon) of specified shipping documents and determine whether such dates were subsequent to December 31, 20XX.	No shipment dates shown on the sample of shipping documents were subsequent to December 31, 20XX.	Nothing came to my attention as a result of applying that procedure.

Procedures Agreed Upon	Appropriate Description of Findings	Inappropriate Description of Findings
Calculate the number of miles of streets paved during the year ended September 30, 20XX, shown on contractors' certificates of completion; compare the resultant number to the number in an identified chart of performance statistics.	The number of miles of streets paved in the chart of performance was X miles more than the number calculated from the contractors' certificates of completion.	The number of miles of streets paved approximated the number of miles included in the chart of performance statistics.
Calculate the rate of return on a specified investment (according to an agreed-upon formula) and verify that the resultant percentage agrees to the percentage in an identified schedule.	No exceptions were found as a result of applying the procedure.	The resultant percentage approximated the predetermined percentage in the identified schedule.
Inspect the quality standards classification codes in identified performance test documents for products produced during a specified period; compare the codes to those shown in an identified computer printout.	All classification codes inspected in the identified documents were the same as those shown in the computer printout except for the following: [List all exceptions]	All classification codes appeared to comply with such performance documents.
Trace all outstanding checks appearing on a bank reconciliation as of a certain date to checks cleared in the bank statement of the subsequent month.	All outstanding checks appearing on the bank reconciliation were cleared in the subsequent month's bank statement except for the following: [List all exceptions]	Nothing came to my attention as a result of applying the procedure.
Compare the amounts of the invoices included in the "over 90 days" column shown in an identified schedule of aged accounts receivable of a specific customer as of a	All outstanding invoice amounts agreed with the amounts shown on the schedule in the "over 90 days" column, and the dates shown on the invoices preceded the date stated on the	The outstanding invoice amounts agreed within approximation of the amounts shown on the schedule in the "over 90 days" column, and nothing came to my attention that the dates

Procedures Agreed Upon	Appropriate Description of Findings	Inappropriate Description of Findings
certain date to the amount and invoice date shown on the outstanding invoice and determine whether or not the invoice dates precede the date stated on the schedule by more than 90 days.	schedule by more than 90 days.	shown on such invoices preceded the date stated on the schedule by more than 90 days.

Negative Assurance

The practitioner should not provide negative assurance about whether a subject matter or assertion is fairly stated based on the criteria. For example, the practitioner should *not* include a statement in his or her report that "nothing came to my attention that caused me to believe that the [*identify subject matter*] is not presented based on [*identify criteria*]."

Explanatory Language

The practitioner may include explanatory language in the report. This language may include matters such as the following:

- Disclosure of stipulated facts, assumptions, or interpretations (including their source) used in the application of the agreed-upon procedures.
- Description of the condition of records, controls, or data to which the procedures were applied.
- Explanation that the practitioner has no responsibility to update his or her report.
- Explanation of sampling risk.

Restricting the Report

Chapter 2 of SSAE-10 (AT 201.04) requires that agreed-upon procedures reports be restricted. The purpose of the restriction on the use of the reports is to restrict their use to only those parties that have agreed upon the procedures performed and taken responsibility for the sufficiency of the procedures.

Subsequent Events

Events or transactions that have a material effect on the subject matter sometimes occur subsequent to the point in time or period of time of the subject matter to which procedures are being applied but prior to the date of the practitioner's report. These occurrences are referred to as "subsequent events." The practitioner has no responsibility to detect subsequent events (unless doing so is one of the procedures that have been agreed upon). However, he or she should inquire of the responsible party (and his or her client if the client is not the responsible party) as to whether they are aware of any subsequent events, through the date of the practitioner's report, that would have a material effect on the subject matter or the assertion. If the practitioner has obtained a representation letter, the letter would ordinarily include a representation concerning subsequent events.

The practitioner has no responsibility to keep informed of events subsequent to the date of his or her report. However, the practitioner may later become aware of conditions that existed at that date that might have affected the practitioner's report had he or she been aware of them. In such circumstances, the practitioner may wish to consider the guidance in AU Section 561 (Subsequent Discovery of Facts Existing at the Date of the Auditor's Report).

Scope Limitations

When circumstances impose restrictions on the performance of agreed-upon procedures, the practitioner should attempt to obtain agreement from the specified parties for modification of the agreed-upon procedures. When such agreement cannot be obtained (for example, when the agreed-upon procedures are published by a regulatory agency that will not modify the procedures), the practitioner should describe any restrictions on the performance of the procedures in his or her report or withdraw from the engagement.

APPENDIX 9A
ENGAGEMENT LETTER

[*date*]

[*name of client (and other specified parties)*]
[*address*]

We are pleased to confirm our understanding of the nature and limitations of the services we are to provide for [*client's legal name*].

We will apply agreed-upon procedures that [*specified parties have specified, listed in the attached schedule*] to [*describe subject matter or related assertion*] of [*name of *responsible party*] as of [*date*], prepared in accordance with [*criteria*]. Our engagement to apply agreed-upon procedures will be conducted in accordance with attestation standards established by the American Institute of Certified Public Accountants. The sufficiency of the procedures is solely the responsibility of those parties specified in the report. Consequently, we make no representation regarding the sufficiency of the procedures described in the attached schedule either for the purpose for which the report has been requested or for any other purpose. If, for any reason, we are unable to complete the procedures, we will describe any restrictions on the performance of the procedures in our report, or will not issue a report as a result of this engagement.

Because the agreed-upon procedures listed in the attached schedule do not constitute an examination, we will not express an opinion on [*describe subject matter*]. In addition, we have no obligation to perform any procedures beyond those listed in the attached schedule.

We will submit a report listing the procedures performed and our findings. This report is intended solely for the use of [*specified parties*], and should not be used by those who did not agree upon the procedures and take responsibility for the sufficiency of the procedures for their purposes. Our report will contain a paragraph stating that had we performed additional procedures, other matters may have come to our attention that would have been reported to you.

We plan to begin our procedures on approximately [*date*] and, unless unforeseeable problems are encountered, the engagement should be completed by [*date*]. At the conclusion of our engagement, we will require a representation letter from management that, among other things, will confirm management's responsibility for the presentation of the [*describe subject matter*] in accordance with [*describe criteria*].

We estimate that our fees for these services will range from $_____ to $_____. You will also be billed for travel and other out-of-pocket costs such as report production, typing, postage, etc. Additional expenses are estimated to be $_____. The fee estimate is based on anticipated cooperation from your personnel and the assumption that unexpected circumstances will not be encountered during the engagement. If significant additional time is necessary, we will discuss it with you and arrive at a new fee estimate before we incur the additional costs. Our invoices for these services will be rendered each month as work progresses and are payable on presentation. In accordance with our firm policies, work may be suspended if your account becomes _____ days or more overdue and will not be resumed until your account is paid in full. If we elect to terminate our services for nonpayment, our engagement will be deemed to have been completed upon written notification of termination, even if we have not completed our report. You will be obligated to compensate us for all time extended and to reimburse us for all out-of-pocket expenditures through the date of termination.

We appreciate the opportunity to be of service to you and believe this letter accurately summarizes the significant terms of our engagement. If you have any questions, please let us know. If you agree with the terms of our engagement as described in this letter, please sign the enclosed copy and return it to us. If the need for additional services arises, our agreement with you will need to be revised. It is customary for us to enumerate these revisions in an addendum to this letter. If additional specified parties of the report are added, we will require that they acknowledge in writing their responsibility for the sufficiency of the procedures.

Very truly yours,

[*CPA firm's name*]

Response

This letter correctly sets forth the understanding of [*client and other specified parties*].

By:

Title:

Date:

APPENDIX 9B ENGAGEMENT LETTER ADDENDUM

[*date*]

[*name of client (and other specified parties)*]
[*address*]

This letter constitutes an addendum to our original engagement letter dated [*date*]. The purpose of this letter is to outline additional procedures you wish us to perform in connection with that agreed-upon procedures engagement.

The additional procedures are:

[*List additional procedures.*]

All the terms of our original engagement letter will apply to this addendum. This addendum will become effective when you sign and date the original and copy of this letter and return the signed copy to us.

Very truly yours,

[*CPA firm's name*]

Response:

This letter correctly sets forth the understanding of [*name of client and other specified parties*].

By:

Title:

Date:

APPENDIX 9C
REQUEST FOR SPECIFIED PARTY'S COMMENTS ON PROCEDURES

[*date*]

[*name of client (and other specified parties)*]
[*address*]

We have been requested by [*client's legal name*] to apply agreed-upon procedures listed in the attached engagement letter. The sufficiency of the requested procedures is solely the responsibility of the specified parties of the report. Consequently, we make no representation regarding the sufficiency of the procedures for the purpose for which this report has been requested or for any other purpose.

Because the agreed-upon procedures listed in the attached engagement letter do not constitute an examination, we will not express an opinion on the [*describe subject matter*]. In addition, we have no obligation to perform any procedures that go beyond those listed in the attached engagement letter.

As a specified user of the report, please review the proposed procedures and acknowledge the sufficiency of the procedures by signing the enclosed copy of this letter and returning it to us. If the procedures are not considered to be sufficient, or are not in accordance with your understanding, please provide comments in the space provided below.

Very truly yours,

[*CPA firm's name*]

Response:

The procedures listed in the attached engagement letter are_____ (are not_____) sufficient for our purposes.

Comments:

By:

Title:

Date:

APPENDIX 9D
AGREED-UPON PROCEDURES CHECKLIST

Client Name: ______________ Date of Subject Matter: ______________
Completed by: ______________ Date Completed: ______________

	Completed by	N/A
1. Complete the Client Acceptance and Retention Evaluation Form.	_______	_______
2. If the engagement was originally intended to be another type of engagement (for example, examination, review, or consulting engagement), document the considerations of:	_______	_______
a. Whether the procedures performed as part of another type of engagement are appropriate for an agreed-upon procedures engagement.	_______	_______
b. The reasons given for the client's request to change the engagement, particularly the implications of a restriction on the scope of the original engagement.	_______	_______
c. The additional effort required to complete the original engagement.	_______	_______
d. Where applicable, any reasons for changing from a general-use report to a restricted-use report.	_______	_______
3. Communicate directly with all specified parties and obtain their acknowledgement of the sufficiency of the procedures for their purposes. If direct communication is not possible, perform one of the following procedures:	_______	_______
a. Distribute a draft of the report or a copy of the engagement letter to the specified parties and obtain their agreement.	_______	_______
b. Compare the procedures to be applied to written requirements of the specified parties.	_______	_______
c. Discuss the procedures to be applied with appropriate representatives (such as legal counsel) of the specified parties.	_______	_______
d. Review relevant contracts with or correspondence from the specified parties.	_______	_______
4. Consider the procedures being requested and determine whether those procedures are appropriate for an agreed-upon procedures engagement.	_______	_______

	Completed by	N/A
5. Establish and document an understanding with the client, preferably in an engagement letter. If an engagement letter will not be obtained, the oral understanding should be documented in a memo.	______	______
6. Obtain an understanding of the client and the engagement.	______	______
7. If the client is not the responsible party, obtain evidence of the responsible party's responsibility for the subject matter.	______	______
8. Obtain an understanding of the subject matter.	______	______
9. Perform any additional services needed to assist the responsible party in developing the subject matter or related assertion.	______	______
10. Determine that the scheduling and staffing are adequate to perform the engagement.	______	______
11. Obtain the engagement partner's approval of the overall engagement plan.	______	______
12. If other services have been performed for the responsible party, review relevant workpapers and any related reports for indications of matters that contradict the subject matter or related assertion.	______	______
13. Include in the workpapers a list of all procedures that were agreed upon in the engagement letter or a copy of the engagement letter.	______	______
14. Perform the agreed-upon procedures and summarize the findings.	______	______
15. If it is considered necessary, obtain a written assertion and a representation letter from the responsible party.	______	______
16. Draft the agreed-upon procedures report.	______	______
17. Consider other reporting issues:	______	______
a. Report all findings, unless a materiality threshold was agreed upon.	______	______
b. A description of any materiality limits that were agreed upon.	______	______
c. Reporting other matters (including subsequent events).	______	______
d. Restrictions on performance of procedures.	______	______
e. Refusal to provide a representation letter.	______	______
f. Explanations of sampling risk.	______	______

	Completed by	N/A
g. Disclosure of stipulated facts, assumptions, or interpretations used in the application of the procedures.	______	______
h. Description of the condition of records, controls, or data to which the procedures were applied.	______	______
i. Explanation that the practitioner has no responsibility to update his or her report.	______	______
j. Description of the nature of any assistance provided by a specialist.	______	______
18. If any additional specified parties are added, obtain their acknowledgement for the sufficiency of the procedures.	______	______
19. Read for inconsistencies other information in a client-prepared document that contains the agreed-upon procedures report.	______	______
20. If any situations have occurred that require consultation, determine that such consultation has been properly documented.	______	______
21. If there were differences of professional opinion among members of the engagement team or between the engagement team and a specialist, determine that the differences were properly resolved and documented.	______	______
22. Determine that all questions, exceptions, or notes, if any, posed during the engagement have been followed up and resolved.	______	______
23. Determine that all required forms, questionnaires, and checklists have been completed.	______	______
24. Ensure that the workpapers the agreed-upon procedures report have been reviewed in accordance with firm policy.	______	______
25. Obtain engagement partner's review and approval for issuance of the report.	______	______

APPENDIX 9E
AGREED-UPON PROCEDURES ENGAGEMENT: PROCEDURES AND FINDINGS FORM

Client Name: ______________ Date of Subject Matter: ______________

Completed by: ______________ Date Completed: ______________

Instructions

This form can be used to record findings as each procedure is performed. Use a separate form for each procedure performed and document each procedure and finding as precisely as possible. Include all findings in the agreed-upon procedures report (unless materiality limits have been established and agreed upon by the specified parties.

Subject matter to which the procedure was applied:

Describe procedure:

Workpaper Reference	Finding

Discussed with responsible party:

Position: Date:

APPENDIX 9F
ILLUSTRATIVE REPRESENTATION LETTER

[*date—No earlier than date of the accountant's report*]

[*name of client (and other specified parties)*]
[*address*]

In connection with your engagement to apply agreed-upon procedures to the [*describe subject matter*] as of [*date of subject matter*], we confirm, to the best of our knowledge and belief, the following representations made to you during your engagement:

- We are responsible for the presentation of [*describe subject matter*] in accordance with [*describe criteria*].
- As of [*date of subject matter*], the [*describe subject matter*] is presented in accordance with [*describe criteria*].
- We are responsible for selecting the criteria and for determining that the criteria are appropriate for our purposes.
- We have disclosed to you all information that we are aware of that may contradict the [*describe subject matter*], and we have disclosed to

you all communications from regulatory agencies affecting [*describe subject matter*].

- We have disclosed to you all events subsequent to [*date of subject matter*] that would contradict the [*describe subject matter*].
- We have made available to you all records relevant to [*describe subject matter*].
- We have responded fully to all inquiries made to us by you during the engagement.
- Your report is intended solely for the information and use of [*specified parties*] and is not intended to be and should not be used by anyone other than those specified parties.

Signature: Signature:

Title: Title:

APPENDIX 9G
CLIENT REPRESENTATION LETTER: CLIENT NOT RESPONSIBLE PARTY

[*date—No earlier than date of the accountant's report*]

[*name of client (and other specified parties)*]
[*address*]

In connection with your engagement to apply agreed-upon procedures to [*describe subject matter*] as of [*date of subject matter*], we confirm, to the best of our knowledge and belief, the following representations made to you during the course of your engagement:

- We have disclosed to you all information, including events subsequent to [*date of subject matter*] of which we are aware that would contradict the [*describe subject matter*].
- We are responsible for selecting the criteria and for determining that the criteria are appropriate for our purposes.
- We have responded fully to all inquiries made to us by you during the engagement.
- Your report is intended solely for the information and use of [*specified parties*] and is not intended to be and should not be used by anyone other than those specified parties.

Signature:

Title:

APPENDIX 9H
REPORT ON APPLYING AGREED-UPON PROCEDURES

Independent Accountant's Report

To the Audit Committees and Managements of
ABC Company and XYZ Fund
[*city, state*]

We have performed the procedures enumerated below, which were agreed to by the audit committees and managements ofABC Company and XYZ Fund, solely to assist you in evaluating the accompanying Schedule of Investment Performance Statistics of XYZ Fund (prepared in accordance with the criteria specified therein) for the year ended December 31, 20XX. XYZ Fund's management is responsible for the schedule of investment performance statistics. This agreed-upon procedures engagement was conducted in accordance with attestation standards established by the American Institute of Certified Public Accountants. The sufficiency of these procedures is solely the responsibility of those parties specified in this report. Consequently, we make no representation regarding the sufficiency of the procedures described below either for the purpose for which this report has been requested or for any other purpose.

[*Include paragraphs to enumerate procedures and findings.*]

We were not engaged to and did not conduct an examination, the objective of which would be the expression of an opinion on the accompanying Schedule of Investment Performance Statistics of XYZ Fund. Accordingly, we do not express such an opinion. Had we performed additional procedures, other matters might have come to our attention that would have been reported to you.

This report is intended solely for the information and use of the audit committees and managements of ABC Company and XYZ Fund, and is not intended to be and should not be used by anyone other than those specified parties.

[*firm's signature*]

[*city, state*]

[*date*]

APPENDIX 9I
REPORT IN CONNECTION WITH A PROPOSED ACQUISITION

Independent Accountant's Report

To the Board of Directors and Management of
XYZ Company
[*city, state*]

We have performed the procedures enumerated below, which were agreed to by the board of directors and management of XYZ Company, solely to assist you in connection with the acquisition of ABC Company as of December 31, 20XX. XYZ Company is responsible for its cash and accounts receivable records. This agreed-upon procedures engagement was conducted in accordance with attestation standards established by the American Institute of Certified Public Accountants. The sufficiency of these procedures is solely the responsibility of those parties specified in this report. Consequently, we make no representation regarding the sufficiency of the procedures described below either for the purpose for which this report has been requested or for any other purpose.

The procedures and associated findings are as follows:

Cash

1. We obtained confirmation of the cash on deposit from the following banks, and agreed the confirmed balance to the amount shown on the bank reconciliations maintained by XYZ Company. We mathematically checked the bank reconciliations and compared the resultant cash balances per book to the respective general ledger account balances.

Bank	General Ledger Account Balances as of 12/31/XX
ABC National Bank	$ 5,000
DEF State Bank	3,776
XYZ Trust Company regular account	86,912
XYZ Trust Company payroll account	5,000
	$110,688

We found no exceptions as a result of the procedures.

Accounts Receivable

2. We added the individual customer account balances shown in an aged trial balance of accounts receivable (identified as Exhibit A) and compared the resultant total with the balance in the general ledger account.

   We found no difference.

3. We compared the individual customer account balances shown in the aged trial balance of accounts receivable (Exhibit A) as of December 31, 20XX, to the balances shown in the accounts receivable subsidiary ledger.

   We found no exceptions as a result of the comparisons.

4. We traced the aging (according to invoice dates) for 50 customer account balances, shown in Exhibit A, to the details of outstanding invoices in the accounts receivable subsidiary ledger. The balances selected for tracing were determined by starting at the eighth item and selecting every fifteenth item thereafter.

We found no exceptions in the aging of the 50 customer account balances selected. The sample size traced was 9.8 percent of the aggregate amount of customer account balances.

5. We mailed confirmations directly to the customers representing the 150 largest customer account balances selected from the accounts receivable trial balance, and we received responses as indicated below. We also traced the items constituting the outstanding customer account balance to invoices and supporting shipping documents for customers from whom there was no reply. As agreed, any individual differences in a customer account balance of less than $300 were to be considered minor, and no further procedures were performed.

   Of the 150 customer balances confirmed, we received responses from 140 customers; 10 customers did not reply. No exceptions were identified in 120 of the confirmations received. The differences disclosed in the remaining 20 confirmation replies were either minor in amount (as defined above) or were reconciled to the customer account balance without proposed adjustment thereto. A summary of the confirmation results according to the respective aging categories is as follows:

Accounts Receivable
December 31, 20XX

Aging Category	Customer Account Balance	Confirmations Requested	Confirmations Received
Current	$156,000	$76,000	$ 65,000
Past due:			
Less than 1 month	60,000	30,000	19,000
1 to 3 months	36,000	18,000	10,000
Over 3 months	48,000	48,000	8,000
	$300,000	$172,000	$102,000

We were not engaged to and did not conduct an audit, the objective of which would be the expression of an opinion on cash and accounts receivable. Accordingly, we do not express such an opinion. Had we performed additional procedures, other matters might have come to our attentions that would have been reported to you.

This report is intended solely for the information and use of the board of directors and management of XYZ Company and is not intended to be and should not be used by anyone other than these specified parties.

[*firm's signature*]

[*city, state*]

[*date*]

APPENDIX 9J
REPORT IN CONNECTION WITH CLAIMS OF CREDITORS

Independent Accountant's Report

To the Trustee of
XYZ Company
[*city, state*]

We have performed the procedures enumerated below, which were agreed to by the trustee of XYZ Company, with respect to the claims of creditors solely to assist you in determining the validity of claims of XYZ Company as of May 31, 20XX, as set forth in the accompanying Schedule A. XYZ Company is responsible for maintaining records of claims submitted by creditors of XYZ Company. This agreed-upon procedures engagement was conducted in accordance with attestation standards established by the American Institute of Certified Public Accountants. The sufficiency of these procedures is solely the responsibility of those parties specified in this report. Consequently, we make no representation regarding the sufficiency of the procedures described below either for the purpose for which this report has been requested or for any other purpose.

The procedures and associated findings are as follows:

1. Compare the total of the trial balance of accounts payable at May 31, 20XX, prepared by XYZ Company, to the balance in the related general ledger account.

   The total of the accounts payable trial balance agreed with the balance in the related general ledger account.

2. Compare the amounts for claims received from creditors (as shown in claim documents provided by XYZ Company) to the respective amounts shown in the trial balance of accounts payable. Using the data included in the claims documents and in XYZ Company's accounts payable detail records, reconcile any differences found to the accounts payable trial balance.

   All differences noted are presented in column 3 of Schedule A. Except for those amounts shown in column 4 of Schedule A, all such differences were reconciled.

3. Obtain the documentation submitted by creditors in support of the amounts claimed and compare it to the following documentation in XYZ Company's files: invoices, receiving reports, and other evidence of receipt of goods or services.

   No exceptions were found as a result of these comparisons.

We were not engaged to and did not conduct an audit, the objective of which would be the expression of an opinion on the claims of creditors set forth in the accompanying Schedule A. Accordingly, we do not express such an opinion. Had we performed additional procedures, other matters might have come to our attentions that would have been reported to you.

This report is intended solely for the information and use of the trustee of XYZ Company, and is not intended to be and should not be used by anyone other than those specified parties.

[*firm's signature*]

[*city, state*]

[*date*]

CHAPTER 10
COMPLIANCE ENGAGEMENTS

CONTENTS

OVERVIEW

This chapter discusses the planning and performance of engagements related to an entity's compliance with specified laws, regulations, rules, contracts, and grants. Two types of engagements are covered: agreed-upon procedures engagements and examination engagements.

INTRODUCTION

Chapter 6 of SSAE-10 (AT 601) provides guidance for engagements related to either (1) an entity's compliance with requirements of specified laws, regulations, rules, contracts, or grants or (2) the effectiveness of an entity's internal control over compliance with specified requirements. Throughout this chapter an entity's compliance with requirements of specified laws, regulations, rules, contracts, or grants is referred to as "compliance with specified requirements." This chapter covers only engagements related to an entity's compliance with specified requirements. Attestation engagements related to an entity's internal control over compliance is discussed in Chapter 11, "Internal Control Engagements." Compliance requirements may be either financial or nonfinancial in nature. A compliance engagement should comply with the general, fieldwork, and reporting standards in Chapter 1 of SSAE-10 (AT 101).

TYPES OF COMPLIANCE ENGAGEMENTS

The practitioner may be engaged to perform agreed-upon procedures to assist users in evaluating the entity's compliance with specified requirements or a written assertion on the requirements. The practitioner may also be engaged to examine an entity's compliance with specified requirements or a written assertion on them.

An important consideration in determining the type of engagement to be performed is the expectations by users of the practitioner's report. Because the users decide the procedures to be performed in an agreed-upon procedures engagement, it is often in the best interests of the practitioner and the users (including the client) to have an agreed-upon procedures engagement rather than an examination.

The attestation standards do not allow for a review of an entity's compliance with specified requirements. In other words, the practitioner may not provide negative assurance with respect to an entity's compliance with specified requirements.

A practitioner may be engaged to provide other types of services in connection with an entity's compliance with specified requirements. For example, a practitioner may be engaged by management to provide recommendations on how to improve the entity's compliance or related internal control. A practitioner engaged to provide such nonattest services should refer to the guidance in the Statement on Standards for Consulting Services (SSCS) (CS 100) (Consulting Services: Definitions and Standards).

AGREED-UPON PROCEDURES ENGAGEMENTS

Engagement Planning

In an agreed-upon procedures engagement, the practitioner performs specific procedures and reports findings. The practitioner does not perform an examination or provide an opinion.

Attestation Standard Requirements

Chapter 6 of SSAE-10 (AT 601.09) requires that certain conditions be met for the practitioner to perform an agreed-upon procedures engagement related to an entity's compliance with specified requirements:

- The responsible party accepts responsibility for the entity's compliance with specified requirements and the effectiveness of the entity's internal control over compliance.
- The responsible party evaluates the entity's compliance with specified requirements.

In addition, Chapter 2 of SSAE-10 (AT 201.06) requires that certain conditions be met in agreed-upon procedures engagements:

- The practitioner must be independent.
- One of the following conditions must be met:
  - — The party wishing to engage the practitioner is responsible for the subject matter or has a reasonable basis for providing a written assertion about the subject matter when the nature of the subject matter is such that a responsible party does not otherwise exist (see discussion in Chapter 3, "Engagement Planning and Administration").
  - — The party wishing to engage the practitioner is not responsible for the subject matter but is able to provide the practitioner, or have a third party who is responsible for the subject matter provide the practitioner, with evidence of the third party's responsibility for the subject matter.
- The practitioner and the specified parties must agree upon the procedures performed or to be performed by the practitioner.
- The specified parties must take responsibility for the sufficiency of the agreed-upon procedures for their purposes.
- The specific subject matter that the procedures are applied to must be subject to reasonably consistent measurement.
- The criteria to be used in the determination of findings must be agreed upon between the practitioner and the specified parties.
- The procedures to be applied to the specific subject matter must be expected to result in reasonably consistent findings using the criteria.
- Evidential matter related to the specified subject matter that the procedures are applied to must be expected to exist to provide a reasonable basis for expressing the findings expressed in the practitioner's report.

- Where applicable, the practitioner and the specified parties must agree on any materiality limits for reporting purposes.
- Use of the report must be restricted to the specified parties.

Responsibilities of the Responsible Party

The responsible party is responsible for ensuring that the entity complies with the requirements applicable to its activities. In most cases, in an engagement to apply agreed-upon procedures related to an entity's compliance with specified requirements, the responsible party is the management of the entity. The responsible party's responsibility includes

- Identifying applicable compliance requirements.
- Establishing and maintaining internal control to provide reasonable assurance that the entity complies with the requirements.
- Evaluating and monitoring the entity's compliance.
- Specifying reports that satisfy legal, regulatory, or contractual requirements.

The responsible party's evaluation may include documentation such as accounting and statistical data, entity policy manuals, accounting manuals, narrative memoranda, procedural write-ups, flowcharts, completed questionnaires, and internal auditors' reports. The form and extent of the documentation varies depending on the nature of the compliance requirements and the size and complexity of the entity. The responsible party may engage the practitioner to gather information to assist it in evaluating the entity's compliance.

> **OBSERVATION:** Regardless of the procedures performed by the practitioner, the responsible party must accept responsibility for its assertion and must not base such assertion solely on the practitioner's procedures.

Written Assertion

As part of the engagement, the practitioner should obtain from the responsible party a written assertion about compliance with specified requirements. The responsible party may present its written assertion in either of the following two forms:

1. A separate report that will accompany the practitioner's report
2. A representation letter to the practitioner

The responsible party's written assertion about compliance with specified requirements may take many forms. For example, the phrase "responsible party's assertion that W Company complied with [*specify compliance requirement*] as of [*date*]," illustrates such an assertion. Other phrases may also be used. However, the practitioner should not accept an assertion that is so subjective (for example, "very effective" compliance) that people having competence in and using the same or similar criteria would not ordinarily be able to arrive at similar conclusions.

In an agreed-upon procedures engagement, if the practitioner's client is the responsible party, the responsible party's refusal to provide a written assertion requires the practitioner to withdraw from the engagement. However, withdrawal is not required if the engagement is required by law or regulation. If the practitioner's client is not the responsible party, the practitioner is not required to withdraw from the engagement; however, he or she should consider the effects of the responsible party's refusal on the engagement and his or her report.

Compliance Criteria

In accordance with Chapter 1 of SSAE-10 (AT 101.23), the practitioner cannot accept an engagement unless he or she has reason to believe that the subject matter is capable of reasonably consistent evaluation against criteria that are suitable and available to users. The criteria used in engagements related to an entity's compliance with specified requirements are usually easy to identify. The criteria are usually spelled out in the compliance requirements themselves. For example, a regulation might require an entity to maintain $100,000 in equity. However, sometimes the compliance requirements are not defined clearly enough to allow consistent measurement. For example, a regulation might state that an entity must maintain "adequate" equity without specifying a specific dollar amount. In such cases, the practitioner should obtain a more objective definition of "adequate" in order to perform the appropriate procedures. The definition of a term such as "adequate" should also be confirmed in the representation letter and disclosed in the practitioner's report.

Independence

Independence is the foundation of the attest function. Third-party users rely on the CPA's opinion in an audit or attest engagement because they believe the conclusion is impartial and unbiased. Chapter 1 of SSAE-10 (AT 101.36) states, "The practitioner should maintain the intellectual honesty and impartiality necessary to reach an unbiased conclusion about the subject matter or the assertion."

In the final analysis, independence in mental attitude means objective consideration of facts, unbiased judgments, and honest neutrality on the part of the CPA in forming and expressing conclusions. Independence in mental attitude presumes an undeviating concern for an unbiased conclusion about the subject matter or assertion no matter what the subject matter or assertion may be.

Engagement Performance

The objective of the practitioner's agreed-upon procedures is to present specific findings to assist users in evaluating the entity's compliance with specified requirements, based on procedures agreed upon by the users of the report.

Terms and Conditions of the Engagement

A practitioner may perform an agreed-upon procedures engagement related to an entity's compliance with specified requirements if the following conditions are met:

- The responsible party accepts responsibility for the entity's compliance with specified requirements and the effectiveness of the entity's internal control over compliance.
- The responsible party evaluates the entity's compliance with specified requirements.

Responsibilities of the Specified Parties

The client engages the practitioner to assist other interested parties in evaluating subject matter or an assertion as a result of a need or needs of the parties. These parties, including the client, are referred to as "specified parties." As a consequence of the role of the specified parties in agreeing upon the procedures performed or to be performed, a practitioner's report on the engagement should clearly state that its use is restricted to the specified parties.

The specified parties are responsible for the sufficiency (nature, timing, and extent) of the agreed-upon procedures because they best understand their own needs. The specified parties assume the risk that the procedures might be insufficient for their purposes. In addition, the specified parties assume the risk that they might misunderstand or otherwise inappropriately use the findings properly reported by the practitioner.

Responsibilities of the Practitioner

The second general standard requires that the practitioner have adequate knowledge of the subject matter. This knowledge can be obtained through formal or continuing education or practical experience. The adequacy of a practitioner's knowledge of the subject matter varies with the type of engagement from common sense to complex subjects such as actuarial data. In general, the practitioner's knowledge of the subject matter should be sufficient to allow the practitioner to form an objective conclusion about the subject matter.

SSAE-10 (AT 101.22) clarifies that the practitioner does not have to personally acquire all of the knowledge in the subject matter to be qualified to apply agreed-upon procedures to it. These knowledge requirements can be met, in part, through the use of one or more specialists on a particular engagement if the practitioner has sufficient knowledge of the subject matter to

- Communicate the objectives of the work to the specialist; and
- Evaluate the specialist's work to determine whether objectives were met.

The practitioner assumes the risk that misapplication of the procedures might result in inappropriate findings being reported. Furthermore, the practitioner assumes the risk that appropriate findings might not be reported or reported inaccurately. The practitioner's risks can be reduced through adequate planning and supervision and due professional care in performing the procedures, determining the findings, and preparing the report.

The practitioner has no responsibility to determine the differences between the agreed-upon procedures to be performed and the procedures that the practitioner would have determined to be necessary had he or she been engaged to perform another form of attest engagement. The procedures that the practitioner agrees to perform may be more or less extensive than the procedures that he or she would determine to be necessary to perform another form of engagement.

Appropriate Procedures

The procedures that the practitioner and the specified parties agree upon may be as limited or as extensive as the specified parties desire. In some circumstances, the procedures evolve or are modified over the course of the engagement. In general, there is flexibility in determining the procedures as long as the specified parties acknowledge responsibility for the sufficiency of the procedures for their purposes. Matters that should be agreed upon include the nature, timing, and extent of the procedures.

The practitioner should obtain evidential matter from applying the agreed-upon procedures to provide a reasonable basis for the finding or findings expressed in his or her report, but he or she need not perform additional procedures outside the scope of the engagement to gather additional evidential matter.

The procedures that the practitioner and specified parties agree upon may be as limited or extensive as the specified parties desire. However, mere reading of an assertion or specified information about the subject matter does not constitute a procedure sufficient to permit a practitioner to report on the results of applying agreed-upon procedures. In addition, the practitioner should not agree to perform procedures that are overly subjective and thus possibly open to varying interpretations. Terms of uncertain meaning (such as "general review," "limited review," "check," or "test") should not be used in describing the procedures unless they are defined within the agreed-upon procedures.

Materiality and Sampling

The concept of materiality is normally not relevant in an agreed-upon procedures engagement. In an agreed-upon procedures engagement, the practitioner is engaged to perform specific procedures that are requested by the specified parties, and the practitioner should report all findings from the application of these procedures. Any materiality levels used in performing the procedures should be determined by the specified parties, agreed to in the engagement letter, and described in the practitioner's report.

Engagement Letters

The attestation standards require the practitioner to establish an understanding with the client. The standards state that a written engagement letter is preferred but not necessarily required. Although not specifically required by the SSAEs, a written engagement letter is strongly recommended. Most practitioners believe that a written engagement letter can effectively reduce misunderstandings between the practitioner and the client over the nature and limitations of the engagement. Engagement letters are particularly important in attestation engagements because of the increased risk of misunderstanding the nature of the practitioner's responsibilities (although clients may be familiar with traditional financial statement audits, they might not understand the nature and limitations of attestation engagements). The written engagement letter commonly includes the items such as the following:

- A description of the nature of the engagement: The practitioner should address the nature of the engagement and any limitations of the engagement. For example, the nature of an agreed-upon procedures engagement is to present in the form of findings the results of applying agreed-upon procedures to specific subject matter.

- An identification of the subject matter, the responsible party, and the criteria to be used.
- An identification of specified parties.
- The specified parties' acknowledgement of their responsibility for the sufficiency of the procedures.
- The practitioner's responsibilities: The practitioner's responsibility is to carry out the procedures and report the findings in accordance with the general, fieldwork, and reporting standards.
- A reference to attestation standards established by the American Institute of Certified Public Accountants.
- An agreement on procedures by enumerating (or referring to) the procedures.
- Disclaimers expected to be included in the practitioner's report.
- Use restrictions.
- A description of assistance to be provided to the practitioner: The practitioner should determine whether the client has the necessary personnel and expertise to develop the subject matter. In addition, this understanding should include arrangements concerning the conduct of the engagement, such as timing, client assistance, and the availability of documents.
- A description of the involvement of a specialist.
- A description of the agreed-upon materiality limits.

Appendix 10A is an illustrative engagement letter for an agreed-upon procedures engagement. When a written engagement letter is not obtained, the understanding of the engagement should be obtained and documented in the workpapers.

> **OBSERVATION:** When a written engagement letter is used, it should be addressed to the client and, in some circumstances, also to all specified parties.

Agreement on and Sufficiency of Procedures

To satisfy the requirements that the practitioner and the specified parties agree upon the procedures performed or to be performed and that the specified parties take responsibility for the sufficiency of the agreed-upon procedures for their purposes, ordinarily the practitioner should communicate directly with and obtain affirmative acknowledgement from each of the specified parties.

> **OBSERVATION:** Reaching agreement may be accomplished by meeting with the specified parties or by distributing a draft of the anticipated report or a copy of an engagement letter to the specified parties and obtaining their agreement.

If the practitioner is not able to communicate directly with all of the specified parties, he of she may satisfy these requirements by applying one or more of the following or similar procedures:

- Compare the procedures to be applied to written requirements of the specified parties.
- Discuss the procedures to be applied with appropriate representatives of the specified parties.
- Review relevant contracts with or correspondence from the specified parties.

The practitioner should not report on an engagement when specified parties do not agree upon the procedures performed or to be performed and do not take responsibility for the sufficiency of the procedures for their purposes.

Adding Specified Parties

Subsequent to the completion of the agreed-upon procedures engagement, the practitioner may be asked to consider the addition of another party as a specified party (referred to as a "nonparticipant party"). The practitioner may agree to add a nonparticipant party, based on the consideration of such factors as the identity of the nonparticipant party and the intended use of the report.

> **OBSERVATION:** When considering whether to add a nonparticipant party, the guidance in SAS-1 (AU 530) (Dating of the Independent Auditor's Report) is helpful.

If the practitioner does agree to add the nonparticipant party, he or she should obtain affirmative acknowledgement, preferably in writing, from the nonparticipant party agreeing to the procedures performed and of its taking responsibility for the sufficiency of the procedures. If the nonparticipant party is added after the report is issued, the report may be reissued or the practitioner may provide other written acknowledgement that the nonparticipant party has been added as a specified party. If the practitioner provides written acknowledgement that the nonparticipant party has been added as a specified party, the written acknowledgement should state that no additional procedures have been performed subsequent to the date of the report.

> **OBSERVATION:** If the report is reissued, the original report date should not be changed.

Understanding the Specified Compliance Requirements

In an engagement to perform agreed-upon procedures on an entity's compliance with specified requirements, the practitioner is required to perform only those procedures that have been agreed to by the users. However, prior to performing the procedures, the practitioner should obtain an understanding of the specified compliance requirements.

To obtain an understanding of the specified compliance requirements, the practitioner should consider the following:

- Laws, regulations, rules, contracts, and grants that pertain to the specified compliance requirements, including published requirements.
- Knowledge about the specified compliance requirements obtained through prior engagements and regulatory reports.
- Knowledge about the specified compliance requirements obtained through discussions with appropriate individuals within the entity (for example, chief financial officer, internal auditors, legal counsel, compliance officer, or grant or contract administrators).
- Knowledge about the specified compliance requirements obtained through discussions with appropriate individuals outside the entity (for example, a regulator or a third-party specialist).

Representation Letter

In an agreed-upon procedures engagement related to an entity's compliance with specified requirements, Chapter 6 of SSAE-10 (AT 601.68) requires the practitioner to obtain written representations from the responsible party. These representations include the following:

- A statement acknowledging the responsible party's responsibility for complying with the specified requirements.

- A statement acknowledging the responsible party's responsibility for establishing and maintaining effective internal control over compliance.
- A statement that the responsible party has performed an evaluation of (1) the entity's compliance with specified requirements or (2) the entity's controls for ensuring compliance and detecting noncompliance with requirements, as applicable.
- A statement of the responsible party's assertion about the entity's compliance with the specified requirements based on the stated or established criteria.
- A statement acknowledging that the responsible party has disclosed to the practitioner all known noncompliance.
- A statement acknowledging that the responsible party has made available all documentation related to compliance with the specified requirements.
- A statement of the responsible party's interpretation of any compliance requirements that have varying interpretations.
- A statement that the responsible party has disclosed any communications from regulatory agencies, internal auditors, and other practitioners concerning possible noncompliance with the specified requirements, including communications received between the end of the period addressed in the written assertion and the date of the practitioner's report.
- A statement that the responsible party has disclosed any known noncompliance occurring subsequent to the period for which, or date as of which, the responsible party selects to make its assertion.

The representation letter should be dated no earlier than the date of the practitioner's report, which should coincide with the end of fieldwork. The letter should be addressed to the practitioner and signed by members of management whom the practitioner believes are responsible for and knowledgeable, directly or through others in the organization, about the matters covered by the representations. Normally, the CEO should sign the letter. It should also be signed by the highest ranking officer under whose responsibility the subject matter falls. For example, if the subject matter is financial, the CFO should also sign the letter.

When the practitioner is performing agreed-upon procedures and the practitioner's client is the responsible party, the responsible party's refusal to furnish all appropriate written representations constitutes a limitation on the scope of the engagement sufficient to cause the practitioner to withdraw. When the practitioner's client is not the responsible party, the practitioner is not required to withdraw but should consider the effects of the responsible party's refusal on his or her report. In addition, the practitioner should consider the effects of the responsible party's refusal on his or her ability to rely on other representations of the responsible party.

When the client is not the responsible party, the practitioner should also consider obtaining a representation letter from the client. For example, when the practitioner's client has entered into a contract with a third party (responsible party) and the practitioner is engaged to perform agreed-upon procedures related to the responsible party's compliance with that contract, the practitioner may want to obtain written representations from his or her client as to their knowledge of any noncompliance.

Appendix 10D and Appendix 10E are illustrative representation letters for agreed-upon procedures engagements.

Use of Client Personnel and Internal Auditors

According to Chapter 2 of SSAE-10 (AT 201.22), the agreed-upon procedures to be enumerated or referred to in the practitioner's report are to be performed entirely by the practitioner. However, internal auditors or other client personnel may prepare schedules and accumulate data or provide other information for the practitioner's use in performing the agreed-upon procedures. Furthermore, internal auditors may perform and report separately on procedures that they have carried out. Such procedures may be similar to the procedures that the practitioner performs.

A practitioner may agree to perform procedures on information documented in the workpapers of internal auditors. For example, the practitioner may agree to

- Repeat some or all of the procedures.
- Determine whether the internal auditors' workpapers contain documentation of procedures performed and whether the findings documented in the workpapers are presented in a report prepared by the internal auditors.

However, it is inappropriate for the practitioner to

- Agree to merely read the internal auditors' report solely to describe or repeat their findings.
- Take responsibility for all or a portion of any procedures performed by internal auditors by reporting those findings as the practitioner's own.
- Report in any manner that implies shared responsibility for the procedures with the internal auditors.

Documentation

The documentation of an agreed-upon procedures engagement is the principal record of procedures applied, information obtained, and findings reached by the practitioner in the engagement. The quantity, type, and content of documentation are matters of the practitioner's professional judgment. Documentation serves mainly to

- Provide the principal support for the practitioner's report, including the representation regarding observance of the standards of fieldwork, which is implicit in the reference in the report to attestation standards.
- Aid the practitioner in the conduct and supervision of the engagement.

Documentation should be sufficient to (1) enable members of the engagement team with supervision and review responsibilities to understand the nature, timing, extent, and results of procedures performed and the information obtained and (2) identify the engagement team member(s) who performed and reviewed the work.

Examples of documentation are work programs, analyses, memoranda, letters of confirmation and representation, abstracts or copies of entity documents, and schedules or commentaries prepared or obtained by the practitioner. Ordinarily, documentation includes

- Documentation of the engagement acceptance or continuance decision.
- An engagement letter.
- Documentation of how the specified parties determined the procedures to be performed.
- Documentation for planning considerations.
- Procedures checklist.
- A list of the procedures agreed to with a cross reference to documentation of performance.
- Summary of findings.
- Agreed-upon procedures report.
- A discussion of unusual matters encountered and their resolution.
- A representation letter.
- Documentation that the workpapers were reviewed.

Documentation may be in paper form, electronic form, or other media. The practitioner has an ethical, and in some situations a legal, obligation to maintain the confidentiality of client information or information of the responsible party. Because documentation often contains confidential information, the practitioner should adopt reasonable procedures to maintain the confidentiality of the information. The practitioner should also adopt reasonable procedures to prevent unauthorized access to documentation.

Reporting

General

The practitioner's report on agreed-upon procedures should be in the form of procedures and findings. The practitioner's report should contain the following elements:

- A title that includes the word "independent."
- Identification of the specified parties.
- Identification of the subject matter (or the written assertion) and the character of the engagement.
- Identification of the responsible party.
- A statement that the subject matter is the responsibility of the responsible party.
- A statement that the procedures, which were those agreed to by the specified parties identified in the report, were performed to assist the specified parties in evaluating the entity's compliance with specified requirements.
- A statement that the agreed-upon procedures engagement was conducted in accordance with attestation standards established by the AICPA.
- A statement that the sufficiency of the procedures is solely the responsibility of the specified parties and a disclaimer of responsibility for the sufficiency of those procedures.
- A list of the procedures performed (or reference to the list) and related findings.
- Where applicable, a description of any agreed-upon materiality limits.
- A statement that the practitioner was not engaged to and did not conduct an examination of the entity's compliance with specified requirements, the objective of which would be an expression of an opinion, a disclaimer of opinion thereon, and a statement that if the practitioner had performed additional procedures, other matters might have come to his or her attention that would have been reported.

- A statement of restrictions on the use of the report because it is intended to be used solely by the specified parties.
- Where applicable, reservations or restrictions concerning procedures or findings.
- Where applicable, a description of the nature of the assistance provided by a specialist.
- The manual or printed signature of the practitioner's firm.
- The date of the report.

Exhibit 10-1 is an example of an agreed-upon procedures report on an entity's compliance with specified requirements in which the procedures and findings are enumerated rather than referenced.

EXHIBIT 10-1
ILLUSTRATIVE AGREED-UPON PROCEDURES REPORT REGARDING COMPLIANCE

[*addressee*]
[*city, state*]

We have performed the procedures enumerated below, which were agreed to by [*list of specified parties*], solely to assist the specified parties in evaluating [*name of entity*]'s compliance with [*list specified requirements*] during the [*period*] ended [*date*]. Management is responsible for [*name of entity*]'s compliance with those requirements. This agreed-upon procedures engagement was conducted in accordance with attestation standards established by the American Institute of Certified Public Accountants. The sufficiency of these procedures is solely the responsibility of those parties specified in this report. Consequently, we make no representation regarding the sufficiency of the procedures described below either for the purpose for which this report has been requested or for any other purpose.

[*Include paragraphs to enumerate procedures and findings.*]

We were not engaged to and did not conduct an examination, the objective of which would be the expression of an opinion on compliance. Accordingly, we do not express such an opinion. Had we performed additional procedures, other matters might have come to our attention that would have been reported to you.

This report is intended solely for the information and use of [*list or refer to specified parties*] and is not intended to be and should not be used by anyone other than these specified parties.

[*firm's signature*]

[*city, state*]

[*date*]

Description of Procedures

The practitioner should present the results of applying the agreed-upon procedures to specific subject matter in the form of findings. The practitioner should report all findings from application of the agreedupon procedures and he or she should avoid vague or ambiguous language in reporting the findings.

Significant Interpretations

Evaluating compliance with certain requirements may require interpretation of the laws, regulations, rules, contracts, or grants that establish those requirements. In such situations, the practitioner should consider whether he or she is provided with the suitable criteria required to evaluate an assertion under the third general attestation standard. If these interpretations are significant, the practitioner may include a paragraph stating the description and source of interpretations made by the entity's management. An example of such a paragraph, which should precede the procedures and findings paragraph(s), is as follows:

> We have been informed that, under [*name of entity*]'s interpretation of [*identify the compliance requirement*], [*explain the nature and source of the relevant interpretation*].

Noncompliance

The practitioner might become aware of noncompliance that occurs subsequent to the period addressed by the practitioner's report but before the date of the report. In this case, the practitioner should consider including information regarding such noncompliance in his or her report. However, the practitioner has no responsibility to perform procedures to detect such noncompliance other than obtaining the responsible party's representation about noncompliance in the subsequent period.

Scope Limitations

When circumstances impose restrictions on the performance of the agreed-upon procedures, the practitioner should attempt to obtain agreement from the specified parties for modification of the agreed upon procedures. When such agreement cannot be obtained (for example, when the agreed-upon procedures are published by a regulatory agency that will not modify the procedures), the practitioner should describe any restrictions on the performance of the procedures in his or her report or withdraw from the engagement.

EXAMINATION ENGAGEMENTS

The objective of the practitioner's examination procedures applied to an entity's compliance with specified requirements is to express an opinion on an entity's compliance (or an assertion related to its compliance), based on the specified criteria. To express such an opinion, the practitioner accumulates sufficient evidence about the entity's compliance with specified requirements, thereby restricting attestation risk to an appropriately low level.

Engagement Acceptance

A practitioner may perform an examination engagement related to an entity's compliance with specified requirements if the following conditions are met:

- The responsible party accepts responsibility for the entity's compliance with specified requirements and the effectiveness of the entity's internal control over compliance.
- The responsible party evaluates the entity's compliance with specified requirements.
- Sufficient evidential matter exists or could be developed to support management's evaluation.

Written Assertion

As part of the engagement, the practitioner should obtain from the responsible party a written assertion about compliance with specified requirements. The responsible party may present its written assertion in either of two forms:

- A separate report that will accompany the practitioner's report.
- A representation letter to the practitioner.

The responsible party's written assertion about compliance with specified requirements may take many forms. For example, the phrase "responsible party's assertion that W Company complied with [*specify compliance requirement*] as of [*date*]" illustrates such an assertion. Other phrases may also be used. However, the practitioner should not accept an assertion that is so subjective (for example, "very effective" compliance) that people having competence in and using the same or similar criteria would not ordinarily be able to arrive at similar conclusions.

Regardless of whether the practitioner's client is the responsible party, the responsible party's refusal to furnish a written assertion as part of an examination engagement should cause the practitioner to withdraw from the engagement. However, an exception is provided if an examination of an entity's compliance with specified requirements is required by law or regulation. In that instance, the practitioner should disclaim an opinion on compliance unless he or she obtains evidential matter that warrants expressing an adverse opinion. If the practitioner expresses an adverse opinion, the practitioner's report should be restricted as to use.

Compliance Criteria

In accordance with Chapter 1 of SSAE-10 (AT 101.23) the practitioner cannot accept an engagement unless he or she has reason to believe that the subject matter is capable of reasonably consistent evaluation against criteria that are suitable and available to users. The criteria used in engagements related to an entity's compliance with specified requirements are usually easy to identify. The criteria are usually spelled out in the compliance requirements themselves. For example, a regulation might require an entity to maintain $100,000 in equity. However, sometimes the compliance requirements are not defined clearly enough to allow consistent measurement. For example, a regulation might state that the entity must maintain "adequate" equity without specifying a specific dollar amount. In such cases, the practitioner should obtain a more objective definition of "adequate" in order to perform the appropriate procedures. The definition of a term such as "adequate" should also be confirmed in the representation letter and disclosed in the practitioner's report.

Engagement Planning

Materiality

In an examination of an entity's compliance with specified requirements, the practitioner's consideration of materiality differs from that of an audit of financial statements in accordance with generally accepted auditing standards. In an examination of an entity's compliance with specified requirements, the practitioner's consideration of materiality is affected by (1) the nature of the compliance requirements (which may or may not be quantifiable in monetary terms), (2) the nature and frequency of noncompliance identified with appropriate consideration of sampling risk, and (3) qualitative considerations, including the needs and expectations of users.

Attestation Risk

In an engagement to examine compliance with specified requirements, the practitioner seeks to obtain reasonable assurance that the entity complied, in all material respects, based on the specified criteria. This includes designing the examination to detect both intentional and unintentional material noncompliance. Absolute assurance is not attainable, because of factors such as the need for judgment, the use of sampling, and the inherent limitations of internal control over compliance and because much of the evidence available to the practitioner is persuasive rather than conclusive in nature. Futhermore, procedures that are effective for detecting noncompliance that is unintentional might be ineffective for detecting noncompliance that is intentional and concealed through collusion between the personnel of the entity and a third party or among management or employees of the entity.

Attestation risk is the risk that the practitioner may unknowingly fail to modify appropriately his or her opinion. This is analogous to the concept of audit risk explained in SAS-47 (AU 312) (Audit Risk and Materiality in Conducting an Audit). In an examination engagement, the practitioner is required to reduce attestation risk to a low level.

Attestation risk, like audit risk, is composed of inherent risk, control risk, and detection risk. For purposes of a compliance examination, these components are defined as follows:

- *Inherent risk* The risk (IR) that material noncompliance with specified requirements could occur, assuming there are no related controls
- *Control risk* The risk (CR) that material noncompliance that could occur will not be prevented or detected on a timely basis by the entity's controls
- *Detection risk* The risk (DR) that the practitioner's procedures will lead him or her to conclude that material compliance does not exist when, in fact, such noncompliance does exist

This combination is multiplicative and is usually stated as follows:

$$AR = IR \times CR \times DR$$

Inherent Risk

In assessing inherent risk, the practitioner should consider factors affecting risk similar to those an auditor would consider when planning an audit of financial statements. Such factors are discussed in SAS-99 (AU 230, AU316, AU333) (Consideration of Fraud in a Financial Statement Audit). In addition, the practitioner should consider factors relevant to compliance engagements, such as

- The complexity of the specified compliance requirements.
- The length of time the entity has been subject to the specified compliance requirements.

- Prior experience with the entity's compliance.
- The potential impact of noncompliance.

Control Risk

The practitioner should assess control risk as discussed below in the discussion of Internal Controls. Assessing control risk contributes to the practitioner's evaluation of the risk that material noncompliance exists. The process of assessing control risk (together with assessing inherent risk) provides evidential matter about the risk that such noncompliance may exist. The practitioner uses this evidential matter as part of the reasonable basis for his or her opinion.

Detection Risk

Detection risk is a measure of the risk that attestation procedures will fail to detect material noncompliance. The practitioner controls detection risk through selection and application of tests. Detection risk arises because all items that make up the subject matter are not examined (sampling error) and attest procedures are not properly applied (nonsampling error). Restating the above formula illustrates the importance of detection risk (DR) as it relates to the performance of the engagement:

$$DR = \frac{AR}{IR \times CR}$$

Whereas inherent risk and control risk are not under the control of the practitioner, detection risk can be controlled by the practitioner because it relates to attest procedures, which can be changed at the practitioner's discretion. Inherent risk and control risk exist, and the practitioner can only assess them. If the assessment of inherent risk and control risk is high, the practitioner's tests must be sufficiently effective to reduce detection risk and adequately control attestation risk. When inherent risk and control risk are lower, the practitioner may do correspondingly less work to reduce detection risk.

Inherent risk and control risk can be assessed separately or in combination, and they can be assessed quantitatively or qualitatively. Although both approaches are acceptable, the approach used in this book is qualitative because it is considered highly effective and efficient. The practitioner can use the matrix in Exhibit 10-2 to express the combined assessments of inherent risk and control risk in qualitative terms: maximum, moderate, or low.

EXHIBIT 10-2
COMBINING INHERENT RISK AND CONTROL RISK

Inherent Risk	x	Control Risk	=	Risk of Material Noncompliance
High		Maximum		High
High		Moderate		High
High		Low		Moderate
Moderate		Maximum		Moderate
Moderate		Moderate		Low
Moderate		Low		Low
Low		Maximum		Moderate
Low		Moderate		Low
Low		Low		Low

Internal Control Consideration

The practitioner should obtain an understanding of relevant portions of internal control over compliance to plan the engagement and to assess control risk for compliance with specified requirements. In planning the examination, such knowledge should be used to identify types of potential noncompliance, to consider factors that affect the risk of material noncompliance, and to design appropriate tests of compliance.

Obtaining an Understanding of Controls over Compliance

The practitioner generally obtains an understanding of the design of specific controls by performing the following:

- Inquiries of appropriate management, supervisory, and staff personnel.
- Inspection of the entity's documents.
- Observation of the entity's activities and operations.

The nature and extent of procedures that a practitioner performs vary from entity to entity and are influenced by factors such as

- The newness and complexity of specified requirements.
- The practitioner's knowledge of internal control over compliance obtained in previous professional engagements.

- The nature of the specified compliance requirements.
- An understanding of the industry in which the entity operates.
- Judgments about materiality.

When seeking to assess control risk below the maximum, the practitioner should perform tests of controls to obtain evidence to support the assessed level of control risk.

Tests of Controls

If the practitioner decides to assess control risk below the maximum, Chapter 6 of SSAE-10 (AT 601.46) requires that tests of controls be performed. In most situations, it is more efficient to test compliance directly rather than test controls over compliance. However, in some situations, tests of controls are required by the terms of the engagement. To be effective, the controls must be designed to ensure compliance or detect noncompliance and they should be in effect for the period that affects the assertions. In order to test controls, the practitioner may apply inquiry, observation, inspection, or reperformance procedures to determine how, by whom, and how consistently a control procedure was applied.

Communication of Significant Deficiencies

During the course of an examination engagement, the practitioner might become aware of significant deficiencies in the design or operation of internal control over compliance that could adversely affect the entity's ability to comply with specified requirements. A practitioner's responsibility to communicate these deficiencies in an examination of an entity's compliance with specified requirements is similar to the auditor's responsibility described in SAS-60 (AU 325) (Communication of Internal Control Related Matters Noted in an Audit). If, in a multiple-party arrangement, the practitioner's client is not the responsible party, the practitioner has no responsibility to communicate reportable conditions to the responsible party.

Communication of Reportable Condition

If the practitioner is engaged by his or her client (ABC Company) to examine the compliance of another entity (XYZ Company), the practitioner has no obligation to communicate any reportable condition that he or she becomes aware of to XYZ Company. However, the practitioner is not precluded from making such a communication.

Consideration of Internal Audit Function

When planning the engagement, the practitioner should consider whether the entity has an internal audit function and the extent to which internal auditors are involved in monitoring compliance with the specified requirements. The practitioner should consider the guidance in SAS-65 (AU 322) (The Auditor's Consideration of the Internal Audit Function in an Audit of Financial Statements) when addressing the competence and objectivity of internal auditors; the nature, timing, and extent of work to be performed; and other related matters.

Obtaining Evidence

The practitioner should apply procedures to provide reasonable assurance of detecting material noncompliance. Determining these procedures and evaluating the sufficiency of the evidence obtained are matters of professional judgment. When exercising such judgment, the practitioner should consider the guidance contained in SAS-39 (AU 350) (Audit Sampling).

The second standard of fieldwork states, "Sufficient evidence shall be obtained to provide a reasonable basis for the conclusion that is expressed in the report." Selecting and applying procedures that will accumulate evidence that is sufficient in the circumstances to provide a reasonable basis for the level of assurance to be expressed in the examination report requires careful exercise of professional judgment. A wide variety of procedures may be applied in an attest engagement. According to SSAE-10 (AT 101.52) in establishing the proper combination of procedures to appropriately restrict attestation risk, the practitioner should consider the following presumptions, keeping in mind that they are not mutually exclusive and might be subject to exceptions:

- Evidence obtained from independent sources outside an entity provides greater assurance about the subject matter or the assertion than evidence secured solely from within the entity.
- Information obtained from the independent attester's direct personal knowledge (such as through physical examination, observation, computation, operating tests, or inspection) is more persuasive than information obtained indirectly.
- The more effective the controls over the subject matter, the more assurance they provide about the subject matter or the assertion.

Therefore, in the hierarchy of available attest procedures, those that involve search and verification (e.g., inspection, confirmation, and observation), particularly when using independent sources outside the entity, are generally more effective in restricting attestation risk than those involving internal inquiries and comparisons of internal information (e.g., analytical procedures and discussions with individuals responsible for the subject matter or assertion). However, internal inquiries and comparisons of internal information are generally less costly to apply.

Planning the Procedures

In the hierarchy of available attest procedures, those that involve search and verification (e.g., inspection, confirmation, and observation), particularly when using independent sources outside the entity, are generally more effective in restricting attestation risk than those involving internal inquiries and comparisons of internal information (e.g., analytical procedures and discussions with individuals responsible for the subject matter or assertion). The extent to which attestation procedures are performed should be based on the level of assurance to be provided and the practitioner's consideration of

- The nature and materiality of the information to be tested to the subject matter or the assertion taken as a whole.
- The likelihood of noncompliance.
- Knowledge obtained during current and previous engagements.
- The responsible party's competence in the subject matter.
- The extent to which the information is affected by the asserter's judgment.
- Inadequacies in the responsible party's underlying data.

For engagements involving compliance with regulatory requirements, the practitioner's procedures should include reviewing reports of significant examinations and related communications between regulatory agencies and the entity and, when appropriate, making inquiries of the regulatory agencies, including inquiries about examinations in progress.

Subsequent Events

The practitioner's consideration of subsequent events in an examination of an entity's compliance with specified requirements is similar to the auditor's consideration of subsequent events in a financial statement audit, as outlined in SAS-1 (AU 560) (Subsequent Events). The practitioner should consider information about such events that comes to his or her attention after the end of the period addressed by the practitioner's report and prior to the issuance of his or her report.

Two types of subsequent events require consideration by the responsible party and evaluation by the practitioner. The first type consists of events that provide additional information about the entity's compliance with specified requirements during the period addressed by the practitioner's report and may affect the practitioner's report. For the period from the end of the reporting period (or point in time) to the date of the practitioner's report, the practitioner should perform procedures to identify such events that provide additional information about compliance during the reporting period. Such procedures should include, but might not be limited to, inquiring about and considering the following information:

- Relevant internal auditors' reports issued during the subsequent period.
- Other practitioners' reports identifying noncompliance issued during the subsequent period.
- Regulatory agencies' reports on the entity's noncompliance issued during the subsequent period.
- Information about the entity's noncompliance obtained through other professional engagements with the entity.

The second type of subsequent event consists of noncompliance that occurs subsequent to the period being reported on but before the date of the practitioner's report. The practitioner has no responsibility to detect such noncompliance. However, should the practitioner become aware of such noncompliance, it may be of such a nature and significance that its disclosure is required to prevent users from being misled. In such cases, the practitioner should include in his or her report an explanatory paragraph describing the nature of the noncompliance.

Representation Letters

In an examination engagement, the practitioner should obtain written representations from the responsible party. The written representations should

- Acknowledge the responsible party's responsibility for complying with the specified requirements.
- Acknowledge the responsible party's responsibility for establishing and maintaining effective internal control over compliance.
- State that the responsible party has performed an evaluation of the entity's compliance with specified requirements.
- State the responsible party's assertion about the entity's compliance with the specified requirements.

- State that the responsible party has disclosed to the practitioner all known noncompliance.
- State that the responsible party has made available all documentation related to compliance with the specified requirements.
- State the responsible party's interpretation of all compliance requirements that have varying interpretations.
- State that the responsible party has disclosed all communications from regulatory agencies, internal auditors, and other practitioners concerning possible noncompliance with the specified requirements, including communications received between the end of the period addressed in the written assertion and the date of the practitioner's report.
- State that the responsible party has disclosed all known noncompliance occurring subsequent to the period which, or date as of which, the responsible party selects to make its assertion.

The responsible party's refusal to furnish all appropriate written representations in an examination engagement constitutes a limitation on the scope of the engagement sufficient to preclude an unmodified opinion. In most cases, this refusal is sufficient to cause the practitioner to disclaim an opinion or withdraw from the engagement. However, based on the nature of the representations not obtained or the circumstances of the refusal, the practitioner may conclude that a qualified opinion is appropriate.

When the practitioner's client is not the responsible party, the practitioner may also want to obtain written representations from the client. For example, when a practitioner's client has entered into a contract with a third party (responsible party) and the practitioner is engaged to examine the responsible party's compliance with that contract, the practitioner may want to obtain written representations from his or her client regarding their knowledge of any noncompliance.

Reporting

The practitioner may examine and report directly on the entity's compliance or on the responsible party's assertion.

Standard Report

According to SSAE-10 (AT 601.35), the practitioner's examination report on compliance, which is ordinarily addressed to the entity, should include the following:

- A title that includes the word "independent."
- Identification of the specified compliance requirements, including the period covered, and the responsible party.

When reporting on management's assertion, the report should include instead an identification of (1) the responsible party's assertion about the entity's compliance with specified requirements, including the period covered by the assertion, and (2) the responsible party. When the responsible party's assertion does not accompany the report, the first paragraph of the report should also include a statement of the assertion.

- A statement that compliance with the specified requirements is the responsibility of the entity's management.
- A statement that the practitioner's responsibility is to express an opinion on the entity's compliance with those requirements (or on management's assertion about the compliance) based on his or her examination.
- A statement that the examination was conducted in accordance with attestation standards established by the American Institute of Certified Public Accountants and, accordingly, included examining, on a test basis, evidence about the entity's compliance with those requirements and performing such other procedures as the practitioner deemed necessary in the circumstances.
- A statement that the practitioner believes the examination provides a reasonable basis for his or her opinion.
- A statement that the examination does not provide a legal determination on the entity's compliance.
- The practitioner's opinion on whether the entity complied, is all material respects, with specified requirements (or whether management's assertion about compliance with specified requirements is fairly stated in all material respects), based on the specified criteria.
- A statement restricting the use of the report to the specified parties under the following circumstances:
  - When the criteria used to evaluate compliance are determined by the practitioner to be appropriate only for a limited number of parties who either participated in their establishment or can be presumed to have an adequate understanding of the criteria.
  - When the criteria used to evaluate compliance are available only to specified parties.
- The manual or printed signature of the practitioner's firm.
- The date of the examination report.

Exhibit 10-3 is an example of an examination report on an entity's compliance with specified requirements. Exhibit 10-4 presents an example of an examination report on management's assertion about compliance with specified requirements.

EXHIBIT 10-3
ILLUSTRATIVE COMPLIANCE EXAMINATION REPORT: REPORT DIRECTLY ON ENTITY'S COMPLIANCE WITH SPECIFIED REQUIREMENTS

[*addressee*]
[*city, state*]

We have examined [*name of entity*]'s compliance with [*list of specified compliance requirements*] during the [*period*] ended [*date*]. Management is responsible for [*name of entity*]'s compliance with those requirements. Our responsibility is to express an opinion on [*name of entity*]'s compliance based on our examination.

Our examination was conducted in accordance with attestation standards established by the American Institute of Certified Public Accountants and, accordingly, included examining, on a test basis, evidence about [name of entity]'s compliance with those requirements and performing such other procedures as we considered necessary in the circumstances. We believe that our examination provides a reasonable basis for our opinion. Our examination does not provide a legal determination on [*name of entity*]'s compliance with specified requirements.

In our opinion, [*name of entity*] complied, in all material respects, with the aforementioned requirements for the [*period*] ended [*date*].

[*firm's signature*]

[*city, state*]

[*date*]

EXHIBIT 10-4
ILLUSTRATIVE COMPLIANCE EXAMINATION REPORT: REPORT ON MANAGEMENT'S ASSERTION ABOUT COMPLIANCE WITH SPECIFIED REQUIREMENTS

[*addressee*]
[*city, state*]

We have examined management's assertion, included in the accompanying [title of management report], that [*name of entity*] complied with [*list of specified compliance requirements*] during the [*period*] ended [*date*]. Management is responsible for [*name of entity*]'s compliance with those requirements. Our responsibility is to express an opinion on [*name of entity*]'s compliance based on our examination.

Our examination was conducted in accordance with attestation standards established by the American Institute of Certified Public Accountants and, accordingly, included examining, on a test basis, evidence about [*name of entity*]'s compliance with those requirements and performing such other procedures as we considered necessary in the circumstances. We believe that our examination provides a reasonable basis for our opinion. Our examination does not provide a legal determination on [*name of entity*]'s compliance with specified requirements.

In our opinion, management's assertion that [*name of entity*] complied with the aforementioned requirements during the [*period*] ended [*date*] is fairly stated, in all material respects.

[*firm's signature*]

[*city, state*]

[*date*]

Compliance Criteria

Generally, compliance criteria are set forth in the specified compliance requirements. When this is the case, it is not necessary to disclose the compliance criteria in the report, because they are incorporated by reference to the compliance requirements. However, if the criteria are not included in the compliance requirements, they should be disclosed in the report. For example, if a compliance requirement states that an entity must maintain equity of at least $50,000, it is not necessary to state that in the report. However, if the compliance requirement states that the entity must maintain "adequate" equity, the report should disclose the criteria used to determine "adequate" equity. This disclosure can be made in an explanatory paragraph or in an attachment. The following is an example of an opinion paragraph with a reference to an attachment:

> In our opinion, management's assertion that [*name of entity*] complied with the aforementioned requirements for the year ended December 31, 20XX, is fairly stated, in all material respects, based on the criteria set forth in [*reference to criteria, such as* "in the following paragraph" *or* "in Attachment A"].

Restricting the Use of the Report

According to the fourth reporting standard, the practitioner's examination report must be restricted to specified parties under the following circumstances:

- When the criteria used to evaluate compliance are determined by the practitioner to be appropriate only for a limited number of parties who either participated in their establishment or can be presumed to have an adequate understanding of the criteria.
- When the criteria used to evaluate compliance are available only to specified parties.

In certain situations, however, criteria that have been specified by management and other report users may still be suitable for general use.

> **OBSERVATION:** Normally, when the responsible party refuses to provide a written assertion, the practitioner should withdraw from the engagement. However, an exception is provided if an examination of an entity's compliance with specified requirements is required by law or regulation. In that instance, the practitioner should disclaim an opinion on compliance unless he or she obtains evidential matter that warrants expressing an adverse opinion. If the practitioner expresses an adverse opinion, the practitioner's report should be restricted as to use.

Disclosure of Significant Interpretations

Evaluating compliance with certain requirements might require interpretation of the laws, regulations, rules, contracts, or grants that establish the requirements. In such situations, the practitioner should consider whether he or she is provided with the criteria required to evaluate an assertion under the third general attestation standard. If the interpretations are significant, the practitioner may include a paragraph stating the description and source of interpretations made by the entity's management. An example of such a paragraph, which should precede the procedures and findings paragraph(s), follows:

> We have been informed that, under [*name of entity*]'s interpretation of [*identify the compliance requirement*], [*explain the nature and source of the relevant interpretation*].

Material Noncompliance

Chapter 6 of SSAE-10 (AT 601.64) requires the practitioner to express a qualified or adverse opinion when an examination of an entity's compliance with specified requirements discloses material noncompliance with the applicable requirements. The decision of whether to express a qualified or adverse opinion is a matter of professional judgment. The practitioner should consider the overall significance and pervasiveness of the noncompliance and its effect on the entity's compliance with the specified requirements.

If the practitioner concludes that the material noncompliance is not so significant or pervasive as to keep the entity from complying overall with the specified requirements, then a qualified opinion would be appropriate. The following is an example of an explanatory paragraph for a qualified examination report:

> Our examination disclosed the following material noncompliance with [*type of compliance requirement*] applicable to [*name of entity*] during the [*period*] ended [*date*]. [*Describe noncompliance.*]

The following is an example of an opinion paragraph for a qualified examination report:

> In our opinion, except for the material noncompliance described in the third paragraph, [*name of entity*] complied, in all material respects, with the aforementioned requirements for the [*period*] ended [*date*].

If the practitioner concludes that the material noncompliance is severe enough to prevent the entity from complying with the specified requirements, the practitioner should express an adverse opinion. The following is an example of an explanatory paragraph for an adverse examination report:

> Our examination disclosed the following material noncompliance with [*type of compliance requirement*] applicable to [*name of entity*] during the [*period*] ended [*date*]. [*Describe noncompliance.*]

The following is an example of an opinion paragraph for an adverse examination report:

> In our opinion, because of the effect of the material noncompliance described in the third paragraph, [*name of entity*] has not complied with the aforementioned requirements for the [*period*] ended [*date*].

Immaterial Noncompliance

In some situations, the terms of the engagement require that all instances of noncompliance, regardless of materiality, be reported. This type of reporting is merely supplemental and is done as an accommodation to the client or specified parties. This situation would not cause the practitioner to issue a qualified opinion if he or she does not believe that the aggregate effect of the noncompliance is material.

Scope Limitations

The third standard of reporting states, "The report shall state all of the practitioner's significant reservations about the engagement, the subject matter, and if applicable, the assertion thereto." The phrase "reservations about the engagement" refers to any unresolved problem that the practitioner had in complying with the attestation standards or interpretive standards. Typically, these types of problems are referred to as "scope limitations."

Scope limitations fall into two categories: (1) those imposed by the client or the responsible party and (2) those imposed by other circumstances:

1. *Client- or responsible party-imposed scope limitations* When the client or responsible party imposes a scope limitation, the practitioner should generally qualify or disclaim an opinion or withdraw from the engagement.

2. *Other scope limitation* When a scope limitation is imposed by circumstances beyond the control of the client or responsible party, then the practitioner may issue a qualified opinion or a disclaimer of opinion, depending on the nature and magnitude of the potential effects of the matters in question and on their significance to the subject matter or assertion.

Reservations about the Subject Matter or the Assertion

The phrase "reservations about the subject matter or the assertion" refers to any unresolved reservation about the conformity of the subject matter with the criteria, including the adequacy of the disclosure of material matters. These reservations may relate to the measurement, form, arrangement, content, or underlying judgments and assumptions applicable to the subject matter and its appended notes. Examples include reservations about:

- The terminology used.
- The amount of detail given.
- The classification of items.
- The bases of amounts set forth.

The existence of these reservations can result in either a qualified or an adverse opinion, depending upon the materiality of the departures from the criteria.

APPENDIX 10A ENGAGEMENT LETTER: AGREED-UPON PROCEDURES ENGAGEMENT

[*date*]

[*name of client (and other specified parties)*]
[*address*]

We are pleased to confirm our understanding of the nature and limitations of the services we are to provide for [*client's legal name*].

We will apply agreed-upon procedures that [*specified parties have specified, listed in the attached schedule*] to [*describe subject matter or related assertion*] of [*name of responsible party*] as of [*date*], prepared in accordance with [*criteria*]. Our engagement to apply agreed-upon procedures will be conducted in accordance with attestation standards established by the American Institute of Certified Public Accountants. The sufficiency of the procedures is solely the responsibility of those parties specified in the report. Consequently, we make no representation regarding the sufficiency of the procedures described in the attached schedule either for the purpose for which the report has been requested or for any other purpose. If, for any reason, we are unable to complete the procedures, we will describe any restrictions on the performance of the procedures in our report, or will not issue a report as a result of this engagement.

Because the agreed-upon procedures listed in the attached schedule do not constitute an examination, we will not express an opinion on [*describe subject matter*]. In addition, we have no obligation to perform any procedures beyond those listed in the attached schedule.

We will submit a report listing the procedures performed and our findings. This report is intended solely for the use of [*specified parties*], and should not be used by those who did not agree upon the procedures and take responsibility for the sufficiency of the procedures for their purposes. Our report will contain a paragraph stating that had we performed additional procedures, other matters may have come to our attention that would have been reported to you.

We plan to begin our procedures on approximately [*date*] and, unless unforeseeable problems are encountered, the engagement should be completed by [*date*]. At the conclusion of our engagement, we will require a representation letter from management that, among other things, will confirm management's responsibility for the presentation of the [describe subject matter] in accordance with [*describe criteria*].

We estimate that our fees for these services will range from $_____ to $_____. You will also be billed for travel and other out-of-pocket costs such as report production, typing, postage, etc. Additional expenses are estimated to be $_____. The fee estimate is based on anticipated cooperation from your personnel and the assumption that unexpected circumstances will not be encountered during the engagement. If significant additional time is necessary, we will discuss it with you and arrive at a new fee estimate before we incur the additional costs. Our invoices for these services will be rendered each month as work progresses and will be payable on presentation. In accordance with our firm policies, work may be suspended if your account becomes _____ days or more overdue and will not be resumed until your account is paid in full. If we elect to terminate our services for nonpayment, our engagement will be deemed to have been completed upon written notification of termination, even if we have not completed our report. You will be obligated to compensate us for all time extended and to reimburse us for all out-of-pocket expenditures through the date of termination.

We appreciate the opportunity to be of service to you and believe this letter accurately summarizes the significant terms of our engagement. If you have any questions, please let us know. If you agree with the terms of our engagement as described in this letter, please sign the enclosed copy and return it to us. If the need for additional services arises, our agreement with you will need to be revised. It is customary for us to enumerate these revisions in an addendum to this letter. If additional specified parties of the report are added, we will require that they acknowledge in writing their responsibility for the sufficiency of the procedures.

Very truly yours,

[*CPA firm's name*]

Response

This letter correctly sets forth the understanding of [*client and other specified parties*].

By:

Title:

Date:

APPENDIX 10B
ENGAGEMENT LETTER ADDENDUM: AGREED-UPON PROCEDURES ENGAGEMENT

[*date*]

[*name of client (and other specified parties)*]
[*address*]

This letter constitutes an addendum to our original engagement letter dated [*date*]. The purpose of this letter is to outline additional procedures you wish us to perform in connection with that agreed-upon procedures engagement.

The additional procedures include:

[*List additional procedures.*]

All the terms of our original engagement letter will apply to this addendum. This addendum will become effective when you sign and date the original and copy of this letter and return the signed copy to us. Very truly yours,

[CPA firm's name]

Response

This letter correctly sets forth the understanding of [*client and other specified parties*].

By:

Title:

Date:

APPENDIX 10C
REQUEST FOR SPECIFIED PARTY'S COMMENTS ON PROCEDURES: AGREED-UPON PROCEDURES ENGAGEMENT

[*date*]

[*specified party's name*]
[*address*]

We have been requested by [*client's legal name*] to apply agreed-upon procedures listed in the attached engagement letter. The sufficiency of the requested procedures is solely the responsibility of the specified parties of the report. Consequently, we make no representation regarding the sufficiency of the procedures for the purpose for which this report has been requested or for any other purpose.

Because the agreed-upon procedures listed in the attached engagement letter do not constitute an examination, we will not express an opinion on the [*describe subject matter*]. In addition, we have no obligation to perform any procedures that go beyond those listed in the attached engagement letter.

As a specified user of the report, please review the proposed procedures and acknowledge the sufficiency of the procedures by signing the enclosed copy of this letter and returning it to us. If the procedures are not considered to be sufficient or are not in accordance with your understanding, please provide comments in the space provided below.

Very truly yours,

[*CPA firm's name*]

Response

The procedures listed in the attached engagement letter are_____ (are not_____) sufficient for our purposes.

Comments:

By:

Title:

Date:

APPENDIX 10D
AGREED-UPON PROCEDURES CHECKLIST: COMPLIANCE ENGAGEMENT

Client Name: _______________ Date of Subject Matter: _______________

Completed by: _______________ Date Completed: _______________

	Completed by	N/A
1. Complete the Client Acceptance and Retention Evaluation Form.	________	________
2. If the engagement was originally intended to be another type of engagement (for example, examination or consulting engagement), document the considerations of:		
a. Whether the procedures performed as part of another type of engagement are appropriate for an agreed-upon procedures engagement.	________	________
b. The reasons given for the client's request to change the engagement, particularly the implications of a restriction on the scope of the original engagement.	________	________
c. The additional effort required to complete the original engagement.	________	________
d. Where applicable, any reasons for changing from a general-use report to a restricted-use report.	________	________

	Completed by	N/A
3. Communicate directly with all specified parties and obtain their acknowledgement of the sufficiency of the procedures for their purposes. If direct communication is not possible, perform one of the following procedures:		
a. Distribute a draft of the report or a copy of the engagement letter to the specified parties and obtain their agreement.	________	________
b. Compare the procedures to be applied with the written requirements of the specified parties.	________	________
c. Discuss the procedures to be applied with appropriate representatives (such as legal counsel) of the specified parties.	________	________
d. Review relevant contracts with or correspondence from the specified parties.	________	________
4. Consider the procedures being requested and determine whether they are appropriate for an agreed-upon procedures engagement.	________	________
5. Establish and document an understanding with the client, preferably in an engagement letter. If an engagement letter will not be obtained, the oral understanding should be documented in a memo.	________	________
6. Obtain an understanding of the client and the engagement.	________	________
7. If the client is not the responsible party, obtain evidence of the responsible party's responsibility for the subject matter.	________	________
8. Obtain an understanding of the specified compliance requirements.	________	________
9. Perform any additional services needed to assist the responsible party in developing the subject matter or related assertion.	________	________
10. Determine that the scheduling and staffing are adequate to perform the engagement.	________	________
11. Obtain the engagement partner's approval of the overall engagement plan.	________	________
12. If other services have been performed for the responsible party, review relevant workpapers and any related reports for indications of matters that contradict the assertion.	________	________
13. Include in the workpapers a list of all procedures agreed upon in the engagement letter or include a copy of the engagement letter.	________	________

	Completed by	N/A
14. Perform the agreed-upon procedures and summarize the findings.	________	________
15. Obtain a written assertion and a representation letter from the responsible party.	________	________
16. Draft the agreed-upon procedures report.	________	________
17. Consider other reporting issues:		
a. Reporting all findings, unless a materiality threshold was agreed upon.	________	________
b. A description of any materiality limits agreed upon.	________	________
c. Reporting other matters (including subsequent events).	________	________
d. Restrictions on performance of procedures.	________	________
e. Refusal to provide a representation letter.	________	________
f. Explanations of sampling risk.	________	________
g. Disclosure of stipulated facts, assumptions, or interpretations used in the application of the procedures.	________	________
h. Description of the condition of records, controls, or data to which the procedures were applied.	________	________
i. Explanation that the practitioner has no responsibility to update his or her report.	________	________
j. Description of the nature of any assistance provided by a specialist.	________	________
18. If any additional specified parties are added, obtain their acknowledgement for the sufficiency of the procedures.	________	________
19. Read other information in a client-prepared document that contains the agreed-upon procedures report for inconsistencies.	________	________
20. If any situations have occurred that require consultation, determine that such consultation has been properly documented.	________	________
21. If there were differences of professional opinion among members of the engagement team or between the engagement team and a specialist, determine that the differences were properly resolved and documented.	________	________
22. Determine that all questions, exceptions, or notes, if any, posed during the engagement have been followed up and resolved.	________	________

		Completed by	N/A
23.	Determine that all required forms, questionnaires, and checklists have been completed.	______	______
24.	Ensure that the workpapers and agreed-upon procedures report have been reviewed in accordance with firm policy.	______	______
25.	Obtain engagement partner's review and approval for issuance of report.	______	______

APPENDIX 10E
AGREED-UPON PROCEDURES ENGAGEMENT: PROCEDURES AND FINDINGS FORM

Client Name: ______________ Date of Subject Matter: ______________

Completed by: ______________ Date Completed: ______________

Instructions

This form can be used to record findings as each procedure is performed. Use a separate form for each procedure performed and document each procedure and finding as precisely as possible. Include all findings in the agreed-upon procedures report, unless materiality limits have been established and agreed upon by the specified parties.

Subject matter to which the procedure was applied:

Describe procedure:

Workpaper Reference	Finding

Discussed with responsible party:

Position: Date:

APPENDIX 10F
REPRESENTATION LETTER: AGREED-UPON PROCEDURES ENGAGEMENT

[*date—No earlier than date of the accountant's report*]

[*CPA firm's name*]
[*address*]

In connection with your engagement to apply agreed-upon procedures to the [*describe subject matter*] as of [*date of subject matter*], we confirm, to the best of our knowledge and belief, the following representations made to you during your engagement:

- We are responsible for complying with [*describe specified requirements*].
- We are responsible for establishing and maintaining effective internal control over compliance.
- We have performed an evaluation of the Company's compliance with [*describe specified requirements*].
- [*Recite the responsible party's assertion.*]
- We have disclosed to you all known noncompliance with [*describe specified requirements*], including noncompliance occurring after [*date of subject matter*].
- We have made available to you all documentation and other information related to compliance with [*describe specified requirements*].
- Out interpretation of [*provision of specified requirements*] is as follows:
  — [*Recite responsible party's interpretation of provision of specified requirements.*]
- There have been no communications from regulatory agencies, internal auditors, or other independent accountants or consultants regarding possible noncompliance with [*describe specified requirements*], including communications received between [*date of subject matter*] and [*date of representation letter*].
- We have responded fully to all inquiries made to us by you during the engagement.
- Your report is intended solely for the information and use of [*specified parties*] and is not intended to be and should not be used by anyone other than those specified parties.

Signature:	Signature:
Title:	Title:

APPENDIX 10G
CLIENT REPRESENTATION LETTER: AGREED-UPON PROCEDURES ENGAGEMENT, CLIENT NOT RESPONSIBLE PARTY

[*date—No earlier than date of the accountant's report*]

[*CPA firm's name*]
[*address*]

In connection with your engagement to apply agreed-upon procedures to [*describe subject matter*] as of [*date of subject matter*], we confirm, to the best of our knowledge and belief, the following representations made to you during the course of your engagement:

- We are responsible for complying with [*describe specified requirements*].

- We are responsible for establishing and maintaining effective internal control over compliance.
- We have performed an evaluation of the Company's compliance with [*describe specified requirements*].
- [*Recite the responsible party's assertion.*]
- We have disclosed to you all known noncompliance with [*describe specified requirements*], including noncompliance occurring after [*date of subject matter*].
- We have made available to you all documentation and other information related to compliance with [*describe specified requirements*].
- Out interpretation of [*provision of specified requirements*] is as follows:
  — [*Recite responsible party's interpretation of provision of specified requirements.*]
- There have been no communications from regulatory agencies, internal auditors, or other independent accountants or consultants regarding possible noncompliance with [*describe specified requirements*], including communications received between [*date of subject matter*] and [*date of representation letter*].
- We have responded fully to all inquiries made to us by you during the engagement.
- Your report is intended solely for the information and use of [*specified parties*] and is not intended to be and should not be used by anyone other than those specified parties.

Signature:

Title:

APPENDIX 10H STANDARD AGREED-UPON PROCEDURES REPORT ON COMPLIANCE WITH SPECIFIED REQUIREMENTS

Independent Accountant's Report

To the Board of Directors of
[*client name*]
[*city, state*]

We have performed the procedures enumerated below, which were agreed to by [*list of specified parties*], solely to assist the specified parties in evaluating [*name of entity*]'s compliance with [*list specified requirements*] during the [*period*] ended [*date*]. Management is responsible for [*name of entity*]'s compliance with those requirements. This agreed-upon procedures engagement was conducted in accordance with attestation standards established by the American Institute of Certified Public Accountants. The sufficiency of these procedures is solely the responsibility of those parties specified in this report. Consequently, we make no representation regarding the sufficiency of the procedures described below either for the purpose for which this report has been requested or for any other purpose.

[*Include paragraphs to enumerate procedures and findings.*]

We were not engaged to and did not conduct an examination, the objective of which would be the expression of an opinion on compliance. Accordingly, we do not express such an opinion. Had we performed additional procedures, other matters might have come to our attention that would have been reported to you.

This report is intended solely for the information and use of [list or refer to specified parties] and is not intended to be and should not be used by anyone other than these specified parties.

[*firm's signature*]

[*city, state*]

[*date*]

APPENDIX 10I
ENGAGEMENT LETTER: EXAMINATION ENGAGEMENT

[*date*]

[*client's name*]
[*address*]

We are pleased to confirm our understanding of the services we are to provide for [*client's legal name*].

We will examine the [*describe subject matter or related assertion*] of [*name of client*] as of [*date*]. Our examination will be conducted in accordance with attestation standards established by the American Institute of Certified Public Accountants. Accordingly, it will include tests of your records and other procedures we consider necessary to enable us to express an opinion as to whether your [*describe subject matter*] is presented, in all material respects, in conformity with [*describe criteria*] or whether [*describe assertion*] is fairly stated, in all material respects based on conformity with [*describe criteria*]. If, for any reason, we are unable to complete the examination, we will not issue a report as a result of this engagement.

[*Describe restrictions on the use of the report, if any.*]

Our engagement will not include a detailed inspection of every transaction and cannot be relied upon to disclose all material errors, fraud, or other illegal acts, that may exist. However, we will inform you of any material errors or fraud that comes to our attention. We will also inform you of any other illegal acts that come to our attention, unless clearly inconsequential.

We understand that you will provide us with the basic information required for our examination and that you are responsible for the accuracy and completeness of that information. We may advise you about appropriate criteria or assist in the development of the subject matter, but the responsibility for the subject matter remains with you. At the end of the engagement, we will require a representation letter from management.

We expect to begin our examination on approximately [*date*]. We estimate that our fees for these services will range from $_____ to $_____. You will also be billed for travel and other out-of-pocket costs such as report production, typing, postage, etc. Additional expenses are estimated to be $_____. The fee estimate is based on anticipated cooperation from your personnel and the assumption that unexpected circumstances will not be encountered during the examination. If significant additional time is necessary, we will discuss it with you and arrive at a new fee estimate before we incur the additional costs. Our invoices for these services will be rendered each month as work progresses and are payable on presentation. In accordance with our firm policies, work may be suspended if your account becomes _____ days or more overdue and will not be resumed until your account is paid in full. If we elect to terminate our services for nonpayment, our engagement will be deemed to have been completed upon written notification of termination, even if we have not completed our report. You will be obligated to compensate us for all time extended and to reimburse us for all out-of-pocket expenditures through the date of termination.

We appreciate the opportunity to be of service to you and believe this letter accurately summarizes the significant terms of our engagement. If you have any questions, please let us know. If you agree with the terms of our engagement as described in this letter, please sign the enclosed copy and return it to us.

Very truly yours,

[*CPA firm's name*]

Response:

This letter correctly sets forth the understanding of [*client's name*].

By:

Title:

Date:

APPENDIX 10J
EXAMINATION PROCEDURES CHECKLIST: COMPLIANCE ENGAGEMENT

Client Name: _______________ Date of Subject Matter: _______________

Completed by: _______________ Date Completed: _______________

	Completed by	N/A
1. Complete the Client Acceptance and Retention Evaluation Form.	_________	_________

	Completed by	N/A
2. Establish and document an understanding with the client, preferably in an engagement letter. If an engagement letter will not be obtained, the oral understanding should be documented in a memo.	________	________
3. Obtain an understanding of the client and the engagement, including the relevant aspects of internal control over compliance.	________	________
4. If the client is not the responsible party, obtain evidence of the responsible party's responsibility for the subject matter.	________	________
5. Obtain an understanding of the specified compliance requirements.	________	________
6. Perform any additional services needed to assist the responsible party in developing the subject matter or related assertion.	________	________
7. Determine that the scheduling and staffing are adequate to perform the engagement.	________	________
8. Make a preliminary assessment of materiality for attest purposes.		
9. Obtain the engagement partner's approval of the overall engagement plan.	________	________
10. If other services have been performed for the responsible party, review relevant workpapers and any related reports for indications of matters that contradict the subject matter or related assertion.	________	________
11. Develop and perform procedures necessary to evaluate the subject matter based on the criteria (attach a program or memo to this checklist).	________	________
12. For engagements involving compliance with regulatory requirements, read reports of significant examinations and related communications between the entity and the applicable regulatory agencies. If necessary make inquiries of agencies, including inquiries about examinations in progress.	________	________
13. Review the results of the preceding procedures and evaluate whether (a) the entity complied, in all material respects, with the specified requirements or (b) the assertion is presented, in all material respects, in conformity with the specified criteria. If the procedures reveal instances of noncompliance, assess the significance of the noncompliance and its effect on the examination report.	________	________

		Completed by	N/A
14.	Consider whether events have occurred after the date of the subject matter but before the end of fieldwork that affect the presentation of the subject matter.	________	________
15.	Obtain a representation letter and written assertion from the responsible party (and the client, if the client is not the responsible party).	________	________
16.	Draft the examination report.	________	________
17.	Read for inconsistencies with the report and material misstatements of fact other information in a client-prepared document that contains the examination report.	________	________
18.	If any situations have occurred that require consultation, determine that such consultation has been properly documented.	________	________
19.	If there were differences of professional opinion among members of the engagement team or between the engagement team and a specialist, determine that the differences were properly resolved and documented.	________	________
20.	Determine that all questions, exceptions, or notes, if any, posed during the engagement have been followed up and resolved.	________	________
21.	Determine that all required forms, questionnaires, and checklists have been completed.	________	________
22.	Ensure that the workpapers and examination report have been reviewed in accordance with firm policy.	________	________
23.	Obtain engagement partner's review and approval for issuance of report.	________	________

APPENDIX 10K
ENGAGEMENT ACCEPTANCE ADDENDUM: COMPLIANCE EXAMINATION ENGAGEMENT

Client Name: ______________ Date of Subject Matter: ______________

Completed by: ______________ Date Completed: ______________

Instructions

This form is an addendum to the Client Acceptance and Retention Evaluation Form. This addendum may be used to document acceptance considerations for compliance examinations.

		Yes	No
1.	Will the responsible party accept responsibility for the entity's compliance with the specified requirements and the effectiveness of the entity's internal control over compliance?	___	___
2.	Will the responsible party evaluate the entity's compliance with the specified requirements?	___	___
3.	Will the responsible party make a written assertion about the entity's compliance with the specified requirements?	___	___

APPENDIX 10L
REPRESENTATION LETTER: EXAMINATION ENGAGEMENT

[*date—No earlier than date of the accountant's report*]

[*CPA firm's name*]
[*address*]

In connection with your examination engagement of [*describe subject matter*] as of [*date of subject matter*], we confirm, to the best of our knowledge and belief, the following representations made to you during your engagement.

- We are responsible for complying with [*describe specified requirements*].
- We are responsible for establishing and maintaining effective internal control over compliance.
- We have performed an evaluation of the Company's compliance with [*describe specified requirements*].
- [*Recite the responsible party's assertion.*]
- We have disclosed to you all known noncompliance with [*describe specified requirements*], including noncompliance occurring after [*date of subject matter*].
- We have made available to you all documentation and other information related to compliance with [*describe specified requirements*].
- Out interpretation of [*provision of specified requirements*] is as follows:
  — [*Recite responsible party's interpretation of provision of specified requirements.*]
- There have been no communications from regulatory agencies, internal auditors, or other independent accountants or consultants regarding possible noncompliance with [*describe specified requirements*], including communications received between [*date of subject matter*] and [*date of representation letter*].
- We have responded fully to all inquiries made to us by you during the engagement.

Signature:	Signature:
Title:	Title:

APPENDIX 10M
CLIENT REPRESENTATION LETTER: EXAMINATION ENGAGEMENT, CLIENT NOT RESPONSIBLE PARTY

[*date—No earlier than date of the accountant's report*]

[*CPA firm's name*]
[*address*]

In connection with your examination of [*describe subject matter*] as of [*date of subject matter*], we confirm, to the best of our knowledge and belief, the following representations made to you during the course of your engagement:

- We are responsible for complying with [*describe specified requirements*].
- We are responsible for establishing and maintaining effective internal control over compliance.
- We have performed an evaluation of the Company's compliance with [*describe specified requirements*].
- [*Recite the responsible party's assertion.*]
- We have disclosed to you all known noncompliance with [*describe specified requirements*], including noncompliance occurring after [*date of subject matter*].
- We have made available to you all documentation and other information related to compliance with [*describe specified requirements*].
- Out interpretation of [*provision of specified requirements*] is as follows:
  — [*Recite responsible party's interpretation of provision of specified requirements.*]
- There have been no communications from regulatory agencies, internal auditors, or other independent accountants or consultants regarding possible noncompliance with [*describe specified requirements*], including communications received between [*date of subject matter*] and [*date of representation letter*].
- We have responded fully to all inquiries made to us by you during the engagement.

Signature:

Title:

APPENDIX 10N
STANDARD EXAMINATION REPORT ON COMPLIANCE WITH SPECIFIED REQUIREMENTS

Independent Accountant's Report

To the Board of Directors of
XYZ Company
[*city, state*]

We have examined [*name of entity*]'s compliance with [*list of specified compliance requirements*] during the [*period*] ended [*date*]. Management is responsible for [*name of entity*]'s compliance with those requirements. Our responsibility is to express an opinion on [*name of entity*]'s compliance based on our examination.

Our examination was conducted in accordance with attestation standards established by the American Institute of Certified Public Accountants and, accordingly, included examining, on a test basis, evidence about [*name of entity*]'s compliance with those requirements and performing such other procedures as we considered necessary in the circumstances. We believe that our examination provides a reasonable basis for our opinion. Our examination does not provide a legal determination on [*name of entity*]'s compliance with specified requirements.

In our opinion, [*name of entity*] complied, in all material respects, with the aforementioned requirements for the [*period*] ended [*date*] is fairly stated, all material respects

[*firm's signature*]

[*city, state*]

[*date*]

APPENDIX 10O
STANDARD EXAMINATION REPORT ON MANAGEMENT'S ASSERTION ABOUT COMPLIANCE WITH SPECIFIED REQUIREMENTS

Independent Accountant's Report

To the Board of Directors of
XYZ Company
[*city, state*]

We have examined management's assertion, included in the accompanying [*title of management report*], that [*name of entity*] complied with [*list of specified compliance requirements*] during the [*period*] ended [*date*]. Management is responsible for [*name of entity*]'s compliance with those requirements. Our responsibility is to express an opinion on [*name of entity*]'s compliance based on our examination.

Our examination was conducted in accordance with attestation standards established by the American Institute of Certified Public Accountants and, accordingly, included examining, on a test basis, evidence about [*name of entity*]'s compliance with those requirements and performing such other procedures as we considered necessary in the circumstances. We believe that our examination provides a reasonable basis for our opinion. Our examination does not provide a legal determination on [*name of entity*]'s compliance with specified requirements.

In our opinion, management's assertion that [*name of entity*] complied with the aforementioned requirements during the [*period*] ended [*date*] is fairly stated, all material respects.

[*firm's signature*]

[*city, state*]

[*date*]

APPENDIX 10P
COMPLIANCE EXAMINATION REPORT: REPORT QUALIFIED FOR NONCOMPLIANCE

Independent Accountant's Report

To the Board of Directors of
XYZ Company
[*city, state*]

We have examined [*name of entity*]'s compliance with [*list of specified compliance requirements*] during the [*period*] ended [*date*]. Management is responsible for [*name of entity*]'s compliance with those requirements. Our responsibility is to express an opinion on [*name of entity*]'s compliance based on our examination.

Our examination was conducted in accordance with attestation standards established by the American Institute of Certified Public Accountants and, accordingly, included examining, on a test basis, evidence about [*name of entity*]'s compliance with those requirements and performing such other procedures as we considered necessary in the circumstances. We believe that our examination provides a reasonable basis for our opinion. Our examination does not provide a legal determination on [*name of entity*]'s compliance with specified requirements.

Our examination disclosed the following material noncompliance with [*type of compliance requirement*] applicable to [*name of entity*] during the [*period*] ended [*date*]. [*Describe noncompliance.*]

In our opinion, except for the material noncompliance described in the third paragraph, [*name of entity*] complied, in all material respects, with the aforementioned requirements for the [*period*] ended [*date*].

[*firm's signature*]

[*city, state*]

[*date*]

APPENDIX 10Q
COMPLIANCE EXAMINATION REPORT: ADVERSE OPINION

Independent Accountant's Report

To the Board of Directors of
XYZ Company
[*city, state*]

We have examined [*name of entity*]'s compliance with [*list of specified compliance requirements*] during the [*period*] ended [*date*]. Management is responsible for [*name of entity*]'s compliance with those requirements. Our responsibility is to express an opinion on [*name of entity*]'s compliance based on our examination.

Our examination was conducted in accordance with attestation standards established by the American Institute of Certified Public Accountants and, accordingly, included examining, on a test basis, evidence about [*name of entity*]'s compliance with those requirements and performing such other procedures as we considered necessary in the circumstances. We believe that our examination provides a reasonable basis for our opinion. Our examination does not provide a legal determination on [*name of entity*]'s compliance with specified requirements.

Our examination disclosed the following material noncompliance with [*type of compliance requirement*] applicable to [*name of entity*] during the [*period*] ended [*date*]. [*Describe noncompliance.*]

In our opinion, because of the effect of the material noncompliance described in the third paragraph, [*name of entity*] has not complied with the aforementioned requirements for the [*period*] ended [*date*].

[*firm's signature*]

[*city, state*]

[*date*]

CHAPTER 11
INTERNAL CONTROL ENGAGEMENTS

CONTENTS

OVERVIEW

This chapter discusses the various types of attestation engagements related to internal control. Internal control is a broad topic. However, the primary focus of this chapter is on engagements to examine the effectiveness of an entity's internal control over financial reporting. In addition, the chapter discusses engagements related to effectiveness of an entity's internal control over compliance (examination and agreed-upon procedures engagements).

INTRODUCTION

Revision of AT 501

Chapter 5 of SSAE-10 (AT 501) provides guidance to practitioners engaged to examine the effectiveness of an entity's internal control over financial reporting. Specifically, guidance is provided regarding the following:

- Conditions that must be met for the practitioner to accept an engagement to examine the effectiveness of any entity's internal control.
- Engagements to examine the design and operating effectiveness of an entity's internal control.
- Engagements to examine the design and operating effectiveness of a segment of an entity's internal control.
- Engagements to examine only the suitability of design of an entity's internal control (no assertion is made about the operating effectiveness).
- Engagements to examine the design and operating effectiveness of an entity's internal control based on criteria established by a regulatory agency.

Although not addressed in Chapter 5 of SSAE-10 (AT 501), this chapter of this guide discusses engagements to examine controls over operations and compliance with laws and regulations, as well as agreed-upon procedures engagements.

On March 18, 2003, the AICPA's Auditing Standards Board (ASB) issued an exposure draft of a proposed revision of Chapter 5 of SSAE-10 (AT 501) (Reporting on an Entity's Internal Control Over Financial Reporting). That exposure draft was included in a document that also contained (1) a proposed Statement on Auditing Standards (SAS) (Auditing an Entity's Internal Control over Financial Reporting in Conjunction with the Financial Statement Audit) and (2) an amendment of SAS-100 (AU 722) (Interim Financial Information).

The AT 501 Task Force (task force) of the ASB has been charged with revising AT 501 to reflect

- Comments received on the exposure draft of AT 501 issued on March 18, 2003.
- PCAOB Auditing Standard No. 2 (AS-2).
- The views of regulators of insurance companies and financial institutions, as well as the Government Accountability Office (GAO), which all use AT 501 to report on internal control.

Alternatives for the Revision of AT 501

The AT 501 Task Force is considering the following alternatives in revising AT 501:

- The starting point for revising AT 501: PCAOB AS-2 or AT 501.
- If the task force begins with PCAOB AS-2, there are additional alternatives for revising or replacing AT 501:
    a. Adopting PCAOB AS-2 with changes to reflect the fact that the entity undergoing the examination is a nonissuer.
    b. Alternative "a" plus modifying management's internal control requirements from evaluating and reporting on internal control to making an assertion about internal control and monitoring it using suitable control criteria. Chapter 6, "Monitoring," of "Internal Control—Integrated Framework" issued by the Committee of Sponsoring Organizations of the Treadway Commission (COSO) describes monitoring, in part, as assessing the quality of an entity's internal control over time. Such monitoring is needed because of possible change in internal control, such as change in the way controls are applied or in the relevance of controls. If the ASB adopted this approach, it would need to determine what work management would be required to perform to support its representations regarding the effectiveness of the entity's internal control and how that work would compare with the work performed by the practitioner.

c. Revising AT 501 to address the needs of regulators of insurance companies, financial institutions, as well as the Government Accountability Office.

SAS-60 (Communication of Internal Control Related Matters Noted in an Audit)

The task force is also recommending that the definition of "significant deficiency" used in PCAOB AS-2 replace the term "reportable condition" used in SAS-60 (AU 325) (Communication of Internal Control Related Matters Noted in an Audit). In addition, the task force is considering the order in which to revise SAS-60 and AT 501. The rationale for conforming these two standards is that it would be illogical for internal control to be adequate for a financial statement audit but not for an examination of internal control.

The task force is also considering the following concepts related to the terms "deficiency," "significant deficiency," and "material weakness" in PCAOB AS-2:

- Inadequate documentation of the design of controls.
- Ineffective oversight by audit committee as a strong indicator of a material weakness.
- The terms "likelihood," "magnitude," "potential," and "prudent official."
- Indicators of deficiencies.
- The following indicators of at least a significant deficiency and a strong indicator of a material weakness:
  - Restatement
  - Auditor found material misstatements
  - Ineffective audit committee
  - Ineffective internal audit or risk assessment process
  - Ineffective regulatory compliance
  - Fraud by senior management
  - Uncorrected significant deficiencies
  - Ineffective control environment
- Required communications in writing about audit committee and external auditor.

Terminology for the Practitioner's Responsibilities

PCAOB AS-2 uses the terms "all," "must," and "shall" in expressing the auditor's responsibilities. This differs from the terms used in the ASB's standards, for example, "should" and "may." The task force is considering whether the ASB should adopt the terms used in the PCAOB's standards.

Other Issues

Other issues being considered by the task force include

- Reporting issues
- Reliance on others
- Public perception of an internal control standard that differs from PCAOB AS-2
- Changes in reporting
- What regulators need in a revised AT 501/PCAOB AS-2

An exposure draft of a proposed SSAE is expected to be issued by the ASB in 2005.

COMMITTEE OF SPONSORING ORGANIZATIONS (COSO)

One of the conditions for engagement performance set forth in Chapter 5 of SSAE-10 (AT 501.04) is that the responsible party evaluates the effectiveness of the entity's internal control using suitable criteria. According to SSAE-10 (AT 501.04), criteria established by groups composed of experts that follow due-process procedures, including exposure of proposed criteria for public comment, usually should be considered suitable criteria for this purpose. Specifically, SSAE-10 (AT 501.04) cites the Committee of Sponsoring Organizations (COSO) report, "Internal Control—Integrated Framework," as an example of suitable criteria.

COSO is a voluntary private-sector organization dedicated to improving the quality of financial reporting through business ethics, effective internal controls, and corporate governance. COSO was originally formed in 1985 to sponsor the National Commission on Fraudulent Financial Reporting, an independent private-sector initiative that studied the causal factors that can lead to fraudulent financial reporting and developed recommendations for public companies and their independent auditors, for the SEC and other regulators, and for educational institutions.

The National Commission was jointly sponsored by the five major financial professional associations in the United States, the American Accounting Association, the American Institute of Certified Public Accountants, the Financial Executives Institute, the Institute of Internal Auditors, and the National Association of Accountants (now the Institute of Management Accountants). The Commission was wholly independent of each of the sponsoring organizations, and it comprised representatives from industry, public accounting, investment firms, and the New York Stock Exchange.

Definition of Internal Control

Internal control is a process, effected by an entity's board of directors, management and other personnel, designed to provide reasonable assurance regarding the achievement of objectives in the following categories:

- Effectiveness and efficiency of operations.
- Reliability of financial reporting.
- Compliance with applicable laws and regulations.

This definition reflects certain fundamental concepts:

- Internal control is a process. It is a means to an end, not an end in itself.
- Internal control is effected by people. It is not merely policy manuals and forms, but also people at every level of an organization.
- Internal control can be expected to provide only reasonable assurance, not absolute assurance, to an entity's management and board.
- Internal control is geared to the achievement of objectives in one or more separate but overlapping categories.

Objectives

Every entity sets out on a mission, establishing objectives it wants to achieve and strategies for achieving them. Objectives may be set for the entity as a whole or aimed at specific activities within the entity. Many objectives are specific to a particular entity, others are widely shared. Objectives common to virtually all entities are achieving and maintaining a positive reputation within the business and consumer communities, providing reliable financial statements to stakeholders, and operating in compliance with laws and regulations.

For this chapter, objectives fall into three categories:

1. *Operations* Relating to the effective and efficient use of the entity's resources.
2. *Financial reporting* Relating to preparation of reliable published financial statements.
3. *Compliance* Relating to the entity's compliance with applicable laws and regulations.

This categorization system separates aspects of internal control. These distinct but overlapping categories (a particular objective can fall under more than one category) address different needs that could be the direct responsibility of different executives. This categorization also allows distinguishing between what can be expected from each category of internal control.

An internal control system can and cannot be expected to provide reasonable assurance of obtaining objectives relating to the reliability of financial reporting and compliance with laws and regulations. The achievement of those objectives, which are based largely on standards imposed by external parties, depends on how activities within an entity's control are performed.

Achievement of operations objectives—such as a particular return on investment, market share, or entry into new product lines—is not always within the entity's control. Internal control cannot prevent bad judgments or decisions or external events that can cause a business to fail to achieve operations goals. For these objectives, the internal control system can provide reasonable assurance only that management (and in its oversight role the board) is made aware, in a timely manner, of the extent to which the entity is moving toward those objectives.

Components

Internal control consists of five interrelated components, which are derived from the way management runs a business and are integrated with management process:

1. *Control environment* The core of any business is its people—their individual attributes, including integrity, ethical values and competence—and the environment in which they operate. They are the engine that drives the entity and the foundation on which everything rests.
2. *Risk assessment* The entity must be aware of and deal with the risks it faces. It must set objectives, integrated with the sales, production, marketing, financial, and other activities, so that the parts of the organization operate in concert. The organization must also establish mechanisms to identify, analyze, and manage the related risks.
3. *Control activities* Control policies and procedures must be established and executed to help ensure that the actions identified by management as necessary to address risks to achievement of the entity's objectives are effectively carried out.
4. *Information and communication* Information and communication systems, enable the entity's people to capture and exchange the information needed to conduct, manage, and control the entity's operations.
5. *Monitoring* The entire process must be monitored, and modifications made as necessary. In this way, the system can react dynamically, changing as conditions warrant.

These internal control components are linked, and internal control systems are dynamic: The assessment of risks not only influences the control activities, but can also highlight the need to reconsider information and communication needs or the entity's monitoring activities. Internal control is not a serial process in which one component affects only the next; rather, it is a multidirectional iterative process in which almost any component can and will influence any other.

No two entities will, or should, have the same internal control system. Companies and their internal control needs differ dramatically by industry and size, and by culture and management philosophy. Although all entities need each of the components to maintain control over their activities, one company's internal control system will likely look very different from from that of another.

SARBANES-OXLEY ACT

On July 30, 2002, President George W. Bush signed into law the Sarbanes-Oxley Act of 2002 (the Act). The Act, which applies in general to publicly held companies and their audit firms, dramatically affects the accounting profession. Section 404 of the Act requires the Securities and Exchange Commission (SEC) to issue rules to require that each annual report of a publicly held company contain an internal control report that

- States the responsibility of management for establishing and maintaining an adequate internal control structure and procedures for financial reporting; and
- Contains an assessment, as of the end of the most recent fiscal year, of the effectiveness of such structure and procedures.

In addition, Section 404 of the Act requires the public company's external auditor to attest to, and report on, the internal control assessment made by the management of the issuer in accordance with the standards for attestation engagements adopted by the new Public Company Accounting Oversight Board (PCAOB) established under the Act.

In June 2004, the SEC approved the PCAOB Auditing Standard No. 2 (AS-2) (An Audit of Internal Control over Financial Reporting Performed in Conjunction with an Audit of Financial Statements), which addresses both the work that is required in order to audit internal control over financial reporting and the relationship of that audit to the audit of the financial statements. An audit of internal control includes, among other things, evaluating the process management used to perform its assessment of internal control effectiveness, evaluating the effectiveness of both the design and operation of the internal control, and forming an opinion about whether internal control over financial reporting is effective.

AUDIT OF INTERNAL CONTROL OVER FINANCIAL REPORTING

Section 404, "Management Assessment of Internal Controls," of the Sarbanes-Oxley Act of 2002 (SOX) requires the management of a public company to include in its annual report to shareholders

- An assessment of the effectiveness of internal control over financial reporting as of the end of the company's most recent fiscal year and
- Management's conclusion as a result of that assessment about whether the company's internal control is effective.

SOX directs the Public Company Accounting Oversight Board (PCAOB) to establish professional standards for independent auditors of public companies to attest to, and report on, management's assessment of the effectiveness of the company's internal control. A public company is required to file the auditor's attestation report as part of its annual report.

In response to these requirements, the PCAOB issued Auditing Standard No. 2 (AS-2) (An Audit of Internal Control over Financial Reporting Performed in Conjunction with an Audit of Financial Statements). AS-2 addresses the work that is required to audit internal control over financial reporting and the relationship of that audit to the audit of the financial statements. The audit of management's assessment of internal control cannot be undertaken as a separate engagement, because the objectives and work involved in such an engagement are closely intertwined with those of an audit of the financial statements. For this reason, the audit of management's assessment of internal control must be integrated with the audit of the company's financial statements. Accordingly, the auditor of a public company issues two audit opinions: one on the company's financial statements and one on the company's internal control over financial reporting.

> **OBSERVATION:** It should be emphasized that AS-2 applies only to audits of public companies. However, the release accompanying AS-2 states that "nothing in the Board's rules would preclude an accounting firm from conducting an audit of a company that is not an issuer in accordance with the Board's standards and so stating in its audit report. This is true regardless of whether or not the accounting firm performing the audit is registered with the Board."

The PCAOB has issued a series of Q&As on AS-2, one of which addresses the situation of whether a nonissuer's internal control over financial reporting must be audited pursuant to AS-2 if it elects to have its financial statements audited pursuant to PCAOB standards. The PCAOB notes that only certain issuers that are subject to Section 404 of SOX are required to include within the scope of the audit an audit of internal control over financial reporting. Although the PCAOB's standards provide for an integrated audit of financial statements and internal control for those issuers that are subject to Section 404 of SOX, the PCAOB's standards also permit auditors to conduct a financial-statement-only audit under circumstances, for example, when Section 404 of SOX is not applicable. Therefore, a nonissuer is not required to undergo an audit of internal control if it elects to have its financial statements audited pursuant to PCAOB standards. Appendix 11W is a summary of the PCAOB Q&A document.

> **OBSERVATION:** The term "issuer" means an issuer as defined in Section 3 of the Securities Exchange Act of 1934 whose securities are registered under Section 12 of the act or who is required to file reports under Section 15(d) of the act or who files or has filed a registration statement with the Securities and Exchange Commission that has not yet become effective under the Securities Act of 1933 that it has not withdrawn. The term "nonissuer" generally means a nonpublic entity.

Applicability of AS-2

AS-2 addresses both the work that is required to audit internal control over financial reporting and the relationship of that audit to the audit of the financial statements. An audit of internal control includes evaluating the process management used to perform its assessment of internal control effectiveness, evaluating the effectiveness of both the design and operation of the internal control, and forming an opinion about whether internal control over financial reporting is effective.

When an auditor is engaged to audit a company's financial statements and management's assessment of internal control over financial reporting, the requirements of AS-2 apply. Pursuant to SEC rules adopted under Section 404(a) of SOX, all companies subject to the Securities Exchange Act of 1934 are required to include in their annual report a report of management on the company's internal control over financial reporting. This report must include management's assessment of the effectiveness of the company's internal control over financial reporting as of the end of the company's most recent fiscal year. Section 404(b) of SOX further requires the company's auditor to attest to and report on management's assessment, and the company is required to file the auditor's report as part of its annual report.

Objective of an Audit of Internal Control over Financial Reporting

The auditor's objective in an audit of internal control over financial reporting is to express opinions on management's assessment of the effectiveness of the company's internal control over financial reporting and on whether the company maintained effective internal control over financial reporting. To express such an opinion, the auditor must plan and perform the audit to obtain reasonable assurance about whether the company maintained, in all material respects, effective internal control over financial reporting as of the date specified in management's assessment. The auditor must also audit the company's financial statements as of the specified date because the information obtained during the financial statement audit is relevant to the auditor's conclusions about the effectiveness of the company's internal control over financial reporting. To obtain reasonable assurance, the auditor evaluates the assessment performed by management and obtains evidence about whether the internal control over financial reporting is designed and operating effectively for all relevant financial statement assertions related to all significant accounts and disclosures in the financial statements.

The auditor is required to obtain evidence of operating effectiveness of controls over relevant assertions for significant accounts and disclosures each year; that is, the audit evidence obtained each year should stand alone. However, the nature, timing, and extent of audit testing directed toward relevant assertions should vary from year to year. These variations are based on prior years' findings, changes in the company's internal control, and/or changes in management.

According to AS-2, the auditor should be aware that the persons who rely on the information concerning internal control over financial reporting include investors, creditors, the board of directors and its audit committee, and regulators in specialized industries such as banking and insurance. The auditor should be aware that external users of financial statements are interested in information on internal control over financial reporting because it enhances the quality of financial reporting and increases their confidence in financial information. This includes financial information issued between annual reports, such as quarterly information. Information on internal control over financial reporting is also intended to provide an early warning to those inside and outside the company (such as the audit committee and regulators in specialized industries) who are in a position to insist on improvements in internal control over financial reporting. Additionally, Section 302 of SOX requires management, with the participation of the principal executive and financial officers, to make quarterly and annual certifications with respect to the company's internal control over financial reporting.

Management's Responsibilities

According to AS-2, for the auditor to satisfactorily complete an audit of internal control over financial reporting, management must do the following:

- Accept responsibility for the effectiveness of the company's internal control over financial reporting.
- Evaluate the effectiveness of the company's internal control over financial reporting, using suitable control criteria.
- Support its evaluation with sufficient evidence, including documentation.
- Present a written assessment of the effectiveness of the company's internal control over financial reporting as of the end of the company's most recent fiscal year.

If management has not fulfilled the responsibilities noted above, the auditor is required to communicate, in writing, to management and the audit committee that the audit of internal control over financial reporting cannot be satisfactorily completed and that, furthermore, he or she, is required to disclaim an opinion.

Management should fulfill its responsibilities by undertaking a comprehensive approach that includes thorough planning and evaluation of its system of internal controls. Once management has identified significant controls, it can document them and proceed with testing their effectiveness.

Evaluation of Management's Assessment Process

In conjunction with planning the audit of internal control over financial reporting, the auditor evaluates management's process for assessing the effectiveness of the entity's internal control over financial reporting, which provides the auditor with evidence that management has a basis to support its assertion on the effectiveness of internal control over financial reporting. The evaluation also helps the auditor understand the entity's internal control over financial reporting, plan the work necessary to complete the audit, and it provides some of the evidence the auditor will use to support the opinion.

The auditor must obtain an understanding of management's process for assessing the effectiveness of the company's internal control over financial reporting and evaluate whether management has determined the appropriate controls to be tested. These controls include controls over all relevant assertions related to all significant accounts and disclosures in the financial statements, including

- Controls over initiating, authorizing, recording, processing, and reporting significant accounts and disclosures and related assertions embodied in the financial statements.

- Controls over the selection and application of accounting policies that are in conformity with generally accepted accounting principles.
- Antifraud programs and controls.
- Controls, including information technology general controls, that other controls are dependent on.
- Controls over significant nonroutine and nonsystematic transactions, such as accounts involving judgments and estimates.
- Company-level controls, including the control environment and controls over the period-end financial reporting process; including controls over procedures used to enter transaction totals into the general ledger; to initiate, authorize, record, and process journal entries in the general ledger; and to record recurring and nonrecurring adjustments to the financial statements (for example, consolidating adjustments, report combinations, and reclassifications).

In addition to determining which controls should be tested, the auditor evaluates the likelihood that failure of a particular control could result in a misstatement, the magnitude of such a misstatement, and the degree to which other controls, if effective, achieve the same control objectives. For a company with multiple locations or business units, the auditor considers management's process for determining the locations or business units to include in its evaluation. Once determined, the auditor also evaluates the design and operating effectiveness at such locations. The auditor also must understand and evaluate management's process for evaluating and communicating deficiencies in internal control over financial reporting that are of such a magnitude and likelihood of occurrence that they constitute significant deficiencies or material weaknesses.

Although AS-2 points out that inquiry of management and others is the beginning point for obtaining an understanding of internal control over financial reporting, inquiry alone is not adequate for reaching a conclusion on any aspect of internal control over financial reporting effectiveness.

Management's Documentation

Documentation of a company's internal control over financial reporting is an essential part of management's evaluation process. It provides evidence that controls related to management's assertion—including changes to those controls—have been identified, can be communicated to those responsible for their performance, and can be monitored. Documentation that provides reasonable support for management's assessment of the effectiveness of internal control over financial reporting includes, but is not limited to

- The design of controls over all relevant assertions related to all significant accounts and disclosures in the financial statements. The documentation should include the five components of internal control over financial reporting, including the control environment and company-level controls.
- Information about how significant transactions are initiated, authorized, recorded, processed, and reported.
- Sufficient information about the flow of transactions to identify the points at which material misstatements due to error or fraud could occur.
- Controls designed to prevent or detect fraud, including who performs the controls and the related segregation of duties.
- Controls over the period-end financial reporting process.
- Controls over safeguarding of assets.
- The results of management's testing and evaluation.

Documentation of controls may take many forms, such as paper, electronic files, or other media and can include a variety of information, including policy manuals, process models, flowcharts, job descriptions, documents, and forms. No one kind of documentation is required and the extent and form of documentation will vary, depending on the size, nature, and complexity of the company.

Inadequate documentation of the design of controls over relevant assertions related to significant accounts and disclosures is a deficiency in the company's internal control over financial reporting, the severity of which is subject to the auditor's professional judgment. The auditor might conclude that the deficiency is only minor. On the other hand, the auditor might conclude that the deficiency represents a significant deficiency or a material weakness. AS-2 states that in evaluating the significance of the deficiency, the auditor should determine whether management is able to demonstrate the monitoring component of the company's internal control over financial reporting. Inadequate documentation could also cause the auditor to conclude that there is a limitation on the scope of the engagement.

Scope of Tests

AS-2 states "Internal control over financial reporting is effectively designed when the controls, if complied with, would be expected to prevent or detect errors or fraud that could result in material misstatements in the financial statements." After obtaining an understanding of internal control over financial reporting, the auditor evaluates the design and operating effectiveness of those controls. By understanding the company's control objectives in each area, identifying the controls that satisfy each objective, and determining whether the controls, if operating properly, can effectively prevent or detect errors or fraud that could result in material misstatements in the financial statements, the auditor determines whether the company has controls to meet the objectives of its control criteria.

Testing and Evaluating Design Effectiveness

The auditor performs procedures to test and evaluate design effectiveness by using inquiry, observation, walkthroughs, and inspection of relevant documentation. In addition, the auditor evaluates whether the controls are likely to prevent or detect misstatements due to error or fraud if they are operated as prescribed by appropriately qualified persons.

The procedures the auditor performs in evaluating management's assessment process and obtaining an understanding of internal control over financial reporting also provide the auditor with evidence about the design effectiveness of internal control over financial reporting. The procedures the auditor performs to test and evaluate design effectiveness may also provide evidence about operating effectiveness.

Testing and Evaluating Operating Effectiveness

In evaluating operating effectiveness, the auditor considers whether the control is operating as designed and whether the person performing the control possesses the necessary authority and qualifications to perform the control effectively.

Nature of Tests of Controls

Tests of controls over operating effectiveness may include a mix of inquiries of appropriate personnel, inspection of relevant documentation, observation of the company's operations, and reperformance of the application of the control. As a example, the auditor might observe the procedures for opening the mail and processing cash receipts to test the operating effectiveness of controls over cash receipts. The auditor should supplement observations with inquiries of company personnel and inspections of documentation about the operation of the controls at other times because an observation is pertinent only at the point in time at which it is made. AS-2 indicates that these inquiries might be made concurrently by performing walkthroughs.

Inquiry is a procedure that consists of seeking information, both financial and nonfinancial, of knowledgeable persons throughout the company. Inquiry is used extensively throughout the audit and often is complementary to performing other procedures. Inquiries may range from formal written inquiries to informal oral inquiries.

Evaluating responses to inquiries is an integral part of the inquiry procedure. Examples of information that inquiries might provide include the skill and competency of those performing a control, the relative sensitivity of a control to prevent or detect errors or fraud, and the frequency with which the control operates to prevent or detect errors or fraud. Responses to inquiries can provide the auditor with corroborative evidence and information he or she has not previously possessed. Alternatively, responses might provide information that differs significantly from other information the auditor obtains (such as information regarding the possibility of management override of controls). In some cases, responses to inquiries provide a basis for the auditor to modify or perform additional procedures.

Because inquiry alone does not provide sufficient evidence to support the operating effectiveness of a control, the auditor should perform additional tests of controls. For example, if the company implements a control activity in which its sales manager reviews and investigates reports of invoices that have unusually high or low gross margins, inquiry of the sales manager about whether he or she investigates discrepancies would not be adequate. To obtain sufficient evidence about the operating effectiveness of the control, the auditor should corroborate the sales manager's responses by performing other procedures, such as inspecting reports or other documentation used in or generated by the performance of the control, and evaluate whether appropriate actions were taken regarding discrepancies.

The nature of a control also influences the nature of the tests of controls that the auditor can perform. For example, the auditor can examine documents pertaining to controls for which documentary evidence exists. However, documentary evidence for some aspects of the control environment, such as management's philosophy and operating style, might not exist. In circumstances where documentary evidence of controls or the performance of controls does not exist and is not expected to exist, the auditor's tests of controls would consist of inquiries of appropriate personnel and observation of company activities.

Example 11-1: Nature of control

A signature on a voucher package indicating that the signer approved it does not necessarily mean that the person carefully reviewed the package before signing. The package may have been signed based on only a cursory review or without any review. As a result, the quality of the evidence regarding the effective operation of the control might not be sufficiently persuasive. If that is the case, the auditor should reperform the control (for example, checking prices, extensions, and additions) as part of the test of the control. In addition, the auditor might inquire of the person responsible for approving voucher packages what he or she looks for when approving packages and how many errors have been found within voucher packages. The auditor also might inquire of supervisors whether they have any knowledge of errors that the person responsible for approving the voucher packages failed to detect.

Timing of Tests of Controls

The auditor must perform tests of controls over a period of time that is adequate to determine whether, as of the date specified in management's report, the controls necessary for achieving the objectives of the control criteria are operating effectively. The period of time over which the auditor performs tests of controls varies with the nature of the controls being tested as well as the frequency with which specific controls operate and specific policies are applied. Some controls operate continuously (for example, controls over sales); others operate only at certain times (for example, controls over the preparation of monthly or quarterly financial statements and controls over physical inventory counts). The auditor's testing of the operating effectiveness of controls should occur at the time the controls are operating. Controls "as of" a specific date encompass controls that are relevant to the company's internal control over financial reporting "as of" that specific date, even though such controls might not operate until after that specific date.

Example 11-2: Timing of tests of controls

Some controls over the period-end financial reporting process normally operate only after the "as of" date. Therefore, if controls over the December 31, 20X4 period-end financial reporting process operate in January 20X5, the auditor should test the control operating in January 20X5 to have sufficient evidence of operating effectiveness "as of" December 31, 20X4.

When the auditor reports on the effectiveness of controls "as of" a specific date and obtains evidence about the operating effectiveness of controls at an interim date, he or she should determine what additional evidence to obtain concerning the operation of the control for the remaining period. In making that determination, the auditor should evaluate

- The specific controls tested prior to the "as of" date and the results of those tests
- The degree to which evidence about the operating effectiveness of the controls was obtained

- The length of the remaining period
- The possibility that there have been any significant changes in internal control over financial reporting subsequent to the interim date

For controls over significant nonroutine transactions, controls over accounts or processes with a high degree of subjectivity or judgment in measurement, or controls over the recording of period-end adjustments, the auditor should perform tests of controls closer to or on the "as of" date rather than at an interim date. However, the auditor should balance performing the tests of controls closer to the "as of" date with the need to obtain sufficient evidence of operating effectiveness.

Prior to the date specified in management's report, management might implement changes to the company's controls to make them more effective, more efficient, or to address control deficiencies. In that case, the auditor might not need to evaluate controls that have been superseded. For example, if the auditor determines that the new controls achieve the related objectives of the control criteria and have been in effect for a sufficient period to permit the auditor to assess their design and operating effectiveness by performing tests of controls, he or she will not need to evaluate the design and operating effectiveness of the superseded controls for purposes of expressing an opinion on internal control over financial reporting.

However, the auditor must communicate all identified significant deficiencies and material weaknesses in controls to the audit committee in writing. In addition, the auditor should evaluate how the design and operating effectiveness of the superseded controls relates to the auditor's reliance on controls for financial statement audit purposes.

Extent of Tests of Controls

Each year the auditor must obtain sufficient evidence about whether the company's internal control over financial reporting, including the controls for all internal control components, is operating effectively. This means that each year the auditor must obtain evidence about the effectiveness of controls for all relevant assertions related to all significant accounts and disclosures in the financial statements. The auditor also should vary from year to year the nature, timing, and extent of testing controls, to introduce unpredictability into the testing and respond to changes in circumstances. For example, each year the auditor might test the controls at a different interim period, increase or reduce the number and types of tests performed, or change the combination of procedures used.

In determining the extent of procedures to perform, the auditor should design the procedures to provide a high level of assurance that the control being tested is operating effectively. In making this determination, the auditor should assess the following factors.

Nature of the Control

The auditor should subject manual controls to more extensive testing than automated controls. In some circumstances, testing a single operation of an automated control may be sufficient to obtain a high level of assurance that the control operates effectively, provided that information technology general controls also are operating effectively. For manual controls, sufficient evidence about the operating effectiveness of the controls is obtained by evaluating multiple operations of the control and the results of each operation. The auditor should also assess the complexity of the controls, the significance of the judgments that must be made in connection with their operation, and the level of competence of the person performing the controls that is necessary for the controls to operate effectively. As the complexity and level of judgment increase or the level of competence of the person performing the control decreases, the extent of the auditor's testing should increase.

Frequency of Operation

Generally, the more frequently a manual control operates, the more operations of the control the auditor should test. For example, for a manual control that operates in connection with each transaction, the auditor should test multiple operations of the control over a sufficient period of time to obtain a high level of assurance that the control operates effectively. For controls that operate less frequently, such as monthly account reconciliations and controls over the period-end financial reporting process, the auditor may test significantly fewer operations of the control. However, the auditor's evaluation of each operation of those controls operating less frequently is likely to be more extensive. For example, when evaluating the operation of a monthly exception report, the auditor should evaluate whether the judgments made with regard to the disposition of the exceptions were appropriate and adequately supported.

Importance of the Control

Controls that are relatively more important should be tested more extensively. Some controls may address multiple financial statement assertions and certain period-end detective controls might be considered more important than related preventive controls. The auditor should test more operations of such controls or, if such controls operate infrequently, evaluate each operation of the control more extensively.

Use of Internal Auditors and Others

In all audits of internal control over financial reporting, the auditor must perform enough of the testing him- or herself so that the principal evidence for his or her opinion is the auditor's own work. The auditor may, however, use the work of others to alter the nature, timing, or extent of the work he or she otherwise would have performed. For these purposes, the work of others includes relevant work performed by internal auditors, company personnel (in addition to internal auditors), and third parties working under the direction of management or the audit committee, that provides information about the effectiveness of internal control over financial reporting.

The auditor should evaluate whether to use the work performed by others in the audit of internal control over financial reporting. To determine the extent to which are auditor may use the work of others to alter the nature, timing, or extent of the work he or she would have otherwise performed in addition to obtaining the principal evidence for his or her opinion, the auditor should

- Evaluate the nature of the controls subjected to the work of others.
- Evaluate the competence and objectivity of the individuals who performed the work.
- Test some of the work performed by others to evaluate the quality and effectiveness of their work.

> **OBSERVATION:** SAS-65 (AU 322) (The Auditor's Consideration of the Internal Audit Function in an Audit of Financial Statements) applies to using the work of internal auditors in an audit of the financial statements. The auditor may apply the relevant concepts described in SAS-65 to using the work of others in the audit of internal control over financial reporting.

The auditor must obtain sufficient evidence to support his or her opinion. Judgments about the sufficiency of evidence obtained and other factors affecting the auditor's opinion, such as the significance of identified control deficiencies, should be made by the auditor. Evidence obtained through the auditor's direct personal knowledge, observation, reperformance, and inspection is generally more persuasive than information obtained indirectly from others, such as internal auditors, other company personnel, or third parties working under the direction of management.

The requirement that the auditor's own work provide the principal evidence for his or her opinion is one of the boundaries an auditor works within when determining what work he or she must perform him- or herself in an audit of internal control over financial reporting. Regardless of the auditor's determination of the work that he or she must perform him- or herself, it is solely the auditor's responsibility to report on the effectiveness of internal control over financial reporting. This responsibility cannot be shared with the other individuals whose work the auditor uses. Therefore, when the auditor uses the work of others, the auditor is responsible for the results of their work.

Evaluating the Nature of the Controls Subjected to the Work of Others

The auditor should examine the following factors when evaluating the nature of the controls subjected to the work of others. As these factors increase in significance, the need for the auditor to perform his or her own work on those controls increases. As these factors decrease in significance, the need for the auditor to perform his or her own work on those controls decreases. Items to examine include

- The materiality of the accounts and disclosures that the control addresses and the risk of material misstatement
- The degree of judgment required to evaluate the operating effectiveness of the control (i.e., the degree to which evaluation of the effectiveness of a control requires evaluation of subjective factors rather than objective testing)
- The pervasiveness of the control
- The level of judgment or estimation required in the account or disclosure
- The potential for management override of the control

Because of the nature of the controls in the control environment, the auditor should not use the work of others to reduce the amount of work he or she performs on controls in the control environment. The auditor should, however, consider the results of work performed in this area by others because it might indicate the need for the auditor to increase his or her work.

The control environment encompasses the following factors:

- Integrity and ethical values
- Commitment to competence
- Participation by board of directors or audit committee
- Management's philosophy and operating style
- Organizational structure
- Assignment of authority and responsibility
- Human resource policies and procedures

Controls that are part of the control environment include, but are not limited to, those specifically established to prevent and detect fraud that is at least reasonably possible to result in material misstatement of the financial statements.

The auditor should perform walkthroughs him- or herself because of the degree of judgment required in performing this work. However, to provide additional evidence, the auditor may also review the work of others who have performed and documented walkthroughs. In evaluating whether his or her own evidence provides the principal evidence, the auditor's own work on the control environment and in performing walkthroughs constitutes an important part of his or her duties.

Evaluating the Competence and Objectivity of Others

The extent to which the auditor may use the work of others depends on the degree of competence and objectivity shown by the individuals performing the work. The higher the degree of competence and objectivity, the greater use the auditor may make of the work. Conversely, the lower the degree of competence and objectivity, the less use the auditor may make of the work. The auditor should not use the work of individuals who have a low degree of objectivity, regardless of their level of competence. Likewise, the auditor should not use the work of individuals who have a low level of competence, regardless of their degree of objectivity.

When evaluating the competence and objectivity of the individuals performing the tests of controls, the auditor should obtain information (or update it from prior years) about the individuals' qualifications, experience, and duties. The auditor should determine whether to test the existence and quality of such factors and, if so, the extent to which such testing should be done, based on the intended effect of the work of others on the audit of internal control over financial reporting.

More specifically, factors concerning the competence of the individuals performing the tests of controls include

- Their educational level and professional experience
- Their professional certification and continuing education
- Practices regarding the assignment of individuals to work areas
- Supervision and review of their activities
- Quality of the documentation of their work, including any reports or recommendations issued
- Evaluation of their performance

Factors concerning the objectivity of the individuals performing the tests of controls include

- The organizational status of the individuals responsible for the work of others (testing authority) in testing controls, including
  - Whether the testing authority reports to an officer of sufficient status to ensure sufficient testing coverage, as well as adequate consideration of, and action on, the findings and recommendations of the individuals performing the testing
  - Whether the testing authority has direct access and reports regularly to the board of directors or the audit committee
  - Whether the board of directors or the audit committee oversees employment decisions related to the testing authority
- Policies to maintain the individuals' objectivity about the areas being tested, including
  - Policies prohibiting individuals from testing controls in areas where relatives are employed in important or internal-control-sensitive positions
  - Policies prohibiting individuals from testing controls in areas they have recently been assigned to or are scheduled to be assigned to upon completion of their controls testing responsibilities

Internal auditors are normally expected to have greater competence and objectivity than other company personnel with regard to internal control over financial reporting. Therefore, the auditor may be able to use their work to a greater extent than the work of other company personnel. This is particularly true in the case of internal auditors who follow the International Standards for the Professional Practice of Internal Auditing, issued by the Institute of Internal Auditors. If internal auditors have performed an extensive amount of relevant work and the auditor determines they possess a high degree of competence and objectivity, the auditor might use their work to the greatest extent an auditor could possibly use the work of others. On the other hand, if the internal audit function reports solely to management, which would reduce internal auditors' objectivity, or if limited resources allocated to the internal audit function result in very limited testing procedures on its part or reduced competency of the internal auditors, the auditor should use their work to a much lesser extent and perform more of the testing him- or herself.

When determining how the work of others will alter the nature, timing, or extent of the auditor's work, the auditor should assess the interrelationship of the nature of the controls and the competence and objectivity of those who performed the work. As the significance of the factors increases, the ability of the auditor to use the work of others decreases at the same time that the necessary level of competence and objectivity of those who perform the work increases. For example, for some pervasive controls, the auditor may determine that using the work of internal auditors to a limited degree is appropriate and that using the work of other company personnel is not appropriate, because other company personnel do not have a high enough degree of objectivity as it relates to the nature of the controls.

Testing the Work of Others

The auditor should test some of the work of others to evaluate the quality and effectiveness of the work. The auditor's tests of the work of others may be accomplished by either testing some of the controls that others tested or testing similar controls not actually tested by others. The nature and extent of the tests depend on the effect of the work of others on the auditor's procedures but should be sufficient to enable the auditor to make an evaluation of the overall quality and effectiveness of the work he or she is considering. The auditor also should assess whether this evaluation has an effect on his or her conclusions about the competence and objectivity of the individuals performing the work.

In evaluating the quality and effectiveness of the work of others, the auditor should evaluate factors such as whether the

- Scope of work is appropriate to meet the objectives
- Work programs are adequate
- Work performed is adequately documented, including evidence of supervision and review
- Conclusions are appropriate in the circumstances
- Reports are consistent with the results of the work performed

Material Weaknesses

The auditor must evaluate identified control deficiencies and determine whether individually or in combination they are significant deficiencies or material weaknesses.

AS-2 defines a "significant deficiency" as a control deficiency or combination of control deficiencies that adversely affects the company's ability to initiate, authorize, record, process, or report external financial data reliably in accordance with generally accepted accounting principles, such that there is more than a remote likelihood that a misstatement of the company's annual or interim financial statements that is more than inconsequential will not be prevented or detected.

A "material weakness" is defined as a significant deficiency or combination of significant deficiencies that results in a more than a remote likelihood that a material misstatement of the annual or interim financial statements will not be prevented or detected.

The term "remote likelihood" as used in the definitions of significant deficiency and material weakness has the same meaning as the term "remote" as used in FAS-5 (Accounting for Contingencies). Paragraph 3 of FAS-5 states the following:

> When a loss contingency exists, the likelihood that the future event or events will confirm the loss or impairment of an asset or the incurrence of a liability can range from probable to remote. This Statement uses the terms probable, reasonably possible, and remote to identify three areas within that range, as follows:
>
> - Probable: The future event or events are likely to occur.
> - Reasonably possible: The chance of the future event or events occurring is more than remote but less than likely.
> - Remote: The chance of the future events or events occurring is slight.

In evaluating whether a control deficiency exists and whether any control deficiencies, either individually or in combination with other control deficiencies, are significant deficiencies or material weaknesses, the auditor should consider the aforementioned definitions. The evaluation of the materiality of the control deficiency should include both quantitative and qualitative considerations. Qualitative factors that might be important in this evaluation include the nature of the financial statement accounts and assertions involved and the reasonably possible future consequences of the deficiency. Furthermore, in determining whether a control deficiency or combination of deficiencies is a significant deficiency or a material weakness, the auditor should evaluate the effect of compensating controls and whether such compensating controls are effective.

The auditor should initially evaluate the significance of a deficiency in internal control over financial reporting by determining the following:

- The likelihood that a deficiency, or a combination of deficiencies, could result in a misstatement of an account balance or disclosure
- The magnitude of the potential misstatement resulting from the deficiency or deficiencies

The significance of a deficiency in internal control over financial reporting depends on the potential for a misstatement, not on whether a misstatement actually has occurred.

Several factors affect the likelihood that a deficiency, or a combination of deficiencies, could result in a misstatement of an account balance or disclosure. These factors include, but are not limited to

- The nature of the financial statement accounts, disclosures, and assertions involved. For example, suspense accounts and related-party transactions involve greater risk.
- The susceptibility of the related assets or liability to loss or fraud: greater susceptibility increases risk.
- The subjectivity, complexity, or extent of judgment required to determine the amount involved: The greater subjectivity, complexity, or judgment (such as that related to an accounting estimate), the greater the risk.
- The cause and frequency of known or detected exceptions for the operating effectiveness of a control. For example, a control with an observed nonnegligible deviation rate is a deficiency.
- The interaction or relationship of the control with other controls, i.e., the interdependence or redundancy of the control.
- The interaction of the deficiencies. For example, when evaluating a combination of two or more deficiencies, whether they could affect the same financial statement accounts and assertions.
- The possible future consequences of the deficiency.

When evaluating the likelihood that a deficiency or combination of deficiencies could result in a misstatement, the auditor should evaluate how the controls interact with other controls. There are controls, such as information technology general controls, that other controls depend on. Some controls function together as a group. Other controls overlap, in the sense that other controls achieve the same objective.

Several factors affect the magnitude of the misstatement that could result from a deficiency or deficiencies in controls, including

- The financial statement amounts or total of transactions exposed to the deficiency.
- The volume of activity in the account balance or class of transactions exposed to the deficiency that has occurred in the current period or that is expected in future periods.

In evaluating the magnitude of the potential misstatement, the auditor should recognize that the maximum amount that an account balance or total of transactions can be overstated is generally the recorded amount. However, the recorded amount is not a limitation on the amount of potential understatement. The auditor should also recognize that the risk of misstatement might be different for the maximum possible misstatement than for lower possible amounts.

When evaluating the significance of a deficiency in internal control over financial reporting, the auditor should also determine the level of detail and degree of assurance that would satisfy prudent officials, in the conduct of their own affairs, that they have reasonable assurance that transactions are recorded as necessary to permit the preparation of financial statements in conformity with generally accepted accounting principles. If the auditor determines that the deficiency would prevent prudent officials, in the conduct of their own affairs, from concluding that they have reasonable assurance, then the auditor should deem the deficiency to be at least a significant deficiency. Having determined in this manner that a deficiency represents a significant deficiency, the auditor must further evaluate the deficiency to determine whether individually, or in combination with other deficiencies, the deficiency is a material weakness.

Inadequate documentation of the design of controls and the absence of sufficient documented evidence to support management's assessment of the operating effectiveness of internal control over financial reporting are control deficiencies. As with other control deficiencies, the auditor should evaluate these deficiencies as to their significance.

The interaction of qualitative considerations that affect internal control over financial reporting with quantitative considerations ordinarily results in deficiencies in the following areas being at least significant deficiencies in internal control over financial reporting:

- Controls over the selection and application of accounting policies that are in conformity with generally accepted accounting principles
- Antifraud programs and controls
- Controls over nonroutine and nonsystematic transactions
- Controls over the period-end financial reporting process, including controls over procedures used to enter transaction totals into the general ledger; to initiate, authorize, record, and process journal entries into the general ledger; and to record recurring and nonrecurring adjustments to the financial statements

Each of the following circumstances should be regarded as at least a significant deficiency and as a strong indicator that a material weakness in internal control over financial reporting exists:

- Restatement of previously issued financial statements to reflect the correction of a misstatement.

OBSERVATION: The correction of a misstatement includes misstatements due to error or fraud. It does not include restatements to reflect a change in accounting principles to comply with a new accounting principle or a voluntary change from one generally accepted accounting principle to another.

- The identification by the auditor of a material misstatement in financial statements in the current period that was not initially identified by the company's internal control over financial reporting is a strong indicator of a material weakness even if management subsequently corrects the misstatement.
- Ineffective oversight of the company's external financial reporting and internal control over financial reporting by the company's audit committee.
- Ineffectiveness of the internal audit function or the risk assessment function, at a company for which such a function needs to be effective for the company to have an effective monitoring or risk assessment component, such as for very large or highly complex companies.

OBSERVATION: The evaluation of the internal audit or risk assessment functions is similar to the evaluation of the audit committee, (i.e., the evaluation is made within the context of the monitoring and risk assessment components). The auditor is not required to make a separate evaluation of the effectiveness and performance of these functions. Instead, he or she should base his or her evaluation on evidence obtained as part of evaluating the monitoring and risk assessment components of internal control over financial reporting.

- An ineffective regulatory compliance function for complex entities in highly regulated industries. This circumstance relates solely to those aspects of the ineffective regulatory compliance function in which associated violations of laws and regulations could have a material effect on the reliability of financial reporting.
- Identification of fraud of any magnitude on the part of senior management.

OBSERVATION: The auditor is required to plan and perform procedures to obtain reasonable assurance that material misstatement caused by fraud is detected by the auditor. However, for the purposes of evaluating and reporting deficiencies in internal control over financial reporting, the auditor should evaluate fraud on the part of senior management of any magnitude (including fraud resulting in immaterial misstatements) that he or she is aware of. Furthermore, for the purposes of this circumstance, "senior management" includes the principal executive and financial officers signing the company's certifications as required under Section 302 of SOX, as well as any other member of management who plays a significant role in the company's financial reporting process.

- Significant deficiencies that have been communicated to management and the audit committee but which remain uncorrected after some reasonable period of time.
- An ineffective control environment.

Reporting

The auditor's report on management's assessment of the effectiveness of internal control over financial reporting must

- Give the report a title that includes the word "independent."
- Identify management's conclusion about the effectiveness of the company's internal control over financial reporting as of a specified date based on the control criteria (for example, criteria established in *Internal Control—Integrated Framework,* issued by the Committee of Sponsoring Organizations of the Treadway Commission [COSO]).
- Identify the title of the management report that includes management's assessment (the auditor should use the same description of the company's internal control over financial reporting as management uses in its report).
- State that the assessment is the responsibility of management.
- State that the auditor's responsibility is to express an opinion on the assessment and an opinion on the company's internal control over financial reporting based on his or her audit.
- Define internal control over financial reporting.
- State that the audit was conducted in accordance with the standards of the Public Company Accounting Oversight Board (United States).
- State that the standards of the Public Company Accounting Oversight Board require that the auditor plan and perform the audit to obtain reasonable assurance about whether effective internal control over financial reporting was maintained in all material respects.
- State that an audit process includes obtaining an understanding of internal control over financial reporting, evaluating management's assessment, testing and evaluating the design and operating effectiveness of internal control, and performing such other procedures as the auditor considers necessary in the circumstances.
- State that the auditor believes the audit provides a reasonable basis for his or her opinions.
- Provide a paragraph stating that, because of inherent limitations, internal control over financial reporting may not prevent

or detect misstatements and that projections of any evaluation of effectiveness to future periods are subject to the risk that controls may become inadequate because of changes in conditions or that the degree of compliance with the policies or procedures may deteriorate.

- Provide the auditor's opinion on whether management's assessment of the effectiveness of the company's internal control over financial reporting as of the specified date is fairly stated, in all material respects, based on the control criteria.
- Provide the auditor's opinion on whether the company maintained, in all material respects, effective internal control over financial reporting as of the specified date, based on the control criteria.
- Provide the manual or printed signature of the auditor's firm.
- Give the city and state (or city and country, in the case of non-U.S. auditors) where the auditor's report has been issued.
- Date the audit report.

Appendix 11X is an illustrative auditor's report for an unqualified opinion on management's assessment of the effectiveness of the company's internal control over financial reporting and an unqualified opinion on the effectiveness of the company's internal control over financial reporting.

Separate or Combined Reports

The auditor may choose to issue a combined report (i.e., one report containing both an opinion on the financial statements and the opinions on internal control over financial reporting) or separate reports on the company's financial statements and on internal control over financial reporting.

If the auditor chooses to issue a separate report on internal control over financial reporting, he or she should add the following paragraph to the auditor's report on the financial statements:

> We also have audited, in accordance with the standards of the Public Company Accounting Oversight Board (United States), the effectiveness of W Company's internal control over financial reporting as of December 31, 20X3, based on [*identify control criteria*] and our report, dated [*date of report, which should be the same as the date of the report on the financial statements*] expressed [*include nature of opinions*].

The auditor should also add the following paragraph to the report on internal control over financial reporting:

> We have also audited, in accordance with the standards of the Public Company Accounting Oversight Board (United States),

the [*identify financial statements*] of W Company and our report, dated [*date of report, which should be the same as the date of the report on the effectiveness of internal control over financial reporting*] expressed [*include nature of opinion*].

Report Date

The auditor cannot audit internal control over financial reporting without also auditing the financial statements. Therefore, the reports should both be given the same date.

When the auditor elects to issue a combined report on the audit of the financial statements and the audit of internal control over financial reporting, the audit opinion will address multiple reporting periods for the financial statements presented but only the end of the most recent fiscal year for the effectiveness of internal control over financial reporting and management's assessment of the effectiveness of internal control over financial reporting.

Report Modifications

The auditor should modify the standard report if any of the following conditions exist:

- Management's assessment is inadequate or management's report is inappropriate.
- There is a material weakness in the company's internal control over financial reporting.
- There is a restriction on the scope of the engagement.
- The auditor decides to refer to the report of other auditors as the basis, in part, for the auditor's own report.
- A significant subsequent event has occurred since the date being reported on.
- There is other information contained in management's report on internal control over financial reporting.

Management's Assessment Inadequate or Report Inappropriate

If the auditor determines that management's process for assessing internal control over financial reporting is inadequate, he or she should modify his or her opinion for a scope limitation. If the auditor determines that management's report is inappropriate, he or she should modify his or her report to include, at a minimum, an explanatory paragraph describing the reasons for this conclusion.

Material Weaknesses

If there are significant deficiencies that, individually or in combination, result in one or more material weaknesses, management is precluded from concluding that internal control over financial reporting is effective. In these circumstances, the auditor must express an adverse opinion on the company's internal control over financial reporting.

When expressing an adverse opinion on the effectiveness of internal control over financial reporting because of a material weakness, the auditor's report must

- Define a material weakness.
- State that a material weakness has been identified and included in management's assessment. If the material weakness has not been included in management's assessment, this sentence should be modified to state that the material weakness has been identified but not included in management's assessment. In this case, the auditor also is required to communicate in writing to the audit committee that the material weakness was not disclosed or identified as a material weakness in management's report.
- Describe any material weaknesses identified in a company's internal control over financial reporting. This description should provide the users of the audit report with specific information about the nature of any material weakness, and its actual and potential effect on the presentation of the company's financial statements issued during the existence of the weakness.

Depending on the circumstances, the auditor may express both an unqualified opinion and an other-than-unqualified opinion within the same report on internal control over financial reporting.

Example 11-3: Different opinions in same report

If management makes an adverse assessment because a material weakness has been identified and not corrected ("internal control over financial reporting is not effective"), the auditor would express an unqualified opinion on management's assessment ("management's assessment that internal control over financial reporting is not effective is fairly stated, in all material respects"). At the same time, the auditor would express an adverse opinion about the effectiveness of internal control over financial reporting ("In our opinion, because of the effect of the material weakness described . . . the company's internal control over financial reporting is not effective.").

Scope Limitations

The auditor can express an unqualified opinion on management's assessment of internal control over financial reporting and an unqualified opinion on the effectiveness of internal control over financial reporting only if he or she has been able to apply all the procedures necessary in the circumstances. If there are restrictions on the scope of the engagement imposed by the circumstances, the auditor should withdraw from the engagement, disclaim an opinion, or express a qualified opinion. The auditor's decision depends on his or her assessment of the importance of the omitted procedure(s) to his or her ability to form an opinion on management's assessment of internal control over financial reporting, as well as an opinion on the effectiveness of the company's internal control over financial reporting. However, when restrictions are imposed by management, the auditor should withdraw from the engagement or disclaim an opinion on management's assessment of internal control over financial reporting and the effectiveness of internal control over financial reporting.

Example 11-4: Scope limitation

Management might have identified a material weakness in its internal control over financial reporting prior to the date specified in its report and implemented controls to correct it. If management believes that the new controls have been operating for a sufficient period of time to determine that they are both effectively designed and operating, management would be able to include in its assessment its conclusion that internal control over financial reporting is effective as of the date specified. However, if the auditor disagrees with the sufficiency of the time period, he or she would be unable to obtain sufficient evidence that the new controls have been operating effectively for a sufficient period. In that case, due to a scope limitation, the auditor should modify his or her opinion on the effectiveness of internal control over financial reporting and the opinion on management's assessment of internal control over financial reporting.

When an auditor plans to disclaim an opinion and the limited procedures performed by the auditor caused him or her to conclude that a material weakness exists, his or her report should

- Define a material weakness.
- Describe all material weaknesses identified in the company's internal control over financial reporting. The description should provide the users of the audit report with specific information about the nature of each material weakness and its actual and potential effect on the presentation of the company's financial statements issued during the existence of the weakness.

Opinions Based in Part on the Report of Another Auditor

When another auditor has audited the financial statements and internal control over financial reporting of one or more subsidiaries, divisions, branches, or components of a company, the auditor should determine whether he or she might serve as the principal auditor and use the work and reports of the other auditor as a partial basis for his or her opinions. AU 543 (Part of Audit Performed by Other Independent Auditors) provides direction on the auditor's decision on whether to serve as the principal auditor of the financial statements. If the auditor decides it is appropriate to serve as the principal auditor of the financial statements, then he or she should also be the principal auditor of the company's internal control over financial reporting, a relationship results from the requirement that an audit of the financial statements be performed in order to audit internal control over financial reporting. Only the principal auditor of the financial statements can be the principal auditor of internal control over financial reporting. The principal auditor of the financial statements needs to participate sufficiently in the audit of internal control over financial reporting to provide a basis for serving as the principal auditor of internal control over financial reporting.

When serving as the principal auditor of internal control over financial reporting, an auditor should decide whether to make reference in the report on internal control over financial reporting to the audit of internal control over financial reporting performed by the other auditor. In these circumstances, the auditor's decision is based on factors similar to those of the independent auditor who uses the work and reports of other independent auditors when reporting on a company's financial statements as described in AU 543.

The decision about whether to make reference to another auditor in the report on the audit of internal control over financial reporting might differ from the corresponding decision as it relates to the audit of the financial statements. For example, the audit report on the financial statements may make reference to the audit of a significant equity investment performed by another independent auditor, but the report on internal control over financial reporting might not make a similar reference because management's evaluation of internal control over financial reporting ordinarily would not extend to controls at the equity method investee.

When an auditor decides to make reference to the report of another auditor as a partial basis for his or her opinions, he or she should refer to the report of the other auditor when describing the scope of the audit and when expressing the opinions.

Subsequent Events

Changes in internal control over financial reporting or other factors that might significantly affect internal control over financial reporting might occur subsequent to the date for which internal control over financial reporting is being audited but before the date of the auditor's report. The auditor should inquire of management whether there were any such changes or factors. The auditor should obtain written representations from management relating to such matters. Additionally, to obtain information about whether changes have occurred that might affect the effectiveness of the company's internal control over financial reporting and, therefore, the auditor's report, the auditor should inquire about and examine, for this subsequent period, the following:

- Relevant internal audit reports (or similar functions, such as loan review in a financial institution) issued during the subsequent period
- Independent auditor reports (if other than the auditor's) of significant deficiencies or material weaknesses
- Regulatory agency reports on the company's internal control over financial reporting
- Information about the effectiveness of the company's internal control over financial reporting obtained through other engagements

The auditor could inquire about and examine other documents for the subsequent period. AU 560 (Subsequent Events) provides direction on subsequent events for a financial statement audit that can also be helpful to the auditor performing an audit of internal control over financial reporting.

If the auditor obtains knowledge about subsequent events that materially and adversely affect the effectiveness of the company's internal control over financial reporting as of the date specified in the assessment, the auditor should issue an adverse opinion on the effectiveness of internal control over financial reporting and an adverse opinion on management's assessment of internal control over financial reporting if management's report does not appropriately assess the effect of the subsequent event. If the auditor is unable to determine the effect of the subsequent event on the effectiveness of the company's internal control over financial reporting, he or she should disclaim opinions. The auditor should disclaim an opinion on management's disclosures about corrective actions taken by the company after the date of management's assessment, if any.

The auditor may obtain knowledge about subsequent events with respect to conditions that did not exist at the date specified in the assessment but arose subsequent to that date. If a subsequent event of this type has a material effect on the company, the auditor should include in his or her report an explanatory paragraph that describes the event and its effects or that directs the reader's attention to the event and its effects as disclosed in management's report. Management's consideration of such events to be disclosed in its report should be limited to a change that has materially affected, or is reasonably likely to materially affect, the company's internal control over financial reporting.

Additional Information Contained in Management's Report

Management's report on internal control over financial reporting may contain information in addition to management's assessment of the effectiveness of its internal control over financial reporting. Such information might include, for example

- Disclosures about corrective actions taken by the company after the date of management's assessment
- The company's plans to implement new controls
- A statement that management believes the cost of correcting a material weakness would exceed the benefits to be derived from implementing new controls

If management's assessment includes such additional information, the auditor should disclaim an opinion on the information. For example, the auditor should use the following language as the last paragraph of the report to disclaim an opinion on management's cost-benefit statement:

> We do not express an opinion or any other form of assurance on management's statement referring to the costs and related benefits of implementing new controls.

If the auditor believes that management's additional information contains a material misstatement of fact, he or she should discuss the matter with management. If the auditor concludes that there is a valid basis for concern, he or she should propose that management consult with some other party whose advice might be useful, such as the company's legal counsel. If, after discussing the matter with management and those who management has consulted, the auditor concludes that a material misstatement of fact remains, the auditor should notify management and the audit committee, in writing, of his or her views concerning the information. The auditor also should consider consulting his or her legal counsel about further actions to be taken, including the auditor's responsibility under Section 10A of the Securities Exchange Act of 1934.

OBSERVATION: If management makes the types of disclosures described above outside its report on internal control over financial reporting and includes them elsewhere within its annual report on the company's financial statements, the auditor would not need to disclaim an opinion. However, in that situation, the auditor's responsibilities are the same as those described above if he or she believes that the additional information contains a material misstatement of fact.

TYPES OF ENGAGEMENTS

Internal control is a process by which management attempts to meet its objectives in the categories of financial reporting, operations, and compliance. A practitioner may be engaged to perform an engagement regarding internal control related to any one of those objectives. In addition, there are various types of engagements that may be performed with respect to these different internal control objectives. However, the practitioner should not perform a review engagement related to internal control.

Examination Engagement

A practitioner may examine the effectiveness of an entity's internal control. Generally, an examination engagement is performed on the effectiveness of internal control over financial reporting. The primary focus of this chapter is on such engagements. However, the practitioner may also examine the effectiveness of internal control over compliance, which is discussed later in this chapter, in the "Internal Controls over Compliance" section. Authoritative guidance for an examination of the effectiveness of an entity's internal control over financial reporting is contained in Chapter 5 of SSAE-10 (AT 501). Authoritative guidance for an examination of an entity's internal control over compliance is contained in Chapter 6 of SSAE-10 (AT 601).

Agreed-Upon Procedures Engagement

A practitioner may perform agreed-upon procedures related to the effectiveness of an entity's internal control. Chapter 2 of SSAE-10 (AT 201) contains the authoritative guidance for agreed-upon procedures related to the effectiveness of internal control over financial reporting. Chapter 6 of SSAE-10 (AT 601) contains the authoritative guidance for agreed-upon procedures related to the effectiveness of internal control over compliance. Engagements related to internal control over compliance are discussed later in this chapter in the "Internal Controls over Compliance" section.

Consulting Engagement

A client may engage a practitioner to provide certain nonattest services in connection with the entity's internal control. For example, a client may engage a practitioner to provide recommendations on improvements to the entity's internal control. In addition, most engagements related to internal control over operations are performed in consulting engagements. The authoritative guidance for all such nonattest services is contained in Statement on Standards for Consulting Services (SSCS) (CS 100) (Consulting Services: Definitions and Standards). These types of nonattest services are not discussed in this guide.

EXAMINATION OF AN ENTITY'S INTERNAL CONTROL OVER FINANCIAL REPORTING

The practitioner's objective in an engagement to examine the effectiveness of the entity's internal control is to express an opinion on (1) the effectiveness of the entity's internal control, in all material respects, based on the control criteria or (2) whether the responsible party's written assertion about the effectiveness of internal control is fairly stated, in all material respects, based on the control criteria. The practitioner's opinion relates to the effectiveness of the entity's internal control taken as a whole, and not to the effectiveness of each individual component (control environment, risk assessment, control activities, information and communication, and monitoring) of the entity's internal control. Therefore, the practitioner considers the interrelationship of the components of the entity's internal control in achieving the objectives of the control criteria. To express an opinion, the practitioner accumulates sufficient evidence about the design effectiveness and operating effectiveness of the entity's internal control, thereby restricting attestation risk to an appropriately low level.

Performing an examination of the effectiveness of an entity's internal control involves

- Planning the engagement.
- Obtaining an understanding of internal control.
- Evaluating the design effectiveness of the controls.
- Testing and evaluating the operating effectiveness of the controls.

- Forming an opinion on the effectiveness of the entity's internal control, or the responsible party's assertion on it, based on the control criteria.

ENGAGEMENT PLANNING AND ADMINISTRATION

Conditions for Acceptance

A practitioner may examine the effectiveness of an entity's internal control if the following conditions are met:

1. Management of the entity accepts responsibility for the effectiveness of the entity's internal control.
2. Management of the entity evaluates the effectiveness of the entity's internal control using suitable criteria. Such criteria are referred to as "control criteria."
3. Sufficient evidential matter exists or could be developed to support management's evaluation.

Written Assertion

As part of performing the engagement, the practitioner should obtain a written assertion from management about the effectiveness of the entity's internal control. Management may present its written assertion in either of the following forms:

- A separate report that accompanies the practitioner's report.
- A representation letter to the practitioner.

The responsible party's written assertion about the effectiveness of an entity's internal control may take many forms. For example, the phrase "management's assertion that W Company maintained effective internal control over financial reporting as of [*date*]" is such an assertion. Other phrases may also be used. However, the practitioner should not accept an assertion that is so subjective (for example, "very effective" internal control) that people having competence in and using the same or similar criteria would not ordinarily be able to arrive at similar conclusions.

Regardless of whether the practitioner's client is the responsible party, the responsible party's refusal to furnish a written assertion as part of an examination engagement should cause the practitioner to withdraw from the engagement. However, an exception is provided if an examination of an entity's compliance with specified requirements is required by law or regulation. In that instance, the practitioner should disclaim an opinion on compliance unless he or she obtains evidential matter that warrants expressing an adverse opinion. If the practitioner expresses an adverse opinion, the practitioner's report should be restricted as to use.

Control Criteria

In accordance with Chapter 1 of SSAE-10 (AT 101.23), the practitioner cannot accept an engagement unless he or she has reason to believe that the subject matter is capable of reasonably consistent evaluation against criteria that are suitable and available to users. The responsible party evaluates the effectiveness of the entity's internal control using suitable criteria. Such criteria are referred to as "control criteria."

Chapter 5 of SSAE-10 (AT 501.04) states that criteria issued by the AICPA, regulatory agencies, and other groups composed of experts that follow due-process procedures, including exposure of the proposed criteria for public comment, should ordinarily be considered suitable criteria. For example, the COSO Report provides suitable criteria against which management may evaluate and report on the effectiveness of the entity's internal control. Criteria established by management, industry associations, or other groups that do not follow due-process procedures may also be considered suitable criteria. The practitioner should determine whether such criteria are suitable for general-use reporting by evaluating them against the attributes in Chapter 1 of SSAE-10 (AT 101.24) (discussed in Chapter 5, "Planning and Administration for Attestation Engagements"). If the practitioner determines that such criteria are suitable for general-use reporting, the criteria should also be available to users. If the practitioner concludes that the criteria are appropriate for only a limited number of parties or are available only to specified parties, his or her report should be restricted to those specified parties.

Independence

Independence is the foundation of the attest function. Third-party users rely on the CPA's opinion in an audit or attest engagement because they believe the conclusion is impartial and unbiased. Chapter 1 of SSAE-10 (AT 101.36) states, "The practitioner should maintain the intellectual honesty and impartiality necessary to reach an unbiased conclusion about the subject matter or the assertion."

Independence in mental attitude means objective consideration of facts, unbiased judgments, and honest neutrality on the part of the CPA in forming and expressing conclusions. Independence in mental attitude presumes an undeviating concern for an unbiased conclusion about the subject matter or an assertion no matter what the subject matter or assertion may be.

Other Planning Considerations

Planning an engagement to examine the effectiveness of an entity's internal control involves developing an overall strategy for the scope and performance of the engagement. When developing an overall strategy for the engagement, the practitioner should consider factors such as

- Matters affecting the industry in which the entity operates, such as financial reporting practices, economic conditions, laws and regulations, and technological changes.
- Knowledge of the entity's internal control obtained during other professional engagements.
- Matters relating to the entity's business, including its organization, operating characteristics, capital structure, and distribution methods.
- The extent of recent changes, if any, in the entity, its operations, or its internal control.
- The responsible party's method of evaluating the effectiveness of the entity's internal control based upon control criteria.
- Preliminary judgments about materiality, inherent risk, and other factors relating to the determination of material weaknesses.
- The type and extent of evidential matter pertaining to the effectiveness of the entity's internal control.
- The nature of specific controls designed to achieve the objectives of the control criteria, and their significance to internal control taken as a whole.
- Preliminary judgments about the effectiveness of internal control.

Multiple Locations

If the entity has multiple locations, the practitioner should consider factors similar to those he or she would consider in performing an audit of the financial statements of an entity with multiple locations. It might not be necessary to understand and test controls at each location. In addition to the factors listed above, the selection of locations should be based on factors such as the following:

- The similarity of business operations and internal control at the various locations.
- The degree of centralization of records.

- The effectiveness of the control environment, particularly management's direct control over the exercise of authority delegated to others and its ability to effectively supervise activities at the various locations.
- The nature and amount of transactions executed and related assets at the various locations.

Internal Audit Function

Another factor the practitioner should consider when planning the engagement is whether the entity has an internal audit function. An important responsibility of the internal audit function is to monitor the performance of an entity's controls. One way internal auditors monitor such performance is by performing tests that provide evidence about the effectiveness of the design and operation of specific controls.

> **OBSERVATION:** The practitioner should consider the guidance in SAS-65 (AU 322) (The Auditor's Consideration of the Internal Audit Function in an Audit of Financial Statements) when assessing the competence and objectivity of internal auditors, the extent of work to be performed, and other matters.

Documentation of Internal Control

Controls and the control objectives that they were designed to achieve should be appropriately documented to serve as a basis for the responsible party's assertion and the practitioner's report. Such documentation is generally prepared by the responsible party. However, the practitioner may assist in preparing or gathering such documentation. This documentation may take various forms, such as entity policy manuals, accounting manuals, narrative memoranda, flowcharts, decision tables, procedural write-ups, or completed questionnaires.

Documenting Engagement Acceptance

SSAE-10 (AT 101.46) requires the practitioner to establish an understanding with the client regarding the services to be performed for each engagement. That understanding should include

- *The objectives of the engagement* The practitioner should address the objectives and any limitations of the engagement. For example, the objective of an examination engagement is to express an opinion on the effectiveness of the entity's internal control or the responsible party's written assertion on it.

- *Management's responsibilities* In an examination engagement, management must select the control criteria and determine that it is appropriate for its purposes. Management is also responsible for the effectiveness of the entity's internal control and for evaluating the effectiveness.
- *Practitioner's responsibilities* The practitioner's responsibility is to perform the engagement in accordance with professional standards. More specifically, to avoid misunderstandings the practitioner should describe the services that he or she will provide as precisely as possible.
- *Limitations of the engagement* The limitations that should be addressed relate to two aspects of the engagement: (1) limitations of the type of services to be performed and (2) use limitations based on the type of service. For example, the practitioner might wish to document that the engagement does not provide absolute assurance. In addition, the client should understand that in some cases the use of the report would be limited. For example, if the practitioner determines that the control criteria are appropriate for only a limited number of parties or are available only to specified parties, the practitioner's report should be restricted to those parties.

Other matters that practitioners should consider discussing with the client include

- *Criteria* The control criteria to be used must be both suitable and available to users. (See discussion in Chapter 5, "Planning and Administration for Attestation Engagements.")
- *Users of the report* Knowing who the potential users are helps the practitioner assess the risks in the engagement and provides information regarding the appropriateness of the service to be provided.
- *Logistics* The practitioner should determine whether the client has the necessary personnel and expertise to develop the subject matter. In addition, this understanding should include arrangements concerning the conduct of the engagement, such as timing, client assistance, and the availability of documents. Additional matters might include arrangements concerning involvement of specialists and conditions under which access to the workpapers may be granted to others.
- *Fees* The practitioner should determine that the fee and billing arrangements are appropriate.

Engagement Letters

The attestation standards require the practitioner to establish an understanding with the client. The standards state that a written engagement letter is preferred but not necessarily required. Although not specifically required by the SSAEs, a written engagement letter is strongly recommended. Most practitioners believe that a written engagement letter can effectively reduce misunderstandings between the practitioner and the client over the nature and limitations of the engagement. Engagement letters are particularly important in attestation engagements because of the increased risk of misunderstanding the nature of the practitioner's responsibilities (although clients may be familiar with traditional financial statement audits, they might not understand the nature and limitations of attestation engagements). The written engagement letter commonly includes the items discussed in the preceding section. Appendix 11A is an illustrative engagement letter for an examination engagement. When a written engagement letter is not obtained, the understanding of the engagement should be obtained and documented in the workpapers.

ENGAGEMENT PERFORMANCE

Obtaining an Understanding of Internal Control

The practitioner should obtain an understanding of the internal control over financial reporting. The understanding should include each of the components of internal control. For example, using the internal control framework in the COSO Report, the practitioner should obtain an understanding of each of the following components:

- Control environment
- Risk assessment
- Control activities
- Information and communication
- Monitoring

The practitioner generally obtains an understanding of the design of specific controls by making inquiries of appropriate management, supervisory, and staff personnel; by inspecting documents; and by observing entity activities and operations.

Evaluating the Design and Effectiveness of Controls

Any of the components of internal control may include controls designed to achieve the objectives of the control criteria. Some controls might have a pervasive effect on achieving many overall objectives of these criteria. For example, computer general controls over program development, program changes, computer operations, and access to programs and data help ensure that specific controls over the processing of transactions are operating effectively. In contrast, other controls are designed to achieve specific objectives of the control criteria. For example, management generally establishes specific controls, such as accounting for all shipping documents, to ensure that all valid sales are recorded.

The practitioner should focus on the significance of controls in achieving the objectives of the control criteria rather than on specific controls in isolation. The absence or inadequacy of a specific control designed to achieve the objectives of a specific criterion might not be a deficiency if other controls specifically address the criterion. Furthermore, when one or more controls achieve the objectives of a specific criterion, the practitioner might not need to consider other controls designed to achieve the same objectives.

Procedures to evaluate the effectiveness of the design of a specific control are concerned with whether the control is suitably designed to prevent or detect material misstatements in specific financial statement assertions. Such procedures vary depending upon the nature of the specific control, the nature of the entity's documentation of the specific control, and the complexity and sophistication of the entity's operations and systems.

Testing and Evaluating the Operating Effectiveness of Controls

To evaluate the operating effectiveness of an entity's internal control, the practitioner performs tests of relevant controls to obtain sufficient evidence to support the opinion in the report. Tests of operating effectiveness of a control are concerned with how the control was applied, the consistency with which it was applied, and by whom it was applied.

Selecting Controls for Testing

Once the significant control objectives are identified, the practitioner should apply tests to those controls that are important in achieving each control objective. There are two basic strategies for identifying key controls:

1. *Client identification* The client might have identified key controls and tested their operating effectiveness. The practitioner may select the same controls for testing.

2. *Independent selection* The practitioner may decide to make an independent selection of key controls rather than testing the controls identified by management.

Nature of Tests

Tests of controls ordinarily include procedures such as inquiries of appropriate personnel, inspection of relevant documentation, observation of the entity's operations, and reapplication or reperformance of the control. Inquiry and observation are generally used for controls whose application do not have a paper trail. Inspection and reperformance are generally used for controls whose performance is documented by the client.

Extent of Tests

The type of test performed influences the extent of tests. Inspection and reperformance lend themselves to sampling; inquiry and observation do not. The extent of testing is based on the practitioner's judgment about the following factors:

- *Significance of the control* The significance of the control is based on the risk that noncompliance would result in a material weakness in internal control. The more significant the control, the higher the level of operating effectiveness needed and the greater the extent of testing needed. Factors to consider in assessing significance include
  - — The likelihood that material misstatements that must be prevented or detected by the control will occur. This is similar to inherent risk in a financial statement audit.
  - — Whether more than one control achieves a specific objective. The level of operating effectiveness needed from one control is less if other controls tested accomplish the same objective.
  - — The degree to which the effectiveness of other controls depends on the effectiveness of the control being tested.
- *Control risk* In this context, control risk refers to the level of work the client has done to assure itself that the control is working.
- *Risk of noncompliance with the control* The risk of noncompliance with the control is the risk that deviations from the control will occur. As the risk of noncompliance increases,

the extent of testing needed generally increases. Factors to consider in assessing the risk of noncompliance include:

- The complexity of the control activity. Complex policies and procedures are generally more susceptible to deviations than simple, routine activities.
- Whether the control relies on performance by an individual or by electronic means. An automated control is generally more effective than a manual control.
- The degree to which the control relies on the effectiveness of other controls. An effective control environment, for example, tends to enhance the operating effectiveness of control activities, and vice versa.
- Whether there have been changes in the control. Changes in internal control can influence the effectiveness of a control. For example, changes in the volume or nature of transactions might adversely affect control design or operating effectiveness.

- *Evidence obtained from other procedures* Evidence obtained from procedures performed in other engagements (such as a financial statement audit) may be used to support the practitioner's conclusions about the effectiveness of a control.

The practitioner should consider the preceding factors and arrive at an overall judgment about the extent of tests of controls that is needed. When sampling is used to test the operating effectiveness of a control, the sample size is determined based on the following factors:

- *Level of effectiveness needed* The level of effectiveness needed is based on the factors listed above. The higher the level of effectiveness needed, the greater the sample size required.
- *Number of deviations* The number of deviations can be estimated based on the practitioner's experience with the client, as well as evidence from other sources (such as the internal auditor's work or results of tests of controls in a financial statement audit). The greater the expected number of deviations, the greater the required sample size.

Timing of Tests

The period of time over which the practitioner should perform tests of controls is a matter of judgment. It varies with the nature of the controls being tested and with the frequency with which specific controls operate and specific policies are applied. Some controls operate continuously (for example, controls over sales) and others operate only at certain times (for example, controls over the preparation of interim financial statements and controls over physical inventory counts).

The practitioner should perform tests of controls over a period of time that is adequate to determine whether, as of the date specified in the assertion, the controls necessary for achieving the objectives of the control criteria are operating effectively.

Written Representations

The practitioner should obtain written representations from management

- Acknowledging management's responsibility for establishing and maintaining effective internal control.
- Stating that management has performed an evaluation of the effectiveness of the entity's internal control and specifying the control criteria.
- Stating management's assertion about the effectiveness of the entity's internal control based on the control criteria as of a specified date.
- Stating that management has disclosed to the practitioner all significant deficiencies in the design or operation of internal control which could adversely affect the entity's ability to initiate, record, process, and report financial data consistent with the assertions of management in the financial statements and has identified deficiencies that it believes to be material weaknesses in internal control.
- Describing any material fraud and any other fraud that, although not material, involves management or other employees who have a significant role in the entity's internal control.
- Stating whether there were, subsequent to the date being reported on, any changes in internal control or other factors that might significantly affect internal control, including any corrective actions taken by management with regard to significant deficiencies and material weaknesses.

The representation letter should be dated as of the end of fieldwork. Appendix 11D provides an illustrative representation letter.

According to Chapter 5 of SSAE-10 (AT 501.45), management's refusal to furnish all appropriate written representations constitutes a limitation on the scope of the examination sufficient to preclude an unqualified opinion and is ordinarily sufficient to cause the practitioner to disclaim an opinion or withdraw from the engagement. However, based on the nature of the representations not obtained or the circumstances of the refusal, the practitioner may conclude that a qualified opinion is appropriate. Furthermore, the practitioner should consider the effects of management's refusal on his or her ability to rely on other representations.

Evaluation of Results

After evaluating the design and operating effectiveness of internal control, the practitioner should consider all of the evidence obtained to evaluate the effectiveness of internal control. If the tests disclose no deviations from controls or other deficiencies (and the practitioner is not aware of any such problems from other sources), he or she can generally conclude that internal control is effective.

However, if deviations are found, the practitioner should determine whether the deviations indicate that the related control is ineffective. When sampling is used, this determination can be accomplished by comparing the number of deviations detected with the number allowed for the sample. If the number of deviations found exceeds the number allowed, the practitioner normally concludes that the control is not effective. However, even if the number of deviations detected is less than the number allowed, the practitioner should consider the following before concluding that the deviations do not indicate a material weakness:

- The nature and cause of the deviations.
- The possibility that the deviation rate in the total population exceeds that in the sample.

An ineffective control is considered to be a deficiency in internal control. The practitioner should determine whether the deficiency constitutes a material weakness. SAS-60 (AU 325) (Communication of Internal Control Related Matters Noted in an Audit) defines a "material weakness" as

> [A] condition in which the design or operation of one or more of the internal control components does not reduce to a relatively low level the risk that misstatements caused by error or fraud in amounts that would be material in relation to the financial statements may occur and not be detected within a timely period by employees in the normal course of performing their assigned functions.

Deciding whether a deficiency (or a combination of deficiencies) constitutes a material weakness is a matter of professional judgment. Factors to consider in evaluating deficiencies include the following:

- *Compensating controls* If other controls are identified and determined to be effective, the ineffective control would generally not be considered to be a material weakness.
- *Effect of other components of internal control* Certain other components of internal control, such as a strong control environment, may help compensate for a particular deficiency in internal control.

- *Effect of the deficiency* When evaluating whether a deficiency is a material weakness, the practitioner should recognize that the amount of misstatements caused by error or fraud that occur and remain undetected range from zero to more than the gross financial statement amounts or transactions that are exposed to the deficiency. The risk of misstatement is likely to be different for the different possible amounts within that range. For example, risk might be higher for smaller misstatements, and vice versa.
- *Effect of other deficiencies* In evaluating whether the combined effect of deficiencies results in a material weakness, the practitioner should consider (1) the range or distribution of the amounts of misstatement that may result during the same accounting period from two or more individual deficiencies and (2) the joint risk or probability that such a combination of misstatements would be material.

The presence of a material weakness will preclude the practitioner from concluding that the entity has effective internal control and will require him or her to modify the examination report. However, depending on the significance of the material weakness and its effect on the achievement of the objectives of the control criteria, the practitioner may qualify his or her opinion (that is, express an opinion that internal control is effective "except for" the material weakness noted) or express an adverse opinion.

Communicating Reportable Conditions and Material Weaknesses

Even if the practitioner concludes that a deficiency does not represent a material weakness in internal control, it may be a reportable condition. SAS-60 (AU 325) defines a reportable condition as

> matters coming to an auditor's attention that represent significant deficiencies in the design or operation of internal control that could adversely affect the entity's ability to initiate, record, process, and report financial data consistent with the assertions of management in the financial statements.

A practitioner engaged to examine the effectiveness of an entity's internal control should communicate reportable conditions to the client's audit committee (or, if there is no audit committee, to an individual or group that takes overall responsibility for financial reporting in the entity). The practitioner should also identify the reportable conditions considered to be material weaknesses. Chapter 5 of SSAE-10 (AT 501.41) states that this communication should preferably be in writing.

When communicating reportable conditions in writing, the practitioner's report should include the following:

- A definition of "reportable conditions."
- A description of the reportable conditions noted.
- An identification of any reportable conditions that are also considered to be material weaknesses.

Because of the potential for misinterpretation of the limited degree of assurance associated with the practitioner issuing such a report, Chapter 5 of SSAE-10 (AT 501.41) prohibits the practitioner from issuing a report stating that no reportable conditions were noted.

The practitioner should communicate reportable conditions on a timely basis, either during the course of the engagement or after the engagement is concluded. The decision about whether an interim communication should be issued would be influenced by the relative significance of the matters noted and the urgency of follow-up action.

Appendix 11G and Appendix 11H are illustrative communications of reportable conditions.

REPORTING

The practitioner may examine and report directly on the entity's effectiveness of internal control or examine and report on management's written assertion.

Standard Reports

The practitioner's examination report should include the following:

- A title that includes the word "independent."
- An identification of the subject matter (internal control over financial reporting) and the responsible party (i.e., management). (When reporting on an assertion, rather than directly on the effectiveness of internal control, the report should identify management's assertion about the effectiveness of the entity's internal control over financial reporting as of a specified date. If the assertion does not accompany the report, the first paragraph of the report should contain a statement of management's assertion.
- A statement that the responsible party is responsible for maintaining effective internal control over financial reporting (when reporting on the assertion, a statement that the assertion is the responsibility of management should be included).
- A statement that the practitioner's responsibility is to express an opinion on the effectiveness of an entity's internal control (or management's assertion) based in his or her examination.

- A statement that the examination was conducted in accordance with attestation standards established by the American Institute of Certified Public Accountants and, accordingly, included obtaining an understanding of internal control over financial reporting, testing and evaluating the design and operating effectiveness of internal control, and performing such other procedures as the practitioner considered necessary in the circumstances.
- A statement that the practitioner believes the examination provides a reasonable basis for his or her opinion.
- A paragraph stating that, because of inherent limitations of any internal control, misstatements due to errors or fraud might occur and not be detected (in addition, the paragraph should state that projections of any evaluation of internal control over financial reporting to future periods are subject to the risk that internal control might become inadequate because of changes in conditions, or that the degree of compliance with the policies and procedures might deteriorate).
- The practitioner's opinion on whether (1) the entity has maintained, in material respects, effective internal control over financial reporting as of the specified date based on the control criteria or (2) management's assertion about the effectiveness of the entity's internal control over financial reporting as of a specified date is fairly stated, in all material respects, based on the control criteria.
- A statement restricting the use of the report to the specified parties under the following circumstances:
  - When the criteria used to evaluate internal control over financial reporting are determined by the practitioner to be appropriate for only a limited number of parties who either participated in their establishment or can be presumed to have an adequate understanding of the criteria.
  - When the criteria used to evaluate internal control over financial reporting are available only to specified parties.
- The manual or printed signature of the practitioner's firm.
- The date of the examination report.

When reporting on management's assertion, the practitioner should identify the management report examined by referring to the title used by management in its report. The language used to describe management's assertion in the report should be the same as the language used by management in its assertion. Furthermore, the report should use the same description of the entity's internal control that management uses in its report, including types of controls that management reports on.

The examination report should be dated as of the end of fieldwork. Exhibit 11-1 is a standard examination report in which the practitioner expresses an opinion directly on the effectiveness of internal control. Exhibit 11-2 is a standard examination report in which the practitioner expresses an opinion on management's assertion about the effectiveness of internal control.

> **OBSERVATION:** Chapter 5 of SSAE-10 (AT 501.52) notes that nothing precludes the practitioner from restricting the use of any report.

EXHIBIT 11-1 STANDARD EXAMINATION REPORT: REPORTS DIRECTLY ON THE EFFECTIVENESS OF INTERNAL CONTROL OVER FINANCIAL REPORTING

Independent Accountant's Report

[*addressee*]
[*city, state*]

We have examined the effectiveness of XYZ Company's internal control over financial reporting as of December 31, 20XX, based on criteria established in *Internal Control—Integrated Framework,* issued by the Committee of Sponsoring Organizations of the Treadway Commission (COSO). XYZ Company's management is responsible for maintaining effective internal control over financial reporting. Our responsibility is to express an opinion on the effectiveness of internal control based on our examination

Our examination was conducted in accordance with attestation standards established by the American Institute of Certified Public Accountants and, accordingly, included obtaining an understanding of the internal control over financial reporting, testing, and evaluating the design and operating effectiveness of the internal control, and performing such other procedures as we considered necessary in the circumstances. We believe our examination provides a reasonable basis for our opinion.

Because of inherent limitations in any internal control, misstatements due to error or fraud may occur and not be detected. Also, projections of any evaluation of the internal control over financial reporting to future periods are subject to the risk that internal control may become inadequate because of changes in conditions, or that the degree of compliance with the policies and procedures may deteriorate.

In our opinion, XYZ Company maintained, in all material respects, effective internal control over financial reporting as of December 31, 20XX, based on criteria established in *Internal Control—Integrated Framework,* issued by the Committee of Sponsoring Organizations of the Treadway Commission (COSO).

[*firm's signature*]

[*city, state*]

[*date*]

EXHIBIT 11-2
STANDARD EXAMINATION REPORT: REPORTS ON MANAGEMENT'S ASSERTION ABOUT THE EFFECTIVENESS OF INTERNAL CONTROL OVER FINANCIAL REPORTING

Independent Accountant's Report

[*addressee*]
[*city, state*]

We have examined management's assertion, included in the accompanying [*title of management report*], that XYZ Company maintained effective internal control over financial reporting as of December 31, 20XX, based on criteria established in *Internal Control—Integrated Framework,* issued by the Committee of Sponsoring Organizations of the Treadway Commission (COSO). XYZ Company's management is responsible for maintaining effective internal control over financial reporting. Our responsibility is to express an opinion on management's assertion based on our examination

Our examination was conducted in accordance with attestation standards established by the American Institute of Certified Public Accountants and, accordingly, included obtaining an understanding of the internal control over financial reporting, testing, and evaluating the design and operating effectiveness of the internal control, and performing such other procedures as we considered necessary in the circumstances. We believe our examination provides a reasonable basis for our opinion.

Because of inherent limitations in any internal control, misstatements due to error or fraud may occur and not be detected. Also, projections of any evaluation of the internal control over financial reporting to future periods are subject to the risk that internal control may become inadequate because of changes in conditions, or that the degree of compliance with the policies and procedures may deteriorate.

In our opinion, management's assertion that XYZ Company maintained effective internal control over financial reporting as of December 31, 20XX is fairly stated, in all material respects, based on criteria established in *Internal Control—Integrated Framework,* issued by the Committee of Sponsoring Organizations of the Treadway Commission (COSO).

[*firm's signature*]

[*city, state*]

[*date*]

Report Modifications

There are a number of situations that require modification of the standard examination report. The practitioner should modify the standard report if any of the following conditions exist:

- There is a material weakness in the entity's internal control.

- There is a restriction on the scope of the engagement.
- The practitioner decides to refer to the report of another practitioner as the basis, in part, for the practitioner's own report.
- A significant subsequent event has occurred since the date being reported on.
- The engagement relates to examining and reporting on the effectiveness of only a segment of the entity's internal control.
- The engagement only relates to examining and reporting on the suitability of design of the entity's internal control.
- The criteria are not suitable for general use.

Material Weaknesses

If the examination discloses conditions that, individually or in combination, result in one or more material weaknesses, the practitioner should modify the report. Chapter 5 of SSAE-10 (AT 501.54) requires practitioners to express either a qualified or adverse opinion directly on the subject matter (i.e., an opinion directly on the effectiveness of internal control over financial reporting) when there is a material weakness. The purpose of that requirement is to highlight the fact that there is a material weakness that impacts the effectiveness of the entity's internal control.

The decision of whether to issue a qualified or adverse opinion is a matter of professional judgment. The practitioner should consider the significance of the material weakness and its effect on the achievement of the control objectives.

If the practitioner concludes that the material weakness is not so pervasive that it keeps the entity's internal control from achieving the control objectives, a qualified opinion is appropriate. Exhibit 11-3 is an example of a report with a qualified opinion. If, however, in the practitioner's judgment, the material weakness(es) is (are) so pervasive that the entity's internal control over financial reporting does not achieve the control objectives, an adverse opinion should be expressed. Exhibit 11-4 is an example of a report with an adverse opinion.

EXHIBIT 11-3
EXAMINATION REPORT WHEN THERE IS A MATERIAL WEAKNESS QUALIFIED OPINION

Independent Accountant's Report

[*addressee*]
[*city, state*]

We have examined the effectiveness of XYZ Company's internal control over financial reporting as of December 31, 20XX, based on criteria established in *Internal Control—Integrated Framework*, issued by the Committee of Sponsoring Organizations of the Treadway Commission (COSO). XYZ

Company's management is responsible for maintaining effective internal control over financial reporting. Our responsibility is to express an opinion on the effectiveness of internal control based on our examination

Our examination was conducted in accordance with attestation standards established by the American Institute of Certified Public Accountants and, accordingly, included obtaining an understanding of the internal control over financial reporting, testing, and evaluating the design and operating effectiveness of the internal control, and performing such other procedures as we considered necessary in the circumstances. We believe our examination provides a reasonable basis for our opinion.

Because of inherent limitations in any internal control, misstatements due to error or fraud may occur and not be detected. Also, projections of any evaluation of the internal control over financial reporting to future periods are subject to the risk that internal control may become inadequate because of changes in conditions, or that the degree of compliance with the policies and procedures may deteriorate.

[*Include sentence(s) describing the material weakness and its effect on the achievement of the objectives of the control criteria.*] We believe such condition represents a material weakness. A material weakness is a condition that precludes the entity's internal control from providing reasonable assurance that material misstatements in the financial statements will be prevented or detected on a timely basis.

In our opinion, except for the effect of the material weakness described in the preceding paragraph on the achievement of the objectives of the control criteria, XYZ Company maintained, in all material respects, effective internal control over financial reporting as of December 31, 20XX, based on criteria established in *Internal Control—Integrated Framework* issued by the Committee of Sponsoring Organizations of the Treadway Commission (COSO).

[*firm's signature*]

[*city, state*]

[*date*]

EXHIBIT 11-4
EXAMINATION REPORT:
MATERIAL WEAKNESS, ADVERSE OPINION

Independent Accountant's Report

[*addressee*]
[*city, state*]

We have examined the effectiveness of XYZ Company's internal control over financial reporting as of December 31, 20XX, based on criteria established in *Internal Control—Integrated Framework* issued by the Committee of Sponsoring Organizations of the Treadway Commission (COSO). XYZ Company's management is responsible for maintaining effective internal control over financial reporting. Our responsibility is to express an opinion on the effectiveness of internal control based on our examination

Our examination was conducted in accordance with attestation standards established by the American Institute of Certified Public Accountants and, accordingly, included obtaining an understanding of the internal control over financial reporting, testing, and evaluating the design and operating effectiveness of the internal control, and performing such other procedures as we considered necessary in the circumstances. We believe our examination provides a reasonable basis for our opinion.

Because of inherent limitations in any internal control, misstatements due to error or fraud may occur and not be detected. Also, projections of any evaluation of the internal control over financial reporting to future periods are subject to the risk that internal control may become inadequate because of changes in conditions, or that the degree of compliance with the policies and procedures may deteriorate.

[*Include sentence(s) describing the material weakness and its effect on the achievement of the objectives of the control criteria.*] We believe such condition represents a material weakness. A material weakness is a condition that precludes the entity's internal control from providing reasonable assurance that material misstatements in the financial statements will be prevented or detected on a timely basis.

In our opinion, because of the effect of the material weakness described above on the achievement of the objectives of the control criteria, XYZ Company has not maintained, in all material respects, effective internal control over financial reporting as of December 31, 20XX, based on criteria established in *Internal Control—Integrated Framework* issued by the Committee of Sponsoring Organizations of the Treadway Commission (COSO).

[*firm's signature*]

[*city, state*]

[*date*]

When the practitioner issues either a qualified or adverse opinion, the report is modified as follows:

- An explanatory paragraph is inserted before the opinion paragraph that (1) Describes the material weakness and its effect on the achievement of the control objectives and (2) defines the condition as a material weakness. The following is an example of such an explanatory paragraph:

  > [*Include sentence(s) describing the material weakness and its effect on the achievement of the objectives of the control criteria.*] We believe such condition represents a material weakness. A material weakness is a condition that precludes the entity's internal control from providing reasonable assurance that material misstatements in the financial statements will be prevented or detected on a timely basis.

- The opinion paragraph should be modified by including a reference to the material weakness. In addition, the practitioner would use the appropriate language to express either a qualified or adverse opinion directly on the effectiveness of the entity's internal control over financial reporting.

If the written assertion accompanying the practitioner's report contains a statement that management believes the cost of correcting the weakness would exceed the benefits to be derived from implementing new controls, the practitioner should disclaim an opinion on management's cost-benefit statement. The following is an example of such a disclaimer (inserted as the last paragraph in the report):

> We do not express an opinion or any other form of assurance on management's cost-benefit statement.

If the practitioner has performed a financial statement audit and an examination of internal control, and both reports are presented in the same document, the following language should be added to the paragraph that describes the material weakness:

> These conditions were considered in determining the nature, timing, and extent of audit tests applied in our audit of the 20XX financial statements, and this report does not affect our report dated [*date of auditor's report*] on these financial statements.

Scope Limitations

Restrictions on the scope of the engagement, whether imposed by the client, the responsible party, or the circumstances, might require the practitioner to withdraw from the engagement, disclaim an opinion, or express a qualified opinion. The practitioner's decision depends on his or her assessment of the importance of the omitted procedure(s) to his or her ability to form an opinion on the effectiveness of internal control.

As discussed earlier, Chapter 5 of SSAE-10 (AT 501.44) requires a written representation letter in an examination of internal control. Management's refusal to provide all appropriate representations constitutes a scope limitation sufficient to preclude an unqualified opinion and is ordinarily sufficient to cause the practitioner to disclaim an opinion or withdraw from the engagement. Furthermore, the practitioner should consider the effects of management's refusal on his or her ability to rely on other representations.

When the examination report expresses a qualified opinion because of a scope limitation, the report should include a scope paragraph, an explanatory paragraph that describes the scope limitation, and a modified opinion paragraph that contains a qualified opinion. The following is an example of a scope paragraph:

> Except as described below, our examination was conducted in accordance with attestation standards established by the American Institute of Certified Public Accountants and, accordingly, included obtaining an understanding of the internal control over financial reporting, testing, and evaluating the design and operating effectiveness of the internal control, and performing such other procedures as we considered necessary in

> the circumstances. We believe our examination provides a reasonable basis for our opinion.

The following is an example of an example explanatory paragraph:

> Prior to December 20, 20XX, XYZ Company had an inadequate system for recording cash receipts, which could have prevented the Company from recording cash receipts on accounts receivable completely and properly. Therefore, cash received could have been diverted for unauthorized use, lost, or otherwise not properly recorded to accounts receivable. We believe this condition was a material weakness in the design or operation of the internal control of XYZ Company in effect at [*date*]. A material weakness is a condition that precludes the entity's internal control from providing reasonable assurance that material misstatements in the financial statements will be prevented or detected on a timely basis. Although the Company implemented a new cash receipts system on December 20, 20XX, the system has not been in operation for a sufficient period of time to enable us to obtain sufficient evidence about its operating effectiveness.

The following is an example of an example opinion paragraph:

> In our opinion, except for the effect of matters we may have discovered had we been able to examine evidence about the effectiveness of the new cash receipts system, XYZ Company maintained, in all material respects, effective internal control over financial reporting as of December 31, 20XX, based on [*identify criteria*].

When restrictions that significantly limit the scope of the examination are imposed by the client or the responsible party, the practitioner generally should disclaim an opinion. In a disclaimer, the practitioner's report refers to the scope limitation in the introductory paragraph, eliminates the scope paragraph and inherent limitations paragraph, includes an explanatory paragraph to describe the scope limitation, and disclaims an opinion in the final paragraph.

Opinion Based on Report of Another Practitioner

When another practitioner has examined the effectiveness of internal control of one or more subsidiaries, divisions, branches, or components of the entity, the practitioner should consider whether he or she may serve as the principal practitioner and use the work and reports of the other practitioner as a basis, in part, for his or her opinion. If the practitioner decides it is appropriate for him or her to serve as the principal practitioner, he or she then should decide whether to make reference in the examination report to the report of the other practitioner.

OBSERVATION: In these cases, the practitioner's considerations are similar to those of an independent auditor who uses the work and reports of other auditors when reporting on an entity's financial statements. SAS-1 (AU 543) (Part of Audit Performed by Other Independent Auditors) provides guidance on this topic.

If the practitioner decides to refer to the report of the other practitioner as a basis, in part, for his or her opinion, the scope and opinion paragraphs of the standard report should be modified by referring to the other practitioner's report. Appendix 11I contains an example of a report that refers to another practitioner's report.

Subsequent Events

Changes in internal control or other factors that might significantly affect internal control might occur subsequent to the date as of which internal control is being examined but before the date of the practitioner's report. To obtain information about whether changes have occurred that might affect the effectiveness of the entity's internal control and, therefore, the examination report, the practitioner should inquire about and examine, for this subsequent period, the following:

- Relevant internal auditor reports issued during the subsequent period.
- Independent auditor reports of reportable conditions or material weaknesses.
- Regulatory agency reports on the entity's internal control.
- Information about the effectiveness of the entity's internal control obtained through other professional engagements.

If the practitioner obtains knowledge about subsequent events that he or she believes significantly affects the entity's internal control, he or she should take the following actions:

- If the event significantly affects the effectiveness of the entity's internal control as of the date specified in the assertion, the practitioner should report directly on the effectiveness of internal control (as opposed to reporting on management's assertion) and issue a qualified or adverse opinion. In this case, if the practitioner cannot determine the effect, he or she should issue a disclaimer.
- If the event affects internal control only after the date specified in the assertion, the practitioner should consider including an explanatory paragraph in the report describing or directing the reader's attention to the effects of the event.

Other Reports

Reporting on a Segment of an Entity's Internal Control

The practitioner may be engaged to examine the effectiveness of only a segment of an entity's internal control, such as a single division or a single account (such as accounts receivable). In that case, the practitioner should apply the guidance in Chapter 5 of SSAE-10 (AT 501) to the portion of internal control he or she is to report on.

Appendix 11J is an example of an examination report on a segment of an entity's internal control.

Reporting on the Design of Internal Control

The practitioner may be engaged to examine the suitability of the design of an entity's internal control for preventing or detecting material misstatements on a timely basis. For example, prior to granting a new casino a license to operate, a regulatory agency might request a report on whether the internal control that management plans to implement will provide reasonable assurance that the control objectives will be achieved. In such an engagement, the practitioner should obtain an understanding of the components of internal control and asses the suitability of the design (as discussed earlier in this chapter). Appendix 11K is an illustrative report; the actual form of the report should be modified by the practitioner as appropriate to fit the circumstances.

When the internal control has already been placed in operation, the practitioner should make it clear that no tests of operating effectiveness have been performed. In that case, the practitioner should modify his or her report by adding the following to the scope paragraph of the report:

> We were not engaged to examine and report on the operating effectiveness of XYZ Company's internal control over financial reporting as of December 31, 20XX, and, accordingly, we express no opinion on operating effectiveness.

Criteria Specified by a Regulatory Agency

A governmental or other agency that exercises regulatory, supervisory, or other public administrative functions may establish its own criteria and require reports on the internal control of entities subject to its jurisdiction. Criteria established by a regulatory agency may be set forth in audit guides, questionnaires, or other publications. The criteria may encompass specified aspects of an entity's internal control and specified aspects of administrative control or compliance with grants, regulations, or statutes. If such criteria have been subjected to due process procedures, including the distribution of proposed criteria for public comment, and the criteria are available to users, the standard form of examination report is appropriate.

Chapter 5 of SSAE-10 (AT 501.72) states that if the regulatory criteria have not been subjected to due process procedures or are not available to users, and the practitioner has determined that the criteria are only suitable for a limited number of users who agreed to the criteria or who can be presumed to understand them, the report must be restricted to the use of the specified parties (for example, the client and the regulatory agency).

For purposes of these reports, a material weakness is

- A condition in which the design or operation of one or more of the specific internal control components does not reduce to a relatively low level the risk that misstatements due to error or fraud in amounts that would be material in relation to the applicable grant or program might occur and not be detected on a timely basis by employees in the normal course of performing their assigned functions.
- A condition in which the lack of conformity with the regulatory agency's criteria is material in accordance with any guidelines for determining materiality that are included in such criteria.

Appendix 11L is an illustrative restricted-use report for this type of engagement.

Other Information in a Client-Prepared Document Containing the Report on the Effectiveness of Internal Control

A client may publish various documents that contain information in addition to the practitioner's report. The practitioner's responsibility with respect to the other information does not extend beyond the information identified in the examination report, and the practitioner has no obligation to perform any procedures to corroborate any other information contained in the document. However, the practitioner should read the other information not covered by the examination report and consider whether it, or the manner of its presentation, is materially consistent with the information appearing in the examination report.

If the practitioner believes that the other information is inconsistent with the information appearing in the examination report, the practitioner should

- Consider whether the examination report requires revision, or
- Request the client to revise the other information to eliminate the inconsistency

If the other information is not revised to eliminate the inconsistency, the practitioner should consider other actions, such as:

- Revising the examination report to include an explanatory paragraph describing the material inconsistency
- Withholding the use of the examination report
- Withdrawing from the engagement

If while reading the other information the practitioner becomes aware of information that he or she believes is a material misstatement of fact that is not a material inconsistency as described above, he or she should discuss the matter with the client. If, after discussing the matter, the practitioner concludes that a material misstatement of fact remains, the action the practitioner takes will depend on his or her judgment in the circumstances. The practitioner should consider steps such as notifying the client's management and audit committee in writing of his or her views concerning the information and consulting his or her legal counsel about further appropriate action in the circumstances.

INTERNAL CONTROL OVER COMPLIANCE

Practitioners may be engaged to report on internal control over compliance. These engagements may be either agreed-upon procedures engagements or examinations. Chapter 6 of SSAE-10 (AT 601) provides guidance for engagements to perform agreed-upon procedures relating to internal control over compliance. However, engagements to examine an entity's internal control over compliance are not specifically addressed in the attestation standards. For guidance on this type of engagement, the practitioner should look to the general guidance contained in Chapter 1 of SSAE-10 (AT 101) and the guidance related to engagements to examine an entity's internal control over financial reporting (contained in Chapter 5 of SSAE-10) (AT 501).

Examination Engagements

Examinations of internal control over compliance can be complex because of the difficulty in obtaining suitable control criteria. In addition, the practitioner might have concerns regarding materiality in an examination engagement. That is, if it is difficult to determine what is material, it is also difficult to determine a material weakness and, therefore, difficult to assess internal controls over compliance. Given these concerns, most practitioners will agree to examine an entity's internal control over compliance only when (1) such an engagement is required for regulatory purposes and (2) the practitioner's concerns over criteria and materiality can be alleviated.

Agreed-Upon Procedures Engagements

The objective of an agreed-upon procedures engagement is to assist specified parties in evaluating the effectiveness of internal control over compliance. The specified parties and the practitioner agree upon the procedures to be performed that the specified parties believe are appropriate.

Attestation Standard Requirements

Chapter 6 of SSAE-10 (AT 601.09) requires that certain conditions be met for the practitioner to perform an agreed-upon procedures engagement related to the effectiveness of an entity's internal control over compliance with specified requirements. These conditions are as follows:

- The responsible party accepts responsibility for the entity's compliance with specified requirements and the effectiveness of the entity's internal control over compliance.
- The responsible party evaluates the effectiveness of the entity's internal control over compliance with specified requirements.

In addition, Chapter 2 of SSAE-10 (AT 201.06) requires that certain conditions be met for any agreed-upon procedures engagement:

- The practitioner is independent.
- One of the following conditions is met:
  - — The party wishing to engage the practitioner is responsible for the subject matter or has a reasonable basis for providing a written assertion about the subject matter when the nature of the subject matter is such that a responsible party does not otherwise exist (see discussion in Chapter 5, "Planning and Administration for Attestation Engagements," of this guide).
  - — The party wishing to engage the practitioner is not responsible for the subject matter but is able to provide the practitioner, or have a third party who is responsible for the subject matter provide the practitioner, with evidence of the third party's responsibility for the subject matter.
- The practitioner and the specified parties agree upon the procedures performed or to be performed by the practitioner.
- The specified parties take responsibility for the sufficiency of the agreed-upon procedures for their purposes.
- The specific subject matter to which the procedures are to be applied is subject to reasonably consistent measurement.

- Criteria to be used in the determination of findings are agreed upon between the practitioner and the specified parties.
- The procedures to be applied to the specific subject matter are expected to result in reasonably consistent findings using the criteria.
- Evidential matter related to the specified subject matter to which the procedures are applied is expected to exist to provide a reasonable basis for expressing the findings in the practitioner's report.
- Where applicable, the practitioner and the specified parties agree on any materiality limits for reporting purposes.
- Use of the report is restricted to the specified parties.

Responsibilities of the Responsible Party

The responsible party is responsible for ensuring that the entity complies with the requirements applicable to its activities. (In most cases, in an engagement to apply agreed-upon procedures related to the effectiveness of an entity's internal control over compliance with specified requirements, the responsible party is the management of the entity.) That responsibility includes

- Identifying applicable compliance requirements.
- Establishing and maintain internal control to provide reasonable assurance that the entity complies with those requirements.
- Evaluating and monitor the entity's compliance.
- Specifying reports that satisfy legal, regulatory, or contractual requirements.

The responsible party's evaluation may include documentation such as accounting or statistical data, entity policy manuals, accounting manuals, narrative memoranda, procedural writeups, flowcharts, completed questionnaires, or internal auditors' reports. The form and extent of the documentation will vary depending on the nature of the compliance requirements and the size and complexity of the entity. The responsible party may engage the practitioner to gather information to assist it in evaluating the entity's compliance.

OBSERVATION: Regardless of the procedures performed by the practitioner, the responsible party must accept responsibility for its assertion and must not base such assertion solely on the practitioner's procedures.

Written Assertion

As part of the engagement, the practitioner should obtain from the responsible party a written assertion about internal control over compliance with specified requirements. The responsible party may present its written assertion in either of the following forms:

- A separate report that will accompany the practitioner's report.
- A representation letter to the practitioner.

The responsible party's written assertion about internal control over compliance with specified requirements may take many forms. For example, the phrase "responsible party's assertion that W Company maintained effective internal control over compliance with [*specify compliance requirement*] as of [*date*]," illustrates such an assertion. Other phrases may also be used. However, the practitioner should not accept an assertion that is so subjective (for example, "very effective" compliance) that people having competence in and using the same or similar criteria would not ordinarily be able to arrive at similar conclusions.

In an agreed-upon procedures engagement, if the practitioner's client is the responsible party, a refusal to provide a written assertion requires the practitioner to withdraw from the engagement. However, withdrawal is not required if the engagement is required by law or regulation. If the practitioner's client is not the responsible party, the practitioner is not required to withdraw from the engagement but should consider the effects of the responsible party's refusal on the engagement and his or her report.

Control Criteria

In accordance with Chapter 1 of SSAE-10 (AT 101.23), the practitioner cannot accept an engagement unless he or she has reason to believe that the subject matter is capable of reasonably consistent evaluation against criteria that are suitable and available to users. The criteria used in engagements related to the effectiveness of an entity's internal control over compliance with specified requirements may be difficult to develop. If the control criteria are not specified by a regulatory agency, then alternative sources of criteria must be develop and used.

Chapter 6 of SSAE-10 (AT 601.06) states that criteria used by regulatory agencies and other groups composed of experts that follow due-process procedures, including exposure of the proposed criteria for public comment, should ordinarily be considered suitable criteria. For example, the COSO Report provides suitable criteria against which management may evaluate and report on the effectiveness of the entity's internal control. However, more detailed criteria relative to specific compliance requirements may have to be developed and an appropriate threshold for measuring the severity of control deficiencies needs to be developed in order to apply the concepts of the COSO Report to internal control over compliance.

Independence

Independence is the foundation of the attest function. Third-party users rely on the CPA's opinion in an audit or attest engagement because they believe the conclusion is impartial and unbiased. Chapter 1 of SSAE-10 (AT 101.36) states, "The practitioner should maintain the intellectual honesty and impartiality necessary to reach an unbiased conclusion about the subject matter or the assertion."

Independence in mental attitude means objective consideration of facts, unbiased judgments, and honest neutrality on the part of the CPA in forming and expressing conclusions. Independence in mental attitude presumes an undeviating concern for an unbiased conclusion about the subject matter or an assertion no matter what the subject matter or assertion may be.

Engagement Performance

The objective of the practitioner's agreed-upon procedures is to present specific findings to assist users in evaluating the entity's internal control over compliance with specified requirements, based on procedures agreed upon by the users of the report.

Terms and Conditions of the Engagement

A practitioner may perform an agreed-upon procedures engagement related to an entity's internal control over compliance with specified requirements if the following conditions are met:

- The responsible party accepts responsibility for the entity's compliance with specified requirements and the effectiveness of the entity's internal control over compliance.
- The responsible party evaluates the entity's compliance with specified requirements.

Responsibilities of the Specified Parties

The client engages the practitioner to assist other interested parties in evaluating subject matter or an assertion as a result of a need or needs of these parties. These parties, including the client, are referred to as "specified parties." As a consequence of the role of the specified parties in agreeing upon the procedures performed or to be performed, a practitioner's report on such engagements should clearly state that its use is restricted to the specified parties.

The specified parties are responsible for the sufficiency (nature, timing, and extent) of the agreed-upon procedures because they best understand their own needs. The specified parties assume the risk that such procedures might be insufficient for their purposes. In addition, the specified parties assume the risk that they might misunderstand or otherwise inappropriately use the findings properly reported by the practitioner.

Responsibilities of the Practitioner

The second general standard requires that the practitioner have adequate knowledge of the subject matter. This knowledge can be obtained through formal or continuing education or practical experience. The adequacy of a practitioner's knowledge of the subject matter varies with the type of engagement, from common sense to complex subjects, such as actuarial data. In general, the knowledge of the subject matter should be sufficient to allow the practitioner to form an objective conclusion about it.

SSAE-10 (AT 101.22) clarifies that the practitioner does not have to personally acquire all of the knowledge in the subject matter to be qualified to apply agreed-upon procedures to it. The knowledge requirement can be met, in part, through the use of one or more specialists on a particular engagement if the practitioner has sufficient knowledge of the subject matter to

- Communicate the objectives of the work to the specialist; and
- Evaluate the specialist's work to determine if objectives were met.

The practitioner assumes the risk that misapplication of the procedures might result in inappropriate findings being reported. Furthermore, the practitioner assumes the risk that appropriate findings might not be reported or might be reported inaccurately. The practitioner's risks can be reduced through adequate planning and supervision and due professional care in performing procedures, determining findings, and preparing the report.

The practitioner has no responsibility to determine the differences between the agreed-upon procedures to be performed and the procedures that the practitioner would have determined to be necessary had he or she been engaged to perform another form of attest engagement. The procedures that the practitioner agrees to perform may be more or less extensive than the procedures that he or she would determine to be necessary to perform another form of engagement.

Appropriate Procedures

The procedures that the practitioner and the specified parties agree upon may be as limited or as extensive as the specified parties desire. In some circumstances, the procedures evolve or are modified over the course of the engagement. In general, there is flexibility in determining the procedures as long as the specified parties acknowledge responsibility for the sufficiency of such procedures for their purposes. Matters that should be agreed upon include the nature, timing, and extent of the procedures.

The practitioner should obtain evidential matter from applying the agreed-upon procedures to provide a reasonable basis for the finding or findings expressed in his or her report, but he or she need not perform additional procedures outside the scope of the engagement to gather additional evidential matter.

As mentioned above, the procedures that the practitioner and specified parties agree upon may be as limited or as extensive as the specified parties desire. However, mere reading of an assertion or specified information about the subject matter does not constitute a procedure sufficient to permit a practitioner to report on the results of applying agreed-upon procedures. In addition, the practitioner should not agree to perform procedures that are overly subjective and thus possibly open to varying interpretations. Terms of uncertain meaning (such as "general review," "limited review," "check," or "test") should not be used in describing the procedures unless they are defined within the agreed-upon procedures.

Materiality and Sampling

The concept of materiality is normally not relevant in an agreed-upon procedures engagement. In an agreed-upon procedures engagement, the practitioner is engaged to perform specific procedures that are requested by the specified parties and the practitioner should report all findings from application of these procedures. Any materiality levels used in performing the procedures should be determined by the specified parties, agreed to in the engagement letter, and described in the practitioner's report.

Engagement Letters

The attestation standards require the practitioner to establish an understanding with the client. The standards state that a written engagement letter is preferred but not necessarily required. Although not specifically required by the SSAEs, a written engagement letter is strongly recommended. Most practitioners believe that a written engagement letter can effectively reduce misunderstandings between the practitioner and the client over the nature and limitations of the engagement. Engagement letters are particularly important in attestation engagements because of the increased risk of misunderstanding the nature of the practitioner's responsibilities (although clients might be familiar with traditional financial statement audits, they might not understand the nature and limitations of attestation engagements). Written engagement letters commonly include items such as the following:

- Description of the nature of the engagement. The practitioner should address the nature of the engagement and any limitations of the engagement. For example, the nature of an agreed-upon procedures engagement is to present the results of applying agreed-upon procedures to specific subject matter in the form of findings.
- Identification of the subject matter, the responsible party, and the criteria to be used.
- Identification of specified parties.
- Specified parties' acknowledgement of their responsibility for the sufficiency of the procedures.
- Practitioner's responsibilities. The practitioner's responsibility is to carry out the procedures and report the findings in accordance with the general, fieldwork, and reporting standards.
- Reference to attestation standards established by the American Institute of Certified Public Accountants.
- Agreement on procedures by enumerating (or referring to) the procedures.
- Disclaimers expected to be included in the practitioner's report.
- Use restrictions.
- Assistance to be provided to the practitioner. The practitioner should determine whether the client has the necessary personnel and expertise to develop the subject matter. In addition, this understanding should include arrangements concerning the conduct of the engagement, such as timing, client assistance, and the availability of documents.
- Involvement of a specialist.
- Agreed-upon materiality limits.

Appendix 11M is an illustrative engagement letter for an agreedupon procedures engagement. When a written engagement letter is not obtained, the understanding of the engagement should be obtained and documented in the workpapers.

OBSERVATION: When a written engagement letter is used, it should be addressed to the client, and in some circumstances, also to all specified parties.

Agreement on and Sufficiency of Procedures

To satisfy the requirements that the practitioner and the specified parties agree upon the procedures performed or to be performed and that the specified parties take responsibility for the sufficiency of the agreed-upon procedures for their purposes, the practitioner should ordinarily communicate directly with and obtain affirmative acknowledgement from each of the specified parties.

OBSERVATION: This agreement may be accomplished by meeting with the specified parties or by distributing a draft of the anticipated report or a copy of an engagement letter to the specified parties and obtaining their agreement.

If the practitioner is not able to communicate directly with all of the specified parties, he or she may satisfy these requirements by applying any one or more of the following or similar procedures:

- Compare the procedures to be applied to the written requirements of the specified parties.
- Discuss the procedures to be applied with appropriate representatives of the specified parties.
- Review relevant contracts with or correspondence from the specified parties.

The practitioner should not report on an engagement when specified parties do not agree upon the procedures performed or to be performed and do not take responsibility for the sufficiency of the procedures for their purposes.

Adding Specified Parties

Subsequent to the completion of the agreed-upon procedures engagement, the practitioner might be asked to consider the addition of another party as a specified party (referred to as a "nonparticipant party"). The practitioner may agree to add a nonparticipant party, based on the consideration of such factors as the identity of the nonparticipant party and the intended use of the report.

OBSERVATION: When considering whether to add a nonparticipant party, the guidance in SAS-1 (AU 530) (Dating of the Independent Auditor's Report) is helpful.

If the practitioner does agree to add the nonparticipant party, he or she should obtain affirmative acknowledgement, preferably in writing, from the nonparticipant party agreeing to the procedures performed and of its taking responsibility for the sufficiency of the procedures. If the nonparticipant party is added after the report is issued, the report may be reissued or the practitioner may provide other written acknowledgement that the nonparticipant party has been added as a specified party. If the practitioner provides written acknowledgement that the nonparticipant party has been added as a specified party, the written acknowledgement should state that no additional procedures have been performed subsequent to the date of the report.

> **OBSERVATION:** If the report is reissued, the original report date should not be changed.

Understanding the Specified Compliance Requirements

In an engagement to perform agreed-upon procedures on an entity's internal control over compliance with specified requirements, the practitioner is required to perform only those procedures that have been agreed to by the users. However, prior to performing such procedures, the practitioner should obtain an understanding of the specified compliance requirements.

To obtain an understanding of the specified compliance requirements, the practitioner should consider the following:

- Laws, regulations, rules, contracts, and grants that pertain to the specified compliance requirements, including published requirements.
- Knowledge about the specified compliance requirements obtained through prior engagements and regulatory reports.
- Knowledge about the specified compliance requirements obtained through discussions with appropriate individuals within the entity (for example, chief financial officer, internal auditors, legal counsel, compliance officer, or grant or contract administrators).
- Knowledge about the specified compliance requirements obtained through discussions with appropriate individuals outside the entity (for example, a regulator or third-party specialist).

Representation Letter

In an agreed-upon procedures engagement related to an entity's internal control over compliance with specified requirements,

Chapter 6 of SSAE-10 (AT 601.68) requires the practitioner to obtain written representations from the responsible party, including the following:

- A statement acknowledging the responsible party's responsibility for complying with the specified requirements.
- A statement acknowledging the responsible party's responsibility for establishing and maintaining effective internal control over compliance.
- A statement that the responsible party has performed an evaluation of the entity's controls for ensuring compliance and detecting noncompliance with requirements, as applicable.
- A statement of the responsible party's assertion about the effectiveness of the entity's internal control over compliance with the specified requirements based on the stated or established criteria.
- A statement acknowledging that the responsible party has disclosed to the practitioner all known noncompliance.
- A statement acknowledging that the responsible party has made available all documentation related to compliance with the specified requirements.
- A statement of the responsible party's interpretation of any compliance requirements that have varying interpretations.
- A statement that the responsible party has disclosed any communications from regulatory agencies, internal auditors, and other practitioners concerning possible noncompliance with the specified requirements, including communications received between the end of the period addressed in the written assertion and the date of the practitioner's report.
- A statement that the responsible party has disclosed any known noncompliance occurring subsequent to the period for which, or date as of which, the responsible party selects to make its assertion.

The representation letter should be dated no earlier than the date of the practitioner's report, which should coincide with the end of fieldwork. The letter should be addressed to the practitioner and signed by members of management whom the practitioner believes are responsible for and knowledgeable, directly or through others in the organization, about the matters covered by the representations. Normally, the CEO should sign the letter. It should also be signed by the highest ranking officer under whose responsibility the subject matter falls. For example, if the subject matter is financial, the CFO should also sign the letter.

When the practitioner is performing agreed-upon procedures and the practitioner's client is the responsible party, the responsible party's refusal to furnish all appropriate written representations constitutes a limitation on the scope of the engagement sufficient to cause the practitioner to withdraw. When the practitioner's client is not the responsible party, the practitioner is not required to withdraw but should consider the effects on his or her report of the responsible party's refusal. In addition, the practitioner should consider the effects of the responsible party's refusal on his or her ability to rely on other representations of the responsible party.

When the client is not the responsible party, the practitioner should also consider obtaining a representation letter from the client. For example, when the practitioner's client has entered into a contract with a third party (responsible party) and the practitioner is engaged to perform agreed-upon procedures related to the responsible party's internal control over compliance with the contract, the practitioner might want to obtain written representations from his or her client as to their knowledge of any noncompliance.

Appendix 11R and Appendix 11S are illustrative representation letters for agreed-upon procedures engagements.

Use of Client Personnel and Internal Auditors

According to Chapter 2 of SSAE-10 (AT 201.22), the agreed-upon procedures to be enumerated or referred to in the practitioner's report are to be performed entirely by the practitioner. However, internal auditors or other client personnel may prepare schedules and accumulate data or provide other information for the practitioner's use in performing the agreed-upon procedures. Also, internal auditors may perform and report separately on procedures that they have carried out. Such procedures may be similar to the procedures that the practitioner performs.

A practitioner may agree to perform procedures on information documented in the workpapers of internal auditors. For example, the practitioner may agree to:

- Repeat some or all of the procedures.
- Determine whether the internal auditors' workpapers contain documentation of procedures performed and whether the findings documented in the workpapers are presented in a report prepared by the internal auditors.

However, it is inappropriate for the practitioner to

- Agree to merely read the internal auditors' report solely to describe or repeat their findings.
- Take responsibility for all or a portion of any procedures performed by internal auditors by reporting those findings as the practitioner's own.
- Report in any manner that implies shared responsibility for the procedures with the internal auditors.

Documentation

Documentation of the agreed-upon procedures engagement is the principal record of procedures applied, information obtained, and findings reached by the practitioner in the engagement. The quantity, type, and content of documentation are matters of the practitioner's professional judgment. Documentation serves mainly to

1. Provide the principal support for the practitioner's report, including the representation regarding observance of the standards of fieldwork, which is implicit in the reference in the report to attestation standards.
2. Aid the practitioner in conducting and supervising the engagement.

Documentation should be sufficient to (1) enable members of the engagement team with supervision and review responsibilities to understand the nature, timing, extent, and results of procedures performed and the information obtained and (2) identify the engagement team member(s) who performed and reviewed the work.

Examples of documentation are work programs, analyses, memoranda, letters of confirmation and representation, abstracts or copies of entity documents, and schedules or commentaries prepared or obtained by the practitioner. Ordinarily, documentation includes

- Documentation of the engagement acceptance or continuance decision.
- An engagement letter.
- Documentation of how the specified parties determined the procedures to be performed.
- Documentation for planning considerations.
- Procedures checklist.
- A list of the procedures agreed to with a cross reference to documentation of performance.
- Summary of findings.
- Agreed-upon procedures report.
- A discussion of unusual matters encountered and their resolution.
- A representation letter.
- Documentation that the workpapers were reviewed.

Documentation may be in paper form, electronic form, or other media. The practitioner has an ethical, and in some situations a legal, obligation to maintain the confidentiality of client information or information of the responsible party. Because documentation often contains confidential information, the practitioner should adopt reasonable procedures to maintain the confidentiality of that information. The practitioner should also adopt reasonable procedures to prevent unauthorized access to documentation.

Reporting

General

The practitioner's report on agreed-upon procedures should be in the form of procedures and findings. The practitioner's report should contain the following elements:

- A title that includes the word "independent."
- Identification of the specified parties.
- Identification of the subject matter (or the written assertion) and the character of the engagement.
- Identification of the responsible party.
- A statement that the subject matter is the responsibility of the responsible party.
- A statement that the procedures, which were those agreed to by the specified parties identified in the report, were performed to assist the specified parties in evaluating the entity's internal control over compliance with specified requirements.
- A statement that the agreed-upon procedures engagement was conducted in accordance with attestation standards established by the AICPA.
- A statement that the sufficiency of the procedures is solely the responsibility of the specified parties and a disclaimer of responsibility for the sufficiency of those procedures.
- A list of the procedures performed (or reference thereto) and related findings.
- Where applicable, a description of any agreed-upon materiality limits.
- A statement that the practitioner was not engaged to and did not conduct an examination, of the entity's internal control over compliance with specified requirements, the objective of which would be an expression of an opinion, a disclaimer of opinion thereon, and a statement that if the practitioner had performed additional procedures, other matters might have come to his or her attention that would have been reported.
- A statement of restrictions on the use of the report because it is intended to be used solely by the specified parties.
- Where applicable, reservations or restrictions concerning procedures or findings.
- Where applicable, a description of the nature of the assistance provided by a specialist.
- The manual or printed signature of the practitioner's firm.
- The date of the report.

Exhibit 11-5 is an example of an agreed-upon procedures report on an entity's internal control over compliance with specified requirements in which the procedures and findings are enumerated rather than referenced.

EXHIBIT 11-5
AGREED-UPON PROCEDURES REPORT REGARDING COMPLIANCE

[*addressee*]
[*city, state*]

We have performed the procedures enumerated below, which were agreed to by [*list of specified parties*], solely to assist the specified parties in evaluating the effectiveness of [*name of entity*]'s internal control over compliance with [*list specified requirements*] during the [*period*] ended [*date*]. Management is responsible for [*name of entity*]'s internal control over compliance with those requirements. This agreed-upon procedures engagement was conducted in accordance with attestation standards established by the American Institute of Certified Public Accountants. The sufficiency of these procedures is solely the responsibility of those parties specified in this report. Consequently, we make no representation regarding the sufficiency of the procedures described below either for the purpose for which this report has been requested or for any other purpose.

[*Include paragraphs to enumerate procedures and findings.*]

We were not engaged to and did not conduct an examination, the objective of which would be the expression of an opinion on the effectiveness of internal control over compliance. Accordingly, we do not express such an opinion. Had we performed additional procedures, other matters might have come to our attention that would have been reported to you.

This report is intended solely for the information and use of [*list or refer to specified parties*] and is not intended to be and should not be used by anyone other than these specified parties.

[*firm's signature*]

[*city, state*]

[*date*]

Description of Procedures

The practitioner should present the results of applying the agreed-upon procedures to specific subject matter in the form of findings. The practitioner should report all findings from application of the agreedupon procedures and he or she should avoid vague and ambiguous language in reporting the findings.

Significant Interpretations

Evaluating compliance with certain requirements might require interpretation of the laws, regulations, rules, contracts, or grants that establish those requirements. In such situations, the practitioner should consider whether he or she is provided with the suitable criteria required to evaluate an assertion under the third general attestation standard. If these interpretations are significant, the practitioner may include a paragraph stating the description and source of interpretations made by the entity's management. An example of such a paragraph, which should precede the procedures and findings paragraph(s), is as follows:

> We have been informed that, under [*name of entity*]'s interpretation of [*identify the compliance requirement*], [*explain the nature and source of the relevant interpretation*].

Noncompliance

The practitioner might become aware of noncompliance that occurs subsequent to the period addressed by the practitioner's report but before the date of the report. In this case, the practitioner should consider including information regarding such noncompliance in his or her report. However, the practitioner has no responsibility to perform procedures to detect such noncompliance other than obtaining the responsible party's representation about noncompliance in the subsequent period.

Scope Limitations

When circumstances impose restrictions on the performance of the agreed-upon procedures, he or she should attempt to obtain agreement from the specified parties for modification of the agreed-upon procedures. When agreement cannot be obtained (for example, when the agreed-upon procedures are published by a regulatory agency that will not modify the procedures), the practitioner should describe any restrictions on the performance of the procedures in his or her report or withdraw from the engagement.

INTERNAL CONTROL OVER OPERATIONS

Engagements related to internal control over operations are not addressed in Chapter 5 of SSAE-10 (AT501).A practitioner engaged to examine the effectiveness of internal control over operations should refer to the general guidance applicable to examinations in Chapter 1 of SSAE-10 (AT 101). A practitioner engaged to perform agreed-upon procedures related to an entity's internal control over operations should refer to the general guidance applicable to agreed-upon procedures engagements in Chapter 2 of SSAE-10 (AT 201).

However, engagements to assess internal controls over operations are generally performed as consulting engagements and thus are governed by SSCS. In this type of engagement, the practitioner is engaged to analyze and make recommendations on an entity's internal control but not provide assurance regarding its effectiveness. Exhibit 11-6 presents an illustration of a consulting report on internal control over operations.

EXHIBIT 11-6
CONSULTING REPORT ON INTERNAL CONTROL OVER OPERATIONS

[*addressee*]
[*city, state*]

The accompanying report presents our analysis of XYZ Company's controls over the financial reporting of sales. In performing our analysis and accompanying recommendations, we identified:

- Significant transaction streams within the sales department.
- Points in the transactions cycle where economic events take place.
- Areas in the processing of accounting information where transactions could be lost or processed incorrectly.
- Internal controls that help deal with whether:
  - — All recorded transactions are valid.
  - — All valid transactions are recorded.
  - — Transactions are properly valued.
  - — Transactions are recorded in the proper period in a timely manner.
  - — Transactions are properly included in subsidiary records and correctly summarized.
- Places where controls should exist but are missing.

These procedures were accomplished by interviewing company management, departmental personnel, and accounting personnel to determine the flow of accounting information and controls placed in operation. The scope of our engagement did not include testing the operating effectiveness of such controls.

Our analysis was not designed to express an opinion on the operations and controls over sales taken as a whole, and we do not express such an opinion. As you know, because of inherent limitations of any internal control, errors or fraud may occur and not be prevented or detected by internal controls.

[*firm's signature*]

[*city, state*]

[*date*]

APPENDIX 11A
ENGAGEMENT LETTER: EXAMINATION OF AN ENTITY'S INTERNAL CONTROL OVER FINANCIAL REPORTING

[*date*]

[*name of client*]
[*address*]

We are pleased to confirm our understanding of the nature and limitations of the services we are to provide for [*client's legal name*].

We will examine the effectiveness of the internal control over financial reporting (internal control) of [*name of client*] as of [*date*]. Our examination will be conducted in accordance with attestation standards established by the American Institute of Certified Public Accountants and, accordingly, will include obtaining an understanding of the internal control, testing and evaluating the design and operating effectiveness of the internal control, and performing such other procedures as we consider necessary to enable us to express an opinion about whether the entity has maintained, in all material respects, effective internal control over financial reporting based on the control criteria [*or management's assertion is fairly stated, in all material respects, based on the control criteria*]. If our opinion is other than unqualified, we will discuss the reasons with you in advance. If, for any reason, we are unable to complete the examination, we will not issue a report as a result of this engagement.

[*Describe limitations on the use of the report, if any.*]

Because of inherent limitations in any internal control, misstatements due to error or fraud may occur and not be detected. Also, projections of any evaluation of the internal control to future periods are subject to the risk that the internal control may become inadequate because of changes in conditions, or that the degree of compliance with the controls may deteriorate. However, during the examination, if we become aware of reportable conditions that are significant deficiencies in the design or operation of the internal control, we will communicate them to you in a separate letter.

We understand that you will present your assertion about the effectiveness of the internal control in a written report. You are responsible for establishing and maintaining effective internal control, as well as evaluating the effectiveness of those controls. We may advise you about appropriate criteria or assist in the development of the assertion, but the responsibility for establishing and maintaining effective internal control remains with you. At the conclusion of our examination, we will require certain representations from you about the effectiveness of the internal control and related matters.

We understand that you will provide us with the information required for our examination and that you are responsible for the accuracy and completeness of that information.

We plan to begin our examination on approximately [*date*] and issue our report no later than [*date*]. We estimate that our fees for these services will range from $_____ to $_____. You will also be billed for travel and other out-of-pocket costs such as report production, typing, postage, etc. Additional expenses are estimated to be $_____. The fee estimate is based on anticipated cooperation from your personnel and the assumption that unexpected circumstances will not be encountered during the examination. If significant additional time is necessary, we will discuss it with you and arrive at a new fee estimate before we incur the additional costs. Our invoices for these fees will be rendered each month as work progresses and are payable on presentation. In accordance with our firm policies, work may be suspended if your account becomes ___ days or more overdue and will not be resumed until your account is paid in full. If we elect to terminate our services for nonpayment, our engagement will be deemed to have been completed upon written notification of termination, even if we have not completed our report. You will be obligated to compensate us for all time expended and to reimburse us for all out-of-pocket expenditures through the date of termination.

We appreciate the opportunity to be of service to you and believe this letter accurately summarizes the significant terms of our engagement. If you have any questions, please let us know. If you agree with the terms of our engagement as described in this letter, please sign the enclosed copy and return it to us.

Very truly yours,

[*CPA firm's name*]

Response:

This letter correctly sets forth the understanding of [*name of client*].

By:

Title:

Date:

APPENDIX 11B
EXAMINATION ENGAGEMENT CHECKLIST: INTERNAL CONTROL OVER FINANCIAL REPORTING

Client Name: ______________ Date of Subject Matter: ________________

Completed by: ______________ Date Completed: ____________________

	Completed by	N/A
1. Complete the Client Acceptance and Retention Evaluation Form.	________	_______
2. Establish and document an understanding with the client, preferably in an engagement letter. If an engagement letter will not be obtained, the oral understanding should be documented in a memo.	________	_______
3. Obtain an understanding of the client and the effectiveness of the entity's internal control.	________	_______
4. If the client is not the responsible party, obtain evidence of the responsible party's responsibility for the effectiveness of internal control over financial reporting (subject matter).	________	_______
5. If necessary, assist management in gathering information to evaluate internal control.	________	_______

		Completed by	N/A
6.	Determine that the scheduling and staffing are adequate to perform the engagement.	________	________
7.	Obtain the engagement partner's approval of the overall engagement plan.	________	________
8.	If other services have been performed for the responsible party, review relevant workpapers and any related reports for indications of matters that contradict the evaluation of internal control.	________	________
9.	Review any regulatory reports, internal audit reports, reports from independent accountants, or other relevant reports for indications of deficiencies in internal control.	________	________
10.	Obtain an understanding of internal control.	________	________
11.	Test and evaluate the design and operating effectiveness of the entity's controls.	________	________
12.	Review the results of the preceding procedures and evaluate the design and operating effectiveness of internal control. If the procedures reveal deficiencies, assess the significance of deficiencies and their effect on the examination report.	________	________
13.	Consider whether events have occurred after the date of the subject matter but before the end of fieldwork that affect internal control over financial reporting.	________	________
14.	Obtain a representation letter and written assertion from the responsible party (and the client, if the client is not the responsible party).	________	________
15.	Draft the examination report.	________	________
16.	Summarize reportable conditions for communication to the client.	________	________
17.	Read for inconsistencies with the report and material misstatements of fact other information in a client-prepared document that contains the examination report.	________	________
18.	If any situations have occurred that require consultation, determine that such consultation has been properly documented.	________	________
19.	If there were differences of professional opinion among members of the engagement team or between the engagement team and a specialist, determine that the differences were properly resolved and documented.	________	________
20.	Determine that all questions, exceptions, or notes, if any, posed during the engagement have been followed up and resolved.	________	________

		Completed by	N/A
21.	Determine that all required forms, questionnaires, and checklists have been completed.	________	________
22.	Ensure that the workpapers and examination report have been reviewed in accordance with firm policy.	________	________
23.	Obtain engagement partner's review and approval for issuance of report.	________	________

APPENDIX 11C
TESTS OF CONTROLS SAMPLING PLANNING AND EVALUATION FORM

Client Name: ______________ Date of Subject Matter: ________________

Completed by: _____________ Date Completed: ______________________

Instructions

This form can be used to test the operating effectiveness of control activities.

1. Describe the control(s) to be tested:

Control to Be Tested	Control Objective	Documentary Evidence

2. Describe the test to be performed:

Test to Be Performed	Workpaper Reference	Deviation Definition

3. Describe how the completeness of the population was considered:
4. Assess the level of effectiveness needed from this control:
   a. High _____
   b. Moderate _____
   c. Low _____
5. Determine the required sample size using the following table.
   Sample size __________________

Matrix for Determining Sample Size for Attribute Sampling

Expected Number of Deviations	Level of Effectiveness Needed: High	Moderate	Low
0	50	30	25
1	80	45	35
2	—*	60	50
3	—*	75	60

* In these situations, the control is generally not effective enough to achieve the control objectives.

6. Document the sample selection method:
   a. Haphazard ____
   b. Random ____
   c. Systemic ____
7. Document the results of the tests
   Number of deviations detected: ________
   Describe deviations below:

Deviation	Cause

8. Compare the number of deviations detected to the number of expected deviations and the level of effectiveness needed from the control. The practitioner should make a qualitative assessment of the nature and cause of any deviations detected before reaching a conclusion about the effectiveness of the controls. Check one of the following to indicate the conclusion about the effectiveness of the controls tested:
   — Controls are sufficiently effective.
   — Controls are NOT sufficiently effective.
9. Describe the effects of these results on the examination (generally, the practitioner should either test other controls that accomplish the same control objectives or consider the effect of the lack of effective controls on the examination report):

APPENDIX 11D
REPRESENTATION LETTER: EXAMINATION OF AN ENTITY'S INTERNAL CONTROL OVER FINANCIAL REPORTING

[*date—No earlier than date of the accountant's report*]

[*CPA firm's name*]
[*address*]

In connection with your examination of the effectiveness of our internal control over financial reporting (internal control) as of [*date of subject matter*], for the purpose of expressing an opinion as to whether the entity maintained, in all material respects, effective internal control over financial reporting based on [*describe control criteria*] (or the assertion is fairly stated, in all material respects, based on [*describe control criteria*]), we confirm, to the best of our knowledge and belief, the following representations made to you during the course of your examination:

- We are responsible for establishing and maintaining effective internal control over financial reporting.
- We have performed an evaluation of the effectiveness of the company's internal control based on [*control criteria*].
- [*Management's assertion about internal control.*]

- We have disclosed to you all information we are aware of that may contradict the effectiveness of internal control, and we have disclosed to you all communications from regulatory agencies affecting internal control.
- There are no:
  - — Material weaknesses in internal control.
  - — Significant deficiencies in the design or operation of internal control that could adversely affect the company's ability to record, process, summarize, and report financial data consistent with the assertions of management in the financial statements.
- There has been no:
  - — Fraud that could have a material effect on the financial statements.
  - — Other fraud involving management or other employees who have significant roles in internal control.
- We have disclosed to you all events subsequent to [*date of subject matter*] that might significantly affect internal control, including any corrective actions taken by management regarding significant deficiencies and material weaknesses.
- We have made available to you all records relevant to the effectiveness of internal control.
- We intend to distribute your report only to [*describe restrictions, if any*].

Signature:	Signature:
Title:	Title:

APPENDIX 11E STANDARD EXAMINATION REPORT DIRECTLY ON THE EFFECTIVENESS OF THE ENTITY'S INTERNAL CONTROL OVER FINANCIAL REPORTING

Independent Accountant's Report

To the Board of Directors of
[*client name*]
[*city, state*]

We have examined the effectiveness of XYZ Company's internal control over financial reporting as of December 31, 20XX, based on criteria established in *Internal Control—Integrated Framework* issued by the Committee of Sponsoring Organizations of the Treadway Commission (COSO). XYZ Company's management is responsible for maintaining effective internal control over financial reporting. Our responsibility is to express an opinion on the effectiveness of internal control based on our examination

Our examination was conducted in accordance with attestation standards established by the American Institute of Certified Public Accountants and, accordingly, included obtaining an understanding of the internal control over financial reporting, testing, and evaluating the design and operating effectiveness of the internal control, and performing such other procedures as we considered necessary in the circumstances. We believe our examination provides a reasonable basis for our opinion.

Because of inherent limitations in any internal control, misstatements due to error or fraud may occur and not be detected. Also, projections of any evaluation of the internal control over financial reporting to future periods are subject to the risk that internal control may become inadequate because of changes in conditions or that the degree of compliance with the policies and procedures may deteriorate.

In our opinion, XYZ Company maintained, in all material respects, effective internal control over financial reporting as of December 31, 20XX, based on criteria established in *Internal Control—Integrated Framework* issued by the Committee of Sponsoring Organizations of the Treadway Commission (COSO).

[*firm's signature*]

[*city, state*]

[*date*]

APPENDIX 11F
STANDARD EXAMINATION REPORT ON MANAGEMENT'S ASSERTION ABOUT THE EFFECTIVENESS OF THE ENTITY'S INTERNAL CONTROL OVER FINANCIAL REPORTING

Independent Accountant's Report

To the Board of Directors of
[*client name*]
[*city, state*]

We have examined management's assertion, included in the accompanying [*title of management report*] that XYZ Company maintained effective internal control over financial reporting as of December 31, 20XX, based on criteria established in *Internal Control—Integrated Framework* issued by the Committee of Sponsoring Organizations of the Treadway Commission (COSO). XYZ Company's management is responsible for maintaining effective internal control over financial reporting. Our responsibility is to express an opinion on management's assertion based on our examination

Our examination was conducted in accordance with attestation standards established by the American Institute of Certified Public Accountants and, accordingly, included obtaining an understanding of the internal control over financial reporting, testing, and evaluating the design and operating effectiveness of the internal control, and performing such other procedures as we considered necessary in the circumstances. We believe our examination provides a reasonable basis for our opinion.

Because of inherent limitations in any internal control, misstatements due to error or fraud may occur and not be detected. Also, projections of any evaluation of the internal control over financial reporting to future periods are subject to the risk that internal control may become inadequate because of changes in conditions or that the degree of compliance with the policies and procedures may deteriorate.

In our opinion, management's assertion that XYZ Company maintained effective internal control over financial reporting as of December 31, 20XX is fairly stated, in all material respects, based on criteria established in *Internal Control—Integrated Framework* issued by the Committee of Sponsoring Organizations of the Treadway Commission (COSO).

[*firm's signature*]

[*city, state*]

[*date*]

APPENDIX 11G
COMMUNICATION OF REPORTABLE CONDITIONS NOTED IN AN EXAMINATION ENGAGEMENT, INDICATION THAT NONE IS A MATERIAL WEAKNESS

To the Audit Committee of
[*client name*]

In performing our examination of the effectiveness of internal control over financial reporting (internal control) of [*client*] as of [*date*], we noted certain matters involving internal control and its operation that we consider to be reportable conditions under standards established by the American Institute of Certified Public Accountants. Reportable conditions involve matters coming to our attention relating to significant deficiencies in the design or operation of the internal control that, in our judgment, could adversely affect the organization's ability to record, process, summarize, and report financial data consistent with the assertions of management in the financial statements.

[*Describe the reportable conditions noted, none of which is a material weakness.*]

A material weakness is a reportable condition in which the design or operation of one or more of the internal control components does not reduce to a relatively low level the risk that misstatements caused by error or fraud in amounts that would be material in relation to the financial statements may occur and not be detected within a timely period by employees in the normal course of performing their assigned functions. None of the reportable conditions described above is believed to be a material weakness.

This report is intended solely for the information and use of the audit committee of [*client name*] and is not intended to be and should not be used by anyone other than these specified parties.

[*firm's signature*]

[*city, state*]

[*report date*]

APPENDIX 11H
COMMUNICATION OF REPORTABLE CONDITIONS NOTED IN AN EXAMINATION ENGAGEMENT, IDENTIFICATION OF MATERIAL WEAKNESSES

To the Audit Committee of
[*client name*]

In performing our examination of the effectiveness of internal control over financial reporting (internal control) of [*client*] as of [*date*], we noted certain matters involving internal control and its operation that we consider to be reportable conditions under standards established by the American Institute of Certified Public Accountants. Reportable conditions involve matters coming to our attention relating to significant deficiencies in the design or operation of the internal control that, in our judgment, could adversely affect the organization's ability to record, process, summarize, and report financial data consistent with the assertions of management in the financial statements.

A material weakness is a reportable condition in which the design or operation of one or more of the internal control components does not reduce to a relatively low level the risk that misstatements caused by error or fraud in amounts that would be material in relation to the financial statements may occur and not be detected within a timely period by employees in the normal course of performing their assigned functions.

In performing our examination, we noted the following reportable conditions that we believe to be material weaknesses.

[*Describe the material weaknesses noted.*]

We also noted the following reportable conditions that are not believed to be material weaknesses.

[*Describe the reportable conditions noted that are not considered material weaknesses.*]

This report is intended solely for the information and use of the audit committee of [*client name*] and is not intended to be and should not be used by anyone other than these specified parties.

[*firm's signature*]

[*city, state*]

[*report date*]

APPENDIX 11I
EXAMINATION REPORT ON EFFECTIVENESS OF INTERNAL CONTROL, REFERENCE TO REPORT OF ANOTHER PRACTITIONER

Independent Accountant's Report

To the Board of Directors of
[*client name*]
[*city, state*]

We have examined the effectiveness of XYZ Company's internal control over financial reporting as of December 31, 20XX, based on criteria established in *Internal Control—Integrated Framework* issued by the Committee of Sponsoring Organizations of the Treadway Commission (COSO). XYZ Company's management is responsible for maintaining effective internal control over financial reporting. Our responsibility is to express an opinion on the effectiveness of internal control based on our examination. We did not examine the effectiveness of the internal control over financial reporting of D Company, a wholly owned subsidiary, whose financial statements reflect total assets and revenues constituting 25 percent and 35 percent, respectively, of the related consolidated financial statement amounts as of and for the year ended December 31, 20XX. The effectiveness of D Company's internal control over financial reporting was examined by other accountants whose report has been furnished to us, and our opinion, insofar as it relates to the effectives of D Company's internal control over financial reporting, is based solely on the report of the other accountants.

Our examination was conducted in accordance with attestation standards established by the American Institute of Certified Public Accountants and, accordingly, included obtaining an understanding of the internal control over financial reporting, testing, and evaluating the design and operating effectiveness of the internal control and performing such other procedures as we considered necessary in the circumstances. We believe our examination provides a reasonable basis for our opinion.

Because of inherent limitations in any internal control, misstatements due to error or fraud may occur and not be detected. Also, projections of any evaluation of the internal control over financial reporting to future periods are subject to the risk that internal control may become inadequate because of changes in conditions or that the degree of compliance with the policies and procedures may deteriorate.

In our opinion, based on our examination and the report of the other accountants, XYZ Company maintained, in all material respects, effective internal control over financial reporting as of December 31, 20XX, based on criteria established in *Internal Control—Integrated Framework*, issued by the Committee of Sponsoring Organizations of the Treadway Commission (COSO).

[*firm's signature*]

[*city, state*]

[*date*]

APPENDIX 11J
EXAMINATION REPORT ON THE EFFECTIVENESS OF A SEGMENT OF INTERNAL CONTROL

Independent Accountant's Report

To the Board of Directors of
[*client name*]
[*city, state*]

We have examined the effectiveness of XYZ Company's internal control over financial reporting for its retail division as of December 31, 20XX, based on criteria established in *Internal Control—Integrated Framework,* issued by the Committee of Sponsoring Organizations of the Treadway Commission (COSO). XYZ Company's management is responsible for maintaining effective internal control over financial reporting. Our responsibility is to express an opinion on the effectiveness of internal control based on our examination

Our examination was conducted in accordance with attestation standards established by the American Institute of Certified Public Accountants and, accordingly, included obtaining an understanding of the internal control over financial reporting, testing, and evaluating the design and operating effectiveness of the internal control, and performing such other procedures as we considered necessary in the circumstances. We believe our examination provides a reasonable basis for our opinion.

Because of inherent limitations in any internal control, misstatements due to error or fraud may occur and not be detected. Also, projections of any evaluation of the internal control over financial reporting to future periods are subject to the risk that internal control may become inadequate because of changes in conditions or the degree of compliance with the policies and procedures may deteriorate.

In our opinion, XYZ Company's retail division maintained, in all material respects, effective internal control over financial reporting as of December 31, 20XX, based on criteria established in *Internal Control—Integrated Framework,* issued by the Committee of Sponsoring Organizations of the Treadway Commission (COSO).

[*firm's signature*]

[*city, state*]

[*date*]

APPENDIX 11K
EXAMINATION REPORT ON THE DESIGN OF THE ENTITY'S INTERNAL CONTROL OVER FINANCIAL REPORTING

Independent Accountant's Report

To the Board of Directors of
[*client name*]
[*city, state*]

We have examined the suitability of design of XYZ Company's internal control over financial reporting to prevent or detect misstatements in the financial statements on a timely basis as of December 31, 20XX, based on criteria established in *Internal Control—Integrated Framework,* issued by the Committee of Sponsoring Organizations of the Treadway Commission (COSO). XYZ Company's management is responsible for the suitable design of internal control over financial reporting. Our responsibility is to express an opinion on the design of internal control based on our examination.

Our examination was conducted in accordance with attestation standards established by the American Institute of Certified Public Accountants and, accordingly, included obtaining an understanding of the internal control over financial reporting, evaluating the design of the internal control, and performing such other procedures as we considered necessary in the circumstances. We believe our examination provides a reasonable basis for our opinion.

Because of inherent limitations in any internal control, misstatements due to error or fraud may occur and not be detected. Also, projections of any evaluation of the internal control over financial reporting to future periods are subject to the risk that internal control may become inadequate because of changes in conditions or the degree of compliance with the policies and procedures may deteriorate.

In our opinion, XYZ Company's internal control over financial reporting is suitably designed, in all material respects, to prevent or detect material misstatements in the financial statements on a timely basis as of December 31, 20XX, based on criteria established in *Internal Control—Integrated Framework*, issued by the Committee of Sponsoring Organizations of the Treadway Commission (COSO).

[*firm's signature*]

[*city, state*]

[*date*]

APPENDIX 11L EXAMINATION REPORT ON THE EFFECTIVENESS OF INTERNAL CONTROL, CRITERIA SPECIFIED BY A REGULATORY AGENCY THAT ARE NOT SUITABLE FOR GENERAL USE

Independent Accountant's Report

To the Board of Directors of
[*client name*]
[*city, state*]

We have examined the adequacy of XYZ Company's internal control over financial reporting as of December 31, 20XX, based on [*identify criteria, for example, the criteria established by* _________ *agency, as set forth in its audit guide dated* _________]. XYZ Company's management is responsible for maintaining adequate internal control over financial reporting. Our responsibility is to express an opinion on whether the internal control is adequate to meet such criteria based on our examination.

Our examination was conducted in accordance with attestation standards established by the American Institute of Certified Public Accountants and, accordingly, included obtaining an understanding of the internal control over financial reporting, testing, and evaluating the design and operating effectiveness of the internal control, and performing such other procedures as we considered necessary in the circumstances. We believe our examination provides a reasonable basis for our opinion.

Because of inherent limitations in any internal control, misstatements due to error or fraud may occur and not be detected. Also, projections of any evaluation of the internal control over financial reporting to future periods are subject to the risk that internal control may become inadequate because of changes in conditions, or that the degree of compliance with the policies and procedures may deteriorate. We understand that the agency considers the controls over financial reporting that meet the criteria referred to in the first paragraph of this report adequate for its purpose. In our opinion, based on this understanding and on our examination, XYZ Company's internal control over financial reporting is adequate, in all material respects, based on the criteria established by [*agency*].

This report is intended solely for the information and use of the board of directors and management of XYZ Company and [*agency*] and is not intended to be and should not be used by anyone other than these specified parties.

[*firm's signature*]

[*city, state*]

[*date*]

APPENDIX 11M
ENGAGEMENT LETTER: AGREED-UPON PROCEDURES RELATED TO INTERNAL CONTROL OVER COMPLIANCE

[*date*]

[*name of client (and other specified parties)*]
[*address*]

We are pleased to confirm our understanding of the nature and limitations of the services we are to provide for [*client's legal name*].

We will apply agreed-upon procedures [that specified parties have specified, listed in the attached schedule,] to [*describe subject matter or related assertion*] of [*name of responsible party*] as of [*date*], prepared in accordance with [*criteria*]. Our engagement to apply agreed-upon procedures will be conducted in accordance with attestation standards established by the American Institute of Certified Public Accountants. The sufficiency of the procedures is solely the responsibility of those parties specified in the report. Consequently, we make no representation regarding the sufficiency of the procedures described in the attached schedule either for the purpose for which the report has been requested or for any other purpose. If, for any reason, we are unable to complete the procedures, we will describe any restrictions on the performance of the procedures in our report or not issue a report as a result of this engagement.

Because the agreed-upon procedures listed in the attached schedule do not constitute an examination, we will not express an opinion on [*describe subject matter*]. In addition, we have no obligation to perform any procedures beyond those listed in the attached schedule.

We will submit a report listing the procedures performed and our findings. This report is intended solely for the use of [*specified parties*], and should not be used by those who did not agree upon the procedures and take responsibility for the sufficiency of the procedures for their purposes. Our report will contain a paragraph stating that had we performed additional procedures, other matters may have come to our attention that would have been reported to you.

We plan to begin our procedures on approximately [*date*] and, unless unforeseeable problems are encountered, the engagement should be completed by [*date*]. At the conclusion of our engagement, we will require a representation letter from management that, among other things, will confirm management's responsibility for the presentation of the [*describe subject matter*] in accordance with [*describe criteria*].

We estimate that our fees for these services will range from $_____ to $_____. You will also be billed for travel and other out-of-pocket costs such as report production, typing, postage, etc. Additional expenses are estimated to be $_____. The fee estimate is based on anticipated cooperation from your personnel and the assumption that unexpected circumstances will not be encountered during the engagement. If significant additional time is necessary, we will discuss it with you and arrive at a new fee estimate before we incur the additional costs. Our invoices for these services will be rendered each month as work progresses and are payable on presentation. In accordance with our firm policies, work may be suspended if your account becomes _____ days or more overdue and will not be resumed until your account is paid in full. If we elect to terminate our services for nonpayment, our engagement will be deemed to have been completed upon written notification of termination, even if we have not completed our report. You will be obligated to compensate us for all time extended and to reimburse us for all out-of-pocket expenditures through the date of termination.

We appreciate the opportunity to be of service to you and believe this letter accurately summarizes the significant terms of our engagement. If you have any questions, please let us know. If you agree with the terms of our engagement as described in this letter, please sign the enclosed copy and return it to us. If the need for additional services arises, our agreement with you will need to be revised. It is customary for us to enumerate these revisions in an addendum to this letter. If additional specified parties of the report are added, we will require that they acknowledge in writing their responsibility for the sufficiency of the procedures.

Very truly yours,

[*CPA firm's name*]

Response

This letter correctly sets forth the understanding of [*client and other specified parties*].

By:

Title:

Date:

APPENDIX 11N
ENGAGEMENT LETTER ADDENDUM: AGREED-UPON PROCEDURES RELATED TO INTERNAL CONTROL OVER COMPLIANCE

[*date*]

[*name of client (and other specified parties)*]
[*address*]

This letter constitutes an addendum to our original engagement letter dated [*date*]. The purpose of this letter is to outline additional procedures you wish us to perform in connection with that agreed-upon procedures engagement.

The additional procedures include:

[*List additional procedures.*]

All the terms of our original engagement letter will apply to this addendum. This addendum will become effective when you sign and date the original and copy of this letter and return the signed copy to us.

Very truly yours,

[*CPA firm's name*]

Response

This letter correctly sets forth the understanding of [*client and other specified parties*].

By:

Title:

Date:

APPENDIX 11O
REQUEST FOR SPECIFIED PARTY'S COMMENTS ON PROCEDURES: AGREED-UPON PROCEDURES RELATED TO INTERNAL CONTROL OVER COMPLIANCE

[*date*]

[*specified party's name*]
[*address*]

We have been requested by [*client's legal name*] to apply agreed-upon procedures listed in the attached engagement letter. The sufficiency of the requested procedures is solely the responsibility of the specified parties of the report. Consequently, we make no representation regarding the sufficiency of the procedures for the purpose for which this report has been requested or for any other purpose.

Because the agree-upon procedures listed in the attached engagement letter do not constitute an examination, we will not express an opinion on the [*describe subject matter*]. In addition, we have no obligation to perform any procedures that go beyond those listed in the attached engagement letter.

As a specified user of the report, please review the proposed procedures and acknowledge the sufficiency of the procedures by signing the enclosed copy of this letter and returning it to us. If the procedures are not considered to be sufficient or are not in accordance with your understanding, please provide comments in the space provided below.

Very truly yours,

[*CPA firm's name*]

Response

The procedures listed in the attached engagement letter are_____ (are not_____) sufficient for our purposes.

Comments:

By:

Title:

Date:

APPENDIX 11P
AGREED-UPON PROCEDURES CHECKLIST: INTERNAL CONTROL OVER COMPLIANCE

Client Name: ______________ Date of Subject Matter: ________________

Completed by: ______________ Date Completed: ____________________

	Completed by	N/A
1. Complete the Client Acceptance and Retention Evaluation Form.	________	________
2. If the engagement was originally intended to be another type of engagement (for example, examination or consulting engagement), document the considerations of:	________	________
a. Whether the procedures performed as part of another type of engagement are appropriate for an agreed-upon procedures engagement.	________	________
b. The reasons given for the client's request to change the engagement, particularly the implications of a restriction on the scope of the original engagement.	________	________
c. The additional effort required to complete the original engagement.	________	________
d. Where applicable, any reasons for changing from a general-use report to a restricted-use report.	________	________

	Completed by	N/A
3. Communicate directly with all specified parties and obtain their acknowledgement of the sufficiency of the procedures for their purposes. If direct communication is not possible, perform one of the following procedures:	_______	_______
a. Distribute a draft of the report or a copy of the engagement letter to the specified parties and obtain their agreement.	_______	_______
b. Compare the procedures to be applied to written requirements of the specified parties.	_______	_______
c. Discuss the procedures to be applied with appropriate representatives (such as legal counsel) of the specified parties.	_______	_______
d. Review relevant contracts with or correspondence from the specified parties.	_______	_______
4. Consider the procedures being requested and determine whether those procedures are appropriate for an agreed-upon procedures engagement.	_______	_______
5. Establish and document an understanding with the client, preferably in an engagement letter. If an engagement letter will not be obtained, the oral understanding should be documented in a memo.	_______	_______
6. Obtain an understanding of the client and the engagement.	_______	_______
7. If the client is not the responsible party, obtain evidence of the responsible party's responsibility for the subject matter.	_______	_______
8. Obtain an understanding of the specified compliance requirements.	_______	_______
9. Perform any additional services needed to assist the responsible party in developing the subject matter or related assertion.	_______	_______
10. Determine that the scheduling and staffing are adequate to perform the engagement.	_______	_______
11. Obtain the engagement partner's approval of the overall engagement plan.	_______	_______
12. If other services have been performed for the responsible party, review relevant workpapers and any related reports for indications of matters that contradict the assertion.	_______	_______
13. Include in the workpapers a list of all procedures agreed upon in the engagement letter or include a copy of the engagement letter.	_______	_______

		Completed by	N/A
14.	Perform the agreed-upon procedures and summarize the findings.	______	______
15.	Obtain a written assertion and a representation letter from the responsible party.	______	______
16.	Draft the agreed-upon procedures report.	______	______
17.	Consider other reporting issues:		
	a. Reporting all findings, unless a materiality threshold was agreed upon.	______	______
	b. A description of any materiality limits agreed upon.	______	______
	c. Reporting other matters (including subsequent events).	______	______
	d. Restrictions on performance of procedures.	______	______
	e. Refusal to provide a representation letter.	______	______
	f. Explanations of sampling risk.	______	______
	g. Disclosure of stipulated facts, assumptions, or interpretations used in the application of the procedures.	______	______
	h. Description of the condition of records, controls, or data to which the procedures were applied.	______	______
	i. Explanation that the practitioner has no responsibility to update his or her report.	______	______
	j. Description of the nature of any assistance provided by a specialist.	______	______
18.	If any additional specified parties are added, obtain their acknowledgement for the sufficiency of the procedures.	______	______
19.	Read for inconsistencies other information in a client-prepared document that contains the agreed-upon procedures report.	______	______
20.	If any situations have occurred that require consultation, determine that such consultation has been properly documented.	______	______
21.	If there were differences of professional opinion among members of the engagement team or between the engagement team and a specialist, determine that the differences were properly resolved and documented.	______	______
22.	Determine that all questions, exceptions, or notes, if any, posed during the engagement have been followed up and resolved.	______	______

	Completed by	N/A
23. Determine that all required forms, questionnaires, and checklists have been completed.	________	________
24. Ensure that the workpapers the agreed-upon procedures report have been reviewed in accordance with firm policy.	________	________
25. Obtain engagement partner's review and approval for issuance of the report.	________	________

APPENDIX 11Q
AGREED-UPON PROCEDURES ENGAGEMENT: PROCEDURES AND FINDINGS FORM

Client Name: ______________ Date of Subject Matter: ______________

Completed by: ______________ Date Completed: __________________

Instructions

This form can be used to record findings as each procedure is performed. Use a separate form for each procedure performed and document each procedure and finding as precisely as possible. Include all findings in the agreed-upon procedures report, unless materiality limits have been established and agreed upon by the specified parties.

Subject matter to which the procedure was applied:

Describe procedure:

Workpaper Reference	Finding

Discussed with responsible party:

Position: Date:

APPENDIX 11R
REPRESENTATION LETTER: AGREED-UPON PROCEDURES RELATED TO INTERNAL CONTROL OVER COMPLIANCE

[*date—No earlier than date of the accountant's report*]

[*CPA firm's name*]
[*address*]

In connection with your engagement to apply agreed-upon procedures to the [*describe subject matter*] as of [*date of subject matter*], we confirm, to the best of our knowledge and belief, the following representations made to you during your engagement:

- We are responsible for complying with [*describe specified requirements*].
- We are responsible for establishing and maintaining effective internal control over compliance.
- We have performed an evaluation of the Company's compliance with [*describe specified requirements*].
- [*Recite the responsible party's assertion.*]
- We have disclosed to you all known noncompliance with [*describe specified requirements*], including noncompliance occurring after [*date of subject matter*].
- We have made available to you all documentation and other information related to compliance with [*describe specified requirements*].
- Our interpretation of [*provision of specified requirements*] is as follows:
  — [*Recite responsible party's interpretation of provision of specified requirements.*]
- There have been no communications from regulatory agencies, internal auditors, or other independent accountants or consultants regarding possible noncompliance with [*describe specified requirements*], including communications received between [*date of subject matter*] and [*date of representation letter*].
- We have responded fully to all inquiries made to us by you during the engagement.
- Your report is intended solely for the information and use of [*specified parties*] and is not intended to be and should not be used by anyone other than those specified parties.

Signature:	Signature:
Title:	Title:

APPENDIX 11S CLIENT REPRESENTATION LETTER: AGREED-UPON PROCEDURES ENGAGEMENT, CLIENT NOT RESPONSIBLE PARTY

[*date—No earlier than date of the accountant's report*]

[*CPA firm's name*]
[*address*]

In connection with your engagement to apply agreed-upon procedures to [*describe subject matter*] as of [*date of subject matter*], we confirm, to the best of our knowledge and belief, the following representations made to you during the course of your engagement:

- We are responsible for complying with [*describe specified requirements*].
- We are responsible for establishing and maintaining effective internal control over compliance.
- We have performed an evaluation of the Company's compliance with [*describe specified requirements*].
- [*Recite the responsible party's assertion.*]
- We have disclosed to you all known noncompliance with [*describe specified requirements*], including noncompliance occurring after [*date of subject matter*].
- We have made available to you all documentation and other information related to compliance with [*describe specified requirements*].
- Our interpretation of [*provision of specified requirements*] is as follows:
  — [*Recite responsible party's interpretation of provision of specified requirements.*]
- There have been no communications from regulatory agencies, internal auditors, or other independent accountants or consultants regarding possible noncompliance with [*describe specified requirements*], including communications received between [*date of subject matter*] and [*date of representation letter*].
- We have responded fully to all inquiries made to us by you during the engagement.
- Your report is intended solely for the information and use of [*specified parties*] and is not intended to be and should not be used by anyone other than those specified parties.

Signature:

Title:

APPENDIX 11T STANDARD AGREED-UPON PROCEDURES REPORT ON INTERNAL CONTROL OVER COMPLIANCE WITH SPECIFIED REQUIREMENTS

Independent Accountant's Report

To the Board of Directors of
[*client name*]
[*city, state*]

We have performed the procedures enumerated below, which were agreed to by [*list of specified parties*], solely to assist the specified parties in evaluating the effectiveness of [*name of entity*]'s internal control over compliance with [*list specified requirements*] as of [*date*]. Management is responsible for [name of entity]'s internal control over compliance with those requirements. This agreed-upon procedures engagement was conducted in accordance with attestation standards established by the American Institute of Certified Public Accountants. The sufficiency of these procedures is solely the responsibility of those parties specified in this report. Consequently, we make no representation regarding the sufficiency of the procedures described below either for the purpose for which this report has been requested or for any other purpose.

[*Include paragraphs to enumerate procedures and findings.*]

We were not engaged to and did not conduct an examination, the objective of which would be the expression of an opinion on the effectiveness of [*name of entity*]'s internal control over compliance. Accordingly, we do not express such an opinion. Had we performed additional procedures, other matters might have come to our attention that would have been reported to you.

This report is intended solely for the information and use of [*list or refer to specified parties*] and is not intended to be and should not be used by anyone other than these specified parties.

[*firm's signature*]

[*city, state*]

[*date*]

APPENDIX 11U
OVERVIEW OF INTERNAL CONTROL

Introduction

There is always the risk in discussing internal controls that the discussion will turn into a piecemeal discussion of specific control-related policies and procedures. When this occurs, it is easy to become confused, because individual controls can appear isolated and unrelated to one another. However, internal controls are actually a coordinated set of policies and procedures that reflect a comprehensive strategy for achieving management objectives. When viewed from this perspective, it is much easier to understand how individual controls function and work together. This appendix provides just such a conceptual overview of internal controls—what they are and who is responsible for them. This overview serves, in turn, as the framework for the more detailed discussion to be found in the chapters that follow.

Management's Responsibilities and the Internal Control Framework

Any entity, be it a government, a business, or a not-for-profit organization, exists to achieve some purpose. It is the role of management to provide the leadership needed for an entity to realize that purpose. Furthermore, management is not free to simply act in any way it chooses to achieve the entity's goals. Rather, management's options and actions are circumscribed by constraints and expectations, both implicit and explicit. Therefore, any analysis of management's fundamental responsibilities needs to address all of the following:

- *Effectiveness* Ultimately, success must be judged on the basis of whether an entity is achieving its objectives. That is to say, effort is no substitute for results. Yet, it is very easy for management to focus so intensely on the handling of day-to-day activities that it loses sight of whether those activities are actually achieving their intended purpose.
- *Efficiency* The modern study of economics is based upon the axiom of the scarcity of resources. Given that there are legitimate and conflicting demands for scarce resources, management has a responsibility to make optimal use of the scarce resources placed under its control. It should also be noted in this regard that there is a clear link between efficiency and effectiveness. "Effectiveness" and "efficiency" are known collectively as "operations" objectives. It is possible for an activity to meet its objectives but be too expensive (i.e., an activity can be effective but inefficient). On the other hand, it is not possible for an activity to be both economical and ineffective (i.e., an activity, no matter how inexpensive, cannot be economical if it does not accomplish what it is supposed to accomplish). Therefore, any intent to assess efficiency must also take into account effectiveness. An ineffective program is no bargain at any price.
- *Compliance* Management does not have unlimited authority over the resources under its control. Rather, management's control over resources is typically limited to some degree by policy, law, or regulation. It is a condition of management's stewardship of resources that it strictly comply with such restrictions.
- *Financial reporting* Managers are also financial decision makers. The best decision, however, is only as good as the data upon which it is based. Thus, it is critical that managers have in place a system of accounting and financial reporting that provides the types of information managers need to make financial decisions when they need it. Likewise, managers must also be accountable to individuals and groups outside the entity for their management of the entity's resources. Managers meet this responsibility by preparing financial statements for the benefit of those without direct access to the entity's accounting system.

If effectiveness, efficiency, compliance, and financial reporting are all responsibilities of management, then internal controls should be seen as the framework that management establishes to ensure that it meets those responsibilities. The comprehensiveness of an entity's internal control framework can be assessed on the basis of whether it does all of the following:

- *Provides a favorable control environment* Modern sociology has demonstrated that interactions among individuals are profoundly affected by the social structure that those interactions take place in, as well as by a variety of spoken and unspoken expectations. This complex mix of factors is sometimes referred to as a business's "corporate culture." Thus, controls do not function in a vacuum. Instead, internal controls are necessarily and profoundly influenced by the environment in which they operate. Consequently, the first and most important step in establishing an effective framework of internal controls is for senior management to create a favorable control environment. A favorable control environment is one in which management is (1) knowledgeable about internal controls, (2) is committed to establishing and maintaining controls, and (3) communicates its support for internal controls to staff at all levels. Attempting to make internal controls function effectively in a hostile or indifferent environment is likely to be a frustrating and futile endeavor.

- *Continually assesses risk* A variety of risks can hamper or prevent management from fulfilling its responsibilities and achieving its goals. Some of these risks can arise from within the entity itself (e.g., a change and personnel), and others can originate outside the entity (e.g., a change in the marketplace). When management is able to anticipate such risks, it is better prepared to manage them. Accordingly, a sound internal control framework must provide for the ongoing identification and assessment of potential risks.
- *Establishes and maintains effective control-related policies and procedures* Once management has identified and assessed potential risks, it needs to take action to compensate for them. In practice, a variety of specific policies and procedures have been developed as tools for achieving this goal (e.g., prior authorization and approval of transactions, properly designed records, appropriate security over assets and records, segregation of incompatible duties, periodic reconciliations, periodic verifications, analytical review and the timely preparation of financial statements). In some cases, the policies and procedures are themselves adequate to prevent undesired actions and events. (e.g., appropriate physical security over assets prevents some thefts). In other cases, the goal of such policies and procedures is to alert management to undesired actions and events in time for them to take effective corrective action (e.g., a periodic bank reconciliation could alert management to a kiting scheme).
- *Effectively communicates information* Information must be reliable if it is to be of use to decision makers. The selection, format, timeliness, and accessibility of information are also crucial factors. Accordingly, a sound framework of internal controls ensures that the right information is provided to the right individuals at the right time and in the right format. Furthermore, there must be adequate means of ongoing communication both within and between various levels and activities of the entity, as well as with those outside the entity (e.g., customers, suppliers).
- *Monitors the effectiveness of control policies and procedures as well as the resolution of potential problems identified by controls* Once appropriate controls are in place, care must be taken to ensure that they continue to function properly. Most often, this monitoring takes place on an ongoing basis. Sometimes special reviews are undertaken of all or a portion of an entity's control-related policies and procedures. Not only must the effectiveness of internal controls themselves be monitored, but management must also monitor the effectiveness of its own response to potential problems identified by the controls (e.g., does management follow up on discrepancies disclosed by periodic reconciliations?).

In brief, internal controls are the varied means used by management to achieve management objectives and to meet management responsibilities. Unfortunately, those unfamiliar with internal controls are sometimes unaware of the necessary and integral connection between internal controls and management. As a result, such individuals might mistakenly come to view internal controls as little more than accounting bells and whistles, and might even come to see internal controls as hindering management rather than helping it to achieve its goals. Alternatively, such individuals might appreciate the importance of internal controls but believe erroneously that internal controls are principally the concern of accountants and auditors rather than of management. In fact, internal controls are essentially management techniques that are an integral and inextricable part of how management conducts business.

Limitations of Internal Controls

Any technique, of its very nature, is a means to an end rather than an end in itself. Consequently, internal controls must be modified at the point where they start to hinder rather than to help (i.e., the costs of internal controls never should exceed the benefits they provide). Accordingly, one limitation of internal control is that considerations of cost prevent management from ever installing a perfect system. Instead, management properly chooses to run certain risks because the cost of mitigating them cannot be justified, just as an automobile owner does not insure against all possible losses but instead arranges for a deductible in the insurance contract.

A second important limitation of internal controls is that they are potentially subject to management override. That is to say, if management has the power to establish a given control policy or procedure, it probably also has the ability to override it. For example, management might generally require adequate documentation and review of travel claims, but it could wrongfully direct that its own travel claims be processed without such documentation or review.

A third limitation of internal controls is the risk of collusion. Often, internal controls are designed so that one employee functions as a check on another employee's work (e.g., segregation of duties). However, there is always the risk that employees who are supposed to serve as checks on one another might instead work together to circumvent controls.

It should be noted that as a basic rule more is not better in the case of internal controls. Even if does the cost of excessive or redundant controls does not exceed the benefits, the perception of excessiveness or redundancy can have a serious negative effect on how employees view controls in general (e.g., as red tape), thus adversely affecting the overall control environment.

Responsibility for Internal Controls

Internal controls are essentially management techniques, an inextricable part of how management conducts its business. Accordingly, management (not the internal or external auditors) is primarily responsible for the effectiveness of internal controls, just as management is accountable for all other aspects of its performance. Furthermore, it is a basic principle of good management that authority and responsibility should not be separated. Because management alone is in a position to both establish and maintain internal controls, it is management that must be held primarily accountable for their proper functioning.

Management's performance is subject to oversight by the entity's governing board. Therefore, although management is primarily responsible for internal controls, the governing board is ultimately responsible for ensuring that management fulfills this duty. The governing board's role in this regard is particularly important because of management's ability to override controls.

Audit professionals, both the independent auditors of the entity's financial statements and the members of the entity's internal audit staff, can play a valuable role in helping management and the board to fulfill their respective responsibilities for internal controls. Nevertheless, auditors cannot themselves assume primary or ultimate responsibility for internal controls.

Management's responsibilities for internal controls can be categorized as follows:

- *Design* Management should use the framework of internal controls to design control-related policies and procedures tailored to the entity's individual circumstances.
- *Implementation* Management should ensure that control-related policies and procedures are actually installed as designed.
- *Monitoring* Management should ensure that after installation controls function as designed and that they are modified or enhanced as needed to conform to changes in the entity's operating environment.
- *Reporting* Management should keep the board informed of how internal controls are functioning.

In many cases, management makes use of the services of internal auditors to monitor the continued effectiveness of control-related policies and procedures on an ongoing basis. Management, itself might also directly evaluate the effectiveness of internal controls from time to time.

Typically, entities engage the services of an independent audit firm to render an opinion on the fair presentation of the entity's financial statements. Independent auditors must gain an understanding of the entity's internal control framework as part of the process of assessing audit risk. Accordingly, management sometimes reaches the (understandable) conclusion that the audit of the financial statements is sufficient to ensure that internal controls are adequately designed and functioning properly. In fact, however, the purpose and scope of the independent auditor's assessment of internal controls are limited.

The objective of the independent audit is to provide assurance to potential users of financial statements that they can reasonably rely upon the statements to be free of material misstatement. Accordingly, a properly conducted financial statement audit should uncover internal control weaknesses that could have a major impact on financial reporting (referred to by auditors as "material weaknesses"). However, most internal control weaknesses, although important to management, are not of such magnitude as to potentially affect a user's overall assessment of an entity's finances. Consequently, there is no assurance that all immaterial weaknesses will be uncovered. An independent auditor's assessment of internal controls should not be viewed as a substitute for management's own ongoing monitoring of the effectiveness of control-related policies and procedures.

APPENDIX 11V
INTERNAL CONTROL EVALUATION WORKSHEET

Client Name: ______________ Date of Subject Matter: ______________

Completed by: ______________ Date Completed: ______________

Instructions

This worksheet is designed to assist the practitioner in evaluating internal control. Listed below are issues the practitioner might consider in evaluating an entity's internal control. This list is not all-inclusive, nor will every item apply to every entity. However, these issues can serve as a starting point. This list has been adapted from COSO's "Internal Control—Integrated Framework" and is organized according to the COSO internal control components. This form should be prepared by the engagement personnel in charge of fieldwork (senior or supervisory staff) and reviewed and approved by the engagement executive for all attestation engagements.

Internal Control Component/Issue	Comment
Evaluation of the Control Environment	
The practitioner should consider each control environment factor in determining whether a positive control environment exists. Although some of the items are highly subjective and require considerable judgment, generally they are relevant to control environment effectiveness.	________
Integrity and Ethical Values	
Existence of and implementation of codes of conduct and other policies regarding acceptable business practice, conflicts of interest, and expected standards of ethical and moral behavior.	________
Dealings with employees, suppliers, customers, investors, creditors, insurers, competitors, and auditors, etc. (e.g., whether management conducts business on a high ethical plane, and insists that others do so, or pays little attention to ethical issues).	________

Internal Control Component/Issue	Comment
Pressure to meet unrealistic performance targets—particularly for short-term results—and extent to which compensation is based on achieving those performance targets.	________
Commitment to Competence	
Formal or informal job descriptions or other means of defining tasks that comprise particular jobs.	________
Analyses of the knowledge and skills needed to perform jobs adequately.	________
Board of Directors or Audit Committee	
Independence from management such that necessary, even difficult and probing, questions are raised.	________
Frequency and timeliness of meetings held with chief financial officer and/or accounting officers, internal auditors, and external auditors.	________
Sufficiency and timeliness of information provided to board or committee members to allow monitoring of management's objectives and strategies, the entity's financial position and operating results, and terms of significant agreements.	________
Sufficiency and timeliness with which the board or audit committee is apprised of sensitive information, investigations, and improper acts (e.g., travel expenses of senior officers, significant litigation, investigations by regulatory agencies, defalcations, embezzlement or misuse of corporate assets, violations of insider trading rules, political payments, illegal payments).	________
Management's Philosophy and Operating Style	
Nature of business risks accepted (e.g., whether management often enters into particularly high-risk ventures or is extremely conservative in accepting risks).	________
Frequency of interaction between senior management and operating management, particularly when operating from geographically removed locations.	________
Attitudes and actions toward financial reporting, including disputes over application of accounting treatments (e.g., selection of conservative versus liberal accounting policies; whether accounting principles have been misapplied, important financial information not disclosed, or records manipulated or falsified).	________

Internal Control Component/Issue	Comment
Organizational Structure	
Appropriateness of the entity's organizational structure and its ability to provide the necessary information flow to manage its activities.	________
Adequacy of definition of key managers' responsibilities and their understanding of these responsibilities.	________
Adequacy of knowledge and experience of key managers in light of responsibilities.	________
Assignment of Authority and Responsibility	
Assignment of responsibility and delegation of authority to deal with organizational goals and objectives, operating functions, and regulatory requirements, including responsibility for information systems and authorizations for changes.	________
Appropriateness of control-related standards and procedures, including employee job descriptions.	________
Appropriate numbers of people, particularly with respect to data processing and accounting functions, with the requisite skill levels relative to the size of the entity and the nature and complexity of activities and systems.	________
Human Resource Policies and Practices	
Extent to which policies and procedures for hiring, promoting, and compensating employees are in place.	________
Appropriateness of remedial action taken in response to departures from approved policies and procedures.	________
Adequacy of background checks for employee candidates, particularly with regard to prior actions or activities considered to be unacceptable by the entity.	________
Adequacy of employee retention and promotion criteria and information-gathering techniques (e.g., performance evaluations) and relation to the code of conduct or other behavioral guidelines.	________
Evaluation of Risk Analysis	
An evaluator will focus on management's process for setting objectives, risk analysis, and managing change, including its linkages and relevance to business activities.	________
Entity-Wide Objectives	
The extent to which the entity-wide objectives provide sufficiently broad statements and guidance on what	

Internal Control Component/Issue	Comment
the entity desires to achieve yet are specific enough to relate directly to the entity.	________
Effectiveness with which the entity-wide objectives are communicated to employees and board of directors.	________
Consistency of strategies and their relation to entity-wide objectives.	________
Consistency of business plans and budgets with entity-wide objectives, strategic plans, and current conditions.	________
Activity-Level Objectives	
The linkage between activity-level objectives and entity-wide objectives and strategic plans.	________
Consistency of activity-level objectives with each other.	________
Relevance of activity-level objectives to all significant business processes.	________
Specificity of activity-level objectives.	________
Adequacy of resources relative to objectives.	________
Identification of objectives that are important (critical success factors) to achievement of entity-wide objectives.	________
Involvement of all levels of management in setting objectives and extent to which all levels of management are committed to the objectives.	________
Risks	
Adequacy of mechanisms to identify risks arising from external sources.	________
Adequacy of mechanisms to identify risks arising from internal sources.	________
Identification of significant risks for each significant activity-level objective.	________
Thoroughness and relevance of the risk analysis process, including estimating the significance of risks, assessing the likelihood of their occurring, and determining needed actions.	________
Managing change	
Existence of mechanisms to anticipate, identify, and react to routine events or activities that affect achievement of activity-level or entity objectives (usually implemented by managers responsible for	

Internal Control Component/Issue	Comment
the activities that would be most affected by the changes).	________
Existence of mechanisms to identify and react to changes that can have a dramatic and pervasive effect on the entity and that demand the attention of top management.	________
Evaluation of Information and Communication	
An evaluator will consider the appropriateness of information and communication systems to the entity's needs.	________
Information	
Obtaining external and internal information and providing management with necessary reports on the entity's performance relative to established objectives. Providing information to the right people in sufficient detail and on time to enable them to carry out their responsibilities efficiently and effectively.	________
Development or revision of information systems based on a strategic plan for information systems that is linked to the entity's overall strategy and is responsive to achieving entity-wide and activity-level objectives.	________
Management's support for the development of necessary information systems is demonstrated by the commitment of appropriate resources, both human and financial.	________
Communication	
Effectiveness with which employees' duties and control responsibilities are communicated.	________
Establishment of channels of communication for people to report suspected improprieties.	________
Receptivity of management to employee suggestions of ways to enhance productivity, quality, or other improvements.	________
Adequacy of communication across the organization (for example, between procurement and production activities) and the completeness and timeliness of information and its sufficiency to enable people to discharge their responsibilities effectively.	________
Openness and effectiveness of channels with customers, suppliers, and other external parties for communicating information on changing customer needs.	________

Internal Control Component/Issue	Comment
Extent to which outside parties have been made aware of the entity's ethical standards.	________
Timely and appropriate follow-up action by management resulting from communications received from customers, vendors, regulators, or other external parties.	________
Evaluation of Monitoring	
In considering the extent to which the continued effectiveness of internal control is monitored, both ongoing monitoring activities and separate evaluations of the internal control system (or portions of it) should be considered.	________
Ongoing Monitoring	
Extent to which personnel, in carrying out their regular activities, obtain evidence about whether the system of internal control continues to function.	________
Extent to which communications from external parties corroborate internally generated information or indicate problems.	________
Periodic comparison of amounts recorded by the accounting system with physical assets.	________
Responsiveness to internal and external auditor recommendations on means to strengthen internal controls.	________
Extent to which training seminars, planning sessions, and other meetings provide feedback to management on whether controls operate effectively.	________
Whether personnel are asked periodically to state whether they understand and comply with the entity's code of conduct and regularly perform critical control functions.	________
Effectiveness of internal audit activities.	________
Separate Evaluations	
Scope and frequency of separate evaluations of the internal control system.	________
Appropriateness of the evaluation process.	________
Whether the methodology for evaluating a system is logical and appropriate.	________
Appropriateness of the level of documentation.	________

Internal Control Component/Issue	Comment
Reporting Deficiencies	
Existence of mechanism for capturing and reporting identified internal control deficiencies.	________
Appropriateness of reporting protocols.	________
Appropriateness of follow-up actions.	________

APPENDIX 11W
PCAOB STAFF Q&AS RELATED TO AUDITS OF FINANCIAL STATEMENTS OF NON-ISSUERS PERFORMED PURSUANT TO THE STANDARDS OF THE PCAOB

The Public Company Accounting Oversight Board (PCAOB) Staff Questions and Answers publications set forth the staff's opinions on issues related to the implementation of the standards of the PCAOB. The staff publishes questions and answers to help auditors implement, and the PCAOB staff administer, the PCAOB's standards. The statements contained in the staff questions and answers are not rules of the PCAOB, nor have they been approved by the PCAOB.

The Sarbanes-Oxley Act of 2002 (SOX) directs the PCAOB to establish auditing and related attestation, quality control, ethics, and independence standards to be used by registered public accounting firms in the preparation and issuance of audit reports of issuers. SOX and PCAOB rules require audits of issuers to be conducted in accordance with PCAOB standards. When issuing an audit report on the financial statements of an issuer, PCAOB Auditing Standard No. 1 (AS-1) requires registered public accounting firms to include a reference to "the standards of the Public Company Accounting Oversight Board (United States)." In contexts other than an audit of the financial statements of an issuer, however, auditors, whether registered or not, may be legally required, or may agree voluntarily, to perform an engagement in accordance with PCAOB standards or some portion of those standards. Auditors and other interested persons have raised questions about the implications of AS-1, as well as SOX and other PCAOB rules, for such engagements. The following staff questions and answers seek to answer some of those questions:

Q1. Must a public accounting firm be registered with the PCAOB to perform an audit of a non-issuer according to PCAOB standards?

A1. No. The Sarbanes-Oxley Act requires only that those public accounting firms that prepare or issue, or participate in the preparation or issuance of, audit reports on the financial statements of issuers be registered.

Q2. The PCAOB's Auditing Standard No. 1 requires the auditor to include a reference to "the standards of the Public Company Accounting Oversight Board (United States)" in audit reports on the financial statements of issuers. May an auditor refer to "the auditing standards of the Public Company Accounting Oversight Board (United States)" rather than to "the standards of the Public Company Accounting Oversight Board (United States)" in an audit report on an audit of the financial statements of a non-issuer that was performed in accordance with the Board's auditing standards?

A2. Yes. In an audit of the financial statements of a non-issuer, an auditor may wish to be clear that he or she adhered to only the auditing standards of the PCAOB; accordingly, the auditor may include the word "auditing" in the reference to the standards of the PCAOB. Registered public accounting firms, however, are not permitted to limit their reference to the "auditing standards" of the PCAOB in their audit reports on the financial statements of issuers.

Q3. What standards are included in a reference to "the standards of the Public Company Accounting Oversight Board (United States)"?

A3. A reference to "the standards of the Public Company Accounting Oversight Board (United States)" includes the standards of the Board that are applicable in the circumstances of the engagement. For example, in an audit of financial statements that does not involve the use of a specialist, the auditor would not be expected to follow the Board's interim auditing standard, Statement of Auditing Standards No. 73, "Using the Work of a Specialist." Similarly, in an audit of an entity that has immaterial inventory balances, the auditor would not be expected to follow the Board's interim auditing standard, AU Section 331, "Inventories" of Statement on Auditing Standards No. 1, "Codification of Auditing Standards and Procedures." On the other hand, the Board's interim auditing standard, Statement on Auditing Standards No. 99, "Consideration of Fraud in a Financial Statement Audit," would be applicable in all audits of financial statements conducted pursuant to the Board's standards. As another example, quality control standards generally apply to a firm's system of quality control over its accounting and auditing practice and not to individual audit engagements. Thus, a breakdown in the system of quality control does not necessarily mean that a particular audit was not conducted in accordance with the standards of the PCAOB. However, such a breakdown might result in a deficient audit if it caused or contributed to an audit deficiency. In addition, an auditor who states that he or she has performed the audit in accordance with the standards of the PCAOB must be in compliance with the applicable interim independence standards of the Board. These are examples only, and not an exhaustive list of standards that may be applicable to an engagement. While not required by PCAOB rules, auditors of issuers and other entities subject to the SEC's jurisdiction are reminded that they must also comply with applicable Commission requirements, including the Commission's auditor independence requirements.

Q4. By referring to "the auditing standards of the Public Company Accounting Oversight Board (United States)" in an audit report on the financial statements of a non-issuer, does the auditor represent that he or she has adhered to the Board's interim independence standards?

A4. No. Auditors of the financial statements of non-issuers, including nonprofit organizations, government agencies, municipalities and other governments, should look to relevant state and federal laws and regulations relating to auditor independence. Auditors of nonpublic companies should bear in mind, however, that any company that becomes an issuer, as defined in Section 2(a)(7) of [SOX], must file with the SEC an audit report prepared and issued by an independent registered public accounting firm, and therefore it may behoove an auditor of a nonpublic company that intends to become an issuer to comply with SEC and PCAOB independence requirements.

Q5. By referring to "the auditing standards of the Public Company Accounting Oversight Board (United States)" or to "the standards of the Public Company Accounting Oversight Board (United States)" in an audit report on the financial statements of a non-issuer, does the auditor represent that he or she has complied with the Commission's auditor independence requirements?

A5. No. A Note to the PCAOB's rule on interim independence standards, PCAOB Rule 3600T, reminds auditors of issuers and other entities subject to the SEC's jurisdiction of their separate obligations under the SEC's rule on auditor independence. The PCAOB's rule on interim independence standards does not, however, incorporate the SEC's auditor independence requirements.

Q6. What are the PCAOB's independence requirements and to whom do they apply?

A6. The PCAOB adopted interim independence standards when it adopted PCAOB Rule 3600T, which is a temporary rule in effect until the Board adopts permanent independence standards. Rule 3600T requires that, when a registered public accounting firm conducts an audit of the financial statements of an issuer, the firm comply with Rule 101 of the AICPA's Code of Professional Conduct, and interpretations and rulings thereunder, as in existence on April 16, 2003; and Standards Nos. 1, 2 and 3, and Interpretations 99-1, 00-1, and 00-2, of the Independence Standards Board.

Registered public accounting firms must also comply with SEC requirements, including its Rule 2-01 of Regulation S-X, relating to auditor independence, when they conduct audits required by the federal securities laws, including audits of financial statements of issuers. The Board did not adopt the SEC's Rule 2-01 because that rule already governs auditor independence from issuers. As a Note to Rule 3600T makes clear, however, in an audit of the financial statements of an issuer, to the extent that a provision of the SEC's rule is more restrictive—or less restrictive—than the Board's interim independence standards, a registered public accounting firm must comply with the more restrictive rule.

Q7. Does a reference to "the auditing standards of the Public Company Accounting Oversight Board (United States)" or to "the standards of the Public Company Accounting Oversight Board (United States)" in an auditor's report on the financial statements of a non-issuer imply that the non-issuer is subject to, or otherwise complied with, some or all of the provisions of [SOX] and other securities laws or the Commission's rules and regulations thereunder?

A7. No. An auditor's reference to PCAOB standards in an audit report on the financial statements of a non-issuer does not subject the auditor or the non-issuer to any laws that the auditor or the non-issuer would not otherwise have been required to comply with. Unless the non-issuer is involved in an activity that subjects it to [SOX] or other securities laws, such as the laws governing broker-dealers, compliance by the auditor or the non-issuer with [SOX] or other securities laws would be strictly voluntary.

Q8. Does inclusion of a reference to the Board's standards in an auditor's report on the financial statements of a non-issuer cause the audit to become eligible for review as a part of a Board inspection?

A8. No. An audit of the financial statements of a non-issuer does not become subject to PCAOB inspection solely because the auditor performed and reported on the audit in accordance with the standards of the PCAOB. Auditors of the financial statements of non-issuers may, nevertheless, be subject to various forms of state and federal oversight, such as review by federal banking regulators, the U.S. General Accounting Office, or a state board of accountancy.

Q9. If a non-issuer elects to have its financial statements audited pursuant to the Board's standards, must it also have its internal control over financial reporting audited pursuant to the Board's Auditing Standard No. 2, "An Audit of Internal Control Over Financial Reporting Conducted in Conjunction with an Audit of Financial Statement"?

A9. No. Only certain issuers that are subject to Section 404 of [SOX] are required to include within the scope of the audit an audit of internal control over financial reporting. Although the Board's standards provide for an integrated audit of financial statements and internal control for those issuers that are subject to Section 404 of [SOX], the Board's standards also permit auditors to conduct a financial statement-only audit under circumstances, for example, when Section 404 of [SOX] is not applicable.

Q10. If an auditor refers to either "the standards of the Public Company Accounting Oversight Board (United States)" or "the auditing standards of the Public Company Accounting Oversight Board (United States)" in an audit report on an audit of the financial statements of a non-issuer, is the auditor also required to subject the audit to a "concurring partner review" as required by the Board's adoption of certain of the requirements of the AICPA's former Securities and Exchange Commission Practice Section (SECPS)?

A10. No. The Board may at some time adopt a standard requiring the performance of a second partner review. At this time, however, the PCAOB interim quality control standards only require registered firms that were members of the SECPS as of April 16, 2003, to have a concurring partner review on audits of issuers. (See PCAOB Release No. 2003-006.)

APPENDIX 11X ILLUSTRATIVE REPORT EXPRESSING AN UNQUALIFIED OPINION ON MANAGEMENT'S ASSESSMENT OF THE EFFECTIVENESS OF INTERNAL CONTROL OVER FINANCIAL REPORTING AND AN UNQUALIFIED OPINION ON THE EFFECTIVENESS OF INTERNAL CONTROL OVER FINANCIAL REPORTING

Report of Independent Registered Public Accounting Firm

To the Board of Directors
W Company
[*city, state*]

[*Introductory paragraph*]
We have audited management's assessment, included in the accompanying [*title of management's report*], that W Company maintained effective internal control over financial reporting as of December 31, 20X3, based on [*identify control criteria, for example,* criteria established in *Internal Control—Integrated Framework,* issued by the Committee of Sponsoring Organizations of the Treadway Commission (COSO)]. W Company's management is responsible for maintaining effective internal control over financial reporting and for its assessment of the effectiveness of internal control over financial reporting.

Our responsibility is to express an opinion on management's assessment and an opinion on the effectiveness of the company's internal control over financial reporting, based on our audit.

[*Scope paragraph*]
We conducted our audit in accordance with the standards of the Public Company Accounting Oversight Board (United States). Those standards require that we plan and perform the audit to obtain reasonable assurance about whether effective internal control over financial reporting was maintained in all material respects. Our audit included obtaining an understanding of internal control over financial reporting, evaluating management's assessment, testing and evaluating the design and operating effectiveness of internal control, and performing such other procedures as we considered necessary in the circumstances. We believe that our audit provides a reasonable basis for our opinion.

[*Definition paragraph*]
A company's internal control over financial reporting is a process designed to provide reasonable assurance regarding the reliability of financial reporting and the preparation of financial statements for external purposes in accordance with generally accepted accounting principles. A company's internal control over financial reporting includes those policies and procedures that (1) pertain to the maintenance of records that, in reasonable detail, accurately and fairly reflect the transactions and dispositions of the assets of the company; (2) provide reasonable assurance that transactions are recorded as necessary to permit preparation of financial statements in accordance with generally accepted accounting principles, and that receipts and expenditures of the company are being made only in accordance with authorizations of management and directors of the company; and (3) provide reasonable assurance regarding prevention or timely detection of unauthorized acquisition, use, or disposition of the company's assets that could have a material effect on the financial statements.

[*Inherent limitations paragraph*]
Because of its inherent limitations, internal control over financial reporting may not prevent or detect misstatements. Also, projections of any evaluation of effectiveness to future periods are subject to the risk that controls may become inadequate because of changes in conditions or that the degree of compliance with the policies or procedures may deteriorate.

[*Opinion paragraph*]
In our opinion, management's assessment that W Company maintained effective internal control over financial reporting as of December 31, 20X3, is fairly stated, in all material respects, based on [*identify control criteria, for example,* criteria established in *Internal Control—Integrated Framework,* issued by the Committee of Sponsoring Organizations of the Treadway Commission (COSO).]. Also, in our opinion W Company maintained, in all material respects, effective internal control over financial reporting as of December 31, 20X3, based on [*identify control criteria, for example,* criteria established in *Internal Control—Integrated Framework,* issued by the Committee of Sponsoring Organizations of the Treadway Commission (COSO)].

[*Explanatory paragraph*]
We have also audited, in accordance with the standards of the Public Company Accounting Oversight Board (United States), the [*identify financial statements*] of W Company and our report, dated [*date of report, which should be the same as the date of the report on the effectiveness of internal control over financial reporting*], expressed [*include nature of opinion*].

[*signature*]

[*city and state or country*]

[*date*]

CHAPTER 12
DUE DILIGENCE ENGAGEMENTS

CONTENTS

OVERVIEW

This chapter discusses the various ways in which practitioners may be involved with the acquisition of one company by another. The guidance in this chapter is directed at the role that accountants can play in situations in which a client is considering an acquisition or merger. These engagements are generally of a fact-finding nature and can involve a study of financial information and accounting practices, analysis of financial statements, review of working papers of other accountants, inspection of tax returns, and discussions with target or buyer management and their independent accountants. The practitioner may be involved with pro forma financial information or prospective financial information. This chapter focuses primarily on engagements related to pro forma financial information. Engagements related to prospective financial information are discussed in Chapter 13, "Prospective Financial Information."

INTRODUCTION

Practitioners may be involved in various ways in the acquisition of one company by another. Due diligence engagements refer to assistance provided to a buyer in connection with a potential acquisition or merger. The nature and extent of the services are generally tailored to the needs of the client. Depending on how the due diligence engagement is structured, it can contain aspects of a consulting engagement, an agreed-upon procedures engagement, or an examination or review engagement. Thus, the applicable professional standards for a due diligence engagement ordinarily include the Statement on Standards for Consulting Services (SSCS) as well as any of the following standards:

- Chapter 2 (AT 201) (Agreed-Upon Procedures Engagements) of SSAE-10
- Chapter 3 (AT 301) (Financial Forecasts and Projections) of SSAE-10
- Chapter 4 (AT 401) (Reporting on Pro Forma Financial Information) of SSAE-10
- SSARS-14 (AR 120) (Compilation of Pro Forma Financial Information)

The primary focus of this chapter is on engagements related to pro forma financial information. Agreed-upon procedures engagements are discussed in Chapter 9, "Agreed-Upon Procedures Engagements," and financial forecasts and projections are discussed in Chapter 13, "Prospective Financial Information."

PRO FORMA FINANCIAL INFORMATION

The objective of pro forma financial information is to show what the significant effects on historical information might have been had a consummated or proposed transaction (or event) occurred at an earlier date. Pro forma financial information is commonly used to show the effects of transactions such as

- Business combinations.
- Change in capitalization.

- Disposition of a significant portion of the business.
- A change in the form of business organization or status as an autonomous entity.
- A proposed sale of securities and application of the proceeds.

This objective is achieved primarily by applying pro forma adjustments to historical financial information. Pro forma adjustments are based on management's assumptions and should give effect to all significant effects directly attributable to the transaction or event.

A practitioner might be associated with pro forma financial information in several ways. Usually, the practitioner is engaged to examine or review pro forma financial information. However, the practitioner may be engaged to perform services that are less than an examination or review. For example, the practitioner may be engaged to compile the pro forma financial information or assist the client in assembling the pro forma financial information. Chapter 4 of SSAE-10 (AT 401) provides guidance for engagements to examine or review pro forma financial information. SSARS-14 (AR 120) (Compilation of Pro Forma Financial Information) provides guidance for engagements to compile pro forma financial information.

EXAMINATION AND REVIEW ENGAGEMENTS

According to Chapter 4 of SSAE-10 (AT 401.07), the practitioner may report on an examination or review of pro forma financial information only if the following conditions are met:

- The document that contains the pro forma financial information includes (or incorporates by reference) complete historical financial statements of the entity for the most recent year (or for the preceding year if the financial statements for the most recent year are not yet available) and, if pro forma financial information is presented for an interim period, the document also includes (or incorporates by reference) historical interim financial information for that period (which may be presented in condensed form).
- The historical financial statements of the entity (or, in the case of a business combination, of each significant constituent part of the combined entity) on which the pro forma financial information is based have been audited or reviewed. Chapter 4 of SSAE-10 (AT 401.07) states that a review performed under SAS-100 (AU 722), (Interim Financial Information), for public companies, or SSARS-1 (AR 100) (Compilation and Review of Financial Statements), for nonpublic companies, is acceptable. The practitioner's attestation risk relating to the pro

forma financial information is affected by the scope of the engagement that provides the practitioner with assurance about the underlying historical financial statements. Therefore, the level of assurance given on the pro forma financial information should be limited to the level of assurance provided on the historical financial statements. For example, if the underlying historical financial statements have been audited at year-end and reviewed at an interim date, the practitioner may perform an examination or review of the pro forma financial information at year-end but is limited to a review of the pro forma financial information at the interim date.

- A practitioner who is reporting on pro forma financial information should have an appropriate level of knowledge of the accounting and financial reporting practices of the entity. This knowledge is ordinarily obtained by the practitioner's auditing or reviewing the historical financial statements of the entity. If another practitioner performed the audit or review of the historical financial statements, the need for an understanding of the entity's accounting and financial reporting practices is not diminished. In this case, the practitioner should determine whether he or she can acquire sufficient knowledge of these matters to perform the procedures necessary to report on the pro forma financial information.

Engagement Performance

The practitioner's objective in an examination of pro forma financial information is to provide reasonable assurance as to whether

- Management's assumptions provide a reasonable basis for presenting the significant effects directly attributable to the underlying transaction (or event).
- The related pro forma adjustments give appropriate effect to those assumptions.
- The pro forma column reflects the proper application of those adjustments to the historical financial statements.

The objective of the practitioner's review of pro forma financial information is to provide negative assurance as to whether any information came to the practitioner's attention to cause him or her to believe that

- Management's assumptions do not provide a reasonable basis for presenting the significant effects directly attributable to the underlying transaction (or event).

- The related pro forma adjustments do not give appropriate effect to those assumptions.
- The pro forma column does not reflect the proper application of those adjustments to the historical financial statements.

Chapter 4 of SSAE-10 (AT 401.01) states that engagements to examine or review pro forma financial information should comply with the general and fieldwork standards set forth in Chapter 1 of SSAE-10 (AT 101). These standards require that

- The engagement be performed by a practitioner having adequate technical training and proficiency in the attest function.
- The engagement be performed by a practitioner having adequate knowledge of the subject matter.
- The practitioner perform the engagement only if he or she has reason to believe that the subject matter is capable of evaluation against criteria that are suitable and available to users.
- In all matters relating to the engagement, an independence in mental attitude be maintained by the practitioner.
- Due professional care be exercised in the planning and performance of the engagement.
- The work be adequately planned and assistants, if any, shall be properly supervised.
- Sufficient evidence be obtained to provide a reasonable basis for the conclusion that is expressed in the report.

In addition, Chapter 4 of SSAE-10 (AT 401.10) sets forth specific procedures to be performed for either an examination or a review of pro forma financial information. These procedures include the following (in addition to these procedures, the historical financial statements on which the pro forma financial information is based must be audited or reviewed):

- Establish the terms of the engagement with the client. Illustrative engagement letters are included in Appendix 12A and Appendix 12B.
- Obtain an understanding of the underlying transaction (or event), for example, by reading relevant contracts and minutes of meetings of the board of directors and by making inquiries of appropriate officials of the entity and, in cases of acquisition, the entity acquired or to be acquired.
- Obtain a level of knowledge of each constituent part of the combined entity in a business combination sufficient to enable the practitioner to perform the required procedures. Procedures to obtain this knowledge may include communicating with other

practitioners who have audited or reviewed the historical financial statements that the pro forma financial information is based on. Matters that may be considered include the accounting principles and financial reporting practices followed, transactions between the entities, and material contingencies.

- Discuss with management their assumptions regarding the effects of the transaction (or event).
- Evaluate whether pro forma adjustments are included for all significant effects directly attributable to the transaction (or event).
- Obtain sufficient evidence in support of such adjustments. The evidence required to support the level of assurance given is a matter of professional judgment. The practitioner typically obtains more evidence in an examination engagement than in a review engagement. Examples of evidence that the practitioner might consider obtaining are purchase, merger, or exchange agreements; appraisal reports; debt agreements; employment agreements; actions of the board of directors; and existing or proposed legislation or regulatory actions.
- Evaluate whether management's assumptions that underlie the pro forma adjustments are presented in a sufficiently clear and comprehensive manner. Also evaluate whether the pro forma adjustments are consistent with each other and with the data used to develop them.
- Determine that computations of pro forma adjustments are mathematically correct and that the pro forma column reflects the proper application of those adjustments to the historical financial statements.
- Obtain written representations from management (illustrative representation letters are included in Appendix 12G and Appendix 12H) concerning their
  - — Responsibility for the assumptions used in determining the pro forma adjustments.
  - — Assertion that the assumptions provide a reasonable basis for presenting all of the significant effects directly attributable to the transaction (or event), that the related pro forma adjustments give appropriate effect to those assumptions, and that the pro forma column reflects the proper application of those adjustments to the historical financial statements.
  - — Assertion that the significant effects directly attributable to the transaction (or event) are appropriately disclosed in the pro forma financial information.

- Read the pro forma financial information and evaluate whether
  - The underlying transaction (or event), the proforma adjustments, the significant assumptions and the significant uncertainties, if any, about those assumptions, have been appropriately described.
  - The source of the historical financial information that the pro forma financial information is based on has been appropriately identified.

Presentation

Pro forma financial information should be labeled as such to distinguish it from historical financial information. This presentation should include the following:

- A description of the transaction (or event) that is reflected in the pro forma financial information.
- The source of the historical financial information on which it is based.
- Significant assumptions used in developing the pro forma adjustments.
- Any significant uncertainties about those assumptions.

The presentation should also state that the pro forma financial information should be read in conjunction with related historical financial information and that the pro forma financial information is not necessarily indicative of the results (such as financial position and results of operations, as applicable) that would have been attained had the transaction (or event) actually taken place earlier.

Reporting

According to Chapter 4 of SSAE-10 (AT 401.11), the practitioner's report on pro forma financial information may be a separate report or it may be added to the practitioner's report on the historical financial statements.

Examination

The practitioner's examination report on pro forma financial information should include the following:

- A title that includes the word "independent."

- An identification of the pro forma financial information.
- A reference to the financial statements that the historical financial information is derived from and a statement that the financial statements were audited (the report on the pro forma financial information should refer to all modifications in the audit report on the historical financial statements).
- An identification of the responsible party and a statement that the responsible party is responsible for the pro forma financial information.
- A statement that the practitioner's responsibility is to express an opinion on the pro forma financial information based on his or her examination.
- A statement that the examination of the pro forma financial information was conducted in accordance with attestation standards established by the American Institute of Certified Public Accountants and, accordingly, included such procedures as the practitioner considered necessary in the circumstances.
- A statement that the practitioner believes that the examination provides a reasonable basis for his or her opinion.
- A separate paragraph explaining the objective of pro forma financial information and its limitations.
- The practitioner's opinion as to whether:
  - — Management's assumptions provide a reasonable basis for presenting the significant effects directly attributable to the transaction (or event).
  - — The related pro forma adjustments give appropriate effect to those assumptions.
  - — The pro forma column reflects the proper application of those adjustments to the historical financial statements.
- The manual or printed signature of the practitioner's firm.
- The date of the examination report.

Appendix 12I is an example examination report on pro forma financial information.

Review

A practitioner's review report on pro forma financial information should include the following:

- A title that includes the word "independent."
- An identification of the pro forma financial information.

- A reference to the financial statements that the historical financial information is derived from and a statement that the financial statements were audited or reviewed (the report on the pro forma financial information should refer to all modifications in the audit or review report on the historical financial statements).
- An identification of the responsible party and a statement that the responsible party is responsible for the pro forma financial information.
- A statement that the review of the pro forma financial information was conducted in accordance with attestation standards established by the American Institute of Certified Public Accountants.
- A statement that a review is substantially less in scope than an examination, the objective of which is the expression of an opinion on the pro forma financial information and, accordingly, the practitioner does not express such an opinion.
- A separate paragraph explaining the objective of pro forma financial information and its limitations.
- The practitioner's conclusion as to whether any information came to the practitioner's attention to cause him or her to believe that:
  - — Management's assumptions do not provide a reasonable basis for presenting the significant effects directly attributable to the transaction (or event).
  - — The related pro forma adjustments do not give appropriate effect to those assumptions.
  - — The pro forma column does not reflect the proper application of those adjustments to the historical financial statements.
- The manual or printed signature of the practitioner's firm.
- The date of the review report.

Appendix 12J is an example review report on pro forma financial information.

Restrictions

A representation letter is required for engagements to examine or review pro forma financial information. Because the representation letter contains a written assertion, the written assertion is required for such engagements. According to Chapter 1 of SSAE-10 (AT 101.78), if a nonclient responsible party refuses to provide a written assertion, the report should be restricted to the use of the specified parties. Although Chapter 4 of SSAE-10 (AT 401.14) does not address that situation in pro forma engagements, it does state that nothing precludes the practitioner from restricting the use of any examination or review report on pro forma financial information.

Dating

The practitioner's report should be dated as of the completion of the examination or review procedures. If the report on the pro forma financial information is added to the report on the historical financial statements, and the date of completion of the examination or review procedures is after the date of completion of the audit or review of the historical financial statements, the combined report should be dual-dated. For example, the report would be dated as follows:

> February 15, 20XX, except for the paragraphs regarding pro forma financial information, as to which the date is March 20, 20XX.

Modifications

In an engagement to examine or review pro forma financial information, the following situations may result in a qualified opinion, adverse opinion, disclaimer of opinion, or withdrawal from the engagement:

- Restrictions on the scope of the engagement.
- Reservations about the propriety of the assumptions and the conformity of the presentation with those assumptions.
- Inadequate disclosure of significant matters.
- Other reservations.

The type of report modification that is necessary will depend on the circumstances of the engagement. When a report modification is necessary, the practitioner should disclose all substantive reasons for the modification.

Scope Restrictions

Restrictions on the scope of an examination engagement may require the practitioner to qualify the opinion, disclaim an opinion, or withdraw from the engagement. The decision on the best course of action depends on an assessment of the significance of the matter that caused the scope restriction. If the significance of the matter is pervasive to the pro forma financial information or the assertion, a disclaimer or withdrawal is more likely to be appropriate. When the scope restriction is imposed by the client or the responsible party, the practitioner should generally disclaim an opinion or withdraw from the engagement.

In a review engagement, if there is a scope restriction, the practitioner should withdraw from the engagement.

Chapter 4 of SSAE-10 (AT 401.10) requires a representation letter in an engagement to examine or review pro forma financial information. If a representation letter is not obtained in an examination, Chapter 1 of SSAE-10 (AT 101.62) states that there is a limitation on the scope of the engagement sufficient to preclude an unqualified opinion. Ordinarily, the inability to obtain a representation letter would be sufficient to cause the practitioner to disclaim an opinion or withdraw from the engagement. However, based on the nature of the representations not obtained or the circumstances of the refusal, the practitioner may conclude, in an examination, that a qualified opinion is appropriate. The practitioner should consider the effects of the refusal on his or her ability to rely on other representations. If a representation letter is not obtained in a review engagement, the practitioner should withdraw from the engagement.

Other Considerations

Subsequent Events

Events or transactions that have a material effect on the subject matter sometimes occur subsequent to the point in time or period of time of the subject matter being tested but prior to the date of the practitioner's report. These occurrences are referred to as "subsequent events." The practitioner has no responsibility to detect subsequent events. However, he or she should inquire of the responsible party (and his or her client if the client is not the responsible party) as to whether they are aware of any subsequent events, through the date of the practitioner's report, that would have a material effect on the subject matter or the assertion. If the practitioner has obtained a representation letter, the letter would ordinarily include a representation concerning subsequent events.

Two types of subsequent events require consideration by the practitioner:

1. Events that provide additional information with respect to conditions that existed at the point in time or during the period of time of the subject matter being tested. This information should be used by the practitioner in considering whether the subject matter is presented in conformity with

the criteria and may affect the presentation of the subject matter, the assertion, or the examination report.

2. Events that provide information with respect to conditions that arose subsequent to the point in time or period of time of the subject matter being tested that are of such a nature and significance that their disclosure is necessary to keep the subject matter from being misleading. This type of information will not normally affect the practitioner's report if the information is appropriately disclosed.

The practitioner has no responsibility to keep informed of events subsequent to the date of his or her report. However, the practitioner might later become aware of conditions that existed at that date that might have affected the practitioner's report had he or she been aware of them. In such circumstances, the practitioner may wish to consider the guidance in AU Section 561 (Subsequent Discovery of Facts Existing at the Date of the Auditor's Report).

Documentation

Attest documentation is the principal record of attest procedures applied, information obtained, and conclusions or findings reached by the practitioner in an engagement. The quantity, type, and content of attest documentation are matters of the practitioner's professional judgment. Attest documentation serves mainly to:

- Provide the principal support for the practitioner's report, including the representation regarding observance of the standards of fieldwork, which is implicit in the reference in the report to attestation standards.
- Aid the practitioner in the conduct and supervision of the attest engagement.

Attest documentation should be sufficient to (1) enable members of the engagement team with supervision and review responsibilities to understand the nature, timing, extent, and results of attest procedures performed and the information obtained and (2) identify the engagement team member(s) who performed and reviewed the work.

Examples of attest documentation are work programs, analyses, memoranda, letters of confirmation and representation, abstracts or copies of entity documents, and schedules or commentaries prepared or obtained by the practitioner. Ordinarily, attest documentation includes:

- Documentation of the engagement acceptance or continuance decision.
- An engagement letter.

- A planning form documenting the practitioner's knowledge of the client and consideration of attestation risk.
- Documentation of the procedures performed.
- Support for data in the presentation.
- A discussion of unusual matters encountered and their resolution.
- A representation letter.
- Copies of reports from other accountants, if any, who have examined a component of the subject matter.
- Documentation that the workpapers were reviewed.

Attest documentation may be in paper form, electronic form, or other media.

The practitioner has an ethical, and in some situations a legal, obligation to maintain the confidentiality of client information or information of the responsible party. Because attest documentation often contains confidential information, the practitioner should adopt reasonable procedures to maintain the confidentiality of that information. The practitioner should also adopt reasonable procedures to prevent unauthorized access to attest documentation.

Use of a Specialist

The practitioner might need specialized assistance on the engagement and may decide to rely on the work of an expert. When the practitioner uses the work of a specialist, the attestation standards require that he or she have sufficient knowledge of the subject matter to (1) communicate to the specialist the objectives of the work and (2) evaluate the specialist's work to determine if the objectives were achieved.

Before using and relying on the work of a specialist, the practitioner should be satisfied with the specialist's qualifications in the particular field. SAS-73 (AU 336) (Using the Work of a Specialist) provides guidance on using the work of a specialist. SAS-73 (AU 336) recommends that the practitioner consider the following in connection with his or her evaluation of a specialist's qualifications:

- The professional certification, license, or other recognition of the competence of the specialist.
- The reputation and standing of the specialist in the views of peers and others familiar with his or her work.
- The specialist's experience in the type of work that the practitioner is considering using the specialist for.

If the specialist is related to the client, the practitioner should assess the risk that the specialist's objectivity might be impaired. If the practitioner believes the specialist's objectivity might be impaired, he or she should either:

- Engage another specialist who is unrelated to the client; or
- Perform additional procedures to test the specialist's assumptions, methods, or findings (or engage another specialist to do so).

COMPILATION ENGAGEMENTS

SSARS-14 (AR 120) (Compilation of Pro Forma Financial Information) provides guidance on the standards and procedures that are applicable when an accountant is engaged to compile or issues a compilation report on pro forma financial information. The engagement must also follow the general compilation performance requirements found in SSARS-1 (AR 100) (Compilation and Review of Financial Statements). This section is an overview of the major considerations pertaining to and steps performed in compiling pro forma financial information. For a complete discussion of compilation engagements, including checklists and practice aids that can be adapted to pro forma financial information, see *Miller Compilations & Reviews*.

Although SSARS-14 (AR 120) provides guidance for compiling pro forma financial information, nothing precludes an accountant from preparing or assisting in the preparation of pro forma financial information and submitting the presentation to the client without the issuance of a compilation report. However, when an accountant prepares or assists a client in preparing a presentation of pro forma financial information, he or she should consider how the presentation will be used. The accountant should consider the potential that he or she will be associated with the presentation and that the user may inappropriately infer, through that association, an unintended level of assurance. If the accountant believes that he or she will be associated with the information, he or she should consider issuing a compilation report so that users will not infer a level of assurance that does not exist.

> **OBSERVATION:** When the accountant is engaged to compile pro forma financial information, he or she is required to report on the compiled pro forma financial information.

A compilation of pro forma financial information is limited to presenting financial information that is the representation of management (or the owners) without undertaking to express any assurance on it. However, the accountant might consider it necessary to perform other accounting services in order to compile the pro forma financial information.

An engagement to compile pro forma financial information may be undertaken as a separate engagement or in conjunction with a compilation of financial statements.

Conditions for Compiling Pro Forma Financial Information

According to SSARS-14 (AR 120), the practitioner may report on a compilation of pro forma financial information only if the following conditions are met:

- The document that contains the pro forma financial information includes (or incorporates by reference) complete historical financial statements of the entity for the most recent year (or for the preceding year if the financial statements for the most recent year are not yet available) and, if pro forma financial information is presented for an interim period, the document also includes (or incorporates by reference) historical interim financial information for that period (which may be presented in condensed form).
- The historical financial statements of the entity (or, in the case of a business combination, of each significant constituent part of the combined entity) that the pro forma financial information is based on have been compiled, reviewed, or audited. The accountant's compilation or review report or the auditor's report should be included (or incorporated by reference) in the document containing the pro forma financial information.

Establishing an Understanding with the Entity

When engaged to compile pro forma financial information, the accountant should establish an understanding with the entity, preferably in writing, regarding the services to be performed. The understanding should include a description of the nature and limitations of the services to be performed and a description of the report. The understanding should also state that

- The engagement cannot be relied upon to disclose errors, fraud, or illegal acts
- The accountant will inform the appropriate level of management of any material errors, of any evidence or information that comes to his or her attention during the engagement that fraud or an illegal act may have occurred.

OBSERVATION: The accountant need not report any matters regarding illegal acts that may have occurred that are clearly inconsequential and may reach agreement in advance with the entity on the nature of matters to be communicated.

OBSERVATION: "Fraud" is an intentional act that results in a misstatement in compiled specified elements, accounts, or items of a financial statement. "Illegal acts" are violations of laws or government regulations, excluding fraud.

OBSERVATION: Whether an act is, in fact, fraudulent or illegal is a determination that is normally beyond the accountant's professional competence. According to SSARS-14 (AR 120), an accountant, in reporting on pro forma financial information, presents him- or herself as one who is proficient in accounting and compilation services. The accountant's training, experience, and understanding of the client and its industry may provide a basis for recognition that some client acts coming to his or her attention may be fraudulent or illegal. However, the determination of whether a particular act is fraudulent or illegal is generally based on the advice of an informed expert qualified to practice law, and it may have to await final determination by a court of law.

Responsibility for Fraud and Illegal Acts

When the accountant is engaged to compile pro forma financial information and evidence or information comes to his or her attention during the engagement that fraud or an illegal act may have occurred, the accountant must adhere to the communication requirements contained in SSARS-1 (AR 100.61–.62), as amended.

AR 100.61 states that when evidence or information comes to the accountant's attention during the performance of compilation procedures that fraud or an illegal act may have occurred, the matter should be brought to the attention of the appropriate level of management. The accountant is not required to report matters regarding illegal acts that are clearly inconsequential and may reach agreement in advance with the client on the nature of items to be communicated.

When the fraud or illegal act involves senior management, the accountant should report the matter to an individual or group at a higher level within the entity, such as the manager (owner) or the board of directors. The communication may be oral or written. If the communication is oral, the accountant should document it. When the fraud or illegal act involves an owner of the business, the accountant should consider resigning from the engagement.

Additionally, the accountant should consider consulting with his or her legal counsel and insurance provider whenever evidence or information that fraud or an illegal act may have occurred comes to his or her attention during the performance of compilation procedures, unless the illegal act is clearly inconsequential.

The disclosure to parties other than the client's senior management (or the client's board of directors, if applicable) of any evidence or information that comes to the accountant's attention during the performance of compilation procedures that fraud or an illegal act may have occurred is not ordinarily part of the accountant's responsibility; ordinarily it would be precluded by the accountant's ethical or legal obligations of confidentiality. The accountant should recognize, however, that in the following circumstances a duty to disclose to parties outside of the entity may exist:

- To comply with certain legal and regulatory requirements
- To a successor accountant when the successor decides to communicate with the predecessor accountant in accordance with SSARS-4 (AR 400) (Communications between Predecessor and Successor Accountants), as amended, regarding acceptance of an engagement to compile or review the financial statements of a nonpublic entity
- In response to a subpoena

Because potential conflicts between the accountant's ethical and legal obligations for confidentiality of client matters may be complex, the accountant may wish to consult with legal counsel before discussing matters regarding fraud or illegal acts with parties outside the client.

Performance Requirements

When an accountant is engaged to compile or issues a compilation report on pro forma financial information, he or she must adhere to the compilation performance requirements contained in SSARS-1 (AR 100.07–.11), as amended, including the following:

1. The accountant should possess a level of knowledge of the accounting principles and practices of the industry the entity operates in that will enable him or her to compile pro forma financial information that is appropriate in form for an entity operating in that industry. An accountant is not precluded from accepting a compilation engagement for an entity in an industry that the accountant has no previous experience in. The requirement does, however, place upon the accountant a responsibility to obtain a sufficient level of knowledge. The accountant may do so this by consulting AICPA guides, industry publications, financial statements of other entities in the industry, textbooks and periodicals, and individuals knowledgeable about the industry.

2. To compile pro forma financial information, the accountant should possess a general understanding of the nature of the entity's business transactions, the form of its accounting records, the stated qualifications of its accounting personnel, the accounting basis on which the pro forma financial information is to be presented, and the form and content of the pro forma financial information. The accountant ordinarily obtains knowledge of these matters through experience with the entity or inquiry of the entity's personnel. On the basis of that understanding, the accountant should consider whether it will be necessary to perform other accounting services, such as assisting in adjusting the books of account or consulting on accounting matters, when he or she compiles the pro forma financial information.
3. The accountant is not required to make inquiries or perform other procedures to verify, corroborate, or review information supplied by the entity. However, the accountant may have made inquiries or performed other procedures. The results of such inquiries or procedures, knowledge gained from prior engagements, or the pro forma financial information on its face may cause the accountant to become aware that information supplied by the entity is incorrect, incomplete, or otherwise unsatisfactory. If any evidence or information comes to the accountant's attention regarding fraud or an illegal act that may have occurred, he or she should request that management consider the effect of the matter on the pro forma financial information. Additionally, the accountant should consider the effect of the matter on his or her compilation report. In circumstances where the accountant believes that the pro forma financial information is materially misstated, the accountant should obtain additional or revised information. If the entity refuses to provide additional or revised information, the accountant should withdraw from the engagement.
4. Before issuance of a compilation report on pro forma financial information, the accountant should read the compiled pro forma financial information, including the summary of significant assumptions, and consider whether the information appears to be appropriate in form and free of obvious material errors. In this context, the term "error" refers to mistakes in the compilation of the pro forma financial information, including arithmetical or clerical mistakes, and mistakes in the application of accounting principles, including disclosures, if presented.

OBSERVATION: The accountant may not report on compiled pro forma financial information if the summary of significant assumptions is not presented. However, as with compiled financial statements, management may elect to omit substantially all disclosures. In other words, the summary of significant assumptions is a *required* part of the presentation of pro forma financial information.

Presentation

Pro forma financial information should be labeled as such to distinguish it from historical financial information. This presentation should include the following:

- Description of the transaction (or event) that is reflected in the pro forma financial information
- Source of the historical financial information it is based on
- Significant assumptions used in developing the pro forma adjustments
- Any significant uncertainties about those assumptions.

The presentation should also state that the pro forma financial information should be read in conjunction with related historical financial information and that the pro forma financial information is not necessarily indicative of the results (such as financial position and results of operations, as applicable) that would have been attained had the transaction (or event) actually taken place earlier.

Reporting Requirements

When an accountant is engaged to compile and issues a compilation report on pro forma financial information, the basic elements of the report are as follows:

- An identification of the pro forma financial information.
- A statement that the compilation was performed in accordance with Statements on Standards for Accounting and Review Services issued by the American Institute of Certified Public Accountants.
- A reference to the financial statements that the historical financial information is derived from and a statement on whether the financial statements were compiled, reviewed, or audited. The report on the pro forma financial information should refer to any modifications in the accountant's or auditor's report on the historical financial statements.
- A statement that the pro forma financial information was compiled. If the compilation was performed in conjunction with a compilation of the company's financial statements, the

paragraph should state this and state the date of the accountant's compilation report on those financial statements. Furthermore, any departure from the standard report on those statements should also be disclosed if it is considered relevant to the presentation of the pro forma financial information.

- A description of the basis that the pro forma financial information is presented on if the basis is not generally accepted accounting principles and a statement that the basis of accounting is a comprehensive basis of accounting other than generally accepted accounting principles.
- A statement that a compilation is limited to presenting pro forma financial information that is the representation of management (or the owners).
- A statement that the pro forma financial information has not been audited or reviewed and, accordingly, the accountant does not express an opinion or any other form of assurance on it.
- A signature of the accounting firm or the accountant as appropriate. (The signature may be manual, stamped, electronic, or typed.)
- The date of the compilation report. (The date of completion of the compilation should be used as the date of the accountant's report.)

Any other procedures that the accountant might have performed before or during the compilation engagement should not be described in the report.

Each page of the compiled pro forma financial information should include a reference, such as "See Accountant's Compilation Report."

In cases where one set of historical financial statements is audited or reviewed and the other is audited, reviewed, or compiled, wording similar to the following is appropriate in the compilation report:

> The historical condensed financial statements are derived from the historical financial statements of XYZ Company, which were compiled by me (us), and of ABC Company, which were reviewed by another (other) accountant(s), appearing elsewhere herein (or incorporated by reference).

An accountant is not precluded from issuing a compilation report on pro forma financial information for an entity that the accountant is not independent of. If the accountant is not independent, he or she should specifically disclose the lack of independence. However, the reason for the lack of independence should not be described. When the accountant is not independent, the following should be included as the last paragraph of the report:

> I am (we are) not independent with respect to XYZ Company.

If the presentation of pro forma financial information does not include all applicable disclosures, the following paragraph should be added:

> Management has elected to omit all of the disclosures ordinarily included in pro forma financial information. The omitted disclosures might have added significant information regarding the company's pro forma financial position and results of operations. Accordingly, this pro forma financial information is not designed for those who are not informed about such matters.

Note, however, that the accountant may not report on compiled pro forma financial information if the summary of significant assumptions is not presented.

Appendix 12N is an example of a compilation report on pro forma financial information.

CONSULTING ENGAGEMENTS

Due diligence engagements may be structured as consulting engagements if they do not involve providing assurance on the financial or nonfinancial information. Common services performed in due diligence engagements include the following:

- Practitioner accompanying client on visits to the target company facilities.
- Practitioner studying documents, correspondence, and financial information related to the acquisition.
- Practitioner meeting with target company management.
- Practitioner providing specific services such as observing target company operations, interviewing target company personnel, and reporting on the results of those services.

Other services provided by the practitioner might include the following:

- Applying agreed-upon procedures to financial or nonfinancial information (see Chapter 9, "Agreed-Upon Procedures Engagements").
- Auditing, reviewing, or compiling the target company's financial statements (see applicable guidance in SASs and SSARSs).
- Developing and/or reporting on pro forma financial information (see the discussion earlier in this chapter).
- Developing and/or reporting on prospective financial information (see Chapter 13, "Prospective Financial Information").
- Reporting on the target company's internal control (see Chapter 11, "Internal Control Engagements").

Engagement Planning and Administration

Professional standards do not require any specific procedures before accepting a consulting engagement. However, before accepting a due diligence engagement that will be structured as a consulting engagement, the practitioner should consider

- The prospective client's reputation.
- The nature of services to be provided.
- The practitioner's ability to provide those services.
- Potential independence issues or conflicts of interest.
- The integrity and reputation of the target company.
- The expected use of the report (if one is to be issued).
- Fee arrangements.

Prospective Client's Reputation

Often the client in a due diligence engagement is a current client of the firm. In those cases, the client's reputation will be known to the practitioner. If the prospective client is new to the firm, the following are potential sources of information about the client that should be considered before accepting the engagement:

- Discussions with other CPAs or other professionals (lawyers, bankers, etc.).
- Inquiry of commercial credit agencies and business groups, such as the Better Business Bureau.
- Review of the prospective client's most recent financial statements, tax returns, and reports to regulatory agencies.

Nature of Services

Because the procedures performed in a due diligence engagement vary depending on the circumstances, a preliminary discussion with the prospective client is usually necessary to become familiar with the services that are required. Deciding what is best for the client is a matter of proper communication.

Ability to Provide the Services

Rule 201 of the AICPA Code of Professional Conduct requires that practitioners undertake only those services that they "can reasonably expect to be completed with professional competence." Other issues that should be considered include:

- Reporting deadlines and staffing requirements.
- Specialized skills or knowledge required.
- Potential independence issues or conflicts of interest.

Independence

Independence standards generally apply to audit and attestation engagements. The professional standards do not require independence for consulting services engagements. However, when performing consulting services for audit or attestation clients, practitioners should ensure that they avoid activities that would impair their independence.

Conflicts of Interest

SSCS requires the practitioner to inform the client of any conflicts of interest that may occur pursuant to the interpretations of Rule 102 of the AICPA Code of Professional Conduct. Interpretation 102-2 states:

> A conflict of interest may occur if a member performs a professional service for a client or employer and the member or his or her firm has a relationship with another person, entity, product, or service that could, in the member's professional judgment, be viewed by the client, employer, or other appropriate parties as impairing the member's objectivity. If the member believes that the professional service can be performed with objectivity, and the relationship is disclosed to and consent is obtained from such client, employer, or other appropriate parties, the rule shall not operate to prohibit the performance of the professional service . . .

Integrity of the Target Company

The effectiveness of the practitioner's services is generally affected by the cooperation of the target company and the quality of information provided. Therefore, the integrity and reputation of the target company should at least be considered in the acceptance decision.

Expected Use of the Report

SSCS does not require a written report as a result of performing consulting services. However, if a written report is issued in a due diligence engagement, it should not be approved for general use. The restriction on the use of the report should be communicated to the client prior to acceptance of the engagement.

Fee Arrangements

Fee arrangements should be discussed with the client prior to acceptance of the engagement and documented in the engagement letter. Because a due diligence engagement is an "as needed" service, there is the risk that the service will no longer be needed before the engagement is completed (for example, if negotiations with the target company are terminated). For this reason, many practitioners require a retainer before they commence work.

Avoiding Liability

Due diligence engagements represent one of the most common sources of litigation against CPAs. The very nature of the engagement creates the risk that a client believes it is getting more than the practitioner is engaged to provide. For this reason, it is critical that practitioners effectively communicate what the services do and do not entail. To avoid unnecessary liability in a due diligence engagement, the following points should be considered:

- Define the engagement clearly and specifically in a written engagement letter.
- Obtain a supplemental engagement letter when the services change or additional services are added.
- Maintain complete work papers.
- Do not leave unanswered questions, unresolved issues, extraneous notes or comments in the work papers.
- Restrict the use of the report.
- Adhere to AICPA professional standards.
- Avoid representing both the buyer and the target company.

Engagement Letters

Although SSCS only requires that the practitioner establish an understanding with the client concerning the services to be performed, it is a good business practice to use a written engagement letter. Matters that are ordinarily covered in an engagement letter include

- Objectives of the engagement.
- Nature of the services to be performed.

- Scope of the services, including limitations or constraints, if any.
- Respective roles, responsibilities, and relationships of the practitioner, the client, and the target.
- A limitation on the use of the report.
- Fee arrangements.
- Indemnification clause.
- Potential conflicts of interest, if any.

Appendix 12O is an illustrative consulting services engagement letter.

Engagement Procedures

Generally, in a consulting services engagement, the procedures are selected based on discussions and communications between the practitioner and the client. In providing the services requested by the client, the practitioner should avoid acting in the role of management by making management decisions or concluding on the merit of the transaction. Instead, the practitioner should maintain an impartial role of client assistance. The client's objective is usually to find out as much as possible about the target company in a timely and cost-effective manner. Consequently, the procedures from one engagement to the next vary based on clients' needs.

Many procedures in a due diligence engagement are similar to those performed in an audit. However, the due diligence engagement is generally less extensive than an audit, consists of procedures selected by the client, and provides no assurance regarding the information supplied by the target company. The practitioner simply applies his or her business knowledge in looking over the information and attempting to identify any critical areas that the client should be aware of.

Reporting

SSCS-1 requires communication to the client of the findings of a consulting services engagement. The final report may be written or oral. The decision of whether a written or oral report is provided is generally a matter of the client's preference. If a written report is not issued, the practitioner should include a summary of the engagement result in the work papers and document any other communications to the client. Whether oral or written, SSCS-1 specifies the following requirements for the final report:

- The significant engagement findings and events should be communicated, together with significant reservations concerning the scope or benefits of the engagement or other qualifications.

- The report should specify any conflicts of interest.

The consulting standards do not specify any particular report format or wording. Appendix 12S is an illustrative report for a consulting services engagement.

PROSPECTIVE FINANCIAL INFORMATION

Due diligence engagements sometimes involve the target's prospective financial information, such as forecasts, projections, and partial presentations. In a due diligence engagement, the practitioner's involvement with prospective financial information can range from compiling or assembling the information to examining the information or applying agreed-upon procedures. Any such engagement should be performed in accordance with the standards in Chapter 3 of SSAE-10 (AT 301). These engagements are discussed in Chapter 13, "Prospective Financial Information."

APPENDIX 12A
ENGAGEMENT LETTER: EXAMINATION OF PRO FORMA FINANCIAL INFORMATION

[*date*]

[*name of client*]
[*address*]

We are pleased to confirm our understanding of the nature and limitations of the services we are to provide for [*client's legal name*].

We will examine, from information management provides, the pro forma balance sheet of [*client*] as of [*date*] and the pro forma income statement for the [*period*] then ended. Our examination will be conducted in accordance with attestation standards established by the American Institute of Certified Public Accountants and, accordingly, will include procedures as we consider necessary to enable us to express an opinion as to whether (a) management's assumptions provide a reasonable basis for presenting the significant effects directly attributable to [*describe transaction or event*], (b) the related pro forma adjustments give appropriate effect to those assumptions, and (c) the pro forma presentation reflects the proper application of those adjustments to the Company's historical financial statements. If, for any reason, we are unable to complete the examination, we will describe any restrictions on the examination in our report or we will not issue a report as a result of this engagement.

Our report will detail the nature of reservations, if any, we have with respect to the pro forma financial information. Should any such reservations develop, we will discuss them with you before the report is issued.

The objective of pro forma financial information is to show what the significant effects on historical financial information might have been had a transaction or event occurred at an earlier date. However, pro forma financial information is not necessarily indicative of the results that would have been attained had the transaction or event actually occurred earlier.

Management is responsible for the pro forma financial information and for the assumptions used in the presentation. We may assist in the preparation of the pro forma presentation, but the responsibility for the presentation remains with you. At the conclusion of the engagement, management agrees to supply us with a representation letter, which, among other things, will confirm management's responsibility for the pro forma presentation and underlying assumptions and management's belief that the significant effects directly attributable to [*describe transaction or event*] are appropriately disclosed in the pro forma financial information.

We understand that the pro forma financial information and our report thereon will be used only for [*state the intended limited use*]. If management intends to reproduce and publish pro forma financial information and our report thereon, they must be reproduced in their entirety, and both the first and subsequent corrected drafts of the document containing the pro forma financial information and any accompanying material must be submitted to us for approval.

We plan to begin our examination on approximately [*date*] and issue our report no later than [*date*].

We estimate that our fees for these services will range from $_____ to $_____. You will also be billed for travel and other out-of-pocket costs such as report production, typing, postage, etc. Additional expenses are estimated to be $_____. The fee estimate is based on anticipated cooperation from your personnel and the assumption that unexpected circumstances will not be encountered during the examination. If significant additional time is necessary, we will discuss it with you and arrive at a new fee estimate before we incur the additional costs. Our invoices for these fees will be rendered each month as work progresses and are payable on presentation. In accordance with our firm policies, work may be suspended if your account becomes ___ days or more overdue and will not be resumed until your account is paid in full. If we elect to terminate our services for nonpayment, our engagement will deemed to have been completed upon written notification of termination, even if we have not completed our report. You will be obligated to compensate us for all time expended and to reimburse us for all out-of-pocket expenditures through the date of termination.

We appreciate the opportunity to be of service to you and believe this letter accurately summarizes the significant terms of our engagement. If you have any questions, please let us know. If you agree with the terms of our engagement as described in this letter, please sign the enclosed copy and return it to us.

Very truly yours,

[*CPA firm's name*]

Response:

This letter correctly sets forth the understanding of [*client*].

By:

Title:

Date:

APPENDIX 12B ENGAGEMENT LETTER: REVIEW OF PRO FORMA FINANCIAL INFORMATION

[*date*]

[*name of client*]
[*address*]

We are pleased to confirm our understanding of the nature and limitations of the services we are to provide for [*client's legal name*].

We will review, from information management provides, the pro forma balance sheet of [*client*] as of [*date*] and the pro forma income statement for the [*period*] then ended. Our review will be conducted in accordance with attestation standards established by the American Institute of Certified Public Accountants. Accordingly, it will consist primarily of inquiries of Company personnel and analytical procedures applied to data. We will not perform an examination, the objective of which is the expression of an opinion as to whether (a) management's assumptions provide a reasonable basis for presenting the significant effects directly attributable to [*describe transaction or event*], (b) the related pro forma adjustments give appropriate effect to those assumptions, and (c) the pro forma presentation reflects the proper application of those adjustments to the Company's historical financial statements. Accordingly, we will not express such an opinion.

Our report on the pro forma financial information is presently expected to read as follows:

> We have reviewed the pro forma adjustments reflecting the transaction (event) described in Note 1 and the application of those adjustments to the historical amounts in the accompanying pro forma balance sheet of [*client*] as of [*date*], and the pro forma statement of income for the year then ended. These historical financial statements are derived from the historical unaudited financial statements of [*client*], which were reviewed by us, appearing elsewhere herein (incorporated by reference). Such pro forma adjustments are based on management's assumptions as described in Note 2. [*client*]'s management is responsible for the pro forma financial information.
>
> Our review was conducted in accordance with attestation standards established by the American Institute of Certified Public Accountants. A review is substantially less in scope than an examination, the objective of which is the expression of an opinion on

> management's assumptions, the pro forma adjustments, and the application of those adjustments to the Company's historical financial statements. Accordingly, we do not express such an opinion.
>
> The objective of this pro forma financial information is to show what the significant effects on historical financial information might have been had a transaction or event occurred at an earlier date. However, the pro forma financial statements are not necessarily indicative of the results of operations or related effects on financial position that would have been attained had the above-mentioned transaction (event) actually occurred earlier.
>
> Based on our review, nothing came to our attention that caused us to believe that management's assumptions do not provide a reasonable basis for presenting the significant effects directly attributable to the above-mentioned transaction (event) described in Note 1, that the related pro forma adjustments do not give appropriate effect to those assumptions, or that the pro forma column does not reflect the proper application of those adjustments to the historical financial statement amounts in the pro forma balance sheet as of [*date*] and the pro forma statement of income for the year then ended.

If, for any reason, we are unable to complete the review, we will describe any restrictions on the performance of the review in our report or will not issue a report as a result of this engagement.

Our engagement will not include obtaining corroborating evidential matter and certain other procedures performed during an examination. Thus, a review does not provide assurance that we will become aware of all significant matters that would be disclosed in an examination. However, our report will detail the nature of reservations, if any, we have with respect to the pro forma financial information. Should any such reservations develop, we will discuss them with you before the report is issued.

The objective of pro forma financial information is to show what the significant effects on historical financial information might have been had a transaction or event occurred at an earlier date. However, pro forma financial information is not necessarily indicative of the results that would have been attained had the transaction or event actually occurred earlier.

Management is responsible for the pro forma financial information and for the assumptions used in the presentation. We may assist in the preparation of the pro forma presentation, but the responsibility for the presentation remains with you. At the conclusion of the engagement, management agrees to supply us with a representation letter, which, among other things, will confirm management's responsibility for the pro forma presentation and underlying assumptions and management's belief that the significant effects directly attributable to [*describe transaction or event*] are appropriately disclosed in the pro forma financial information.

We understand that the pro forma financial information and our report thereon will be used only for [*state the intended limited use*]. If management intends to reproduce and publish pro forma financial information and our report thereon, they must be reproduced in their entirety, and both the first and subsequent corrected drafts of the document containing the pro forma financial information and any accompanying material must be submitted to us for approval.

We plan to begin our examination on approximately [*date*] and issue our report no later than [*date*].

We estimate that our fees for these services will range from $_____ to $_____. You will also be billed for travel and other out-of-pocket costs such as report production, typing, postage, etc. Additional expenses are estimated to be $_____. The fee estimate is based on anticipated cooperation from your personnel and the assumption that unexpected circumstances will not be encountered during the examination. If significant additional time is necessary, we will discuss it with you and arrive at a new fee estimate before we incur the additional costs. Our invoices for these fees will be rendered each month as work progresses and are payable on presentation. In accordance with our firm policies, work may be suspended if your account becomes ____ days or more overdue and will not be resumed until your account is paid in full. If we elect to terminate our services for nonpayment, our engagement will deemed to have been completed upon written notification of termination, even if we have not completed our report. You will be obligated to compensate us for all time expended and to reimburse us for all out-of-pocket expenditures through the date of termination.

We appreciate the opportunity to be of service to you and believe this letter accurately summarizes the significant terms of our engagement. If you have any questions, please let us know. If you agree with the terms of our engagement as described in this letter, please sign the enclosed copy and return it to us.

Very truly yours,

[*CPA firm's name*]

Response:

This letter correctly sets forth the understanding of [*client*].

By:

Title:

Date:

APPENDIX 12C
ENGAGEMENT LETTER: COMPILATION OF PRO FORMA FINANCIAL INFORMATION

[*date*]

[*name of client*]
[*address*]

This letter is to confirm our understanding of the terms and objectives of our engagement and the nature and limitations of the services we will provide.

We will perform the following services:

We will compile, from information you provide, the pro forma financial information of [*client*] as of [*date*].

We will compile the pro forma financial information and issue an accountant's report thereon in accordance with Statements on Standards for Accounting and Review Services. A compilation is limited to presenting financial information that is the representation of management (owners). We will not audit or review the pro forma financial information and, accordingly, will not express an opinion or any other form of assurance on it.

Our engagement cannot be relied upon to disclose errors, fraud, or illegal acts that may exist. However, we will inform the appropriate level of management of any material errors, and of any evidence or information that comes to our attention during the performance of our compilation procedures, that fraud may have occurred. In addition, we will report to you any evidence or information that comes to our attention during the performance of our compilation procedures regarding illegal acts that may have occurred, unless they are clearly inconsequential.

As part of our engagement, we will also (list any nonattest services to be performed, if applicable, such as income tax preparation and bookkeeping services).

You are responsible for:

(a) Making all management decisions and performing all management functions;

(b) Designating an individual who possesses suitable skill, knowledge, and/or experience, preferably within senior management, to oversee the services;

(c) Evaluating the adequacy and results of the services performed;

(d) Accepting responsibility for the results of the services; and

(e) Establishing and maintaining internal controls, including monitoring ongoing activities.

If, for any reason, we are unable to complete the compilation of your pro forma financial information, we will not issue a report on such information as a result of this engagement.

Our fees for this work will be at our regular hourly rates for the individuals involved plus direct out-of-pocket expenses. Payment for service is due when rendered, and interim billings may be submitted as work progresses and expenses are incurred.

Billings become delinquent if not paid within [*number*] days of the invoice date. If billings are past due in excess of [*number*] days, we will stop all work until your account is brought current, or withdraw from this engagement. [*Client*] acknowledges and agrees that we are not required to continue work in the event of [*client's*] failure to pay on a timely basis for services rendered as required by this engagement letter. [*Client*] further acknowledges and agrees that in the event we stop work or withdraw from this engagement as a result of [*client's*] failure to pay on a timely basis for services rendered as required by this engagement letter, we shall not be liable to [*client*] for any damages that occur as a result of our ceasing to render services.

We will require a retainer of $[*amount*], which will be applied to current billings as registered.

We shall be pleased to discuss this letter with you at any time.

If the foregoing is in accordance with your understanding, please sign the copy of this letter in the space provided and return it to us.

Sincerely,

____

[*CPA firm name*]

Acknowledged:

____

[*client*]

____

Date

APPENDIX 12D
EXAMINATION ENGAGEMENT CHECKLIST: PRO FORMA FINANCIAL INFORMATION

Client Name: ____________________ Date of Subject Matter: ____________

Completed by: ____________________ Date Completed: ________________

	Completed by	N/A
1. Complete the Client Acceptance and Retention Evaluation Form.	________	_______
2. Establish and document an understanding with the client, preferably in an engagement letter. If an engagement letter will not be obtained, the oral understanding should be documented in a memo.	________	_______

		Completed by	N/A
3.	Obtain an understanding of the client and the engagement.	______	______
4.	If the client is not the responsible party, obtain evidence of the responsible party's responsibility for the pro forma financial information.	______	______
5.	Determine that the scheduling and staffing are adequate to perform the engagement.	______	______
6.	Consider planning materiality.	______	______
7.	Obtain the engagement partner's approval of the overall engagement plan.	______	______
8.	Discuss with management their assumptions regarding the effects of the transaction or event that is reflected in the pro forma presentation.	______	______
9.	Evaluate whether pro forma adjustments are included for all significant effects that are directly attributable to the underlying transaction or event.	______	______
10.	Develop and perform procedures necessary to obtain sufficient evidence to support the pro forma adjustments.	______	______
11.	Evaluate whether the pro forma adjustments are consistent with each other and with the data used to develop them.	______	______
12.	Determine that the pro forma adjustments are mathematically correct and that the pro forma column reflects the proper application of the adjustments to the historical financial statements.	______	______
13.	Review the results of the preceding procedures and evaluate whether:		
	a. Management's assumptions provide a reasonable basis for presenting the significant effects that are directly attributable to the underlying transaction or event.	______	______
	b. The pro forma adjustments give appropriate effect to the assumptions.	______	______
	c. The pro forma presentation reflects the proper application of the pro forma adjustments to the historical financial statements.	______	______
14.	Read the pro forma financial information and evaluate whether it:		
	a. Appropriately labeled to distinguish it from historical or prospective information.	______	______

	Completed by	N/A
b. Describes the purpose for which it was prepared.	________	________
c. Describes the source of the historical financial information on which it is based.	________	________
d. Describes the transaction or event that is reflected in the pro forma presentation.	________	________
e. Describes the significant assumptions used in developing the pro forma adjustments and any significant uncertainties about those assumptions.	________	________
f. Describes the pro forma adjustments.	________	________
g. Warns readers that the pro forma financial information should be read in conjunction with the related historical information and that the pro forma financial information is not necessarily indicative of the results that would have been attained if the transaction or event had actually taken place during the period depicted.	________	________
h. Discloses significant accounting policies used in the preparation of the pro forma information or references to such disclosure in the historical financial statements.	________	________
15. Obtain a representation letter.	________	________
16. Draft the examination report.	________	________
17. Read other information in a client-prepared document that contains the examination report for inconsistencies with the report and material misstatements of fact.	________	________
18. If any situations have occurred that require consultation, determine that such consultation has been properly documented.	________	________
19. If there were differences of professional opinion among members of the engagement team or between the engagement team and a specialist, determine that the differences were properly resolved and documented.	________	________
20. Determine that all questions, exceptions, or notes, if any, posed during the engagement have been followed up and resolved.	________	________
21. Determine that all required forms, questionnaires, and checklists have been completed.	________	________
22. Ensure that the workpapers and examination report have been reviewed in accordance with firm policy.	________	________
23. Obtain engagement partner's review and approval for issuance of report.	________	________

APPENDIX 12E
REVIEW ENGAGEMENT CHECKLIST:
PRO FORMA FINANCIAL INFORMATION

Client Name: ____________________ Date of Subject Matter: __________

Completed by: ____________________ Date Completed: ______________

	Completed by	N/A
1. Complete the Client Acceptance and Retention Evaluation Form.	________	________
2. If the engagement was originally intended to be an examination, document the consideration as to:		
a. The reasons given for the client's request to change the engagement to a review, particularly the implications of a restriction on the scope of the examination, whether imposed by the client or circumstances.	________	________
b. The additional effort required to complete the examination.	________	________
c. The estimated additional cost to complete the examination.	________	________
3. Establish and document an understanding with the client, preferably in an engagement letter. If an engagement letter will not be obtained, the oral understanding should be documented in a memo.	________	________
4. Obtain an understanding of the client and the engagement.	________	________
5. If the client is not the responsible party, obtain evidence of the responsible party's responsibility for the pro forma financial information.	________	________
6. Determine that the scheduling and staffing are adequate to perform the engagement.	________	________
7. Consider planning materiality.	________	________
8. Obtain the engagement partner's approval of the overall engagement plan.	________	________
9. Discuss with management their assumptions regarding the effects of the transaction or event that is reflected in the pro forma presentation.	________	________
10. Evaluate whether pro forma adjustments are included for all significant effects that are directly attributable to the underlying transaction or event.	________	________
11. Develop and perform procedures necessary to provide limited assurance in support of the pro forma adjustments.	________	________

	Completed by	N/A
12. Evaluate whether the pro forma adjustments are consistent with each other and with the data used to develop them.	______	______
13. Determine that the pro forma adjustments are mathematically correct and that the pro forma column reflects the proper application of the adjustments to the historical financial statements.	______	______
14. If there is an indication that the presentation may be incomplete or inaccurate, perform additional procedures as deemed necessary.	______	______
15. Review the results of the preceding procedures and evaluate any conditions that indicate that:		
a. Management's assumptions do not provide a reasonable basis for presenting the significant effects that are directly attributable to the underlying transaction or event.	______	______
b. The pro forma adjustments do not give appropriate effect to the assumptions.	______	______
c. The pro forma presentation does not reflect the proper application of the pro forma adjustments to the historical financial statements.	______	______
16. Read the pro forma financial information and evaluate whether it:		
d. Is appropriately labeled to distinguish it from historical or prospective information.	______	______
e. Describes the purpose for which it was prepared.	______	______
f. Describes the source of the historical financial information on which it is based.	______	______
g. Describes the transaction or event that is reflected in the pro forma presentation.	______	______
h. Describes the significant assumptions used in developing the pro forma adjustments and any significant uncertainties about those assumptions.	______	______
i. Describes the pro forma adjustments.	______	______
j. Warns readers that the pro forma financial information should be read in conjunction with the related historical information and that the pro forma financial information is not necessarily indicative of the results that would have been attained if the transaction or event		

		Completed by	N/A
	had actually taken place during the period depicted.	______	______
	k. Discloses significant accounting policies used in the preparation of the pro forma information or references to such disclosure in the historical financial statements.	______	______
17.	Obtain a representation letter.	______	______
18.	Draft the review report.	______	______
19.	Read other information in a client-prepared document that contains the review report for inconsistencies with the report and material misstatements of fact.	______	______
20.	If any situations have occurred that require consultation, determine that such consultation has been properly documented.	______	______
21.	If there were differences of professional opinion among members of the engagement team or between the engagement team and a specialist, determine that the differences were properly resolved and documented.	______	______
22.	Determine that all questions, exceptions, or notes, if any, posed during the engagement have been followed up and resolved.	______	______
23.	Determine that all required forms, questionnaires, and checklists have been completed.	______	______
24.	Ensure that the workpapers and review report have been reviewed in accordance with firm policy.	______	______
25.	Obtain engagement partner's review and approval for issuance of report.	______	______

APPENDIX 12F
COMPILATION ENGAGEMENT CHECKLIST: PRO FORMA FINANCIAL INFORMATION

Use the following procedures as a guide for performing a compilation of pro forma financial information. The compilation program is only a guide, and professional judgment should be exercised to determine how the procedures should be revised or added to.

Initial and date each procedure as it is completed. If a procedure is not relevant to this particular compilation engagement, place "N/A" (not applicable) in the space provided for initials and cross-reference the omitted procedure to another workpaper that explains why the procedure was omitted.

Client Name: ______________________________

Date of Presentation: ______________________________

		Initials	Date
1.	Acquire an adequate understanding of the accounting principles and practices of the client's industry.	______	______
2.	Develop a general understanding of the nature of the client's business transactions.	______	______
3.	Develop a general understanding of the stated qualifications of the client's accounting personnel.	______	______
4.	Develop a general understanding of the accounting basis used to prepare the pro forma financial information.	______	______
5.	Develop a general understanding of the form and content of the pro forma financial information.	______	______
6.	Consider whether other professional services are needed in order to complete the compilation engagement.	______	______
7.	If any evidence or information regarding fraud or an illegal act that may have occurred is discovered:		
	a. Request that management consider the effect of the matter on the specified element.	______	______
	b. Consider the effect of the matter on the compilation report.	______	______
8.	Read the pro forma financial information.	______	______
9.	On the basis of information collected using other compilation procedures and/or information that otherwise has come to our attention, consider whether additional or revised information must be obtained.	______	______
10.	Other compilation procedures used:		

____

____

____

Reviewed By: ______________________________

Date: ______________________________

APPENDIX 12G
REPRESENTATION LETTER: EXAMINATION OF PRO FORMA FINANCIAL INFORMATION

[*date—No earlier than date of the accountant's report*]

[*CPA firm's name*]
[*address*]

In connection with your examination of the pro forma balance sheet of [*client*] as of [*date*] and the pro forma income statement for the period then ended, we make the following representations:

- We are responsible for the assumptions used in determining the pro forma adjustments.
- We believe the assumptions provide a reasonable basis for presenting all the significant effects directly attributable to [*describe transaction or event*].
- We believe the pro forma adjustments give appropriate effect to our assumptions.
- We believe that the pro forma financial information reflects the proper application of the pro forma adjustments to the Company's historical financial statements.
- We believe that the significant effects directly attributable to [*describe transaction or event*] are appropriately disclosed in the pro forma financial information.
- We have made available to you all significant information that we believe is relevant to the pro forma financial information, and we are not aware of any information not previously disclosed to you that significantly contradicts the [*describe transaction or event*].
- We have responded fully to all inquiries made to us by you during the examination.
- We intend to use this pro forma financial information only for [*describe the intended limited use*].

Signature:	Signature:
Title:	Title:

APPENDIX 12H
REPRESENTATION LETTER: REVIEW OF PRO FORMA FINANCIAL INFORMATION

[*date—No earlier than date of the accountant's report*]

[*CPA firm's name*]
[*address*]

In connection with your review for the purpose of expressing limited assurance on the pro forma balance sheet of [*client*] as of [*date*] and the pro forma income statement for the period then ended, we make the following representations:

- We are responsible for the assumptions used in determining the pro forma adjustments.
- We believe the assumptions provide a reasonable basis for presenting all the significant effects directly attributable to [*describe transaction or event*].
- We believe the pro forma adjustments give appropriate effect to our assumptions.
- We believe that the pro forma financial information reflects the proper application of the pro forma adjustments to the Company's historical financial statements.
- We believe that the significant effects directly attributable to [*describe transaction or event*] are appropriately disclosed in the pro forma financial information.
- We have made available to you all significant information that we believe is relevant to the pro forma financial information, and we are not aware of any information not previously disclosed to you that significantly contradicts the [*describe transaction or event*].
- We have responded fully to all inquiries made to us by you during the examination.
- We intend to use this pro forma financial information only for [*describe the intended limited use*].

Signature:	Signature:
Title:	Title:

APPENDIX 12I
STANDARD EXAMINATION REPORT ON PRO FORMA FINANCIAL INFORMATION

Independent Accountant's Report

To the Board of Directors of
XYZ Company
[*city, state*]

We have examined the pro forma adjustments reflecting the transaction (event) described in Note 1 and the application of those adjustments to the historical amounts in the accompanying pro forma balance sheet of XYZ Company as of December 31, 20XX, and the pro forma statement of income for the year then ended. These historical financial statements are derived from the historical financial statements of XYZ Company, which were audited by us, and of ABC Company, which were audited by other accountants, appearing elsewhere herein (incorporated by reference). Such pro forma adjustments are based on management's assumptions as described in Note 2. XYZ Company's management is responsible for the pro forma financial information. Our responsibility is to express an opinion on the pro forma financial information based on our examination.

Our examination was conducted in accordance with attestation standards established by the American Institute of Certified Public Accountants and, accordingly, included such procedures as we considered necessary in the circumstances. We believe that our examination provides a reasonable basis for our opinion.

The objective of this pro forma financial information is to show what the significant effects on historical financial information might have been had the transaction (event) occurred at an earlier date. However, the pro forma financial statements are not necessarily indicative of the results of operations or related effects on financial position that would have been attained had the above-mentioned transaction (event) actually occurred earlier.

In our opinion, management's assumptions provide a reasonable basis for presenting the significant effects directly attributable to the above-mentioned transaction (event) described in Note 1, that the related pro forma adjustments give appropriate effect to those assumptions, and the pro forma column reflects the proper application of those adjustments to the historical financial statement amounts in the pro forma balance sheet as of December 31, 20XX, and the pro forma statement of income for the year then ended.

[*firm's signature*]

[*city, state*]

[*date*]

APPENDIX 12J
STANDARD REVIEW REPORT ON PRO FORMA FINANCIAL INFORMATION

Independent Accountant's Report

To the Board of Directors of
XYZ Company
[*city, state*]

We have reviewed the pro forma adjustments reflecting the transaction (event) described in Note 1 and the application of those adjustments to the historical amounts in the accompanying pro forma balance sheet of XYZ Company as of December 31, 20XX, and the pro forma statement of income for the year then ended. These historical financial statements are derived from the historical unaudited financial statements of XYZ Company, which were reviewed by us, and of ABC Company, which were reviewed by other accountants, appearing elsewhere herein (incorporated by reference). Such pro forma adjustments are based on management's assumptions as described in Note 2. XYZ Company's management is responsible for the pro forma financial information.

Our review was conducted in accordance with attestation standards established by the American Institute of Certified Public Accountants. A review is substantially less in scope than an examination, the objective of which is the expression of an opinion on management's assumptions, the pro forma adjustments, and the application of those adjustments to the Company's historical financial statements. Accordingly, we do not express such an opinion.

The objective of this pro forma financial information is to show what the significant effects on historical financial information might have been had a transaction or event occurred at an earlier date. However, the pro forma financial statements are not necessarily indicative of the results of operations or related effects on financial position that would have been attained had the above-mentioned transaction (event) actually occurred earlier.

Based on our review, nothing came to our attention that caused us to believe that management's assumptions do not provide a reasonable basis for presenting the significant effects directly attributable to the above-mentioned transaction (event) described in Note 1, that the related pro forma adjustments do not give appropriate effect to those assumptions, or that the pro forma column does not reflect the proper application of those adjustments to the historical financial statement amounts in the pro forma balance sheet as of December 31, 20XX, and the pro forma statement of income for the year then ended.

[*firm's signature*]

[*city, state*]

[*date*]

APPENDIX 12K EXAMINATION REPORT: QUALIFIED BECAUSE OF A SCOPE LIMITATION

Independent Accountant's Report

To the Board of Directors of
XYZ Company
[*city, state*]

We have examined the pro forma adjustments reflecting the transaction (event) described in Note 1 and the application of those adjustments to the historical amounts in the accompanying pro forma balance sheet of XYZ Company as of December 31, 20XX, and the pro forma statement of income for the year then ended. These historical financial statements are derived from the historical financial statements of XYZ Company, which were audited by us, and of ABC Company, which were audited by other accountants, appearing elsewhere herein (incorporated by reference). Such pro forma adjustments are based on management's assumptions as described in Note 2. XYZ Company's management is responsible for the pro forma financial information. Our responsibility is to express an opinion on the pro forma financial information based on our examination.

Except as described below, our examination was conducted in accordance with attestation standards established by the American Institute of Certified Public Accountants and, accordingly, included such procedures as we considered necessary in the circumstances. We believe that our examination provides a reasonable basis for our opinion.

We were unable to perform the examination procedures we considered necessary with respect to assumptions relating to the proposed loan described in Adjustment E in Note 2.

The objective of this pro forma financial information is to show what the significant effects on historical financial information might have been had the transaction (event) occurred at an earlier date. However, the pro forma financial statements are not necessarily indicative of the results of operations or related effects on financial position that would have been attained had the above-mentioned transaction (event) actually occurred earlier.

In our opinion, except for the effects of such changes, if any, as might have been determined to be necessary had we been able to satisfy ourselves as to the assumptions relating to the proposed loan, management's assumptions provide a reasonable basis for presenting the significant effects directly attributable to the above-mentioned transaction (event) described in Note 1, that the related pro forma adjustments give appropriate effect to those assumptions, and the pro forma column reflects the proper application of those adjustments to the historical financial statement amounts in the pro forma balance sheet as of December 31, 20XX, and the pro forma statement of income for the year then ended.

[*firm's signature*]

[*city, state*]

[*date*]

APPENDIX 12L EXAMINATION REPORT: QUALIFIED BECAUSE OF RESERVATIONS ABOUT THE PROPRIETY OF ASSUMPTIONS ON AN ACQUISITION TRANSACTION

Independent Accountant's Report

To the Board of Directors of
XYZ Company
[*city, state*]

We have examined the pro forma adjustments reflecting the transaction (event) described in Note 1 and the application of those adjustments to the historical amounts in the accompanying pro forma balance sheet of XYZ Company as of December 31, 20XX, and the pro forma statement of income for the year then ended. These historical financial statements are derived from the historical financial statements of XYZ Company, which were audited by us, and of ABC Company, which were audited by other accountants, appearing elsewhere herein (incorporated by reference). Such pro forma adjustments are based on management's assumptions as described in Note 2. XYZ Company's management is responsible for the pro forma financial information. Our responsibility is to express an opinion on the pro forma financial information based on our examination.

Our examination was conducted in accordance with attestation standards established by the American Institute of Certified Public Accountants and, accordingly, included such procedures as we considered necessary in the circumstances. We believe that our examination provides a reasonable basis for our opinion.

The objective of this pro forma financial information is to show what the significant effects on historical financial information might have been had the transaction (event) occurred at an earlier date. However, the pro forma financial statements are not necessarily indicative of the results of operations or related effects on financial position that would have been attained had the above-mentioned transaction (event) actually occurred earlier.

As discussed in Note 2 to the pro forma financial statements, the pro forma adjustments reflect management's assumption that X Division of the acquired company will be sold. The net assets of this division are reflected at their historical carrying amount; generally accepted accounting principles require these net assets to be recorded at estimated net realizable value.

In our opinion, except for the inappropriate valuation of the net assets of X Division, management's assumptions provide a reasonable basis for presenting the significant effects directly attributable to the above-mentioned transaction (event) described in Note 1, that the related pro forma adjustments give appropriate effect to those assumptions, and the pro forma column reflects the proper application of those adjustments to the historical financial statement amounts in the pro forma balance sheet as of December 31, 20XX, and the pro forma statement of income for the year then ended.

[*firm's signature*]

[*city, state*]

[*date*]

APPENDIX 12M
DISCLAIMER OF OPINION BECAUSE OF A SCOPE LIMITATION

Independent Accountant's Report

To the Board of Directors of
XYZ Company
[*city, state*]

We were engaged to examine the pro forma adjustments reflecting the transaction (event) described in Note 1 and the application of those adjustments to the historical amounts in the accompanying pro forma balance sheet of XYZ Company as of December 31, 20XX, and the pro forma statement of income for the year then ended. These historical financial statements are derived from the historical financial statements of XYZ Company, which were audited by us, and of ABC Company, which were audited by other accountants, appearing elsewhere herein (incorporated by reference). Such pro forma adjustments are based on management's assumptions as described in Note 2. XYZ Company's management is responsible for the pro forma financial information. Our responsibility is to express an opinion on the pro forma financial information based on our examination.

As discussed in Note 2 to the pro forma financial statements, the pro forma adjustments reflect management's assumptions that the elimination of duplicate facilities would have resulted in a 30 percent reduction in operating costs. Management could not supply us with sufficient evidence to support this assertion.

The objective of this pro forma financial information is to show what the significant effects on historical financial information might have been had the transaction (event) occurred at an earlier date. However, the pro forma financial statements are not necessarily indicative of the results of operations or related effects on financial position that would have been attained had the above-mentioned transaction (event) actually occurred earlier.

Because we were unable to evaluate management's assumptions regarding the reduction in operating costs and other assumptions related thereto, the scope of our work was not sufficient to express and, therefore, we do not express an opinion on the pro forma adjustments, management's underlying assumptions regarding those assumptions and the application of those adjustments to the historical financial statement amounts in the pro forma balance sheet as of December 31, 20XX, and the pro forma statement of income for the year then ended.

[*firm's signature*]

[*city, state*]

[*date*]

APPENDIX 12N COMPILATION REPORT ON PRO FORMA FINANCIAL INFORMATION

To the Board of Directors of
XYZ Company
[*city, state*]

(I) We have compiled the accompanying pro forma financial information as of and for the year ended December 31, 20XX, reflecting the business combination of the Company and ABC Company in accordance with Statements on Standards for Accounting and Review Services issued by the American Institute of Certified Public Accountants. The historical condensed financial statements are derived from the historical unaudited financial statements of XYZ Company, which were compiled by me (us), and of ABC Company, which were compiled by another (other) accountant(s).

A compilation is limited to presenting pro forma financial information that is the representation of management (owners). I (we) have not audited or reviewed the accompanying pro forma financial information and, accordingly, do not express an opinion or any other form of assurance on it.

The objective of this pro forma financial information is to show what the significant effects on the historical financial information might have been had the transaction (or event) occurred at an earlier date. However, the pro forma financial information is not necessarily indicative of the results of operations or related effects on financial position that would have been attained had the above-mentioned transaction (or event) actually occurred earlier.

[*firm's signature*]

[*city, state*]

[*date*]

APPENDIX 12O
ENGAGEMENT LETTER: ACQUISITION ASSISTANCE ENGAGEMENT, CONSULTING SERVICES

[*date*]

[*name of client*]
[*address*]

We are pleased to confirm our understanding of the terms and objectives of our engagement and the nature and limitations of the services we are to provide for [*client's legal name*].

The objective of our engagement is to assist you with your investigation and analysis of [*target*]. We will perform inquiries and analyses based on the information made available to us. Our assistance will be directed to those business activities, operational areas, and financial information that you have identified as being of concern to you. In performing our services, we will be relying on the sufficiency, accuracy, and reliability of information provide by [*target*].Also, our ability to complete our work will depend on the cooperation of the management of [*target*].

We will perform the procedures listed in Exhibit 1 to this letter. The sufficiency of the procedures is solely your responsibility. Our procedures are limited to those which you have determined will best meet your informational needs and may not necessarily disclose all significant errors, fraud, or illegal acts that may exist.

At the conclusion of our engagement, we will require a representation letter from [*target*]. We will also ask you to provide a representation letter stating that the procedures performed were consistent with the procedures you requested and that you have made available to us all financial records and data received from [*target*].

At the conclusion of our engagement, we will present our findings to you in an oral report.We will also report to you in writing our comments and observations based on the results of our procedures. Furthermore, it will state that we will not independently verify the information gathered or contained in our report and, accordingly, that our report will include a statement that the information is presented based on discussions with and information provided by [*target*]. Our procedures will not constitute an audit, review, or compilation of the information provided and, accordingly, we will not express a conclusion or provide any other form of assurance on the completeness or accuracy of the information.

Our report is suitable for use only by those who have participated in determining the procedures. Consequently, our report will be restricted to your internal use only. We have no responsibility to update our report for events and circumstances that occur after the date of its issuance. If for any reason we are unable to complete the engagement, we will not issue a report as a result of the engagement.

We plan to begin our procedures on approximately [*date*] and, unless unforeseeable problems are encountered, the engagement should be completed by [*date*].

We estimate that our fees for these services will range from $____ to $____. You will also be billed for travel and other out-of-pocket costs such as report production, typing, postage, etc. Additional expenses are estimated to be $____. The fee estimate is based on anticipated cooperation from your personnel, personnel of [*target*], and the assumption that unexpected circumstances will not be encountered during the engagement. If significant additional time is necessary, we will discuss it with you and arrive at a new fee estimate before we incur the additional costs. Payment of our fees is not in any way contingent on the final outcome of the proposed transaction.

We will require a retainer of $____ at the execution of this agreement. Our invoices for these services will be rendered each month as work progresses and are payable on presentation. In accordance with our firm policies, work may be suspended if your account becomes ____ days or more overdue and will not be resumed until your account is paid in full. If we elect to terminate our services for nonpayment, our engagement will be deemed to have been completed upon written notification of termination, even if we have not completed our report. You will be obligated to compensate us for all time extended and to reimburse us for all out-of-pocket expenditures through the date of termination.

We appreciate the opportunity to be of service to you and believe this letter accurately summarizes the significant terms of our engagement. If you have any questions, please let us know. If you agree with the terms of our engagement as described in this letter, please sign the enclosed copy and return it to us. If the need for additional services arises, our agreement with you will need to be revised. It is customary for us to enumerate these revisions in an addendum to this letter.

Very truly yours,

[*CPA firm's name*]

Response:

This letter correctly sets forth the understanding of [*client*].

By:

Title:

Date:

APPENDIX 12P
PROCEDURES CHECKLIST: ACQUISITION ASSISTANCE ENGAGEMENT, CONSULTING SERVICES

Client Name: ____________________ Date of Subject Matter: ____________

Completed by: ____________________ Date Completed: ________________

	Completed by	N/A
1. Conduct a pre-engagement meeting with the client:		
a. Determine the scope of the engagement.	________	________
b. Determine whether a written report will be issued.	________	________
c. Obtain and read relevant documentation related to the proposed acquisition (such as the purchase agreement, the selling memorandum, other correspondence related to the proposed acquisition, or other information or data provided to the client by the target).	________	________
2. Complete the Client Acceptance and Retention Evaluation Form.	________	________
3. Establish in an engagement letter an understanding with the client regarding the nature, scope, and limitations of the services to be performed.	________	________
4. Ensure that any conflicts of interest have been disclosed to and accepted by the client.	________	________

		Completed by	N/A
5.	Determine that the scheduling and staffing are adequate to perform the engagement.	______	______
6.	Obtain the engagement partner's approval of the overall engagement plan.	______	______
7.	Include in the workpapers a list of all procedures referenced in the engagement letter, or include a copy of the engagement letter.	______	______
8.	Perform the procedures and summarize the findings.	______	______
9.	If the nature or scope of the engagement is changed, obtain the client's written approval of the change.	______	______
10.	Draft the report.	______	______
11.	Determine that all questions, exceptions, or notes, if any, posed during the engagement have been followed up and resolved.	______	______
12.	Determine that all required forms, questionnaires, and checklists have been completed.	______	______
13.	Ensure that the workpapers and report have been reviewed in accordance with firm policy.	______	______
14.	Obtain engagement partner's review and approval for issuance of report.	______	______

APPENDIX 12Q
TARGET REPRESENTATION LETTER: ACQUISITION ASSISTANCE ENGAGEMENT, CONSULTING SERVICES

[*date—No earlier than date of the accountant's report*]

[*CPA firm's name*]
[*address*]

In connection with your engagement to assist [*client*] with its investigation and analysis of [*target*], we confirm to the best of our knowledge and belief, the following representations made to you during the course of your engagement:

- We are responsible for the fair presentation in the financial statements of financial position, results of operations, and cash flows in conformity with generally accepted accounting principles and all representations made to you during the course of your engagement, whether oral or written.
- We have made available to you all:
  - — Financial records and related data.
  - — Minutes of the meetings of stockholders, directors, and committees of directors, or summaries of actions of recent meetings for which minutes have not yet been prepared.

- There have been no:
  - — Fraudulent financial reporting or misappropriation of assets involving management or employees who have significant roles in internal control.
  - — Fraudulent financial reporting or misappropriation of assets involving other employees that could have a material effect on the financial statements.
  - — Communications from regulatory agencies concerning noncompliance with, or deficiencies in, financial reporting practices.
- We have no plans or intentions that may materially affect the carrying value or classification of assets and liabilities.
- The following have been properly recorded or disclosed to you:
  - — Related-party transactions and related accounts receivable or payable, including sales, purchases, loans, transfers, leasing arrangements, and guarantees.
  - — Guarantees, whether written or oral, under which the company is liable.
  - — Capital stock repurchase options or agreements or capital stock reserved for options, warrants, conversions, or other requirements.
  - — Arrangements with financial institutions involving compensating balances or other arrangements involving restrictions on cash balances and lines of credit or similar arrangements.
  - — Agreements to repurchase assets previously sold.
- There are no:
  - — Violations or possible violations of laws or regulations whose effect should be considered for disclosure in the financial statements or as a basis for recording a loss contingency.
  - — Other liabilities or gain or loss contingencies that are required to be accrued or disclosed by Statement of Financial Accounting Standards No. 5.
- There are no unasserted claims or assessments that our lawyer has advised us are probable of assertion and must be disclosed in accordance with Statement of Financial Accounting Standards No. 5.
- There are no material transactions that have not been properly recorded in the accounting records underlying the financial statements.
- Provision, when material, has been made to reduce excess or obsolete inventories to their estimated net realizable value.
- The company has satisfactory title to all owned assets, and there are no liens or encumbrances on such assets nor has any asset been pledged.
- Provision has been made for any material loss to be sustained in the fulfillment of, or from inability to fulfill, any sales commitments.
- Provision has been made for any material loss to be sustained as a result of purchase commitments for inventory quantities in excess of normal requirements or at prices in excess of prevailing market prices.

- We have complied with all aspects of contractual agreements that would have a material effect on the financial statements in the event of noncompliance.
- We have identified all accounting estimates that could be material to the financial statements, including the key factors and significant assumptions underlying those estimates, and we believe the estimates are reasonable in the circumstances.
- There are no such estimates that may be subject to material change in the near term that have not been properly disclosed in the financial statements. We understand that near term means the period within one year of the date of the financial statements.
- No events have occurred subsequent to the balance sheet date that would require adjustment to, or disclosure in, the most recently available financial statements.
- We have been provided with a copy of your draft report to [*client*] dated [*date*], and we are not aware of any significant errors or misstatements contained in that report.
- We understand that the report is for the information and use of management and the board of directors of [*client*] and that the report should not be used by anyone other than these specified parties.

Signature:	Signature:
Title:	Title:

APPENDIX 12R
CLIENT REPRESENTATION LETTER: ACQUISITION ASSISTANCE ENGAGEMENT, CONSULTING SERVICES

[*date—No earlier than date of the accountant's report*]

[*CPA firm's name*]
[*address*]

In connection with your engagement to assist us with our investigation and analysis of [*target*], we confirm to the best of our knowledge and belief, the following representations made to you during the course of your engagement:

- We have made available to you all financial records and related data received from [*target*].
- The procedures you performed were consistent with the procedures we requested.
- The sufficiency of the procedures is solely our responsibility.
- Your procedures were limited to those that we determined would best need our informational needs and may not necessarily disclose all significant errors, fraud, or illegal acts that may exist.

- Your report is suitable for use only by those who have participated in determining the procedures. Consequently, your report will be restricted to our internal use only.
- We have responded fully to all inquiries made to us by you during your engagement.
- We have reviewed a copy of your draft report dated [*date*], and we are not aware of any significant errors or misstatements contained in that report.
- We understand that the report is for the information and use of management and the board of directors of [*client*] and that the report should not be used by anyone other than these specified parties.

Signature:	Signature:
Title:	Title:

APPENDIX 12S
ACQUISITION ASSISTANCE ENGAGEMENT: CONSULTING SERVICES REPORT

[*date of report*]

To the Board of Directors of
[*name of client*]
[*city, state*]

Introduction

We have concluded our engagement to assist you with your investigation and analysis of [*target*]. This report presents our comments and recommendations based on the results of our procedures.

Nature of the Information

The information presented is based on discussions with and information provided by [*target*]. We have not independently verified the information gathered or contained in this report and, accordingly, our procedures do not constitute an audit, review, or compilation of the information provided. Thus, we do not express a conclusion or provide any other form of assurance on the completeness or accuracy of the information.

Our assistance was directed to those business activities, operational areas, and financial information that you identified as being of concern to you. In performing our services, we performed inquiries and analyses based on the information made available to us, and we relied on the sufficiency, accuracy, and reliability of information provided by [*buyer*].

Procedures Performed

We performed the procedures enumerated in the engagement letter dated [*date*]. A copy of the engagement letter is presented in Attachment A. The procedures were limited to those which you determined best met your informational needs and cannot be relied upon to disclose all significant matters about [*target*] or to disclose errors, fraud, or other illegal acts that may exist. Had we performed additional procedures or had we conducted an audit or review of the financial statements, other matters might have come to our attention that would have been reported to you.

You reviewed a draft of our report in order to confirm that the procedures performed were consistent with those requested by you. In addition, we have made our workpapers available to you and you have obtained copies as you determined appropriate. We have also reviewed a draft of our report with [*target*] in order to confirm its factual accuracy.

The financial statements presented in Attachment B have not been audited, reviewed, or compiled by us and, accordingly, we assume no responsibility for them.

Use of the Report

Due to its special nature, our report may not be suitable for any purpose other than to assist you in your evaluation of [*target*]. Consequently, our report is for your information and use only and should not be used by anyone else. In addition, our report is based on current circumstances. Given the fact that many aspects of the transaction either have not been finalized or are not yet documented, certain changes may materially affect the financial events and circumstances that occur after [*date of report*].

Sincerely,

[*firm's signature*]

[*city, state*]

[*date*]

Comments and Recommendations

Source of Information

The information presented is based on discussions with and information provided by [*target*]. Members of [*target*] management interviewed included:

[*name*]—President

[*name*]—Treasurer and Controller

[*name*]—Senior Accountant

[*name*]—Materials Manager

Background and History

Terms of the Acquisition

[*Describe the terms of the proposed acquisition.*]

History

[*Discuss relevant information pertaining to target's history.*]

Organizational Structure

[*Describe organizational structure of ownership and management.*]

Operating Characteristics

[*Describe operating characteristics such as locations, major products, major customers, marketing methods, major suppliers, and financing sources.*]

Industry

[*Provide a brief overview of the industry.*]

*Analysis of [*target*]*

Balance Sheet

- Cash
- Accounts Receivable
- Inventory
- Prepaid Assets
- Property, Plant, and Equipment
- Intangible Assets
- Accounts Payable
- Accrued Expenses
- Notes Payable
- Long-Term Debt

Income Statement

- Sales
- Cost of Goods Sold
- Operating Expenses

Commitments and Contingencies

Related-Party Transactions

Information Systems

Workforce

CHAPTER 13 PROSPECTIVE FINANCIAL INFORMATION

CONTENTS

OVERVIEW

This chapter discusses engagements related to prospective financial statements. Prospective financial statements include both financial forecasts and financial projections. Three types of engagements are covered in this chapter: compilation engagements, examination engagements, and agreed-upon procedures engagements. In addition, partial presentations are discussed, along with reporting implications when prospective financial statements are included in documents containing other information.

INTRODUCTION

Chapter 3 of SSAE-10 (AT 301) sets forth the standards for engagements related to prospective financial statements. Prospective financial statements are prospective financial information that presents financial position, results of operations, and cash flows. There are two kinds of prospective financial statements: (1) financial forecasts and (2) financial projections. In addition, the practitioner may be involved with partial presentations. A partial presentation is a presentation of prospective financial information that excludes one or more of the minimum items required for prospective financial statement presentations. A practitioner may also be engaged to prepare a financial analysis of a potential project where the engagement includes obtaining the information, making appropriate assumptions, and assembling the presentation. Such an analysis is not a forecast or projection and should not be called, or used, as such (unless the client adopts the assumptions and takes responsibility for them).

Chapter 3 of SSAE-10 (AT301.02) states that the practitioner should perform an examination, compilation, or agreed-upon procedures engagement, whenever he or she

- Submits to his or her client or others prospective financial statements that the practitioner has assembled or assisted in assembling that are or reasonably might be expected to be used by another (third) party; or

- Reports on prospective financial statements that are or reasonably might be expected to be used by another (third) party.

In deciding whether the prospective financial statements are or reasonably might be expected to be used by a third party, the practitioner may rely on either the written or oral representations of the responsible party, unless information comes to his or her attention that contradicts the responsible party's representation.

> **OBSERVATION:** If third-party use of the prospective financial statements is not reasonably expected, the provisions of Chapter 3 of SSAE-10 are not applicable, unless the practitioner has been engaged to examine, compile, or apply agreed-upon procedures to the prospective financial statements. In other words, the practitioner can assemble prospective financial statements without reporting on them if the prospective financial statements are not reasonably expected to be used by a third party.

In reporting on prospective financial statements, the practitioner may assist the responsible party in identifying assumptions, gathering information, or assembling the statements. The responsible party is nonetheless responsible for the preparation and presentation of the prospective financial statements because the prospective financial statements are dependent on the actions, plans, and assumptions of the responsible party, and only the responsible party can take responsibility for the assumptions. Accordingly, the practitioner's engagement should not be characterized in his or her report as including "preparation" of the prospective financial statements. A practitioner may be engaged to prepare a financial analysis of a potential project, including obtaining the information, making appropriate assumptions, and assembling the presentation. Such an analysis is not and should not be characterized as a forecast or projection and would not be appropriate for general use. However, if the responsible party reviewed and adopted the assumptions and presentation, or based its assumptions and presentation on the analysis, the practitioner could perform one of the engagements described in this chapter and issue a general-use report.

The concept of materiality affects the application of the professional standards to prospective financial statements just as materiality affects the application of generally accepted auditing standards to historical financial statements. Materiality is a concept that is judged in light of the expected range of reasonableness of the information; therefore, users should not expect prospective information to be as precise as historical information.

TYPES OF PROSPECTIVE FINANCIAL STATEMENTS

There are two kinds of prospective financial statements: (1) financial forecasts and (2) financial projections.

Forecast

Forecasts present, to the best of the responsible party's knowledge and belief, an entity's expected financial position, results of operations, and cash flows. A financial forecast is based on the responsible party's assumptions reflecting the conditions it expects to exist and the course of action it expects to take. A financial forecast may be expressed in specific monetary amounts as a single point estimate of forecasted results or as a range, where the responsible party selects key assumptions to form a range within which it reasonably expects the item or items to fall.

Projection

Projections present, to the best of the responsible party's knowledge and belief, given one or more hypothetical assumptions, an entity's expected financial position, results of operations, and cash flows. A financial projection is sometimes prepared to present one or more hypothetical courses of action for evaluation, as in response to a question such as "What would happen if . . .?" A financial projection is based on the responsible party's assumptions reflecting conditions it expects would exist and the course of action it expects would be taken, given one or more hypothetical assumptions. A projection, like a forecast, may contain a range.

Case Study 13-1: Forecast versus Projection

Scenario 1 Facts

Connor Manufacturing is in the process of searching for long-term financing, which management expects it will receive. In addition to traditional historical financial statements, creditors also wish to review information about the company's financial prospects for the future.

Based on current industry conditions and its marketing plans, management believes that sales will increase 2% in the upcoming two-year period. This increase in sales will not require any additions to its manufacturing capacity. The company's relationship with its major suppliers is stable, and there are no signs of any significant shortages. The company's labor contract covers most of its employees and will be in effect for another two years. Additionally, management expects that it will be able to obtain an extension of its existing short-term line of credit.

Scenario 2 Facts

Assume the same facts as in Scenario 1 except that the company is considering the construction of a new plant. In order to secure this financing, lenders have asked for financial statements that would show the company's financial position if it received the financing and if it successfully completed the construction of the plant.

Scenario 1 Analysis

Connor Manufacturing should prepare a financial forecast.

Scenario 2 Analysis

Connor should prepare a financial projection. The construction of the plant is not an action that management expects to take but, rather, an action it would take if it received the financing. In effect, the lenders have asked "What would the company's financial position look like if . . . we grant financing and the project gets built?"

USES OF PROSPECTIVE FINANCIAL STATEMENTS

General Use

The term "general use" refers to the use of prospective financial statements by persons that the responsible party is not negotiating with directly (for example, in an offering statement of an entity's debt or equity securities). Recipients of prospective financial statements distributed for general use are unable to ask the responsible party directly about the presentation. Therefore, the presentation most useful to them is the one that portrays, to the best of the responsible party's knowledge and belief, the expected results. Thus, only a financial forecast is appropriate for general use.

Limited Use

The term "limited use" refers to the use of prospective financial statements by the responsible party alone or the responsible party and third parties that the responsible party is negotiating with directly. Examples include use in negotiations for a bank loan, submission to a regulatory agency, and use solely within the entity. Third-party recipients of prospective financial statements intended for limited use can ask questions of the responsible party and negotiate directly with it. Any type of prospective financial statements that would be useful in the circumstances would normally be appropriate for limited use. Thus, the presentation may be a financial forecast or a financial projection.

DEFINITIONS

For purposes of Chapter 3 of SSAE-10 (AT 301), the following definitions apply:

- *Prospective financial statements* Either financial forecasts or financial projections including the summaries of significant assumptions and accounting policies. Although prospective financial statements may cover a period that has partially expired, statements for periods that have completely expired are not considered to be prospective financial statements. Pro forma financial statements and partial presentations are not considered to be prospective financial statements.
- *Partial presentation* A presentation of financial information that excludes one or more of the items required for prospective financial statements as described below.
- *Entity* Any unit, existing or to be formed, for which financial statements could be prepared in accordance with GAAP or an other comprehensive basis of accounting. For example, an entity can be an individual, partnership, corporation, trust, estate, association, or governmental unit.
- *Hypothetical assumption* An assumption used in a financial projection to present a condition or course of action that is not necessarily expected to occur, but is consistent with the purpose of the projection.
- *Responsible party* The person or persons who are responsible for the assumptions underlying the prospective financial statements. The responsible party usually is management, but it can be persons outside of the entity who do not currently have the authority to direct operations (for example, a party considering acquiring an entity).

- *Assembly* The manual or computer processing of mathematical or other clerical functions related to the presentation of the prospective financial statements. Assembly does not refer to the mere reproduction and collation of such statements or to the responsible party's use of the practitioner's computer processing hardware or software.
- *Key factors* The significant matters on which the entity's future results are expected to depend. Such factors are basic to the entity's operations and thus encompass matters that affect, among other things, the entity's sales, production, service, and financing activities. Key factors serve as a foundation for prospective financial statements and are the bases for the assumptions.

PRESENTATION

Minimum Presentation Guidelines

Prospective information presented in the format of historical financial statements facilitates comparisons with financial position, results of operations, and cash flows of prior periods, as well as those actually achieved for the prospective period. Accordingly, Chapter 3 of SSAE- 10 (AT 301.68) states that prospective financial statements should preferably be in the format of historical financial statements that would be issued for the period(s) covered unless there is an agreement between the responsible party and potential users specifying another format. Prospective financial statements may take the form of complete basic financial statements or be limited to the following minimum items (which would be presented for historical financial statements for the period):

- Sales or gross revenue.
- Gross profit or cost of sales.
- Unusual or infrequently occurring items.
- Provision for income taxes.
- Discontinued operations or extraordinary items.
- Income from continuing operations.
- Net income.
- Basic and diluted earnings per share.
- Significant changes in financial position.
- A description of what the responsible party intends the prospective financial statements to present, a statement that the assumptions are based on the responsible party's judgment

at the time the prospective information was prepared, and a caveat that the prospective results might not be achieved.

- Summary of significant assumptions.
- Summary of significant accounting policies.

A presentation that omits one or more of the applicable minimum items above is a partial presentation, which would not ordinarily be appropriate for general use.

OBSERVATION: The minimum items that constitute a presentation of a financial forecast or projection are specified in the AICPA Audit and Accounting Guide *Guide for Prospective Financial Information,* which includes complete presentation guidelines along with illustrative presentations.

OBSERVATION: The usual footnotes associated with historical financial statements need not be included as such. However, significant assumptions and accounting policies should be disclosed.

OBSERVATION: Similar types of financial information should be presented for entities for which these terms do not describe operations. Further, similar items should be presented if a comprehensive basis of accounting other than GAAP is used to present the prospective financial statements. For example, if the cash basis was used, "cash receipts" would be used in the statement instead of "sales or gross receipts."

OBSERVATION: The responsible party should disclose significant cash flows and other significant changes in balance sheet accounts during the period. However, neither a balance sheet nor a statement of cash flows is required.

Partial Presentations

A presentation that omits one or more of the applicable items listed above is a partial presentation. A partial presentation is ordinarily not appropriate for general use; accordingly, partial presentations should be restricted for use by specified parties who will be negotiating directly with the responsible party. The practitioner's procedures on partial presentations may be affected by the nature of the information presented. Many elements of prospective financial statements are interrelated. According to Chapter 3 of SSAE-10 (AT 301.57), when a practitioner has been engaged to examine or compile a partial presentation, he or she should give appropriate consideration to whether key factors affecting elements, accounts, and interrelated items have been considered. This consideration includes key factors that might not necessarily be obvious to the partial presentation (for example, productive capacity relative to a sales forecast). The practitioner should also consider whether all significant assumptions have been disclosed.

Because partial presentations are generally appropriate only for limited use, reports on partial presentations of both forecasted and projected information should include a description of any limitations on the usefulness of the presentation.

TYPES OF ENGAGEMENTS

Chapter 3 of SSAE-10 (AT 301) provides standards and procedures for three types of engagements that may be performed on prospective financial statements: (1) examinations, (2) compilations, and (3) agreed-upon procedures engagements.

Examination

An examination of prospective financial statements involves

- Evaluating the preparation of the prospective financial statements.
- Evaluating the support underlying the assumptions.
- Evaluating the presentation of the prospective financial statements for conformity with AICPA presentation guidelines detailed in the AICPA Audit and Accounting Guide *Guide for Prospective Financial Information.*
- Issuing and examination report.

As a result of his or her examination, the practitioner has a basis for reporting on whether, in his or her opinion

- The prospective financial statements are presented in conformity with AICPA guidelines.
- The assumptions provide a reasonable basis for the responsible party's forecast.
- The assumptions provide a reasonable basis for the responsible party's projection given the hypothetical assumptions.

Compilation

A compilation of prospective financial statements involves

- Assembling, to the extent necessary, the prospective financial statements based on the responsible party's assumptions.

- Performing the required compilation procedures, including reading the prospective financial statements with their summaries of significant assumptions and accounting policies, and considering whether they appear to be presented in conformity with AICPA presentation guidelines and are not obviously inappropriate.
- Issuing a compilation report.

A compilation is not intended to provide assurance on the prospective financial statements or the assumptions underlying the statements. Because of the limited nature of the practitioner's procedures, a compilation does not provide assurance that the practitioner will become aware of significant matters that might be disclosed by more extensive procedures, for example in an examination.

Agreed-Upon Procedures

An agreed-upon procedures engagement is one in which a practitioner is engaged by a client to issue a report of findings based on specific procedures performed on the prospective financial statements. Generally, in an engagement to apply agreed-upon procedures to prospective financial statements, the practitioner's procedures may be as limited or as extensive as the specified parties desire, as long as the specified parties take responsibility for their sufficiency.

COMPILATION OF PROSPECTIVE FINANCIAL STATEMENTS

A compilation of prospective financial statements involves

- Assembling, to the extent necessary, the prospective financial statements based on the responsible party's assumptions.
- Performing the required compilation procedures, including reading the prospective financial statements with their summaries of significant assumptions and accounting policies, and considering whether they appear to be presented in conformity with AICPA presentation guidelines and are not obviously inappropriate.
- Issuing a compilation report.

A compilation is not intended to provide assurance on the prospective financial statements or the assumptions underlying the statements.

Standards

The following standards apply to a compilation of prospective financial statements and to the resulting report:

- The compilation should be performed by a person or persons having adequate technical training and proficiency to compile prospective financial statements.
- Due professional care should be exercised in the performance of the compilation and the preparation of the report.
- The work should be adequately planned, and assistants, if any, should be properly supervised.
- Applicable compilation procedures should be performed as a basis for reporting on the compiled prospective financial statements.
- The report based on the practitioner's compilation of prospective financial statements should conform to the applicable guidance in Chapter 3 of SSAE-10 (AT 301.18).

The summary of significant assumptions is essential to the reader's understanding of prospective financial statements. Accordingly, the practitioner should not compile prospective financial statements that exclude disclosure of the summary of significant assumptions. Also, the practitioner should not compile a financial projection that excludes either (1) an identification of the hypothetical assumptions or (2) a description of the limitations on the usefulness of the presentation.

Training and Proficiency, Planning, and Procedures

Training and Proficiency

The practitioner should be familiar with the guidelines for the preparation and presentation of prospective financial statements. The guidelines are contained in the AICPA Audit and Accounting Guide *Guide for Prospective Financial Information*.

The practitioner should posses or obtain a level of knowledge of the industry and the accounting principles and practices of the industry that the entity operates in or will operate in sufficient to enable him or her to compile prospective financial statements that are appropriate in form for an entity operating in that industry.

Planning the Compilation Engagement

To compile the prospective financial statements of an existing entity, the accountant should obtain a general knowledge of the nature of the entity's business transactions and the key factors that its future financial results appear to depend on. He or she should also obtain an understanding of the accounting principles and practices of the entity to determine whether they are comparable to those used within the industry that the entity operates in.

To compile the prospective financial statements of a proposed entity, the practitioner should obtain knowledge of the proposed operations and the key factors that its future results appear to depend on and that have affected the performance of entities in the same industry.

Compilation Procedures

In performing a compilation of prospective financial statements, the practitioner should, where applicable

- Establish an understanding with the client, preferably in writing, regarding the services to be performed. The understanding should include the objectives of the engagement, the client's responsibilities, the accountant's responsibilities, and the limitations of the engagement. The practitioner should document the understanding in the workpapers, preferably through a written communication with the client. If the accountant believes an understanding with the client has not been established, he or she should decline to accept or perform the engagement. Appendix 13A is an illustrative engagement letter for a compilation of prospective financial statements.
- Inquire about the accounting principles used in the preparation of the prospective financial statements:
  - — For existing entities, compare the accounting principles used will those used in preparation of previous historical financial statements and inquire whether the principles are the same as those expected to be used in the historical financial statements covering the prospective period.
  - — For entities to be formed or entities formed that have not commenced operations, compare specialized industry accounting principles used, if any, with those typically used in the industry. Inquire about whether the accounting principles used for the prospective financial statements are those that are expected to be used when, or if, the entity commences operations.
- Ask how the responsible party identifies the key factors and develops its assumptions.
- List, or obtain a list of, the responsible party's significant assumptions providing the basis for the prospective financial statements and consider whether there are any obvious omissions in light of the key factors that the prospective results of the entity appear to depend on.

- Consider whether there appear to be any obvious internal inconsistencies in the assumptions.
- Perform, or test the mathematical accuracy of, the computations that translate the assumptions into prospective financial statements.
- Read the prospective financial statements, including the summary of significant assumptions, and consider whether
  - — The statements, including the disclosures of assumptions and accounting policies, appear not to be presented in conformity with the AICPA presentation guidelines for prospective financial statements.
  - — The statements, including the summary of significant assumptions, appear not to be obviously inappropriate in relation to the accountant's knowledge of the entity and its industry and
    - (i) For a financial forecast, the expected conditions and course of action in the prospective period.
    - (ii) For a financial projection, the purpose of the presentation.
- If a significant part of the prospective period has expired, inquire about the results of operations or significant portions of the operations (such as sales volume), and significant changes in financial position, and consider their effect in relation to the prospective financial statements. If historical financial statements have been prepared for the expired portion of the period, the practitioner should read the statements and consider those results in relation to the prospective financial statements.
- Confirm his or her understanding of the statements (including assumptions) by obtaining written representations from the responsible party. Because the amounts reflected in the statements are not supported by historical books and records but, rather, by assumptions, the practitioner should obtain representations in which the responsible party states its responsibility for the assumptions. The representations should be signed by the responsible party at the highest level of authority who the practitioner believes is responsible for and knowledgeable, directly or through others, about matters covered by the representations:
  - — For a financial forecast, the representations should include a statement that the financial forecast presents, to the best of the responsible party's knowledge and belief, the expected financial position, results of operations, and cash flows for the forecast period and that the forecast reflects the responsible party's judgment, based on present circumstances, of the expected conditions and its expected course of action. If the forecast contains a range, the representation

should also include a statement that, to the best of the responsible party's knowledge and belief, the items subject to the assumption are expected to actually fall within the range and that the range was not selected in a biased or misleading manner.

— For a financial projection, the representations should include a statement that the financial projection presents, to the best of the responsible party's knowledge and belief, the expected financial position, results of operations, and cash flows for the projection period given the hypothetical assumptions, and that the projection reflects its judgment based on present circumstances, of expected conditions and its expected course of action given the occurrence of the hypothetical events. The representations should also (1) identify the hypothetical assumptions and describe the limitations on the usefulness of the presentation, (2) state that the assumptions are appropriate, (3) state whether the hypothetical assumptions are improbable, and (4) if the projection contains a range, include a statement that, to the best of the responsible party's knowledge and belief, given the hypothetical assumptions, the item or items subject to the assumption are expected to actually fall within the range and that the range was not selected in a biased or misleading manner. The representations should also include a statement that the projection is presented in conformity with guidelines for presentation of a projection established by the American Institute of Certified Public Accountants.

Appendix 13K is an illustrative representation letter.

- Consider, after applying the above procedures, whether he or she has received representations or other information that appears to be obviously inappropriate, incomplete, or otherwise misleading and, if so, attempt to obtain additional or revised information. If the practitioner does not receive such information, her or she should ordinarily withdraw from the compilation engagement. The practitioner need not withdraw from the engagement if the effect of such information on the prospective financial statements does not appear to be material. (Note that the omission of disclosures, other than those relating to significant assumptions, would not require the practitioner to withdraw.)

Case Study 13-2: Key Factors

Facts

Chandler Builders is a developer of apartment complexes. The company is about to begin construction of a new 300-unit complex. Debt financing will be required to finance 70% of the construction cost. After construction, Chandler will lease the individual units. The company would like to prepare a three-year forecast that includes a balance sheet, a statement of income, and a statement of cash flows.

Analysis

Several key factors would be identified, including the following:

- The cost of developing the project will determine the most significant asset on the balance sheet and also depreciation expense (a significant expense). Cost will also indirectly determine the amount of financing, which will be the most significant liability.
- The financing amount and terms will determine debt classification, expense, and cash flow for interest expense.
- Rental rates will determine the maximum amount of revenue that can be generated from the project.
- The lease-up period (how quickly the property will achieve full occupancy) together with rental rates will determine expected revenue and cash inflow during the forecast period.

For each of these key factors, Chandler will need to make assumptions in order to develop its forecast.

Reporting

The practitioner's standard report on a compilation of prospective financial statements should include the following:

- An identification of the prospective financial statements presented by the responsible party.
- A statement that the practitioner has compiled the prospective financial statements in accordance with attestation standards established by the American Institute of Certified Public Accountants.
- A statement that a compilation is limited in scope and does not enable the practitioner to express an opinion or any other form of assurance on the prospective financial statements or the assumptions.
- A caveat that the prospective results might not be achieved
- A statement that the practitioner assumes no responsibility to update the report for events and circumstances occurring after the date of the report.
- The manual or printed signature of the practitioner's firm.
- The date of the compilation report.

Exhibit 13-1 is the form of the standard compilation report on a forecast that does not contain a range:

EXHIBIT 13-1
STANDARD COMPILATION REPORT: FORECAST

[*addressee*]
[*city, state*]

We have compiled the accompanying forecasted balance sheet, statements of income, retained earnings, and cash flows of XYZ Company as of December 31, 20XX, and for the year then ending, in accordance with attestation standards established by the American Institute of Certified Public Accountants.

A compilation is limited to presenting in the form of a forecast information that is the representation of management and does not include an evaluation of the support for the assumptions underlying the forecast. We have not examined the forecast and, accordingly, do not express an opinion or any other form of assurance on the accompanying statements or assumptions. Furthermore, there will usually be differences between the forecasted and actual results, because events and circumstances frequently do not occur as expected, and those differences may be material. We have no responsibility to update this report for events and circumstances occurring after the date of this report.

[*firm's signature*]

[*city, state*]

[*date*]

When the presentation is a projection, the compilation report should include all of the report elements above. In addition, the report should include a statement describing the special purpose for which the projection was prepared as well as a separate paragraph that restricts the use of the report. Exhibit 13-2 is the form of the standard compilation report on a projection that does not contain a range:

EXHIBIT 13-2
STANDARD COMPILATION REPORT: PROJECTION

[*addressee*]
[*city, state*]

We have compiled the accompanying projected balance sheet, statements of income, retained earnings, and cash flows of XYZ Company as of December 31, 20XX, and for the year then ending, in accordance with attestation standards established by the American Institute of Certified Public Accountants. The accompanying projection was prepared for [*state special purpose, for example,* the purpose of negotiating a loan to expand XYZ Company's plant].

A compilation is limited to presenting in the form of a projection information that is the representation of management and does not include an evaluation of the support for the assumptions underlying the projection. We have not examined the projection and, accordingly, do not express an opinion or any other form of assurance on the accompanying statements or assumptions. Furthermore, even if [*describe hypothetical assumption, for example,* the loan is granted and the plant is expanded], there will usually be differences between the projected and actual results, because events and circumstances frequently do not occur as expected, and those differences may be material. We have no responsibility to update this report for events and circumstances occurring after the date of this report.

The accompanying projection and this report are intended solely for the information and use of [*identify specified parties, for example,* XYZ Company and DEF Bank] and are not intended to be and should not be used by anyone other than these specified parties.

[*firm's signature*]

[*city, state*]

[*date*]

Prospective Financial Statements with a Range

When the prospective financial statements contain a range, the practitioner's standard report should include a separate paragraph that states that the responsible party has elected to portray the expected results of one or more assumptions as a range. The following is an example of the separate paragraph to be added when the prospective financial statements, in this case a forecast, contain a range:

> As described in the summary of significant assumptions, management of XYZ Company has elected to portray forecasted [*describe financial statement element or elements for which the expected results of one or more assumptions fall within a range, and identify the assumptions expected to fall within a range, for example,* revenue at the amounts of $X,XXX and $Y,YYY, which is predicated upon occupancy rates of XX percent and YY percent of available apartments,] rather than as a single point estimate. Accordingly, the accompanying forecast presents forecasted financial position, results of operations, and cash flows [*describe one or more assumptions expected to fall within a range, for example,* at such occupancy rates]. However, there is no assurance that the actual results will fall within the range of [describe one or more assumptions expected to fall within a range, for example, "occupancy rates"] presented.

Dating the Report

The date of completion of the practitioner's compilation procedures should be used as the date of the report.

Independence

A practitioner may compile prospective financial statements for an entity that he or she is not independent of. In such circumstances, the practitioner should specifically disclose his or her lack of independence; however, the reason for the lack of independence should not be described. When the practitioner is not independent, the following sentence should be added to the compilation report after the last paragraph:

> We are not independent with respect to XYZ Company.

> **OBSERVATION:** In making a judgment about independence, the practitioner should consult the AICPA Code of Professional Conduct, along with related ethics interpretations and rulings.

Prospective Financial Statements Included with Historical Financial Statements

Prospective financial statements may be included in a document that also contains historical financial statements and the practitioner's report on them. In addition, the historical financial statements that appear in the document may be summarized and presented with the prospective financial statements for comparative purposes. An example of the reference to the practitioner's report on the historical financial statements when he or she audited, reviewed, or compiled those statements is presented below. This reference would be included after the last paragraph in the compilation report:

> The historical financial statements for the year ended December 31, 20XX, [from which the historical data are derived] and our report thereon are set forth on pages XX–XX of this document.

Emphasis of a Matter

In some circumstances, the practitioner might wish to expand his or her report to emphasize a matter regarding the prospective financial statements. Such information may be presented in a separate paragraph of the compilation report. However, the practitioner should exercise care that emphasizing such a matter does not give the impression that he or she is expressing assurance or expanding the degree of responsibility he or she is taking with respect to such information. For example, the practitioner should not include statements in the compilation report about the mathematical accuracy of the statements or their conformity with presentation guidelines.

Report Modifications

An entity may request a practitioner to compile prospective financial statements that contain certain deficiencies or omit disclosures other than those relating to significant assumptions. The practitioner may compile such prospective financial statements provided the deficiency or omission is clearly stated in his or her report and is not, to his or her knowledge, undertaken with the intention of misleading the user(s) of the prospective financial statements.

The following is an example of a paragraph that should be added to the compilation report, in this case a financial forecast, in which the summary of significant accounting policies has been omitted:

> Management has elected to omit the summary of significant accounting policies required by the guidelines for presentation of a forecast established by the American Institute of Certified Public Accountants. If the omitted disclosures were included in the forecast, they might influence the user's conclusions about the Company's financial position, results of operations, and cash flows for the forecast period. Accordingly, this forecast is not designed for those who are not informed about such matters.

If the compiled prospective financial statements are presented on a comprehensive basis of accounting other than GAAP and do not include disclosure of the basis of accounting used, the basis should be disclosed in the compilation report.

EXAMINATION OF PROSPECTIVE FINANCIAL STATEMENTS

An examination of prospective financial statements involves

- Evaluating the preparation of the prospective financial statements.
- Evaluating the support underlying the assumptions.
- Evaluating the presentation of the prospective financial statements for conformity with AICPA presentation guidelines detailed in the AICPA Audit and Accounting Guide *Guide for Prospective Financial Information.*
- Issuing and examination report.

As a result of his or her examination, the practitioner has a basis for reporting on whether, in his or her opinion

- The prospective financial statements are presented in conformity with AICPA guidelines.
- The assumptions provide a reasonable basis for the responsible party's forecast, or whether the assumptions provide a reasonable basis for the responsible party's projection given the hypothetical assumptions.

The practitioner should follow the general, fieldwork, and reporting standards for attestation engagements as set forth in Chapter 1 of SSAE-10 (AT 101), in addition to the specific requirements set forth in Chapter 3 of SSAE-10 (AT 301) for examination of prospective financial statements.

Training and Proficiency, Planning, and Procedures

Training and Proficiency

The practitioner should be familiar with the guidelines for the preparation and presentation of prospective financial statements. The guidelines are contained in the AICPA Audit and Accounting Guide *Guide for Prospective Financial Information*.

The practitioner should posses or obtain a level of knowledge of the industry and the accounting principles and practices of the industry in which the entity operates or will operate that will enable him or her to examine prospective financial statements that are appropriate in form for an entity operating in that industry.

Planning an Examination Engagement

Planning the examination engagement involves developing an overall strategy for the expected scope and conduct of the engagement. To develop such a strategy, the practitioner needs to have sufficient knowledge to enable him or her to adequately understand the events, transactions, and practices that, in his or her judgment, have a significant effect on the prospective financial statements.

Factors to be considered by the practitioner in planning the examination include the following:

- The accounting principles to be used and the type of presentation.
- The anticipated level of attestation risk related to the prospective financial statements. Attestation risk is the risk that the practitioner might unknowingly fail to appropriately modify his or her examination report on prospective financial statements that are materially misstated, that is, that are not presented in conformity with AICPA presentation guidelines or have assumptions that do not provide a reasonable basis for management's forecast, or management's projection given the hypothetical assumptions. It consists of (a) the risk (consisting of inherent risk and control risk) that the prospective financial statements contain errors that could be material and (b) the risk (detection risk) that the practitioner will not detect such errors.
- Preliminary judgments about materiality levels.

- Items within the prospective financial statements that are likely to require revision or adjustment.
- Conditions that might require extension or modification of the practitioner's examination procedures.
- Knowledge of the entity's business and its industry.
- The responsible party's experience in preparing prospective financial statements.
- The length of the period covered by the prospective financial statements.
- The process by which the responsible party develops its prospective financial statements.

The practitioner should obtain knowledge of the entity's business, accounting principles, and the key factors that its future financial results appear to depend on. The practitioner should focus on areas such as the following:

- The availability and cost of resources needed to operate (principal items usually include raw materials, labor, short- and long-term financing, and plant and equipment).
- The nature and condition of markets in which the entity sells its goods and services, including final consumer markets if the entity sells to intermediate markets.
- Factors specific to the industry, including competitive conditions, sensitivity to economic conditions, accounting policies, specific regulatory requirements, and technology.
- Patterns of past performance for the entity or comparable entities, including trends in revenue and costs, turnover of assets, uses and capacities of physical facilities, and management policies.

Examination Procedures

The practitioner should establish an understanding with the responsible party regarding the services to be performed. The understanding should include the objectives of the engagement, the responsible party's responsibilities, the practitioner's responsibilities, and limitations of the engagement. The practitioner should document the understanding in the workpapers, preferably through a written communication with the responsible party. If the practitioner believes an understanding with the responsible party has not been established, he or she should decline to accept or perform the engagement. If the responsible party is different from the client, the practitioner should establish an understanding with both the client and the responsible party, and the understanding should also include the client's responsibilities. Appendix 13B is an illustrative engagement letter for an examination of prospective financial statements.

The practitioner's objective in an examination of prospective financial statements is to accumulate sufficient evidence to restrict attestation risk to a level that is, in his or her professional judgment, appropriate for the level of assurance that may be imparted by his or her examination report. In a report on an examination of prospective financial statements, the practitioner provides assurance only about whether the prospective financial statements are presented in conformity with AICPA presentation guidelines and whether the assumptions provide a reasonable basis for management's forecast, or a reasonable basis for management's projection given the hypothetical assumptions. The practitioner does not provide assurance about the achievability of the prospective results, because events and circumstances frequently do not occur as expected and achievement of the prospective results is dependent on the actions, plans, and assumptions of the responsible party.

In his or her examination of prospective financial statements, the practitioner should select from all available procedures—that is, procedures that assess inherent and control risk and restrict detection risk—any combination that can restrict attestation risk to an appropriate level. The extent to which examination procedures are to be performed should be based on the practitioner's consideration of the following:

- The nature and materiality of the information to the prospective financial statements taken as a whole.
- The likelihood of misstatements.
- Knowledge obtained during current and previous engagements.
- The responsible party's competence with respect to prospective financial statements.
- The extent to which the prospective financial statements are affected by the responsible party's judgment, for example, its judgment in selecting the assumptions used to prepare the prospective financial statements.
- The adequacy of the responsible party's underlying data.

The practitioner should perform those procedures he or she considers necessary in the circumstances to report on whether the assumptions provide a reasonable basis for the following:

- *Financial forecast* The practitioner can form an opinion that the assumptions provide a reasonable basis for the forecast if the responsible party represents that the presentation reflects, to the best of its knowledge and belief, its estimate of expected financial position, results of operations, and cash flows for the prospective period (if the forecast contains a range, the representation should also include a statement that, to the best of the responsible party's knowledge and belief, the item or items subject to the assumption are expected to actually fall within the range and that the range was not selected in a biased or misleading manner) and the practitioner concludes, based on his or her examination, (1) that the responsible party has explicitly identified all factors expected to materially affect the operations of the entity during the prospective period and has developed appropriate assumptions with respect to the factors (it is not feasible to list all assumptions; some basic assumptions that have enormous potential impact are considered to be implicit, such as conditions of peace and absence of natural disasters) and (2) that the assumptions are suitably supported.

- *Financial projection given the hypothetical assumptions* The practitioner can form an opinion that the assumptions provide a reasonable basis for the projection given the hypothetical assumptions if the responsible party represents that the presentation reflects, to the best of its knowledge and belief, expected financial position, results of operations, and cash flows for the prospective period given the hypothetical assumptions (if the projection contains a range, the representation should also include a statement that, to the best of the responsible party's knowledge and belief, given the hypothetical assumptions, the item or items subject to the assumption are expected to actually fall within the range and that the range was not selected in a biased or misleading manner) and the practitioner concludes, based on his or her examination that
  - The responsible party has explicitly identified all factors that would materially affect the operations of the entity during the prospective period if the hypothetical assumptions were to materialize and has developed appropriate assumptions with respect to such factors; and
  - The other assumptions are suitably supported given the hypothetical assumptions. However, as the number and significance of the hypothetical assumptions increase, the practitioner may not be able to satisfy himself or herself about the presentation as whole by obtaining support for the remaining assumptions.

The practitioner should evaluate the support for the assumptions:

- *Financial forecast* The practitioner can conclude that assumptions are suitably supported if the preponderance of information supports each significant assumption.

- *Financial projection* In evaluating support for assumptions other than hypothetical assumptions, the practitioner can conclude that they are suitably supported if the preponderance of information supports each significant assumption given the hypothetical assumptions. The practitioner need not obtain support for the hypothetical assumptions, although he or she should consider whether they are consistent with the purpose of the presentation.

In evaluating the support for the assumptions, the practitioner should consider

- Whether sufficient pertinent sources of information about the assumptions have been considered. Examples of external sources the practitioner might consider are government publications, industry publications, economic forecasts, existing or proposed legislation, and reports of changing technology. Examples of internal sources are budgets, labor agreements, patents, royalty agreements and records, sales backlog records, debt agreements, and actions of the board of directors involving entity plans.
- Whether the assumptions are consistent with the sources they are derived from.
- Whether the assumptions are consistent with each other.
- Whether the historical financial information and other data used in developing the assumptions are sufficiently reliable for that purpose. Reliability can be assessed by inquiry and analytical or other procedures, some of which may have been completed in past audits or reviews of the historical financial statements. If historical financial statements have been prepared for an expired part of the prospective period, the practitioner should consider the historical data in relation to the prospective results for the same period, where applicable. If the prospective financial statements incorporate such historical financial results and that period is significant to the presentation, the practitioner should make a review of the historical information in conformity with the applicable standards for a review.
- Whether the historical financial information and other data used in developing the assumptions are comparable over the periods specified or the effects of any lack of comparability were considered in developing the assumptions.
- Whether the logical arguments or theory, considered with the data supporting the assumptions, are reasonable.

Case Study 13-3: Reasonably Objective Basis

Scenario 1 Facts

Suppose in Case Study 13-2 that Chandler is an experienced developer of apartment complexes. The financing amount and terms Chandler is seeking are consistent with those that currently exist in the marketplace. Further, assume that the apartments will be built in a familiar location that is not overbuilt and where the supply and demand for apartments is in general equilibrium.

Scenario 2 Facts

Suppose that one or more of the following conditions exists:

- Chandler is a developer of office buildings. They have never built an apartment complex before.
- The financing terms are not normal for the current lending market. For example, assume most lenders will not loan more than 50% of the construction cost of an apartment complex.
- The apartment complex is being built in an unfamiliar location in a market that is saturated.

Analysis

In Scenario 1, Chandler would seem to have a basis for developing sufficiently objective assumptions for each of the key factors previously identified.

Analysis

But in Scenario 2, important questions arise about the company's ability to develop appropriate assumptions:

- If the entity has never built an apartment complex, how will it develop an appropriate assumption for the construction cost?
- If no one is lending at the terms required,howcan the company forecast debt financing?
- If the market is overbuilt and the location is unfamiliar, how will the company develop appropriate estimates of rental rates and the lease-up period? Current leasing conditions might not be a good source of information; by the time the project is built and ready for occupancy, conditions may have changed dramatically.

In evaluating the preparation and presentation of the prospective financial statements, the practitioner should perform procedures that will provide reasonable assurance as to the following:

- The presentation reflects the identified assumptions.
- The computations made to translate the assumptions into prospective amounts are mathematically accurate.
- The assumptions are internally consistent.
- Accounting principles used in the
  - Financial forecast are consistent with the accounting principles expected to be used in the historical financial statements covering the prospective period and those used in the most recent historical financial statements, if any.
  - Financial projection are consistent with the accounting principles expected to be used in the prospective period and those used in the most recent historical financial statements, if any, or that they are consistent with the purpose of the presentation.
- The presentation of the prospective financial statements follows the AICPA guidelines applicable to such statements.
- The assumptions have been adequately disclosed based on AICPA presentation guidelines for prospective financial statements.

The practitioner should consider whether the prospective financial statements, including related disclosures, should be revised because of any of the following:

- Mathematical errors
- Unreasonable or internally inconsistent assumptions
- Inappropriate or incomplete presentation
- Inadequate disclosure

The practitioner should obtain written representations from the responsible party acknowledging its responsibility for both the presentation and the underlying assumptions. The representations should be signed by the responsible party at the highest level of authority who the practitioner believes is responsible for and knowledgeable, directly or through others, about matters covered by the representations

- For a financial forecast, the representations should include a statement that the financial forecast presents, to the best of the responsible party's knowledge and belief, the expected financial position, results of operations, and cash flows for the forecast period and that the forecast reflects the responsible party's judgment, based on present circumstances, of the expected conditions and its expected course of action. If the forecast contains a range, the representation should also include a statement that, to the best of the responsible party's knowledge and belief, the items subject to the assumption are expected to actually fall within the range and that the range was not selected in a biased or misleading manner.

- For a financial projection, the representations should include a statement that the financial projection presents, to the best of the responsible party's knowledge and belief, the expected financial position, results of operations, and cash flows for the projection period given the hypothetical assumptions, and that the projection reflects its judgment based on present circumstances, of expected conditions and its expected course of action given the occurrence of the hypothetical events. The representations should also (1) identify the hypothetical assumptions and describe the limitations on the usefulness of the presentation, (2) state that the assumptions are appropriate, (3) indicate if the hypothetical assumptions are improbable, and (4) if the projection contains a range, include a statement that, to the best of the responsible party's knowledge and belief, given the hypothetical assumptions, the item or items subject to the assumption are expected to actually fall within the range and that the range was not selected in a biased or misleading manner. The representations should also include a statement that the projection is presented in conformity with guidelines for presentation of a projection established by the American Institute of Certified Public Accountants.

Appendix 13L is an illustrative representation letter.

Reporting

The practitioner's standard examination report on prospective financial statements should include the following:

- A title that includes the word "independent."
- An identification of the prospective financial statements presented.
- An identification of the responsible party and a statement that the prospective financial statements are the responsibility of the responsible party.
- A statement that the practitioner's responsibility is to express an opinion on the prospective financial statements based on his or her examination.

- A statement that the examination of the prospective financial statements was conducted in accordance with attestation standards established by the American Institute of Certified Public Accountants and, accordingly, included such procedures as the practitioner considered necessary in the circumstances.
- A statement that the practitioner believes that the examination provides a reasonable basis for his or her opinion.
- The practitioner's opinion that the prospective financial statements are presented in conformity with AICPA presentation guidelines and that the underlying assumptions provide a reasonable basis for the forecast or a reasonable basis for the projection given the hypothetical assumptions.
- A caveat that the prospective results might not be achieved.
- A statement that the practitioner assumes no responsibility to update the report for events and circumstances occurring after the date of the report.
- The manual or printed signature of the practitioner's firm.
- The date of the examination report.

Exhibit 13-3 is the form of a standard examination report on a forecast that does not contain a range.

EXHIBIT 13-3
STANDARD EXAMINATION REPORT: FORECAST

[*addressee*]
[*city, state*]

We have examined the accompanying forecasted balance sheet, statements of income, retained earnings, and cash flows of XYZ Company as of December 31, 20XX, and for the year then ending. XYZ Company's management is responsible for the forecast. Our responsibility is to express an opinion on the forecast based on our examination.

Our examination was conducted in accordance with attestation standards established by the American Institute of Certified Public Accountants and, accordingly, included such procedures as we considered necessary to evaluate both the assumptions used by management and the preparation and presentation of the forecast. We believe that our examination provides a reasonable basis for our opinion.

In our opinion, the accompanying forecast is presented in conformity with guidelines for the presentation of a forecast established by the American Institute of Certified Public Accountants, and the underlying assumptions provide a reasonable basis for management's forecast. However, there will usually be differences between the forecasted and actual results, because events and circumstances frequently do not occur as expected, and those differences may be material. We have no responsibility to update this report for events and circumstances occurring after the date of this report.

[*firm's signature*]

[*city, state*]

[*date*]

When the presentation is a projection, the opinion regarding the assumptions should be conditioned on the hypothetical assumptions; that is, the practitioner should express an opinion on whether the assumptions provide a reasonable basis for the projection given the hypothetical assumptions. The examination report should include all of the report elements above. In addition, the report should include a statement describing the special purpose for which the projection was prepared as well as a separate paragraph that restricts the use of the report. Exhibit 13-4 is the form of the standard examination report on a projection that does not contain a range.

EXHIBIT 13-4
STANDARD EXAMINATION REPORT: PROJECTION

[*addressee*]
[*city, state*]

We have examined the accompanying projected balance sheet, statements of income, retained earnings, and cash flows of XYZ Company as of December 31, 20XX, and for the year then ending. XYZ Company's management is responsible for the projection, which was prepared for [*state special purpose, for example,* the purpose of negotiating a loan to expand XYZ Company's plant]. Our responsibility is to express an opinion on the projection based on our examination.

Our examination was conducted in accordance with attestation standards established by the American Institute of Certified Public Accountants and, accordingly, included such procedures as we considered necessary to evaluate both the assumptions used by management and the preparation and presentation of the projection. We believe that our examination provides a reasonable basis for our opinion.

In our opinion, the accompanying projection is presented in conformity with guidelines for the presentation of a forecast established by the American Institute of Certified Public Accountants, and the underlying assumptions provide a reasonable basis for management's projection [*describe hypothetical assumption, for example,* assuming the granting of the requested loan for the purpose of expanding XYZ Company's plant as described in the summary of significant assumptions]. However, even if [*describe hypothetical assumption, for example,* the loan is granted and the plant is expanded], there will usually be differences between the projected and actual results, because events and circumstances frequently do not occur as expected, and those differences may be material. We have no responsibility to update this report for events and circumstances occurring after the date of this report.

The accompanying projection and this report are intended solely for the information and use of [*identify specified parties, for example,* XYZ Company and DEF Bank] and are not intended to be and should not be used by anyone other than these specified parties.

[*firm's signature*]

[*city, state*]

[*date*]

Prospective Financial Statements with a Range

When the prospective financial statements contain a range, the practitioner's standard report should include a separate paragraph that states that the responsible party has elected to portray the expected results of one or more assumptions as a range. The following is an example of the separate paragraph to be added when the prospective financial statements, in this case a forecast, contain a range:

> As described in the summary of significant assumptions, management of XYZ Company has elected to portray forecasted [*describe financial statement element or elements for which the expected results of one or more assumptions fall within a range, and identify the assumptions expected to fall within a range, for example,* revenue at the amounts of $X,XXX and $Y,YYY, which is predicated upon occupancy rates of XX percent and YY percent of available apartments,] rather than as a single point estimate. Accordingly, the accompanying forecast presents forecasted financial position, results of operations, and cash flows [*describe one or more assumptions expected to fall within a range, for example,* at such occupancy rates]. However, there is no assurance that the actual results will fall within the range of [*describe one or more assumptions expected to fall within a range, for example,* occupancy rates] presented.

Dating the Report

The date of completion of the practitioner's examination procedures should be used as the date of the report.

Modification of the Opinion

The following circumstances result in the following types of modified opinions in the examination report:

- If, in the practitioner's opinion, the prospective financial statements depart from the AICPA presentation guidelines, he or she should express a qualified opinion or an adverse opinion. However, if the presentation departs from the presentation guidelines because it fails to disclose assumptions that appear to be significant, the practitioner should express an adverse opinion.

- If the practitioner believes one or more significant assumptions do not provide a reasonable basis for the forecast, or a reasonable basis for the projection given the hypothetical assumptions, he or she should express an adverse opinion.
- If the practitioner's examination is affected by conditions that preclude application of one or more procedures he or she considers necessary in the circumstances, he or she should disclaim an opinion and describe the scope limitation in the his or her report.

Qualified Opinion

In a qualified opinion, the practitioner should state, in a separate paragraph, all substantive reasons for modifying his or her opinion and describe the departure from AICPA presentation guidelines. The opinion should include the words "except" or "exception" as the qualifying language and should refer to the separate explanatory paragraph.

> **OBSERVATION:** Because of the nature, sensitivity, and interrelationship of prospective information, a reader would have difficulty interpreting an examination report qualified for a measurement departure, the reasonableness of underlying assumptions, or a scope limitation. (An example of a measurement departure is the failure to capitalize a capital lease in a forecast where historical financial statements for the prospective period are expected to be presented in conformity with GAAP.) Accordingly, Chapter 3 of SSAE-10 prohibits the use of a qualified opinion for these circumstances. Instead, an adverse opinion or disclaimer of opinion should be used.

Exhibit 13-5 is an example of an examination report on a forecast that is at variance with AICPA presentation guidelines.

EXHIBIT 13-5
EXAMINATION REPORT: FORECAST, AT VARIANCE WITH AICPA GUIDELINES

[*addressee*]
[*city, state*]

We have examined the accompanying forecasted balance sheet, statements of income, retained earnings, and cash flows of XYZ Company as of December 31, 20XX, and for the year then ending. XYZ Company's management is responsible for the forecast. Our responsibility is to express an opinion on the forecast based on our examination.

Our examination was conducted in accordance with attestation standards established by the American Institute of Certified Public Accountants and, accordingly, included such procedures as we considered necessary to evaluate both the assumptions used by management and the preparation and presentation of the forecast. We believe that our examination provides a reasonable basis for our opinion.

The forecast does not disclose significant accounting policies. Disclosure of such policies is required by guidelines established by the American Institute of Certified Public Accountants.

In our opinion, except for the omission of the disclosure of significant accounting policies discussed in the preceding paragraph, the accompanying forecast is presented in conformity with guidelines for the presentation of a forecast established by the American Institute of Certified Public Accountants, and the underlying assumptions provide a reasonable basis for management's forecast. However, there will usually be differences between the forecasted and actual results, because events and circumstances frequently do not occur as expected, and those differences may be material. We have no responsibility to update this report for events and circumstances occurring after the date of this report.

[*firm's signature*]

[*city, state*]

[*date*]

Adverse Opinion

In an adverse opinion, the practitioner should state, in a separate paragraph, all of the substantive reasons for the adverse opinion

- If the presentation departs from AICPA presentation guidelines, the opinion should state that the presentation is not in conformity with presentation guidelines and refer to the explanatory paragraph.
- If the assumptions do not provide a reasonable basis for the prospective financial statements, the opinion paragraph should state that in the practitioner's opinion the assumptions do not provide a reasonable basis for the prospective financial statements.

Exhibit 13-6 is an example of an adverse opinion on an examination of a forecast.

EXHIBIT 13-6
ADVERSE OPINION: FORECAST

[*addressee*]
[*city, state*]

We have examined the accompanying forecasted balance sheet, statements of income, retained earnings, and cash flows of XYZ Company as of December 31, 20XX, and for the year then ending. XYZ Company's management is responsible for the forecast. Our responsibility is to express an opinion on the forecast based on our examination.

Our examination was conducted in accordance with attestation standards established by the American Institute of Certified Public Accountants and, accordingly, included such procedures as we considered necessary to evaluate both the assumptions used by management and the preparation and presentation of the forecast. We believe that our examination provides a reasonable basis for our opinion.

As discussed under the caption "Sales" in the summary of significant forecast assumptions, the forecasted sales include, among other things, revenue from the Company's federal defense contracts continuing at the current level. The Company's present federal defense contracts will expire in March 20XX. No new contracts have been signed and no negotiations are under way for new federal defense contracts. Furthermore, the federal government has entered into contracts with another company to supply the items being manufactured under the Company's present contracts.

In our opinion, the accompanying forecast is not presented in conformity with guidelines for the presentation of a forecast established by the American Institute of Certified Public Accountants, because management's assumptions, as discussed in the preceding paragraph, do not provide a reasonable basis for management's forecast. We have no responsibility to update this report for events and circumstances occurring after the date of this report.

[*firm's signature*]

[*city, state*]

[*date*]

If the presentation, including the summary of significant assumptions fails to disclose assumptions that at the time appear to be significant, the practitioner should describe the assumptions in his or her report and express an adverse opinion. The practitioner should not examine a presentation that omits all disclosures of assumptions. Also, the practitioner should not examine a financial projection that omits (1) an identification of the hypothetical assumptions or (2) a description of the limitations on the usefulness of the presentation.

Disclaimer of Opinion

In a disclaimer of opinion, the practitioner's report should state, in a separate paragraph, the respects in which the examination did not comply with the standards for an examination. The practitioner should state that the scope of the examination was not sufficient to enable him or her to express an opinion with respect to the presentation or the underlying assumptions, and his or her disclaimer of opinion should include a direct reference to the explanatory paragraph. Exhibit 13-7 is an example of a report on an examination of prospective financial statements, in this case a financial forecast, for which a significant assumption could not be evaluated.

EXHIBIT 13-7
FINANCIAL FORECAST: UNDERLYING ASSUMPTION NOT EVALUATED

[*addressee*]
[*city, state*]

We have examined the accompanying forecasted balance sheet, statements of income, retained earnings, and cash flows of XYZ Company as of December 31, 20XX, and for the year then ending. XYZ Company's management is responsible for the forecast. Our responsibility is to express an opinion on the forecast based on our examination.

As discussed under the caption "Income from Investee" in the summary of significant forecast assumptions, the forecast includes income from an equity investee constituting 23 percent of forecasted net income, which is management's estimate of the Company's share of the investee's income to be accrued for 20XX. The investee has not prepared a forecast for the year ending December 31, 20XX, and we were therefore unable to obtain suitable support for this assumption.

Because, as described in the preceding paragraph, we were unable to evaluate management's assumption regarding income from an equity investee and other assumptions that depend thereon, the scope of our work was not sufficient to express, and we do not express, an opinion with respect to the presentation of or the assumptions underlying the accompanying forecast. We have no responsibility to update this report for events and circumstances occurring after the date of this report.

[*firm's signature*]

[*city, state*]

[*date*]

When there is a scope limitation and the practitioner also believes there are material departures from the presentation guidelines, those departures should be described in the report.

Case Study 13-4: Modification of the Opinion

Facts

Gazoogle is an Internet start-up company that derives revenue from the sale of its products and "click-through" advertising it places on its Web site. The company is in the process of raising additional capital and as part of that process it will prepare a financial forecast of its expected statement of position, results of operations, and cash flows for the next twelve months. Historically, potential investors have focused primarily on revenue growth to asses the merits of companies like Gazoogle. The company engages a CPA to perform an examination of its financial forecast.

In performing the examination procedures, the practitioner discovers that the company's accounting policy for recognizing revenue from advertising sales does not comply with a recently issued accounting pronouncement. Management of Gazoogle explains that previous financial statements and the financial statements of competitors used the previous accounting standards and that they believe it is important not to change their accounting policies.

AICPA guidelines on the preparation of prospective financial statements require entities to use the accounting principles expected to be used in the historical financial statements covering the prospective period. Management of Gazoogle decided to not change their financial forecast to comply with this requirement.

Analysis

The attestation standards require modification of the opinion whenever there are reservations about the assertion or the subject matter. In this case, the subject matter (the financial forecast) is not in conformity with the criteria (guidelines for preparation of a financial forecast published by the AICPA). Therefore, the practitioner must express either a qualified or an adverse opinion.

Deciding which of the two opinions to express depends on the materiality of the departure from the criteria. The practitioner's consideration of materiality should include both quantitative and qualitative factors. For example, suppose that advertising revenues comprise 50% of total forecast revenues during the prospective period. In that situation, the magnitude of the departure would be so significant, particularly given the importance of revenue forecasts to potential investors, that the practitioner probably would be inclined to express an adverse opinion.

On the other hand, suppose that advertising revenues comprised only 10% of forecasted revenues. The smaller magnitude of the departure in and of itself might not change the opinion. The practitioner should also consider the qualitative aspects of the departure and how they might affect the decisions of potential investors (for example, the practitioner should consider whether the departure results in forecasted net income when a loss would otherwise have been forecasted if the subject matter was in conformity with the AICPA's guidelines). After considering these qualitative factors, and given the dollar magnitude of the company's departure from the criteria, the practitioner might be more inclined to express a qualified opinion in these circumstances.

Other Report Modifications

The circumstances describe below, although not necessarily resulting in modifications to the practitioner's opinion, would result in modifications to the standard examination report.

Emphasis of a Matter

In some circumstances, the practitioner may wish to emphasize a matter regarding the prospective financial statements but nevertheless intends to express an unqualified opinion. Chapter 3 of SSAE-10 (AT 301.46) states that the practitioner may present other information and comments he or she wishes to include, such as explanatory comments or other informative material, in a separate paragraph of his or her report.

Evaluation Based in Part on a Report of Another Practitioner

When more than one practitioner is involved in the examination, the guidance provided for that situation in connection with examinations of historical financial statements is generally applicable. When the principal practitioner decides to refer to the report of another practitioner as a basis, in part, for his or her own opinion, he or she should disclose that fact in stating the scope of the examination and should refer to the report of the other practitioner in expressing his or her opinion. Such a reference states the division of responsibility for the performance of the examination.

Comparative Historical Financial Information

Prospective financial statements may be included in a document that also contains historical financial statements and a practitioner's report on them. In addition, the historical financial statements that appear in the document may be summarized and presented with the prospective financial statements for comparative purposes. An example of the reference to the practitioner's report on the historical financial statements when he or she audited, reviewed, or compiled those statements is presented below. This reference would be included after the last paragraph in the examination report:

> The historical financial statements for the year ended December 31, 20XX, [from which the historical data are derived] and our report thereon are set forth on pages XX–XX of this document.

APPLYING AGREED-UPON PROCEDURES TO PROSPECTIVE FINANCIAL STATEMENTS

An agreed-upon procedures engagement is one in which a practitioner is engaged by a client to issue a report of findings based on specific procedures performed on the prospective financial statements. The practitioner should follow the general, fieldwork, and reporting standards for attest engagements set forth in Chapter 1 of SSAE-10 (AT 101) and the guidance in Chapter 2 of SSAE-10 (AT 201), related to agreed-upon procedures engagements.

Conditions

The practitioner may perform an agreed-upon procedures engagement on prospective financial statements provided that

- The practitioner is independent.
- The practitioner and the specified parties agree upon the procedures performed or to be performed by the practitioner.
- The specified parties take responsibility for the sufficiency of the agreed-upon procedures for their purposes.
- The prospective financial statements include a summary of significant assumptions.
- The prospective financial statements to which the procedures are to be applied are subject to reasonably consistent evaluation against criteria that are suitable and available to the specified parties.
- Criteria to be used in the determination of findings are agreed upon between the practitioner and the specified parties.
- The procedures to be applied to the prospective financial statements are expected to result in reasonably consistent findings using the criteria.
- Evidential matter related to the prospective financial statements to which the procedures are applied is expected to exist to provide a reasonable basis for expressing the findings in the practitioner's report.
- Where applicable, the practitioner and the specified parties agree on any materiality limits for reporting purposes.
- Use of the report is restricted to the specified parties.

Engagement Procedures

Agreement on and Sufficiency of Procedures

To satisfy the requirements that the practitioner and the specified parties agree upon the procedures performed or to be performed and that the specified parties take responsibility for the sufficiency of the agreed-upon procedures for their purposes, ordinarily the practitioner should communicate directly with and obtain affirmative acknowledgement from each of the specified parties.

> **OBSERVATION:** This agreement may be accomplished by meeting with the specified parties or by distributing a draft of the anticipated report or a copy of an engagement letter to the specified parties and obtaining their agreement.

If the practitioner is not able to communicate directly with all of the specified parties, the practitioner may satisfy these requirements by applying any one or more of the following or similar procedures:

- Compare the procedures to be applied to written requirements of the specified parties.
- Discuss the procedures to be applied with appropriate representatives of the specified parties.
- Review relevant contracts with or correspondence from the specified parties.

The practitioner should not report on an engagement when specified parties do not agree upon the procedures performed or to be performed and do not take responsibility for the sufficiency of the procedures for their purposes.

Appendix 13E is an illustrative letter that requests the specified parties' comments on the agreed-upon procedures.

Adding Specified Parties

Subsequent to the completion of the agreed-upon procedures engagement, the practitioner may be asked to consider the addition of another party as a specified party (referred to as a "nonparticipant party"). The practitioner may agree to add a nonparticipant party, based on the consideration of such factors as the identity of the nonparticipant party and the intended use of the report.

> **OBSERVATION:** When considering whether to add a nonparticipant party, the guidance in SAS-1 (AU 530) (Dating of the Independent Auditor's Report) is helpful.

If the practitioner does agree to add the nonparticipant party, he or she should obtain affirmative acknowledgement, preferably in writing, from the nonparticipant party agreeing to the procedures performed and of its taking responsibility for the sufficiency of the procedures. If the nonparticipant party is added after the report is issued, the report may be reissued or the practitioner may provide other written acknowledgement that the nonparticipant party has been added as a specified party. If the practitioner provides written acknowledgement that the nonparticipant party has been added as a specified party, the written acknowledgement should state that no additional procedures have been performed subsequent to the date of the report.

The illustrative letter in Appendix 13E is a request for specified party's comments on procedures, which may be used to obtain affirmative acknowledgement from the nonparticipant party of responsibility and sufficiency of procedures.

> **OBSERVATION:** If the report is reissued, the original report date should not be changed.

Designing Procedures

The specified parties are responsible for the sufficiency (nature, timing, and extent) of the agreed-upon procedures because they best understand their own needs. The specified parties assume the risk that the procedures might be insufficient for their purposes. In addition, the specified parties assume the risk that they might misunderstand or otherwise inappropriately use the findings properly reported by the practitioner.

The practitioner assumes the risk that misapplication of the procedures might result in inappropriate findings being reported. Furthermore, the practitioner assumes the risk that appropriate findings might not be reported or might be reported inaccurately. The practitioner's risks can be reduced through adequate planning and supervision and due professional care in performing the procedures, determining the findings, and preparing the report.

The practitioner has no responsibility to determine the differences between the agreed-upon procedures to be performed and the procedures that the practitioner would have determined to be necessary had he or she been engaged to perform another form of attest engagement. The procedures that the practitioner agrees to perform may be more or less extensive than the procedures that he or she would determine to be necessary in order to perform another form of engagement.

Appropriate Procedures

The procedures that the practitioner and the specified parties agree upon may be as limited or as extensive as the specified parties desire. In some circumstances, the procedures evolve or are modified over the course of the engagement. The practitioner may use an addendum to the agreement reached in the original engagement letter to document the modified or additional procedures. Appendix 13D is an illustrative engagement letter addendum. In general, there is flexibility in determining the procedures as long as the specified parties acknowledge responsibility for the sufficiency of the procedures for their purposes. Matters that should be agreed upon include the nature, timing, and extent of the procedures.

The practitioner should obtain evidential matter through applying the agreed-upon procedures in order to provide a reasonable basis for the finding or findings expressed in his or her report but need not perform additional procedures outside the scope of the engagement to gather additional evidential matter.

Inappropriate Procedures

The procedures that the practitioner and specified parties agree upon may be as limited or as extensive as the specified parties desire. However, mere reading of an assertion or specified information about the subject matter does not constitute a procedure sufficient to permit a practitioner to report on the results of applying agreed-upon procedures. In addition, the practitioner should not agree to perform procedures that are overly subjective and thus possibly open to varying interpretations. Terms of uncertain meaning (such as "general review," "limited review," "check," or "test") should not be used in describing the procedures unless they are defined within the agreed-upon procedures.

Change in Type of Engagement

A practitioner who has been engaged to perform another form of attest engagement or a nonattest service engagement might before the engagement's completion be requested to change the engagement to an agreed-upon procedures engagement. A request to change the engagement can result from a change in circumstances affecting the client's requirements, a misunderstanding about the nature of the original services or the alternative services originally available, or a restriction on the performance of the original engagement, whether imposed by the client or caused by circumstances.

Before a practitioner changes the engagement to an agreed-upon procedures engagement, he or she should consider the following:

- The possibility that certain procedures performed as part of another type of engagement are not appropriate for inclusion in an agreed-upon procedures engagement.
- The reason given for the request, particularly the implications of a restriction on the scope of the original engagement or the matters to be reported.
- The additional effort required to complete the original engagement.

- If applicable, the reasons for changing from a general-use report to a restricted-use report.

If the specified parties acknowledge agreement to the procedures performed or to be performed and assume responsibility for the sufficiency of the procedures to be included in the agreed-upon procedures engagement, either of the following two situation would be considered a reasonable basis for requesting a change in the engagement:

1. A change in circumstances that requires another form of engagement.
2. A misunderstanding concerning the nature of the original engagement or the available alternatives.

In all circumstances, if the original engagement procedures are substantially complete or the effort to complete such procedures is relatively insignificant, the practitioner should consider the propriety of accepting a change in the engagement.

If the practitioner concludes, based on his or her professional judgment, that there is reasonable justification to change the engagement, and provided he or she complies with the standards applicable to an agreed-upon procedures engagement, he or she should issue an appropriate agreed-upon procedures report.

> **OBSERVATION:** The report should not refer to either the original engagement or the performance limitations that resulted in the changed engagement.

Reporting

The practitioner's report on the results of applying agreed-upon procedures should be in the form of procedures and findings. The practitioner's report should contain the following elements:

- A title that includes the word "independent."
- Identification of the specified parties.
- Reference to the prospective financial statements and the character of the engagement.
- A statement that the procedures performed were those agreed to by the specified parties identified in the report.
- Identification of the responsible party and a statement that the prospective financial statements are the responsibility of the responsible party.

- A statement that the agreed-upon procedures engagement was conducted in accordance with attestation standards established by the AICPA.
- A statement that the sufficiency of the procedures is solely the responsibility of the specified parties and a disclaimer of responsibility for the sufficiency of those procedures.
- A list of the procedures performed (or a reference to them) and related findings.
- Where applicable, a description of any agreed-upon materiality limits.
- A statement that the practitioner was not engaged to and did not conduct an examination of the prospective financial statements; a disclaimer of opinion on whether the presentation of the prospective financial statements is in conformity with AICPA presentation guidelines and on whether the underlying assumptions provide a reasonable basis for the forecast, or a reasonable basis for the projection given the hypothetical assumptions; and a statement that if the practitioner had performed additional procedures, other matters might have come to his or her attention that would have been reported.
- A statement of restrictions on the use of the report because it is intended to be used solely by the specified parties.
- Where applicable, reservations or restrictions concerning procedures or findings.
- A caveat that the prospective results might not be achieved.
- A statement that the practitioner assumes no responsibility to update the report for events and circumstances occurring after the date of the report.
- Where applicable, a description of the nature of the assistance provided by a specialist.
- The manual or printed signature of the practitioner's firm.
- The date of the report.

DOCUMENTATION

Attest documentation is the principal record of attest procedures applied, information obtained, and conclusions or findings reached by the practitioner in the engagement. The quantity, type, and content of attest documentation are matters of the practitioner's professional judgment. Attest documentation serves mainly to

- Provide the principal support for the practitioner's report, including the representation regarding observance of the standards of fieldwork, which is implicit in the reference in the report to attestation standards.

- Aid the practitioner in the conduct and supervision of the attest engagement.

Attest documentation should be sufficient to (1) enable members of the engagement team with supervision and review responsibilities to understand the nature, timing, extent, and results of attest procedures performed and the information obtained and (2) identify the engagement team member(s) who performed and reviewed the work.

Examples of attest documentation are work programs, analyses, memoranda, letters of confirmation and representation, abstracts or copies of entity documents, and schedules or commentaries prepared or obtained by the practitioner. Ordinarily, attest documentation includes

- Documentation of the engagement acceptance or continuance decision.
- An engagement letter.
- Documentation of how the specified parties determined the procedures to be performed.
- A planning form documenting the practitioner's knowledge of the client and consideration of attestation risk.
- Documentation of the procedures performed.
- Support for data in the presentation.
- A list of the procedures agreed to with a cross reference to documentation of performance.
- Summary of findings.
- A discussion of unusual matters encountered and their resolution.
- A representation letter.
- Copies of reports from other accountants, if any, who have examined a component of the subject matter.
- Documentation that the workpapers were reviewed.

Attest documentation may be in paper form, electronic form, or other media.

The practitioner has an ethical, and in some situations a legal, obligation to maintain the confidentiality of client information or information of the responsible party. Because attest documentation often contains confidential information, the practitioner should adopt reasonable procedures to maintain the confidentiality of the information. The practitioner should also adopt reasonable procedures to prevent unauthorized access to attest documentation.

OTHER INFORMATION ACCOMPANYING PROSPECTIVE FINANCIAL STATEMENTS

Budget Information

According to Chapter 3 of SSAE-10 (AT 301.59), when a practitioner compiles, reviews, or audits historical financial statements that are included in a practitioner-submitted document containing prospective financial statements, the practitioner should either examine, compile, or apply agreed-upon procedures to the prospective financial statements and report accordingly. However, an exception to this requirement applies if

- The prospective financial statements are labeled as a "budget."
- The budget does not extend beyond the end of the current fiscal year.
- The budget is presented with interim historical financial statements for the current year.

In such circumstances, the practitioner need not examine, compile, or apply agreed-upon procedures to the budget. However, he or she should report on the budget, and

- State that he or she did not examine or compile the budget.
- Disclaim an opinion or any other form of assurance on the budget.

In addition, the budgeted information may omit the summaries of significant assumptions and accounting policies required by the AICPA presentation guidelines, provided

- The omission is not, to the practitioner's knowledge, undertaken with the intention of misleading those who might reasonably be expected to use such budgeted information; and
- The omission is disclosed in the report.

Exhibit 13-8 is the form of report to be used in this circumstance.

EXHIBIT 13-8 BUDGET INFORMATION

[*addressee*]
[*city, state*]

The accompanying budgeted balance sheet, statements of income, retained earnings, and cash flows of XYZ Company as of December 31, 20XX, and for the six months then ending, have not been compiled or examined by us, and, accordingly, we do not express an opinion or any other form of assurance on them.

Management has elected to omit the summaries of significant assumptions and accounting policies required under established guidelines for presentation of prospective financial statements. If the omitted summaries were included in the budgeted information, they might influence the user's conclusions about the company's budgeted information. Accordingly, this budgeted information is not designed for those who are not informed about such matters.

[*firm's signature*]

[*city, state*]

[*date*]

OBSERVATION: Expired budget information presented with historical financial statements can be treated as supplementary information and reported on as such in the CPA's compilation, review, or audit report on the historical financial statements.

Historical Financial Statements

When the practitioner's compilation, review, or audit report on historical financial statements is included in a client-prepared document containing prospective financial statements, the practitioner should not consent to the use of his or her name in the document unless

- He or she has examined, compiled, or applied agreed-upon procedures to the prospective financial statements and his or her report accompanies them.
- The prospective financial statements are accompanied by a statement by the responsible party or the practitioner that the practitioner has not performed such a service on the prospective financial statements and that the practitioner assumes no responsibility for them.
- Another practitioner has examined, compiled, or applied agreed-upon procedures to the prospective financial statements and his or her report is included in the document.

In addition, if the practitioner has audited the historical financial statements and they accompany prospective financial statements that he or she did not examine, compile, or apply agreed-upon procedures to in certain client-prepared documents, he or she should refer to SAS- 8 (AU 550) (Other Information in Documents Containing Audited Financial Statements).

When the practitioner's report on prospective financial statements is included in a client-prepared document containing historical financial statements, the practitioner should not consent to the use of his or her name in the document unless

- He or she has compiled, reviewed, or audited the historical financial statements and his or her report accompanies them.
- The historical financial statements are accompanied by a statement by the responsible party or the practitioner that the practitioner has not performed such a service on the historical financial statements and that the practitioner assumes no responsibility for them.
- Another practitioner has compiled, reviewed, or audited the historical financial statements and his or her report is included in the document.

Other Information in a Client-Prepared Document

A client may publish various documents that contain information other than historical financial statements in addition to the compiled or examined prospective financial statements and the practitioner's report thereon. The practitioner's responsibility with respect to the other information does not extend beyond the financial information identified in the report, and the practitioner has no obligation to perform any procedures to corroborate any other information contained in the document. However, the practitioner should read the other information and consider whether it, or the manner of its presentation, is materially consistent with the information appearing in the prospective financial statements.

Examination Engagement

If, in an examination of the prospective financial statements, the practitioner believes that the other information is inconsistent with the information appearing in the examination report, the practitioner should

- Consider whether the examination report, the prospective financial statements, or both require revision; or
- Request the client to revise the other information to eliminate the inconsistency.

If the other information is not revised to eliminate the inconsistency, the practitioner should consider other actions, such as

- Issuing an adverse opinion.
- Withholding the use of the examination report.
- Withdrawing from the engagement.

Compilation Engagement

If the practitioner compiles the prospective financial statements included in the document containing inconsistent information, he or she should attempt to obtain additional or revised information. If the practitioner does not receive such information, the he or she should withhold the use of the report or withdraw from the compilation engagement.

Material Misstatement of Fact

If, while reading the other information, the practitioner becomes aware of information that he or she believes is a material misstatement of fact that is not a material inconsistency, the practitioner should discuss the matter with the client. If after discussing the matter the practitioner concludes that a material misstatement of fact remains, the action taken will depend on the practitioner's judgment in the circumstances. The practitioner should consider steps such as notifying the responsible party in writing of his or her views concerning the information and consulting his or her legal counsel about further appropriate action in the circumstances.

APPENDIX 13A
ENGAGEMENT LETTER: COMPILATION OF PROSPECTIVE FINANCIAL STATEMENTS

[*date*]

[*name of client*]
[*address*]

We are pleased to confirm our understanding of the nature and limitations of the services we are to provide for [*client's legal name*].

We will compile, from information management provides, the [forecasted *or* projected] balance sheet of [*client*] as of [*date*] and the [forecasted *or* projected] statements of income, retained earnings, and cash flows for the [*period*] then ending. We will not examine or apply agreed-upon procedures to the prospective financial statements. Our report on the prospective financial statements is currently expected to read as follows:

> We have compiled the accompanying [forecasted *or* projected] balance sheet, statements of income, retained earnings, and cash flows of XYZ Company as of December 31, 20XX, and for the year then ending, in accordance with attestation standards established by the American Institute of Certified Public Accountants. [The accompanying projection was prepared for [state special purpose].]

> A compilation is limited to presenting in the form of a [forecast or projection] information that is the representation of management and does not include an evaluation of the support for the assumptions underlying the [forecast or projection]. We have not examined the [forecast or projection] and, accordingly, do not express an opinion or any other form of assurance on the accompanying statements or assumptions. Furthermore, [even if [*describe hypothetical assumption*]], there will usually be differences between the [forecasted *or* projected] and actual results, because events and circumstances frequently do not occur as expected, and those differences may be material. We have no responsibility to update this report for events and circumstances occurring after the date of this report.
>
> [The accompanying projection and this report are intended solely for the information and use of [*identify specified parties*] and is not intended to be and should not be used by anyone other than these specified parties.]

If for any reason, we are unable to complete the compilation of the prospective financial statements, we will not issue a compilation report on such statements as a result of this engagement.

Our engagement cannot be relied upon to disclose errors, fraud, or illegal acts that may exist. However, we will inform the appropriate level of management of any material errors that come to our attention and any fraud or illegal acts that come to our attention, unless they are clearly inconsequential.

Management is responsible for the prospective financial statements and for the assumptions used in the presentation. We may assist in the preparation of the presentation, but the responsibility for the presentation remains with you. At the conclusion of the engagement, management agrees to supply us with a representation letter, which, among other things, will confirm management's responsibility for the prospective financial statements and underlying assumptions.

We plan to begin our compilation on approximately [*date*] and issue our report no later than [*date*].

We estimate that our fees for these services will range from $_____ to $_____. You will also be billed for travel and other out-of-pocket costs such as report production, typing, postage, etc. Additional expenses are estimated to be $_____. The fee estimate is based on anticipated cooperation from your personnel and the assumption that unexpected circumstances will not be encountered during the compilation. If significant additional time is necessary, we will discuss it with you and arrive at a new fee estimate before we incur the additional costs. Our invoices for these fees will be rendered each month as work progresses and are payable on presentation. In accordance with our firm policies, work may be suspended if your account becomes ___ days or more overdue and will not be resumed until your account is paid in full. If we elect to terminate our services for nonpayment, our engagement will deemed to have been completed upon written notification of termination, even if we have not completed our report. You will be obligated to compensate us for all time expended and to reimburse us for all out-of-pocket expenditures through the date of termination.

We appreciate the opportunity to be of service to you and believe this letter accurately summarizes the significant terms of our engagement. If you have any questions, please let us know. If you agree with the terms of our engagement as described in this letter, please sign the enclosed copy and return it to us.

Very truly yours,

[*CPA firm's name*]

Response:

This letter correctly sets forth the understanding of [*client*].

By:

Title:

Date:

APPENDIX 13B
ENGAGEMENT LETTER: EXAMINATION OF PROSPECTIVE FINANCIAL STATEMENTS

[*date*]

[*name of client*]
[*address*]

We are pleased to confirm our understanding of the services we are to provide for [*client's legal name*].

We will examine the [forecasted *or* projected] balance sheet of [*name of client*] as of [*date*] and the [forecasted *or* projected] statements of income, retained earnings, and cash flows, for the [*period*] then ending. Our examination will be conducted in accordance with attestation standards established by the American Institute of Certified Public Accountants. Accordingly, it will include procedures we consider necessary to enable us to express an opinion as to whether the prospective financial statements are presented in conformity with AICPA presentation guidelines and whether the underlying assumptions provide a reasonable basis for the management's forecast [projection, [*describe hypothetical assumption*]]. If, for any reason, we are unable to complete the examination, we will not issue a report as a result of this engagement.

[*Describe restrictions on the use of the report, if it is a projection.*]

Our engagement will not include a detailed inspection of every transaction and cannot be relied upon to disclose all material errors, fraud, or other illegal acts, that may exist. However, we will inform you of any material errors or fraud that comes to our attention. We will also inform you of any other illegal acts that come to our attention, unless clearly inconsequential.

We understand that you will provide us with the basic information required for our examination and that you are responsible for the accuracy and completeness of that information. We may assist in the preparation of the presentation, but the responsibility for the presentation remains with you.

At the conclusion of the engagement, management agrees to supply us with a representation letter, which, among other things, will confirm management's responsibility for the prospective financial statements and underlying assumptions.

We expect to begin our examination on approximately [*date*]. We estimate that our fees for these services will range from $_____ to $_____. You will also be billed for travel and other out-of-pocket costs such as report production, typing, postage, etc. Additional expenses are estimated to be $_____. The fee estimate is based on anticipated cooperation from your personnel and the assumption that unexpected circumstances will not be encountered during the examination. If significant additional time is necessary, we will discuss it with you and arrive at a new fee estimate before we incur the additional costs. Our invoices for these services will be rendered each month as work progresses and are payable on presentation. In accordance with our firm policies, work may be suspended if your account becomes _____ days or more overdue and will not be resumed until your account is paid in full. If we elect to terminate our services for nonpayment, our engagement will be deemed to have been completed upon written notification of termination, even if we have not completed our report. You will be obligated to compensate us for all time extended and to reimburse us for all out-of-pocket expenditures through the date of termination.

We appreciate the opportunity to be of service to you and believe this letter accurately summarizes the significant terms of our engagement. If you have any questions, please let us know. If you agree with the terms of our engagement as described in this letter, please sign the enclosed copy and return it to us.

Very truly yours,

[*CPA firm's name*]

Response:

This letter correctly sets forth the understanding of [*name of client*].

By:

Title:

Date:

APPENDIX 13C ENGAGEMENT LETTER: APPLYING AGREED-UPON PROCEDURES TO PROSPECTIVE FINANCIAL STATEMENTS

[*date*]

[*name of client (and other specified parties)*]
[*address*]

We are pleased to confirm our understanding of the nature and limitations of the services we are to provide for [*client's legal name*].

We will apply agreed-upon procedures which [specified parties have specified, listed in the attached schedule] to [*describe prospective financial statements*] of [*name of responsible party*] as of [*date*], prepared in accordance with [*criteria*]. Our engagement to apply agreed-upon procedures will be conducted in accordance with attestation standards established by the American Institute of Certified Public Accountants. The sufficiency of the procedures is solely the responsibility of those parties specified in the report. Consequently, we make no representation regarding the sufficiency of the procedures described in the attached schedule either for the purpose for which the report has been requested or for any other purpose. If, for any reason, we are unable to complete the procedures, we will describe any restrictions on the performance of the procedures in our report, or will not issue a report as a result of this engagement.

Because the agreed-upon procedures listed in the attached schedule do not constitute an examination, we will not express an opinion on [*describe prospective financial statements*]. In addition, we have no obligation to perform any procedures beyond those listed in the attached schedule.

We will submit a report listing the procedures performed and our findings. This report is intended solely for the use of [*specified parties*], and should not be used by those who did not agree upon the procedures and take responsibility for the sufficiency of the procedures for their purposes. Our report will contain a paragraph stating that had we performed additional procedures, other matters may have come to our attention that would have been reported to you.

We plan to begin our procedures on approximately [*date*] and, unless unforeseeable problems are encountered, the engagement should be completed by [*date*]. At the conclusion of our engagement, we will require a representation letter from management that, among other things, will confirm management's responsibility for the presentation of the [*describe prospective financial statements*] in accordance with [*describe criteria*].

We estimate that our fees for these services will range from $_____ to $_____. You will also be billed for travel and other out-of-pocket costs such as report production, typing, postage, etc. Additional expenses are estimated to be $_____. The fee estimate is based on anticipated cooperation from your personnel and the assumption that unexpected circumstances will not be encountered during the engagement. If significant additional time is necessary, we will discuss it with you and arrive at a new fee estimate before we incur the additional costs. Our invoices for these services will be rendered each month as work progresses and are payable on presentation. In accordance with our firm policies, work may be suspended if your account becomes _____ days or more overdue and will not be resumed until your account is paid in full. If we elect to terminate our services for nonpayment, our engagement will be deemed to have been completed upon written notification of termination, even if we have not completed our report. You will be obligated to compensate us for all time extended and to reimburse us for all out-of-pocket expenditures through the date of termination.

We appreciate the opportunity to be of service to you and believe this letter accurately summarizes the significant terms of our engagement. If you have any questions, please let us know. If you agree with the terms of our engagement as described in this letter, please sign the enclosed copy and return it to us. If the need for additional services arises, our agreement with you will need to be revised. It is customary for us to enumerate these revisions in an addendum to this letter. If additional specified parties of the report are added, we will require that they acknowledge in writing their responsibility for the sufficiency of the procedures.

Very truly yours,

[*CPA firm's name*]

Response:

This letter correctly sets forth the understanding of [*client and other specified parties*].

By:

Title:

Date:

APPENDIX 13D
ENGAGEMENT LETTER ADDENDUM

[*date*]

[*name of client*]
[*address*]

This letter constitutes an addendum to our original engagement letter dated [*date*]. The purpose of this letter is to outline additional procedures you wish us to perform in connection with that agreed-upon procedures engagement.

The additional procedures include:

[*List additional procedures.*]

All the terms of our original engagement letter will apply to this addendum. This addendum will become effective when you sign and date the original and copy of this letter and return the signed copy to us.

Very truly yours,

[*CPA firm's name*]

Response:

This letter correctly sets forth the understanding of [*client and other specified parties*].

By:

Title:

Date:

APPENDIX 13E
REQUEST FOR SPECIFIED PARTY'S COMMENTS ON PROCEDURES

[*date*]

[*client name*]
[*address*]

We have been requested by [*client's legal name*] to apply agreed-upon procedures listed in the attached engagement letter. The sufficiency of the requested procedures is solely the responsibility of the specified parties of the report. Consequently, we make no representation regarding the sufficiency of the procedures for the purpose for which this report has been requested or for any other purpose.

Because the agree-upon procedures listed in the attached engagement letter do not constitute an examination, we will not express an opinion on the [*describe prospective financial statements*]. In addition, we have no obligation to perform any procedures that go beyond those listed in the attached engagement letter.

As a specified user of the report, please review the proposed procedures and acknowledge the sufficiency of the procedures by signing the enclosed copy of this letter and returning it to us. If the procedures are not considered to be sufficient, or are not in accordance with your understanding, please provide comments in the space provided below.

Very truly yours,

[*CPA firm's name*]

Response:

The procedures listed in the attached engagement letter are_____ (are not_____) sufficient for our purposes.

Comments:

By:

Title:

Date:

APPENDIX 13F
PLANNING MATERIALITY CALCULATION FORM

Client Name: _______________ Date of Subject Matter: _______________

Completed by: _______________ Date Completed: ____________________

Instructions

The purposed of this form is to determine and document the materiality amount that will be considered suitable for planning purposes. For engagements related to financial or numeric subject matter, complete Part 1 of this form to determine planning materiality and tolerable misstatement. Part 1 should be completed using amounts as of the date of the subject matter. For nonfinancial and nonnumeric subject matter, complete Part 2 of this form to document the assessed tolerable rate of misstatement or noncompliance for the subject matter. This form should be prepared by the engagement personnel in charge of fieldwork (senior or supervisory staff) and reviewed and approved by the engagement executive for all attestation engagements.

Part 1: Procedures Related to Financial or Numeric Subject Matter

If the total dollar amount of the subject matter (the "base") is:		*Planning materiality is:*
Over	But less than	Amount + (Percent × Base)
$0	$50 thousand	0 + 5.5%
$50 thousand	$100 thousand	1,250 + 3.0%
$100 thousand	$500 thousand	2,250 + 2.0%
$500 thousand	$1 million	7,500 + 1.0%
$1 million	$5 million	9,500 + 0.8%
$5 million	$10 million	19,500 + 0.6%
$10 million	$50 million	40,000 + 0.4%
$50 million	$100 million	115,000 + 0.25%
$100 million		185,000 + 0.18%

Example: If the base amount were $5.5 million, then the planning materiality would be determined as follows:

$\$19,500 + (.006' \$5,500,000) = \$52,500$

Calculations

1. *Planning Materiality*

Amount from Table	+	(Percentage (from Table	×	Base) Amount)	=	Planning Materiality
________		(________	×	________)	=	________

2. *Tolerable Misstatement*

Tolerable misstatement is used in computing sample sizes and in making other scope decisions. As a rule of thumb, tolerable misstatement can be calculated as follows:

Planning Materiality from Above	×	Factor	=	Tolerable Misstatement
____________	×	.75	=	____________

3. Individually Significant Items

The amount used to determine individually significant items can be any amount up to tolerable misstatement.

Part 2: Nonfinancial and Nonnumeric Subject Matter

For nonfinancial and nonnumeric subject matter, materiality is considered to be a tolerable rate of _____ %.

APPENDIX 13G
COMPILATION ENGAGEMENT CHECKLIST: PROSPECTIVE FINANCIAL STATEMENTS

Client Name: ________________ Date of Subject Matter: ________________

Completed by: ________________ Date Completed: ____________________

	Completed by	N/A
1. Complete the Client Acceptance and Retention Evaluation Form.	________	________
2. Establish and document an understanding with the client, preferably in an engagement letter. If an engagement letter will not be obtained, the oral understanding should be documented in a memo.	________	________
3. Obtain an understanding of the guidelines for the preparation and presentation of prospective financial statements, contained in the AICPA Audit and Accounting Guide *Guide for Prospective Financial Information*.	________	________
4. Obtain an understanding of the industry and the accounting principles and practices of the industry in which the client operates.	________	________
5. Obtain an understanding of the client and the engagement, including:	________	________
a. Nature of the client's business transactions.	________	________
b. Key factors upon which its future financial results appear to depend and that have affected the performance of entities in the same industry.	________	________
c. Client's accounting principles and practices and whether they are comparable to other entities in the industry.	________	________
d. Proposed operations of the client.	________	________

	Completed by	N/A
6. Determine that the scheduling and staffing are adequate to perform the engagement.	______	______
7. Obtain the engagement partner's approval of the overall engagement plan.	______	______
8. Inquire about the accounting principles used in the preparation of the prospective financial statements:	______	______
a. For existing entities, compare the accounting principles used to those used in the preparation of previous historical financial statements and inquire whether such principles are the same as those expected to be used in the historical financial statements covering the prospective period.	______	______
b. For entities to be formed or entities formed that have not commenced operations, compare specialized industry accounting principles used, if any, to those typically used in the industry. Inquire about whether the accounting principles used for the prospective financial statements are those that are expected to be used when, or if, the entity commences operations.	______	______
9. Ask how the responsible party identifies the key factors and develops its assumptions.	______	______
10. List, or obtain a list of, the responsible party's significant assumptions providing the basis for the prospective financial statements and consider whether there are any obvious omissions in light of the key factors upon which the prospective results of the entity appear to depend.	______	______
11. Consider whether there appear to be any obvious internal inconsistencies in the assumptions.	______	______
12. Perform, or test the mathematical accuracy of, the computations that translate the assumptions into prospective financial statements.	______	______
13. Read the prospective financial statements, including the summary of significant assumptions, and consider whether:	______	______
a. The statements, including the disclosures of assumptions and accounting policies, appear to be not presented in conformity with the AICPA presentation guidelines for prospective financial statements.	______	______

	Completed by	N/A
b. The statements, including the summary of significant assumptions, appear to be not obviously inappropriate in relation to the accountant's knowledge of the entity and its industry and, for a:	______	______
i. Financial forecast, the expected conditions and course of action in the prospective period.	______	______
ii. Financial projection, the purpose of the presentation.	______	______
14. If a significant part of the prospective period has expired, inquire about the results of operations or significant portions of the operations (such as sales volume), and significant changes in financial position, and consider their effect in relation to the prospective financial statements. If historical financial statements have been prepared for the expired portion of the period, the practitioner should read such statements and consider those results in relation to the prospective financial statements.	______	______
15. Obtain a representation letter.	______	______
16. Consider, after applying the above procedures, whether he or she has received representations or other information that appears to be obviously inappropriate, incomplete, or otherwise misleading.	______	______
17. Draft the compilation report.	______	______
18. If any situations have occurred that require consultation, determine that such consultation has been properly documented.	______	______
19. If there were differences of professional opinion among members of the engagement team or between the engagement team and a specialist, determine that the differences were properly resolved and documented.	______	______
20. Determine that all questions, exceptions, or notes, if any, posed during the engagement have been followed up and resolved.	______	______
21. Determine that all required forms, questionnaires, and checklists have been completed.	______	______
22. Ensure that the workpapers and compilation report have been reviewed in accordance with firm policy.	______	______

	Completed by	N/A
23. Obtain engagement partner's review and approval for issuance of report.	________	________

APPENDIX 13H
EXAMINATION ENGAGEMENT CHECKLIST: PROSPECTIVE FINANCIAL STATEMENTS

Client Name: ______________ Date of Subject Matter: ______________

Completed by: ______________ Date Completed: ______________

	Completed by	N/A
1. Complete the Client Acceptance and Retention Evaluation Form.	________	________
2. Establish and document an understanding with the client, preferably in an engagement letter. If an engagement letter will not be obtained, the oral understanding should be documented in a memo.	________	________
3. Obtain an understanding of the guidelines for the preparation and presentation of prospective financial statements, contained in the AICPA Audit and Accounting Guide *Guide for Prospective Financial Information*.	________	________
4. Obtain an understanding of the industry and the accounting principles and practices of the industry in which the client operates.	________	________
5. In developing an overall strategy for the engagement, consider the following factors:		
a. The accounting principles to be used and the type of presentation.	________	________
b. The anticipated level of attestation risk related to the prospective financial statements. (Attestation risk is the risk that the practitioner may unknowingly fail to appropriately modify his or her examination report on prospective financial statements that are materially misstated, that is, that are not presented in conformity with AICPA presentation guidelines or have assumptions that do not provide a reasonable basis for management's forecast, or management's projection given the hypothetical assumptions. It consists of (1) the risk (consisting of inherent risk and control risk) that the prospective financial statements contain errors that could be material		

	Completed by	N/A
and (2) the risk (detection risk) that the practitioner will not detect such errors.)	________	________
c. Preliminary judgments about materiality levels.	________	________
d. Items within the prospective financial statements that are likely to require revision or adjustment.	________	________
e. Conditions that may require extension or modification of the practitioner's examination procedures.	________	________
f. Knowledge of the entity's business and its industry.	________	________
g. The responsible party's experience in preparing prospective financial statements.	________	________
h. The length of the period covered by the prospective financial statements.	________	________
i. The process by which the responsible party develops its prospective financial statements.	________	________
6. Obtain knowledge of the entity's business, accounting principles, and the key factors upon which its future financial results appear to depend. Focus on areas such as the following:	________	________
a. The availability and cost of resources needed to operate. (Principal items usually include raw materials, labor, short-term and long-term financing, and plant and equipment.)	________	________
b. The nature and condition of markets in which the entity sells its goods and services, including final consumer markets if the entity sells to intermediate markets.	________	________
c. Factors specific to the industry, including competitive conditions, sensitivity to economic conditions, accounting policies, specific regulatory requirements, and technology.	________	________
d. Patterns of past performance for the entity or comparable entities, including trends in revenue and costs, turnover of assets, uses and capacities of physical facilities, and management policies.	________	________
7. Determine that the scheduling and staffing are adequate to perform the engagement.	________	________
8. Consider planning materiality.	________	________
9. Obtain the engagement partner's approval of the overall engagement plan.	________	________

	Completed by	N/A
10. Develop and perform procedures necessary to evaluate the prospective financial statements (attach a program or memo to this checklist).The extent to which examination procedures will be performed should be based on the practitioner's consideration of the following:	________	________
a. The nature and materiality of the information to the prospective financial statements taken as a whole.	________	________
b. The likelihood of misstatements.	________	________
c. Knowledge obtained during current and previous engagements.	________	________
d. The responsible party's competence with respect to prospective financial statements.	________	________
e. The extent to which the prospective financial statements are affected by the responsible party's judgment, for example, its judgment in selecting the assumptions used to prepare the prospective financial statements.	________	________
f. The adequacy of the responsible party's underlying data.	________	________
11. For a financial forecast, form an opinion that the assumptions provide a reasonable basis for the forecast if the responsible party represents that the presentation reflects, to the best of its knowledge and belief, its estimate of expected financial position, results of operations, and cash flows for the prospective period and the practitioner concludes, based on his or her examination, (i) that the responsible party has explicitly identified all factors expected to materially affect the operations of the entity during the prospective period and has developed appropriate assumptions with respect to such factors and (ii) that the assumptions are suitably supported. (If the forecast contains a range, the representation should also include a statement that, to the best of the responsible party's knowledge and belief, the item or items subject to the assumption are expected to actually fall within the range and that the range was not selected in a biased or misleading manner.) (It is not feasible to list all assumptions. Some basic assumptions that have enormous potential impact are considered to be implicit, such as conditions of peace and absence of natural disasters.)	________	________

	Completed by	N/A
12. For a financial projection (given the hypothetical assumptions), form an opinion that the assumptions provide a reasonable basis for the projection given the hypothetical assumptions if the responsible party represents that the presentation reflects, to the best of its knowledge and belief, expected financial position, results of operations, and cash flows for the prospective period given the hypothetical assumptions and the practitioner concludes, based on his or her examination that (if the projection contains a range, the representation should also include a statement that, to the best of the responsible party's knowledge and belief, given the hypothetical assumptions, the item or items subject to the assumption are expected to actually fall within the range and that the range was not selected in a biased or misleading manner:	________	________
a. The responsible party has explicitly identified all factors that would materially affect the operations of the entity during the prospective period if the hypothetical assumptions were to materialize and has developed appropriate assumptions with respect to such factors; and	________	________
b. The other assumptions are suitably supported given the hypothetical assumptions. However, as the number and significance of the hypothetical assumptions increase, the practitioner may not be able to satisfy himself or herself about the presentation as whole by obtaining support for the remaining assumptions.	________	________
13. Evaluate the support for the assumptions:		
a. Financial forecast The practitioner can conclude that assumptions are suitably supported if the preponderance of information supports each significant assumption.	________	________
b. Financial projection In evaluating support for assumptions other than hypothetical assumptions, the practitioner can conclude that they are suitably supported if the preponderance of information supports each significant assumption given the hypothetical assumptions. The practitioner need not obtain support for the hypothetical assumptions, although he or she should consider whether they are consistent with the purpose of the presentation.	________	________

	Completed by	N/A
14. In evaluating the support for the assumptions, consider:	________	________
a. Whether sufficient pertinent sources of information about the assumptions have been considered. Examples of external sources the practitioner might consider are government publications, industry publications, economic forecasts, existing or proposed legislation, and reports of changing technology. Examples of internal sources are budgets, labor agreements, patents, royalty agreements and records, sales backlog records, debt agreements, and actions of the board of directors involving entity plans.	________	________
b. Whether the assumptions are consistent with the sources from which they are derived.	________	________
c. Whether the assumptions are consistent with each other.	________	________
d. Whether the historical financial information and other data used in developing the assumptions are sufficiently reliable for that purpose. Reliability can be assessed by inquiry and analytical or other procedures, some of which may have been completed in past audits or reviews of the historical financial statements. If historical financial statements have been prepared for an expired part of the prospective period, the practitioner should consider the historical data in relation to the prospective results for the same period, where applicable. If the prospective financial statements incorporate such historical financial results and that period is significant to the presentation, the practitioner should make a review of the historical information in conformity with the applicable standards for a review.	________	________
e. Whether the historical financial information and other data used in developing the assumptions are comparable over the periods specified or whether the effects of any lack of comparability were considered in developing the assumptions.	________	________
f. Whether the logical arguments or theory, considered with the data supporting the assumptions, are reasonable.	________	________
15. Evaluate the preparation and presentation of the prospective financial statements, by		

	Completed by	N/A
performing procedures that will provide reasonable assurance as to the following:		
a. The presentation reflects the identified assumptions.	________	________
b. The computations made to translate the assumptions into prospective amounts are mathematically accurate.	________	________
c. The assumptions are internally consistent.	________	________
d. Accounting principles used in the:		
i. Financial forecast are consistent with the accounting principles expected to be used in the historical financial statements covering the prospective period and those used in the most recent historical financial statements, if any.	________	________
ii. Financial projection are consistent with the accounting principles expected to be used in the prospective period and those used in the most recent historical financial statements, if any, or that they are consistent with the purpose of the presentation.	________	________
e. The presentation of the prospective financial statements follows the AICPA guidelines applicable to such statements.	________	________
f. The assumptions have been adequately disclosed based on AICPA presentation guidelines for prospective financial statements.	________	________
16. Consider whether the prospective financial statements, including related disclosures, should be revised because of any of the following:		
a. Mathematical errors.	________	________
b. Unreasonable or internally inconsistent assumptions.	________	________
c. Inappropriate or incomplete presentation.	________	________
d. Inadequate disclosure.	________	________
17. Obtain a representation letter.	________	________
18. Draft the examination report.	________	________
19. Read other information in a client-prepared document that contains the examination report for inconsistencies with the report and material misstatements of fact.	________	________

	Completed by	N/A
20. If any situations have occurred that require consultation, determine that such consultation has been properly documented.	________	________
21. If there were differences of professional opinion among members of the engagement team or between the engagement team and a specialist, determine that the differences were properly resolved and documented.	________	________
22. Determine that all questions, exceptions, or notes, if any, posed during the engagement have been followed up and resolved.	________	________
23. Determine that all required forms, questionnaires, and checklists have been completed.	________	________
24. Ensure that the workpapers and examination report have been reviewed in accordance with firm policy.	________	________
25. Obtain engagement partner's review and approval for issuance of report.	________	________

APPENDIX 13I
AGREED-UPON PROCEDURES ENGAGEMENT CHECKLIST: PROSPECTIVE FINANCIAL STATEMENTS

Client Name: ______________ Date of Subject Matter: ______________

Completed by: ______________ Date Completed: ______________

	Completed by	N/A
1. Complete the Client Acceptance and Retention Evaluation Form.	________	________
2. If the engagement was originally intended to be another type of engagement (for example, examination, compilation, or consulting engagement), document the considerations of:		
a. Whether the procedures performed as part of another type of engagement are appropriate for an agreed-upon procedures engagement.	________	________
b. The reasons given for the client's request to change the engagement, particularly the implications of a restriction on the scope of the original engagement.	________	________
c. The additional effort required to complete the original engagement.	________	________

	Completed by	N/A
d. Where applicable, any reasons for changing from a general-use report to a restricted-use report.	______	______
3. Communicate directly with all specified par ties and obtain their acknowledgement of the sufficiency of the procedures for their purposes. If direct communication is not possible, perform one of the following procedures:	______	______
a. Distribute a draft of the report or a copy of the engagement letter to the specified parties and obtain their agreement.	______	______
b. Compare the procedures to be applied to written requirements of the specified parties.	______	______
c. Discuss the procedures to be applied with appropriate representatives (such as legal counsel) of the specified parties.	______	______
d. Review relevant contracts with or correspondence from the specified parties.	______	______
4. Consider the procedures being requested and determine whether those procedures are appropriate for an agreed-upon procedures engagement.	______	______
5. Establish and document an understanding with the client, preferably in an engagement letter. If an engagement letter will not be obtained, the oral understanding should be documented in a memo.	______	______
6. Obtain an understanding of the guidelines for the preparation and presentation of prospective financial statements, contained in the AICPA Audit and Accounting Guide *Guide for Prospective Financial Information.*	______	______
7. Obtain an understanding of the industry and the accounting principles and practices of the industry in which the client operates.	______	______
8. Perform any additional services needed to assist the responsible party in developing the prospective financial statements or underlying assumptions.	______	______
9. Determine that the scheduling and staffing are adequate to perform the engagement.	______	______
10. Obtain the engagement partner's approval of the overall engagement plan.	______	______
11. If other services have been performed for the responsible party, review relevant		

	Completed by	N/A
workpapers and any related reports for indications of matters that contradict the prospective financial statements or underlying assumptions.	______	______
12. Include in the workpapers a list of all procedures agreed upon in the engagement letter, or include a copy of the engagement letter.	______	______
13. Perform the agreed-upon procedures and summarize the findings.	______	______
14. If considered necessary, obtain a representation letter from the responsible party.	______	______
15. Draft the agreed-upon procedures report.	______	______
16. Consider other reporting issues:		
a. Reporting all findings, unless a materiality threshold was agreed upon.	______	______
b. A description of any materiality limits agreed-upon.	______	______
c. Reporting other matters (including subsequent events).	______	______
d. Restrictions on performance of procedures.	______	______
e. Refusal to provide a representation letter.		
f. Explanations of sampling risk.	______	______
g. Disclosure of stipulated facts, assumptions, or interpretations used in the application of the procedures.	______	______
h. Description of the condition of records, controls, or data to which the procedures were applied.	______	______
i. Explanation that the practitioner has no responsibility to update his or her report.	______	______
j. Description of the nature of any assistance provided by a specialist.	______	______
17. If any additional specified parties are added, obtain their acknowledgement for the sufficiency of the procedures.	______	______
18. Read other information in a client-prepared document that contains the agreed-upon procedures report for inconsistencies.	______	______
19. If any situations have occurred that require consultation, determine that such consultation has been properly documented.	______	______
20. If there were differences of professional opinion among members of the engagement		

	Completed by	N/A
team or between the engagement team and a specialist, determine that the differences were properly resolved and documented.	________	________
21. Determine that all questions, exceptions, or notes, if any, posed during the engagement have been followed up and resolved.	________	________
22. Determine that all required forms, questionnaires, and checklists have been completed.	________	________
23. Ensure that the workpapers and agreed-upon procedures report have been reviewed in accordance with firm policy.	________	________
24. Obtain engagement partner's review and approval for issuance of report.	________	________

APPENDIX 13J AGREED-UPON PROCEDURES ENGAGEMENT: PROCEDURES AND FINDINGS FORM

Client Name: ________________ Date of Subject Matter: ________________

Completed by: ________________ Date Completed: ____________________

Instructions

This form can be used to record findings as each procedure is performed. Use a separate form for each procedure performed and document each procedure and finding as precisely as possible. Include all findings in the agreed-upon procedures report, unless materiality limits have been established and agreed upon by the specified parties.

Subject matter to which the procedure was applied:

Describe procedure:

Workpaper Reference	Finding

Discussed with responsible party:

Position: Date:

APPENDIX 13K
REPRESENTATION LETTER: COMPILATION OF PROSPECTIVE FINANCIAL STATEMENTS

[*date—No earlier than date of the accountant's report*]

[*CPA firm's name*]
[*address*]

In connection with your compilation of the forecasted [projected] balance sheet as of [*date of subject matter*], and the related statements of income, retained earnings, and cash flows for the [*period*] then ending, we confirm, to the best of our knowledge and belief, the following representations made to you during the course of your compilation.

- We are responsible for the assumptions underlying the prospective financial statements.
- The financial forecast [projection] presents expected financial position, results of operations, and cash flows for the forecast [projection] period [given the hypothetical assumptions] and the forecast [projection] reflects our judgment, based on present circumstances, of the expected conditions and our expected course of action [given the occurrence of the hypothetical events].
- The financial forecast [projection] is presented in conformity with guidelines for the presentation of a forecast [projection] established by the American Institute of Certified Public Accountants.
- The assumptions on which the forecast is based are reasonable.
- [*If the forecast or projection contains a range*] [Given the hypothetical assumptions] The item(s) subject to the assumption are expected to actually fall within the range and the range was not selected in a biased or misleading manner.
- [*For a projection*] The projection is based on the hypothetical assumption that [*describe hypothetical assumption*], which is appropriate and not improbable.
- We have disclosed to you all information of which we are aware that may contradict the [forecast *or* projection], and we have disclosed to you all communications from regulatory agencies affecting [forecast *or* projection].
- We have disclosed to you all events subsequent to [*date*] that would have a material effect on [forecast *or* projection].
- We have made available to you all records relevant to the [forecast *or* projection].
- We intend to distribute your report only to [*describe restrictions, if the compilation is a projection*].

Signature:	Signature:
Title:	Title:

APPENDIX 13L
REPRESENTATION LETTER: EXAMINATION OF PROSPECTIVE FINANCIAL STATEMENTS

[*date—No earlier than date of the accountant's report*]

[*CPA firm's name*]
[*address*]

In connection with your examination of the forecasted [projected] balance sheet as of [*date of subject matter*], and the related statements of income, retained earnings, and cash flows for the [*period*] then ending, we confirm, to the best of our knowledge and belief, the following representations made to you during the course of your examination.

- We are responsible for the assumptions underlying the prospective financial statements.
- The financial forecast [projection] presents expected financial position, results of operations, and cash flows for the forecast [projection] period [given the hypothetical assumptions] and the forecast [projection] reflects our judgment, based on present circumstances, of the expected conditions and our expected course of action [given the occurrence of the hypothetical events].
- The financial forecast [projection] is presented in conformity with guidelines for the presentation of a forecast [projection] established by the American Institute of Certified Public Accountants.
- The assumptions on which the forecast is based are reasonable.
- [*If the forecast or projection contains a range*] [Given the hypothetical assumptions] The item(s) subject to the assumption are expected to actually fall within the range and the range was not selected in a biased or misleading manner.
- [*For a projection*] The projection is based on the hypothetical assumption that [*describe hypothetical assumption*], which is appropriate and not improbable.
- We have disclosed to you all information of which we are aware that may contradict the [forecast *or* projection], and we have disclosed to you all communications from regulatory agencies affecting [forecast or projection].
- We have disclosed to you all events subsequent to [*date*] that would have a material effect on [forecast *or* projection].
- We have made available to you all records relevant to the [forecast *or* projection].
- We intend to distribute your report only to [*describe restrictions, if the examination is a projection*].

Signature:	Signature:
Title:	Title:

APPENDIX 13M
REPRESENTATION LETTER: AGREED-UPON PROCEDURES ENGAGEMENTS

[*date—No earlier than date of the accountant's report*]

[*CPA firm's name*]
[*address*]

In connection with your engagement to apply agreed-upon procedures to the forecasted [projected] balance sheet as of [*date of subject matter*], and the related statements of income, retained earnings, and cash flows for the [*period*] then ending, we confirm, to the best of our knowledge and belief, the following representations made to you during the course of your engagement:

- We are responsible for the assumptions underlying the prospective financial statements.
- The financial forecast [projection] presents expected financial position, results of operations, and cash flows for the forecast [projection] period [given the hypothetical assumptions] and the forecast [projection] reflects our judgment, based on present circumstances, of the expected conditions and our expected course of action [given the occurrence of the hypothetical events].
- The financial forecast [projection] is presented in conformity with guidelines for the presentation of a forecast [projection] established by the American Institute of Certified Public Accountants.
- The assumptions on which the forecast is based are reasonable.
- [*If the forecast or projection contains a range*] [Given the hypothetical assumptions] The item(s) subject to the assumption are expected to actually fall within the range and the range was not selected in a biased or misleading manner.
- [*For a projection*] The projection is based on the hypothetical assumption that [*describe hypothetical assumption*], which is appropriate and not improbable.
- We have disclosed to you all information of which we are aware that may contradict the [forecast *or* projection], and we have disclosed to you all communications from regulatory agencies affecting [forecast *or* projection].
- We have disclosed to you all events subsequent to [*date*] that would have a material effect on [forecast *or* projection].
- We have made available to you all records relevant to the [forecast *or* projection].
- Your report is intended solely for the information and use of [*specified parties*] and is not intended to be and should not be used by anyone other than those specified parties.

Signature:	Signature:
Title:	Title:

CHAPTER 14 MANAGEMENT'S DISCUSSION AND ANALYSIS

CONTENTS

OVERVIEW

This chapter discusses the various types of attestation engagements related to management's discussion and analysis. AT 701 sets forth attestation standards and provides guidance to practitioners performing attest engagements with respect to management's discussion and analysis prepared pursuant to the rules and regulations adopted by the Securities and Exchange Commission and presented in annual reports to shareholders and in other documents.

INTRODUCTION

Chapter 7 of SSAE-10 (AT 701) (Management's Discussion and Analysis) is applicable when a practitioner is engaged to examine or review management's discussion and analysis (MD&A). The engagement may be performed for

- A public entity that prepares MD&A in accordance with Securities and Exchange Commission (SEC) rules and regulations.
- A nonpublic entity that prepares an MD&A presentation and whose management provides a written assertion that the presentation has been prepared using SEC rules and regulations.

TYPES OF ENGAGEMENTS

There are four types of engagements that CPAs can perform on MD&A presentations:

1. Examination
2. Review
3. Agreed-upon procedures
4. Letters for underwriters

Examination Engagements

To express an opinion about whether (1) the MD&A presentation includes, in all material respects, the required elements of the rules and regulations adopted by the SEC, (2) the historical financial amounts have been accurately derived, in all material respects, from the entity's financial statements, and (3) the underlying information, determinations, estimates, and assumptions of the entity provide a reasonable basis for the disclosures contained therein, the practitioner seeks to obtain reasonable assurance by accumulating sufficient evidence in support of the disclosures and assumptions, thereby restricting attestation risk to an appropriately low level. Authoritative guidance for examining MD&A is found in Chapter 7 of SSAE-10 (AT 701), which is discussed later in this chapter.

Review Engagements

The objective of a review engagement, including a review of MD&A for an interim period, is to accumulate sufficient evidence to provide the practitioner with a basis for reporting whether any information came to the practitioner's attention to cause him or her to believe that (1) the MD&A presentation does not include, in all material respects, the required elements of the rules and regulations adopted by the SEC, (2) the historical financial amounts included the presentation have not been accurately derived, in all material respects, from the entity's financial statements, or (3) the underlying information, determinations, estimates, and assumptions of the entity do not provide a reasonable basis for the disclosures contained the presentation. Authoritative guidance for reviewing specified elements is found in Chapter 7 of SSAE-10 (AT 701), which is discussed later in this chapter.

Agreed-Upon Procedures Engagements

An agreed-upon procedures engagement is one in which a practitioner is engaged by a client to issue a report of findings based on specific procedures performed on the MD&A presentation. The client engages the practitioner to assist specified parties in evaluating the MD&A presentation as a result of a need or needs of the specified parties. Because the specified parties require that findings be independently derived, the services of a practitioner are obtained to perform procedures and report on his or her findings. The specified parties and the practitioner agree upon the procedures to be performed. These are the procedures that the specified parties believe are appropriate. Because the needs of the specified parties can vary widely, the nature, timing, and extent of the procedures can vary as well. Consequently, the specified parties assume responsibility for the sufficiency of the procedures because they best understand their own needs. Authoritative guidance for agreed-upon procedures engagements is found in Chapter 2 of SSAE-10 (AT 201). Agreed-upon procedures engagements are covered in Chapter 9, "Agreed-Upon Procedures Engagements," of this guide.

Letters for Underwriters

Letters for underwriters and certain other requesting parties (commonly referred to as "comfort letters") are issued by CPAs in connection with financial statements and financial statement schedules contained in registration statements filed with the SEC under the Securities Act of 1933 and other securities offerings. The service of accountants providing letters for underwriters developed following enactment of the 1933 Act. Section 11 of the 1933 Act provides that underwriters, among others, could be liable if any part of a registration statement contains material omissions or misstatements. The 1933 Act also provides for an affirmative defense for underwriters if it can be demonstrated that the underwriter has reasonable grounds, after a reasonable investigation, to believe that there were no material omissions or misstatements. Consequently, underwriters request accountants to assist them in developing a record of reasonable investigation. An accountant issuing a comfort letter is one of a number of procedures that may be used to establish that an underwriter has conducted a reasonable investigation. Authoritative guidance for comfort letters is found in SAS-72 (AU 634) (Letters for Underwriters and Certain Other Requesting Parties), as amended. Letters for underwriters are not addressed in this chapter. For additional guidance on issuing comfort letters, see the *Miller GAAS Practice Manual.*

Other Engagements

Exhibit 14-1 illustrates other types of engagements for which AT 701 does not apply.

EXHIBIT 14-1
ENGAGEMENTS FOR WHICH AT 701 DOES NOT APPLY

Type of Engagement	Applicable Guidance
Engagements to perform agreed-upon procedures on MD&A	AT 201 (Agreed-Upon Procedures Engagements)
Engagements to provide attest services with respect to an MD&A presentation that is prepared based on criteria other than the SEC rules and regulations	AT 101 (Attest Engagements) or AT 201 (Agreed-Upon Procedures Engagements)
Engagements to provide recommendations on how to improve the MD&A rather than to provide assurance	Statement on Standards for Consulting Services No. 1 (SSCS-1) (Consulting Services: Definitions and Standards).
Engagements to perform agreed-upon procedures on MD&A and to report on it in a letter for underwriters	AU 634 (Letters for Underwriters and Certain Other Requesting Parties)

EXAMINATION ENGAGEMENTS

To express an opinion about whether (1) the presentation includes, in all material respects, the required elements of the rules and regulations adopted by the SEC, (2) the historical financial amounts have been accurately derived, in all material respects, from the entity's financial statements, and (3) the underlying information, determinations, estimates, and assumptions of the entity provide a reasonable basis for the disclosures, the practitioner seeks to obtain reasonable assurance by accumulating sufficient evidence in support of the disclosures and assumptions, thereby restricting attestation risk to an appropriately low level.

Planning

In planning an examination of MD&A, the practitioner should consider factors such as the following:

- The anticipated level of attestation risk related to assertions embodied in the MD&A.
- Preliminary judgments about materiality.
- The items within the MD&A presentation that are likely to require revision or adjustment.
- Conditions that may require extension or modification of attest procedures.

Before accepting an engagement to examine MD&A, the practitioner should consider whether management, and others involved in the preparation of MD&A (e.g., legal counsel), have appropriate knowledge of the SEC rules and regulations relating to MD&A. In addition, in order to perform such an engagement, all the conditions summarized below should be met.

Conditions for Performing an Examination of MD&A

Before accepting an engagement to examine the MD&A of a public or nonpublic entity, the practitioner should observe the following conditions:

- The practitioner must audit, in accordance with GAAS (for engagements in accordance with PCAOB standards, "in accordance with the standards of the Public Company Accounting Oversight Board"), the financial statements for at least the latest period the MD&A presentation relates to.
- The financial statements for the other periods covered by the MD&A presentation must have been audited by the practitioner or a predecessor auditor.
- If a predecessor auditor has audited the financial statements for a prior period covered by the MD&A, the practitioner (successor auditor) should consider whether he or she can

acquire sufficient knowledge of the entity's business, and accounting and financial reporting practices for the period to enable him or her to

— Identify types of potential material misstatements in the MD&A and consider the likelihood of their occurrence.

— Perform the necessary procedures in order to express an opinion on whether the MD&A presentation includes the required elements of the rules and regulations adopted by the SEC.

— Perform the procedures necessary to express an opinion on the MD&A presentation with respect to whether the historical financial amounts have been accurately derived from the entity's financial statements for such period.

— Perform the necessary procedures in order to express an opinion on whether the underlying information, determinations, estimates, and assumptions of the entity provide a reasonable basis for the disclosures contained therein.

Materiality

The practitioner should consider the concept of materiality in planning and performing the engagement. The practitioner should consider the omission or misstatement of an individual assertion to be material if its magnitude is such that a reasonable person using the MD&A presentation would be influenced by the inclusion or correction of the individual assertion.

Internal Control

The practitioner is required to document his or her understanding of the entity's internal control applicable to the preparation of MD&A used to plan the examination and the assessment of the level of control risk. The form and extent of this documentation is influenced by the size and complexity of the entity, as well as the nature of the entity's controls applicable to the preparation of MD&A.

If during the course of the examination engagement, the practitioner becomes aware of significant deficiencies in the design or operation of internal control applicable to the preparation of MD&A, the practitioner should consider the impact of the deficiencies on his or her ability to rely on management's representations and the comparisons to summary accounting records. The practitioner's responsibility to communicate these control deficiencies in an examination of MD&A is similar to the auditor's responsibility described in AU 325 (Communication of Internal Control Related Matters Noted in an Audit) and AU 380 (Communication with Audit Committees).

Procedures in an Examination Engagement

The practitioner should perform the following procedures when engaged to examine an entity's MD&A:

1. Obtain an understanding of the SEC rules and regulations for MD&A and management's method for the preparation its MD&A.
2. Plan the examination engagement.
3. Consider relevant portions of the entity's internal control applicable to the preparation of MD&A.
4. Obtain sufficient evidence, including testing completeness.
5. Consider the effect of events subsequent to the balance-sheet date.
6. Obtain written representations from management.
7. Form an opinion on the examination of MD&A.

In addition to complying with the specific requirements discussed above, the practitioner should comply with the five general standards, the two fieldwork standards, and the four reporting standards described in AT 101. These standards are discussed in Chapter 3, "Pre-Engagement Considerations."

Appendix 14A is a procedures checklist for engagements to examine MD&A.

Management Representations

In an examination engagement, the practitioner should obtain written representations from management. The specific written representations needed depend on the circumstances of the engagement and the nature of the MD&A presentation. Specific representations should relate to the following matters:

- Management's acknowledgment of its responsibility for the preparation of MD&A and management's assertion that the MD&A presentation has been prepared in accordance with the rules and regulations adopted by the SEC for MD&A
- A statement that the historical financial amounts included in the MD&A have been accurately derived from the entity's financial statements
- Management's belief that the underlying information, determinations, estimates, and assumptions of the entity provide a reasonable basis for the disclosures contained in the MD&A

- A statement that management has made available all significant documentation related to compliance with SEC rules and regulations for MD&A
- Completeness and availability of all minutes of meetings of stockholders, directors, and committees of directors
- For a public entity, whether any communications from the SEC were received concerning noncompliance with or deficiencies in MD&A reporting practices
- Whether any events occurred subsequent to the latest balance-sheet date that would require disclosure in the MD&A
- If forward-looking information is included, a statement that
  - — The forward-looking information is based on management's best estimate of expected events and operations and is consistent with budgets, forecasts, or operating plans prepared for the periods in question
  - — The accounting principles expected to be used for the forward-looking information are consistent with the principles used in preparing the historical financial statements
  - — Management has provided the latest version of the budgets, forecasts, or operating plans and informed the practitioner of anticipated changes or modifications to the information that could affect the disclosures contained in the MD&A presentation
- If voluntary information is included that is subject to the rules and regulations adopted by the SEC (for example, information required by Item 305 "Quantitative and Qualitative Disclosures About Market Risk"), a statement that the voluntary information has been prepared in accordance with the related rules and regulations adopted by the SEC for such information
- If pro forma information is included, a statement that
  - — Management is responsible for the assumptions used in determining the pro forma adjustments
  - — Management believes that the assumptions provide a reasonable basis for presenting all the significant effects directly attributable to the transaction or event, that the related pro forma adjustments give appropriate effect to those assumptions, and that the pro forma column reflects the proper application of those adjustments to the historical financial statements
  - — Management believes that the significant effects directly attributable to the transaction or event are appropriately disclosed in the pro forma financial information

In an examination, management's refusal to furnish written representations constitutes a limitation on the scope of the engagement sufficient to preclude an unqualified opinion and is ordinarily sufficient to cause a practitioner to disclaim an opinion or withdraw from the examination engagement. However, based on the nature of the representations not obtained or the circumstances of the refusal, the practitioner may conclude that a qualified opinion is appropriate in an examination engagement.

If the practitioner is precluded from performing procedures he or she considers necessary in the circumstances with respect to a matter that is material to the MD&A presentation, even though management has made representations concerning the matter, there is a limitation on the scope of the engagement, and the practitioner should qualify his or her opinion or disclaim an opinion in an examination engagement.

Documentation

Attest documentation is the principal record of attest procedures applied, information obtained, and conclusions or findings reached by a practitioner in an engagement. The quantity, type, and content of attest documentation are matters of the practitioner's professional judgment. Attest documentation serves mainly to

- Provide the principal support for the practitioner's report, including the representation regarding observance of the standards of fieldwork, which is implicit in the reference in the report to attestation standards.
- Aid the practitioner in the conduct and supervision of the attest engagement.

Attest documentation should be sufficient to (1) enable members of the engagement team with supervision and review responsibilities to understand the nature, timing, extent, and results of attest procedures performed and the information obtained and (2) indicate the engagement team member(s) who performed and reviewed the work.

Examples of attest documentation are work programs, analyses, memoranda, letters of confirmation and representation, abstracts or copies of entity documents, and schedules or commentaries prepared or obtained by the practitioner. Ordinarily, attest documentation includes

- Documentation of the engagement acceptance or continuance decision
- An engagement letter
- A planning form documenting the practitioner's knowledge of the client and consideration of attestation risk

- Documentation of the procedures performed
- Support for data in the presentation
- A discussion of unusual matters encountered and their resolution
- A representation letter
- Copies of reports from other accountants, if any, who have examined a component of the subject matter
- Documentation that the workpapers were reviewed

Attest documentation may be in paper form, electronic form, or other medium. The practitioner has an ethical, and in some situations a legal, obligation to maintain the confidentiality of client information or information of the responsible party. Because attest documentation often contains confidential information, the practitioner should adopt reasonable procedures to maintain the confidentiality of that information. The practitioner should also adopt reasonable procedures to prevent unauthorized access to attest documentation.

Reporting on an Examination Engagement

In order for the practitioner to issue a report on an examination of MD&A, the financial statements for the periods covered by the MD&A presentation and the related auditor's report(s) should accompany the MD&A presentation. For a public entity, alternatively, the financial statements for the periods covered by the MD&A presentation and the related auditor's report(s) may be incorporated in the document containing the MD&A by reference to information filed with a regulatory agency. In addition, if the entity is a nonpublic entity, either (1) a statement should be included in the body of the MD&A presentation saying that it has been prepared using the rules and regulations adopted by the SEC or (2) a separate written assertion should accompany the MD&A presentation or be included in a representation letter from the entity.

The practitioner's report on an examination of MD&A should include all of the following elements:

- A title that includes the word "independent."
- An identification of the MD&A presentation, including the period covered.
- A statement that management is responsible for the preparation of the MD&A pursuant to the SEC rules and regulations, and a statement that the practitioner's responsibility is to express an opinion on the presentation based on his or her examination.

- A reference to the auditor's report on the related financial statements, and if the report was other than a standard report, the substantive reasons for that.
- A statement that the examination was made in accordance with attestation standards established by the AICPA [or, for engagements performed in accordance with PCAOB standards, "in accordance with the standards of the Public Company Accounting Oversight Board (United States)"] and a description of the scope of an examination of MD&A.
- A statement that the practitioner believes that his or her examination provides a reasonable basis for his or her opinion.
- A paragraph stating that
  - — The preparation of MD&A requires management to interpret the criteria, make determinations as to the relevancy of information to be included, and make estimates and assumptions that affect reported information.
  - — Actual results in the future may differ materially from management's present assessment of information regarding the estimated future impact of transactions and events that have occurred or are expected to occur, expected sources of liquidity and capital resources, operating trends, commitments, and uncertainties.
- If the entity is a nonpublic entity, a statement that although the entity is not subject to the rules and regulations of the SEC, the MD&A presentation is intended to be a presentation in accordance with the SEC rules and regulations.
- The practitioner's opinion on whether
  - — The presentation includes, in all material respects, the required elements of the SEC rules and regulations.
  - — The historical financial amounts have been accurately derived, in all material respects, from the entity's financial statements.
  - — The underlying information, determinations, estimates, and assumptions of the entity provide a reasonable basis for the disclosures it contains.
- Manual or printed signature of the practitioner's firm.
- Date of the examination report, which is the date as of the completion of the examination procedures (the date should not precede the date of the auditor's report on the latest historical financial statements covered by the MD&A).
- For engagements in accordance with the standards of the Public Company Accounting Oversight Board, the city and state (or city and country, for non-U.S. practitioners) where the practitioner's report has been issued.

Appendix 14C is an example of a standard examination report on MD&A.

Report Modifications

The practitioner should modify the standard examination report if any of the following conditions exist:

- The MD&A presentation excludes a material element required under the SEC rules and regulations (see Appendix 14D).
- The historical financial amounts have not been accurately derived, in all material respects, from the entity's financial statements.
- The underlying information, determinations, estimates, and assumptions used by management do not provide the entity with a reasonable basis for the disclosure in the MD&A presentation (see Appendix 14E).
- There is a restriction on the scope of the engagement.
- The practitioner decides to refer to the report of another practitioner as the basis, in part, for his or her report (see Appendix 14F).
- The practitioner is engaged to examine the MD&A presentation after it has been filed with the SEC or other regulatory agency.

REVIEW ENGAGEMENTS

The objective of a review engagement, including a review of MD&A for an interim period, is to accumulate sufficient evidence to provide the practitioner with a basis for reporting whether any information came to his or her attention to cause him or her to believe that (1) the MD&A presentation does not include, in all material respects, the required elements of the rules and regulations adopted by the SEC, (2) the historical financial amounts included therein have not been accurately derived, in all material respects, from the entity's financial statements, or (c) the underlying information, determinations, estimates, and assumptions of the entity do not provide a reasonable basis for the disclosures contained therein. MD&A for an interim period may be a freestanding presentation or combined with the MD&A presentation for the most recent fiscal year. Procedures for conducting a review of MD&A are generally limited to inquiries and analytical procedures, rather than also including search and verification procedures, concerning factors that have a material effect on financial condition, including liquidity and capital resources, results of operations, and cash flows.

Planning

In planning an review of MD&A, the practitioner should consider factors such as the following:

- The anticipated level of attestation risk related to assertions embodied in the MD&A.
- Preliminary judgments about materiality.
- The items within the MD&A presentation that are likely to require revision or adjustment.
- Conditions that may require extension or modification of attest procedures.

Before accepting an engagement to review MD&A, the practitioner should consider whether management, and others involved in the preparation of MD&A (e.g., legal counsel), have appropriate knowledge of the SEC rules and regulations relating to MD&A. In addition, in order to perform an engagement to review MD&A, all the applicable conditions summarized below should be met.

Conditions for Performing a Review of MD&A

Before accepting an engagement to review the MD&A of a public or nonpublic entity, the practitioner should observe the following conditions.

Public Entities

For annual periods:

- The practitioner has audited, in accordance with PCAOB standards, the financial statements for at least the latest annual period that the MD&A presentation relates to.
- The financial statements for the other periods covered by the MD&A presentation have been audited by the practitioner or a predecessor auditor.
- If a predecessor auditor has audited the financial statements for a prior period covered by the MD&A, the practitioner (successor auditor) should consider whether he or she can acquire sufficient knowledge of the entity's business and accounting and financial reporting practices for the period to enable him or her to
    - — Identify types of potential material misstatements in the MD&A and consider the likelihood of their occurrence.

— Perform the procedures that will provide the practitioner with a basis for reporting whether any information has come to his or her attention to cause him or her to believe any of the following:

The MD&A presentation does not include the required elements of the SEC rules and regulations.

The historical financial amounts included have not been accurately derived from the entity's financial statements for the period.

The underlying information, determinations, estimates, and assumptions of the entity do not provide a reasonable basis for the disclosures.

For interim periods:

- The practitioner performs either of the following:
  - A review of the historical financial statements for the related comparative interim periods and issues a review report on them in accordance with AU 722 (Interim Financial Information).
  - An audit of the interim financial statements.
- The MD&A presentation for the most recent fiscal year has been or will be examined or reviewed by either the practitioner or a predecessor auditor.

Nonpublic Entities

For annual periods:

- The annual financial statements for the periods covered by the MD&A presentation have been or will be audited and the practitioner has audited or will audit the most recent year.
- If a predecessor auditor has audited the financial statements for a prior period covered by the MD&A, the practitioner should consider whether he or she can acquire sufficient knowledge of the entity's business, and accounting and financial reporting practices for the period to enable him or her to
  - Identify types of potential material misstatements in the MD&A and consider the likelihood of their occurrence.
  - Perform the procedures that will provide the practitioner with a basis for reporting whether any information has come to his or her attention to cause him or her to believe any of the following:

    The MD&A presentation does not include the required elements of the SEC rules and regulations.

The historical financial amounts included in the MD&A have not been accurately derived from the entity's financial statements for such period.

The underlying information, determinations, estimates, and assumptions of the entity do not provide a reasonable basis for the disclosures.

- Management will provide a written assertion that the presentation has been prepared using the SEC rules and regulations as the criteria.

For interim periods:

- The practitioner performs one of the following:
  - — A review of the historical financial statements for the related interim periods under the Statements on Standards for Accounting and Review Services and issues a review report on them.
  - — A review of the condensed interim financial information for the related interim periods under AU 722 (Interim Financial Information) and issues a review report on it, and the interim financial information is accompanied by complete audited annual financial statements for the most recent fiscal year.
  - — An audit of the interim financial statements.
- The MD&A presentation for the most recent fiscal year has been or will be examined or reviewed.
- Management will provide a written assertion stating that the presentation has been prepared using the SEC rules and regulations as the criteria.

Materiality

The practitioner should consider the concept of materiality in planning and performing the engagement. The practitioner should consider the omission or misstatement of an individual assertion to be material if its magnitude is such that a reasonable person using the MD&A presentation would be influenced by the inclusion or correction of the individual assertion.

Procedures in a Review Engagement

The practitioner should perform the following procedures when engaged to review an entity's MD&A:

1. Obtain an understanding of the published SEC rules and regulations for MD&A and management's method for the preparation of MD&A.

2. Plan the review engagement.
3. Consider relevant portions of the entity's internal control applicable to the preparation of MD&A.
4. Apply analytical procedures to the financial statements and related MD&A and make inquiries of management and others.
5. Consider the effect of events subsequent to the balance-sheet date.
6. Obtain written representations from management.
7. Form a conclusion on the MD&A presentation.

In addition to complying with the specific requirements discussed above, the practitioner should comply with the five general standards, the two fieldwork standards, and the four reporting standards described in AT 101. These standards are discussed in Chapter 3, "Pre-Engagement Considerations."

Appendix 14B is a procedures checklist for engagements to review MD&A.

If the practitioner is unable to perform the inquiry and analytical procedures considered necessary for the MD&A review, the review is incomplete and the practitioner does not have a basis for issuing a review report. When the practitioner is unable to complete a review because of a scope limitation, he or she should consider the implications of that limitation with respect to possible misstatements of the MD&A presentation. In such circumstances, the practitioner should also refer to the guidance discussed below in the section headed "Communications with Audit Committee."

Management Representations

In a review engagement, the practitioner should obtain written representations from management. The specific written representations needed by the practitioner depend on the circumstances of the engagement and the nature of the MD&A presentation. Specific representations should relate to the following matters:

- Management's acknowledgment of its responsibility for the preparation of MD&A and management's assertion that the MD&A presentation has been prepared in accordance with the rules and regulations adopted by the SEC for MD&A
- A statement that the historical financial amounts included in the MD&A have been accurately derived from the entity's financial statements
- Management's belief that the underlying information, determinations, estimates, and assumptions of the entity provide a reasonable basis for the disclosures contained in the MD&A

- A statement that management has made available all significant documentation related to compliance with SEC rules and regulations for MD&A
- Completeness and availability of all minutes of meetings of stockholders, directors, and committees of directors
- For a public entity, whether any communications from the SEC were received concerning noncompliance with or deficiencies in MD&A reporting practices
- Whether any events occurred subsequent to the latest balance-sheet date that would require disclosure in the MD&A
- If forward-looking information is included, a statement that
  - — The forward-looking information is based on management's best estimate of expected events and operations and is consistent with budgets, forecasts, or operating plans prepared for the periods in question
  - — The accounting principles expected to be used for the forward-looking information are consistent with the principles used in preparing the historical financial statements
  - — Management has provided the latest version of that budgets, forecasts, or operating plans and informed the practitioner of any anticipated changes or modifications to the information that could affect the disclosures contained in the MD&A presentation
- If voluntary information is included that is subject to the rules and regulations adopted by the SEC (for example, information required by Item 305, "Quantitative and Qualitative Disclosures About Market Risk"), a statement that the voluntary information has been prepared in accordance with the related rules and regulations adopted by the SEC for such information
- If pro forma information is included, a statement that
  - — Management is responsible for the assumptions used in determining the pro forma adjustments
  - — Management believes that the assumptions provide a reasonable basis for presenting all the significant effects directly attributable to the transaction or event, that the related pro forma adjustments give appropriate effect to those assumptions, and that the pro forma column reflects the proper application of those adjustments to the historical financial statements
  - — Management believes that the significant effects directly attributable to the transaction or event are appropriately disclosed in the pro forma financial information

In a review engagement, management's refusal to furnish written representations constitutes a limitation of the scope of the engagement sufficient to require withdrawal from the review engagement. Further, the practitioner should consider the effects of the refusal on his or her ability to rely on other management representations.

If the practitioner is precluded from performing procedures he or she considers necessary in the circumstances with respect to a matter that is material to the MD&A presentation, even though management has made representations concerning the matter, there is a limitation on the scope of the engagement, and the practitioner should withdraw from a review engagement.

Documentation

Attest documentation is the principal record of attest procedures applied, information obtained, and conclusions or findings reached by a practitioner in an engagement. The quantity, type, and content of attest documentation are matters of the practitioner's professional judgment. Attest documentation serves mainly to

- Provide the principal support for the practitioner's report, including the representation regarding observance of the standards of fieldwork, which is implicit in the reference in the report to attestation standards.
- Aid the practitioner in the conduct and supervision of the attest engagement.

Attest documentation should be sufficient to (1) enable members of the engagement team with supervision and review responsibilities to understand the nature, timing, extent, and results of attest procedures performed and the information obtained and (2) indicate the engagement team member(s) who performed and reviewed the work.

Examples of attest documentation are work programs, analyses, memoranda, letters of confirmation and representation, abstracts or copies of entity documents, and schedules or commentaries prepared or obtained by the practitioner. Ordinarily, attest documentation includes

- Documentation of the engagement acceptance or continuance decision
- An engagement letter
- A planning form documenting the practitioner's knowledge of the client and consideration of attestation risk
- Documentation of the procedures performed
- Support for data in the presentation
- A discussion of unusual matters encountered and their resolution

- A representation letter
- Copies of reports from other accountants, if any, who have examined a component of the subject matter
- Documentation that the workpapers were reviewed

Attest documentation may be in paper form, electronic form, or other medium. The practitioner has an ethical, and in some situations a legal, obligation to maintain the confidentiality of client information or information of the responsible party. Because attest documentation often contains confidential information, the practitioner should adopt reasonable procedures to maintain the confidentiality of that information. The practitioner should also adopt reasonable procedures to prevent unauthorized access to attest documentation.

Reporting on a Review Engagement

In order for the practitioner to issue a report on a review of MD&A for an annual period, the financial statements for the periods covered by the MD&A presentation and the related auditor's report(s) should accompany the MD&A presentation. For a public entity, alternatively, the financial statements for the periods covered by the MD&A presentation and the related auditor's report(s) may be incorporated in the document containing the MD&A by reference to information filed with a regulatory agency.

If the MD&A presentation relates to an interim period and the entity is a public entity, the financial statements for the interim periods covered by the MD&A presentation and the related accountant's review report(s) should accompany the MD&A presentation, or be incorporated in the document containing the MD&A by reference to information filed with a regulatory agency.

If the MD&A presentation relates to an interim period and the entity is a nonpublic entity, the following conditions should be met in order for the practitioner to issue a review report:

- The MD&A presentation for the most recent fiscal year and related accountant's examination or review reports should accompany the interim MD&A presentation.
- The financial statements for the periods covered by the respective MD&A presentations (i.e., most recent fiscal year and interim periods and the related auditor's reports and accountant's review reports) should accompany the interim MD&A presentation.
- One of the following conditions should be met:
  - — A statement should be included in the body of the MD&A presentation that it has been prepared using the SEC rules and regulations.

— A separate written assertion should accompany the MD&A presentation or be included in a representation letter from the entity.

The practitioner's report on a review of MD&A should include all the following elements:

- A title that includes the word "independent."
- An identification of the MD&A presentation, including the period covered.
- A statement that management is responsible for the preparation of the MD&A pursuant to the rules and regulations adopted by the SEC.
- A reference to the auditor's report on the related financial statements, and if the report was other than a standard report, the substantive reasons for that.
- A statement that the review was conducted in accordance with attestation standards established by the AICPA [or, for engagements in accordance with PCAOB standards, "in accordance with the standards of the Public Company Accounting Oversight Board (United States)"].
- A description of the procedures for a review of MD&A.
- A statement that a review of MD&A is substantially less in scope than an examination, the objective of which is an expression of opinion regarding the MD&A presentation, and accordingly, no such opinion is expressed.
- A paragraph stating that
  — The preparation of MD&A requires management to interpret the criteria, make determinations as to the relevancy of information to be included, and make estimates and assumptions that affect reported information.
  — Actual results in the future may differ materially from management's present assessment of information regarding the estimated future impact of transactions and events that have occurred or are expected to occur, expected sources of liquidity and capital resources, operating trends, commitments, and uncertainties.
- If the entity is a nonpublic entity, a statement that, although the entity is not subject to the rules and regulations of the SEC, the MD&A presentation is intended to be a presentation in accordance with the rules and regulations adopted by the SEC.
- A statement about whether any information came to the practitioner's attention that caused him or her to believe that:
  — The MD&A presentation does not include, in all material respects, the required elements of the rules and regulations adopted by the SEC.

  - The historical financial amounts included in the MD&A have not been accurately derived, in all material respects, from the entity's financial statements.
  - The underlying information, determinations, estimates, and assumptions of the entity do not provide a reasonable basis for the disclosures.
- If the entity is a public entity, or a nonpublic entity that is making or has made an offering of securities and it appears that the securities may subsequently be registered or subject to a filing with the SEC or other regulatory agency, a statement of restrictions on the use of the report to specified parties because it is not intended to be filed with the SEC as a report under the 1933 Act or the 1934 Act.
- Manual or printed signature of the practitioner's firm.
- Date of the review report, which is the date as of the completion of the review procedures (the date should not precede the date of the practitioner's report on the latest historical financial statements covered by the MD&A).
- For engagements in accordance with the standards of the Public Company Accounting Oversight Board, the city and state (or city and country, for non-U.S. practitioners) where the practitioner's report has been issued.

Appendix 14G is an example of a standard review report on an annual MD&A presentation. Appendix 14H is a standard review report on an interim MD&A presentation.

Report Modifications

The practitioner should modify the standard review report if any of the following conditions exist:

- The MD&A presentation excludes a material required element of the SEC rules and regulations (see Appendix 14I).
- The historical financial amounts have not been accurately derived, in all material respects, from the entity's financial statements.
- The underlying information, determinations, estimates, and assumptions used by management do not provide the entity with a reasonable basis for the disclosures in the MD&A presentation.
- The practitioner decides to refer to the report of another practitioner as the basis, in part, for his or her report.
- The practitioner is engaged to review the MD&A presentation after it has been filed with the SEC or other regulatory agency.

OTHER ISSUES

Combined Examination and Review Report on MD&A

A practitioner may be engaged both (1) to examine MD&A as of the most recent fiscal year-end and (2) to review a separate MD&A presentation for a subsequent interim period. If the examination and review engagements are completed at the same time, the practitioner may issue a combined report. Appendix 14J is an example of a combined report on an examination of an annual MD&A presentation and the review of a separate MD&A presentation for an interim period.

An entity may prepare a combined MD&A presentation for annual and interim periods in which there is a discussion of liquidity and capital resources only as of the most recent interim period but not as of the most recent annual period. In such circumstances, the practitioner is limited to performing the highest level of service that is provided with respect to the historical financial statements for any of the periods covered by the MD&A presentation. Appendix 14K is an example of a review report on a combined MD&A presentation for annual and interim periods.

Engagement of Practitioner Subsequent to the Filing of MD&A

If the practitioner is engaged to examine or review an MD&A presentation of a public entity that has already been filed with the SEC, or other regulatory agency, he or she should consider whether material subsequent events are appropriately disclosed in a Form 8-K or Form 10-Q or a registration statement that includes or incorporates by reference the MD&A presentation, as follows.

Subsequent Event Disclosed or There Are No Subsequent Events

If subsequent events of a public entity are appropriately disclosed in a Form 8-K or Form 10-Q or in a registration statement or if there have been no material subsequent events, the practitioner should add the following paragraph to his or her examination or review report following the opinion or concluding paragraph:

> The accompanying Management's Discussion and Analysis does not consider events that have occurred subsequent to July 15, 20X3, the date as of which it was filed with the Securities and Exchange Commission.

Subsequent Event Not Disclosed

If there has been a material subsequent event that has not been appropriately disclosed, and if the practitioner determines that it is appropriate to issue a report even though the MD&A presentation has not been updated for the material subsequent event, the practitioner should express a qualified or an adverse opinion (or appropriately modify the review report) on the MD&A presentation. If the material subsequent event is not appropriately disclosed, the practitioner should evaluate (1) whether to resign from the engagement related to the MD&A presentation and (2) whether to remain as the entity's auditor or stand for reelection to audit the entity's financial statements.

Because a nonpublic entity is not subject to the filing requirements of the SEC, an MD&A presentation of a nonpublic entity should be updated for material subsequent events through the date of the practitioner's report.

Situations Involving a Predecessor Auditor Who Has Audited Prior-Period Financial Statements

If a predecessor auditor has audited the financial statements for a prior period covered by the MD&A, the successor practitioner reporting on the MD&A should consider reviewing the predecessor auditor's working papers with respect to audits of financial statements and examinations or reviews of MD&A presentations for such prior periods.

Also, if at the time of the appointment as auditor, the practitioner is also being engaged to examine or review MD&A, he or she should also make specific inquiries of the predecessor auditor regarding matters that may affect the examination or review engagement of MD&A.

Situations Involving Another Auditor of a Significant Part of the Financial Statements

When another auditor audits a significant part of the financial statements, the practitioner may perform the procedures him- or herself directly with respect to the components or request that the other auditor perform procedures with respect to the MD&A. The practitioner should consider whether he or she has sufficient industry expertise and experience with respect to a subsidiary audited by another auditor to take sole responsibility for the consolidated MD&A presentation.

Unless the other auditor issues an examination or a review report on a separate MD&A presentation of components, the principal practitioner should not make reference to the work of the other practitioner on MD&A in his or her report on MD&A. Therefore, if the practitioner has requested the other auditor to perform procedures, the principal practitioner should perform the procedures that he or she considers necessary to take responsibility for the work of the other auditor. Such procedures may include one or more of the following:

- Visit the other auditor and discuss the procedures performed and the results obtained.
- Review the working papers of the other auditor with respect to the component.
- Participate in discussions with the component's management regarding matters that may affect the preparation of MD&A.
- Perform additional tests with respect to the component.

Communications with Audit Committee

The practitioner may become aware of certain matters that require communication with the audit committee, such as the following:

- Material inconsistencies between the MD&A presentation and other information included in the document containing the MD&A presentation.
- Material inconsistencies between the MD&A presentation and the historical financial statements.
- Material omissions.
- Material misstatements of fact.

If management refuses to take corrective action in the circumstances, the practitioner should inform the audit committee, or others with equivalent authority and responsibility. If the MD&A is not revised, the practitioner should consider consulting with his or her legal counsel and evaluate

- Whether to resign from the engagement related to the MD&A.
- Whether to remain as the entity's auditor or stand for reelection to audit the entity's financial statements.

A practitioner who is engaged after the MD&A presentation has been filed with the SEC (or other regulatory agency) may become aware that the MD&A presentation on file has not been revised for a matter that the practitioner has qualified or would qualify his or her opinion for. In such circumstances, the practitioner should discuss the matter with the audit committee and request that the MD&A presentation be revised. If the audit committee fails to take appropriate action, the practitioner should consider whether to resign as the independent auditor of the company. For additional guidance, see AU 317 (Illegal Acts by Clients).

APPENDIX 14A
PROCEDURES CHECKLIST FOR ENGAGEMENTS TO EXAMINE MD&A

	Performed by	Workpaper Reference
1. Consider whether management, and others involved in the preparation of MD&A (e.g., legal counsel), have appropriate knowledge of the SEC rules and regulations relating to MD&A.	________	________
2. Obtain an understanding of the SEC rules and regulations for MD&A and management's method for the preparation of MD&A, and make inquiries about		
a. The sources of the information.	________	________
b. How the information is gathered.	________	________
c. How management evaluates the types of factors having a material effect on financial condition, results of operations, and cash flows.	________	________
d. Whether there have been any changes in the procedures from the prior year.	________	________
3. Obtain an understanding of the entity's internal control applicable to the preparation of MD&A sufficient to plan the engagement and assess control risk, by performing procedures such as the following:		
a. Making inquiries of appropriate management, supervisory, and staff personnel.	________	________
b. Inspecting relevant documents and records.	________	________
c. Observing the entity's relevant activities and operations, including controls over matters discussed in MD&A, nonfinancial data that is included, and management evaluation of the reasonableness of included information.	________	________

	Performed by	Workpaper Reference
4. Develop an overall strategy for the expected scope and performance of the engagement, by considering factors such as the following:		
a. The industry the entity operates in and matters affecting the industry, such as financial reporting practices, economic conditions, laws and regulations, and technological changes.	________	________
b. Knowledge of the entity's internal control applicable to the preparation of MD&A obtained during the audit of the financial statements and subsequent changes.	________	________
c. The entity's business, including its organization structure, operating characteristics, capital structure, and distribution methods.	________	________
d. The types of relevant information that management reports to external analysts, e.g., press releases and presentations to lenders and rating agencies concerning past and future performance.	________	________
e. How the entity analyzes actual performance versus budgets and the types of information provided to the board of directors for day-to-day operations and long-range planning.	________	________
f. The extent of management's knowledge of and experience with the SEC rules and regulations for MD&A.	________	________
g. For nonpublic entities, the intended use of the MD&A presentation.	________	________
h. Preliminary judgments about materiality, inherent risk at the individual assertion level, and factors relating to significant deficiencies in internal control applicable to the preparation of MD&A.	________	________
i. The fraud risk factors or other conditions identified during the audit of the most recent annual financial statements and the practitioner's response to the risk factors.	________	________
j. The type and extent of evidential matter supporting management's assertions and disclosures in the MD&A.	________	________

	Performed by	Workpaper Reference
k. The nature of complex or subjective matters potentially material to the MD&A that may require specialized skill or knowledge or using the work of a specialist to obtain sufficient evidential matter.	________	________
l. The presence of an internal audit function and the extent that internal auditors are involved in directly testing the MD&A presentation, in monitoring the entity's internal control applicable to the preparation of MD&A, or in testing the underlying records supporting disclosures in the MD&A.	________	________
5. Consider the results of the audits of the financial statements for the periods covered by the MD&A on the examination engagement, including matters such as		
a. The availability and condition of the entity's records.	________	________
b. The nature and magnitude of audit adjustments.	________	________
c. Likely misstatements that were not corrected in the financial statements that may affect MD&A disclosures, such as misclassifications between financial statement line items.	________	________
d. Modification of the auditor's report, including matters addressed in explanatory paragraph of the auditor's report.	________	________
6. When MD&A has not previously been examined:		
a. Consider the degree to which the entity has information available for prior periods and the continuity of the entity's personnel and their ability to respond to inquiries with respect to prior periods.	________	________
b. Obtain an understanding of the entity's internal control in prior years that is applicable to the preparation of MD&A.	________	________
7. When the entity has operations in several components (for example, locations, subsidiaries), determine the components		

	Performed by	Workpaper Reference
procedures should be applied to. In such cases, consider factors such as		
a. The relative significance of each component to the applicable MD&A disclosure.	________	________
b. The extent to which pertinent records are centralized.	________	________
c. The effectiveness of controls, particularly oversight controls at the various locations.	________	________
d. The nature and extent of operations conducted at the various components.	________	________
e. The similarity of operations and internal control for the different components.	________	________
8. Read the MD&A presentation and determine whether the information presented is consistent with the audited financial statements, or related accounting records and analyses.	________	________
9. Recompute increases, decreases, and percentages disclosed.	________	________
10. Compare nonfinancial data to the audited financial statements or, if inapplicable, to other records.	________	________
11. Consider whether explanations presented in the MD&A are consistent with information obtained during the audit; for items or explanations that cannot be substantiated by information in the audit working papers, investigate through inquiry of client executives and inspection of relevant records.	________	________
12. Examine internally generated documents (e.g., sales analyses, business plans) and externally generated documents (e.g., contracts, loan agreements) to support the explanations, events, and items disclosed in the MD&A.	________	________
13. Obtain available prospective financial information (e.g., budgets, financial forecasts and projections) and compare it with forward-looking MD&A disclosures; consider whether the underlying information and assumptions provide a reasonable basis for the MD&A disclosures.	________	________

	Performed by	Workpaper Reference
14. Consider obtaining prospective financial information relating to prior periods and comparing actual results with forecasted and projected amounts.	______	______
15. Make inquiries of company officials responsible for operational, financial, and accounting matters about their future plans and expectations that could affect the entity's liquidity and capital resources.	______	______
16. Consider obtaining independent information about industry trends, inflation, and changing prices and comparing it with the related MD&A disclosures.	______	______
17. Compare the information in the MD&A with the rules and regulations adopted by the SEC.	______	______
18. Read the minutes of meetings of the board of directors and other significant committees to identify matters that may affect MD&A and consider whether such matters are appropriately addressed in the MD&A.	______	______
19. Inquire of management about the entity's prior experience with the SEC and the extent of comments received in connection with documents filed with the SEC by the entity; read related correspondence between the entity and the SEC.	______	______
20. Obtain public communications made by the entity (e.g., press releases, quarterly reports) dealing with historical and future results; consider whether the MD&A is consistent with the communications.	______	______
21. Consider obtaining other types of publicly available information (e.g., analyst reports, news articles) and compare it with the MD&A presentation.	______	______
22. If the MD&A presentation includes certain nonfinancial data (e.g., units produced, units sold, major customers, plant utilization, square footage), consider whether		
a. The definitions used by management for the nonfinancial data are reasonable.	______	______

	Performed by	Workpaper Reference
b. Industry standards exist for the non-financial data.	________	________
c. Different methods of measurement may be used and whether such methods could result in materially different results.	________	________
d. The method of measurement selected by management is reasonable and consistent between periods covered by the MD&A presentation.	________	________
23. Consider whether the MD&A discloses matters that could significantly impact future financial condition and results of operations of the entity, as follows:		
a. Inquire of the entity's management about current events, conditions, economic changes, commitments, and uncertainties.	________	________
b. Consider information obtained through the audit of the financial statements.	________	________
c. Obtain other information through procedures performed during the engagement.	________	________
24. Consider information about subsequent events after the end of the period addressed by MD&A and prior to the issuance of the report that may have a material effect on the entity's financial condition (including liquidity and capital resources), changes in financial condition, results of operations, and material commitments for capital resources. Events and matters that should be disclosed in the MD&A include those that		
a. Are reasonably expected to have a material favorable or unfavorable impact on net sales or revenues or income from continuing operations.	________	________
b. Are reasonably likely to result in a material increase or decrease in the entity's liquidity.	________	________
c. Will have a material effect on the entity's capital resources.	________	________

	Performed by	Workpaper Reference
d. Would cause reported financial information not to be necessarily indicative of future operating results or of future financial condition.	________	________
25. Perform the following subsequent events procedures		
a. Read available minutes of meetings of stockholders, directors, and appropriate committees.	________	________
b. Inquire about any recent meetings for which minutes have not yet been prepared. When minutes have not been prepared, inquire of management about matters dealt with at the meetings, and obtain written representation from management regarding the matters that were dealt with.	________	________
c. Read the latest available interim financial statements and compare them with the financial statements for the periods covered by the MD&A. Pay special attention to major changes in the business or environment that the client operates in, and inquire of and discuss with management		
(1) Whether the interim financial statements have been prepared on the same basis as the current period audited financial statements.	________	________
(2) Whether there were any significant changes in the entity's operations, liquidity, or capital resources in the subsequent period.	________	________
(3) The current status of items in the financial statements that the MD&A has been prepared for that were accounted for on the basis of tentative, preliminary, or inconclusive data.	________	________
(4) Whether any unusual adjustments were made during the period from the balance-sheet date to the date of inquiry.	________	________
d. Inquire of management about the current status of litigation, claims, and assessments identified during		

	Performed by	Workpaper Reference
the audit of the financial statements and consider obtaining updated legal letters from legal counsel.	________	________
e. Consider whether there have been any changes in economic conditions or the industry that could have a significant effect on the entity.	________	________
f. Obtain written representations from appropriate officials as to whether events occurred during the subsequent period that require disclosure in the MD&A.	________	________
g. Make additional inquiries or perform additional procedures that are deemed necessary depending on the results of the procedures described above.	________	________
26. Obtain a letter of representation from management that contains the following:		
a. Management's acknowledgment of its responsibility for the preparation of MD&A and their assertion that the MD&A presentation has been prepared in accordance with the rules and regulations adopted by the SEC for MD&A. (For nonpublic entities, also obtain a written assertion that the presentation has been prepared using the rules and regulations adopted by the SEC.)	________	________
b. A statement that the historical financial amounts included in the MD&A have been accurately derived from the entity's financial statements.	________	________
c. A statement that the entity's underlying information, determinations, estimates, and assumptions of the entity provide a reasonable basis for the disclosures contained in the MD&A.	________	________
d. A statement that the entity has made available to the practitioner all significant documentation related to compliance with the SEC rules and regulations for MD&A.	________	________
e. A statement on the completeness and availability of all minutes of meetings of stockholders, directors, and committees of directors.	________	________

	Performed by	Workpaper Reference
f. For public entities, a statement that management has provided to the practitioner communications from the SEC concerning noncompliance with or deficiencies in MD&A reporting practices.	______	______
g. A statement on whether any events occurred subsequent to the latest balance-sheet date that require disclosure in the MD&A.	______	______
h. If forward-looking information is included, a statement saying that		
(1) The forward-looking information is based on management's best estimate of expected events and operations and is consistent with budgets, forecasts, or operating plans prepared for the periods.	______	______
(2) The accounting principles expected to be used for the forward-looking information are consistent with the principles used in preparing the historical financial statements.	______	______
(3) Management has provided the latest version of budgets, forecasts, or operating plans and has informed the practitioner of any anticipated changes or modifications to the information that could affect the disclosures contained in the MD&A presentation.	______	______
i. If voluntary information is included that is subject to the rules and regulations adopted by the SEC (for example, information required by Item 305, "Quantitative and Qualitative Disclosures about Market Risk"), a statement that the voluntary information has been prepared in accordance with the related rules and regulations adopted by the SEC for voluntary information.	______	______
j. If pro forma information is included, a statement that		
(1) Management is responsible for the assumptions used in determining the pro forma adjustments.	______	______

	Performed by	Workpaper Reference
(2) Management believes that the assumptions provide a reasonable basis for presenting all the significant effects directly attributable to the transaction or event, that the related pro forma adjustments give appropriate effect to the assumptions, and that the pro forma column reflects the proper application of the adjustments to the historical financial statements.	______	______
(3) Management believes that the significant effects directly attributable to the transaction or event are appropriately disclosed in the pro forma financial information.	______	______

APPENDIX 14B
PROCEDURES CHECKLIST FOR ENGAGEMENTS TO REVIEW MD&A

	Performed by	Workpaper Reference
1. Consider whether management and others involved in the preparation of MD&A (e.g., legal counsel) have appropriate knowledge of the SEC rules and regulations relating to MD&A.	______	______
2. Obtain an understanding of the SEC rules and regulations for MD&A and management's method for the preparation of MD&A, and make inquiries about		
a. The sources of the information.	______	______
b. How the information is gathered.	______	______
c. How management evaluates the types of factors having a material effect on financial condition, results of operations, and cash flows.	______	______
d. Whether there have been any changes in the procedures from the prior year.	______	______
3. Develop an overall strategy for the expected scope and performance of the		

	Performed by	Workpaper Reference
engagement by considering factors such as the following:		
a. The industry the entity operates in and matters affecting the industry, such as financial reporting practices, economic conditions, laws and regulations, and technological changes.	________	________
b. The entity's business, including its organization structure, operating characteristics, capital structure, and distribution methods.	________	________
c. The types of relevant information that management reports to external analysts (e.g., press releases and presentations to lenders and rating agencies concerning past and future performance).	________	________
d. The extent of management's knowledge of and experience with the SEC rules and regulations for MD&A.	________	________
e. For nonpublic entities, the intended use of the MD&A presentation.	________	________
f. Matters identified during the audit or review of the historical financial statements relating to MD&A reporting, including knowledge of the entity's internal control applicable to the preparation of MD&A and the extent of recent changes, if any.	________	________
g. Matters identified during prior engagements to examine or review MD&A.	________	________
h. Preliminary judgments about materiality.	________	________
i. Any complex or subjective matters potentially material to the MD&A that may require specialized skill or knowledge.	________	________
j. The presence of an internal audit function and the extent to which internal auditors are involved in directly testing the MD&A presentation or underlying records.	________	________
4. Obtain a sufficient understanding of the entity's internal control applicable to the preparation of MD&A in order to:		
a. Identify types of potential misstatements in MD&A, including types of		

	Performed by	Workpaper Reference
material omissions, and consider the likelihood of their occurrence.	________	________
b. Select the inquiries and analytical procedures that will provide a basis for reporting whether		
(1) The MD&A presentation does not include, in all material respects, the required elements of the rules and regulations adopted by the SEC; or the historical financial amounts that are included have not been accurately derived, in all material respects, from the entity's financial statements.	________	________
(2) The underlying information, determinations, estimates, and assumptions of the entity do not provide a reasonable basis for the disclosures.	________	________
5. Read the MD&A presentation and determine whether the information presented is consistent with the audited financial statements (or reviewed interim financial information if the MD&A includes interim information).	________	________
6. Compare financial amounts to the audited or reviewed financial statements or related accounts and analyses.	________	________
7. Recompute the increases, decreases, and percentages disclosed.	________	________
8. Compare nonfinancial data to the audited or reviewed financial statements or, if inapplicable, other records.	________	________
9. Consider whether explanations presented in the MD&A are consistent with information obtained during the audit or the review of interim financial information; make further inquiries of management as necessary.	________	________
10. Obtain available prospective financial information (e.g., budgets, financial forecasts and projections) and compare it with forward-looking MD&A disclosures; consider whether the underlying information, determinations, estimates, and assumptions provide a reasonable basis for the MD&A disclosures of trends, demands, commitments, events, or uncertainties.	________	________

	Performed by	Workpaper Reference
11. Make inquiries of company officials responsible for operational, financial, and accounting matters about their future plans and expectations that could affect the entity's liquidity and capital resources.	________	________
12. Compare the information in the MD&A with the SEC rules and regulations.	________	________
13. Read the minutes of meetings of the board of directors and other significant committees to identify matters that may affect MD&A and consider whether the matters are appropriately addressed in the MD&A.	________	________
14. Inquire of management about the entity's prior experience with the SEC and the extent of comments received in connection with documents filed by the entity with the SEC; read related correspondence between the entity and the SEC.	________	________
15. Inquire of management regarding the nature of public communications (e.g., press releases, quarterly reports) dealing with historical and future results and consider whether the MD&A presentation is consistent with the communications.	________	________
16. If the MD&A presentation includes certain nonfinancial data (e.g., units produced, units sold, major customers, plant utilization, square footage), inquire about whether the definitions used by management for the nonfinancial data are consistent between periods covered by the MD&A presentation.	________	________
17. Consider information about subsequent events after the end of the period addressed by MD&A and prior to the issuance of the report that may have a material effect on the entity's financial condition (including liquidity and capital resources), changes in financial condition, results of operations, and material commitments for capital resources. Events and matters that should be disclosed in the MD&A include those that		
a. Are reasonably expected to have a material favorable or unfavorable		

	Performed by	Workpaper Reference
impact on net sales or revenues or income from continuing operations.	______	______
b. Are reasonably likely to result in a material increase or decrease in the entity's liquidity.	______	______
c. Will have a material effect on the entity's capital resources.	______	______
d. Would cause reported financial information not to be necessarily indicative of future operating results or of future financial condition.	______	______
18. Perform the following subsequent-events procedures:		
a. Read available minutes of meetings of stockholders, directors, and appropriate committees.	______	______
b. Inquire about any recent meetings for which minutes have not yet been prepared. When minutes have not been prepared, inquire of management about matters dealt with at the meetings and obtain written representation from management regarding the matters.	______	______
c. Read the latest available interim financial statements and compare them with the financial statements for the periods covered by the MD&A. Pay special attention to major changes in the business or environment that the client operates in and inquire of and discuss with management		
(1) Whether the interim financial statements have been prepared on the same basis as the current period audited financial statements.	______	______
(2) Whether there were any significant changes in the entity's operations, liquidity, or capital resources in the subsequent period.	______	______
(3) The current status of items in the financial statements for which the MD&A has been prepared that were accounted for on the basis of tentative, preliminary, or inconclusive data.	______	______

	Performed by	Workpaper Reference
(4) Whether any unusual adjustments were made during the period from the balance-sheet date to the date of inquiry.	________	________
d. Inquire of management about the current status of litigation, claims, and assessments identified during the audit of the financial statements and consider obtaining updated legal letters from legal counsel.	________	________
e. Consider whether there have been any changes in economic conditions or the industry that could have a significant effect on the entity.	________	________
f. Obtain written representations from appropriate officials as to whether any events occurred during the subsequent period that would require disclosure in the MD&A.	________	________
g. Make additional inquiries or perform additional procedures that are deemed necessary depending on the results of the procedures described above.	________	________
19. Obtain a letter of representations from management that contains the following:		
a. Management's acknowledgment of its responsibility for the preparation of MD&A and management's assertion that the MD&A presentation has been prepared in accordance with the rules and regulations adopted by the SEC for MD&A. (For nonpublic entities, also obtain a written assertion that the presentation has been prepared using the rules and regulations adopted by the SEC.)	________	________
b. A statement that the historical financial amounts included in the MD&A have been accurately derived from the entity's financial statements.	________	________
c. A statement that the entity's underlying information, determinations, estimates, and assumptions provide a reasonable basis for the disclosures contained in the MD&A.	________	________

	Performed by	Workpaper Reference
d. A statement that the entity has made available to the practitioner all significant documentation related to compliance with the SEC rules and regulations for MD&A.	________	________
e. A statement regarding the completeness and availability of all minutes of meetings of stockholders, directors, and committees of directors.	________	________
f. For public entities a statement that management has provided to the practitioner communications from the SEC concerning noncompliance with or deficiencies in MD&A reporting practices.	________	________
g. A statement on whether any events occurred subsequent to the latest balance-sheet date that require disclosure in the MD&A.	________	________
h. If forward-looking information is included, a statement that		
(1) The forward-looking information is based on management's best estimate of expected events and operations and is consistent with budgets, forecasts, or operating plans prepared for the periods.	________	________
(2) The accounting principles expected to be used for the forward-looking information are consistent with the principles used in preparing the historical financial statements.	________	________
(3) Management has provided the latest version of the budgets, forecasts, or operating plans and has informed the practitioner of any anticipated changes or modifications to the information that could affect the disclosures contained in the MD&A presentation.	________	________
i. If voluntary information is included that is subject to the rules and regulations adopted by the SEC (for example, information required by Item 305, "Quantitative and Qualitative		

	Performed by	Workpaper Reference
Disclosures about Market Risk"), a statement that the voluntary information has been prepared in accordance with the related rules and regulations adopted by the SEC for voluntary information.	________	________
j. If pro forma information is included, a statement that		
(1) Management is responsible for the assumptions used in determining the pro forma adjustments.	________	________
(2) Management believes that the assumptions provide a reasonable basis for presenting all the significant effects directly attributable to the transaction or event, that the related pro forma adjustments give appropriate effect to the assumptions, and that the pro forma column reflects the proper application of the adjustments to the historical financial statements.	________	________
(3) Management believes that the significant effects directly attributable to the transaction or event are appropriately disclosed in the pro forma financial information.	________	________

APPENDIX 14C
STANDARD UNQUALIFIED EXAMINATION REPORT ON MD&A

Independent Accountant's Report

[*for accounting firms registered with the PCAOB, the title should read* "Report of Independent Registered Public Accounting Firm"]

Board of Directors and Stockholders
ABC Company

We have examined ABC Company's Management's Discussion and Analysis taken as a whole, included [incorporated by reference] in the Company's [*insert description of registration statement or document*]. Management is responsible for the preparation of the Company's Management's Discussion and Analysis pursuant to the rules and regulations adopted by the Securities and Exchange Commission. Our responsibility is to express an opinion on the presentation based on our examination. We have audited, in accordance with auditing standards generally accepted in the United States of America [*for engagements performed in accordance with PCAOB standards,* "in accordance with the standards of the Public Company Accounting Oversight Board (United States)"], the financial statements of ABC Company as of December 31, 20X2, and 20X1, and for each of the years in the three-year period ended December 31, 20X2, and in our report dated February 12, 20X3, we expressed an unqualified opinion on those financial statements.[1]

Our examination of Management's Discussion and Analysis was made in accordance with attestation standards established by the American Institute of Certified Public Accountants [*for engagements performed in accordance with PCAOB standards,* "in accordance with the standards of the Public Company Accounting Oversight Board (United States)"] and, accordingly, included examining, on a test basis, evidence supporting the historical amounts and disclosures in the presentation. An examination also includes assessing the significant determinations made by management as to the relevancy of information to be included and the estimates and assumptions that affect reported information. We believe that our examination provides a reasonable basis for our opinion.

The preparation of Management's Discussion and Analysis requires management to interpret the criteria, make determinations as to the relevancy of information to be included, and make estimates and assumptions that affect reported information. Management's Discussion and Analysis includes information regarding the estimated future impact of transactions and events that have occurred or are expected to occur, expected sources of

---

[1] If prior financial statements were audited by other auditors, this sentence would be replaced by the following:

> We have audited, in accordance with auditing standards generally accepted in the United States of America [*for engagements performed in accordance with PCAOB standards,* "in accordance with the standards of the Public Company Accounting Oversight Board (United States)"], the financial statements of ABC Company as of and for the year ended December 31, 20X2, and in our report dated February 12, 20X3, we expressed an unqualified opinion on those financial statements. The financial statements of ABC Company as of December 31, 20X1, and for each of the years in the two-year period then ended were audited by other auditors, whose report dated January 30, 20X2, expressed an unqualified opinion on those financial statements.

If the practitioner's opinion on the financial statements is based on the report of other auditors, this sentence would be replaced by the following:

> We have audited, in accordance with auditing standards generally accepted in the United States of America [*for engagements performed in accordance with PCAOB standards,* "in accordance with the standards of the Public Company Accounting Oversight Board (United States)"], the financial statements of ABC Company as of December 31, 20X2, and 20X1, and for each of the years in the three-year period ended December 31, 20X2, and in our report dated February 12, 20X3, we expressed an unqualified opinion on those financial statements based on our audits and the report of other auditors.

liquidity and capital resources, operating trends, commitments, and uncertainties. Actual results in the future may differ materially from management's present assessment of this information because events and circumstances frequently do not occur as expected.[2]

In our opinion, the Company's presentation of Management's Discussion and Analysis includes, in all material respects, the required elements of the rules and regulations adopted by the Securities and Exchange Commission; the historical financial amounts included therein have been accurately derived, in all material respects, from the Company's financial statements; and the underlying information, determinations, estimates, and assumptions of the Company provide a reasonable basis for the disclosures contained therein.

[*signature*]

[*city and state for U.S. practitioners; city and country for non-U.S. practitioners*]

[*date*]

APPENDIX 14D
EXAMINATION REPORT ON MD&A WITH A QUALIFIED OPINION DUE TO A MATERIAL OMISSION

Independent Accountant's Report

[*for accounting firms registered with the PCAOB, the title should read* "Report of Independent Registered Public Accounting Firm"]

Board of Directors and Stockholders
ABC Company

We have examined ABC Company's Management's Discussion and Analysis taken as a whole, included [incorporated by reference] in the Company's [*insert description of registration statement or document*]. Management is responsible for the preparation of the Company's Management's Discussion and Analysis pursuant to the rules and regulations adopted by the Securities and Exchange Commission. Our responsibility is to express an opinion on the presentation based on our examination. We have audited, in accordance with auditing standards generally accepted in the United States of America [*for engagements performed in accordance with*

[2] If the entity is a nonpublic entity, the following sentence should be added to the beginning of this explanatory paragraph:

> Although ABC Company is not subject to the rules and regulations of the Securities and Exchange Commission, the accompanying Management's Discussion and Analysis is intended to be a presentation in accordance with the rules and regulations adopted by the Securities and Exchange Commission.

PCAOB standards, "in accordance with the standards of the Public Company Accounting Oversight Board (United States)"], the financial statements of ABC Company as of December 31, 20X2, and 20X1, and for each of the years in the three-year period ended December 31, 20X2, and in our report dated February 12, 20X3, we expressed an unqualified opinion on those financial statements.

Our examination of Management's Discussion and Analysis was made in accordance with attestation standards established by the American Institute of Certified Public Accountants [*for engagements performed in accordance with PCAOB standards,* "in accordance with the standards of the Public Company Accounting Oversight Board (United States)"] and, accordingly, included examining, on a test basis, evidence supporting the historical amounts and disclosures in the presentation. An examination also includes assessing the significant determinations made by management as to the relevancy of information to be included and the estimates and assumptions that affect reported information. We believe that our examination provides a reasonable basis for our opinion.

The preparation of Management's Discussion and Analysis requires management to interpret the criteria, make determinations as to the relevancy of information to be included, and make estimates and assumptions that affect reported information. Management's Discussion and Analysis includes information regarding the estimated future impact of transactions and events that have occurred or are expected to occur, expected sources of liquidity and capital resources, operating trends, commitments, and uncertainties. Actual results in the future may differ materially from management's present assessment of this information because events and circumstances frequently do not occur as expected.

Based on information furnished to us by management, we believe that the Company has excluded a discussion of the significant capital outlay required for its plans to expand into the telecommunications industry and the possible effects on the Company's financial condition, liquidity, and capital resources.

In our opinion, except for the omission of the matter described in the preceding paragraph, the Company's presentation of Management's Discussion and Analysis includes, in all material respects, the required elements of the rules and regulations adopted by the Securities and Exchange Commission; the historical financial amounts included therein have been accurately derived, in all material respects, from the Company's financial statements; and the underlying information, determinations, estimates, and assumptions of the Company provide a reasonable basis for the disclosures contained therein.

[*signature*]

[*city and state for U.S. practitioners; city and country for non-U.S. practitioners*]

[*date*]

APPENDIX 14E
EXAMINATION REPORT ON MD&A WITH A QUALIFIED OPINION WHEN OVERLY SUBJECTIVE ASSERTIONS ARE INCLUDED IN MD&A

Independent Accountant's Report

[*for accounting firms registered with the PCAOB, the title should read* "Report of Independent Registered Public Accounting Firm"]

Board of Directors and Stockholders
ABC Company

We have examined ABC Company's Management's Discussion and Analysis taken as a whole, included [incorporated by reference] in the Company's [*insert description of registration statement or document*]. Management is responsible for the preparation of the Company's Management's Discussion and Analysis pursuant to the rules and regulations adopted by the Securities and Exchange Commission. Our responsibility is to express an opinion on the presentation based on our examination. We have audited in accordance with auditing standards generally accepted in the United States of America [*for engagements performed in accordance with PCAOB standards*, "in accordance with the standards of the Public Company Accounting Oversight Board (United States)"], the financial statements of ABC Company as of December 31, 20X2, and 20X1, and for each of the years in the three-year period ended December 31, 20X2, and in our report dated February 12, 20X3, we expressed an unqualified opinion on those financial statements.

Our examination of Management's Discussion and Analysis was made in accordance with attestation standards established by the American Institute of Certified Public Accountants [*for engagements performed in accordance with PCAOB standards*, "in accordance with the standards of the Public Company Accounting Oversight Board (United States)"] and, accordingly, included examining, on a test basis, evidence supporting the historical amounts and disclosures in the presentation. An examination also includes assessing the significant determinations made by management as to the relevancy of information to be included and the estimates and assumptions that affect reported information. We believe that our examination provides a reasonable basis for our opinion.

The preparation of Management's Discussion and Analysis requires management to interpret the criteria, make determinations as to the relevancy of information to be included, and make estimates and assumptions that affect reported information. Management's Discussion and Analysis includes information regarding the estimated future impact of transactions and events that have occurred or are expected to occur, expected sources of liquidity and capital resources, operating trends, commitments, and uncertainties. Actual results in the future may differ materially from management's present assessment of this information because events and circumstances frequently do not occur as expected.

Based on information furnished to us by management, we believe that the underlying information, determinations, estimates, and assumptions used by management do not provide the company with a reasonable basis for the disclosure concerning [*describe*] in the Company's Management's Discussion and Analysis.

In our opinion, except for the disclosure regarding [*describe*] discussed in the preceding paragraph, the Company's presentation of Management's Discussion and Analysis includes, in all material respects, the required elements of the rules and regulations adopted by the Securities and Exchange Commission; the historical financial amounts included therein have been accurately derived, in all material respects, from the Company's financial statements; and the underlying information, determinations, estimates, and assumptions of the Company provide a reasonable basis for the disclosures contained therein.

[*signature*]

[*city and state for U.S. practitioners; city and country for non-U.S. practitioners*]

[*date*]

APPENDIX 14F EXAMINATION REPORT ON MD&A WITH REFERENCE MADE TO THE REPORT OF ANOTHER PRACTITIONER

Independent Accountant's Report

[*for accounting firms registered with the PCAOB, the title should read* "Report of Independent Registered Public Accounting Firm"]

Board of Directors and Stockholders
ABC Company

We have examined ABC Company's Management's Discussion and Analysis taken as a whole, included [incorporated by reference] in the Company's [*insert description of registration statement or document*]. Management is responsible for the preparation of the Company's Management's Discussion and Analysis pursuant to the rules and regulations adopted by the Securities and Exchange Commission. Our responsibility is to express an opinion on the presentation based on our examination.

We did not examine Management's Discussion and Analysis of DEF Corporation, a wholly owned subsidiary, included in DEF Corporation's [*insert description of registration statement or document*]. Such Management's Discussion and Analysis was examined by other accountants, whose report has been furnished to us, and our opinion, insofar as it relates to information included for DEF Corporation, is based solely on the report of the other accountants.

We have audited, in accordance with auditing standards generally accepted in the United States of America [*for engagements performed in accordance with PCAOB standards,* "in accordance with the standards of the Public Company Accounting Oversight Board (United States)"], the consolidated financial statements of ABC Company as of December 31, 20X2, and 20X1, and for each of the years in the three-year period ended December 31, 20X2, and in our report dated February 12, 20X3, we expressed an unqualified opinion on those financial statements based on our audits and the report of other auditors.

Our examination of Management's Discussion and Analysis was made in accordance with attestation standards established by the American Institute of Certified Public Accountants [*for engagements performed in accordance with PCAOB standards,* "in accordance with the standards of the Public Company Accounting Oversight Board (United States)"] and, accordingly, included examining, on a test basis, evidence supporting the historical amounts and disclosures in the presentation. An examination also includes assessing the significant determinations made by management as to the relevancy of information to be included and the estimates and assumptions that affect reported information. We believe that our examination and the report of the other accountants provide a reasonable basis for our opinion.

The preparation of Management's Discussion and Analysis requires management to interpret the criteria, make determinations as to the relevancy of information to be included, and make estimates and assumptions that affect reported information. Management's Discussion and Analysis includes information regarding the estimated future impact of transactions and events that have occurred or are expected to occur, expected sources of liquidity and capital resources, operating trends, commitments, and uncertainties. Actual results in the future may differ materially from management's present assessment of this information because events and circumstances frequently do not occur as expected.[1]

In our opinion, based on our examination and the report of other accountants, the Company's presentation of Management's Discussion and Analysis included [incorporated by reference] in the Company's [*insert description of registration statement or document*] includes, in all material respects, the required elements of the rules and regulations adopted by the Securities and Exchange Commission; the historical financial amounts included therein have been accurately derived, in all material respects, from the Company's financial statements; and the underlying information, determinations,

---

[1] If the entity is a nonpublic entity, the following sentence should be added to the beginning of this explanatory paragraph:

> Although ABC Company is not subject to the rules and regulations of the Securities and Exchange Commission, the accompanying Management's Discussion and Analysis is intended to be a presentation in accordance with the rules and regulations adopted by the Securities and Exchange Commission.

estimates, and assumptions of the Company provide a reasonable basis for the disclosures contained therein.

[*signature*]

[*city and state for U.S. practitioners; city and country for non-U.S. practitioners*]

[*date*]

APPENDIX 14G STANDARD REVIEW REPORT ON AN ANNUAL MD&A PRESENTATION

Independent Accountant's Report

[*for accounting firms registered with the PCAOB, the title should read* "Report of Independent Registered Public Accounting Firm"]

Board of Directors and Stockholders
ABC Company

We have reviewed ABC Company's Management's Discussion and Analysis taken as a whole, included [incorporated by reference] in the Company's [*insert description of registration statement or document*]. Management is responsible for the preparation of the Company's Management's Discussion and Analysis pursuant to the rules and regulations adopted by the Securities and Exchange Commission. We have audited, in accordance with auditing standards generally accepted in the United States of America [*for engagements performed in accordance with PCAOB standards,* "in accordance with the standards of the Public Company Accounting Oversight Board (United States)"], the financial statements of ABC Company as of December 31, 20X2, and 20X1, and for each of the years in the three-year period ended December 31, 20X2, and in our report dated February 12, 20X3, we expressed an unqualified opinion on those financial statements.

We conducted our review of Management's Discussion and Analysis in accordance with attestation standards established by the American Institute of Certified Public Accountants [*for engagements performed in accordance with PCAOB standards,* "in accordance with the standards of the Public Company Accounting Oversight Board (United States)"]. A review of Management's Discussion and Analysis consists principally of applying analytical procedures and making inquiries of persons responsible for financial, accounting, and operational matters. It is substantially less in scope than an examination, the objective of which is the expression of an opinion on the presentation. Accordingly, we do not express such an opinion.

The preparation of Management's Discussion and Analysis requires management to interpret the criteria, make determinations as to the relevancy of information to be included, and make estimates and assumptions that affect reported information. Management's Discussion and Analysis includes information regarding the estimated future impact of transactions and events that have occurred or are expected to occur, expected sources of liquidity and capital resources, operating trends, commitments, and uncertainties. Actual results in the future may differ materially from management's present assessment of this information because events and circumstances frequently do not occur as expected.[1]

Based on our review, nothing came to our attention that caused us to believe that the Company's presentation of Management's Discussion and Analysis does not include, in all material respects, the required elements of the rules and regulations adopted by the Securities and Exchange Commission, that the historical financial amounts included therein have not been accurately derived, in all material respects, from the Company's financial statements, or that the underlying information, determinations, estimates, and assumptions of the Company do not provide a reasonable basis for the disclosures contained therein.

This report is intended solely for the information and use of [*list or refer to specified parties*], and is not intended to be and should not be used by anyone other than the specified parties.

[*signature*]

[*city and state for U.S. practitioners; city and country for non-U.S. practitioners*]

[*date*]

APPENDIX 14H STANDARD REVIEW REPORT ON AN INTERIM MD&A PRESENTATION

Independent Accountant's Report

[*for accounting firms registered with the PCAOB, the title should read* "Report of Independent Registered Public Accounting Firm"]

Board of Directors and Stockholders
ABC Company

We have reviewed ABC Company's Management's Discussion and Analysis taken as a whole, included in the Company's [*insert description of registration*

---

[1] If the entity is a nonpublic entity, the following sentence should be added to the beginning of this explanatory paragraph:

> Although ABC Company is not subject to the rules and regulations of the Securities and Exchange Commission, the accompanying Management's Discussion and Analysis is intended to be a presentation in accordance with the rules and regulations adopted by the Securities and Exchange Commission.

statement or document]. Management is responsible for the preparation of the Company's Management's Discussion and Analysis pursuant to the rules and regulations adopted by the Securities and Exchange Commission. We have reviewed, in accordance with standards established by the American Institute of Certified Public Accountants [*for engagements performed in accordance with PCAOB standards,* "in accordance with the standards of the Public Company Accounting Oversight Board (United States)"], the interim financial information of ABC Company as of June 30, 20X3, and 20X2, and for the three-month and six-month periods then ended, and have issued our report thereon dated July 27, 20X3.

We conducted our review of Management's Discussion and Analysis in accordance with attestation standards established by the American Institute of Certified Public Accountants [*for engagements performed in accordance with PCAOB standards,* "in accordance with the standards of the Public Company Accounting Oversight Board (United States)"]. A review of Management's Discussion and Analysis consists principally of applying analytical procedures and making inquiries of persons responsible for financial, accounting, and operational matters. It is substantially less in scope than an examination, the objective of which is the expression of an opinion on the presentation. Accordingly, we do not express such an opinion.

The preparation of Management's Discussion and Analysis requires management to interpret the criteria, make determinations as to the relevancy of information to be included, and make estimates and assumptions that affect reported information. Management's Discussion and Analysis includes information regarding the estimated future impact of transactions and events that have occurred or are expected to occur, expected sources of liquidity and capital resources, operating trends, commitments, and uncertainties. Actual results in the future may differ materially from management's present assessment of this information because events and circumstances frequently do not occur as expected.[1]

Based on our review, nothing came to our attention that caused us to believe that the Company's presentation of Management's Discussion and Analysis does not include, in all material respects, the required elements of the rules and regulations adopted by the Securities and Exchange Commission, that the historical financial amounts included therein have not been accurately derived, in all material respects, from the Company's financial statements, or that the underlying information, determinations, estimates, and assumptions of the Company do not provide a reasonable basis for the disclosures contained therein.

---

[1] If the entity is a nonpublic entity, the following sentence should be added to the beginning of this explanatory paragraph:

> Although ABC Company is not subject to the rules and regulations of the Securities and Exchange Commission, the accompanying Management's Discussion and Analysis is intended to be a presentation in accordance with the rules and regulations adopted by the Securities and Exchange Commission.

This report is intended solely for the information and use of [*list or refer to specified parties*], and is not intended to be and should not be used by anyone other than the specified parties.

[*signature*]

[*city and state for U.S. practitioners; city and country for non-U.S. practitioners*]

[*date*]

APPENDIX 14I MODIFIED REVIEW REPORT ON AN MD&A PRESENTATION FOR A MATERIAL MISSTATEMENT

Independent Accountant's Report

[*for accounting firms registered with the PCAOB, the title should read* "Report of Independent Registered Public Accounting Firm"]

Board of Directors and Stockholders
ABC Company

We have reviewed ABC Company's Management's Discussion and Analysis taken as a whole, included [incorporated by reference] in the Company's [*insert description of registration statement or document*]. Management is responsible for the preparation of the Company's Management's Discussion and Analysis pursuant to the rules and regulations adopted by the Securities and Exchange Commission. We have audited, in accordance with auditing standards generally accepted in the United States of America [*for engagements performed in accordance with PCAOB standards,* "in accordance with the standards of the Public Company Accounting Oversight Board (United States)"], the financial statements of ABC Company as of December 31, 20X2, and 20X1, and for each of the years in the three-year period ended December 31, 20X2, and in our report dated February 12, 20X3, we expressed an unqualified opinion on those financial statements.

We conducted our review of Management's Discussion and Analysis in accordance with attestation standards established by the American Institute of Certified Public Accountants [*for engagements performed in accordance with PCAOB standards,* "in accordance with the standards of the Public Company Accounting Oversight Board (United States)"]. A review of Management's Discussion and Analysis consists principally of applying analytical procedures and making inquiries of persons responsible for financial, accounting, and operational matters. It is substantially less in scope than an examination, the objective of which is the expression of an opinion on the presentation. Accordingly, we do not express such an opinion.

The preparation of Management's Discussion and Analysis requires management to interpret the criteria, make determinations as to the relevancy of information to be included, and make estimates and assumptions that affect reported information. Management's Discussion and Analysis includes information regarding the estimated future impact of transactions and events that have occurred or are expected to occur, expected sources of liquidity and capital resources, operating trends, commitments, and uncertainties. Actual results in the future may differ materially from management's present assessment of this information because events and circumstances frequently do not occur as expected.[1]

Based on information furnished to us by management, we believe that the Company has excluded a discussion of the significant capital outlay required for its plans to expand into the telecommunications industry and the possible effects on the Company's financial condition, liquidity, and capital resources.

Based on our review, with the exception of the matter described in the preceding paragraph, nothing came to our attention that caused us to believe that the Company's presentation of Management's Discussion and Analysis does not include, in all material respects, the required elements of the rules and regulations adopted by the Securities and Exchange Commission, that the historical financial amounts included therein have not been accurately derived, in all material respects, from the Company's financial statements, or that the underlying information, determinations, estimates, and assumptions of the Company do not provide a reasonable basis for the disclosures contained therein.

This report is intended solely for the information and use of [*list or refer to specified parties*], and is not intended to be and should not be used by anyone other than the specified parties.

[*signature*]

[*city and state for U.S. practitioners; city and country for non-U.S. practitioners*]

[*date*]

APPENDIX 14J
COMBINED REPORT ON AN EXAMINATION OF AN ANNUAL MD&A PRESENTATION AND REVIEW OF MD&A FOR AN INTERIM PERIOD

Independent Accountant's Report

[*for accounting firms registered with the PCAOB, the title should read* "Report of Independent Registered Public Accounting Firm"]

[1] If the entity is a nonpublic entity, the following sentence should be added to the beginning of this explanatory paragraph:

> Although ABC Company is not subject to the rules and regulations of the Securities and Exchange Commission, the accompanying Management's Discussion and Analysis is intended to be a presentation in accordance with the rules and regulations adopted by the Securities and Exchange Commission.

Board of Directors and Stockholders
ABC Company

We have examined ABC Company's Management's Discussion and Analysis taken as a whole for the three-year period ended December 31, 20X2, included [incorporated by reference] in the Company's [*insert description of registration statement or document*]. Management is responsible for the preparation of the Company's Management's Discussion and Analysis pursuant to the rules and regulations adopted by the Securities and Exchange Commission. Our responsibility is to express an opinion on the annual presentation based on our examination. We have audited, in accordance with auditing standards generally accepted in the United States of America [*for engagements performed in accordance with PCAOB standards,* "in accordance with the standards of the Public Company Accounting Oversight Board (United States)"], the financial statements of ABC Company as of December 31, 20X2, and 20X1, and for each of the years in the three-year period ended December 31, 20X2, and in our report dated February 12, 20X3, we expressed an unqualified opinion on those financial statements.

Our examination of Management's Discussion and Analysis was conducted in accordance with attestation standards established by the American Institute of Certified Public Accountants [*for engagements performed in accordance with PCAOB standards,* "in accordance with the standards of the Public Company Accounting Oversight Board (United States)"] and, accordingly, included examining, on a test basis, evidence supporting the historical amounts and disclosures in the presentation. An examination also includes assessing the significant determinations made by management as to the relevancy of information to be included and the estimates and assumptions that affect reported information. We believe that our examination provides a reasonable basis for our opinion.

The preparation of Management's Discussion and Analysis requires management to interpret the criteria, make determinations as to the relevancy of information to be included, and make estimates and assumptions that affect reported information. Management's Discussion and Analysis includes information regarding the estimated future impact of transactions and events that have occurred or are expected to occur, expected sources of liquidity and capital resources, operating trends, commitments, and uncertainties. Actual results in the future may differ materially from management's present assessment of this information because events and circumstances frequently do not occur as expected.[1]

In our opinion, the Company's presentation of Management's Discussion and Analysis for the three-year period ended December 31, 20X2, includes,

---

[1] If the entity is a nonpublic entity, the following sentence should be added to the beginning of the explanatory paragraph:

> Although ABC Company is not subject to the rules and regulations of the Securities and Exchange Commission, the accompanying Management's Discussion and Analysis is intended to be a presentation in accordance with the rules and regulations adopted by the Securities and Exchange Commission.

in all material respects, the required elements of the rules and regulations adopted by the Securities and Exchange Commission; the historical financial amounts included therein have been accurately derived, in all material respects, from the Company's financial statements; and the underlying information, determinations, estimates, and assumptions of the Company provide a reasonable basis for the disclosures contained therein.

We have also reviewed ABC Company's Management's Discussion and Analysis taken as a whole for the six-month period ended June 30, 20X3, included [incorporated by reference] in the Company's [*insert description of registration statement or document*]. We have reviewed, in accordance with standards established by the American Institute of Certified Public Accountants [*for engagements performed in accordance with PCAOB standards,* "in accordance with the standards of the Public Company Accounting Oversight Board (United States)"], the interim financial information of ABC Company as of June 30, 20X3, and 20X2, and for the six-month periods then ended, and have issued our report thereon dated July 27, 20X3.

We conducted our review of Management's Discussion and Analysis in accordance with attestation standards established by the American Institute of Certified Public Accountants [*for engagements performed in accordance with PCAOB standards,* "in accordance with the standards of the Public Company Accounting Oversight Board (United States)"]. A review of Management's Discussion and Analysis consists principally of applying analytical procedures and making inquiries of persons responsible for financial, accounting, and operational matters. It is substantially less in scope than an examination, the objective of which is the expression of an opinion on the presentation. Accordingly, we do not express such an opinion.

Based on our review, nothing came to our attention that caused us to believe that the Company's presentation of Management's Discussion and Analysis for the six-month period ended June 30, 20X3, does not include, in all material respects, the required elements of the rules and regulations adopted by the Securities and Exchange Commission, that the historical financial amounts included therein have not been accurately derived, in all material respects, from the Company's unaudited interim financial statements, or that the underlying information, determinations, estimates, and assumptions of the Company do not provide a reasonable basis for the disclosures contained therein.

This report is intended solely for the information and use of [*list or refer to specified parties*], and is not intended to be and should not be used by anyone other than the specified parties.

[*signature*]

[*city and state for U.S. practitioners; city and country for non-U.S. practitioners*]

[*date*]

APPENDIX 14K
REVIEW REPORT ON A COMBINED ANNUAL AND INTERIM MD&A PRESENTATION

Independent Accountant's Report

[*for accounting firms registered with the PCAOB, the title should read* "Report of Independent Registered Public Accounting Firm"]

Board of Directors and Stockholders
ABC Company

We have reviewed ABC Company's Management's Discussion and Analysis taken as a whole, included [incorporated by reference] in the Company's [*insert description of registration statement or document*]. Management is responsible for the preparation of the Company's Management's Discussion and Analysis pursuant to the rules and regulations adopted by the Securities and Exchange Commission. We have audited, in accordance with auditing standards generally accepted in the United States of America [*for engagements performed in accordance with PCAOB standards,* "in accordance with the standards of the Public Company Accounting Oversight Board (United States)"], the financial statements of ABC Company as of December 31, 20X2, and 20X1, and for each of the years in the three-year period ended December 31, 20X2, and in our report dated February 12, 20X3, we expressed an unqualified opinion on those financial statements.

We have reviewed, in accordance with standards established by the American Institute of Certified Public Accountants [*for engagements performed in accordance with PCAOB standards,* "in accordance with the standards of the Public Company Accounting Oversight Board (United States)"], the interim financial information of ABC Company as of June 30, 20X3, and 20X2, and for the six-month periods then ended, and have issued our report thereon dated July 27, 20X3.

We conducted our review of Management's Discussion and Analysis in accordance with attestation standards established by the American Institute of Certified Public Accountants [*for engagements performed in accordance with PCAOB standards,* "in accordance with the standards of the Public Company Accounting Oversight Board (United States)"]. A review of Management's Discussion and Analysis consists principally of applying analytical procedures and making inquiries of persons responsible for financial, accounting, and operational matters. It is substantially less in scope than an examination, the objective of which is the expression of an opinion on the presentation. Accordingly, we do not express such an opinion.

The preparation of Management's Discussion and Analysis requires management to interpret the criteria, make determinations as to the relevancy of information to be included, and make estimates and assumptions that affect reported information. Management's Discussion and Analysis includes information regarding the estimated future impact of transactions and events that have occurred or are expected to occur, expected sources of liquidity and capital resources, operating trends, commitments, and uncertainties. Actual results in the future may differ materially from management's present assessment of this information because events and circumstances frequently do not occur as expected.[1]

Based on our review, nothing came to our attention that caused us to believe that the Company's presentation of Management's Discussion and Analysis does not include, in all material respects, the required elements of the rules and regulations adopted by the Securities and Exchange Commission, that the historical financial amounts included therein have not been accurately derived, in all material respects, from the Company's financial statements, or that the underlying information, determinations, estimates, and assumptions of the Company do not provide a reasonable basis for the disclosures contained therein.

This report is intended solely for the information and use of [*list or refer to specified parties*], and is not intended to be and should not be used by anyone other than the specified parties.

[*signature*]

[*city and state for U.S. practitioners; city and country for non-U.S. practitioners*]

[*date*]

---

[1] If the entity is a nonpublic entity, the following sentence should be added to the beginning of the explanatory paragraph:

> Although ABC Company is not subject to the rules and regulations of the Securities and Exchange Commission, the accompanying Management's Discussion and Analysis is intended to be a presentation in accordance with the rules and regulations adopted by the Securities and Exchange Commission.

Accounting Resources on the Web

Presented here are World Wide Web URLs of interest to practitioners. Because of the constantly changing nature of the Internet, addresses change and new resources become available every day. To find additional resources, use search engines such as Google (http://www.google.com/) and Yahoo! (http://search.yahoo.com/).

Accounting Research Manager
http://www.AccountingResearchManager.com/

AICPA http://www.aicpa.org

American Accounting Association
http://www.accounting.rutgers.com/

Association of Certified Fraud Examiners (ACFE)
http://www.cfenet.com/

Association of School Business Officials
http://www.asbointl.org/

AuditNet http://www.auditnet.org

BoardSource http://www.boardsource.org/

Bugnosis (Privacy Foundation) http://www.bugnosis.org/

CCH INCORPORATED http://cchgroup.com/

Check Payment Systems Association
http://www.cpsa-checks.org/

"Choosing an External Auditor"
http://www.auditforum.org/mid america/midam_exauditor.htm

Code of Federal Regulations
http://www.access.gpo.gov/nara/cfr/index.html

Electronic Privacy Information Center http://www.epic.org/

FASAB http://www.fasab.gov/

FASB http://www.fasb.org/

Federal Register
http://www.access.gpo.gov/su_docs/aces/aces140.html

Federal Tax Law http://www.taxsites.com/federal.html

Fedworld http://www.fedworld.gov/

FirstGov http://www.firstgov.gov/

GASB http://www.gasb.org/

Governmental Accountability Office http://www.gao.gov/

General Services Administration http://www.gsa.gov/

Government Printing Office http://www.gpo.gov/

Intergovernmental Audit Forums http://www.auditforum.org/

International Accounting Standards Board (formerly International Accounting Standards Committee (IASC)]
http://www.iasb.org.uk/

International Institute of Municipal Clerks (IIMC)
http://www.iimc.com/

Internal Revenue Service http://www.irs.gov/

Learning Center http://cch.learningcenter.com/

The Library of Congress http://www.loc.gov/

National Archives and Records Administration Code of Federal Regulations http://www.access.gpo.gov/nara/cfr/index.html

National Association of College and University Business Officers
http://www.nacubo.org/

National Association of State Agencies for Surplus Property
http://www.nasasp.org/

National Association of State Auditors, Comptrollers and Treasurers (NASACT) http://www.nasact.org/

National Association of State Boards of Accountancy (NASBA)
http://www.nasba.org/

National Center for Charitable Statistics (at the Urban Institute)
http://www.nccs.urban.org/

NACHA—The Electronic Payments Association
http://www.nacha.org/

North American Industry Classification System (NAICS)
http://www.census.gov/ftp/pub/epcd/www/naics.html

Office of Management and Budget
http://www.whitehouse.gov/omb

Privacy Foundation http://www.privacyfoundation.org/

ProSystem *fx* Engagement http://cchgroup.com/

Public Accounting Oversight Board http://www.pcaobus.org

Securities and Exchange Commission http://www.sec.gov/

State and local links http://www.statelocal.gov/

Thomas: Legislative Information http://thomas.loc.gov/

U.S. Census Bureau http://www.census.gov/

U.S. government forms http://www.gsa.gov/forms

U.S. House of Representatives http://www.house.gov/

U.S. House of Representatives Current Floor Proceedings
http://clerkweb.house.gov/floor/current.htm

U.S. Senate http://www.senate.gov/

Index

E

F

J

K

L

N

Q

R

T

U

V

W

X

About the CD-ROM

CD-ROM Instructions

SYSTEM REQUIREMENTS

- IBM PC or compatible computer with CD-ROM drive
- Microsoft Word 7.0 for Windows or compatible word processor and
- 3MB available on hard drive

The CD-ROM provided with *Attestation and Other Special Engagements* contains sample letters, work programs, and other practice aids. The word processing forms are intended to be used in conjunction with your word processing software. The word processing forms have been formatted in RTF.

Subject to the conditions in the license agreement and the limited warranty, which are reproduced at the end of this book, you may duplicate the files on this disc, modify them as necessary, and create your own customized versions. Installing the disc contents and/or using the disc in any way indicates that you accept the terms of the license agreement.

If you experience any difficulties installing or using the files included on this disc and cannot resolve the problem using the information presented in this section, call 1 800 835 0105 or visit our website: http://support.cch.com.

CD-ROM Contents

Disc contents by short file name are listed as shown. For more information about the CD-ROM, please see "CD-ROM Instructions."

Form Name	*File Name*	*File Type*
Resources on the Web	Resource	RTF
Chapter 1. Overview of Attestation and Other Special Engagements		
Exhibit 1-1: Comparison of Attestation, Assurance, and Consulting Services	**01_01**	**RTF**
Exhibit 1-2: Key Differences Between Standards	**01_02**	**RTF**
Exhibit 1-3: Comparison of Requirements for Attestation Engagements	**01_03**	**RTF**
Chapter 2. Marketing Special Engagements		
Exhibit 2-1: Identifying Opportunities with Existing Clients	**02_01**	**RTF**
Exhibit 2-2: Determining Which Type of Engagement to Perform	**02_02**	**RTF**
Exhibit 2-3: Common Types of Nontraditional Engagements	**02_03**	**RTF**
Appendix 2A: New Service Opportunity Checklist	**A02_A**	**RTF**
Appendix 2B: Potential Engagements	**A02_B**	**RTF**
Appendix 2C: Ten Phrases for Positive Client Communication	**A02_C**	**RTF**
Appendix 2D: Ten Suggested Uses for Brochures	**A02_D**	**RTF**
Chapter 3. Professional Standards for the CPA and the Firm		
Exhibit 3-1: Illustrative Audit Report	**03_01**	**RTF**
Chapter 4. Pre-Engagement Considerations		
Exhibit 4-1: Information Release Form	**04_01**	**RTF**
Exhibit 4-2: Dos and Don'ts in Engagement Letters	**04_02**	**RTF**
Appendix 4A: Rule 101 of the AICPA Code of Professional Conduct	**A04_A**	**RTF**
Appendix 4B: Client Acceptance and Retention Evaluation Form	**A04_B**	**RTF**

Form Name	*Name*	*Type*
Appendix 4C: Illustrative Client Consent and Acknowledgement Letter	**A04_C**	**RTF**
Appendix 4D: Illustrative Successor Auditor Acknowledgement Letter	**A04_D**	**RTF**
Appendix 4E: Information Release Form	**A04_E**	**RTF**

Chapter 5. Planning and Administration for Attestation Engagements

Exhibit 5-1: Reporting Implications When Written Assertion is Not Obtained	**05_01**	**RTF**
Exhibit 5-2: Determining Which Type of Engagement to Perform	**05_02**	**RTF**
Exhibit 5-3: Engagement Resignation Letter	**05_03**	**RTF**
Case Study 5-1: Nonclient Responsible Party	**E05_01**	**RTF**
Case Study 5-2: Subject Matter and Responsible Party	**E05_02**	**RTF**
Case Study 5-3: Applicability of Attestation Standards	**E05_03**	**RTF**
Case Study 5-4: Type of Engagement	**E05_04**	**RTF**
Case Study 5-5: Suitability of Criteria	**E05_05**	**RTF**
Case Study 5-6: Suitability of Criteria: Reasonably Consistent Measurement	**E05_06**	**RTF**
Case Study 5-7 Suitability of Criteria: Reasonably Consistent Measurement	**E05_07**	**RTF**
Case Study 5-8: Suitability of Criteria: Objectivity	**E05_08**	**RTF**
Case Study 5-9: Suitability of Criteria: Measurability	**E05_09**	**RTF**
Case Study 5-10: Suitability of Criteria: Completeness	**E05_10**	**RTF**
Case Study 5-11: Choice of Criteria	**E05_11**	**RTF**
Appendix 5A: Frequently Asked Questions	**A05_A**	**RTF**
Appendix 5B: Comparison Between Attestation Standards and Generally Accepted Auditing Standards	**A05_B**	**RTF**

Chapter 6. Examination Engagements

Exhibit 6-1: Guidelines to Calculate Planning Materiality	**06_01**	**RTF**
Exhibit 6-2: Combining Inherent Risk and Control Risk	**06_02**	**RTF**

Form Name	*Name*	*Type*
Exhibit 6-3: Risk Factors	**06_03**	**RTF**
Exhibit 6-4: Matrix for Determining Sample Size for Attribute Sampling	**06_04**	**RTF**
Exhibit 6-5: Illustrative Examination Report: Examination of Subject Matter	**06_05**	**RTF**
Exhibit 6-6: Illustrative Examination Report: Examination of Assertion about the Subject Matter	**06_06**	**RTF**
Case Study 6-1: Nonclient Responsible Party	**E06_01**	**RTF**
Case Study 6-2: Responsibility for Subject Matter	**E06_02**	**RTF**
Case Study 6-3: Materiality	**E06_03**	**RTF**
Case Study 6-4: Nature of Tests	**E06_04**	**RTF**
Case Study 6-5: Emphasis of a Matter	**E06_05**	**RTF**
Case Study 6-6: Scope Limitations	**E06_06**	**RTF**
Appendix 6A: Illustrative Engagement Letter	**A06_A**	**RTF**
Appendix 6B: Planning Materiality Calculation Form	**A06_B**	**RTF**
Appendix 6C: Examination Procedures Checklist	**A06_C**	**RTF**
Appendix 6D: Sampling Worksheet for Substantive Tests	**A06_D**	**RTF**
Appendix 6E: Sampling Planning and Evaluation Form	**A06_E**	**RTF**
Appendix 6F: Attribute Planning and Evaluation Form	**A06_F**	**RTF**
Appendix 6G: Illustrative Representation Letter	**A06_G**	**RTF**
Appendix 6H: Client Representation Letter: Client Not Responsible Party	**A06_H**	**RTF**
Appendix 6I: Standard Examination Report on Subject Matter	**A06_I**	**RTF**
Appendix 6J: Standard Examination Report on an Assertion	**A06_J**	**RTF**
Appendix 6K: Standard Examination Report: Examination of an Assertion; Opinion on Subject Matter	**A06_K**	**RTF**
Appendix 6L: Examination Report: Disclaimer of Opinion because of a Scope Limitation	**A06_L**	**RTF**
Appendix 6M: Examination Report: Restricted Because the Criteria Are Available Only to Specified Parties	**A06_M**	**RTF**

Form Name	*Name*	*Type*
Appendix 6N: Examination Report: Qualified for Material Misstatements or Deviations from the Criteria	**A06_N**	**RTF**
Appendix 6O: Examination Report: Restricted Because No Written Assertion Provided by the Nonclient Responsible Party	**A06_O**	**RTF**

Chapter 7. Review Engagements

Form Name	*Name*	*Type*
Exhibit 7-1: Illustrative Review Report: Review of Subject Matter	**07_01**	**RTF**
Exhibit 7-2: Review Report: Review of Assertion about the Subject Matter	**07_02**	**RTF**
Case Study 7-1: Nonclient Responsible Party	**E07_01**	**RTF**
Case Study 7-2: Responsibility for Subject Matter	**E07_02**	**RTF**
Case Study 7-3: Materiality	**E07_03**	**RTF**
Case Study 7-4: Extent of Procedures	**E07_04**	**RTF**
Case Study 7-5: Emphasis of a Matter	**E07_05**	**RTF**
Appendix 7A: Illustrative Engagement Letter	**A07_A**	**RTF**
Appendix 7B: Planning Materiality Calculation Form	**A07_B**	**RTF**
Appendix 7C: Review Procedures Checklist	**A07_C**	**RTF**
Appendix 7D: Illustrative Representation Letter	**A07_D**	**RTF**
Appendix 7E: Client Representation Letter: Client Not Responsible Party	**A07_E**	**RTF**
Appendix 7F: Standard Review Report on Subject Matter	**A07_F**	**RTF**
Appendix 7G: Standard Review Report on an Assertion	**A07_G**	**RTF**
Appendix 7H: Review Report: Restricted Because No Written Assertion Provided by the Nonclient Responsible Party	**A07_H**	**RTF**

Chapter 8. Specified Elements, Accounts, or Items of a Financial Statement

Form Name	*Name*	*Type*
Exhibit 8-1: Guidelines to Calculate Planning Materiality	**08_01**	**RTF**
Exhibit 8-2: Combining Inherent and Control Risk	**08_02**	**RTF**
Exhibit 8-3: Relationship of Assertions and Objectives for Inventory	**08_03**	**RTF**

Chapter 9. Agreed-Upon Procedures Engagements

Form Name	*Name*	*Type*
Exhibit 9-2: Engagements Excluded from the Standards for Agreed-Upon Procedures	**09_02**	**RTF**
Exhibit 9-3: Description of Findings	**09_03**	**RTF**
Case Study 9-1: Agreement on Sufficiency of Procedures	**E09_01**	**RTF**
Case Study 9-2: Appropriateness of Procedures	**E09_02**	**RTF**
Appendix 9A: Engagement Letter	**A09_A**	**RTF**
Appendix 9B: Engagement Letter Addendum	**A09_B**	**RTF**
Appendix 9C: Request for Specified Party's Comments on Procedures	**A09_C**	**RTF**
Appendix 9D: Agreed-Upon Procedures Checklist	**A09_D**	**RTF**
Appendix 9E: Agreed-Upon Procedures Engagement: Procedures and Findings Form	**A09_E**	**RTF**
Appendix 9F: Illustrative Representation Letter	**A09_F**	**RTF**
Appendix 9G: Client Representation Letter: Client Not Responsible Party	**A09_G**	**RTF**
Appendix 9H: Report on Applying Agreed-Upon Procedures	**A09_H**	**RTF**
Appendix 9I: Report in Connection with a Proposed Acquisition	**A09_I**	**RTF**
Appendix 9J: Report in Connection with Claims of Creditors	**A09_J**	**RTF**
Chapter 10. Compliance Engagements		
Exhibit 10-1: Illustrative Agreed-Upon Procedures Report Regarding Compliance	**10_01**	**RTF**
Exhibit 10-2 Combining Inherent Risk and Control Risk	**10_02**	**RTF**
Exhibit 10-3: Illustrative Compliance Examination Report: Report Directly on Entity's Compliance with Specified Requirements	**10_03**	**RTF**
Exhibit 10-4: Illustrative Compliance Examination Report: Report on Management's Assertion about Compliance with Specified Requirements	**10_04**	**RTF**
Appendix 10A: Engagement Letter: Agreed-Upon Procedures Engagement	**A10_A**	**RTF**

Form Name	*Name*	*Type*
Chapter 11. Internal Control Engagements		
Exhibit 11-1: Standard Examination Report: Reports Directly on the Effectiveness of Internal Control over Financial Reporting	**11_01**	**RTF**
Exhibit 11-2: Standard Examination Report: Reports on Management's Assertion about the Effectiveness of Internal Control over Financial Reporting	**11_02**	**RTF**
Exhibit 11-3: Examination Report When There Is a Material Weakness Qualified Opinion	**11_03**	**RTF**
Exhibit 11-4: Examination Report: Material Weakness, Adverse Opinion	**11_04**	**RTF**
Exhibit 11-5: Agreed-Upon Procedures Report Regarding Compliance	**11_05**	**RTF**
Exhibit 11-6: Consulting Report on Internal Control over Operations	**11_06**	**RTF**
Appendix 11A: Engagement Letter: Examination of an Entity's Internal Control over Financial Reporting	**A11_A**	**RTF**
Appendix 11B: Examination Engagement Checklist: Internal Control over Financial Reporting	**A11_B**	**RTF**
Appendix 11C: Tests of Controls Sampling Planning and Evaluation Form	**A11_C**	**RTF**
Appendix 11D: Representation Letter: Examination of an Entity's Internal Control over Financial Reporting	**A11_D**	**RTF**
Appendix 11E: Standard Examination Report Directly on the Effectiveness of the Entity's Internal Control over Financial Reporting	**A11_E**	**RTF**
Appendix 11F: Standard Examination Report on Management's Assertion about the Effectiveness of the Entity's Internal Control over Financial Reporting	**A11_F**	**RTF**
Appendix 11G: Communication of Reportable Conditions Noted in an Examination Engagement, Indication That None is a Material Weakness	**A11_G**	**RTF**
Appendix 11H: Communication of Reportable Conditions Noted in an Examination Engagement, Identification of Material Weaknesses	**A11_H**	**RTF**

Form Name	*Name*	*Type*
Appendix 11W: PCAOB Staff Q&As Related to Audits of Financial Statements of Non-Issuers Performed Pursuant to the Standards of the PCAOB	**A11_W**	**RTF**
Appendix 11X: Illustrative Report Expressing an Unqualified Opinion on Management's Assessment of the Effectiveness of Internal Control over Financial Reporting and an Unqualified Opinion on the Effectiveness of Internal Control over Financial Reporting	**A11_X**	**RTF**

Chapter 12. Due Diligence Engagements

Form Name	*Name*	*Type*
Appendix 12A: Engagement Letter: Examination of Pro Forma Financial Information	**A12_A**	**RTF**
Appendix 12B: Engagement Letter: Review of Pro Forma Financial Information	**A12_B**	**RTF**
Appendix 12C: Engagement Letter: Compilation of Pro Forma Financial Information	**A12_C**	**RTF**
Appendix 12D: Examination Engagement Checklist: Pro Forma Financial Information	**A12_D**	**RTF**
Appendix 12E: Review Engagement Checklist: Pro Forma Financial Information	**A12_E**	**RTF**
Appendix 12F: Compilation Engagement Checklist: Pro Forma Financial Information	**A12_F**	**RTF**
Appendix 12G: Representation Letter: Examination of Pro Forma Financial Information	**A12_G**	**RTF**
Appendix 12H: Representation Letter: Review of Pro Forma Financial Information	**A12_H**	**RTF**
Appendix 12I: Standard Examination Report on Pro Forma Financial Information	**A12_I**	**RTF**
Appendix 12J: Standard Review Report on Pro Forma Financial Information	**A12_J**	**RTF**
Appendix 12K: Examination Report: Qualified Because of a Scope Limitation	**A12_K**	**RTF**
Appendix 12L: Examination Report: Qualified Because of Reservations About the Propriety of Assumptions on an Acquisition Transaction	**A12_L**	**RTF**

Form Name	*Name*	*Type*
Appendix 12M: Disclaimer of Opinion Because of a Scope Limitation	**A12_M**	**RTF**
Appendix 12N: Compilation Report on Pro Forma Financial Information	**A12_N**	**RTF**
Appendix 12O: Engagement Letter: Acquisition Assistance Engagement, Consulting Services	**A12_O**	**RTF**
Appendix 12P: Procedures Checklist: Acquisition Assistance Engagement, Consulting Services	**A12_P**	**RTF**
Appendix 12Q: Target Representation Letter: Acquisition Assistance Engagement, Consulting Services	**A12_Q**	**RTF**
Appendix 12R: Client Representation Letter: Acquisition Assistance Engagement, Consulting Services	**A12_R**	**RTF**
Appendix 12S: Acquisition Assistance Engagement: Consulting Services Report	**A12 _S**	**RTF**

Chapter 13. Prospective Financial Information

Form Name	*Name*	*Type*
Exhibit 13-1: Standard Compilation Report: Forecast	**13_01**	**RTF**
Exhibit 13-2: Standard Compilation Report: Projection	**13_02**	**RTF**
Exhibit 13-3: Standard Examination Report: Forecast	**13_03**	**RTF**
Exhibit 13-4: Standard Examination Report: Projection	**13_04**	**RTF**
Exhibit 13-5: Examination Report: Forecast, at Variance with AICPA Guidelines	**13_05**	**RTF**
Exhibit 13-6: Adverse Opinion: Forecast	**13_06**	**RTF**
Exhibit 13-7: Financial Forecast: Underlying Assumption Not Evaluated	**13_07**	**RTF**
Exhibit 13-8: Budget Information	**13_08**	**RTF**
Case Study 13-1: Forecast versus Projection	**E13_01**	**RTF**
Case Study 13-2: Key Factors	**E13_02**	**RTF**
Case Study 13-3: Reasonably Objective Basis	**E13_03**	**RTF**
Case Study 13-4: Modification of the Opinion	**E13_04**	**RTF**
Appendix 13A: Engagement Letter: Compilation of Prospective Financial Statements	**A13_A**	**RTF**

Form Name	*Name*	*Type*
Appendix 13B: Engagement Letter: Examination of Prospective Financial Statements	**A13_B**	**RTF**
Appendix 13C: Engagement Letter: Applying Agreed-Upon Procedures to Prospective Financial Statements	**A13_C**	**RTF**
Appendix 13D: Engagement Letter Addendum	**A13_D**	**RTF**
Appendix 13E: Request for Specified Party's Comments on Procedures	**A13_E**	**RTF**
Appendix 13F: Planning Materiality Calculation Form	**A13_F**	**RTF**
Appendix 13G: Compilation Engagement Checklist: Prospective Financial Statements	**A13_G**	**RTF**
Appendix 13H: Examination Engagement Checklist: Prospective Financial Statements	**A13_H**	**RTF**
Appendix 13I: Agreed-Upon Procedures Checklist: Prospective Financial Statements	**A13_I**	**RTF**
Appendix 13J: Agreed-Upon Procedures Engagement: Procedures and Findings Form	**A13_J**	**RTF**
Appendix 13K: Representation Letter: Compilation of Prospective Financial Statements	**A13_K**	**RTF**
Appendix 13L: Representation Letter: Examination of Prospective Financial Statements	**A13_L**	**RTF**
Appendix 13M: Representation Letter: Agreed-Upon Procedures Engagements	**A13_M**	**RTF**
Chapter 14. Management's Discussion and Analysis		
Exhibit 14-1: Engagements for Which AT 701 Does Not Apply	**14_01**	**RTF**
Appendix 14A: Procedures Checklist for Engagements to Examine MD&A	**A14_A**	**RTF**
Appendix 14B: Procedures Checklist for Engagements to Review MD&A	**A14_B**	**RTF**
Appendix 14C: Standard Unqualified Examination Report on MD&A	**A14_C**	**RTF**
Appendix 14D: Examination Report on MD&A with Qualified Opinion Due to a Material Omission	**A14_D**	**RTF**

Form Name	Name	Type
Appendix 14E: Examination Report on MD&A with a Qualified Opinion When Overly Subjective Assertions Are Included in MD&A	**A14_E**	**RTF**
Appendix 14F: Examination Report on MD&A with Reference Made to the Report of Another Practitioner	**A14_F**	**RTF**
Appendix 14G: Standard Review Report on an Annual MD&A Presentation	**A14_G**	**RTF**
Appendix 14H: Standard Review Report on an Interim MD&A Presentation	**A14_H**	**RTF**
Appendix 14I: Modified Review Report on an MD&A Presentation for a Material Misstatement	**A14_I**	**RTF**
Appendix 14J: Combined Report on an Examination of an Annual MD&A Presentation and Review of MD&A for an Interim Period	**A14_J**	**RTF**
Appendix 14K: Review Report on a Combined Annual and Interim MD&A Presentation	**A14_K**	**RTF**

CCH, a Wolters Kluwer Business

SOFTWARE LICENSE AGREEMENT FOR ELECTRONIC FILES TO ACCOMPANY 20[illegible]6 ATTESTATION AND OTHER SPECIAL ENGAGEMENTS (THE "BOOK").

READ THE TERMS AND CONDITIONS OF THIS LICENSE AGREEMENT CAREFULLY BEFORE INSTALLING THE SOFTWARE (THE "PROGRAM") TO ACCOMPANY ATTESTATION AND OTHER SPECIAL ENGAGEMENTS. THE PROGRAM IS COPYRIGHTED AND LICENSED (NOT SOLD). BY INSTALLING THE PROGRAM, YOU ARE ACCEPTING AND AGREEING TO THE TERMS OF THIS LICENSE AGREEMENT. IF YOU ARE NOT WILLING TO BE BOUND BY THE TERMS OF THIS LICENSE AGREEMENT, YOU SHOULD PROMPTLY RETURN THE PACKAGE IN RESELLABLE CONDITION AND YOU WILL RECEIVE A REFUND OF YOUR MONEY. THIS LICENSE AGREEMENT REPRESENTS THE ENTIRE AGREEMENT CONCERNING THE PROGRAM BETWEEN YOU AND CCH (REFERRED TO AS "LICENSOR"), AND IT SUPERSEDES ANY PRIOR PROPOSAL, REPRESENTATION, OR UNDERSTANDING BETWEEN THE PARTIES.

1. License Grant. Licensor hereby grants to you, and you accept, a nonexclusive license to use the Program CD-ROM and the computer programs contained therein in machine-readable, object code form only (collectively referred to as the "Software"), and the accompanying User Documentation, only as authorized in this License Agreement. The Software may be used only on a single computer owned, leased, or otherwise controlled by you; or in the event of the inoperability of that computer, on a backup computer selected by you. Neither concurrent use on two or more computers nor use in a local area network or other network is permitted without separate authorization and the possible payment of other license fees. You agree that you will not assign, sublease, transfer, pledge, lease, rent, or share your rights under the License Agreement. You agree that you may not reverse engineer, decompile, disassemble, or otherwise adapt, modify, or translate the Software.

Upon loading the Software into your computer, you may retain the Software CD-ROM for backup purposes. In addition, you may make one copy of the Software on a set of diskettes (or other storage medium) for the purpose of backup in the event the Software files are damaged or destroyed. You may make one copy of any additional User Documentation (such as the README.TXT file or the "About the Computer Disc" section of the Book) for backup purposes. Any such copies of the Software or the User Documentation shall include the Licensor's copyright and other proprietary notices. Except as authorized under this paragraph, no copies of the Software or any portions thereof may be made by you or any person under your authority or control.

2. Licensor's Rights.You acknowledge and agree that the Software and the User Documentation are proprietary products of Licensor protected under U.S. copyright law. You further acknowledge and agree that all right, title, and interest in and to the Software, including associated intellectual property rights, are and shall remain with Licensor. This License Agreement does not convey to you an interest in or to the Software, including associated intellectual property rights, which are and shall remain with Licensor. This License Agreement does not convey to you an interest in or to the Software, but only a limited right of use revocable in accordance with the terms of this License Agreement.

3. License Fees. The license fees paid by you are paid in consideration of the licenses granted under this License Agreement.

4. Term. This License Agreement is effective upon your installing this software and shall continue until terminated. You may terminate this License Agreement at any time by removing all copies of the Software and returning the CD-ROM to Licensor. Licensor may terminate this License Agreement upon the breach by you of any term hereof. Upon such termination by Licensor, you agree to return to Licensor the Software and all copies and portions thereof.

5. Limited Warranty. Licensor warrants, for our benefit alone, for a period of 90 days from the date of commencement of this License Agreement (referred to as the "Warranty Period") that the Program CD-ROM in which the software is contained is free from defects in material and workmanship. If during the Warranty Period, a defect appears in the Program CD-ROM, you may return the Program to Licensor for either replacement or, at Licensor's option, refund of amounts paid by you under this License Agreement. You agree that the foregoing constitutes your sole and exclusive remedy for breach by Licensor of any warranties made under this Agreement. EXCEPT FOR THE WARRANTIES SET FORTH ABOVE, THE PROGRAM, AND THE SOFTWARE CONTAINED THEREIN, ARE LICENSED "AS-IS," AND LICENSOR DISCLAIMS ANY AND ALL OTHER WARRANTIES, WHETHER EXPRESS OR IMPLIED, INCLUDING, WITHOUT LIMITATION, ANY IMPLIED WARRANTIES OF MERCHANTABILITY OR FITNESS FOR A PARTICULAR PURPOSE.

6. Limitation of Liability. Licensor's cumulative liability to you or any other party for any loss or damages resulting from any claims, demands, or actions arising out of or relating to this Agreement shall not exceed the license fee paid to Licensor for the use of the Program. IN NO EVENT SHALL LICENSOR BE LIABLE FOR ANY INDIRECT, INCIDENTAL,CONSEQUENTIAL, SPECIAL OR EXEMPLARY DAMAGES (INCLUDING, BUT NOT LIMITED TO, LOSS OF DATA, BUSINESS INTERRUPTION, OR LOST PROFITS) EVEN IF LICENSOR HAS BEEN ADVISED OF THE POSSIBILITY OF SUCH DAMAGES.

7. Miscellaneous. The License Agreement shall be construed and governed in accordance with the laws of the State of Delaware. Should any term of this License Agreement be declared void or unenforceable by any court of competent jurisdiction, such declaration shall have no effect on the remaining terms hereof. The failure of either party to enforce any rights granted hereunder or to take action against the other party in the event of any breach hereunder shall not be deemed a waiver by that party as to subsequent enforcement of rights or subsequent actions in the event of future breaches.